Constitutional Law
A Critical Introduction

Constitutional Law
A Critical Introduction

Ian Loveland
Professor of Law, Brunel University

'Wherever the real power in a government lies, there is the danger of oppression. In our Governments the real power lies in the majority of the Community, and the invasion of private rights is chiefly to be apprehended, not from acts of Government contrary to the senses of its constituents, but from acts in which the Government is the mere instrument of the major number of the constituents. This is a truth of great importance, but not yet sufficiently attended to.'

James Madison.

Butterworths
London, Dublin & Edinburgh
1996

United Kingdom   Butterworths, a Division of Reed Elsevier (UK) Ltd, Halsbury House, 35 Chancery Lane, LONDON WC2A 1EL and 4 Hill Street, EDINBURGH EH2 3JZ

Australia   Butterworths, a Divison of Reed International Books Australia Pty Ltd, CHATSWOOD, New South Wales

Canada   Butterworths Canada Ltd, MARKHAM, Ontario

Hong Kong   Butterworths Asia (Hong Kong), HONG KONG

India   Butterworths India, NEW DELHI

Ireland   Butterworth (Ireland) Ltd, DUBLIN

Malaysia   Malayan Law Journal Sdn Bhd, KUALA LUMPER

New Zealand   Butterworths of New Zealand Ltd, WELLINGTON

Singapore   Butterworths Asia, SINGAPORE

South Africa   Butterworths Publishers (Pty) Ltd, DURBAN

USA   Lexis Law Publishing, CHARLOTTESVILLE, Virginia

Reprinted 1997 and 1998

A CIP Catalogue record for this book is available from the British Library.

ISBN 0 406 04968 8

Photoset by Intype London Ltd
Printed in Great Britain by Antony Rowe Ltd, Chippenham, Wiltshire

Visit us at our website: http//www.butterworths.co.uk

Preface

There are already many textbooks, some of them admirable, on the subject of constitutional law. This volume is intended to add to, rather than supplant, the existing literature. In writing the book, I have tried to draw far more heavily on sources in the areas of political science and political history than the authors of most other constitutional law texts. This is in part because I have assumed that the constitution has a story to tell, a story which is incomplete if shorn of its political and historical components. That assumption was itself structured by my undergraduate and doctoral education, which was undertaken (at Warwick University and Nuffield College, Oxford) in environments which presented law as just one (and by no means the most important one) of the many social sciences. This book reflects that 'realist' or 'socio-legal' approach to legal scholarship. Whether that approach is per se desirable, and whether this book uses the approach effectively, are questions I leave others to answer.

It should also be stressed that this book is written from a particular party political standpoint. I can make no claim for thorough-going 'neutrality' or 'objectivity' in the pages that follow, although I have tried to avoid advocacy of a narrowly partisan line of argument. My own political preferences, and thence my view of the constitution, float around the centre-left of the political spectrum. It will readily become apparent that I regard this country's current constitutional arrangements as entirely unsatisfactory. As of late 1995, I am a reluctant member of the Labour party, somewhat perturbed to find that Paddy Ashdown's Liberal party advances a far more innovative (and in my opinion desirable) agenda for constitutional reform than Tony Blair's shadow cabinet. I should also add, for the sake of completeness, that I can discern little merit in any of the policies pursued by the Thatcher and Major governments which have controlled this country since 1979.

I should also emphasise that the book is intended as an

introductory text, primarily for first year law and political science students. The contents are loosely based on the present syllabus for the London University LLB, and buried somewhere within each chapter is the outline of a lecture I have delivered to students taking that degree in the past few years. I therefore make no grand claims for the book's thoroughness – what is offered here is a very selective viewpoint – nor for the sophistication of its analysis.

Readers who are already familiar with British public law will no doubt find parts of the text unduly simplistic, even crude, in tone and content. This is due in part to my attempts to impose a chronological structure on the course of the narrative: I have tried (in the main) to resist the temptation to analyse older case law in the light of later and more elaborate administrative law principles. But it is also due to the aforementioned introductory nature of the text: I have assumed that readers new to the subject might sensibly be given an opportunity to trace the historical process through which basic principles have assumed a more complex identity, rather than be presented at the outset with the myriad complications of the contemporary public law landscape. I have also tried to make both the substance of the ideas that are presented, and the language in which they are expressed, increasingly elaborate as the book progresses: I would hope that the text takes novice readers up a fairly rapid learning curve, and equips them, should their interest have been aroused by the topic, with a sufficient grounding in its basic points to move fruitfully on to rather more demanding texts, particularly Martin Loughlin's *Public Law and Political Theory* and Paul Craig's *Public Law and Democracy in Britain and the USA*.

Experienced readers will also no doubt find some of the ideas advanced in the book rather unorthodox, bizarre, or even, as Oliver Sanders has suggested to me in respect of my views on the incorporation of Treaties into domestic law, 'just plain wrong'. For this reason, the discerning student would be well advised not to rely solely on this work as her source for knowledge on constitutional law; Munro's *Studies in Constitutional Law*, Turpin's *British Government and the Constitution*, and Ewing and Bradley's *Constitutional and Administrative Law* would all offer a valuable counter-position to the arguments advanced here. I have taken many of Oliver Sanders' criticisms on board in producing the final version of the text. I would nevertheless hope that some of the 'wrong' ideas that I have chosen to retain may have sufficient merit to promote other scholars to explore them in rather greater depth, if only to demonstrate that they rest on an entirely fanciful basis.

Despite the kind attentions of the various people who have read parts of the book during the early stages of its life, I do not doubt that the text contains errors. I look forward to having them pointed out to me (ideally by students – who will then have learned never fully to trust what supposed authorities tell them), and hope to be able to correct them if the book is sufficiently successful to merit a second edition. There is however one very substantial omission in the current text which should be adverted to here – namely a detailed consideration of the impact wrought on the development of British constitutional law by this country's relationship with Ireland. This question is touched on tangentially at various stages in the book, but is too complex an issue to be addressed without the benefit of long and careful study. That is also something I would hope to remedy in a second edition.

Ian Loveland
London, Spring 1996.

Acknowledgments

As is always the case in a project of this kind, the list of people who are properly owed considerable thanks for helpful contributions is too long to be written in full. Successive years of students at Lady Margaret Hall, Oxford University and Queen Mary College, London University have lent the greatest assistance, with particular thanks owed to Andy Sharland and Oliver Sanders who spent three years showing me how little I knew of the subjects about which we were learning. Further thanks are owed to Oliver Sanders for helping me out in the final stages of the book's preparation and offering me a vigorous critique of its contents (and to Roger Cotterrell at QMW and Michael Sterling at Brunel for making funds available for that purpose). I also owe a great debt to Hazel Genn, who when Head of Department at QMW allowed me appreciable space to indulge some rather unusual ideas.

Joanne Scott offered me the benefit of her much more extensive (than mine) knowledge of the EC by commenting on chapters 12 and 13. Carol Vincent also lent me the benefit of her advice on the entire text at various stages of its development, for which I am most grateful.

My thanks finally to the editorial staff at Butterworths for being so enthusiastic in support of this project, and relatedly to several unknown reviewers of the original proposal for confirming that what I had to say on this subject might be worth listening to. I hope they are not disappointed with the end product.

Contents

Chapter 3. The rule of law and the separation of powers   63
I. The Diceyan perspective: the rule of law
    in the pre-welfare state   64
    Entick v Carrington (1765)   66
    Dicey's rule of law – process or substance?   70
    The 'independence of the judiciary'   71
II. The rule of law in the welfare state   73
    Hayek – *The road to serfdom*   74
    Jones – the rule of law in the welfare state   76
III. Judicial regulation of government behaviour: the
    constitutional rationale   79
    The meaning of words: *Liversidge v Anderson* (1942)   83
    Principles of statutory interpretation   87
    Stare decisis   90
IV. Parliamentary sovereignty v the rule of law   92
    Anisminic v Foreign Compensation Commission (1969)   93
    Burmah Oil Co (Burma Trading) Ltd v Lord Advocate (1965)   96
    M v Home Office (1994)   98
Conclusion   101

Chapter 4. The royal prerogative   102
    The source of prerogative powers   103
    Post-1688 – the revolutionary settlement   108
I. The relationship between statute, the prerogative and the
    rule of law   111
    A-G v De Keyser's Royal Hotel Ltd (1920)   112
    Laker Airways Ltd v Department of Trade (1977)   113
    *R v Secretary of State for the Home Department, ex p
    Fire Brigades Union* (1995)   115
II. The traditional perspective on judicial review
    of prerogative powers: and its erosion   116
    R v Criminal Injuries Compensation Board, ex p Lain (1967)   117
    Gouriet v Union of Post Office Workers (1978)   118
III. The acceptance of full reviewability – the *GCHQ* affair   121
IV. Post-*GCHQ* developments – the shifting nature of
    'justiciability'   123
    The *ZAPU* case (1986)   124
    *R v Secretary of State for the Home Department, ex p
    Northumbria Police Authority* (1988)   125
    Foreign affairs?   127
    Excluded categories: a shrinking list?   129
V. 'Justiciability' revisited – are all statutory powers
    reviewable?   130
Conclusion   132

xvi   *Contents*

Table of statutes

References in this table to *Statutes* are to Halsbury's Statutes of England (Fourth Edition) showing the volume and page at which the annotated sections of the Act may be found.

Table of treaties and agreements

List of cases

Decisions of the European
Court of Justice are listed
below numerically. These
decisions are also included
in the preceding
alphabetical list.

CHAPTER ONE

Defining the constitution

'We hold these truths to be self-evident. That all men are created equal. That they are endowed by their creator with certain inalienable rights. That among these are life, liberty and the pursuit of happiness. That to secure these rights, governments are instituted among men, deriving their just powers from the consent of the governed. That whenever any form of government becomes destructive of those ends, it shall be the right of the people to alter or abolish it, and to institute new government, laying its foundations upon such principles, and organising its powers in such form, as shall seem to them most likely to effect their safety and happiness.'
Thomas Jefferson, Philadelphia, July 4 1776.

It may initially seem odd to begin a textbook analysing the law and politics of the British constitution by quoting several sentences from the United States' Declaration of Independence, a document drafted by Thomas Jefferson in 1776. The Declaration of Independence was of course written because the American colonists, most of whom were then the descendants of British emigrés, had *rejected* the British constitutional system under which they had previously been governed. Jefferson's words were intended firstly to provide an explanation for and justification of the American colonists' decision to rebel against British rule, and secondly to outline the broad moral and political principles that the revolutionaries would try to preserve in the new country they intended to create.

This book begins with Jefferson's words in part because there is much common ground between American and British perceptions as to the moral principles which should be served by a country's constitutional arrangements.[1] However, they have been

1 See Harlow C (1995) 'A special relationship? American influences on judicial review in England'; and Allan T (1995) 'Equality and moral independence: public law and private morality', both in Loveland I (ed) *A Special Relationship?* (Oxford: Clarendon Press).

chosen primarily because it may plausibly be argued that, some two hundred and twenty years after they were written, they continue to provide the most succinct and eloquent statement of the issues and ideas with which constitutional lawyers in any modern democratic country should be concerned.

We might contrast the sentiments of the Declaration with the various definitions of the British constitution offered by the authors of several recent textbooks. Colin Turpin suggests that the constitution is: 'a body of rules, conventions and practices which regulate or qualify the organisation and operation of government in the United Kingdom'; deSmith's classic introductory text regards the constitution as 'a central, but not the sole feature, of the rules regulating the system of government', while, in a somewhat circular fashion, David Hughes and David Pollard define it as 'how a state is constituted and functions'.[2] A slightly longer version is offered by Vernon Bogdanor, for whom the constitution is:

> 'a code of rules which aspire to regulate the allocation of functions, powers and duties among the various agencies and officers of government, and defines the relationship between these and the public.'[3]

These authors seem to be trying to tell us what the constitution is – to *describe* the *form* that it takes. Jefferson, in contrast, is trying to tell us in the Declaration what a constitution is *for* – to *analyse* the *functions* it performs. This book follows the Jeffersonian approach in attempting to present a functionalist view of the British constitution – it is concerned more with the 'How?' and the 'Why?' than with the 'What?' of contemporary arrangements; it assumes that the purpose of a constitution is to articulate and preserve its society's fundamental moral principles. This is not to suggest that a knowledge of the form that the constitution takes is unimportant, nor that issues of form and function are unrelated phenomena; it is simply to stress that one cannot understand the law of the constitution without looking beyond and behind its surface image.

The book does not, however, seek to offer a one-sentence 'defi-

2 Respectively in (2nd edn, 1990) *British Government and the Constitution* p 3 (London: Weidenfield and Nicolson); Street H and Brazier R (5th edn, 1985), *deSmith's Constitutional and Administrative Law* p 15 (Harmondsworth: Penguin); *Cases and Materials on Constitutional and Administrative Law* p 1 (London: Butterworths).
3 Bogdanor V (1988) 'Introduction' p 4 in Bogdanor V (ed) *Constitutions in Democratic Politics* (Aldershot: Dartmouth Publishing).

nition' of the constitution, on the grounds that such a task cannot sensibly be performed. Rather, the entire book may be seen as a 'definition'. But one should stress at the outset that this book amounts to only *one* definition, which is no more or less conclusive than any other formula that a student may encounter. In the United Kingdom, constitutional law is a subject as much concerned with social history and political practice as with legal rules; in consequence, definitive answers to particular problems are almost invariably elusive, and it is almost always possible to advance plausible alternatives to the solutions that have apparently been adopted. The two broad questions which are generally before us are firstly; 'Which alternative solution is the most convincing?'; and secondly; 'What factors have led us to that conclusion?' Whether this book offers more or less *authoritative* responses to those questions than other academic commentaries is something which only its readers are in a position to judge.

This introductory chapter is intended merely to identify certain evaluative criteria which readers might wish to keep in mind when considering the description and analysis of Britain's current constitutional arrangements presented in the rest of the book. The following pages explore several abstract questions concerning the functions that a constitution might perform in order to illustrate the complex nature of the subject we are studying. We also devote some attention to the solutions which the American revolutionaries adopted to resolve the constitutional difficulties which they faced when the United States became an independent country. This is not a comparative book, nor is it suggested that the American solution is necessarily 'better' in any particular sense than the British model. The British and American systems are however very different in the form that they take. This is highly significant for our purposes, because Jefferson and his colleagues claimed that their revolution was fought not against the political and moral principles of the British constitution, but against the corruption of those principles by the British Parliament, the British government, the British judiciary, and the British people.

We will return to these historical matters shortly. Before doing so, however, we might usefully spend some time considering the meaning of what we might (from a late twentieth-century vantage point) intuitively regard as the most important function a constitution should perform – to ensure that a country is governed in accordance with 'democratic principles'.

Defining the constitution

I. THE MEANING(S) OF 'DEMOCRACY'?

For many readers of this book, the notion that modern Britain is a democratic country is perhaps a contemporary example of a 'self-evident truth': the point is possibly so obvious that few observers would ever feel a need to question it. But if we start to dig beneath the surface of such widely held assumptions, we may find that we hold rather different views about the essential features of a democratic state.[4] We might also find that we would reach different conclusions about *how* democratic a country Britain actually is.

That, however, is a judgment best reserved to the book's concluding chapter. At this point, we might more sensibly ask what yardsticks we might use in attempting to answer the question. The following hypothetical example assumes that the constitutions of the countries concerned provide simply that laws shall be made by referendums, in which all adult citizens are granted one vote each. A law is passed if 50% + 1 of those citizens who vote support the proposal. Let us assume that a majority of citizens in both countries A and B decide that they are not prepared to tolerate the poverty caused by an economic depression which has left 20% of the adult population unemployed.

In country A, the law is amended to provide for a very generous scheme of unemployment benefits, which are financed by heavy income taxes on the wealthiest 30% of the population. In doing this, the law frees the poorest members of society from the threat or reality of starvation and homelessness. But it also deprives the richest citizens of a substantial slice of their income, which they had planned to spend in pursuit of their own favoured forms of happiness.

In country B, the law is amended to require the government to deport unemployed citizens to an inhospitable, uninhabited island where they are left to survive according to their own devices. The cost of the scheme is met by fining the deportees themselves for being unemployed. In doing this, the law rids the country of the problem of unemployment at no financial cost to the majority of the population, but exposes the formerly unemployed citizens to the dangers and isolation of a new homeland.

How would we decide if either or both of these laws were 'democratic'? Should we ask only if the law has majority support,

---

4 For an introduction see Bealey F (1988) *Democracy in the Contemporary State* esp chs 1 and 2 (Oxford: Clarendon Press); Holden B (1988) *Understanding Liberal Democracy* esp ch 1 (Oxford: Phillip Allan).

and if the answer is yes, go no further? If so, both laws (and presumably the constitutional arrangements under which they were passed) would be democratic. Or should we demand that there be an inter-relationship between the level of support a law attracts and the severity of its consequences for particular minorities – the more severe the law, the greater the degree of support it must attract to be democratic? If we accepted that principle, could we then agree that deporting the unemployed is more 'severe' than imposing heavy taxes on the rich? If so, could we further agree that deportation would be 'democratic' if it enjoyed 55% (or 66% or 75% or 100%) support, while 50% + 1 would be sufficient to 'democratise' swingeing tax increases? Or thirdly, should we conclude that there are some laws whose consequences would be so severe that they may never be enacted by a democratic society, even if they attract the consent of 100% of the population? If so, would either deportation or large tax increases fall into that category?

Alternatively, let us suppose that country C declares war on countries D, E, and F. Country D immediately passes a law forbidding any criticism of its government's war effort and providing for the execution of citizens who do so, for fear that such freedom of speech could undermine morale and so increase the risk of defeat. Country E enacts a law which allows the government to imprison (without trial, and for an indefinite period, but in humane conditions) anybody suspected by a designated group of government employees of having connections with the enemy country, for fear that such people might be spies or saboteurs. Both laws achieve the desired effect, and country C's attacks are repelled. In country F, the majority decides that it must accord priority to freedom of speech and liberty of the person, and enacts neither of those measures. Subsequently, enemy agents (whose sympathies are suspected but unproven) succeed in sabotaging miltary facilities and undermining the citizenry's morale to such an extent that country F is defeated.

Which country has acted in a democratic fashion here? Does a desire to preserve the country's independence justify interference with freedom of speech and physical liberty? Does the answer to this question depend on the severity of the interference – or on the severity of the threat from the aggressor? Or on the outcome of the war? Would one again wish to know the *size* of the majority supporting each measure before deciding if it was democratic?

We can rapidly make the questions raised by such 'laws' more elaborate by bringing the hypothetical law-making process under closer scrutiny. Would our conclusions about 'democracy' alter if it transpired that the law enacted in country A was supported by the 70% of the population who would not have to pay extra taxes to finance it, but opposed by the 30% who would suffer reduced income if the new system was introduced? Or alternatively, that it was supported by all of the richest 30% but opposed by many of the unemployed, who regarded it as a patronising erosion of their dignity and self-respect? Similarly, would our views as to the democratic nature of the new law made in country B change if we learned that it had been enthusiastically supported by the overwhelming majority of the people who were to be sent overseas? Or, to introduce a further variable, would either law become more or less democratic in our eyes if we discover that neither country permits unemployed people to cast votes in the law-making process?

Constitutions as a social and political contract?

We might readily agree that the issue of 'consent' permeates the many plausible answers that might be offered to those hypothetical questions. As a statement of general principle, it is difficult to find fault with Jefferson's suggestion that 'government derives its just powers from the consent of the governed'. Problems begin to arise when we go rather further and ask 'Who is doing the consenting?'; 'What is it they are consenting to?'; and 'In what ways must that consent be expressed?'.

The notion of a constitution as some form of 'contract', negotiated either among the citizenry themselves, or between the citizenry and their rulers, was not a novel idea, if only in philosophical terms, in 1776. The French philosopher Jean-Jacques Rousseau had explored the concept of 'direct democracy' through an idealised small city state, in which all citizens participated personally in fashioning the laws under which they lived.[5] In such a society, the legitimacy of all laws would rest on the citizenry's constant, express consent to the process of government. Rousseau rejected the idea of a divine, or natural system of government; his men and women were not sculpted by their creator and endowed with those 'inalienable rights' that the American revolutionaries were so keen to defend. Rousseau's social order resulted from agreements between every individual citizen and the citizenry as a whole, from which government was formed. All government action therefore had a 'contractual' base; the citizens' rights and obligations under their constitution derived from covenants that they willingly made.

5 Rousseau J (1987) *The Social Contract* (edited and translated by C Betts) (Oxford: OUP).

John Locke's celebrated *Two Treatises of Government*, first published in 1690, pursued the concept of constitutions as contracts in a slightly different form. Unlike Rousseau, Locke maintained that society was subject to a form of natural or divine law which imposed limits on individual behaviour. Government existed in order to provide mechanisms for enforcing the substance of such natural laws, the terms of which would serve as the constitution within which the government operated:

> 'It is unreasonable for Men to be Judges in their own Cases . . . Self-love will make Men partial to themselves and their friends. And on the other side, . . . Ill Nature, Passion and Revenge will carry them too far in punishing others. And hence nothing but Confusion or Disorder will follow, and therefore God hath certainly appointed Government to restrain the partiality and violence of Men.'[6]

Locke and Rousseau were of course engaging in an exercise in abstract, academic philosophising: they were sketching ideal solutions to hypothetical problems, rather than offering a detailed programme capable of immediate implementation in their respective countries.[7] Indeed, in the early eighteenth century it was rather difficult to identify any historical examples of such idealised sentiments being put into practice. Thus David Hume's famous 1748 essay on the formation of constitutions and governments, entitled 'Of the Original Contract', was able to record that

> 'Almost all governments which exist at present, or of which there remains any record in story, have been founded originally either on usurpation or conquest, or both, without any pretence of a fair consent or voluntary subjection of the people.'[8]

This is not to suggest that academic speculation is without value. Students of the French and American revolutions will appreciate that the writings of Locke and Rousseau provided an important frame of reference for those revolutionaries whose armed struggle was waged so that their countries might try to construct a new, 'ideal' form of constitutional order. The suggestion that 'there is nothing so powerful as an idea whose time has come' may be a cliché, but it is not without considerable force in the context of

---

6 Laslett P (ed) (1988) Locke *Two Treatises of Government*, II para 13 (Cambridge: CUP).
7 Although there is a lively debate among Lockean scholars as to whether the *Second Treatise* was written as an ex post facto justification for the 1688 English revolution, of which more will be said in chapter two; see Laslett P (1988) '*Two Treatises of Government* and the revolution of 1688', in Laslett P (ed) *op cit*.
8 Reproduced in Hume D (1994) *Political Writings* p 168 (edited by Warner D and Livingston D) (Cambridge: Hackett).

constitutional reform. We will return to this point shortly. But even at a hypothetical, abstract level, the idea of constitutions as political contracts or covenants raises major difficulties, the foremost among which is, as Rousseau recognised, 'to determine what those covenants are'.

Locke presented the emergence of government as a prerequisite for protecting individual citizens' 'property', a concept which he construed broadly as encompassing their lives, their physical and spiritual liberty, and their land and possessions.[9] These matters could thus be construed as entitlements which citizens derived from 'natural law', and are an obvious source of inspiration for Jefferson's notion of 'inalienable rights'. The terms are clearly too vague to permit any exhaustive definition of their content. Nevertheless, by focusing on the specific grievances and objectives of the American revolutionaries we can gain some indication of the issues they might encompass.

If we study the Declaration of Independence, we find that the Americans' complaints against the British government concerned both the way that laws were made and their content. The overall thrust of the argument was that Britain was seeking to establish 'an absolute Tyranny over these States', but the general accusation was made up of many more specific complaints. Jefferson accused the British of, for example, 'imposing taxes on us without our consent' and '[keeping] among us, in times of peace, standing armies without the consent of our legislatures'. Jefferson is not arguing here that the levying of taxation or the maintenance of an army in peace-time are per se unacceptable features of government power, but that they are acceptable only if 'the people' affected by the measures have agreed to them.

At other points in the Declaration, in contrast, Jefferson identified British actions which apparently were unacceptable per se. The British had, for instance:

> 'dissolved Representative Houses repeatedly.... [and] refused for a long time, after dissolutions, to cause others to be elected.... [and] refused to pass laws for the accommodation of large districts of people, unless those people would relinquish the right of Representation in the Legislature, a right inestimable in them and formidable to tyrants only.'[10]

9 This book makes no attempt to explore the subtleties of Lockean philosophy. A useful introduction to Locke's use of 'property' is offered in Laslett P (1988) 'The social and political theory of *Two Treatises of Government*', in Laslett (ed) *op cit.*
10 For the Lockean roots of this complaint see the *Two Treatises of Government*, II paras 215–216.

That this grievance was so keenly felt suggests that Jefferson considered that no part of the government process can be acceptable if 'the people' are not able to choose their preferred lawmakers at regular intervals. In the absence of this power of choice, the people could not have 'consented' to the laws under which they were governed, and therefore those laws could not be 'just'.

Yet a third category of complaints seems to suggest that there were some laws to which 'the people' could not give their consent even if they wished to. The Americans were outraged, for example, that Britain had subjected them to laws which; 'depriv[ed] us in many cases of the benefits of Trial by Jury' and 'transport[ed] us beyond seas to be tried for pretended offences'. The presumption that one's guilt in criminal matters be established by a jury of one's peers, and that the scope of the criminal law be clear and stable, were seemingly regarded as fundamental principles of social organisation by the colonists. One might attach similar importance to Jefferson's claim that the British King had:

> 'obstructed the Administration of Justice, by refusing his Assent to Laws for establishing Judiciary powers. He has made Judges dependent on his Will alone, for the tenure of their offices, and the amount and payment of their salaries.'

But it is perhaps easier to identify precisely those aspects of government behaviour which the revolution was fought against, than those it was fought for. The rhetoric of 'All men being created equal' and sharing 'inalienable rights to life, liberty and the pursuit of happiness' is beguiling, almost perhaps bewitching. We might (again intuitively) regard such sentiments as integral ingredients of a democratic constitutional order. But what do such concepts mean? Their concern, broadly stated, appears to be with the nature both of the legal powers that a government possesses and of the processes through which that power is exercised. The bulk of this book explores those concerns in the British context, but we might first dwell on the answers which Jefferson and his contemporaries offered to these questions.

II. THE FIRST 'MODERN' CONSTITUTION?

The following pages offer a simplistically drawn picture of the constitutional settlement at which the American revolutionaries finally arrived in 1791.[11] It is intended to operate not as a yardstick

---

11 Readers seeking a more detailed introduction might usefully refer to McKay D (1989) *American Politics and Society* chs 3 and 4 (Oxford: Basil Blackwell).

against which to measure the adequacy of the details of the British constitution, which we will examine in subsequent chapters, but as a comparator which indicates alternative ways in which modern societies might organise their constitutional structures. Whether aspects of the American system are in any sense preferable to features of the British model is an issue to which we shall return in the final chapter.

The problem – majoritarianism

The central principle informing the deliberations of the framers of the American constitution could cynically be described as a pervasive distrust of human nature. This sentiment was best expressed by one of Jefferson's contemporaries, James Madison, in *The Federalist Papers No 10:*

> 'As long as the reason of man continues fallible, and he is at liberty to exercise it, different opinions will be formed. . . . A zeal for different opinions concerning religion, concerning government and [above all] the unequal distribution of property. . . . have, in turn, divided man-kind into parties, inflamed them with mutual animosity, and rendered them much more disposed to vex and oppress each other than to co-operate for their common good.'[12]

Madison saw no merit in trying to suppress diversity of opinion per se. That men would take different views on all manner of questions was an inevitable and indispensable component of both individual and collective liberty. He was however greatly concerned to draw lessons from history concerning the dangers that a country faced from within its own borders by the combination of citizens sharing the same 'vexatious' or 'oppressive' sentiments into distinct political 'factions', a faction being:

> 'a number of citizens, whether amounting to a majority or minority of the whole, who are united and actuated by some common impulse

---

12 *The Federalist Papers* were a collection of essays written by James Madison, Alexander Hamilton and John Jay in the mid- to late-1780s and published in serial form. The US Constitution which exists today was not in fact adopted until 1789, and was the second Constitution which the revolutionaries adopted after having won the War of Independence. *The Federalist Papers* were part of an intense argument between advocates of the new Constitution and defenders of the then extant first Constitution, which was known as the Articles of Confederation. We will examine the perceived inadequacies of the Articles both later in this chapter and in chapter ten.

of passion, or of interest, adverse to the rights of other citizens, or to the permanent and aggregate interests of the community.'[13]

A form of government in which laws were passed to express the wishes of the majority of the population would ensure that any irrational or oppressive schemes favoured by minority factions would not be given legal effect. But, Madison suggested, this 'majoritarian' system of law-making offered no protection to society when oppressive or irrational ideas were favoured by a majority of the population. The mere fact that an idea enjoyed majority support did not necessarily make the idea conducive to the 'public good': majorities might proceed on the basis of false information, be temporarily persuaded to abandon their better judgement by the seductive rhetoric of charismatic leaders, or simply be prepared to sacrifice their country's long-term welfare to gain a short-term, sectional advantage. Consequently, Madison argued that perhaps the most important characteristic of the Constitution he was urging his fellow Americans to adopt was its attempt to ensure that 'the majority . . . be rendered unable to concert and carry into effect schemes of oppression'.

The solutions – representative government, federalism, a separation of powers, and supra-legislative 'fundamental' rights

Madison suggested that the dangers of faction could be reduced by adopting a form of 'representative government', in which laws would be made not directly by the people themselves, but by representatives who the people had chosen to exercise law-making power on their behalf in a legislative assembly. Madison hoped:

'to refine and enlarge the public views by passing them through the medium of a chosen body of citizens, whose wisdom may best discern the true interest of their country and whose patriotism and love of justice will be least likely to sacrifice it to temporary or partial considerations.'

We might take something of a diversion at this point, and wonder how Madison's notions of 'wise' legislators fits with contemporary understandings of 'democratic' government. Let us return to countries A and B, and assume that laws are made not by the people directly, but by 100 legislators who are selected by the people to act on their behalf; a law is enacted if a simple majority of legislators support it. We may further assume that for the

13 *Ibid.*

purposes of selecting its legislators, both countries are divided into electoral districts with equal populations, each of which returns one member to the legislature; all adult citizens have one vote in choosing their representatives, and the legislative seat is won by whichever candidate receives the most votes.

Would we consider the new tax law enacted in country A as democratic if we learned, firstly, that 10 of the 55 legislators who voted for it represented areas where the majority of electors opposed any tax increase, and secondly that the ten legislators concerned had promised their electors they would vote against any such measure? Would it make any difference to our answer if the reason for the 10 legislators' change of heart was the force of the arguments presented in favour of the law during a debate in the legislature prior to the vote? The answer to this question presumably depends on how we would answer the logically pre-cedent question of whether we accept that the role of a legislator is simply to transmit the wishes of her electors into law, or is rather to exercise her judgement as to the 'best' response to particular issues and act accordingly, even if her electors would wish her to reach a different conclusion?

A constitution in which law-making power is delegated or entrusted to a small number of citizens makes the task of judging the democratic nature of laws infinitely more complex, for we immediately become concerned not just with the merits of the particular law per se, but also with the merits of those laws which determine the way that legislators are selected and the ways that they behave during the legislature's law-making process. Might we question the 'democratic' basis of *every* law country A enacted, for example, if it transpired that some electoral districts contained twice as many electors as others, but still returned only one member? Or, to revisit a familiar question, if unemployed people were not allowed to stand for election to the legislature, or were not permitted to vote in the electoral process? Similarly, would a law to the effect that candidates for election were not permitted to advocate large tax increases compromise the constitution's democratic base? Might we also feel uneasy about the law-making process if we learned that many seats in the legislature had been contested by four or five candidates, all of whom attracted approxi-mately equal electoral support, with the result that the winner was voted for by barely 30% of the people in that electoral district?

A less contentious matter, at least from the American revolution-aries' perspective, was the presumption that the people's represen-tatives, once elected, should enjoy unimpeded freedom to discuss any subject they chose, and to cast their law-making votes in any manner they wished. The colonists' aforementioned complaints over British interference with the operation of their colonial legislatures have clear philosophical roots in Locke's suggestion that 'consent' to government demanded that the people's legislature should not be hindered by any legal rules. If prevented:

> 'from assembling in its due time, or from acting freely, pursuant to those ends for which it was constituted, the Legislative is altered. For tis not a certain number of men, no nor their meeting, unless they have also Freedom of Debating, and Leisure of perfecting, what is for the good of the Society wherein the Legislature exists. . . . For it is not Names that Constitute governments, but the use and exercise of those powers that were intended to accompany them . . .'[14]

The issue of representative government invites us to consider further dimensions of the concept of liberty adverted to in the Declaration. Jefferson's condemnation of imprisonment for 'pretended offences' addresses liberty in a physical and individual sense. Yet the Declaration also suggests that liberty bears more abstract and collective meanings, particularly in respect of matters concerning freedom of speech and conscience.

This leads us once again to consider the notion of 'consent' to government. Jefferson and his contemporaries assumed that 'man' was a rational, autonomous being; the preservation of his liberty demanded that 'he' make decisions on the basis of full and accurate knowledge. Consent had to be *informed* consent. The American revolutionaries thus placed a considerable premium on safeguarding individual citizens' freedom of conscience and expression in relation to moral and political matters. Consequently, the restrictions which Britain had placed on the activities of representative colonial legislatures were perceived by the colonists as an intolerable infringement of their collective liberty.

It is readily apparent both that this particular strand of 'liberty' can be compromised in many ways, and that it is intimately tied to our contemporary understandings of 'democratic government'. Would we conclude, for example, that no law made by the legislative assembly of our hypothetical country A could be democratic if it was a criminal offence for any person to reveal details of legislators' speeches or votes on the proposals before them? In such circumstances, electors would not know which legislators had supported or opposed tax increases, and so could not make informed choices as to their preferred candidate at the next election. Would we draw the same conclusion about country

14 Locke *op cit* II para 215.

B if we learned that it was a crime in that society for anyone to
voice criticisms of the laws enacted by the majority in the legislature, with a view to convincing electors to choose different representatives at the next election? The Americans' initial response
to this issue is considered further below,[15] for it is obviously of
major significance to any attempt to gauge the adequacy of the
mechanism through which legislatures are elected.

At this point, however, we might note that Madison's particular
vision of 'representative government' clearly demands that one
accept the desirability of fostering a certain degree of élitism in
one's governors, and as such demands that law-makers ignore the
irrational or oppressive sentiments of the citizens they represent.
But this élitism may substantially dilute the 'representativeness' of
the laws enacted. The preamble to the US Constitution begins
with the words: 'We the people of the United States, in order to
form a more perfect union . . .'. Yet it is evident that 'The People'
who chose the legislators who framed the Constitution comprised
barely 10% of the populace of the colonies.[16] Voters were all male,
almost all were white, and the great majority were atypically well
educated and affluent. The consent of the poor, the uneducated,
and women was not presumed to be necessary to the establishment
of the United States' newly created form of government, seemingly
because the framers of the Constitution doubted that such groups,
which comprised the mass of the populace, could be relied upon
to support rational constitutional provisions.

Such discriminatory principles might lead us to conclude that
the 'consent' which the revolutionaries sought was somewhat
illusory, on the basis that consent should be a universal rather
than selective phenomenon. This question is one to which we will
frequently return in the context of British constitutional history
and practice. Yet we may also consider it prudent to be concerned
with the powers that legislators might wield once they have
assumed (in accordance with whatever notion of popular consent
determines their selection) their law-making powers. Madison
recognised that it was by no means a complete answer to the
spectre of tyranny simply to hope that a system of representative
government, in which legislators were selected by an elitist electorate, would invariably produce rulers who would have the wisdom

---

15 At p 18, fn 1 and accompanying text.
16 See, for contrasting views, Beard C (1990) 'An economic interpretation of the
   Constitution', in Ollman B and Birnbaum J (eds) *The United States Constitution*
   (New York: New York University Press) and Brown R (1987) 'The Beard thesis
   attacked: a political approach', in Levy L (ed) *The Making of the Constitution*
   (New York: OUP).

and capacity always to forswear sectional or irrational objectives favoured by factions of the population. One could not always rely on 'patriotism and love of justice' rather than 'temporary and partial considerations' being the dominant forces in the minds of one's chosen law-making representatives, no matter how carefully they were chosen. Madison considered that it was:

'In vain to say that enlightened statesmen will be able to adjust... clashing interests and render them all subservient to the public good. Enlightened statesmen will not always be at the helm.'[17]

In those circumstances, the problem of majoritarianism was simply displaced from the arena of the 'people' themselves to the much smaller number of citizens who served as legislators. For the designers of the US Constitution, this indicated that preserving 'the public good' might demand that the helmsmen steering the ship of state either be precluded from embarking on voyages to certain undesirable destinations, or at the very least, be subject to constraints that made such journeys very difficult to undertake.

Federalism and the separation of powers

At the time of the revolution, the American colonists' sense of themselves as citizens of a single nation was not well developed. Each colony had been created, in the legal sense, by 'Charters' granted by the British monarchy.[18] These had been awarded at different times, and on rather different terms. In consequence, by 1776, the (then) thirteen colonies (from a British perspective) or States (in the revolutionaries' eyes) had developed distinctive political and social cultures, which were expressed in their respective laws.[19] Yet the colonists also shared many common practical and philosophical concerns. The most pressing was obviously justifying and then succeeding in their revolutionary war against British rule: this was a task that could be achieved only if the colonies acted in a co-ordinated manner, in pursuit of shared objectives; aspects of their individual identities would have to be surrendered to a 'national' military and political project. But having won their independence through such unified action,

---

17 *Federalist Papers No 10*.
18 The grant of Charters was a part of what were known as the Monarch's 'prerogative' powers. We shall examine these powers more closely in chapters 2–4.
19 See Bailyn B (1967) *The Ideological Origins of the American Revolution* pp 191–193 (Cambridge, Mass: Harvard UP). A contemporaneous perspective is offered by Madison in *The Federalist Papers No 39*.

the revolutionaries then faced the dilemma of how best to structure the inter-relationships between the nation, the States and
the people. Their eventual solution was to fashion a 'federal'
constitution.

In the modern era, 'federalism' is a concept that may bear many
meanings. As perceived by the American revolutionaries, their
federal constitution would have the positive virtue of creating a
multiplicity of powerful political societies within a single nation
state, each wielding significant political powers within precisely
defined geographical boundaries. However, the Constitution
placed limits on the political autonomy of each State by granting
sole responsibility for certain types of governmental power to the
newly created national government. Those matters which had
been left within the sole competence of the States, while important
in themselves, were not regarded as crucial to the well-being of
the nation as a whole. It would not therefore be dangerous to
allow the people of each State to devise their own 'internal' constitutional arrangements to determine their respective preferences
on these issues: if they chose to indulge factional sentiment within
their own border, so be it; but their choices would have no legal
force in the other States within the country. Each State could
quite lawfully enact different laws to deal with matters within their
geographical and functional jurisdictions.

The principle underlying the creation of a federal nation again
derives from a particular view of the meaning of 'consent'. It
assumes that a 'people' within which divergent factions held differing views on major (if not fundamental) political matters would
be more likely to agree to live under a constitutional order which
offered many opportunities for those views to be given legal effect
at the same time, albeit within limited geographical areas, than a
system which allowed a majority of the entire population, acting
through a national legislature, to impose its preferences on all
issues on the entire country.

Even if one accepts this principle as desirable, however, there
remains the problem of deciding which powers should be allocated to which level of government. This is a question to which
the many federal constitutions which now exist have given quite
different answers. The American revolutionaries initially adopted
a constitution known as the Articles of Confederation, which gave
virtually no powers to the national government. The Articles were
rejected within ten years, in favour of a new constitutional settlement which granted the national government considerably more

authority.[20] The national government would be empowered to conduct foreign policy, to grant national citizenship, to maintain military forces and wage war, to issue the national currency, to impose customs duties on imported and exported goods, to levy sales taxes (but not income taxes) on a uniform basis throughout the country, to run the nation's postal service and to regulate trade among the States and with foreign nations.[21] The States were not permitted to enact laws concerning these matters.

Thus, if our hypothetical countries A, D and E were organised on the same federal lines as the United States' constitution, country A's central legislature would apparently have been unable to introduce its proposed anti-unemployment law, irrespective of how many legislators supported it, since the constitution seemingly did not give it the power to levy income taxes. Alternatively, if we accepted that the laws introduced by countries D and E were an element of the central legislatures' war powers, they could be enacted even if the majority of people in several of the States heartily disapproved of their contents.

Madison's concern with the dangers of faction and majoritarianism was initially directed at placing limits on the power of national government, acting at the behest either of a majority of the people or a majority of the States,[22] to produce irrational or oppressive laws. This safeguard was to be achieved in part by a further development on the theme of representative government. The Constitution eventually devised a representative form of national government which produced a balance between the people as a whole and the people as citizens of their respective States. The framers of the Constitution created an elaborate separation (or fragmentation) of powers within the institutions of the national government. The national legislature, the Congress, would have two component parts. Seats in the House of Representatives were to be apportioned among the States in proportion to their respective populations. In contrast, each State, irrespective of its population size, would have two members in the Senate. The approval of a majority in both chambers would be required to enact

20 See Jensen M (1990) 'The Articles of Confederation', in Birnbaum and Ollman *op cit*; Levy L (1987) 'Introduction – the making of the Constitution 1776–1789', in Levy *op cit.*
21 Article 1, s 8 and Article 2, s 2.
22 Since the States were not of equal (population) size, the two concepts are not coterminous.

laws.[1] Thus, in simple terms, neither a majority of the States nor a majority of the population could impose its wishes on the other. The dual nature of the national legislature did not however exhaust the fragmentation of power to which the Constitution subjected the national government.

The task of implementing congressional legislation was granted not to the Congress itself, but to a separate, 'executive' branch of government headed by an elected President. In addition to possessing a limited array of personal powers, the President was also afforded a significant role in the legislative process. Measures which attracted majority support in both chambers of Congress would become laws only when signed by the President. Should he refuse his assent to the measure, it would be enacted only if it returned to Congress and was then approved by a two-thirds majority in both the Senate and the House. The President was thus empowered to block the law-making preferences of a *small* Congressional majority, but he could not frustrate the wishes of an *overwhelming* majority in both houses. The Framers' initial distrust of populist sentiment was further emphasised by the electoral arrangements made for choosing the President and the legislators who staffed the two chambers of Congress. While members of the House were to be elected directly by the 'people' of each State, Senators would be selected by each State's own legislative assembly, and the President would be chosen by an 'electoral college' of representatives from each State.

Thus two branches of the national government were to be placed in office by what was in effect an 'electorate within an electorate', whose members might be thought likely to (in Madison's words) 'refine and enlarge the public views'. Madison assumed that this élitist process would much reduce the possibility that the occupants of the most important national government offices would be motivated by 'temporary or partial considerations' when they performed the task of enacting and implementing laws made *within* the boundaries of their respective constitutional competences. But the Constitution took one further step in its efforts to guarantee that the federal and institutional separation of powers which the revolutionaries considered fundamental to the nation's long-term security and prosperity would be preserved against the threat of internal factions, even if that fac-

---

1 Jefferson's aforementioned reiteration of Locke's analysis of the prerequisites of effective legislatures was met by the Constitution's requirements that Congress meet at least once every year, and that its proceedings, including the voting behaviour of its members, be published.

tion should prove to be of sufficient size to control the national law-making process.

Fundamental rights and a supra-legislative constitution

It perhaps sounds fatuous to record that the Americans assumed that their Constitution would function as a 'constituent' document, but as we shall see in chapter two, the point is of considerable significance. The Framers of the Constitution regarded the rules they had created as 'the highest form of law' within American society. The Constitution was to be the source of all governmental powers; its terms identified the fundamental or basic moral and political principles according to which society should be managed.

Federalism was clearly a fundamental political value to the Framers of the Constitution. This was evident not only in the proposed allocation of powers between the national and State governments, but also in the procedures through which the Constitution itself was to gain legal force. As Madison explained in *The Federalist Papers No 39*:

> 'Assent and ratification is to be given by the people, not as individuals composing one entire nation, but as composing the distinct and independent States to which they respectively belong. . . . The act, therefore, establishing the Constitution will not be a *national* but a *federal* act' (original emphasis).

The Constitution would come into being, and the Articles of Confederation disappear, only if at least nine of the 13 States agreed to this new allocation of powers.[2] The States would thus willingly surrender some of their previously existing powers to the national government which they themselves created. An individual State might, if its citizens so wished, refuse to consent to the new Constitution. But once that consent had been given, an individual State would not have the legal authority to take any of those powers back.

Madison and the other architects of the Constitution rejected the Lockean notion of 'divine' law in the sense of considering human beings subservient to a rigid set or rules emanating from a deity. Similarly, they were not persuaded that the moral values which they wished to control the government of their new nation should be subject to an eternally fixed code of 'natural' law, which

---

2 The Articles themselves required that all 13 States assent to any amendment. This had led to suggestion that the Constitution was itself a 'revolution', albeit a peaceful one, fought against the United States' initial constitutional order; see Levy *op cit.* Jensen *op cit.*

could never be altered. They nevertheless concluded that once they had succeeded in identifying the mutually acceptable principles according to which the foundations of government should be laid, those 'fundamental laws' of the United States should enjoy a considerable degree of fixity. There was something very 'special' both about the terms of the Constitution and the process through which it was made. In the aftermath of a War of Independence, in the face of the apparent inadequacies of the Articles of Confederation, the greatest political thinkers of the day gathered together to try to reconcile their disparate philosophies as to the ideal form of government. The moral and political principles expressed in the Constitution had not lightly been arrived at: they were not lightly to be discarded; they were not to be left at the mercy of the ordinary institutions of government.

We have already remarked on the élitist nature of the constitution-making process. It is also evident that the framers possessed a considerable degree of arrogance as to the preferability of their proposed fundamental political and moral values to those that might be held by the majority of the populace. They were not, however, *so* arrogant as to assume that the views they held in 1789–1791 amounted to *eternal* truths, which would control the government of American society for all time.

The federal Congress, the federal President, and the various State governments would all be bodies of limited legal competence: they possessed only those powers which 'the people' had granted to them in the Constitution, and had no capacity to create new powers for themselves. The ultimate, or sovereign legal authority, was 'the people'. If the Congress, or the President, or one or more of the States wished to acquire new powers, they would have to persuade 'the people' to amend the Constitution. The Framers of the Constitution decided that 'the people' would express themselves for this purpose through a special law-making process, involving both the Congress and the States, which demanded extremely large majorities in favour of change. Article 5 of the Constitution permits amendments only if the change attracts the support of a two-thirds majority of both houses of Congress[3] *and* three quarters of the states.[4]

'The people' was therefore not a law-making body that would be in constant, or even regular, session. It would act only on those

---

3 Ie the majority needed to overcome a presidential veto in the ordinary legislative process.
4 This somewhat oversimplfes the position, but the description is adequate for our limited purposes.

rare occasions when the overwhelming majority of members of Congress, and an even larger majority of the States, considered that the time had come for aspects of the country's fundamental laws to be altered.

The Constitution was in fact substantially altered almost as soon as it was introduced, although this initiative might more sensibly be regarded as the final stage of the original settlement rather than a rejection of its initial premises. The Constitution was adopted by the requisite number of States on the assumption that Congress' first task would be to formulate amendment proposals to send to the States for their approval.

Ten amendments, colloquially referred to as the 'Bill of Rights', were introduced in 1791. The first eight amendments listed a series of individual liberties (clearly much influenced by the litany of complaints in the Declaration) with which the institutions of national government could not interfere. These need not be listed in their entirety here, but we might note some of their most important provisions. The First Amendment precluded Congress from enacting laws which abridged freedom of speech, the freedom of the press, and freedom of religious belief.[5] The Fourth Amendment forbade national government officials from conducting arbitrary searches of citizens' houses and seizure of their possessions. The Fifth Amendment prevented the national government from appropriating citizens' property, or interfering with their lives or liberty, without 'due process of law', and required that just compensation be paid if such property was taken for public use. The Fifth and Sixth Amendments in combination guaranteed the right to trial by jury in criminal cases,[6] granted the accused the right to legal representation, and excused her from having to provide self-incriminatory evidence; while the Eight Amendment prohibited the infliction of 'cruel and unusual punishments'.

Madison and his supporters had initially argued that the 'Bill of Rights' was superfluous. Congress and the Presidency possessed only those powers which the Constitution had granted them. Since no powers had been given to infringe the 'liberties' later listed in the Bill of Rights, the Constitution implicitly forbade the national government acting in such a manner. The Madisonian 'faction' was later convinced that giving such liberties explicit protection

5 A provision which would call into question the legality of the censorship law enacted by country D.
6 A provision which might conceivably preclude enactment of country E's arbitrary imprisonment law.

was a beneficial course to follow. In part this shift of position was for the tactical reason of assuaging opposition to the new Constitution and thereby facilitating its adoption. However Madison also accepted that the Bill of Rights would have an intrinsic, declaratory value, by laying further emphasis on the basic moral principles the revolution had been fought to defend. These provisions themselves could of course only be altered or abolished in future in accordance with the Article 5 amendment process.

The importance which the Framers accorded to maximising the political autonomy of the States within the Constitution's federal structure is illustrated by their decision to apply the provisions of the Bill of Rights only against the national government, not against the States. If the people of the States wished to impose similar restraints on their respective State governments, they were free to do so. But they were equally free not to do so. Madison himself, once he accepted the desirability in principle of the Bill of Rights, had favoured its extension to State as well as Federal governments. He found little support for this argument either in Congress or among the States; nothing in the text of the first eight amendments indicated that they were to control the States as well as Congress and the Presidency.

The constitutional role of the Supreme Court

The Constitution could be no more than a framework document. It sought to outline the broad principles within which the government process should be conducted, not to promulgate detailed rules which would provide answers to every forseeable (or unforseeable) problem that might arise. The framers anticipated that there would frequently be ambiguity in respect of the national/State separation of powers, over such questions for example as whether a particular State measure affected commerce among the States,[7] or touched only on matters internal to the State.[8] Alternatively, within the context of the Bill of Rights, doubt might arise as to whether a Congressional law or Presidential action 'abridged the freedom of the press', or imposed a 'cruel and unusual punishment', or infringed rights of property without following the 'due process of law'. The framers entrusted the task of answering such questions to the United States Supreme Court.

The intended role of the Supreme Court was outlined by Alexander Hamilton in *The Federalist Papers No 78*. Hamilton envisaged

---

7 And so represented an unconstitutional State intrusion into federal competence.
8 And was thus within the States' competence.

that the court would serve as the ultimate arbiter of the meaning of the Constitution. 'The people' had intended that the Constitution would impose agreed limitations on the powers of government bodies, and in Hamilton's view:

'Limitations of this kind can be preserved in practice no other way than through the medium of courts of justice, whose duty it must be to declare all acts contrary to the manifest tenor of the Constitution void.'

The court would therefore stand:

'between the people and the legislature, to keep the latter within the limits assigned to their authority. . . . A constitution is, in fact, and must be regarded by the judges as fundamental law . . . the Constitution ought to be preferred to the [legislature's] statute, the intention of the people to the intention of their agents.'

But Hamilton took care to stress that this did not mean that the Supreme Court was to be in any sense 'superior' to the Congress:

'It only supposes that the power of the people is superior to both, and that where the will of the legislature [or the Presidency] . . . stands in opposition to that of the people, the judges ought to be governed by the latter and not the former.'

Unlike the Presidency, the legislature, or the States, the court had 'neither sword nor purse'; the effectiveness of its judgments would depend not on any coercive power, but on their legitimacy, which we may construe as their capacity to convince the citizenry that they were in conformity with the meaning of the Constitution.

Great care would thus have to be exercised in selecting the judges who sat on the Supreme Court, for they bore a heavy constitutional burden. Hamilton suggested that:

'There can be but few men in the society who will have sufficient skill in the laws to qualify them for the stations of judges. And making the proper deductions for the ordinary depravity of human nature, the number must be still smaller of those who unite the requisite integrity with the requisite knowledge.'

The Constitution did not specify either the intellectual or moral qualifications that Supreme Court nominees should possess, but involved both the President and the Senate in their selection. The President would nominate candidates for judicial office, but his nominees could assume their seats only after receiving the approval of the Senate. The President could thus not 'pack' the court with appointees who did not enjoy the confidence of the legislature, although it would of course be possible for a President and Senate majority who adhered to the same faction to do so.

Hamilton had placed much emphasis on a pre-revolutionary custom or tradition, developed (as we shall see in chapter three) within the British constitution, but corrupted in the colonies, that both politicians and the judiciary themselves should regard the courts' 'interpretation' of the law (be it a provision of the constitution, or a statute, or the common law) as a matter above and beyond factional politics. Politicians should thus forswear considerations of personal or party advantage in selecting members of the judiciary, while the judges themselves should exclude such considerations from their judgments.

But the Framers did not rely solely on Presidential and Congressional self-restraint to safeguard the independence of the Supreme Court. Once the judges were in office, neither the President nor the Congress would be able to remove them simply because they disapproved of the decisions the court subsequently reached. Unless convicted of criminal offences, or guilty of grossly immoral behaviour, Supreme Court justices were to enjoy lifetime tenure, with payment of their salaries expressly guaranteed in the Constitution itself.[9]

The enormous power and responsibility entrusted to the Supreme Court under the American Constitution can be illustrated by returning to our hypothetical nations. It was suggested earlier that if countries A, D and E had federal constitutions modelled on the initial American settlement, country A's tax-raising law would have been illegal as the national legislature had no power to levy income tax. In contrast, the imprisonment and censorship measures enacted in nations D and E would be constitutional as these actions were part of the legislature's war powers.

Let us suppose, however, that the Supreme Court of country A concluded that the law in question was in reality a measure to regulate commerce among the nation's various States (a matter clearly within the national legislature's competence) by stimulating economic growth, and the tax thereby raised was merely an incidental side effect. As such, the measure would be constitutional. Similarly let us suppose that the Supreme Court of country D decided that the censorship measure contravened the free speech clause of the First Amendment, while in country E the Supreme Court held that the law introducing indefinite imprisonment without trial amounted to cruel and unusual punishment and thereby breached the Eighth Amendment. Would we conclude that such judgments represented a judicial attempt to

---

9 Provisions which obviously met the Declaration's aforementioned complaints as to the pre-revolutionary judiciary's lack of independence.

subvert the fundamental principles of the Constitution, or that they were merely a rather surprising but nevertheless defensible interpretation of an ambiguous constitutional text?

It would be quite misleading to suggest that Supreme Court decisions which frustrated the wishes of the elected Congress or President were necessarily 'undemocratic' simply because the judges themselves were not elected officials. Such accusations would have conclusive force only if one equates 'democracy' with a constitutional order which gives unfettered supremacy to the wishes of a legislative majority. They would be considerably less convincing if one took a view of 'democracy' which entailed the protection of 'higher laws' against the possibly transient and ill-informed views of the greater number of one's legislators. Within that constitutional context, accusations of 'anti-democratic' conduct might just as readily be levelled at the elected politicians who were apparently seeking to subvert the wishes of 'the people' from whom their powers derived. This is however a question, like many of the others broached in this chapter, that can sensibly only be raised, and not in any meaningful sense answered, at this early stage.

CONCLUSION

Two hundred and twenty years ago, it took a revolutionary war for the American colonists to rid themselves of what they considered to be an unacceptable constitutional order. The new Constitution which the United States subsequently fashioned marked a radical departure from traditional British understandings of the appropriate way for a country to regulate the relationship between its people and its government: its principles have been widely copied by many nations who have created or redesigned their own constitutional arrangments in the modern era. Lest it be assumed that the Americans created an 'ideal' constitutional order, we might note that the Framers preserved the institution of negro slavery by leaving its abolition to the individual States. Thus while slaveowners had 'property' (guaranteed by the Fifth Amendment) in their slaves, slaves themselves enjoyed no inalienable rights, either of a physical or spiritual nature. Jefferson, for whom all men were supposedly created equal, was himself a slave-owner. And those framers who found slavery morally abhorrent preferred to tolerate its continued existence in the Southern States rather than take the risk that some States would reject the new constitutional settlement.[10]

But, as we shall begin to see in chapter two, the contemporary British constitution retains many important elements of the system which the Americans rejected as tyrannical and oppressive in 1776. In modern Britain, there is no likelihood of a violent revolution to overhaul our constitutional arrangements. The country has, by and large,[11] avoided the difficulties posed by armed conflict between factions of its population for over three hundred years. For some observers, that basic political reality might be sufficient grounds for concluding that there is no need even to question the adequacy of the constitution, still less to expend energy on proposals advocating fundamental or even partial reforms to its substance. Yet as we approach the end of the twentieth century, the workings of the constitution are the subject of wide-ranging and critical debate. We will examine the sources and nature of that debate throughout the remainder of this book. The modest objective of this opening chapter has been to identify some of the general ideas we might use to evaluate Britain's existing constitutional arrangements. In chapter two, we turn to what many commentators regard as perhaps the most important part of Britain's constitutional heritage – the doctrine of parliamentary sovereignty.

10 See particulary Madison's *Federalist Papers No 54*: Du Bois W (1990) 'Slavery and the Founding Fathers', in Ollman and Birmbaum *op cit*; Kelly A, Harbison W and Belz H (1983) *The American Constitution* ch 14 (New York: W W Norton).
11 As noted in the preface, this book does not address the history of Britain's relationship with Ireland in any systematic way. That history does of course demand that we qualify the notion of internal peace to an appreciable extent.

CHAPTER TWO

Parliamentary sovereignty

For the purposes of analysing the way that constitutions work, it might be helpful to think of 'laws' as a formal way in which a 'democratic' society expresses its consent to the way in which it is governed. If we recall the references made to the American revolution in chapter one, we might say that the US Constitution is a clear example of a society making fundamental changes to its legal and political structures because its people no longer consented to their existing form of government.

The foundations of the USA's constitution reflect its architects' commitment to what is now regarded in many modern western societies as a basic, if contentious, point of democratic theory. Simply put, that principle asserts that in a democratic nation, the more important that a particular law is to the way that society is governed, the more difficult it should be for that law to be changed. One might suggest the reason for this is that it would be undesirable for fundamental features of the way in which a country is run to be vulnerable to reform in a way which does not attract the 'consent' of the governed. The difficult questions that face designers of modern constitutions are: firstly, how much importance should one ascribe to particular values; secondly, how much consent should one need to change those values; and thirdly, in what ways should that consent be expressed?

As noted in chapter one, most of the terms of the United States' Constitution can only be amended with the consent of two-thirds of the members of the federal Congress and the legislatures of three-quarters of the fifty states. Because this level of consent is quite difficult to obtain, the Federal Constitution has been amended fewer than thirty times in over two hundred years. This degree of permanence might justifiably lead us say that the Constitution marks out stable and predictable legal boundaries which define the nature of the American people's consent to the powers of their government. This does not mean that the USA's

Constitution invariably prevents a tyranny of the majority – but it does preclude a tyranny of *small* majorities.

It is also the case that most law-making in the USA takes place *within* the boundaries of consent outlined by the Constitution. These laws affect issues which are not fundamental to society's basic values, and so can be changed in less difficult ways. Some can be altered by the Congress, some fall within the remit of individual States. A straightforward majority vote in the particular legislature is often enough to change those parts of the law which are not regarded as fundamental to society's welfare.

Pre-1688 – natural or divine law

The American system seeks to protect fundamental values by making their reform subject to a cumbersome law-making process requiring extremely high levels of popular consent. An analysis of early seventeenth century English case law reveals several judgments in which the courts suggested that were certain values that were *so fundamental* to the English constitution that they could not be changed by any process at all. These principles are perhaps analogous to the 'inalienable rights' of which Thomas Jefferson spoke in the US Declaration of Independence. Some judges seemed ready to suggest that there was a system of 'natural law' or 'divine law' which placed limits on what the various branches of government might do.

For example in *Dr Bonham's Case*[1] in 1610, Chief Justice Coke had said: 'When an Act of Parliament is against common right or reason, or repugnant, or impossible to be performed, the common law will control it, and adjudge such Act to be void'. Five years later, in *Day v Savadge*,[2] Chief Justice Hobart felt able to conclude that: 'even an Act of Parliament, made against natural equity, as to make a man judge in his own case, is void in itself'. Similarly in the 1653 case of *R v Love*,[3] Keble J had pronounced that: 'Whatsoever is not consonant to the law of God, or to right reason which is maintained by scripture, . . . be it Acts of Parliament, customs, or any judicial acts of the Court, it is not the law of England'.

The facts of these cases need not detain us here. The only point one would want to stress is that there was a time in British

1 (1610) 8 Co Rep 107a at 118a.
2 (1614) Hob 85.
3 (1653) 5 State Tr 825.

constitutional history when it seems that it was widely believed that there were basic moral or political principles that it was not within the power of any number of the people, through any type of law-making process, to change in any way at all.[4]

The Diceyan theory

Such beliefs do not appear to play any part in modern constitutional theory. We no longer seem to recognise the natural law doctrines of the seventeenth century. And unlike the Americans, we have not accepted that our fundamental constitutional values should be safeguarded by a complex and difficult amendment process. The 'basic principle' of the British constitution can be summed up in a fairly bald statement. A statute, that is a piece of legislation produced by Parliament, is generally regarded as the highest form of law within the British constitutional structure. The British Parliament, it is said, is a *sovereign law-maker*.

In describing this concept of parliamentary sovereignty, we are drawing mainly on two sources. The first is the political events of the late seventeenth century, when England experienced its last civil war. The second is a legal theory articulated in the late nineteenth century by an Oxford law professor, A V Dicey. We will return to the late seventeenth century shortly; but it is helpful to begin by looking at Dicey's legal theory.

Dicey wields an enormous influence on British constitutional law. This is in many senses rather unfortunate. Some of Dicey's political views would be considered a little bizarre today. He certainly did not approve of democracy as we understand it. For example, he was very much opposed to allowing women or the working class to vote in Parliamentary elections.[5] Nevertheless, it

4 The cautious language indicates that commentators hold divergent views as to the principles that Coke and his fellow judges were espousing. Several analysts have suggested that *Bonham* is merely advancing an unusual rule of statutory interpretation; see Thorne S (1938) '*Dr Bonham's case I.QR* 543–552; Plucknett T (1928) '*Doctor Bonham's Case* and judicial review' *Harvard LR* 30–70. In contrast see Dike C (1976) 'The case against Parliamentary Sovereignty' *Public Law* 283–297; Maitland F (1908) *The Constitutional History of England* (Cambridge: CUP) at p 300: 'It is always difficult to pin Coke to a theory, but he does seem to claim distinctly that the common law is above the statute'.

5 See McEldowney J (1985) 'Dicey in historical perspective', in McAuslan P and McEldowney J (eds) *Law, Legitimacy and the Constitution* (London: Sweet and Maxwell); Loughlin M (1992) *Public Law and Political Theory* ch 7 (Oxford: Clarendon Press).

is important to understand the basic features of his theory. Dicey suggested that the concept of parliamentary sovereignty has two parts – a positive limb and a negative limb.

The positive and negative limbs of Dicey's theory

The idea contained in the *positive limb* is that Parliament can make or unmake any law whatsoever. If a majority of members of the House of Commons vote in favour of a particular Bill, and this is then approved by both the House of Lords and the Monarch, that Bill becomes an Act, irrespective of its contents. In technical legal terms there are no limits to the substance of statute law; Parliament can make any law that it wishes. Nor does it matter how big the majority in each house is for a particular measure; an Act passed by a majority of one in both the House of Commons and the House of Lords is as authoritative as legislation which receives unanimous support.

The proposition advanced in the *negative limb* is that the legality of an Act of Parliament cannot be challenged in any British court. There is no mechanism within the British constitution for declaring an Act of Parliament legally invalid in any sense. So adherents to Dicey's theory clearly reject the idea that the courts could invoke natural law or divine law to say that a statute was 'unconstitutional'. In the Diceyan theory of the Constitution, there is no higher form of law than the will of Parliament as expressed in the text of an Act.

These two propositions, the negative and positive limbs of Dicey's theory, seem to offer us a simple and straightforward principle upon which to base an analysis of the Constitution. As we examine the subject of parliamentary sovereignty further, it will become evident that the picture is not quite as clear cut as the orthodox theory might lead us to believe. But before examining the criticisms of this orthodox theory, it is useful to devote some attention to the sources on which contemporary adherents to Dicey's thesis rely to support his arguments. Why does it seem that statute is the highest form of law in modern Britain?

The political source of parliamentary sovereignty – the 'glorious revolution'

When trying to make sense of contemporary constitutional practice, it is often helpful to turn our attention to the events of 1688.

One might immediately sound a note of warning here. Readers might quite reasonably ask why events that happened over three hundred years ago, in a pre-industrial society, where hardly anybody had the right to vote, should be regarded as relevant to shaping the constitutional structure of a modern, industrialised and apparently democratic country. That is a question to which we shall constantly be returning in later chapters. For the present, we will simply focus on the question of what is, rather than what should be, and so adopt (briefly) a formalist rather than functionalist approach to our subject.

The central theme of seventeenth-century British political history is a struggle for power between the House of Commons and House of Lords and the Monarchy. In its most acute form, the conflict produced civil war, the execution of Charles I, the brief rule of Oliver Cromwell, the restoration of Charles II to the throne, followed by the overthrow of his brother, James II in 1688, and the installation of William of Orange and his wife Mary as joint monarchs.[6] But in less dramatic terms, seventeenth-century England had been continually beset by squabbles between the King, the Commons and the Lords as to the extent of their respective powers. This argument was waged as frequently in the courts as on the battlefield: both the King and the respective houses of Parliament hoped that the courts would supply rulings which favoured their own preferences. As we shall see in chapter four, the courts tended to switch their allegiance in these disputes as expediency and principle demanded. But on some occasions they struck an independent line; in the natural or divine law cases mentioned earlier, the judges were effectively saying that neither Acts of Parliament nor the actions of the Monarch were supreme. Both were subject to the laws of God and nature, and of course only the judges could identify the content of these immutable principles. In functionalist terms, adoption of this principle would have made the judiciary the 'highest source of law' within the English constitution.

Such reasoning did not commend itself to the Stuart Monarchs, who were firm believers in the doctrine of the divine right of

6 It is not possible to examine the details of this period in any depth in this book. Readers might usefully refer to the following sources for further information: Russell C (1971) *The Crisis of Parliaments* (Oxford: Clarendon Press); Hutton R (1985); *The Restoration* (Oxford: Clarendon Press); Underdown D (1985) *Revel, Riot, and Rebellion* (Oxford: Clarendon Press); Speck W (1986) *Reluctant Revolutionaries* (Oxford: Clarendon Press). A useful, succinct guide to the events of 1688 itself is provided in Miller J (1983) *The Glorious Revolution* (London: Longman)

kings. The doctrine placed complete legal authority in the person
of the King himself. James I explained the rationale behind this
theory thus in 1610:

> 'Kings are not only God's lieutenants on earth . . . but even by God
> himself they are called Gods. . . . [T[hey exercise a manner or resem-
> blance of divine power on earth . . . they make and unmake their
> subjects; they have power of raising and casting down; of life and of
> death; judges over all their subjects, and in all causes, and yet account-
> able to none but God only.'[7]

James I would have rejected any assertion that this claimed power
amounted to tyranny, for he considered himself bound by an oath
he took upon his coronation to exercise his powers in accordance
with the laws of the land. Yet since he also claimed the power to
alter such laws at will, the substantive value of the oath was somewhat limited. The previous Tudor dynasty, in which the foundations of a recognisably modern government structure were laid,[8]
had make no such sweeping claims. Nor, as a consequence, was
James' doctrine uncontested by the House of Commons and the
House of Lords. Both bodies invoked constitutional principles of
considerable antiquity to place limits on the Stuart kings' effective
legal powers.

Since the signing of the Magna Carta in the thirteenth century
it had been accepted that the King could not levy taxation without
'Parliament's' approval.[9] Magna Carta could be compared to the
American revolution in some respects. Both events represented a
severe rupture in the fabric of society's previously dominant political values. They signalled that the present government no longer
commanded the consent of 'the people', and they led to the
digging of new political foundations upon which the constitution's
legal structure was based. This is not to suggest that Magna Carta
was in any sense a democratic document as we understand the
term.[10] It simply transfered some powers from one person, the

7 See Plucknett T (11th edn, 1960) Taswell-Langmead's *English constitutional history* pp 329–333 (London: Sweet and Maxwell).
8 See Elton G (1953) *The Tudor Revolution in Government* (Cambridge: CUP);
Loach J (1990) *Parliament under the Tudors* (Oxford: Clarendon Press).
9 Article 14 of Magna Carta. 'Parliament' did not then exist in a recognisably
modern form; Article 14 refers to 'the archbishops, bishops, abbots, earls, and
greater barons, by writ addressed to each severally, and all other tenants *in
capite* by a general writ addressed to the sheriff of each shire'. One can discern
here the outline of the subsequent distinction between the House of Lords and
the House of Commons.
10 Professor John Millar argued for example that Magna Carta was intended 'to
establish the privileges of a few individuals. A great tyrant on one side [King

King, to the handful of aristocrats who effectively controlled 'Parliament'.[11] Nevertheless, we would have to accept that it broadened, albeit very slightly, the basis of consent required to make law in English society. The Monarch's grip on the reins of constitutional power remained particularly firm because she retained the personal legal power (or 'prerogative') to summon and dissolve Parliament as and when she thought fit.

By the seventeenth century the Commons and Lords had become increasingly reluctant to give approval for the levying of taxes without a guarantee that the Monarch accepted certain limits on his personal powers. Although (as we shall see in chapter four) the Stuart Monarchs on occasion found ways to subvert this principle, Charles II and James II had generally sought to govern the country by proclamation or prerogative powers, bypassing Parliament and entrusting the administration of government to their own appointees. To a degree it was feasible for a Monarch to do this; the difficulty arose whenever the Crown needed money above and beyond its own resources – whenever it wanted to go to war for example.

The Triennial Act of 1641 was a measure passed by Parliament which purportedly required the Monarch to summon Parliament at least once every three years. Yet following the restoration of the Stuart Monarchy in 1660, Charles II did not regard himself as obliged to obey its terms. The long-term causes of the 1688 revolution are many and varied, and cannot sensibly be addressed in any detail in this work. It is nevertheless clear that James II's evident contempt for the (admittedly limited) notion of citizen 'consent' to the government process, which was made apparent by his disinclination to allow Parliament to sit on a regular basis,[12] was a major contributor to his eventual downfall. The complaints of the English revolutionaries were outlined in the 1688 'Declaration of Right'. The broad thrust of the Declaration of Right was that:

'the late King James, by the assistance of diverse evill councellors, judges, and ministers imployed by him, did endeavour to subvert and

---

John], and a set of petty tyrants on the other, seem to have divided the kingdom, and the great body of people, disregarded and oppressed on all hands, were beholden for any privileges bestowed on them, to the jealousy of their masters' (1803) *Historical View* vol II pp 80–81, quoted in Loughlin (1992) *op cit* p 7.

11 An accessible introduction both to the events leading to the signing of Magna Carta, and the terms of the document itself, is provided in Plucknett (1960) *op cit* ch 4.

12 See Plucknett (1960) *op cit* pp 524–526.

extirpate the Protestant religion, and the laws and liberties of this kingdom.'

In the same way as the American revolutionaries' Declaration of Independence, the English revolutionaries' Declaration of Right supported its general accusation with a myriad of specific charges, and it seems that the similarities between the two documents extended to matters of substance as well as mere methodology. James II, it was alleged, had infringed upon the 'liberties' of the English people in, inter alia, the following ways:[13]

'By levying money for and to the use of the Crown by [pretence] of prerogative for other time and in other manner than . . . granted by Parliament;

By assuming and exercising a power of dispensing with and suspending of lawes and the execution of laws without consent to Parliament;

By violating the freedom of elections of members to serve in Parliament;

By raising and keeping a standing army within this kingdom in time of peace without consent of Parliament and quartering soldiers contrary to law;

Corrupt and unqualified persons have been returned and served on juries in trials;

And excessive fines have been imposed and illegal and cruell punishments inflicted.'

The 1688 revolution, like Magna Carta and the Civil War before it, marked the crossing of a political watershed. A new political 'contract'[14] was struck between the Commons, the Lords and the Monarchy, and consequently a new constitutional foundation was laid. In return for the throne, William and Mary accepted that the Crown's ability to govern the English nation though its prerogative powers would be severely limited in future. The Monarch might still be responsible for governing the country, and she could appoint the ministers who would do that job, but those ministers would govern the country according to laws defined by Parliament.

---

13 The following quotations are actually drawn from the Bill of Rights of 1689, the first major statute passed by the post-revolutionary Parliament. The phraseology of the Declaration and the first parts of the Bill are virtually identical; Plucknett (1960) *op cit* pp 447–450.

14 On the notion of the settlement as a 'contract' see Slaughter T (1981) ' "Abdicate"and "contract" in the Glorious Revolution' 24 *The Historical Journal* 323–337; Miller J (1982) 'The Glorious Revolution: "contract" and "abdication" reconsidered' 25 *The Historical Journal* 541–555.

And if Parliament changed the law, the King's government would have to respond accordingly.

The initial 'terms' of the contract were specified in the text of the Bill of Rights produced by the Parliament of 1689. As one might expect, they address directly the complaints made in the Declaration of Right:[15]

'1. That the pretended power of suspending of laws or the execution of laws by regall authority without consent of Parliament is illegal;

13. And that for redresse of all grievances and for the amending, strengthening and preserving of the laws Parliaments ought to be held frequently;

8. That elections of members of Parliament ought to be free;

9. That the freedome of speech, and debates or proceedings in Parliament ought not to be impeached or questioned in any court or place out of Parliament;

4. That levying of money for or to the use of the Crown by pretence of prerogative without grant of Parliament . . . is illegal;

6. That the raising or keeping of a standing army within the kingdom in time of peace unlesse it be with consent of Parliament is against law;

11. That jurors ought to be duly impannelled and returned . . .

10. That excessive bail ought not to be required nor excessive fines imposed nor cruel and unusual punishment inflicted.'

By virtue of their enactment in the Bill of Rights, these moral principles were henceforth to possess a superior legal status to any personal legal powers retained by the Monarchy. Furthermore, in addition to placing the Monarch's prerogative powers beneath statute in the hierarchy of constitutional importance, the 1688 revolution is generally regarded as having settled the question of the relationship between Parliament and the courts. The notion aired in *Dr Bonham's* case and *R v Love* that 'natural' or 'divine' law provided the courts with a constitutional principle of more importance than statute was disregarded. And it was also assumed that the common law was subordinate in terms of its legal authority to legislation. We will examine the constitutional significance of the royal prerogative and the common law in more detail in chapter four; the basic principle one needs to remember at this point is that both are assumed to be less important than statute.

15 The numbers are those used in the Bill itself; they have been re-ordered thematically here.

Despite the evident similarities between the functional under-pinnings of the Declaration of Independence and the Declaration of Right, the English revolutionary settlement expressed in the 1689 Bill of Rights is substantially different from the American settlement articulated in the 1789–1791 Constitution. It is clear, for example, that while the American revolutionaries presumed that sovereignty should lie with the American 'people', their English predecessors assumed that sovereignty would rest with 'Parliament'. Consequently, the terms of the Bill of Rights could not be regarded as a constituent framework for the country's subsequent governance in the legal sense provided for by the Constitution in the United States.

This is not to say that the English revolutionaries were less sincere in the moral principles they expressed than were the Americans. Rather it means that there was nothing 'special' in the legal sense about the terms of the English settlement. Parliament, as the country's sovereign law-making power, was competent to alter, repeal or add to the supposedly 'fundamental' provisions of the Bill of Rights whenever it chose, through exactly the same process as it might enact laws on the most trivial of subjects. The English Bill of Rights was not secured against attack by the national legislature in the same way as its American namesake was protected against infringement by Congress. Parliament was to be the ordinary as well as the extraordinary legislative assembly of the newly created English nation. It would sit in regular, perhaps almost constant session. And it alone would wield all the law-making powers that were subsequently so carefully and elaborately divided by Madison and his colleagues among the Presidency, the Congress, the States and the people of the United States.

Moreover, England was a unitary rather than federal state. If geographically discrete parts of the country wished to be governed in different ways, in order to reflect local traditions or political sentiments, they could do so only with Parliament's permission. It was within Parliament's power to designate the boundaries of any sub-central units of government in England, to determine the powers such bodies might possess, and to specify the manner in which the officials running them were to be appointed or elected. And, of course, Parliament might change its mind on such matters whenever it chose. There were thus to be no constitutional rights which a citizen or group of citizens could expect the English courts to enforce against Parliament, for the wishes of Parliament were 'the highest form of law' known to the English constitution.

That the American revolutionaries framed their rebellion against Britain's post-revolutionary constitution in much the same terms as the architects of that constitution had framed their own complaints against the Stuart Kings some ninety years earlier might suggest that the 1688 settlement had not provided effective protection for 'the liberties of the people'. We might therefore wonder if the sovereignty of Parliament, a constitutional device created to safeguard the nation and its empire against the tyranny of its King, had succeeding merely in transferring tyrannical authority into different hands? In what sense, if any, did the English revolution ensure that the laws of England enjoyed the consent of the governed?

What is (was) 'Parliament'?

The 1688 Parliament was not 'representative' of the English population as we would now understand that term. But it would be rash to dismiss the principles underlying the 1688 settlement too quickly. For in some ways it was based on ideas that we might consider valid today. It is important to clarify what the revolutionaries of 1688 meant by the institution of 'Parliament' for instance Parliament was not a single body, but had three parts, the House of Commons, the House of Lords, and the Monarch. At that time, all three parts of Parliament had equal powers within the law-making process. If one part refused to approve a Bill, that Bill could not become law.

From a modern-day perspective, we might think that the 1688 Parliament simply represented the views of élite groups and effectively excluded the mass of the population from any means of consenting to the law-making process. Nevertheless, many political theorists of the late seventeenth century sincerely believed that a Parliament composed of these three bodies was the most effective way to secure that laws accurately expressed the national interest.[16] We should recall that Jefferson used a very selective definition of 'The People' in the Declaration of Independence; for law-making purposes, many poor men, all women and all slaves were not 'people' in late eighteenth-century America. Similarly, in seventeenth-century England, it was assumed that only the King, the aristocracy, the Church, and the affluent merchant and landowning class which elected members of the House of Commons, had any legitimate role to play in fashioning the laws within which society was governed. Orthodox political theory argued that the

16 See particularly Judson M (1936) 'Henry Parker and the theory of parliamentary sovereignty', in Wittke C (ed) *Essays in History and Political Theory in Honour of Charles Howard McIlwain* (Cambridge, Mass: HUP). For an overview of the debate, on both sides of the Atlantic, see Bailyn *op cit* pp 198–229.

Commons, the Lords, and the Monarch formed the three 'Estates of the Realm'. These estates, acting in concert, were presumed to be the only legitimate arbiters of the national interest.

So the 1688 settlement could be perceived as democratic in a twisted sense of the term; not because it gave all citizens a role in the law-making process, but because it gave such a role to everyone who was presumed to be entitled to participate. This might be seen as a more extreme version of Madison's subsequent advocacy of élitist representative assemblies, staffed only by legislators who could be trusted to act in the national interest. But the 1688 settlement had a further purpose in mind. The objective of the 1688 revolution was to create a 'balanced' law-making process within a 'balanced' constitution.[17] Because Acts of Parliament could only be made if the Commons, Lords, and King were in agreement with each other, the legislature could not produce statutes which represented the interests of only one or two of the three Estates of the Realm.[18] This supposed solution to the problem of potentially tyrannical law-makers did not spring, Athena-like, from the heads of the 1688 revolutionaries. Rather it represented the culmination of a long process of theorisation and practice which had exercised the minds of philosophers and politicians throughout the seventeenth century.[19]

We should also remember that the Parliament of 1688 was not organised along party political lines as it is today. There were some fairly firm party-based alliances among groups of members;[20] but the seventeenth-century Parliament was intended to function as an arena both for local interests to be aired and for discussion of

17 See Vile M (1967) *Constitutionalism and the Separation of Powers* ch 3 (Oxford: Clarendon Press).
18 Contemporary commentators expressed the principle in more hyperbolic language: 'Lest . . . the Crown should lead towards arbitrary government, or the tumultuary licentiousness of the people should incline towards a democracy, the wisdom of our ancestors hath instituted a middle state of nobility. . . . The excellence of this government consists in the due balance of the several constituent parts of it, for if either one of them should be too hard for the other two, there is an actual dissolution of the constitution'; Trenchard J and Moyle W (1697) *An Argument Showing that a Standing Army is Inconsistent with a Free Government*, quoted in Miller J *op cit* p 114.
19 Perhaps the most helpful survey of the ebbs and flows of opinions and events is offered in Sharp A (1983) *Political Ideas of the English Civil War* (London: Longman).
20 Plucknett (1960) *op cit* pp 436–438. For some estimate of the strength of recognisably modern party loyalties in the revolution Parliament see Horwitz H (1974) 'Parliament and the glorious revolution' *Bulletin of the Institute of Historical Research* 36–52; Plumb J (1937) 'Elections to the Convention Parliament of 1689' *Cambridge Historical Journal* 235–254.

national priorities – the House of Commons was initially conceived as the *House of Communities*. Many individual members came to the Commons as representatives not of a political party, but of their town or county.

From a contemporary perspective, one might readily ask how the formal structure of our constitution has responded to changing definitions of 'the people', and to what we might call the growing 'nationalisation' of politics? As chapter seven will explain, it is now a fundamental tenet of modern British society that virtually every adult is entitled to vote in Parliamentary elections. It is also clear that Parliamentary elections are contested by nationally organised politically parties, and are won and lost primarily on national rather than local issues. It might seem obvious that a constitutional structure designed to adduce the consent of a tiny minority of the small population of an agrarian country would be ill-suited to securing the consent of some forty million people in a modern industrialised society. It is perhaps instructive to observe for instance that no other modern democracy has fully copied the British constitutional model: the American system has proved much the more influential blueprint. But in many respects, our formal constitutional principles remain largely unchanged today. And it is probably accurate to say that parliamentary sovereignty is the most important of those unchanged principles. It is therefore important that we begin to consider the ways in which the doctrine has been both criticised and vindicated in rather more recent times.

I. LEGAL AUTHORITY FOR THE PRINCIPLE OF PARLIAMENTARY SOVEREIGNTY

As mentioned earlier, our constitution no longer seems to offer any role for the courts to invoke natural law or common law as having a higher constitutional status than Acts of Parliament. One must look very hard indeed to find any suggestion that after 1688 the courts entertained the idea that statutes might be struck down if they conflicted with natural or divine law. The 1701 case of *City of London v Wood*[21] offers some, albeit confused, support for the *Bonham* principle. At one point in his judgment, Holt CJ argued that:

---

21 (1701) 12 Mod 669 at 687. A very helpful discussion of the case is offered in Plucknett (1928) *op cit.*

'What my Lord Coke says in *Dr Bonham's Case* is far from any extravagancy, for it is a very reasonable and true saying, that if an Act of Parliament should ordain the same person should be party and judge, it would be a void Act of Parliament.'

But having offered this apparent support for Coke's ideas, Holt CJ continued by concluding that 'an Act of Parliament can do no wrong, though it may do several things that look pretty odd'. So contradictory a judgment cannot be considered a powerful authority for natural law ideas. Nor can one find more helpful precedents in later post-revolutionary case law:[1] the principle was last seen in *Forbes v Cochrane* in 1824, when the court suggested it would not enforce a law permitting slavery, as this would be 'against the law of nature and God'.[2]

On the other hand, one will not find much case law prior to 1800 which lends explicit support to the idea of parliamentary sovereignty. In his celebrated *Commentaries*, first published in 1765, Blackstone drew the following conclusion about the constitutional status of legislation:

'I know it is generally laid down . . . that acts of parliament contrary to reason are void. But if the parliament will positively enact a thing to be done which is unreasonable, I know of no power that can control it . . . for that were to set the judicial power above that of the legislature, which would be subversive of all government.'[3]

As we saw in chapter one, the American colonists were contemporaneously trying to fashion a constitutional order which avoided the problem of subversion by setting the power of the people above both legislature and judiciary. Blackstone was manifestly unimpressed by such theorisation, but one might also note that he could find little direct judicial authority for his proposition as to Parliament's supremacy.[4] The dearth of authority may be because everybody took it for granted that this was the way things were; sometimes the most important values are those which go unspoken and therefore unexamined. But that may be a rash assumption to make. However several strands of case law supporting the concept of parliamentary sovereignty appear in the nineteenth century.

---

1 Readers interested in exploring the esoterica of post-revolutionary natural law jurisprudence might consult *R v Cumberland County Inhabitants* (1795) 6 Term Rep 194, and *Leigh v Kent* (1789) 3 Term Rep 362.
2 (1824) 2 B & C 448.   3 Vol I at p 91.
4 One might point to a by no means unambiguous endorsement of this position in *The Duchess of Hamilton's* case (*Thornby d Hamilton (Duchess) v Fleetwood*) (1712) 10 Mod 114. A stronger authority appears in *R v Great Chart Inhabitants* (1742) SC 194, 2 Stra 1173.

The first strand deals with what has been termed 'the enrolled Bill rule'.

Substance or procedure? The enrolled Bill rule

The respondent in *Edinburgh and Dalkeith Rly Co v Wauchope*[5] was a landowner affected by a private Act of Parliament authorising construction of a railway. He claimed that the court should invalidate the legislation because its promoters had not given notice to affected parties in accordance with the House of Commons' standing orders which regulated its internal procedures in respect of such measures. Giving judgment, Lord Campbell thought that assessing the constitutional adequacy of proceedings in either the Commons or the Lords was entirely beyond the court's powers:

> 'All that a court . . . can do is to look to the Parliamentary Roll: if from that it should appear that a Bill has passed both Houses and received the Royal Assent, no court . . . can inquire into the mode in which it was introduced . . . or what passed . . . during its progress in its various stages through Parliament.'[6]

A similar conclusion was reached by the court in the factually similar case of *Lee v Bude and Torrington Junction Rly Co* where Willes J commented that: 'if an Act of Parliament has been obtained improperly it is for the legislature to correct it by repealing it; but so long as it exists as law, the Courts are bound to obey it'.[7]

This principle was also forcefully restated by the House of Lords in the 1974 case of *British Railways Board v Pickin*.[8] The facts of *Pickin* are very similar to the *Wauchope* and *Lee* litigation. Mr Pickin alleged that British Rail had steered a private Bill through Parliament without giving the necessary notices to affected landowners, and had also misled Parliament about the Bill's intentions. Somewhat surprisingly, the Court of Appeal thought this raised a triable issue: Lord Denning indicated that he thought one could draw a valid distinction between public Bills and private Bills.[9] But that view was rapidly overruled by the House of Lords. Lord Reid was quite explicit in denying that the courts had any power to question the legality of a Bill's passage through Parliament. He thought any such investigation by the court would bring it into conflict

5 (1842) 8 Cl & Fin 710, 8 ER 279, HL.
6 *Ibid*, at 285.
7 (1871) LR 6 CP 576 at 582.
8 [1974] AC 765.
9 This distinction is addressed in chapter five.

with Parliament. Lord Reid said that he would only do so if compelled to by clear authority, but he was quite certain that: 'the whole trend of authority for over a century is clearly against permitting such an investigation'.[10] In Lord Simon's opinion:

> 'a concomitant of the sovereignty of Parliament is that the houses of Parliament enjoy certain privileges. . . . Among the privileges of the Houses of Parliament is the exclusive right to determine their own proceeding.'[11]

The enrolled bill rule has been widely construed as offering an unambiguous judicial affirmation of the principle of parliamentary sovereignty. Whether this view is analytically defensible (in either formal or functionalist terms) is a question to which we shall return in subsequent chapters. For the moment, attention turns to a second series of cases, setting out what has come to be known as the 'doctrine of implied repeal', which is also presumed to provide similarly unequivocal support for the theory that Parliament enjoys unlimited legal powers.

The doctrine of implied repeal

The two cases we are concerned with here, *Vauxhall Estates Ltd v Liverpool Corpn* (1932) and *Ellen Street Estates Ltd v Minister of Health* (1934)[12] both focused on the Acquisition of Land Act 1919. That Act was a slum-clearance measure which laid down levels of compensation for property owners whose houses were demolished. The Housing Acts of 1925 and 1930 made these compensation provisions less generous. Not suprisingly, the landowners affected looked for some way to have compensation assessed on the basis used in the 1919 Act.

The landowners seized on s 7 of the 1919 Act. This said that any Act affecting compensation provisions would 'cease to have or *shall not have effect*' (emphasis added) if it was inconsistent with the 1919 legislation. That phraseology is arguably looking towards future Acts as well as those already existing. But the plaintiffs did not argue that the 1919 Act was completely protected from amendment by a subsequent Parliament. Instead they drew a *distinction between express and implied repeal.*

The landowners conceded that if a subsequent Act said expressly

10 [1974] AC 765 at 788.
11 [1974] AC 765 at 788–789. We will address the issue of the 'privileges of Parliament' in some depth in chapter eight.
12 [1932] 1 KB 733 and [1934] 1 KB 590, CA, respectively.

that the 1919 Act was overturned, the courts could not challenge the new Act's effect. However, it was argued that the courts could safeguard the 1919 Act against *accidental or implied repeal;* if Parliament did not expressly say it was changing a statute that seemed to have been intended to prevent future amendment, the court should assume that the original Act should be upheld.

This argument seems to be reaching out towards constitutional principles founded on notions of consent theory. It suggests that it would be unconstitutional to allow legislation to have unintended effects because 'the people' could not have knowingly consented to the law that had been passed. This seems to offer a variation on the theme of 'functionalist' approaches to parliamentary sovereignty; if that function is to ensure that laws enjoy the consent of the governed, it would be logical to assume that the courts should not permit Parliament to enact legislation premised on false information.

The argument reached the Court of Appeal in *Ellen Street* – where it was uncategorically dismissed. The courts rejected any notion of a functionalist interpretation of the parliamentary sovereignty doctrine. The judges adopted instead a 'formalist approach' to parliamentary sovereignty. That formal rule simply demanded that the courts unquestioningly obey the most recent Act of Parliament. And if that Act appeared inconsistent with previous legislation, the previous legislation must give way.[13] Questions about the existence of the people's consent, or Parliament's unspoken intentions, were not something the courts were prepared to entertain.

Despite the vigour with which the Court of Appeal delivered its opinion, it could not draw on much past case law to support its proposition. The main precedent it relied on was the decision in *Vauxhall Estates* two years earlier. That seems a flimsy legal base on which to build so important a constitutional principle as parliamentary sovereignty.[14] We can however find a further line of supportive decisions in cases dealing with the relationship between British statutes and international law.

13 The rule is sometimes expressed in the Latin maxim 'lex posterior derogat priori' (a later Act overrules an earlier one).
14 See Marshall G (1954) 'What is Parliament? The changing concept of Parliamentary Sovereignty' *Political Studies* 193–209. There is also some ambiguity in Maugham LJ's judgment, in that he suggests implied repeal will only be effective 'if Parliament chooses to make it plain that the earlier statute is being to some extent repealed' [1934] 1 KB 590 at 597. This suggests implied repeal will apply in situations where the later Act 'envelops' the former, but not when there is simply an 'overlap' of inconsistent provisions.

Inconsistency with international law

The first case we might consider is *Mortensen v Peters*,[15] decided in 1906. One of the most important areas of international law relates to defining the extent of a country's jurisdiction over the oceans by which it is surrounded. By 1906, most nations had accepted that their respective jurisdictions should extend for some three miles from their coastline and had signed treaties with each other to that effect. In 1899, the British Parliament passed the Herring Fishery (Scotland) Act. This Act gave Scotland's Fishery Board the power to make byelaws to control fishing in the Moray Firth. Much of the Moray Firth is more than three miles from land, so the 1899 Act would seem to be inconsistent with international law to which Britain was supposedly a party.

Mortensen was the captain of a Norwegian trawler. He was arrested for breaching the bye-laws that the Fishery Board had made. His defence was that the Act was 'unconstitutional' because it breached accepted international standards, and therefore could not have any legal effect. The court peremptorily dismissed this argument:

> 'In this Court we have nothing to do with . . . whether an act of the legislature is *ultra vires* as in contravention of generally acknowledged principles of international law. For us, an Act of Parliament duly passed by Lords and Commons and assented to by the King, is supreme, and we are bound to give effect to its terms.'[16]

This conclusion is entirely consistent with both traditional Diceyan theory and the political outcome of the 1688 revolution. Under Britain's constitutional arrangements, treaties are negotiated and formally entered into by the Crown (or 'the government') through its prerogative powers, not by Parliament. Orthodox constitutional theory maintains that a treaty signed by the British government can only have legal effect in Britain if it is *incorporated* into British law by an Act of Parliament. This is a logical consequence of the parliamentary sovereignty doctrine. The 1688 revolution produced an agreement between William of Orange and Parliament which provided that the constitutional role of the King's government was to govern within the laws made by Parliament. The

---

15 (1906) 14 SLT 227.
16 *Ibid*, at 230. The term ultra vires literally means 'beyond the legal powers'. If a body is legally sovereign, nothing can be beyond its powers. The ultra vires doctrine thus could not be applied to Parliament, but as we shall see in subsequent chapters, it has an important role in respect of other governmental organisations.

government itself could not create new laws simply by coming to an agreement with foreign countries. If one allowed that to happen, one would essentially be saying that it is the government rather than Parliament that is the sovereign law-maker.

The principle is further illustrated by the case of *Cheney v Conn*,[17] decided in 1968. Mr Cheney was a taxpayer who appealed against the Inland Revenue's assessment of his income tax liability. The Inland Revenue made its assessment in accordance with the Finance Act 1964. Mr Cheney claimed that some of his tax money was being used to build nuclear weapons, contrary to the principles of the Geneva Convention, a 1957 treaty which the British government had signed.

Parts of the treaty had been incoporated into British law, but these were not helpful to Mr Cheney's argument. His case rested on sections of the treaty that remained unincorporated. Mr Cheney argued that since these parts of the treaty forbade the use of nuclear weapons, it must be illegal for Parliament to enact a statute that raised money so that such weapons could be built. The judge, Ungoed-Thomas J, had no doubt that this was a pointless argument. As far as he was concerned:

> 'What the statute itself enacts cannot be unlawful, because what the statute says is itself the law, and the highest form of law that is known to this country. It is the law which prevails over every other form of law, and it is not for the court to say that a parliamentary enactment, the highest law in this country, is illegal.'[18]

Parliament was at liberty to forbid the manufacture of nuclear weapons in Britain, and should it ever do so the British courts would be obliged to apply that legislation. But an unincorporated Treaty could not have that effect.

Having sketched the basic political and legal foundations of the parliamentary sovereignty doctrine, we turn in the second half of this chapter to the various challenges to the Diceyan theory that have been aired before the courts in recent years. We might say at the outset that none of these challenges has thus far proved effective – but that that does not necessarily mean that one will not become so in the future. We will consider three of these arguments in some detail. Firstly, we will look at the 'manner and form' technique of safeguarding certain basic constitutional values against reform by a simple majority vote in Parliament. Secondly, we will assess the status of the Treaty of Union of 1707 between England

and Scotland. And thirdly, we will explore the notion that there might still be some moral or political values which the courts suggest Parliament can only change through express legislation.

II. ENTRENCHING LEGISLATION – 'CONTINUING' AND 'SELF-EMBRACING' THEORIES OF PARLIAMENTARY SOVEREIGNTY

The positive limb of Dicey's theory seems to say that there is nothing that Parliament cannot do. But there appears to be one basic flaw of logic in Dicey's parliamentary sovereignty concept. Simply put, the problem is how can Parliament have supreme legislative power if there is still one thing it cannot do? That one thing seems to be that Parliament cannot pass an Act which is binding on its successors. If Parliament is truly sovereign, then one would have assumed that it must have the power to give its sovereignty up? This apparent conundrum presents us with the distinction between the *continuing* and *self-embracing* theories of parliamentary sovereignty.[19]

The *continuing* theory maintains that the sovereign Parliament is a *perpetual institution.* Its unconfined legislative power is created anew every time it meets, irrespective of what previous Parliaments have enacted. This is the position which Professor Dicey supported. As far as Dicey was concerned, Parliament need pay no heed at all to what its predecessors have done. And this remains the orthodox interpretation of Parliament's legal powers.

The *self-embracing* theory advocates a radical position. It has aroused much academic interest. As yet it has not had any practical political effect in this country, but it has had considerable influence in countries which used to be British colonies. The self-embracing theory holds that a given Parliament's sovereignty does include the power to bind itself and its successors. Supporters of the self-embracing theory argue that it is possible to enact legislation which is safe from subsequent amendment – that certain measures can be *entrenched* within the legal system and rendered immune from repeal by a future Parliament.

When we talk of entrenchment in the British context, we are not dealing with a single device. The concept simply means any constitutional mechanism which makes some laws immune to repeal by the usual legislative formula of a simple majority vote

19 Winterton G (1976) 'The British grundnorm: parliamentary sovereignty re-examined' 92 *LQR* 591–617.

in the Commons and the Lords plus the Royal Assent. In principle, a particular political value might be entrenched in either a *substantive* or *procedural* sense. *Substantive entrenchment* would entail acceptance of the principle that *Parliament cannot legislate at all* about specific subjects. It implies that there are basic human values which can never be changed. This argument is reminiscent of the old and discredited natural law or divine law ideas, and has not been vigorously pursued in recent times. The obvious drawback to substantive entrenchment would be that a society would be stuck with particular values forever; it is a completely rigid form of safeguarding basic principles.

In the modern era, commentators who oppose Dicey's theory have sought to limit Parliament's power through the device of procedural entrenchment. It is important to stress that *procedural entrenchment would not necessarily produce a rigid constitution* – it produces a relative rather than absolute degree of permanence in respect of certain laws. In theory, one would have entrenched a particular piece of legislation if a majority of two rather than one in the House of Commons was needed to change it. That legislation would not be entrenched very firmly of course; but as one makes reform procedures more rigorous, so legislation becomes more securely entrenched. Constitutional values which could only be changed with the support of, for example 70% of MPs would be quite deeply entrenched; if one required unanimous support, then change might be virtually impossible.[20]

Jennings' critique and the 'rule of recognition'

The starting point for analysis of this theory is to ask ourselves why it is that the courts recognise statutes as the highest form of law? Osensibly, it seems *to be a common law rule* that makes the courts behave in this way. We cannot find the doctrine of parliamentary sovereignty laid down in a statute for example. But the haziness surrounding the legal status of this so-called '*rule of recognition*' has given some assistance to constitutional lawyers opposed to the Diceyan view.[1]

The most forceful exponent of what has come to be known as the '*manner and form*' strategy of procedural entrenchment in the

---

20 One could thus say that most parts of the United States' Constitution are deeply, but not permanently entrenched.

1 The term is that of Professor H Hart; see (1961) *The Concept of Law* p 161 (Oxford: OUP). For an overview of related theories see Winterton (1976) *op cit.*

first half of the twentieth century was Sir Ivor Jennings.[2] Jennings based his critique of the orthodox theory on a version of the self-embracing form of sovereignty. His argument goes through three apparently logical steps. Firstly, the rule of recognition is a common law concept. Secondly, statute is legally superior to the common law. Therefore, thirdly, Parliament can enact legislation changing the rule of recognition and requiring the courts to accept that some Acts of Parliament are protected from repeal by a simple majority vote. There seems to be an obvious legal logic to this argument. It also appears to make sound political sense. If the judges are subordinate to Parliament, then surely Parliament can tell them what rules they should follow when assessing whether or not a statute is unconstitutional?

The manner and form argument draws its theoretical basis largely from Jennings' work. One would be quite justified in assuming however that academic theories are rather less important than case law in assessing the legal status of constitutional ideas. The legal basis of the manner and form argument relies heavily on two cases, both of them rooted in the process of former British colonies gaining independence. The first, *A-G for New South Wales v Trethowan*,[3] was an Australian case decided by the Privy Council in 1932.

A-G for New South Wales v Trethowan

The New South Wales Parliament was created by a British statute, called in New South Wales 'The Constitution Statute 1855'. In many respects, the New South Wales constitution followed the British model. Legislation required the support of a simple majority in an upper house (the Legislative Council) and lower house (the Legislative Assembly), and the Royal Assent provided by the Governor-General qua the Monarch's representative. However, s 5 of a subsequent British statute, the Colonial Laws Validity Act 1865, provided that statutes enacted by all colonial legislatures (including the New South Wales Parliament) which sought to alter their own 'constitution, powers or procedures' would have legal effect only if passed 'in such manner or form' as the law then in force in the colony demanded. The terms of s 5 were left unchanged when the New South Wales' Constitution Act was passed by the New South Wales Legislature in 1902. The 1902 Act, inter alia, made provisions concerning the composition and

2 See especially (5th edn, 1959) *The Law and the Constitution* pp 140–145 (London: Hodder and Stoughton).
3 [1932] AC 526.

respective powers of the two houses.

In 1929, the Liberal Party government, which had majorities in both houses of the NSW Parliament, promoted the Constitution (Legislative Council Amendment) Bill 1929. The Bill was passed by both houses, received the Royal Assent, and thus became an Act. The Act introduced a new s 7A into the Constitution Act 1902, to the effect that a bill seeking to abolish the Legislative Council could not be sent for the Royal Assent unless it had been approved by a majority of both houses and by a majority of the electorate in a special referendum. Section 7(A) therefore seemed to change the 'manner and form' of the legislation needed to abolish the upper chamber, by adding an additional step to the usual legislative process. Furthermore, s 7A (6) provided that s 7A itself could not be repealed unless the repealing legislation had also been approved by a majority of electors in a special referendum. It appeared that the government expected to be defeated in the imminent general election, and wished to ensure that the opposition party could not carry out its stated intention to abolish the upper house without first putting that specific question to the 'people' of New South Wales.

After the New South Wales elections of 1930, the previous opposition party secured a majority in both houses. Both houses thereafter approved bills respectively repealing s 7A and abolishing the Legislative Council. Neither measure was subjected to a referendum before it was submitted for the Royal Assent. Several members of the Legislative Council immediately began an action before the New South Wales courts requesting an injunction to prevent the bills being sent for the Royal Assent; if granted, the injunction would therefore prevent the bills becoming legislation. Their argument, quite simply, was that s 7A could be repealed only in the 'manner and form' which it had itself specified.

The new government argued that successive New South Wales Parliaments, just like the British Parliament, could not be bound by any legislation passed by their predecessors. A Parliament might pass any 'manner and form' provisions it thought fit, but they would cease to have effect when a future Parliament, acting by the 'simple majority plus Royal Assent formula', passed legislation to repeal them. That had indeed happened here, and thus s 7A had been lawfully repealed.

In the High Court of Australia,[4] two of the five judges accepted that argument. However the majority took the view that the court

---

4 (1931) 44 CLR 394. The High Court is Australia's highest domestic court of appeal. At that time, its judgments could be appealed to the British Privy Council.

was bound to prevent any bill dealing with the subect matter of s 7A being sent for the Royal Assent unless it had been approved in a referendum. The special 'manner and form' of s 7A did provide an effective form of procedural entrenchment safeguarding the existence of the Legislative Council. The majority reasoned that, unlike the British Parliament, the New South Wales legislature owed its existence to a clearly visible British statute, the Colonial Laws Validity Act 1865. New South Wales had adopted that Act as the basis of its Constitution, and until s 5 of the 1865 Act was itself repealed, the New South Wales legislature was subject to its terms. The majority saw this as a straightforward *legal* rule, which, Rich J explained (in terms very reminiscent of Madison's warnings as to the dangers of factionalism) served an obvious political purpose:

> 'There is no reason why a Parliament representing the people should be powerless to determine whether the constitutional salvation of the State is to be reached by cautious and well considered steps rather than by rash and ill considered measures.'[5]

On a further appeal to the Privy Council,[6] the majority opinion, and the reasoning underlying it, was upheld unanimously.

Harris v Dönges (Minister of the Interior)[7]

The second case, *Harris v Dönges (Minister of the Interior)*, was decided by the South African Supreme Court in 1952. Once again, the story begins with the slow process of Britain disengaging itself from its former Empire. In 1909 the British Parliament passed the South Africa Act, which united the four South African colonies under a single legislature. The South African Parliament mirrored that of Britain in most respects. It had a House of Assembly and a Senate and retained the King's power of Royal Assent. In respect of almost all laws, South Africa's legislature had the same legal competence as the British Parliament – a bill receiving a simple majority in both the House and the Senate and thereafter receiving the Royal Assent was generally the 'highest form of law' within

---

5 *Ibid*, at 420.
6 Which then served as the ultimate court of appeal for most colonial courts.
7 [1952] 1 TLR 1245. The following pages present a simplified version of a series of complex judgments, all of which merit close study. For comment see particularly Griswold E (1952) 'The "coloured vote case" in South Africa' 65 *Harvard LR* 1361–1374; Note (1952) 68 *Law Quarterly Review* 285–287; Cowen D (1952) and (1953) 'Legislature and judiciary: parts I and II' 15 and 16 *Modern Law Review* 282–296 and 273–298.

South Africa's constitution. However the 1909 Act contained some exceptions to the 'simple majority plus Royal Assent' formula.

Firstly, the South African Parliament could not, under any circumstances, pass laws 'repugnant' to British laws intended to have effect within South Africa. The supremacy of British law vis-à-vis South African law was a substantively entrenched feature of South Africa's 1909 constitutional settlement. Secondly, ss 33–34 of the 1909 Act prevented the South African Parliament altering the composition of the House or the Senate for ten years. Those provisions were thus substantively, but temporarily, entrenched. After the ten years had expired, the composition of the House and Senate could be altered by simple majority legislation. Thirdly, s 35 provided that the right of Cape coloured citizens to be registered on the same electoral roll as whites could not be removed by South African legislation unless that legislation had been supported by a two-thirds majority of the House and Senate sitting in joint session. Fourthly, s 137 provided that the status of both Afrikaans and English as the country's official languages could only be changed by the two-thirds-majority procedure. S 152 thereafter provided that s 35 and s 137 themselves could be amended only by a South African statute also attracting a two-thirds majority in a joint legislative session. S 35 and s 152 imply that the British Parliament in 1909 considered that coloured citizens' 'right' to vote on the same basis as whites was too important a political value to be left at the mercy of a bare legislative majority. It was not an 'inalienable right', but was to be more difficult to change than most other aspects of the South African constitution.[8] It seemed to be a value which was procedurally (and quite firmly) entrenched.

In 1931, the British Parliament passed the Statute of Westminster which recognised South Africa (and several other former colonies) as an independent sovereign state. The entrenchment provided for in ss 33–34 had by then elapsed, and the 1931 statute empowered South Africa's Parliament to enact legislation 'repugnant' to British law if it wished. However the 1931 Act did not expressly repeal ss 35, 137 and 152; indeed, both houses of the South African legislature had requested that the terms of the 1931 Act should 'in no way derogate from the entrenched provisions of the South Africa Act'.[9]

From the late 1940s onwards, the white Afrikaner National

---

8 For insight into why the British Parliament thought this additional protection appropriate see Lewin J (1956) 'The struggle for law in South Africa' 27 *Political Quarterly* 176–181.

9 Cited in *Harris v Dönges (Minister of the Interior)* [1952] 1 TLR 1245 at 1253.

Party possessed a majority in both houses of the legislature. The National Party had committed itself to introducing apartheid, a policy demanding separation of different racial groups. One element of this policy was to create separate electoral registers and voting systems for white and Cape coloured citizens. The Separate Representation of Voters Act was passed in 1951 by a simple majority, with both Houses sitting separately. Its 'constitutionality' was then challenged by several coloured voters, on the basis that the procedures used to enact it did not comply with the 'manner and form' specified in s 35.

Before South Africa's Supreme Court, the South African government argued that this special procedure was no longer necessary. The government maintained that after the Statute of Westminster was passed in 1931 South Africa had become a sovereign state, and therefore its Parliament was not bound by the country's initial constitution, which was enacted while South Africa was still a colony.[10] As a matter of South African constitutional law, the government argued, the South African legislature had thus acquired all the legal attributes of Britain's Parliament: it could enact any law whatsoever by a simple majority; and no domestic court was competent to question the legality of any such Act.

All five of the judges then sitting on South Africa's Supreme Court rejected this argument, and concluded that the Act was unconstitutional. The court did accept that South Africa was a sovereign country. The South African courts would no longer consider British legislation superior to South African statutes. The court also accepted that South Africa had a sovereign Parliament. The Supreme Court nevertheless held that the Separate Representation of Voters Act was an illegal measure.

The judgment hinges on two presumptions. The first is the conclusion that it is *possible to have a sovereign country without having a sovereign legislature.* Pointing to the United States as an example, Centlivres CJ observed it was entirely feasible for a country's constitutional arrangements to withhold some legal powers from its central legislature. As we saw in chapter one, the USA's Constitution reserves control of most its basic principles to the cumbersome 'two-thirds of Congress plus three-quarters of the States' amendment process.

The seond presumption, in respect of which the US model is not a helpful analogy, is that *a country can have a sovereign Parliament*

---

10 There already seemed to have been been a decision by a lower court to this effect; *Ndlwana v Hofmeyr NO* [1937] AD 229 (SA).

without according complete legal competence to a simple majority procedure.
The court held that South Africa had adopted the terms of ss 35
and 152 of the 1909 Act as part of its constitutional settlement
when it gained independence in 1931. Its Parliament therefore
existed in *two forms*. For every purpose but three, Parliament could
pass an Act by a simple majority with the houses sitting separately.
But for those three purposes of repealing s 35, or s 137 or s 152,
Parliament had to act by a two-thirds-majority in joint session.
Until such time as that high percentage of the legislature's members wished to repeal those provisions, they remained entrenched
within South Africa's constitution.

Are *Trethowan* and *Harris* relevant to the British situation?

Initially it might seem that *Harris* and *Trethowan* provide a model
to bind Parliament in Britain. Suppose Parliament enacts a statute
which, for example, fixes income tax at ten pence in the pound,
and adds a clause saying this rate can only be changed if 70% of
MPs vote in favour. If a subsequent Parliament wished to increase
taxes, surely *Harris* and *Trethowan* are precedents for saying that
it could not do so by a simple majority: the 'manner and form'
of 70% support would be required before a British court would
enforce any new statute raising tax levels ? This proposition has
attracted the support of several eminent commentators, in
addition to Jennings himself.[11]

However there would seem to be little force to such arguments.
Much the more persuasive analysis of these cases is that they are
completely irrelevant to questions concerning the sovereignty of
the British Parliament. This position, most forcefully argued by
Wade in 1955,[12] contends that if one transposes these cases to the
British context, they are revealed simply as instances of statutory
bodies created by Parliament acting beyond the confines of the
authority which Parliament granted. In both cases there was a
'higher law' to which the Acts in question were subordinate,
namely an Act of the British Parliament: the New South Wales'
and South African legislatures were acting 'ultra vires' (beyond

11 See Friedmann W (1950) 'Trethowan's case, parliamentary sovereignty and the
limits of legal change' 24 *Australian Law Journal* 103–108; Keir D (6th edn,
1978) *Cases in Constitutional Law* p 7 (Oxford: Clarendon Press); Griswold *op cit*
Heuston R (1964) *Essays in Constitutional Law* ch 1 (London: Stevens). For a
recent overview see Craig P (1991) 'Sovereignty of the United Kingdom Parliament after *Factortame*' *Yearbook of European Law* 221–255.
12 (1955) 'The basis of legal sovereignty' *Cambridge LJ* 172–197.

their legal powers).[13] If these two *subordinate* legislatures had acted beyond the legal limits of the powers which created them, it was quite consistent with the theory of parliamentary sovereignty for the courts to intervene.[14] Indeed, the courts would have to intervene, since they had in effect been ordered to do so by the terms of the initial British statutes.

Britain, in contrast, has no higher source of law than Parliament. Nor is there any colonial master to which the British Parliament owes its existence. Consequently it is not possible for it to exceed its legal authority. Indeed, it is extremely puzzling that the earlier decision in *Trethowan* was ever invoked to suggest that the British Parliament could enact manner and form limitations on its own sovereignty, given the comments of the Australian judges hearing the case. Rich J stated quite clearly that: 'The Legislature of New South Wales is not sovereign, and no analogy can be drawn from the position of the British Parliament'; similarly, in Starke J's opinion: 'the Parliaments of the Dominions or Colonies are not sovereign and omnipotent bodies. They are subordinate bodies; their powers are limited by the Imperial [British] or other Acts which created them', while Dixon J observed that:

> 'The incapacity of the British legislature to limit its own power . . . has been explained as a necessary consequence of a true conception of sovereignty. But in any case it depends on considerations which have no application to the legislature of New South Wales, which is not a sovereign body and has a purely statutory origin.'[15]

The logic of the manner and form argument rests on the assumption made by Professor Jennings that the 'rule of recognition' is a common law principle. But as Professor Wade suggests, that logic disintegrates if one regards the *rule of recognition as a political fact rather than a legal principle*. In Wade's view, the rule of recognition is not part of the common law, but something prior to and superior to the common law. It is in essence a basic political reality, not a technical legal rule. It represents the courts' acceptance of the new political consensus brought about by the 1688 revolution. As a result of that revolution, the political underpinnings of British society were radically changed. Parliament was in a position to

13 Professor Wade put a rather different gloss on *Harris*, suggesting that the South African Supreme Court was effectively in a revolutionary situation, in which its judgment was determined by political rather than legal principles: (1955) *op cit.*
14 A similar argument can be applied to a third, oft-cited case of 'manner and form' entrenchment, emanating from Sri Lanka: *Bribery Comr v Ranasinghe* [1965] AC 172, PC.
15 (1931) 44 CLR 394 at 418, 422 and 425–426 respectively.

establish its superiority over both the King and the courts – and both the King and the courts had no choice but to acquiesce to these new circumstances.

Thus from Wade's 1955 perspective, the theory and practice of parliamentary sovereignty could not be altered by legal means, no matter how ingenious an argument we came up with. The only thing that could have removed the legislative sovereignty of Parliament was another revolution. This need not be a war or a violent insurrection, but it would have to be some momentous break in legal and political continuity, some fundamental redefinition of the way that the country's citizens bestow law-making power on their legislature.

Subsequently, in a series of lectures he delivered in 1980,[16] Wade appeared to adopt a rather different position. He suggested that the only feasible way forward was the very simple device of Parliament introducing legislation to change the judiciary's oath of loyalty. The new oath would require the judges to swear eternal obedience to a statute entrenching certain fundamental rights or liberties that we would never want to have removed, or which could only be removed by a special form of Parliamentary procedure above and beyond a bare majority. If the courts subsequently found themselves presented with a situation analogous to the one that the South African Supreme Court faced in *Harris v Dönges (Minister of the Interior)*, their loyalty to the new oath would require them to declare the so-called legislation unconstitutional.

The obvious drawback of that proposal is that one could envisage a future Parliament introducing legislation to change the oath back again. The idea does indeed look very simple – but perhaps that is because it seems most unlikely that it would work unless it was a part of a more wide-ranging revolutionary overhaul of the constitution that Wade talked of in 1955. It will be suggested in the final chapter of this book that no such 'revolution' is necessary, and that the *Trethowan* and *Harris* episodes do indeed provide the legal tools with which to entrench legislation in Britain, even though one cannot remove Parliament's omnicompetent 'simple majority plus Royal Assent' legislative powers. That argument must however be withheld until we have explored other relevant aspects of Britain's constitutional arrangements. For the moment, however, we might strengthen the case against 'simple' solutions to the entrenchment conundrum by noting the South African government's response to the Supreme Court's judgment in *Harris*.

16 *Constitutional Fundamentals* (London: Stevens).

Harris v Minister of the Interior – the aftermath

The only entrenched clauses remaining in South Africa's constitution in 1952 were s 35, s 137 and s 152. Everything else could seemingly be changed by a simple majority House plus Senate vote.[17] The government decided to use its majorities in the legislature to bypass or overcome the Supreme Court's defence of the constitution. Its first initiative was to enact a measure, the High Court of Parliament Act 1952, which purported to turn the Senate and the House of Assembly into a new court, which would have exclusive powers to determine the consitutionality of legislation. The 'Act' was passed by simple majority. The victorious plaintiffs in *Harris* immediately challenged this legislation, arguing that any such measure could only be enacted through the s 152 procedures. In *Minister of the Interior v Harris*,[18] the South African Supreme Court invalidated the 1952 Act, albeit through a somewhat more inventive strategy than the one it had deployed in *Harris*.

A unanimous court found that s 152 impliedly contained a provision demanding that any legislation dealing with matters protected by s 35 or s 137 be subject to scrutiny by a 'court', which would ensure the Act had been passed in conformity with s 152. This implied term was a necessary inheritance of the British constitutional tradition on which South Africa's own constitution was based. Furthermore, a 'court' in this sense had to be institutionally independent from the legislature and the government, and had to be staffed by legally qualified 'judges'. The supposed 'High Court of Parliament' met neither criteria. It could not be a 'court' simply because a majority of the two houses so labelled it. To entrust such a body with the legal protection of ss 35 and 137 would render that protection illusory. It could therefore only be created via the s 152 procedures.

The government's second strategy was more straightforward. The government had re-introduced the Separate Representation Act in 1953 and 1954. On each occasion, it failed to achieve a two-thirds majority. But the Constitution did not prevent the legislature increasing the size of the Supreme Court. Consequently, the government invited the legislature to enact the 1955 Appeal Court Quorum Act. This legislation added six further judges, appointed by the government, to the existing five. All six were government supporters. Parliament then enacted, again by

17 The South African Parliament had by then enacted legislation compelling the Monarch to grant the Royal Assent to all measures passed by the other two chambers of the legislature.
18 1952 (4) SA 769 (A).

a simple majority process, the Senate Act 1955. This measure enlarged the Senate from 48 to 89 members.[19] The additional Senators were chosen by a method which ensured that they were almost all National Party supporters. The government thereby gained a two-thirds majority when the two houses sat in joint session. A majority of the new eleven-judge Supreme Court promptly held that the Senate Act was constitutional.[20] Then, in 1956, Parliament passed legislation in accordance with the manner and form required by s 35 which placed Cape coloured citizens on a separate electoral register.

All the steps in this process were 'legal' in the formal sense, although we might question their moral acceptability.[1] These events would nevertheless suggest that there is probably no quick and easy way to dispense with the idea of parliamentary sovereignty.[2] A solution imposed at one point in the constitutional structure may simply serve to reveal that there are other entirely legal roots for a bare Parliamentary majority to enact (eventually) whatever legislation it wishes.

Is parliamentary sovereignty a British or English concept?

The mid 1950s were an interesting time for opponents of the parliamentary sovereignty doctrine. As well as producing the *Harris* case, that era also lent a new impetus to a Scots challenge to the legal supremacy of the British Parliament. This chapter has stressed that parliamentary sovereignty initially emerged in *England, not in Britain*. The Glorious Revolution happened in 1688. At that time, England and Scotland shared a King, and had done so since 1603. But each country had its own Parliament. There was no doubt that Scotland and England were at that time both sovereign states, each with its own particular constitutional structure. *Britain* was not created until the Acts of Union of 1707. In those nineteen years between 1688 and 1707, parliamentary sovereignty may have been accepted as the foundation of the

---

19 Which, as we have seen, could not have been done prior to 1919.
20 *Collins v Minister of the Interior* 1957 (1) SA 552 (A). The majority included four of the original five judges.
1 For perspectives from within South Africa see Lewin *op cit*; Le May G (1957) 'Parliament, the Constitution and the doctrine of the mandate' 74 *South African Law Journal* 33–42.
2 For a contemporaneous critique of Wade's proposal see Winterton G (1981) 'Parliamentary supremacy and the judiciary' 97 *LQR* 265–275.

constitution in England, but it is far from certain that the idea enjoyed that status in Scotland.[3]

Orthodox British theory suggests that what happened in 1707 was essentially a *takeover* of the Scots Parliament by the English Parliament. That is to say that the constitution of the newly created country of Great Britain was based on the same principles that underpinned the English constitution between 1688 and 1707. Some Scots theorists would argue however that what happened in 1707 was *not a takeover, but a merger.*[4] They also suggest that the terms of that merger were set out in the Act of Union itself. This means that the Acts of Union were not simply a statute produced by the British Parliament, rather that they were the final Acts of the Scots and English Parliaments through which the British Parliament was created. The argument is therefore that the Acts of Union do provide a form of higher law, a higher law which does place some limits on the legal powers of the British Parliament. These limits are supposedly laid out in the Act of Union produced by the British Parliament, which simply repeats the terms of the identical statutes passed by the Scots and English legislatures.

The great practical weakness to this theory is that most of the provisions of the Act of Union are apparently no longer in force. It seems to have been generally accepted until the 1950s that the legal status of the Act of Union was the same as any other statute – its provisions were open to amendment by either express or implied repeal by subsequent legislation. This is not a conclusive answer to the question, since one might assume that the Scots nation had in some way 'consented' to all these changes. But the 'merger theory' has been tested on several occasions since then in the Scots courts, and the Scots judges have not dismissed it out of hand.

The 1953 case of *MacCormick v Lord Advocate*[5] concerned a challenge to the constitutionality of the Royal Titles Act 1953. Under the terms of this Act, the former Princess Elizabeth succeeded to the British throne with the title of Elizabeth II. MacCormick argued that Britain had never had a Queen Elizabeth I – the woman who stepped on Walter Raleigh's cloak in the sixteenth

3 Smith T (1957) 'The Union of 1707 as fundamental law' *Public Law* 99–121; Munro C (1987) *Studies in Constitutional Law* ch 4 (London: Butterworths); MacCormick N (1978) 'Does the United Kingdom have a constitution?' 29 *Northern Ireland Law Quarterly* 1–20.
4 See especially MacCormick *op cit*.
5 1953 SC 396.

century was *Elizabeth I of England* – and so could not have an Elizabeth II.

The court dismissed MacCormick's claim on the facts, but it offered some unexpected observations on the wider issue of the constitutional status of the Act of Union:

> The principle of the unlimited sovereignty of Parliament is a distinctively English principle which has no counterpart in Scottish constitutional law. . . . Considering that the Union legislation extinguished the Parliaments of Scotland and England and replaced them by a new Parliament, I have difficulty in seeing why it should have been supposed that the new Parliament of Great Britain must inherit all the peculiar characteristics of the English Parliament but none of the Scottish Parliament, as if all that happened in 1707 was that Scottish representatives were admitted to the Parliament of England. That is not what was done.[6]

We should also remember that while many of the terms of the Act of Union have been repealed, some of its most important provisions remain in place. Scotland retains its own legal system for example,[7] and its own established church. It is interesting to speculate how the courts in England and Scotland would respond if Parliament passed legislation changing either of these two features of Scottish society. At present, however, speculating is all we can do.

Women's enfranchisement

The common law also provides one often overlooked example of the courts disapplying orthodox notions of parliamentary sovereignty in defence of traditional moral or political values. As we shall see in chapter seven, the 1832 Great Reform Act extended the Parliamentary franchise to affluent middle class men. Further nineteenth-century reforms gave the right to vote to an increasing percentage of the male population. Parliament declined explicitly to enfranchise women: but in the 1860s, women's suffrage campaigners formulated an argument that Parliament had done so impliedly.

Section 4 of Lord Brougham's Act, passed in 1850, provided that 'in all Acts words importing the masculine gender shall be

---

6 *Ibid*, at 411.
7 For illustrations of the significant differences between the two systems see Richardson T (1995) 'The War Crimes Act 1991', in Loveland I (ed.) *Frontiers of Criminality* (London: Sweet and Maxwell).

deemed and taken to include females . . . unless the contrary as to gender is expressly provided'. The 1867 Reform Act did not expressly exclude women. John Stuart Mill, then an MP and supporter of women's suffrage, had suggested during the Bill's passage that such phraseology impliedly extended the vote to women. The government declined to introduce a clause expressly disapplying Lord Brougham's Act to the franchise issue, suggesting that interpretation of the statute would have to be left to the courts.[8]

In *Chorlton v Lings*,[9] a woman who satisfied all the criteria specified to entitle a man to vote argued that women had indeed been impliedly enfranchised by the 1867 Act. However, the Court of Common Pleas held that Parliament could not possibly have intended to extend the right to vote to women. To do so would overturn centuries of constitutional tradition and practice. Willes J explained the essentially political and moral reasoning behind this practice, in language no doubt considered diplomatic at the time:

> 'The absence of such a right is referable to the fact that . . . chiefly out of respect to women, and a sense of decorum, and not from their want of intellect, or their being for any other reason unfit to take part in the goverment of the country, they have been excused from taking any share in this department of public affairs.'[10]

The court's unanimous rejection of the argument that Parliament could impliedly amend basic constitutional values was most clearly expressed by Keating J: the legislature, 'if desirous of making an alteration so important and extensive, would have said so plainly and distinctly'.[11]

The *Chorlton v Lings* scenario was replayed some forty years later in *Nairn v University of St Andrews*.[12] The Representation of the People (Scotland) Act 1868 extended the franchise in university constituencies to all of the university's graduates. The Universities (Scotland) Act 1889 empowered Scots universities to award degrees to women. Nairn was one of several woman graduates who contended that the 1889 legislation necessarily implied that she was now entitled to vote. The House of Lords saw little merit

---

8 Kent S (1989) *Sex and suffrage in Britain 1860–1914* ch 8 (New Jersey: Princeton University Press).

9 (1868) LR 4 CP 374.

10 *Ibid*, at 392.

11 *Ibid*, at 395.

12 [1909] AC 147. On the background to the case see Leneman L (1991) 'When women were not "persons": the Scottish women graduates case, 1906–1908' *Juridical Review* 109–118.

in such an argument. Lord Loreburn LC was particularly adamant that female suffrage could be introduced only by the *most explicit* of statutory provisions:

'It would require a convincing demonstration to satisfy me that Parliament intended to effect a constitutional change so momentous and far-reaching by so furtive a process.'[13]

Keating J's holding in *Chorlton* that Parliament may introduce 'important and extensive' changes to the nature of a citizen's relationship to the state only through 'plain and distinct' statutory language is a principle of potentially wide application. One could draw the same conclusion about Lord Loreburn's observation that the common law does not permit Parliament to achieve policy objectives through 'furtive' legislative devices.

What the courts appear to be saying in these two cases does not seem easy to reconcile with the legal principles advanced in orthodox interpretations of the decisions in *Vauxhall Estates* and *Ellen Street Estates*, which are assumed to have established the doctrine of implied repeal. However, one can see convincing 'democratic' reasons for preferring the *Chorlton/Nairn* rationale. If we assume that Parliament derives its political authority from the consent of the people, it would seem sensible that Parliament is candid about the objectives it is seeking. Without such honesty in the legislative processs, it would not be possible for citizens to decide whether or not they wished to continue to consent to what Parliament was doing. That is however essentially a political argument rather than a legal one, and as yet it is one that the British courts have not been prepared to accept.

CONCLUSION

We might at this juncture draw some initial conclusions about the status of parliamentary sovereignty within our constitution. Perhaps the most important point to remember is that parliamentary sovereignty was not designed for a modern, democratic society which has large political parties which contest general elections on a nationwide basis. It is a three-hundred-year-old idea.

In order to do justice to Dicey's theorisation of the principle in the 1880s, we ought to note that his concern was to illustrate the relationship between Acts of Parliament and the courts – to stress that as *a matter of legal principle* the courts were invariably subordi-

13 [1909] AC 147 at 161.

nate to the will of Parliament. Dicey took pains to stress that political sovereignty was a very different thing. When it came to the practicalities of government, it was simply nonsense to say that Parliament could enact legislation on any subject it chose. Because one part of Parliament, the House of Commons, was an elected body, and its members could periodically be changed by its citizens, MPs would always have to be conscious of what measures the electorate would accept, and temper the legislation they produce accordingly. Thus, to evaluate the *political acceptability* of Dicey's legal doctrine we must examine long-term changes in other areas of Britain's law-making and government processes. In particular, we must assess the *voting system* through which members of the House of Commons are elected, the *relationship between the House of Commons and the government*, and the *changing balance of power within Parliament* between the Commons, Lords, and Monarch.

These inquiries will repeatedly lead us to a point of considerable importance which frequently resurfaces in any study of the British constitution; namely a *distinction between legal formality and political reality*. These two concepts do not always coincide, and one of the great difficulties facing constitutional lawyers is deciding in what circumstances law gives way to politics, and vice versa. We will often return to this problem in subsequent chapters. But for the present, we might leave our discussion of parliamentary sovereignty with a quotation from the 1969 case of *Madzimbamuto v Lardner-Burke*. Lord Reid observed that:

> 'It is often said that it would be unconstitutional for . . . Parliament to do certain things, meaning that the moral, political and other reasons against doing them are so strong that most people would regard it as highly improper if Parliament did these things. But that does not mean it is beyond the power of Parliament to do such things. If Parliament chose to do any of them, the courts could not hold the Act of Parliament invalid.'[14]

As later chapters suggest, the United Kingdom's accession to the European Economic Community in 1973 has cast considerable doubt on certain aspects of the orthodox theory of parliamentary sovereignty. But it would be an adventurous lawyer who suggested that we can currently find purely *domestic* limitations to the principle that Parliament's legal powers are unconfined.

14 [1969] 1 AC 645 at 723, PC.

CHAPTER THREE

The rule of law and the separation of powers

The 'rule of law' is another element of the British constitution taken for granted. It is often glibly invoked, as is 'democracy', as a means of conveying the essential adequacy of Britain's constitutional arrangements. But on reflection, it is clear that 'the rule of law', in the same way as 'democracy', is not a concept with just *one* accepted meaning. This multiplicity of meanings derives from the fact that 'the rule of law' is not a legal rule, whether in the context of the British constitution or any other, but a political or moral principle. It is trite to observe that people in democratic societies hold different political and moral views. But if we accept that point, and if we accept that the rule of law is a political or moral concept, we must also accept that the rule of law may mean different things to different people according to their particular moral or political positions. In later chapters, we will assess whether one can identify characteristics of 'the rule of law' which traverse party political, national, and chronological boundaries, and we will question whether Britain's model is found wanting when measured against such a yardstick. At present, we will concentrate on exploring the various meanings that the rule of law has been accorded in the post-revolutionary British constitution.

For analytical purposes, it is helpful to view the rule of law as a vehicle for expressing 'the people's' preferences about two essentially political issues. Firstly, it relates to the *substance* of the relationship between the citizen and her government. Secondly, it deals with the *processes* through which that relationship is conducted. That can be rephrased more simply – the rule of law is concerned with what government can do – and how government can do it.

Many legal and political theorists have presented variations on these two themes.[1] In addition to addresssing a series of seminal cases, in which one can discern the varying ways in which principles are put into practice, this chapter deals briefly with three theoretical analyses, those of A V Dicey, Friedrich Hayek, and Harry Jones, which in both chronological and political terms, span the spectrum of mainstream debate about the nature of the rule of law in Britain's twentieth-century constitution.

I. THE DICEYAN PERSPECTIVE: THE RULE OF LAW IN THE PRE-WELFARE STATE

Before examining Dicey's views on the rule of law, we should again recall why we might prudently view his theories with a sceptical eye. Firstly we must remember that Dicey was the product of an undemocratic society in the sense we would understand it: as we shall see in chapter 7, fewer than half the adult population were entitled to vote in Parliamentary elections when Dicey completed his famous *Law of the Constitution* in the 1880s. Dicey himself was also vehemently opposed to the nineteenth-century trend towards increased government intervention in social and economic affairs. He would not have approved of a National Health Service, or of universal state schooling for example.[2] So his ideas about the relationship between government and citizens were not shaped by political values which most modern observers accept as entirely orthodox. Nevertheless, as we saw in respect of parliamentary sovereignty, the British constitution is still built upon a foundation which pre-dates modern concepts of democracy. Consequently, Dicey's theories still provide us with a good place to start our examination of the meaning of the rule of law in modern Britain. There are several elements of Dicey's analysis that we need to address.

Dicey encapsulated his ideas in a single phrase:

> 'No man is punishable or can be lawfully made to suffer in body or goods except for a distinct breach of the law established in the ordinary legal manner before the ordinary courts of the land.'[3]

This definition can be divided into three separate parts. Firstly,

---

1 Perhaps the most helpful introduction is offered in Harlow C and Rawlings R (1984) *Law and Administration* chs 1–2 (London: Weidenfeld and Nicolson). See also Munro (1987) *op cit* ch 9; Thompson E (1975) *Whigs and Hunters* pp 258–266 (London: Penguin); Raz J (1977) 'The rule of law and its virtue' 93 *LQR* 195–211.
2 McEldowney (1985) *op cit.*
3 *Op cit* p 188.

'no man can lawfully be made to suffer in body or goods'. That indicates that Dicey's primary concern is with the protection of individual rights and liberties (and as such is clearly in some respects a more modern restatement of Lockean principles). Dicey stressed that this *protection* had to be effective *against both other citizens and against the government*. Acting in an official capacity did not per se amount to a defence for a civil servant or minister accused, for example, of theft, or being sued for breach of contract, or for trespass on private property. A government official, just like every other citizen, had to find some legal justification for behaving in an apparently unlawful way. Secondly, 'except for a distinct breach of the law . . .'. This reinforces the conclusion that *government has to operate within a framework of laws* which are in some way superior to the mere actions of government officials: behaviour does not become lawful simply because a government official claims it is so. The third factor is that any breach of the law 'must be established in the ordinary legal manner before the ordinary courts of the land'. The implication of this third point is that the courts, rather than the government, have the power to determine whether or not the law has been broken. In combination, these three elements of Dicey's rule of law lead us towards yet another of the taken for granted components of the constitution; namely the principle of the *separation of powers*.

Readers interested in pursuing the philosphical foundations of the principle in the modern era might usefully consult John Locke's *Second Treatise of Civil Government* (1690) and Montesquieu's *Spirit of the Laws* (1748). Such works had a profound influence on theoretical analyses of the British constitution, and, in an obviously different way, on the constitutional principles adopted by the American revolutionaries.[4] For our introductory purposes, the basic point we need to distill from the separation of powers doctrine as it applies to the British constitution is that the governmental function can be divided into three discrete or separate activities.

The first is legislation. One part of government has to make the laws under which people live. If we return to the idea of the British constitution as a social contract discussed in chapter 1, we could say that the legislative function is to produce the terms of the contract under which government is conducted. But if a society drafts a contract, the people must also design some way of carrying that contract out. This second part of government, the carrying

4 An incisive critique of the differential impact of these theories on Britain, France and the United States is provided in Vile *op cit.*

out of the laws, is presumed to be undertaken by the executive. Dicey's version of the rule of law regards the second function of government with great suspicion. The assumption that underpins Dicey's view of the rule of law is that the executive will always be inclined to try to do things that the legislature has not authorised. Consequently, the third arm of government must offer citizens some way of securing a remedy if the executive acts in ways that contravene the laws the legislature has enacted. This third arm is the courts. The citizen can approach the courts for redress if she believes herself to be the victim of a government action conducted without lawful authority.

In the American context, one would add a fourth and fifth element to the separation of powers, namely the constitution itself, sitting above the three other branches of government, and thereafter the 'the people' in the form of the 'two-thirds majority in Congress plus three-quarters of the States' whose consent is needed to amend the constitution. The Madisonian view of the rule of law would assume not only (like Dicey) that the executive might seek to behave in ways not authorised by the legislature, *but also* that the legislature might seek to behave in ways unauthorised by 'the people'. Similarly, in South Africa prior to 1955, a fourth element was provided by the constitutional requirements of ss 35, 137 and 152 of the South Africa Act 1909.[5] In Britain however, we seemingly need to deal only with three component parts of government. The interaction of this threefold division with a Diceyan version of the rule of law can perhaps best be understood by analysing one of the most celebrated early cases in the post-revolutionary era – *Entick v Carrington.*

Entick v Carrington (1765)[6]

The mid-eighteenth century was a turbulent time in British constitutional history. In addition to facing the threat of revolution in the American colonies, the government was under continuous pressure from an indigenous radical movement which accused it of corruption and incompetence, and which advocated far more extensive participation in the electoral process. Technological advances in the printing industry enabled radicals to spread their ideas far and wide. London in the 1760s was awash with numerous

5 See pp 50–57 above.
6 (1765) 19 State Tr 1029.

pamphlets, cartoons and sermons which criticised or satirised the government.

The focus of much of the opposition was a man called John Wilkes. Wilkes was a radical politician who was elected to the House of Commons several times. But on each occasion the Commons had refused to permit him to take his seat.[7] This made him a great hero to many American colonists, who felt he shared with them a noble struggle against an increasingly tyrannical government and an increasingly insensitive Parliament.[8] Obviously, the radicals were not heroes to the British government, which had adopted various draconian tactics to try to stem the flow of critical literature being produced by Wilkes and his colleagues. One technique that the Home Secretary deployed was to issue a 'general warrant' empowering his civil servants to raid the houses or business premises of radicals suspected of producing seditious literature. The warrant purportedly authorised government officials to enter private premises without seeking the owner's permission, and without offering the owner any opportunity to rebut their suspicions, and to seize every document that they found there without providing any form of receipt recording what had been taken. In 1764, the Home Secretary authorised a raid on the home of a Mr Entick. Entick was a printer and Wilkes' sympathiser, who was suspected of producing much of the radicals' literature. The Home Secretary's messengers broke into Entick's house and removed all of his papers.

We might assume at this point that the government's action contravened some of the basic principles of consensual constitutional government discussed in chapters 1 and 2. There was little point in electors choosing Wilkes as their MP if the 'government'[9] prevented him from taking his seat. And it would be difficult for electors to make an informed choice about their law-makers if the government was suppressing radical publications. Since eighteenth-century Britain was not a democratic country in the modern sense, one could not expect government behaviour to respect modern democratic principles. But was it a society subject to the rule of law as Dicey later defined it?

Entick had obviously been made to suffer in goods – his papers had been taken away. But had he committed 'a distinct breach of

7 The basis of this power, and its application to Wilkes and others, is explored further in chapter 8.
8 See Maier P (1963) 'John Wilkes and American disillusionment with Britain' *William and Mary Quarterly* 373–395.
9 The word is used guardedly for reasons addressed in chapter 8.

the law established in the ordinary manner before the ordinary courts'? The answer would seem to be no. He had not been accused nor convicted of a crime. He certainly had not been brought before any court. In contrast, the government's officials appeared to have contravened the common law by trespassing on Mr Entick's property and seizing his papers.

So Mr Entick sued the messengers for trespass to his land and goods. When the case came to trial, the messengers' defence was that the Home Secretary's warrant provided them with a lawful excuse for their actions. However, the defence proved difficult to sustain. The defendants could not point to any legislation in which Parliament had authorised the Home Secretary to take away all Mr Entick's papers in this manner. Such legislation had existed in the past, but had always been enacted for only a limited period, and none of it was any longer in force.[10] Nor did there seem to be any common law precedent in the law reports which made this kind of government activity lawful.

In the absence of a clear statutory or common law authority, the government officials based their defence on two grounds. The first was an argument of 'state necessity'. The Home Secretary essentially claimed that he thought Entick's papers presented a serious threat to public order and social stability; it was necessary to seize the papers in order to prevent political unrest. The second argument might best be described as one of 'acquiescence' or 'custom and tradition'. The Home Secretary pointed out that this power had been used many times in recent years, and had never been challenged by anyone. If no-one had objected, surely the practice could not be unlawful?

Lord Chief Justice Camden was unimpressed by these arguments about necessity or habit. He was not interested in what the government thought was necessary, or in what the government had done in the past. All he was interested in was finding the law.

And at least one element of 'the law' was entirely clear. There was no doubt that:

> 'By the laws of England, every invasion of private property, be it ever so minute is a trespass. No man can set his foot upon my ground without my licence. . . . If he admits the fact, he is bound to show by way of justification, that some positive law has empowered or excused him. . . . If that cannot be done, that is a trespass.'[11]

Furthermore, so 'exorbitant' a power as the one deployed against

---

10 Anson (5th edn, 1922) *The Law and Custom of the Constitution* pp 309–311 (Oxford: Clarendon Press). Plucknett (1960) *op cit* pp 661–666.
11 (1765) 19 State Tr 1029 at 1066.

Mr Entick could be justified only by extremely clear statutory or common law authority. Lord Chief Justice Camden put the point quite simply; 'If it is law, it will be found in our books. If it is not to be found there, it is not law'.[12] The lawyers arguing the messenger's case were unable to find any such authority. In consequence, the messengers' entry to Mr Entick's property and seizure of his papers were straightforward instances of trespass. Mr Entick was thus entitled to recover damages from them to compensate him for his loss. And he was indeed awarded by the jury the then substantial sum of £300.

It was decisions such as *Entick v Carrington* which led one legal philosopher to characterise the courts as the 'lions under the throne' of the British constitution.[13] The aphorism perhaps lends itself to several interpretations, but for our purposes might be seen as conveying the idea that the judges were always ready to spring out and fiercely defend the rights and liberties of individual citizens from unlawful government interference. *Entick v Carrington* therefore provides a classic example of the courts upholding the rule of law in the sense of the theory that Dicey later produced. The theory does not entail that government always acts lawfully, but that the citizen always has a legal remedy when the government acts unlawfully, and that the government respects the courts' judgment when it is held to have breached the law.

But *Entick v Carrington* offers us no more than a partial picture, either of the principle or practice of the rule of law's constitutional role in modern Britain. Lord Camden's reasoning in *Entick* clearly reveals the depths with which Lockean notions of 'property' and 'liberty' were embedded within the eighteenth-century common law tradition. He noted at one point that:

> "The great end, for which men entered into society, was to secure their property. That right is preserved sacred and incommunicable in all instances, where it has not been taken away or abridged by some public law for the good of the whole."[14]

But even if we accept that the defence of 'property' and 'liberty' against arbitrary government is the courts' primary constitutional responsibility, we once again encounter the problem, adverted to in chapters 1 and 2, of just what 'liberty' and 'property' might mean?

12 *Ibid.*
13 See Heuston R (1970) '*Liversidge v Anderson* in retrospect' 86 *LQR* 33–68.
14 (1765) 19 State Tr 1029 at 1066.

Dicey's rule of law – process or substance?

The concept of the separation of powers, coupled with the application of that principle in *Entick*, might lead us to think that the Diceyan theory of the rule of law is *concerned only with the process of the way laws are administered*, and *not with the substance or content* of those laws. However Dicey's overt focus on process went hand in hand with a less visible political view about the 'correct' substance of the laws which the legislature should make. Dicey was much concerned that the laws which government administered had a high degree of *predictability or forseeability*. People needed to know where they stood if they were to run a business, get involved in politics, or start certain types of social relationships. So Dicey thought the rule of law demanded that Parliament did not give government any arbitrary or wide discretionary powers. A statute which said for instance that the Home Secretary can imprison anyone she likes, whenever she likes, for as long as she likes, for whatever reason she likes, would not meet the tests of predictability and forseeability, and would therefore seem to contradict Dicey's version of rule of law.

But we automatically encounter a major problem with this element of the rule of law. Dicey seems to be saying that there are limits to the type of governmental powers which Parliament can create through legislation if society is to remain subject to the rule of law. Yet the theory of parliamentary sovereignty tells us that there are no legal limitations on the statutes which Parliament can enact. One cannot go to court and ask for a statute which (for example) bestows very wide discretionary powers on the Home Secretary to search people's homes and seize their papers to be declared unconstitutional because it contravenes the Diceyan rule of law.[15] It appears from the judgment in *Entick v Carrington*, that had Parliament previously passed a statute authorising the Home Secretary to seize people's papers whenever he thought such action desirable, the civil servants' intrusion into Entick's property would have been lawful, and Entick's suit would have failed. It was suggested earlier that notions of the inviolability of 'property' and 'liberty' were by then 'embedded' in the common law. They were not, of course, 'entrenched' in the constitution, for, as a matter

---

15 One can of course do precisely that in the United States; the Fourth and Fourteenth Amendments of the Constitution place limits on the amount of discretion that Congress and the States can bestow on the executive arms of the federal and State governments; search warrants may only be issued 'upon probable cause . . . and particularly describing the place to be searched and the persons or things to be seized'.

of legal theory, Parliament might impinge upon property rights and personal liberties whenever and however it thought fit. In the aftermath of *Entick*, Parliament could if it had so wished have passed legislation affording 'general warrants' an entirely lawful status.[16]

The logical conclusion would therefore seem to be that the rule of law is a less important constitutional principle than the sovereignty of Parliament. But we must remember that both the Diceyan rule of law and Dicey's theory of parliamentary sovereignty are at root political or moral concepts; perhaps they are both, to borrow Professor Wade's terminology, 'ultimate political facts'. The difficult question which then arises is how can one have two 'ultimate' facts: one value must presumably give way to the other?[17] In later parts of this chapter, and at various points in subsequent chapters, we will consider the ways in which this apparent tension between parliamentary sovereignty and Dicey's rule of law has been addressed. For the moment, we might just note that the two concepts seem theoretically irreconcilable.

The 'independence of the judiciary'

A second contradiction between the rule of law and parliamentary sovereignty appears when we consider the concept of the 'independence of the judiciary'. Before the 1688 revolution, and in the years immediately thereafter, all judges in the English empire held office 'at the King's pleasure'. This meant quite simply that not only did the King appoint the judges, but also that judges who subsequently displeased the King or his government could be sacked. This was the fate that befell Chief Justice Coke in the early seventeenth century; the cumulative effect of judgments such as *Dr Bonham's Case* (and others we consider in chapter four) led Coke into such disfavour with the Crown that he was removed from office.[18]

The continuance of this situation after the 1688 revolution would clearly have presented a threat to the doctrine of parliamen-

16 As indeed it had already done in respect of the American colonies; see Brogan H (1986) *History of the USA* ch 8 (Harmondsworth: Pelican). See particularly the judgment of the US Supreme Court in *Boyd v United States* 116 US 616 (1886). As we shall see in chapter 14, it later did so in the domestic context.

17 An incisive analysis of this conundrum is provided by Allan T (1985) 'Legislative supremacy and the rule of law: democracy and constitutionalism' *Cambridge LJ* 111–143.

18 See Plucknett (1928) *op cit*; Corwin E (1928) 'The "higher law" background of American constitutional law (parts I and II)' *Harvard LR* 149–182 and 365–409.

tary sovereignty, since the King could conceivably have used his dismissal powers to 'persuade' judges to interpret laws in a manner inconsistent with Parliament's intentions. The solution to this problem, adopted in 1701, provides a further example of a 'balanced' constitution. The Act of Settlement 1701 provided that while the Crown had the power to appoint judges, judges would hold office 'during good behaviour'. This means a judge can only be removed by a joint address of the House of Lords and the House of Commons, after the judge has committed a crime or engaged in some particularly gross form of moral misbehaviour. She cannot simply be sacked by the Crown for interpreting the law in a way that the government does not like.

As we saw in chapter 1, one of the chief complaints of the American revolutionaries was that the Act of Settlement did not extend to all of the colonies. Their judges were appointed for limited terms by the colonial governors, acting on behalf of the Crown. And so they could be dismissed if they made decisions of which the governor disapproved. This meant of course that the judiciary was not very independent of the governor; judges wishing to stay in office had to keep one eye over their shoulders when deciding a case to see what the government wanted. In contrast, Lord Camden was able to produce a judgment of which the government disapproved in *Entick v Carrington* in 1765 because, unlike colonial judges, he was not dismissable at the whim of the government. Alexander Hamilton presumably had such principles in mind in *The Federalist Papers No 78*, when he advocated that the United States Supreme Court judges should hold office during good behaviour, noting that: 'The experience of Great Britain affords an illustrious comment on the excellence of the institution'.

One must observe however that the Act of Settlement only secured the independence of the judiciary against the Crown, not against Parliament. Parliamentary sovereignty meant both that an individual judge could be dismissed by a majority in the Commons and the Lords, and that the rules in the Act of Settlement could be changed at any time by new legislation. This theoretical possibility has yet to emerge in reality: only one High Court judge has ever been dismissed (in 1830); and while the Act of Settlement has been subjected to minor modifications, its basic provisions remain intact.[19] We might therefore plausibly conclude that in practice the British constitution affords the judiciary independence (from both government and Parliament) in the tenure of

19 We will consider the reasons for this in chapter 9.

their office. The force of this tradition in the 'British' context is perhaps best illustrated by returning once again to the aftermath of the *Harris* decision in South Africa; not even the National Party government thought that attempting to sack the five obstructive Supreme Court judges was a politically acceptable way to proceed. But those events also show that there may be more to the concept of an 'independent' judiciary than job security. Legislatures (as in South Africa) may create compliant courts by packing them with new judges rather than sacking the existing ones. 'Independence' may thus be as much a question of a judge's state of mind as the fixity of her legal hold on her office. One is thus drawn once again to note the inter-meshing of 'law' and 'politics' within the contemporary constitution.

II. THE RULE OF LAW IN THE WELFARE STATE

As has already been stressed, Dicey formulated his constitutional theories in the Victorian era. His views were shaped by the experience of living in a society in which few citizens were permitted to vote in Parliamentary elections, and in which government performed only a limited number of functions. By the 1950s, Britain was a society in which not only were virtually all adults enfranchised, but also government had assumed a very significant role in the management of economic and social affairs. At around the same time that Dicey was writing his *Law of the Constitution*, Parliament had begun to make greater use of legislation which gave government bodies loosely defined discretionary powers and duties. This trend accelerated markedly in the first half of the twentieth century, and continued to pick up pace in the immediate aftermath of World War II. It is beyond the scope of this book to consider questions of political theory and history in any great depth, but it is important that we at least grasp the rudiments of the arguments which have informed British political life in the modern era. Many of the significant constitutional events of recent years have arisen as a result of the government's attempts to pursue a particular ideological programme. To put things simply, we might suggest that there have been two main currents of opinion as to how best to govern a capitalist society in the post-war era.[20]

The first theory, representing right-wing political views, we

20 The most helpful introduction is perhaps George V and Wilding P (1976) *Ideology and State Welfare* (London: RKP).

might call 'market liberalism', to which Dicey was an early adherent. Its most celebrated defence in the modern era was put forward by an Austrian economist, Friedrich von Hayek, in a 1944 book entitled *The Road to Serfdom*.[1] The second theory, social democracy, emerged from the centre-left of the political spectrum, and from a lawyer's viewpoint is best explained by the American jurist Harry Jones in a 1958 article in the *Columbia Law Review*.[2] Since Parliament is a legally sovereign body, it may pursue liberal market, social democratic or any other brand of economic policy as and when it wishes. Rather different considerations pertained in the United States in the early part of the twentieth century, when Congressional attempts to introduce social democratic policies were held by the Supreme Court to violate various provisions of the Constitution.[3] That the Supreme Court subsequently changed its mind on such matters may indicate that a 'supra-legislative' constitution can be an extremely flexible legal creature. But in the British context, we need only note at this juncture that Parliament should not in theory find any such obstacles placed in the way of its preferences on economic policy issues.[4]

Hayek – *The road to serfdom*

Hayek is essentially a latter day exponent of the orthodox Diceyan viewpoint. For Hayek, the function of the rule of law is to ensure that 'government in all its actions is bound by rules fixed and announced beforehand'.[5] Citizens must be able to predict with a high degree of certainty the *exact limits* of the government's legal powers. This concern encompasses both process and substance.

In respect of process, Hayek follows Dicey in demanding that all citizens must have access to an independent judiciary before which they can challenge the legality of government action; is it the case that what government has done is in accordance with a pre-existing common law or statutory rule? The courts' first and

---

1 (London: RKP).
2 Jones H (1958) 'The rule of law and the welfare state' 58 *Columbia LR* 143–156. For a specifically contextualised explanation of the political objects such a theory should serve see Crosland C (1952) 'The transition from capitalism'; and Jenkins R (1952) 'Equality', both in Crossman R (ed) *New Fabian Essays* (London: Turnstile).
3 See generally Maidment R (1992) *The Supreme Court and the New Deal* (Buckingham: Open University Press).
4 At this juncture, we are not taking account of the impact of the UK's membership of the EC. We will return to this matter in chapters 12 and 13.
5 (1944) *op cit* p 54.

only duty is to protect the citizen against the government; judges must not succumb to the temptation to bend legal rules in order to facilitate the government process. Hayek's reference to 'rules' is of fundamental importance to his analysis. There is minimal scope within his ideal society for laws which give government *discretionary powers*, that is to say laws which made it possible for government to respond in more than one way in a given situation. In such circumstances, it would be impossible for citizens to predict the exact extent of government authority. This preference for a rule-bound government process co-exists with a desire for a *government which is minimalist in substance*. The substance of Hayek's political and economic theories exercised a great deal of influence on the Thatcher administrations which governed Britain between 1979 and 1990.[6] To put the matter crudely, Hayekians believe that society's interests are best served by reducing the power and size of government to a minimum, thereby giving individual citizens as much freedom as possible to organise their social and economic affairs in accordance with their own wishes. Government must provide an army to defend the country from external aggression; it must provide a police force to uphold the criminal law; and it must provide a court system to settle disputes over crimes, contracts, and property. But it should go no further. In its most extreme form, market liberalism would maintain that government should have no role at all in the provision of health services, education, housing, or social security. If such things were beneficial to society, they would be provided by private entrepreneurs and purchased by individual citizens.

Hayek accepts that there will be great inequalities of wealth in such a society. This is considered regrettable, but is regarded as a natural consequence of people's varying attitudes and abilities. Hayek considers such inequality to be a lesser evil than the intrusion upon individual freedom which would result if the government took positive steps to address this 'natural' state of affairs. The bottom line of the Hayekian analysis is that society cannot have both the rule of law and a welfare state. Since Parliament is sovereign, it may choose one value or the other, but it would be quite wrong for legislators to claim that they could simultaneously pursue both ideals. The *rule of law is an absolute value*, which can exist only in constitutions which prevent legislators intervening in social and economic affairs. From this view-

6 A useful introduction is provided by Hall S (1983) 'The great moving right show' and Gough I (1983) 'Thatcherism and the welfare state'; both in Hall S and Jacques M (eds) *The Politics of Thatcherism* (London: Lawrence and Wishart).

point, the rule of law 'has little to do with the question whether all actions of government are legal in the juridical sense', rather 'it implies limits to the scope of legislation'.[7] Hayek denies that the legislature can perform a balancing act between economic equality and the rule of law; 'any policy aiming directly at a substantive ideal of redistributive justice must lead to the destruction of the rule of law'.[8] Parliament cannot 'trade off' a slight reduction in the rule of law to gain a slight increase in economic or social equality.

Jones – the rule of law in the welfare state

While Hayek's theory was very influential in Britain in the 1980s, it enjoyed little support among either the Conservative or Labour parties in the thirty years following World War II. The political consensus in that era fell within the broad confines of a *social democratic approach to government.* The politics of the period are often referred to as 'Butskellism'. This is a combination of the names of R A B Butler and Hugh Gaitskell, who were leading figures in the Conservative and Labour parties respectively, and the term is designed to stress the similarity of the political objectives which the two parties pursued.[9] This perspective assumes firstly that government ought to play an extensive role in the management of economic affairs, and secondly that individuals must accept quite restrictive limits on their autonomy if the legislature deems such restraints to be in the public interest. Social democracy must be distinguished from those forms of socialism and communism which have as their objective absolute economic equality between citizens. Social democracy is concerned with ameliorating, not eliminating inequality.

Some of the earliest examples of this theory of government were introduced by the Gladstone and Disraeli administrations in the late nineteenth century, in legislation which placed limits on the use of child labour for example, or which prevented factories from emptying their effluent into rivers or the streets. The justification for such government intervention comes from two sources. Firstly, it is considered 'just' and 'fair' insofar as it protects individuals from exploitation. Secondly, it is thought to

---

7 *Op cit* at pp 61–62.
8 *Ibid,* at p 59.
9 A helpful introductory guide to these various theories of government is George and Wilding *op cit* chs 2–4.

be rational for society as a whole; for example the cost of ill health and death which might result from not having controls on pollution outweighs the expense involved in disposing of waste in a satisfactory manner.

By the 1950s, this twin rationale underpinned an immense network of government activities; a National Health Service, millions of publicly-owned houses; government control of the coal, steel, water, gas, and electricity industries; old age pensions; unemployment benefits; and free schooling for all children until the age of fifteen. This clearly represented, in Hayek's words, a 'substantive ideal of redistributive justice'. The welfare state also required Parliament to give government officials large numbers of discretionary powers; it was simply not feasible to run a complex welfare state in accordance with legislative 'rules'. Government was now doing so much, and dealing with so many different situations, that it would simply be impossible for legislators to produce a rule for every forseeable situation. This growth in the enactment of discretion-laden legislation necessarily meant that there was some reduction in the degree to which citizens could precisely predict the limits of government's legal authority. However, some constitutional lawyers denied that this meant that society could not be governed in accordance with the rule of law.

In contrast to Hayek, Harry Jones suggests that the *rule of law is a relative rather than absolute political value*. It is possible to dilute the Diceyan model of the rule of law, without removing its basic features. Like Hayek, Jones accepts that 'the rule of law's great purpose is protection of the individual against state power holders'.[10] But he also suggested that the rule of law would continue to exist as long as legislators, government officials, and the judiciary accepted what he termed an 'adjudicative ideal'.

While legislation in Hayekian society would take the form of rigid rules, the statutory basis of a welfare state would also contain flexible standards, permitting government to make various responses to given situations. However the adjudicative ideal demands that although the legislature can bestow wide discretion on government bodies, it may not grant them arbitrary powers. Jones' version of the rule of law does not dismiss the importance of predictability and certainty; rather it accepts that in some areas of government activity it is only necessary that citizens be able to forsee the general boundaries rather than the precise location of government authority.

Nor does Jones' theory reject the need for a separation of

10 *Op cit* at p 145.

powers. Citizens must be able to challenge the legality of government through a 'meaningful day in court'. Jones differs from Hayek in assuming that 'a meaningful day in court' need not entail resort to the 'ordinary courts'; specialist tribunals could serve this purpose in respect of some government functions, since they might be more informal, more expert and less time-consuming and expensive than the normal judicial process.

The task which faces the courts and tribunals in social democratic society is not simply to protect the individual at all costs. Since Parliament has given the government discretionary powers, the courts must accept that the legislature has intended that individuals might suffer some minor detriment or restraint on their autonomy in order to further the public interest. This may present courts with a difficult problem – how much discretion did Parliament intend the government to have? Jones recognised that this set 'a harder and wider task for the rule of law', but he suggested that Hayek was being unduly pessimistic in suggesting that the concept had to be abandoned altogether.

Although the creation of a welfare state may be difficult to reconcile with a Diceyan or Hayekian view of the rule of law, it would seem consistent with some of the notions of democracy in the sense of government by consent discussed in chapter 1. If 'the people' have decided that they are willing to dilute the Diceyan ideal to achieve certain economic or social objectives, there would seem to be no obvious barrier to them doing so. Whether that conclusion is, from a political perspective, a sound one, is a question to which we shall return in later chapters. We might note for instance that it would be quite possible for a society to adhere to Hayek/Dicey's version of the rule of law without being a democracy. A dictator who preserved market autonomy and stuck rigidly to pre-announced limits on her/his powers would pass Hayek's test. Whether one can have a democratic constitution without respect for at least a diluted version of the rule of law is a more difficult question, which we shall pursue at a later stage.

However, from a lawyer's perspective, Jones' and Hayek/Dicey's competing viewpoints about the 'what and the how' of modern government are neatly encapsulated in what Carol Harlow and Richard Rawlings term the 'red light' and 'green light' theories of legal control of executive behaviour.[11] Red light theorists such as Hayek, echoing Dicey's suspicion of the executive, maintain that the rule of law's primary concern should be to *stop government interfering with individual autonomy.* Green light theorists such as

11 *Op cit* chs 1 and 2.

Jones, in contrast, believe that the Diceyan pre-occupation with individual rights is misplaced in modern society. It is assumed that Parliament and the courts should loosen the legal constraints on government discretion, enabling government to *curb individual autonomy in order to promote society's collective well-being*.

We will make repeated forays into the judicial arena in this and subsequent chapters. As we shall see, the reality of court regulation of government action in the modern British constitutional context does not fit neatly into one or other of these theoretical perspectives. Harlow and Rawlings suggest that we can identify a third theoretical position, labelled 'amber light' theory, lying inbetween the two extremes. This does not mean that, in practice, legal controls lie at the precise mid-point of the theoretical continuum, but that individual cases tend to be located at various positions on the spectrum. Sometimes they approach the green light extreme, sometimes the red.

Within this theoretical framework, legal controls are designed to provide government with some flexibility, but not too much flexibility. That naturally raises the question of 'How much is too much?' There is no easy answer to this question; the point is perhaps best illustrated by the gradual accumulation of many examples; a task to which, after a brief schematic diversion, we shall shortly return.

III. JUDICIAL REGULATION OF GOVERNMENT BEHAVIOUR: THE CONSTITUTIONAL RATIONALE

The origins, structure, and powers of the present judicial system is a subject best explored in detail in textbooks dealing with the English legal system. However some very broad points must be made here about the nature both of the court system and the 'judicial law-making process'. All courts in Britain are now in technical terms statutory creations. Prior to the revolution, the legal landscape was littered with a vast array of different courts, each exercising nominally independent but frequently overlapping jurisdictions. An inevitable consequence of the emergence of the parliamentary sovereignty doctrine was that the powers (and indeed even the existence) of particular courts could be amended or abolished by legislation. Numerous piecemeal reforms (such as the Act of Settlement 1701) were introduced during the next two hundred years, but for our purposes the most significant legislative initiative was the passage of the Judicature Acts of 1873 and 1875. These Acts merged the many so-called 'superior' courts into the newly created High Court and Court of Appeal, and defined both the new courts' respective jurisdictions and the qualifications required of the judges who would sit in them. Subsequent statutes confirmed the House of Lords' position (in its judicial capacity) at the apex of the British judicial system, where it functions as the final court of appeal.

However, while Parliament has periodically altered the structure and jurisdiction of the courts, and while the 'common law'[12] is undoubtedly inferior to statute in circumstances where a statutory and common law rule seemingly demand different solutions to a particular problem, Parliament has never enacted legislation which has sought systematically to control either the method or outcome of the judiciary's law-making process. The 1688 revolution did establish that statute could alter or abolish any common law principles whenever Parliament wished, but virtually all of those principles initially remained in place. Thus, in the absence of statutory controls, the content of the common law remains a matter for the courts to determine. And within the present court system, it is the House of Lords in its judicial capacity which is the ultimate arbiter of the substance of common law principles.

Such judicial power is not inconsistent with the notion of parliamentary sovereignty, because it is assumed that Parliament always intends that government will exercise its statutory powers in accordance with the precepts that the common law currently requires. One might say that *common law principles are the implied terms of the government process*, and that Parliament is generally considered to have *contracted in* to these limits on executive autonomy. If Parliament does not want a particular government action to be subject to judicial control, it must say so in the statute which grants the power. Because Parliament is sovereign, it would seem that in theory Parliament can if it wishes *contract out* of the common law principles which allow the court to regulate government activities. Such legislation might seem (to borrow Lord Reid's terminology in *Madzimbamuto v Lardner-Burke*) 'politically or morally improper', insofar as it arguably derogates from orthodox understandings of the rule of law, but there is no legal impediment to Parliament enacting it.

This book will use the term 'administrative law' to encompass the various common law controls that the courts place on the

12 The term is used here in a very loose sense, simply to denote laws made by courts rather than by Parliament. The technical distinctions between common law, equity and other historical forms of judicial law-making are an unnecessary complication for the purposes of this study.

government process. In many instances, administrative law may take the simple form of an action in contract or (as in *Entick v Carrington*) tort against a government body where the government has breached a contract or committed a tortious act. However, the concept of *judical review* is the main component of administrative law. We will not explore that concept in any great depth in this book, but, if one wishes to gain a proper understanding of the basic features of constitutional law, it is necessary to consider the fundamental ingredients of, and justification for the doctrine of judicial review of executive action. Broadly stated, the modern form of judicial review is designed to uphold a certain interpretation of the rule of law and the separation of powers – its function is to *ensure that executive bodies remain within the limits of the powers that the legislature has granted*. In the United States, as we saw in chapter 1, judicial review has a further dimension, for the Supreme Court is also responsible for *ensuring that the legislature remains within the limits of the powers that the Constitution has granted*.

In the more limited British context, the leading case is the 1948 Court of Appeal decision in *Associated Provincial Picture Houses Ltd v Wednesbury Corpn.*[13] *Wednesbury* suggests that there are three grounds on which a court may find that executive action is 'ultra vires', that is to say 'beyond the limits' of parliamentary authority. The first ground could be described as 'illegality'. If Parliament passes a statute for instance which allows the government to provide schools, the government could not invoke that statute as a justification to build houses.

Wednesbury also makes it clear that a government body exceeds its statutory powers if it exercises them in a way that is *unreasonable* or *irrational*. This ground of review is particularly important in respect of discretionary powers. The concept of 'unreasonableness' bears a special meaning in administrative law. An action is only unreasonable if it is so bizarre that no reasonable person could have assumed Parliament would have intended it to happen. As an example, assume that a statute gives government the power to employ teachers in primary schools 'on such terms as it thinks fit'. The exercise of that power would only be unreasonable if it was used in a way that appeared to bear no relation at all to rational objectives: if the government body decided not to employ anyone with red hair for instance. In contrast, reasonable people

---

13 [1948] 1 KB 223. The case did not create any new principles, but merely provided a thorough restatement of well-established concepts; see Sedley S (1994) 'Governments, constitutions and judges', in Genn H and Richardson G (eds) *Administrative Law and Government Action* (Oxford: Clarendon Press).

might reach rather different conclusions about precisely how much teachers should be paid, for example, or what level of qualifications they should have. Such diversity is perfectly lawful: administrative law accepts that when a statute uses a discretionary term, the Parliament which enacted the legislation expects that there will be some variation in the substance of decisions reached. The notion of irrationality functions to ensure that those variations remain within the boundaries of political consensus that Parliament envisaged.

The third point to note is that administrative law requires statutory powers to be exercised through *fair procedures*. Broadly stated, this means firstly that decision-makers should not have a personal interest in the decision being made; and secondly that people affected by the decision should have an opportunity to state their case before a conclusion is reached.[14]

Judicial review is a *supervisory rather than appellate* jurisdiction. A court which holds a government action unlawful will not substitute its own decision for the one made by the government body concerned, but will return the question to the original decision-maker so that the decision can be made again, this time (one assumes) in accordance with legal requirements. In contrast, in an action for (for example) trespass or breach of contract, the court will impose its solution on the dispute before it.

It should again be stressed that the theoretical rationale for judicial control of government behaviour derives from the constitution's 'ultimate political fact' of parliamentary sovereignty. This requires that the government may only perform those tasks that Parliament permits. The courts' constitutional role is therefore to police the boundaries of legislative intent,[15] and ensure that government cannot overstep those boundaries without incurring legal liability.

Yet one should beware of concluding from this that the courts' role is one of mere mechanical obeisance to legislative texts. We will return to this point in more detail below. But here, we might note that since the *Wednesbury* grounds of review are common law concepts, it is entirely legal for the courts to amend, abolish or

14 The concept has generated a vast amount of case law, which is most appropriately addressed in a text dealing exclusively with the detail of administrative law.

15 This point applies as much to legal justifications for government behaviour rooted in common law rather than statute, for one assumes that particular common law rules exist only because Parliament has not seen any need to abolish or amend them. Judicial regulation of the government's common law powers is addressed in chapter 4.

add to those grounds as they think fit. We will shortly, when examining the concept of stare decisis, encounter the moral or political principles which have led the courts to be cautious in developing new grounds of review or redefining existing ones. But until such time as Parliament enacts legislation which seems to 'freeze' aspects of the common law at a particular point in their development, there is no legal impediment to radical judicial reform of its contents.

The extent of the courts' power in this regard is perhaps best illustrated by discussion of another of the seminal constitutional cases. For if *Entick v Carrington* provides an example of the courts upholding the Diceyan principle of the rule of law, *Liversidge v Anderson* presents a judgment seemingly doing precisely the opposite.

The meaning of words: *Liversidge v Anderson* (1942)

Liversidge v Anderson[16] was a case that arose in 1942 out of the Defence Regulations 1939. At the start of World War II, Parliament enacted various measures to strengthen the government's powers to protect the country from sabotage or treason by enemy agents. Regulation 18b of the 1939 Regulations provided that:

> 'If the Home Secretary has reasonable cause to believe any person to be of hostile origins or association . . . , he may make an order against that person directing that he be detained.'

Between May and August 1940, the Home Secretary, Sir John Anderson, used reg 18b to order the detention of around one and a half thousand people. Over eleven hundred detainees were quickly released when it became clear that the government's suspicions about them were not well founded.[17]

One person detained was Robert Liversidge. Liversidge sued Anderson for false imprisonment. Liversidge had obviously been made to 'suffer in body' – he had been confined in prison. The question before the court was whether the executive action which had led to Liversidge's detention was lawful. Was there a statutory or common law power which empowered the government to lock Mr Liversidge up? This situation is in one sense different from *Entick v Carrington*. In the latter case, the Home Secretary had some statutory regulations to which he could point in an attempt

16 [1942] AC 206.
17 See the fascinating study by Simpson A (1991) *In the Highest Degree Odious* (Oxford: Clarendon Press).

to justify his action. However, Liversidge's contention was that athough the Defence Regulations gave the Home Secretary the power to detain people in some circumstances, those circumstances did not exist in this particular case. The detention was therefore illegal in the *Wednesbury* sense.

To understand the judgment in *Liversidge v Anderson*, we must examine the precise wording of reg 18b. It says that the Home Secretary can detain an individual if: 'he has reasonable cause to believe' that person is of hostile origin or association. The insertion of the 'reasonable cause to believe' clause seems to fit with the Diceyan idea of the rule of law which disapproves of any statute in which Parliament grants the government wide discretionary powers. The clause seems to limit the possibility of the Home Secretary using the power arbitrarily. Regulation 18b apparently requires the Home Secretary to show the court the evidence on which his suspicions were based, and to convince the judges that the evidence did indeed amount to a 'reasonable cause'. If there was insufficient evidence to support the conclusion that a detainee had hostile origins, the power could not lawfully be used.

The government itself had acknowledged that this was the correct interpretation of the regulations in the first case challenging their use, *R v Secretary of State for Home Affairs, ex p Lees*.[18] In a subsequent case, *Budd v Anderson*,[19] the court had ordered the plaintiff to be released because the Home Secretary was unable to produce any convincing evidence of his 'hostility'.

However, the government changed its argument in *Liversidge*, and contended that no such evidence need be presented. Four[20] of the five members of the House of Lords agreed with the government's interpretation. They concluded that the Home Secretary could use reg 18b to imprison anyone he thought was of hostile origins. He did not need to offer the court any evidence to show that his belief was reasonable. He could in fact imprison anyone at all. He did not have to say why. And anyone who was detained was wasting her time coming to the courts to challenge the adequacy of the Home Secretary's belief. Lord Wright encapsulated the majority sentiment by concluding that:

> 'All the word "reasonable", then, means is that the minister must not lightly or arbitrarily invade the liberty of the subject, He must be reasonably satisfied before he acts, but it is still his decision, and not

18 [1941] 1 KB 72, CA; discussed in Simpson *op cit* pp 62–63 and ch 14.
19 [1943] 2 All ER 452. See Simpson *op cit* pp 318–321.
20 Viscount Maugham, Lord Macmillan, Lord Wright, and Lord Romer.

the decision of anyone else. . . . No outsider's decision is invoked, nor is the issue within the competence of any court.'[21]

One Law Lord took a different view. Lord Atkin thought that reg 18b could bear only one possible meaning. If Parliament said 'reasonable cause to believe', it must have intended that there be *some* plausible evidence on which that view was based. If legislators had intended to give the Home Secretary an arbitrary power, they would simply have said 'if the Home Secretary believes'. Regulation 18(b)'s parliamentary history seems to support Lord Atkin's view.[1] The original version of the regulation had not included the 'reasonable cause' requirement. It had been inserted as an amendment because MPs had feared that leaving it out would give the Home Secretary an arbitrary power. This suggests that the majority judgment effectively permitted the government both to disregard the principle of parliamentary sovereignty and to contravene Dicey's version of the rule of law.

But despite the apparently 'unconstitutional' nature of the majority judgment, it was Lord Atkin who received considerable criticism from the government, from fellow judges, and from the public at large. In part, this criticism was directed at the substance of his opinion. The country was after all at war. People were greatly concerned about saboteurs, traitors and spies. Atkin was accused of wanting to tie the government's hands in its efforts to root out these potential enemies. Hayekian theory, for example, would accept that the rule of law could legitimately be 'suspended' during war, on the grounds that the most important political value (another 'ultimate political fact'?) was the preservation of the country's very existence as an independent state.[2] From that perspective, Lord Atkin's attachment to rigorous legal principle could almost be construed as treasonable.

However, Lord Atkin also antagonised many people (including

---

21 [1942] AC 206 at 268 and 270.
1 For reasons discussed in chapter 8, courts did not at that time look at the records of Parliamentary debates to assist them in interpreting the meaning of statutes. Cf Lord Macmillan in *Liversidge* at 256: 'I do not know, and it would not be proper for me to inquire, why a change was made . . .'.
2 The principle is sometimes expressed in the latin maxim *salus populi est suprema lex*. See for example Viscount Maugham in *Liversidge* at 218–219, and Lord Macmillan at 251. In contrast, at 244, Lord Atkin argued: 'In this country, amid the clash of arms, the laws are not silent. They may be changed, but they speak the same language in war as in peace. It has always been one of the pillars of freedom, one of the principles of liberty for which on recent authority we are now fighting, that the judges are no respecters of persons and stand between the subject and any attempted encroachments on his liberty by the executive'.

fellow judges) by the language that he used to express his opinions.[3] He accused his four colleagues in the Lords of being 'more executive minded than the executive'.[4] Lord Atkin had found only one possible 'authority' to justify the majority's interpretation of reg 18b. There is a scene in *Alice Through the Looking Glass* where Alice and Humpty Dumpty discuss the use of language:

> ' "When I use a word", Humpty Dumpty said in rather a scornful tone, "it means just what I choose it to mean, neither more nor less". "The question is" said Alice, "whether you can make words mean different things". "The question is", said Humpty Dumpty, "which is to be master – that's all".'[5]

This is not to suggest that the British constitution is built on the Humpty Dumpty theory of the rule of law. That would be a flippant over-statement. But the important inference that we ought to draw from Lord Atkin's dissent is that there is little point in regarding the relationship between citizens and the government as a 'political contract' in which Parliament creates a legal framework to which the people consent, nor to assume that the constitution rests on the twin bedrocks of parliamentary sovereignty and the Diceyan rule of law, if the words that the legislature uses in statutes to express its wishes can be interpreted by the courts to mean things Parliament did not intend. Such an outcome might be seen as a judicial subversion of the power of Parliament. One might meet this point by suggesting that the majority decision in *Liversidge* must have been 'correct', because Parliament took no steps to reverse it. As we shall see on later occasions, that argument rather over-simplifies the nature of the relationship between Parliament and the courts. It also fails to meet the objection that the House of Commons, the House of Lords or the Monarch might seek to mislead each other (or combine to mislead the people) by deliberately passing bills in the expectation that the courts will lend the resultant statute an interpretation that seems to defy accepted understandings as to the meaning of language.

In the aftermath of *Liversidge*, one of Lord Atkin's fellow judges (Stable J) wrote to him to say the majority decision brought the judiciary into disrepute. The judges were no longer 'lions under the throne, but mice squeaking under a chair in the Home Office'.[6] Again, one would be unduly flippant in suggesting that

---

3 See Heuston R (1970) '*Liversidge v Anderson* in retrospect' *LQR* 33–68.
4 [1942] AC 206 at 244.
5 *Ibid*, at 245.
6 Quoted in Heuston (1970) *op cit* at p 51.

Liversidge v Anderson is authority for the proposition that the effective operation of the rule of law in modern Britain rests on a Mickey Mouse theory of judicial integrity. But the case once again suggests that effective functioning of the rule of law, at least as Dicey understood it, requires judges who possess an *independence of mind*, as well as an independence of office.

This necessarily leads us to ask to whom, or to what, does a judge's constitutional loyalty ultimately lie? This is not so much a question of a judge's personal predisposition, but of the principles which the High Court, Court of Appeal and House of Lords deploy when interpreting the meaning of statutes and deciding the content of the common law. Both issues are more appropriately discussed in detail in textbooks on jurisprudence or the English legal system, but they are integral elements of the contemporary constitutional order, and so must be adverted to at least briefly in this work.[7]

Principles of statutory interpretation

While the words of a statute have traditionally been regarded as the 'highest form of law' known to the British constitution, the task of attaching a specific legal meaning to the words that Parliament has used has generally fallen to the courts. The inherent ambiguity and imprecision of language necessarily entails that even legislation which is expressed in the form of rigid rules may sometimes raise questions concerning its applicability to particular situations. Such uncertainty is much increased when Parliament chooses to employ statutory formulae which bestow discretionary powers on government bodies. Since the resolution of such uncertainty is a judicial function, the process of statutory interpretation is thus a crucial element both of the rule of law and the sovereignty of Parliament.

Parliament has on occasion enacted legislation instructing the courts as to the meaning to be accorded to particular words or phrases which constantly reappear in various statutes. We saw one example of a so-called 'Interpretation Act' in chapter two when we looked at the role played by Lord Brougham's Act of 1850 in the *Chorlton v Lings* litigation. However such legislation pertains to technicalities, rather than to sweeping instructions as to broad interpretive techniques. That latter component of the constitution

7 I am much indebted in the following pages to Michael Zander's (1994) *The Law-Making Process* chs 3–4 (London: Butterworths).

is one that has traditionally been controlled by the courts themselves.

Three such techniques, respectively referred to as the 'literal rule', the 'golden rule', and the 'mischief rule' have traditionally been recognised as legitimate. The literal rule, which has been by far the dominant approach, suggests that the court's duty is to attach the orthodox, grammatical meaning to the statute's phraseology, even if that leads to ostensibly unjust or even bizarre results. The literal rule was perhaps most clearly expressed by Lord Esher in 1892 in *R v Judge of the City of London Court*:

> 'If the words of the Act are clear, you must follow them, even though they lead to a manifest absurdity. The court has nothing to do with the question of whether the legislature has committed an absurdity.'[8]

The literal rule betokens a very dogmatic judicial acceptance of the common law's constitutional inferiority to statute. Since Parliament may if it wishes enact 'absurdities', the court would be questioning Parliament's sovereignty if it tried to attach a 'sensible' interpretation to statutory formulae whose literal meaning pointed in a different direction. If the absurdity or unjust result was a mistake rather than an intended consequence, the solution would be for Parliament to enact a new statute amending the meaning of the former Act.

The so-called 'golden rule' credits the legislature with a somewhat greater degree of rationality. The golden rule suggests that when a literal reading of a particular statutory provision would lead to an absurdity, the court should examine the statute in its entirety to see if another, more sensible, meaning might be attached to the relevant words in the light of the legislative context in which they appear.

The third strategy, the 'mischief rule', neatly illustrates the hierarchical relationship between statute and common law. The rule requires that the court ask itself which 'mischief' or defect in the common law (or previous legislation) that the statute was intended to amend, and thereafter to construe it in a manner that minimises the possibility of the mischief recurring. In its initial form, the judges' interpretation of the mischief rule did not empower them to look beyond the statute and the relevant common law rules to ascertain the 'mischief' Parliament was supposedly trying to remove. Thus, if a logical parliamentary intent could not be deduced from the words of the Act itself, the rule could not be applied. By the mid-1970s, the courts had begun to refer to

8 [1892] 1 QB 273 at 290, CA.

government policy documents explaining the policies underlying particular legislative reforms as an aid to interpretation.[9] That initiative certainly enhanced the potency of the mischief rule. But its utility continued to be greatly limited by the courts' presumption that their search for Parliament's intentions did not permit them to clarify the meaning of statutory texts by referring to speeches made about the legislation during its passage through the Commons and the Lords. We will consider the basis and implications of that principle, and the House of Lords' more recent departure from it, at a later stage, for neither can be fully understood until we have examined the nature of the legislative process in rather greater detail.[10]

All three traditional strategies seem to draw a clear distinction between the legislative and judicial role, and emphasise the subordinacy of the latter to the former. They did not, however, find favour with with all members of the judiciary, some of whom thought a rather more radical approach was desirable. Lord Denning, in the 1950 case of *Magor and St Mellons RDC v Newport Corpn*, advanced a rather different understanding of the court's 'interpretive' duty:

> 'We do not sit here to pull the language of Parliament and of Ministers to pieces and make nonsense of it. . . . We sit here to find out the intention of Parliament and of Ministers and carry it out, and we do this better by filling in the gaps and making sense of the enactment than by opening it up to destructive analysis.'[11]

Lord Denning's intiative may be seen as an early example of a fourth interpretive techinque, now known as the 'purposive' or 'teleological' approach. This strategy rejects the presumption that a judge should restrict her search for the meaning of law to the statute itself, but rather tries to imagine what the framers of the legislation would have done if faced with the problem now before the court. The teleological strategy was by then already a common feature of many continental European legal systems, and was widely used in the United States. But Lord Denning's efforts to 'import' it into the English constitutional tradition found little favour with the House of Lords. On further appeal, the House of Lords firmly rebutted Lord Denning's presumptions as to the judiciary's appropriate constitutional role. According to Lord Simonds:

9 *Black-Clawson International Ltd v Papierwerke Waldhof-Aschaffenburg AG* [1975] AC 591.
10 At pp 314–320 below.
11 [1950] 2 All ER 1226 at 1236, CA.

'[T]he general proposition that it is the duty of the court to find out the intention of Parliament – and not only of Parliament but of Ministers also – cannot by any means be supported. The duty of the court is to interpret the words that the legislature has used.'[12]

As to Lord Denning's suggestion that the court might 'fill in the gaps' left by the statute's text, Lord Simonds identified fundamental constitutional objections. For a court to adopt such techniques would be: 'a naked usurpation of the legislative function under the thin guise of interpretation. . . . If a gap is disclosed, the remedy lies in an amending Act'.[13]

Lord Simonds somewhat overstated the 'naked usurpation' criticism. In the absence of legislation specifically forbidding 'purposive' interpretive techniques, the House of Lords (as the ultimate arbiter of common law principles) was in theory quite competent to jettison the three traditional rules and adopt Lord Denning's preferred option. That the majority in *Magor* chose not to do so was an indication that they considered such an innovation 'unconstitutional' in the sense of its political illegitimacy, not of its legal impossibility. Denning's judgment was overturned by the House of Lords not because it *was* unconstitutional in some objective sense, but because the Law Lords *felt that it was* unconstitutional.

The case does however emphasise the point that the dividing line between 'interpretation' and 'legislation' may on occasion be a difficult one to draw. We can confidently state that, as a matter of constitutional theory, Parliament legislates and the courts interpret. It is much more difficult to ascertain whether, as a matter of constitutional practice, that theory is always respected. We will return to the purposive approach in chapters 8 and 11. At this juncture, we might simply observe that, even as late as 1985, it remained a radical (indeed almost subversive) common law doctrine.

Stare decisis

The principle of legal certainty – that citizens be able to predict the limits the law places on individual and governmental behaviour – is an essential ingredient (albeit one respected with varying degrees of stringency) in all theoretical analyses of the rule of law. The principle has only a precarious legal basis in

12 W[1951] 2 All ER 839 at 841.
13 *Ibid.*

the British constitution, since Parliament may at any time change any law in any way whatsoever. For much of the modern era, the common law has, in contrast, possessed an almost absolute degree of legal certainty.

The common law's attachment to an inflexible doctrine of stare decisis (a maxim best translated as meaning 'let the previous decision stand') was confirmed in the 1898 case of *London Tramways Co v LCC*.[14] For a unanimous House of Lords, Lord Halsbury claimed that the judgments of that court bound not only all inferior courts, but also the House of Lords itself. He acknowledged that such rigidity might on occasion produce substantively unjust solutions to given problems because the common law could not be adapted to meet changing social conditions:

> 'but what is that . . . as compared with the inconvenience – the disastrous inconvenience – of having each question subject to being reargued and the dealings of mankind rendered doubtful by reason of different decisions, so that in truth and in fact there would be no final court of appeal.'[15]

Lord Halsbury's reasoning obviously has strong roots in Diceyan perceptions of the need to avoid unpredictability and arbitrariness in the content of the legal framework within which citizens live. It may thus be seen as a legal expression of the political principles underpinning red light variants of the rule of law. It should however be emphasised that the courts' adherence to a rigid stare decisis principle (like its preference for a literal rule of statutory interpretation) was a common law rule, fashioned by the House of Lords itself, not a requirement imposed upon the courts by Parliament. Clearly, in cases involving intolerable injustice in which the House of Lords felt itself bound by a previous decision, Parliament could if it wished pass legislation altering the substantive law. Similarly, Parliament could at any time enact a statute ordering the courts to depart from the *London Tramways* rule in any way on any occasions they thought fit, or to abandon the principle altogether. But furthermore, in the absence of any legislation on the point, the House of Lords itself retained the power to amend or reject the rule: common law rules are as much at the mercy of the final court of appeal as of the legislature.

Lord Halsbury's suggestion that the House of Lords could bind itself is therefore a nonsense, as a matter both of abstract logic and constitutional principle. Binding legal rules depend for their

14 [1898] AC 375.
15 *Ibid*, at 380.

force on the existence of a higher source of law than the rules themselves. The members of the House of Lords qua final court of appeal in 1898 could no more 'bind' their successors than the Parliament of that year could 'bind' future Parliaments. Lord Halsbury might expect his successors to respect his rule because of its intrinsic merits; he could in no legal sense compel them to do so.

In the event, the House of Lords did not avail itself of its undoubted constitutional power to depart from the *London Tramways* principle until 1966. In a *Practice Statement* issued on July 26, the Lord Chancellor announced that the House of Lords would in future modify its approach to stare decisis, and depart from its previous decisions in order to avoid injustice in particular cases and to facilitate the development of common law principles in a way that reflected changing social and economic conditions. The House of Lords has however rarely availed itself of this new power, and has developed quite rigorous criteria which must be met before a previous decision is overruled.[16] The initiative may thus be seen as a classic example of the green light approach to the rule of law, in which red light principles are not abandoned entirely, but are nevertheless appreciably diluted. While important in itself, the significance of the 1966 *Practice Statement* should not be exaggerated. The House of Lords will only infrequently find itself faced by legal problems which cannot in some way be distinguished from previous decisions on similar points. And for constitutional lawyers, the more pressing question is not what the House of Lords will do when faced with a common law rule it considers unpalatable, but what it will do when its distaste is triggered by a statutory provision.

IV. PARLIAMENTARY SOVEREIGNTY v THE RULE OF LAW

Dicey's notions of parliamentary sovereignty and the rule of law only function in the sense that he intended if the courts accept that their allegiance lies to the legislature rather than to the executive. We must stress again that in orthodox constitutional theory, the courts' allegiance is not to the people, nor to a supra-legislative constitution, but simply to the will of Parliament as expressed in the words of a statute. But as our knowledge of the law of the constitution increases, so we come to see that orthodox theory may present a misleading picture. *Liversidge* seemingly pro-

16 See Zander (1994) *op cit* pp 190–199.

vides an example of the courts in effect giving allegiance to the executive rather than to Parliament. Insofar as the constitution places the task of interpreting legislation in the hands of the courts, *Liversidge* respects parliamentary sovereignty because it is only the court which can tell us what Parliament intended. But that is a very formalistic view of 'law'; if we look behind this legal facade to the political principles underpinning traditonal views of the rule of law and the separation of powers, *Liversidge* can plausibly be portrayed as a manifestly 'unconstitutional' decision.

But one can also find episodes in constitutional history when the judiciary apparently considered that its ultimate allegiance lay not to the executive, nor even to Parliament, but rather to a version of the rule of law which possessed a higher constitutional status than the clear words of legislation. Such appears to be the lesson offered by the judgment of the House of Lords in the 1969 case of *Anisminic Ltd v Foreign Compensation Commission*.

Anisminic Ltd v Foreign Compensation Commission (1969)[17]

In the 1950s and 1960s, Parliament made increasing use of statutes purporting to oust the courts' common law power of review. These so-called 'ouster clauses' were a logical ingredient of the drift towards 'green light' theories of administrative law. Often Parliament sought to exclude the courts because the legislation concerned established alternative fora for review, appeal, or inquiry. Relatedly, it was widely felt that much government activity did not lend itself to resolution by judicial methods.[18] Such statutes would contradict the Diceyan version of the rule of law, but since Parliament can make any law whatsoever, there is theoretically no impediment to it passing legislation which excludes the common law power of review.

One might take as an example of this process the system of welfare payments established under the National Insurance (Industrial Injuries) Act 1948. The Act made provision for dissatisfied applicants to appeal to a specialised medical tribunal. Section 36(3) provided that the tribunal's decision 'shall be final', a formula which seemed to remove the individual's right to seek review of the tribunal's decision in the courts. However in *R v Medical Appeal Tribunal, ex p Gilmore* Lord Denning, faced with an apparent

17 [1969] 2 AC 147.
18 See particularly Titmuss R (1971) 'Welfare rights, law and discretion' *Political Quarterly* 113–131.

error of law on the tribunal's part, concluded that, notwithstanding s 36(3)'s apparently unambiguous instruction, judicial review:

'is never to be taken away by any statute except by the most clear and explicit words. The word "final" is not enough. That only means "without appeal". It does not mean without recourse to [review].'[19]

This apparently presents us with a modification to the doctrine of implied repeal, which we discussed in chapter 2. Section 36(3) implies that Parliament had decided to 'contract out' of judicial review with respect to industrial injury compensation. Lord Denning's judgment appears to echo the decisions in *Chorlton v Lings* and *Nairn v St Andrews University* where the courts held that the enfranchisement of women would represent such a fundamental reform to society's political order that Parliament could not effect it through implied or 'furtive' legislative terms. In *Gilmore*, Denning seems to attribute the same high political status to a Diceyan principle of the rule of law – namely that individual citizens should always be able to challenge the decisions of government bodies before 'the ordinary courts'. Denning suggests that Parliament may 'suspend' this principle if it wishes, but only by adopting absolutely unambiguous statutory formulae.

One might have assumed that Parliament had adopted 'the most clear and explicit words' in the ouster clause contained in s 4(4) of the Foreign Compensation Act 1950. The Act established a Commission to distribute limited funds among British nationals whose overseas property had been seized by foreign governments. Section 4(4) provided that the Commission's 'determinations . . . shall not be called in question in any court of law'. The concept of 'calling into question' would appear to reach both appeal and review. Nevertheless, in *Anisminic Ltd v Foreign Compensation Commission*,[20] the House of Lords assumed jurisdiction to review the Commission's activities. It did so on the grounds that the Commission had made an error of law in its decision-making process. Consequently, the decision that the Commission had produced was not a determination, but 'a purported determination'. Since the ouster clause made no reference to 'purported determinations', the court was not challenging parliamentary sovereignty by declaring the Commission's action unlawful.

In much the same way as the majority judgment in *Liversidge*, such reasoning commends itself only to the most formalistic of constitutional analyses. *Gilmore* and *Anisminic* can more plausibly

---

19 [1957] 1 QB 574 at 583, CA.
20 [1969] 2 AC 147.

be presented as examples of the judges steeling themselves to resist orthodox understandings of the hierarchy of legal authority within the constitution in order to safeguard a political principle – that government action might always be subject to judicial review, irrespective of Parliament' intentions. In each case, the judges adopted a rather narrow view of legislative sovereignty. Parliament could indeed exclude judicial review; but it could do so only by initiating the protracted and highly visible process of passing legislation explicitly overturning the courts' decisions. One might say that the House of Lords was rejecting a formal, legalistic interpretation of parliamentary sovereignty in favour of a functionalist, political interpretation – namely to ensure that the exclusion of judicial review really did attract the consent of the people.

The House of Lords' judgment might lead some observers to recall the oft-quoted words of Bishop Hoadly, delivered in a sermon to the King in 1717:

> 'Whoever hath an absolute authority to interpret any written or spoken laws, it is he who is truly the lawgiver, to all intents and purposes, and not the person who first spoke or wrote them.'

Anisminic clearly presented a judicial challenge to Parliament's sovereignty, but that challenge lay in the sphere of the legitimacy rather than legality of Parliamentary intentions. Parliament could if it wished have reversed *Anisminic*, but only at the risk of being seen to abrogate orthodox understandings of the rule of law. The government initially seemed prepared to take that risk, and prepared a bill containing a more extensive ouster clause. Whether the courts would have been prepared to 'defy' that legislation by a further exercise in creative statutory 'interpretation' is a matter for speculation, for the proposal was abandoned in the face of opposition within Parliament, and replaced by a measure granting the Court of Appeal appellate jurisdiction over the Commission's determinations.[1]

Leading constitutional theorists took rather different views of *Anisminic's* implications. Professor John Griffith felt that the courts were intruding in an unconstitutional way on the sovereignty of Parliament.[2] In contrast, Professor Wade suggested that the threat to the constitution came not from the judges' apparent challenge to parliamentary sovereignty, but from Parliament's increas-

---

1 Foreign Compensation Act 1969 s 3. See Wade H R W and Forsyth C (1994) *Administrative Law* pp 734–739 (Oxford: Clarendon Press).
2 (1977) *The Politics of the Judiciary* pp 123–124 (Harmondsworth: Penguin).

ing predisposition to deploy ouster clauses to limit or remove the courts' powers of judicial review. Such legislation showed an unhealthy disrespect for the orthodox principles of the rule of law.[3] Both viewpoints are obviously defensible, a fact which further strengthens the presumption that constitutional analysis must operate as much in the realm of practical politics as of legal theory.

However if the *Anisminic* saga was seen by some constitutional physicians as a symptom that their patient was a little under the weather, the legislative response to the *Burmah Oil* judgment might have suggested that she was in immediate need of a prolonged course of intensive care.

Burmah Oil Co (Burma Trading) Ltd v Lord Advocate (1965)[4]

The objection that Diceyans would make to Parliament's growing preference for granting the executive discretionary powers in statutes is that citizens may find it difficult to predict what government will do. That objection is met only in part by the *Wednesbury* principles of administrative law; those principles may enable the citizen to predict the outer limts of lawful government action, but not to identify the precise point at which a given decision may be located. But unpredictability would be taken to an extreme degree if Parliament enacted legislation which had *retrospective effect*; for example by enacting a statute in 1993 which provided that everybody who had bought a foreign car since 1971 had to pay a 'patriotism levy' of £50; or by introducing legislation in 1993 which made it a criminal offence to have said or written anything critical of government policy before 1992. Since Parliament is sovereign, there is no theoretical impediment to it introducing such legislation. In doing so, however, Parliament would surely be undermining all three versions of the rule of law which have been discussed in this chapter. For students who might suppose Parliament could never do such a thing, the events which followed the 1964 case of *Burmah Oil v Lord Advocate* may come as something of a surprise.

The saga began in 1942, when the British government, acting

---

3 (1969) 'Constitutional and administrative aspects of the *Anisminic* case' 85 *Law Quarterly Review* 198–212; (1980) *Constitutional Fundamentals* pp 65–66 (London: Stevens).
4 [1965] AC 75, HL.

under what it presumed to be a common law power,[5] ordered its army in Burma to destroy one of Burmah Oil's refineries to prevent it falling into the hands of the advancing Japanese forces. After the war, the government offered Burmah Oil an *ex gratia* payment of £4.6 million as compensation. The oil company launched an action in the courts, claiming some £31 million compensation, and arguing that the common law power which the government used required that owners be fully reimbursed by the government for any loss that they suffered. There did not appear to be any clear authority for the House of Lords to follow in this case. The judges thus faced the task of deciding the extent of the government's common law prerogative power to destroy property in time of war. The details of the House of Lords' judgment need not concern us here,[6] suffice it to say that the majority upheld Burmah Oil's claim.

The government was alarmed by this decision, since it might mean that not only Burmah Oil, but also many other individuals or companies whose property had been destroyed in similar circumstances, would be entitled to large sums of compensation. In combination, such claims could have major implications for public expenditure. The government therefore introduced the War Damage Bill into Parliament to reverse the *Burmah Oil* judgment. There could be no objection in terms of constitutional principle to Parliament changing the common law by statute in the sense of providing that *in future* the payment of compensation in such circumstances will be determined by statutory rule *x* rather than common law rule *y*. Such action is permitted by the doctrine of parliamentary sovereignty, and is consistent with all versions of the rule of law. However, the War Damage Bill was intended to overrule the common law not just for future instances of property loss, but also for those which had already happened – the statute was to have retrospective as well as prospective effect.

As stressed above, Diceyan theory tells us that such legislation is entirely consistent with the legal doctrine of parliamentary sovereignty, but utterly inconsistent with the political principle of the rule of law. The Bill was therefore the subject of appreciable controversy as it progressed through Parliament[7]. That it emerged

---

5 These 'royal prerogative powers' are considered in detail in chapter 4. The only point one need note here is that the claimed power had a common law rather than statutory origin.

6 A usefully succinct summary of a very long judgment is provided by Jackson P (1964) 'The royal prerogative' *Modern Law Review* 709–717.

7 See Jackson P (1965) 'War Damage Act 1965' *Modern Law Review* 574–576, and pp 211–212 below.

unscathed as the War Damage Act 1965 provides further compelling evidence that the rule of law, insofar as it can be construed as a moral code entrenching certain political values in Britain's democratic structure, may on occasions be regarded by our sovereign legislature as an expendable rather than indispensible ingredient of Britain's constitutional recipe.

Such considerations take our argument very firmly into the spheres of politics and legitimacy rather than law and legality. To conclude our initial discussion of the rule of law, we might sensibly return to more firmly legal ground, and consider once again the relationship between the courts and the executive.

M v Home Office (1994)[8]

M was a teacher from Zaire who sought political asylum in Britain, claiming that he would be subject to political persecution if he returned to his homeland. The Home Secretary[9] decided he did not qualify for asylum under the relevant legislation, and ordered his deportation. M's counsel then presented new evidence to the court. By this time, M was on his way to Heathrow. The judge, Garland J, considered that the Home Office's counsel had given the court an undertaking that M would not be deported until the new evidence was heard, and made an order (which was in effect an interim injunction) in those terms. However, M was then flown to Paris and placed on a flight to Zaire. M's solicitor then woke up Garland J in the middle of the night, and the judge immediately (by phone) ordered the Home Secretary to return M to Britain. The Home Secretary was then informed by his legal advisers that Garland J had no power to make such an order, and the Home Secretary decided to ignore it. M has not been heard of since.

The case raised several important issues. Much of the argument centres on complex questions of administrative law, which need not concern us here.[10] There are however, two points of constitutional siginificance which we need to address. Firstly, did the High Court have the power to issue an injunction against the Crown, represented here by the Home Office? And if so, was

8 [1994] 1 AC 377, HL.
9 It appears that the decision was actually made by a junior minister, and that the Home Secretary himself, Kenenth Baker, was not familiar with the case.
10 See Gould M (1993) '*M v Home Office*: government and the judges' *Public Law* 568–578.

Kenneth Baker, the Home Secretary, in either his personal or ministerial capacity, in contempt of court for ignoring it? If we recall *Entick* and *Liversidge*, we see that the citizen's legal actions were not against the 'government' (or the Crown), but against individual government officials. In both instances, the government official was being sued for allegedly committing a tortious action: trespass in *Entick* and false imprisonment in *Liversidge*. In neither 1765 nor 1942 was it possible for those actions to be commenced against the Crown per se. As previously noted, while the 1688 revolution had established the supremacy of statute over common law, it did not in itself alter common law principles in any systematic way. One such principle, encapsulated in the aphorism that 'the King could do no wrong', was that the courts had no jurisdiction to entertain suits in tort or contract against the Crown. Citizens could pursue such actions only through a device called 'the petition of right', in which the Crown consented to the initiation of an action against a named official, and undertook to furnish the means for that individual to comply with whatever order the court might make against her. Relatedly, it had always been thought that an injunction could not lie against the Crown per se. A 1901 case, *Nireaha Tamaki v Baker*,[11] had held that injunctions could issue against ministers in their individual capacity, but not against ministers in their ministerial capacity, when they were in theory the Crown itself. Similarly, while an individual government official who deliberately defied an injunction against her would be in contempt of court, the non-availability of such judgment against the Crown would logically imply that there could be nothing in respect of which the Crown per se could be in contempt.

It was not until the Crown Proceedings Act 1947 that Parliament exercised its sovereign legal power to abolish the petition of right device. The Act made it clear that the Crown itself could now be sued in contract or tort. However the Act did not explicitly confirm that injunctions and the contempt jurisidiction could also issue against the Crown per se, rather than just against individual officials. Prior to the *Re M* case, the weight of judicial authority suggested such remedies were not available. In effect, this case law seemingly suggested that remedies which citizens might enforce against other citizens were only available against the Crown when Parliament had explicitly legislated to that effect.

This left something of a gap in the legal regulation of government activity. On the facts of *Re M*, for example, an interim

11 [1901] AC 561, PC.

injunction against Mr Baker in person would not have prevented other Home Office ministers or employees from placing M on the plane to Zaire. Had Mr Baker wilfully defied the courts and breached such an order, he personally would have been in contempt, but that consequence would neither be of assistance to M nor underline the principle that the government as a corporate body must respect court orders. Thus, if the 'rule of law' was not to be undermined in practice, we would have to rely on the integrity of government in never doing anything that might be the subject of an injunction or a contempt order, a reliance that fits uneasily with the Diceyan principle that the rule of law demands that we should always be suspicious of government's bona fides.

The leading judgment in *Re M* was given by Lord Woolf. The other Law Lords unanimously concurred in his opinion, which concluded that the High Court had the power to issue an interim injunction against the Crown, that the Crown was in theory amenable to the contempt jurisdiction, and that, on the facts of this case, such a contempt had been committed. Lord Woolf's judgment is much concerned with technical questions of administrative law. For our purposes, perhaps the key passage in the decision comes from Lord Templeman's speech:

'[T]he argument that there is no power to enforce the law by injunction . . . against a Minister in his official capacity would, if upheld, establish the proposition that the executive obey the law as a matter of grace and not as a matter of necessity, a proposition which would reverse the result of the civil war.'[12]

One assumes that Lord Templeman meant the 1688 revolution rather than the civil war. But the logic of his contention seems unarguable; namely that the revolution had created a situation in which the Crown's legal status was equivalent to that of an ordinary legal person; thus all legal remedies which are available against individuals should be available against the Crown, unless Parliament has clearly provided to the contrary.

Lord Woolf drew on similarly expansive principles in confirming the availability of the contempt jurisdiction. The Home Secretary, in either his personal or official capacity, could be in contempt for disregarding the terms of such an injunction. The only body capable of overturning the order of a High Court judge would be the Court of Appeal; if one allowed ministers to ignore the courts

12 [1994] 1 AC 377 at 395.

on the basis of the advice of their lawyers, the rule of law would clearly be being subverted. As Lord Woolf explained:

'[T]he ability of the court to make a finding of contempt is of great importance. It would demonstrate that a government department has interfered with the administration of justice. It will then be for Parliament to determine what should be the consequences of that finding.'[13]

CONCLUSION

This chapter has suggested that we must exercise caution in assuming that Britain's constitutional tradition rests securely on the three supporting pillars of parliamentary sovereignty, the rule of law and the separation of powers, which are themselves securely rooted in the foundation stone of democracy. Chapters 1 and 2 indicated that our constitution's foundation is itself shifting and unstable; in addition, the theoretical analyses and historical events discussed in this chapter have suggested that those pillars may at times lean in contradictory rather than complementary directions. Whether this is a desirable situation is a question to which we shall return; it may be that one can argue it is preferable for a constitution to bend to the wind of changing times, rather than to stand rigid and so risk destruction in the face of a political or social hurricane. To sustain or refute that argument however, we need to gather more knowledge of the constitution's historical and contemporary make-up. In chapter 4, we begin that task by turning to the issue of the royal prerogative.

13 [1994] 1 AC 377 at 425.

CHAPTER FOUR

The royal prerogative

As a consequence of the British constitution's adoption of the doctrine of parliamentary sovereignty, it is clear that the courts have traditionally been regarded as having no power to review the substance of legislation. The 'common law' is presumed to be subordinate to Parliament in that formal sense. The House of Lords' decision in *Anisminic* does suggest that there are some situations in which the courts seem *in effect* to dispute Parliament's supremacy. But as we saw in that case, the court took great care to root its arguments in a constitutional framework which was *theoretically* legitimate.

The existence of a gap between theoretical and practical legitimacy in judicial behaviour is much less evident in relationship to review of government action taken *under* statute. The decision in *Entick v Carrington* is a prominent example of the courts' use of administrative law to ensure that what the government has done is within the powers that Parliament has granted. This is clearly necessary to maintain the sovereignty of Parliament with respect to the government. If the courts permitted government to do things which exceeded the legal boundaries which Parliament has laid out, they would be saying that it was government action, rather than legislation, which was the most important value in the constitutional hierarchy. As suggested by *Liversidge v Anderson*, one sometimes finds cases where, in practice, the court's interpretation of a statute seems impossible to reconcile with Parliamentary intent as expressed in the words of the Act. In such circumstances, we might plausibly argue that the theory of parliamentary sovereignty is being subverted. But in principle, as Lord Atkin's dissenting judgment in *Liversidge* stressed, such decisions should not happen.

However, as was noted in chapter two, statute is not the only source of the British government's legal authority. The government also possesses a miscellaneous collection of common law powers. Constitutional lawyers gather these powers together under the label of the royal prerogative.

The source of prerogative powers

In initial, pre-1688 form, the 'royal prerogative' comprised the personal powers of the Monarch. In contrast to some European régimes, and despite the apparent wishes of the Stuart kings, the English monarchy was never absolutist – mediaeval kings had neither the financial nor military resoures to rule without the active support of a majority of the nobility. That support was essentially dependent on the Monarch accepting some constraints on her/his power to govern. Those constraints were articulated in both statute and the common law – neither of which the Monarch could change without the support of Parliament or the courts. For example, Richard II was seemingly overthrown in 1399 because he had claimed absolute powers both to govern without Parliament and to ignore the opinions of the judges.[1]

As noted at the outset of this book, we must often look to the seventeenth century for the origins of current constitutional doctrines, and the prerogative is no exception to that rule. We saw in chapter two that this period of constitutional history was marked by a series of disputes between King and Parliament over the distribution of governmental power. There was an ongoing struggle between the King's effort to rule by prerogative powers or 'proclamations', and Parliament's power to restrain the King's autonomy through statute. And until such time as that struggle degenerated into civil war, the courts were usually the site of the battle.

Prerogative cases before the 1688 revolution

The key point to emphasise about the development of legal doctrine in the seventeenth century is that the courts' role was very ambiguous over the issues of how and for what purpose prerogative powers could be used. The crucial question was whether, both in principle and in practice, the Monarch's prerogative powers had a superior constitutional status to Acts of Parliament. Judges tended to produce opinions which adopted inconsistent positions on this question, a fact which, given the political instability of that era, is perhaps readily understandable. In a climate of constant

1 See Plucknett (1960) *op cit* pp 174–177.

'revolution', the ultimate source of legal authority within the constitution was likely to be an unstable phenomenon.[2]

Prior to the 1688 revolution, the courts had on occasion robustly resisted the King's preferences. In the 1607 *Case of Prohibitions*,[3] James I had claimed a divine right to sit as a judge and to develop the common law as he thought appropriate: 'The King said that he thought the law was founded upon reason, and that he and others had reason, as well as the judges'. The common law judges, led by Chief Justice Coke, rejected this claim. While the judges confirmed that the King was not subject to any man, he was subject to the law, and until such time as he had gained sufficient expertise in the law's many rules he had no entitlement to sit as a judge. This expertise was not a matter of 'natural reason' or 'common sense', but demanded mastery of 'an artificial reason . . . which requires long study and experience, before that a man can attain to the cognizance of it'.[4] As well as placing restraints on the Monarch, this ruling enhanced the powers of the courts. We might recall that 'common reason' was the formula invoked in *Dr Bonham*'s case to overrule statute; if that common reason was something that only the judges were competent to discern, one would be saying in effect that the courts were the ultimately authoritative source of law in the pre-revolutionary constitution.

Similarly, in the 1611 *Case of Proclamations*,[5] Chief Justice Coke seemingly placed quite stringent limits on the King's ability to rule by prerogative powers. Firstly, the King only had those prerogative powers which the common law *already recognised*; he could not conjure up new ones from thin air or divine intercession. Secondly, the King could not use prerogative powers to create offences previously unknown to the common law.[6]

However not all judges were as committed to keeping the King's personal powers within legal boundaries as Coke. There are several

---

2 See Wade (1955) *op cit* pp 188–190.

3 (1607) 12 Co Rep 63.

4 *Ibid*, at 65. One sees here an early statement of a pervasive trend in British constitutional theory, subsequently embraced by other countries, which tied the 'independence' of the judiciary to its competence; see for example the sentiments of Alexander Hamilton in *The Federalist Papers No 78* (at pp 23–24 above) and of the South African Supreme Court in *Minister of the Interior v Harris (No 2)* (at pp 56–57 above).

5 (1611) 12 Co Rep 74.

6 Such activities were not the exclusive preserve of the Stuart kings. The decision in *Darcy v Allin (or Allen), The Case of Monopolies* ((1602) 11 Co Rep 84 placed a judicial limit on Elizabeth I's use of prerogative powers, on the grounds that her attempt to create a monopoly in the manufacture and import of playing cards was against the 'public interest'.

examples in the seventeenth century of the judges interpreting prerogative powers in a way that completely undermined the principles laid down in the *Case of Proclamations*.

The *Case of Impositions*,[7] or *Bate*'s case, in 1610, centred on the King's prerogative power to regulate foreign trade, and Parliament's statutory power to prevent the King levying taxation without parliamentary consent. Bate had refused to pay an import duty that the King had placed on currants, his argument being the tax was illegal because it did not have parliamentary approval. The King's response that this was not a tax at all, but a measure to regulate trade. As such it was quite lawful – the money raised was just an incidental side effect of the regulatory power. The integrity of that argument is obviously questionable. However, the court was prepared to accept it, and so provided a back-door route for prerogative powers to override statutory provisions. That was not necessarily unconstitutional at the time; we must remember that the supremacy of statute had not been established by then. Condemnation of this type of monarchical behaviour was subsequently to prove a major component of the 1688 *Declaration of Right*, and as we saw in chapter two, it was expressly prohibited by Article 4 of the Bill of Rights.[8]

A similar scenario arose in the *Case of Ship Money, R v Hampden*[9] in 1637. It was still then accepted that prerogative powers extended to permitting the king to levy a special tax called Ship Money to pay for military expenses necessary to repel a foreign invasion. When Charles I sought to impose such a tax in 1637, a man called John Hampden refused to pay. Hampden accepted that the prerogative power existed, but argued that it could only be invoked when a military emergency was actually happening. In a sense the court agreed with Mr Hampden's argument: *Ship Money could only be levied when an emergency arose*. But the judges went on to say that *only the King was legally competent to judge if such an emergency existed*, and it was not within the court's power to call that judgement into question. So here one is apparently presented with an example of what seems to be a clear constitutional principle, namely that the King needs parliamentary consent to levy taxation, being sabotaged in practice by the courts.

Protection against unlawful taxation was clearly an important element of the citizens' property rights in pre-revolutionary England. It was however perhaps less important than 'property' in one's physical liberty, in the sense of being able to call upon

7 (1610) 2 State Tr 371.
8 See p 35 above. 9 (1637) 3 State Tr 826.

the courts for protection against unlawful arrest or imprisonment. The writ of habeas corpus has common law origins which predate even the Magna Carta. Its purpose, crudely put, was to empower the common law courts to order any person detaining a citizen to bring that person before the court and show lawful authority for the detention. If no such authority could be shown in the gaoler's 'return', the prisoner would be released.

Habeas corpus was, in practice, hedged about with many limitations. Its utiltity was particularly compromised during the reign of Elizabeth I. Elizabeth and her Privy Councillors[10] claimed an entirely arbitrary power to imprison anyone who displeased them, without charge or trial, for as long as they wished. The constitutionality of such commitment was widely questioned, and caused sufficient disquiet for the judges to deliver an opinion to the Crown assessing its legality. The so-called *Resolutions in Anderson* began with what seems a spirited defence of individual liberty: 'her highnesses subjects may not be detained in prison, by commandment of any nobleman or councillor, against the laws of the realm'.[11] This suggests that the judges were claiming authority to examine the justification for any such detention and thereafter pronounce upon its legality. However, the *Resolutions* concluded by accepting that the courts had no power to question the actual basis of a claim by the Crown that the person detained had, in the Crown's view, committed treason. Thus, as long as Privy Councillors complied with this formality, their actions would be within 'the laws of the realm', and their effective powers of arbitrary imprisonment would remain untouched.[12]

Anderson offers an obvious precedent for the *Bate's* case and *Ship money* principle that the Monarch was the sole judge of whether the factual prerequisites of a prerogative power actually existed. Unsurprisingly, Charles I relied upon the opinion as a justification for imprisoning those of his subjects who declined to pay the 'unlawful' taxes that he levied. Sir Thomas Darnel was one of five knights (including John Hampden's cousin, Edmund) who had refused to pay a compulsory loan to the king. Charles I immediately ordered their arrest and imprisonment. In *Darnel's case*,[13] the knights' application for writs of habeas corpus were met by a

10 On the status of the Privy Council see pp 137–138 below.
11 (1593) 1 Anderson 297. See also Lord Camden's discussion of the principle in *Entick* (1765) 19 State Jr 1029 at 1054–1055 and Plucknett (1960) *op cit* pp 308–311.
12 Which, on a cynical view, one might suggest was precisely the conclusion reached by the House of Lords in *Liversidge* in respect of the powers granted to the Home Secretary by reg 18b.
13 (1627) 3 State Tr 1.

return stating simply that they were held 'by special command of the king'. Darnel's counsel argued that this was in itself insufficient justification for committal, since it disclosed no breach of any known law. The court however concluded that the King's power fell within that considered acceptable in the *Resolutions in Anderson*: the judges would not investigate either the factual or legal basis of the King's opinion. In effect, it seemed, the King retained an arbitrary power.

In the aftermath of the Civil War, the Commons and Lords persuaded Charles II and James II to assent to a series of Habeas Corpus Acts which appeared to extend the reach of the remedy, and relatedly, to curb the Crown's capacity to evade it. But, as the principle articulated in the following case suggests, the then uncertain status of statute vis-à-vis the prerogative cast considerable doubt on the efficacy of any such legislation.

James II was particularly eager to take advantage of the court's flexibility to rule by prerogative powers rather than with Parliamentary consent in the 1680s. The case of *Godden v Hales*[14] in 1686 is perhaps the most obvious example of this trend. A central cause of tension between the Commons and Lords and James II was religion; James was a King with strong Catholic sympathies trying to rule a country whose legislative houses were dominated by Protestants. Parliament had passed several Acts disqualifying Catholics from government office. James attempted to override these acts on behalf of a Catholic citizen, Sir Edward Hales, by annoucing that Hales would not have to take an oath of loyalty to the Protestant faith before assuming office. Although this was obviously in direct contradiction of an Act of Parliament, the court held that it was part of the Monarch's prerogative to dispense with laws in particular cases if it was *necessary* to do so. And as in the *Ship Money* case, the King was to be the sole judge of necessity. As we have already seen, such practices were subsequently forbidden by Article 1 of the Bill of Rights, which also made more effective provision to safeguard rights of habeas corpus.[15]

What the courts appeared to be saying in *Godden v Hales*, *Ship Money*, *Bate's* case, and *Darnel's case* was that certain questions

14 (1686) 11 State Tr 1165.
15 See p 35 above. A far more extensive remedy was secured by the Habeas Corpus Act 1816. This should not be seen as in any sense a 'fundamental right'. As we saw in *Liversidge*, Parliament can grant statutory powers which authorise arbitrary detention. Parliament has also passed legislation suspending the 1816 Act. Moreover, as noted in chapter 8, while the post-revolutionary Commons was so enthusiastic to curb the King's powers of arbitrary detention, it proved very slow to accept that it did not have such powers itself; see pp 312–314 below.

raised by the use of prerogative powers were not 'justiciable'. In effect, these cases concluded that some government functions were of so political a nature that they could not be addressed by the judges. One was therefore required to accept that the King was acting in good faith and not trying to circumvent parliamentary power by relying on the courts to manipulate common law doctrines. Such an assumption would not seem compatible with the various theories of the rule of law which subsequently emerged within the British constitutional tradition, and nor, one assumes, could they have survived unscathed the aftermath of the English revolution.

Post-1688 – the revolutionary settlement

It was arguably James II's persistent disregard of parliamentary authority that eventually triggered the 1688 revolution. The Bill of Rights 1689, which we could plausibly regard as the contract of government between William and Mary and the revolutionary Commons and Lords, placed clear statutory limits on the extent of prerogative powers.

Two points of great significance seemed to emerge from the political deal that was struck. Firstly, the *scope of prerogative powers was fixed* – it was not open to the king to claim new ones. What William and Mary received in 1688 was the *residue* of the previous King's powers.[16] That residue has been shrinking ever since. This point was well put by Diplock LJ in the 1965 case of *BBC v Johns*, when he observed that it was:

> '350 years and a civil war too late for the Queen's courts to broaden the prerogative. The limits within which the executive government may impose obligations or restraints on citizens of the UK without any statutory authority are now well settled and incapable of extension.'[17]

One must however note that while it is generally accepted that the 1688 settlement had imbued the prerogative with a residual character, the exact extent of that residue was far from clear. As we saw in *Burmah Oil*,[18] the courts have on occasion been called upon to decide the precise limits of prerogative powers, which, even some three hundred years after the revolution, remain poorly

16 Thus in *Entick v Carrington* the government was unable to claim its actions were conducted under the prerogative power as no trace of a pre-1688 general power of search and seizure could be found.
17 [1965] Ch 32 at 79, CA.
18 Page 97 above.

defined. *Burmah Oil* provides us with another example of the loose fit between the form and the reality of constitutional principles; while there is no mechanism within the constitution through which the Crown can de jure create new prerogative powers or duties, the courts could achieve that result by holding that the Crown had rediscovered a 'forgotten' part of the 1688 residue.

The second point, and the reason why the residue has been getting smaller, is that the 1688 settlement acknowledged that it was *within the power of Parliament to amend or abolish prerogative powers* through legislation. The prerogative was recognised as being a common law power, and so always subordinate to statute. Thus, as in the *Burmah Oil* saga, Parliament may always respond to inconvenient judicial decisions concerning the scope of an existing prerogative power by introducing legislation to alter or reverse the courts' decisions.

Similarly, Parliament may at any time create a statutory framework which limits the ways prerogative powers may be used. This principle is perhaps best illustrated in the immediate post-revolutionary era by legislative regulation of the Monarch's power to summon and dissolve Parliament. We may recall that Article 13 of the Bill of Rights had provided that 'Parlyaments ought to be held frequently'. Parliament defined that timescale more precisely in the Triennial Act 1694. This statute required the King to summon a new Parliament within three years of the dissolution of the previous Parliament, and also obliged him not to permit Parliament to sit for more than three years before the next dissolution. Within these statutory time limits, the Monarch enjoyed unfettered legal power to summon or dismiss the Commons and the Lords; but he/she had no legal power to exceed those periods. Parliament could extend or shorten the time scale if it wished, and indeed in the Septennial Act of 1716 it chose to increase its maximum duration to seven years.

Since 1688, the personal political powers of the Monarch have declined significantly in practical terms. As we shall see in later chapters, the Queen is now largely just a figurehead, performing ceremonial and symbolic functions within the contemporary constitution. But this does not mean that the prerogative powers have disappeared. For most practical purposes, *prerogative powers are exercised on the monarch's behalf by the government.* But before considering a brief list of the residue of prerogative powers which the government can use in the modern era, we ought to make some reference to a *definitional problem.* What was originally meant by the notion of the *personal powers* of the sovereign?

What is the prerogative? A definitional controversy

There are two schools of thought on this point. The first, *narrow or restrictive* interpretation was advanced by Blackstone. As far as Blackstone was concerned, the prerogative powers were only those which were 'singular and eccentrical' to the King himself – that is things which only the King could do. So for example the power to enter into contracts, to lend money, to employ people, should not be considered as part of the prerogative because any other citizen was legally competent to do those things. Only powers such as declaring war, or granting peerages were exclusive to the King, and so correctly labelled as prerogative powers.

The second, *wide* definition comes from Dicey. In Dicey's view everything that government can lawfully do that does not have its roots in a statute, but which could be enforced in the courts, was a prerogative power. Dicey's usage is generally accepted today – although there are still some influential commentators who favour the Blackstone version, Profesor Wade being foremost among them.[19] But assuming we take the wider view as the more authoritative version, which prerogative powers does the government still possess?

The most important one is probably the conduct of foreign affairs and the signing of treaties. In the domestic sphere such actions as the granting of peerages, appointing judges, giving pardons to convicted criminals or stopping criminal proceedings, and the terms and conditions on which civil servants were employed were all components of this residual source of legal authority. This is not an exhaustive list, but it is sufficient to convey the point that the prerogative remains a substantively important source of governmental authority.

All of these powers can be exercised in two ways, either *directly or indirectly*. Direct exercise of the prerogative need not take any documentary form. Foreign policy for example is usually carried on this way. The prerogative is exercised indirectly through a device known as the *Order in Council*, which is in some respects analogous to a statute, in that it often grants ministers the legal authority to exercise a range of discretionary powers. Changes to the terms of employment of civil servants are usually made through this indirect procedure.

Irrespective of the way they are used, the continued existence of prerogative powers really raises two issues – one of which is legal, the other political. The legal issue is essentially the question

---

19 See particularly (1985) 'The civil service and the prerogative' 101 *LQR* 190–199.

of the relationship between the government and the judiciary; which prerogative powers will the courts subject to judical review, and in what circumstances and according to which criteria will the courts intervene to regulate government activity? The political issue centres on the relationship between the government and Parliament. Is it desirable that important political decisions such as going to war, signing treaties, granting pardons and so on should be taken without the explicit prior approval of a majority of MPs? We will return to the political issue at a later stage of the book. In the rest of this chapter we will focus on the fate of the prerogative in the courts during the twentieth century.

I. THE RELATIONSHIP BETWEEN STATUTE, THE PREROGATIVE AND THE RULE OF LAW

In the early twentieth century, the courts produced two forceful opinions curbing the way that prerogative powers could be exercised. One of the most sweeping prerogative powers exercised by Monarchs was to seize property for military reasons in times of war, if the seizure was thought necessary to safeguard national security. The power was invoked frequently during World War I. The government appeared to have no doubts as to the legality of its actions, but not all of the 'victims' of this power shared that view, and some seizures were challenged in the courts.

If we recall the *Ship Money* case, we will remember that the question of deciding what was 'necessary' to protect national security was held to be the sole preserve of the Monarch; it was a non-justiciable issue. In *The Zamora*,[20] the House of Lords adopted a less pliant approach than its seventeenth-century predecessor. The Zamora was a ship from a neutral country carrying a cargo of copper. The government seized the ship and its cargo when it docked at a British port. The court accepted that judges were neither sufficiently expert, nor constitutionally entitled to argue the case with the government as to the adequacy of the national security justification for using this prerogative power. National security was still regarded as a non-justiciable issue. However, in this case the government had not produced any evidence at all that the copper was needed for national security reasons. The court accepted that the prerogative power to seize the ship was available in certain circumstances. But the House of Lords also held that the government had not shown that the *factual prerequiste*

20 [1916] 2 AC 77.

for using the power had arisen. And unless those facts were shown
to exist, no prerogative power came into being. And as a result
the seizure was unlawful.

The *Zamora* seems to display a clear shift from the position
which the courts adopted in *Ship Money* in the seventeenth century.
The decision seems to make essentially the same point as Lord
Atkin's subsequent dissent in *Liversidge*, namely in the absence of
a clear legislative provision to the contrary, the executive must
convince the court that the facts which trigger the use of a legal
power do indeed exist. What is less clear is how much evidence
would be required to confirm that national security issues were
involved. That is a point to which we will devote further attention
later in the chapter.

A-G v De Keyser's Royal Hotel Ltd (1920)[1]

A few years later, again in a case arising out of World War I, the
House of Lords powerfully restated the relationship between
the prerogative and Acts of Parliament. The type of seizure of
property at issue in *The Zamora* was not undertaken without compensation; but any such compensation was generally agreed by
negotiation or through ex gratia payments. However from the
nineteenth century onwards Parliament began to pass a series of
Defence of the Realm Acts which gradually encroached on the
former prerogative powers.

In 1916, the Ministry of Defence invoked the Defence of the
Realm Act 1916 to take over the De Keyser Royal Hotel for use as
officers' accommodation. The hotel owners were not convinced
the Act covered this situation, but gave up the hotel on the understanding they reserved the right to challenge the legality of the
action, and the size of compensation, at a later date. The 1916
Act had laid down rules about compensation, but the owners and
the MoD were unable to agree on the correct sum. Subsequently, the MoD decided that it had seized the hotel under
prerogative powers, and that it need only offer an ex gratia payment which was considerably less than the amount laid down by
the 1916 Act.

When the case came before the courts, the government argued
that the statutory power and the prerogative power existed side
by side, and that the government had the option of choosing
whichever of the two best suited its needs. All five Law Lords

1 [1920] AC 508, HL.

hearing the case rejected this argument. They had no doubt that the government's argument was quite inconsistent with the notion of parliamentary sovereignty. As far as the courts are concerned, the latest statute Parliament enacts is the most authoritative source of law. If a prerogative power is inconsistent with that statute, it has to give way.

So the House of Lords seemed to be saying unequivocally that *prerogative powers and statute cannot exist side by side* as the government claimed. The government does not have a choice about which it should use. If a statute is enacted which covers exactly the same ground as a prerogative power, the prerogative power is extinguished. The *De Keyser* decision is obviously consistent with the *doctrine of implied statutory repeal* that we examined in chapter 2. If statute is a superior form of law to the prerogative, and if existing statutes must give way if they are inconsistent with the latest legislation, it would be a nonsense if an existing prerogative power was considered more authoritative than an inconsistent statute.

Laker Airways Ltd v Department of Trade (1977)[2]

The decision of the Court of Appeal in *Laker Airways* further emphasised the prerogative's inferior constitutional status relative to statutes by a logical extension of the *De Keyser* principle. Following the passage of the Civil Aviation Act 1970, airlines which wished to operate a service between Britain and the USA required two forms of authorisation.

Firstly, the airline had to be granted a licence by the Civil Aviation Authority (CAA). The CAA had been created by the 1970 Act, and awarded licences according to criteria laid down in s 3(1), which required the CAA to promote low fares, high safety standards, and competition on major routes. Under s 3(2) the Department of Trade (DoT) could give the CAA 'guidance' concerning the way it exercised its licensing function. Under s 4(3), the DoT could give the CAA 'directions' concerning matters which affected national security or diplomatic relations with other countries. Secondly, the airline had to be granted landing rights in the USA. These were not statutory rights, but derived from a Treaty called the Bermuda Agreement which the government, using its prerogative powers, had negotiated with the USA.

In 1972 Laker Airways applied for a licence to operate a very cheap London to New York service. At the time, the only British companies flying on these routes were British Airways and British Caledonian. The CAA granted Laker a licence under s 3(1), and the DoT used its prerogative power to make arrangements under the Bermuda Treaty for Laker to be given landing rights in New York. After the 1974 general election, the new Labour government decided that it wanted to protect British Airways and British Caledonian from Laker's competition, and so looked for a way to withdraw Laker's permission to fly. The government could not use s 4(3) to give 'directions' to the CAA to revoke Laker's licence, since no questions of national security or diplomatic relations arose. Consequently, the DoT used its prerogative powers to cancel Laker's landing rights under the Bermuda Treaty, and issued the CAA with 'guidance' under s 3(2) instructing it to withdraw Laker's licence. Laker claimed that both actions were ultra vires.

The Court of Appeal supported Laker's contention; neither the statute nor the prerogative provided a lawful basis for the government's action. Lord Denning first considered the meaning of the word 'guidance' in s 3(2). He felt that Parliament's intention in using this term had been to 'explain', 'amplify' or 'supplement' the policy of the Act, but not to 'reverse' or 'contradict' that policy. However, Lord Denning concluded that the effect of the government's new policy would be to reduce competition and so raise prices on the London-New York route. This was entirely inconsistent with the objectives Parliament had enacted in s 3(1), namely to encourage competition and reduce prices. The policy could not therefore be 'guidance', and so lacked a statutory foundation.

Lord Denning also rejected the argument that the government's prerogative power to negotiate treaties with other states provided a lawful justification for withdrawing Laker's landing rights. He did so on the grounds that the government was trying to use its prerogative powers to contradict a statutory objective. In contrast to *De Keyser*, *Laker* presented a situation in which statutory and prerogative powers were *not overlapping, but interlocking*. The statute therefore was not intended to replace the prerogative, but to be used in conjunction with it. Nevertheless, in such circumstances, the statute's superior constitutional status demanded that the prerogative be exercised only in ways that furthered, rather than obstructed Parliament's intentions. If the government wished to pursue a policy which contradicted the objectives of the 1970 Act, it would have to persuade Parliament to enact new legislation which repealed or amended the limits placed on the DoT's powers by Parliament in 1970.[3]

R v Secretary of State for the Home Department, ex p Fire Brigades Union (1995)[4]

This principle was extended in 1994, in a judgment concerning the administration of the Criminal Injuries Compensation scheme. The Criminal Injuries Compensation Board was established in 1964 to provide compensation to the victims of violent crime or to their dependants. It was not set up under statute, but under the prerogative. The government also publicised a scheme which announced the criteria the Board would use to assess compensation.

Some twenty-four years later, the Criminal Justice Act 1988 s 17(1) empowered the Home Secretary to place the original entitlement criteria on a statutory basis 'on such day as he may appoint'. The government chose not to exercise this power immediately. Some five years later, the government concluded that the existing scheme was proving too expensive. Consequently, rather than exercise his s 17 power, the Home Secretary concluded that he would use his prerogative powers to amend the original scheme and introduce a cheaper system. He argued that he was free to do so, since s 17 had no legal effect until such time as he exercised the power he had been granted.

The Court of Appeal accepted that s 17 did not place the Home Secretary under a duty to place the scheme on a statutory basis by any particular date. However, it did have the effect of 'freezing' the Home Secretary's prerogative powers in respect of the scheme. By enacting s 17, Parliament had in effect given a statutory seal of approval to the way in which the prerogative had been exercised when the CICB was established in 1964. For the Home Secretary to alter the scheme would therefore be inconsistent with Parliament's intention. If the government wished to introduce a different set of entitlement criteria, it would first have to ask Parliament to repeal s 17. The Court of Appeal's decision was subsequently upheld in the House of Lords.[5] Shortly thereafter, the government announced that it would introduce a Bill to modify the existing scheme.

---

3 See Wade W (1977) 'Judicial control of the prerogative' 93 *LQR* 325–327.
4 [1995] 1 All ER 888, CA.
5 [1995] 2 All ER 244.

II. THE TRADITIONAL PERSPECTIVE ON JUDICIAL REVIEW OF PREROGATIVE POWERS: AND ITS EROSION

While *De Keyser* reinforced traditional perceptions of the relationship between Acts of Parliament and prerogative powers, it also confirmed that there was an important distinction to be drawn concerning the extent to which the principles of judicial review applied to government action taken under statute or the prerogative respectively. As we saw in chapter 3, orthodox constitutional theory assumes that Parliament 'contracts in' to administrative law when creating government powers through statute. If Parliament does not wish the implied terms of administrative law to apply to particular statutory activities, it must make that intention clear in the legislation. In the absence of such express 'contracting out', a government body's exercise of statutory power will (according to the *Wednesbury* principles) be ultra vires if no such power has been granted, if the power has been exercised 'unreasonably', or if decisions have been made through 'unfair procedures'.

However, in relation to judicial review of government action taken under the prerogative, the courts traditionally applied only the first of the three *Wednesbury* principles. The judges were, as in *De Keyser* or *BBC v Johns*, willing to say whether or not a claimed prerogative power actually existed. This is clearly consistent with the notion that the prerogative was a collection of residual powers – the courts would not permit the government to claim new ones. The courts were less willing to say in what way, or for what objectives, the powers which did exist should be used. The concepts of 'unreasonableness' or 'procedural fairness' to which statutory powers were subjected by the *Wednesbury* judgment were not applied to the prerogative. Thus while the courts were concerned with the *existence and extent* of a claimed prerogative power, they were not concerned with the way in which that power was *exercised*.[6]

This differential treatment of prerogative and statutory powers would seem difficult to reconcile with orthodox understandings of the function performed by the principle of the rule of law within democratic constitutions – namely to minimise the possibility of government being able lawfully to exercise power in arbitrary, irrational, or procedurally unfair ways. From a functionalist perspective, such a dichotomy would be defensible only if prerogative powers were in some qualitative sense quite distinct from powers exercised under statute. In the absence of such a

---

6 See for example *Hanratty v Butler* (1971) 115 Sol Jo 386; CA; *de Freitas v Benny* [1976] AC 239, PC.

distinction, the common law's varying treatment of these two types of government powers could be justified only on purely formalist grounds – that prerogative powers were not fully reviewable simply because they were prerogative powers. One can thus discern a 'rule of law' as well as a 'parliamentary sovereignty' basis for the *De Keyser* principle which forbade the co-existence of prerogative and statutory powers; to permit co-existence would allow the government to evade the judicial review principles to which it was assumed Parliament had subjected it by passing legislation in an area where executive powers previously derived solely from the prerogative.[7] From the late 1960s onwards, the courts' attachment to this formalist position began to change. There are two cases to which we should pay close attention. The first case is the 1967 High Court decision in *R v Criminal Injuries Compensation Board, ex p Lain*.[8]

R v Criminal Injuries Compensation Board, ex p Lain (1967)

Mrs Lain was the widow of a murdered policeman. She was seeking to argue that the amount of compensation she had been offered had not been properly assessed in accordance with the published criteria. In other words, she was questioning the way in which the Board had exercised its powers. As one might expect, the Board contended that the court had no power to review the exercise of the prerogative.

However, in an apparent break with tradition, the court held that this particular prerogative power should be reviewed as if it derived from a statute. The main reason for this appeared to be that the Board was performing an essentially 'judicial' task. It had the straightforward duty of awarding compensation on the basis of the published rules. The court considered this to be a very 'justiciable' function. Unlike the complex national security question raised in cases like *Ship Money*, this was an issue which the courts were well equipped to decide.

Lain did not attract much attention at the time, even though it apparently made a distinct break with traditional theory. In *Laker Airways*, a decade later, Lord Denning had seemed to approve this conclusion in suggesting that:

---

7 Parliament could of course expressly provide that the statutory power in question was to co-exist with the relevant part of the prerogative; eg Immigration Act 1971 s 33.

8 [1967] 2 QB 864.

'Seeing that the prerogative is a discretionary power to be exercised for the public good, it follows that its exercise can be examined by the courts just as any other discretionary power which is vested in the executive [ie by statute]'.[9]

However, it was not clear from the *Lain* and *Laker Airways* decisions if the courts were saying that all prerogative powers should be fully reviewable, or whether full review should apply only to powers which were justiciable.

Gouriet v Union of Post Office Workers (1978)[10]

The 1978 case of *Gouriet v Union of Post Office Workers* shows that the higher courts adopted different interpretations of the *Lain* decision. One prerogative power exercised on behalf of the government by the Attorney General is the *relator* proceeding. This enables the Attorney General to initiate civil proceedings in defence of the public interest in situations where an individual is either unable or unwilling to take action.

The Post Office Union had decided to boycott mail to and from South Africa for twenty four hours, as a gesture of disapproval of the South African government's apartheid régime. This constituted a criminal offence under the Post Office Acts. However, for political reasons, the government decided that the union would not be prosecuted. Mr Gouriet was a member of a group called the Freedom Association, which greatly disapproved both of the Union's activities, and of the government's failure to start a prosecution. Consequently, Mr Gouriet approached the Attorney General, asking him to initiate a *relator* action for an injunction to stop the mail embargo going ahead. When the Attorney General refused to proceed, Mr Gouriet asked the courts to review his decision.

Before *Gouriet* there was no case law supporting the argument that the *relator* power could be reviewed in the courts. There was however very strong precedent for the converse proposition; namely whether or not to launch *relator* proceedings was a prerogative power solely within the control of the Attorney General. The *Gouriet* case produced a divergence of opinion between Lord Denning in the Court of Appeal and the House of Lords. Denning thought that the time had come to question traditional perceptions of the *relator* action as being completely beyond the

9 [1977] 2 All ER 182 at 193.
10 [1978] AC 435, HL.

supervision of the courts. He was slightly cautious in doing this however. Denning drew a distinction between a situation where the Attorney General launched *relator* proceedings, and circumstances where he refused to do so. In the former case, use of the prerogative power was not open to question in the courts. However a refusal to begin proceedings could be challenged; Denning suggested that if the courts did not intervene in situations like this it would allow the criminal law to be infringed with impunity. In such circumstances, Denning asked himself: 'Are the courts to stand idly by?' In his opinion, the answer was no.

It is important to emphasise that there was nothing unconstitutional, in the legal sense, about Denning's analysis.[11] Since the prerogative is a common law concept, and since the common law is dynamic and open to constant amendment by the courts, Denning's innovative judgment could be thought legally defensible. He was not overriding a statute – but simply saying that an old common law rule should be replaced by a new one. From an orthodox theoretical perspective, Denning's decision was certainly less contentious than *Anisminic* for example. However, as far as the House of Lords was concerned, the courts should indeed stand idly by when this particular prerogative power was being employed – and when it was not being employed. The Law Lords were unanimously critical of Denning's radical judgment. They noted that Denning did not cite any authority for the proposition – it was just an idea he had dreamed up himself. In the House of Lords' opinion, whether or not to launch a *relator* action was a public interest question which only the government was competent to decide. It was another example (like the test of 'necessity' in *Ship Money* perhaps) of a non-justiciable legal power. The judgment suggested that it would be unconstitutional, in the political if not the legal sense, to overturn government policy over this issue.

Denning's perception of constitutionality accorded the highest priority to seeing that the criminal law was not ignored. In contrast, the House of Lords' version was most concerned with not overruling the policy preferences of an elected government. Despite the House of Lords' strong stance, there was a suggestion that the judges' reluctance to intervene owed more to the highly contentious *nature* of the power concerned rather than simply its *source* in the prerogative. In contrast to *Lain*, *Gouriet* raised an

11 Whether it was unconstitutional in a *political* sense is a question to which we shall shortly return.

issue which had immense party political implications. For the court to have told the government that it could not act in the way it wished might have exposed the judges to accusations of subverting the democratic process.

But would the courts be infringing parliamentary sovereignty if they changed the common law in order to place review of the prerogative on the same basis as review of action taken under statute? Clearly, any such alteration in the common law would be unconstitutional if it contradicted a statute. But even in the absence of an expressly contradictory statute, the constitutionality of such a reform to the law could perhaps be questioned. One might argue that if Parliament was unhappy about the courts' traditionally limited competence to review prerogative powers, it could do one of two things. Either it could pass a statute saying that all prerogative powers would henceforth be reviewable in the same way as statutory powers. Or, less radically, it could place specific prerogative powers on a statutory basis, and so make them amenable to full *Wednesbury* review. If the legislature took neither of these steps, it would seem plausible to assume that Parliament approved of the present situation of limited review. Consequently, if the courts changed the common law, they might in effect, if not in theory, be 'usurping the legislative function'.

Nevertheless, the suggestion being floated in the early 1980s was that the time was ripe for the courts to reject the traditional idea that all exercises of the prerogative were beyond judicial supervision. If the courts could say that executive action taken under statute was unlawful in some circumstances, surely the same argument could be applied to the less party politicised aspects of prerogative power. As suggested above, this is another illustration of a constitutional argument rooted in a functionalist rather than formalist conceptual framework. If the function of the rule of law is to protect citizens from arbitrary or unpredictable government activity, why should the source of that government power be of any relevance? Use of the prerogative could impact just as seriously on individuals as action taken under statute. There was no logical, functional reason why the two sources of governmental authority should be distinguished. The scene was set therefore for the courts to question, or perhaps even to overturn, the orthodox constitutional theory. The opportunity for them to do so was provided by *Council of Civil Service Unions v Minister for the Civil Service*, a case which reached the House of Lords in 1985.

III. THE ACCEPTANCE OF FULL REVIEWABILITY – THE GCHQ AFFAIR

Council of Civil Service Unions v Minister for the Civil Service[12] is now the pivotal case in the development of judicial review of the prerogative. The litigation is generally known as the *GCHQ* case, since it concerned employees at the Government Communication Headquarters in Cheltenham. GCHQ was responsible for monitoring radio and satellite transmissions in overseas countries; it was linked in some ill-defined way with the security services. Many of its employees belonged to one or other of the civil service trade unions. At that time, civil servants did not have contracts of employment. Their terms and conditions of work were generally regulated by *Orders in Council*, the *indirect exercise of the prerogative*.[13] One of the terms under which civil servants at GCHQ worked was that their conditions of service should not be altered until the Minister for the Civil Service had consulted with the trade unions about the proposed change.

In the early 1980s, the trade unions engaged in industrial action which to some extent disrupted GCHQ's intelligence gathering activities. The then Prime Minister, Margaret Thatcher, was also Minister for the Civil Service. She decided to respond to the disruption by forbidding GCHQ employees from belonging to a trade union. Employees who refused to resign from their union would be redeployed to less sensitive posts. The Prime Minister did not consult the trade unions before introducing this change.

The trade unions challenged the action on the grounds that the Prime Minister had acted in a procedurally unfair way by failing to consult them. In effect, the unions were asking the courts to apply standards of statutory review to prerogative powers. The government advanced two defences. The first was simply that this was a prerogative power, and thus not subject to review on grounds of procedural unfairness. The second defence was that even if principles of procedural fairness did apply to this prerogative power, the court should not intervene here because the issue concerned 'national security'.

To many people's surprise, the House of Lords rejected the

---

12 [1985] AC 374, HL. For comment see Lee S (1985) 'Prerogative and public law principles' *Public Law* 186–193.

13 For subsequent developments on that point see Morris G and Fredman S (1991) 'Judicial review and civil servants: contracts of employment declared to exist' *Public Law* 485–490.

government's first defence. Lord Fraser perhaps put the point most clearly:

> 'There is no doubt that if the Order in Council of 1982 had been made under the authority of a statute, the power delegated to the Minister would have been . . . subject to a duty to act fairly. I am unable to see why the words conferring the same powers should be construed differently merely because their source was an Order in Council made under the prerogative.'[14]

This point was made with similar force by Lord Roskill, who could not see:

> 'any logical reason why the fact that the source of the power is the prerogative and not statute should today deprive the citizen of that right of challenge to the manner of its exercise which he would possess were the source of power statutory. In either case the act in question is the act of the executive. To talk of that act as the act of the sovereign savours of the archaism of past centuries.'[15]

Such comments confirmed that the availability of judical review in the modern era would depend upon *the nature of government powers, not their source*. But victory on this point of general constitutional principle did not mean that the trade unions were ultimately successful.

The House of Lords' concern with the nature of government powers takes us to the second important part of the *GCHQ* decision. Once again we face the question of justiciability. Lord Diplock suggested that government powers would not be justiciable, and so would not be subject to review, if the dispute was of a sort which does not lend itself to resolution by judicial type methods. The non-justiciable issue is not simply a case of A versus B. Rather it presents a great many competing points of view, all of which have to be weighed and balanced in the search for an overall political solution. Elected politicians, rather than non-elected judges, are the appropriate people to make these kinds of decisions. Lord Diplock described this type of decision as 'a balancing exercise which judges by their upbringing and experience are ill-qualified to perform'.[16] He considered that national security was 'par excellence a non-justiciable question. The judicial processes are totally inept to deal with the sort of problems which it involves'.[17]

14 [1985] AC 374 at 399.
15 *Ibid*, at 417.
16 *Ibid*, at 411.
17 *Ibid*, at 412.

In effect, the House of Lords refused to investigate either the honesty or the reasonableness of the Prime Minister's claim that she had revoked trade union membership without consultation because of national security reasons. If we are looking for old parallels to elements of the *GCHQ* decision, it might be more appropriate to focus on the court's approach to this question of national security. In the pre-revolutionary *Ship Money* case, the court held that the King need not offer any evidence to support his assertion that the security of the realm was in jeopardy. In the 1916 *Zamora* case, in contrast, the court had required at least some evidence that the government had bona fide grounds for believing national security to be threatened. The *GCHQ* decision seems to follow the *Zamora* principle. The court required the government to produce an affidavit confirming that the minister had genuinely considered the issue. But this does not seem to be a very difficult hurdle for the government to clear, and it implies that we have to trust the government never to invoke national security reasons for dishonest or bizarre reasons.

The final important point advanced in *GCHQ* was the court's conclusion that it was not just national security issues which were non-justiciable. Lord Roskill produced a list of what we might call 'excluded' categories – aspects of the prerogative where review would relate only to the existence of the claimed power, not to its exercise. The powers that Lord Roskill had in mind were; 'the making of treaties, the defence of the realm, the prerogative of mercy, the grant of honours, the dissolution of Parliament and the appointment of Ministers'.[18]

This list perhaps suggest that the court's definition of non-reviewable prerogative powers quite closely resembles Blackstone's old notion of the prerogative as consisting solely of those powers which are 'singular and eccentrical to the Crown', which indicates that one may always find a historical precedent for supposedly radical developments in constitutional law.

IV. POST-*GCHQ* DEVELOPMENTS – THE SHIFTING NATURE OF 'JUSTICIABILITY'

Cases which have been decided since 1985 seem to build on rather than contradict the somewhat more functionalist analysis which the House of Lords adopted in *GCHQ*. The central question the case raised, but perhaps could not answer, was whether 'justici-

18 *Ibid*, at 418.

ability' was a concept with a fixed meaning, or whether if, like
other common law principles, it would prove to be an unstable
concept, prone to sudden and substantial change. An initial
answer to that question was offered by the Zimbabwean Supreme
Court in 1986.[19]

The ZAPU case (1986)[20]

When Zimbabwe eventually achieved 'independence'[1] in the early
1980s, it adopted a constitutional structure which retained several
British features. In particular, the President possessed prerogative
powers to issue proclamations analagous to the British government's prerogative powers. We do not need to dwell on the facts
of the case, which concerned a change to the law regulating
general elections. But we should note that the Zimbabwean
Supreme Court seemed to accept exactly the same principles as
the House of Lords in *GCHQ*. Firstly, that government powers were
not excluded from review on the grounds of unreasonableness or
procedural fairness simply because their source was the prerogative rather than statute. And secondly that certain prerogative
powers were non-justiciable. The Supreme Court's list resembled
the one produced by Lord Roskill in *GCHQ*, but also included the
accreditation of diplomats, the declaration of war and the imposition of a state of national emergency.

The *ZAPU* case is at best of persuasive authority in this country.
But it is quite valuable in illustrating the very wide meaning that
can be given to these notions of non-justiciable powers. What is
perhaps most striking about the *ZAPU* case is that the Zimbabwe
Supreme Court laid out its long list of excluded categories, and
then suggested that the circumstances in which review was not
available would be 'now very few and far between'. That seems a
questionable assumption. Some of the powers listed are extremely
important, and if we are concerned to ensure that government's
use of the prerogative is not arbitrary, irrational, or unfair, the
court's reluctance to review such powers is perhaps disturbing.

19 See Walker C (1987) 'Review of the prerogative: the remaining issues' *Public
Law* 63–84.
20 *Patriotic Front-ZAPU v Minister of Justice, Legal and Parliamentary Affairs* 1986 (1)
SA 532.
1 Zimbabwe was formerly known as Rhodesia, a British colony which had
'rebelled' against British rule in the mid-1960s. On the difficulties this de facto
renunciation of parliamentary sovereignty posed for the Wilson government
see Pimlott B (1992) *Harold Wilson* pp 366–381 (London: Harper Collins);
Crossman R (1979) *The Crossman Diaries* pp 151–161 (London: Mandarin).

***R v Secretary of State for the Home Department, ex p Northumbria Police Authority* (1988)**

Some constitutional lawyers were also rather disturbed by the Court of Appeal's 1988 decision in *R v Secretary of State for the Home Department, ex p Northumbria Police Authority*.[2] The legal structure of the police forces in this country is quite complex; but to put the matter simply, some powers rest with central government, some with local police authorities, and some with the Chief Constable of each force.[3]

The *Northumbria* case arose when the central government decided to set up a central supply store for plastic bullets and CS gas, on which Chief Constables could draw when they thought it necessary. Northumbria Police Authority did not want its Chief Constable to use these weapons without its approval, and so it initiated judicial review proceedings in an effort to establish that central government had no legal power to pursue this policy. The government claimed such power emanated from one or both of two sources. Either it came from the Police Act 1964, or it came from the old prerogative power 'to keep the peace'.

The Court of Appeal eventually decided that the 1964 Act did include the power to set up a central weapons depot. That was a controversial conclusion, but we need not dwell on it here. What we do need to consider is the court's answer to the questions of whether there was a prerogative power to keep the peace, and if so, what types of action came within the confines of that power in the mid-1980s ?

Northumbria's case rested on two main contentions. The Police Authority's first argument was that there was no mention in nine-teenth-century textbooks or case law of a prerogative power to keep the peace. This would seem a strong argument in the Police Authority's favour. If we recall Lord Camden's judgment in *Entick v Carrington*, we will remember that he was quite clear about how to determine if the Crown had a legal power to seize Mr Entick's papers; 'If it is law, it will be found in our books. If it is not to be found there, it is not law'. In effect, this argument is saying that the residue of prerogative powers left to the Crown after the 1688 revolution never extended to equipping a police force.

---

2 [1988] 1 All ER 556. See also Bradley A (1988) 'Police powers and the prerogative'*Public Law* 298–303.
3 An excellent analysis is offered in Lustgarten L (1989) *The Governance of Police* (London: Sweet and Maxwell). For a more concise introduction see Marshall G and Loveday B (1994) 'The police: independence and accountability', in Jowell and Oliver *op cit.*

The Court of appeal dismissed this contention. Its somewhat innovative attitude is perhaps best expressed by Nourse LJ:

'[The] scarcity of reference in the books to the prerogative of keeping the peace within the realm does not disprove that it exists. Rather it may point to an unspoken assumption that it does.'[4]

It is not difficult to agree with the first of those sentences; we should be cautious about assuming that eighteenth-century textbooks and law reports offered a comprehensive map of that era's legal landscape.[5] But the meaning of the second sentence seems a little odd. Nourse LJ appears to argue that we can assume a legal power exists becomes no judge or textbook writer has ever recognised it. It seems hard to reconcile that reasoning with definitions of the rule of law which demand predictability and certainty in the scope of government's legal powers. Nevertheless, as we have already stressed, the *Burmah Oil* case serves as a salutary reminder that while there is no doubt that the prerogative is residual, there yet remains considerable doubt that all parts of that residue have thus far been identified. Nourse LJ's anaysis might therefore be defended on the basis that he was perspicacious enough to find a 'lost' power which no other judge had previously managed to spot.

Northumbria's second argument drew on the *De Keyser Hotel* and *Laker Airways* principle. The first police force was created by statute in the early nineteenth century. So Northumbria contended that whatever prerogative powers to keep the peace may have existed in 1688 would have been superseded by any overlapping statutory provisions. Section 4 of the Police Act 1964 granted the power to provide clothing and equipment to the police to Police Authorities. Northumbria argued that if one applied the *De Keyser* principle to s 4, one could only conclude that whatever prerogative power to supply equipment the Home Secretary might have had before 1964 had now been removed.

But the Court of Appeal also rejected this argument. Croom-Johnson LJ held that s 4 did not 'expressly grant a monopoly' in respect of equipment provision to the Police Authority, but rather

---

4 [1988] 1 All ER 556 at 575.
5 Cf Nourse LJ's contention at 574 that: 'It has not at any stage in our history been practicable to identify all the prerogative powers of the Crown. It is only by a process of piecemeal decision over a period of centuries that particular powers are seen to exist or not exist'. The House of Lords' decision in *Burmah Oil* (above) is a pertinent example of what might best be described as a three-hundred year time lag in the judiciary's discovery of a hitherto hidden legal rule.

created a situation in which the Police Authority's statutory power co-existed with the Home Secretary's prerogative power. But unlike the situation in *Laker*, the co-existence appeared to be contradictory rather than interlocking. This is a rather surprising argument, for it seems to be saying that the doctrine of implied repeal, discussed in chapter 2, does not apply to prerogative powers. Croom-Johnson LJ is apparently suggesting that Parliament can only abolish the prerogative through express statutory provisions.[6]

This initially appears to takes us into a seemingly illogical train of thought. Firstly, we accept that statute has a superior legal status to the prerogative. Secondly, we accept that statutes can be impliedly repealed by subsequent, impliedly inconsistent legislation. Thirdly, we accept that prerogative powers cannot be impliedly repealed by subsequent, impliedly inconsistent legislation. The third contention obviously contradicts points one and two. It is difficult to reconcile the Court of Appeal's decision about the status of the prerogative with orthodox constitutional theory, which might perhaps lead us to conclude that if we look hard enough we will usually find that our constitution harbours exceptions to even the most evidently straightforward of rules. On further reflection however, Northumbria's acceptance of the co-existence of statutory and prerogative powers is, post-*GCHQ*, arguably unproblematic. Since the nature of the Crown's prerogative power to keep the peace and the powers afforded to the Home Secretary by the Police Act 1964 is the same, whichever method the government chose to apply its preferred policies would be subject to precisely the same degree of judicial scrutiny. There is thus no longer any functionalist justification for assuming the grant of statutory powers impliedly suspends or abolishes analogous prerogative authority.

Foreign affairs?

Two other recent cases on the prerogative merit a brief mention here. They arguably both fall under the excluded category of 'foreign policy' to which Lord Roskill referred in *GCHQ*.

The first case, *Ex p Molyneaux*,[7] arose from the Anglo-Irish agreement signed by the British and Irish governments in 1985. The

---

6 *Ibid* at 564. This sets a somewhat improbable test; it would presumably have been rather unlikely that the 1964 Parliament would have expended energy on expressly abolishing a prerogative power which was not then known to exist.
7 [1986] 1 WLR 331.

agreement established an Inter-Governmental Conference which would meet to try to develop initiatives which might resolve the problems afflicting Northern Ireland. Molyneaux was one of several Protestant Northern Irish politicians who opposed the Agreement. He sought judicial review of the agreement on the grounds that it implemented policies which could only be achieved through legislation. This was a very speculative argument, and the court dismissed it out of hand. The agreement was a treaty with a foreign state; it was quite clear that the government had a prerogative power to negotiate treaties; and it was equally clear that the exercise of that power was not justiciable.

The court reached a different conclusion in the 1989 case of *R v Secretary of State for Foreign and Commonwealth Affairs, ex p Everett*.[8] Mr Everett was an alleged criminal who had taken up residence in Spain, a country with which Britain did not then have an extradition agreement which covered Mr Everett's alleged offence. When Mr Everett's passport expired, the Foreign Office declined to renew it. The government maintained a policy of not renewing passports when the applicant was the subject of an arrest warrant. The issuance of passports has not been put on a statutory basis, and so was clearly a prerogative power. The Foreign Office's refusal meant that Mr Everett would not be able to leave Spain. The Foreign Office did offer him a one-way trip back to Britain, but since he would have been arrested as soon as he arrived, this was an offer which Mr Everett decided to refuse.[9]

Mr Everett subsequently sought a review of the Foreign Office's decision. The government's primary defence was that the issue and renewal of passports was a question of foreign policy, and so within Lord Roskill's 'excluded categories'. The Court of Appeal rejected this argument. O'Connor LJ held that;

> 'the issue of a passport fell into an entirely different category. [I]t would seem obvious to me that the exercise of the prerogative ... is an area where common sense tells one that, if for some reason a passport is wrongly refused for a bad reason, the court should be able to inquire into it'.[10]

---

8 [1989] QB 811, CA.
9 The alleged crime, incidentally and ironically, related to the provision of forged passports!
10 [1989] 2 WLR 224 at 228. That common sense was the appropriate tool to decide the extent of legal powers was of course the argument advanced by James I in the 1611 *Case of Proclamations*. As noted above, Coke CJ thought common sense (even kingly common sense) a most inapposite device to control legal interpretation.

'Common sense' is perhaps not a very precise legal precedent. Taylor LJ's reasoning is perhaps more helpful. He suggested that non-justiciability in foreign relations issues only extended to questions of 'high policy'. He did not define this precisely, but he seems to mean matters which had national security implications or which directly afffected Britain's relationship with a foreign state. He felt that the grant of a passport was not a matter of high policy, but merely an administrative decision. As such, it should be subject to review.

Excluded categories: a shrinking list?

The prerogative of mercy figured prominently in Lord Roskill's list of non-justiciable prerogative powers in *GCHQ*. But barely ten years later, in *R v Secretary of State for the Home Department, ex p Bentley*,[11] the court effectively extended its power of review to this aspect of the prerogative. Derek Bentley, a nineteen-year-old youth of very limited intellectual capacity, had been convicted of murder in 1952 and was subsequently hanged in 1953. Bentley had been an accomplice to the actual murderer, a sixteen-year-old, who was too young to be sentenced to capital punishment. Despite a recommendation from the jury that Bentley should not be executed, the trial judge imposed the death sentence. The then Home Secretary declined to grant mercy to Bentley, despite advice to that effect from his senior officials.

The *Bentley* case of was one of the final steps in a forty-year campaign fought by Iris Bentley, the accused's sister, to establish either that her brother was innocent of the crime, or, at the very least, that he should not have received a capital sentence. By the early 1990s, Iris Bentley had managed to convince many people that her brother had been unjustly treated, and in 1992 she asked the Home Secretary to grant her brother a posthumous free pardon. The Home Secretary (then Kenneth Clarke) refused to do so. Mr Clarke suggested that he personally believed that Bentley should not have been hanged, but that he was unable to grant a pardon because he had not been presented with any evidence to indicate that Bentley was morally and technically innocent of the murder.

Before the High Court, Iris Bentley argued that the Home Secretary had misdirected himself in law, by failing to appreciate that 'a pardon' could take several forms, not all of which required a presumption of innocence. The Court rejected the Home Sec-

11 [1993] 4 All ER 442.

retary's assertion that this particular prerogative power was per se unreviewable, concluding that Lord Roskill's apparent assertion to that effect in *GCHQ* was simply obiter. The court based its analysis on a seemingly logical extension of the *GCHQ* principle that: 'the powers of the court cannot be ousted merely by invoking the word "prerogative" '.[12] The High Court then turned for guidance to a recent New Zealand decision, in which the New Zealand Court of Appeal held that while the prerogative of mercy was 'peculiar' to the Crown:

> 'it would be inconsistent with the contemporary approach to say that, merely because it is a pure and strict prerogative power, its exercise or non-exercise must be immune from curial challenge. . . . [T]he rule of law requires that challenge shall be permitted in so far as issues arise of a kind with which the courts are competent to deal'.[13]

The issue before the Court in *Bentley* was not the essentially non-justiciable question of how the Home Secretary should have balanced the various moral and political factors involved in determining whether a pardon should be granted in this case, but the eminently 'legal' question of whether the Home Secretary should be required to remake his decision when his original response was based on a fundamental misunderstanding of the scope of his power. In such circumstances, the court saw no constitutional barrier to the availability of review.

But having assumed the power to declare the Mr Clarke's decision was unlawful, the Court then declined to use it. Rather, Watkins LJ 'invited' the Home Secretary to look at the question again and 'devise some formula which would amount to a clear acknowledgment that an injustice was done'.[14] In such circumstances, the distinction between an 'invitation' and an 'order' is perhaps merely semantic: the practical effect of the court's decision was to pull a hitherto legally unregulated aspect of the government process within a recognisably Diceyan notion of the rule of law.

V. 'JUSTICIABILITY' REVISITED – ARE ALL STATUTORY POWERS REVIEWABLE?

Before we leave the royal prerogative, it is important to remember that the notion of justiciability is something of a two-edged sword.

12 *Ibid*, at 452.
13 *Burt v Governor General* [1992] 3 NZLR 672 at 678.
14 [1993] 4 All ER 442 at 455.

If, post-*GCHQ*, the courts' concern is now with the nature of a government power rather than its source, it would not seem implausible to assume that there are some statutory powers whose nature makes them unsuitable for review. Once more, therefore, we are drawn towards a functionalist rather than formalist interpretation of constitutional principle. The 1964 case of *Chandler v DPP*[15] offers an example of this principle being put into practice.

Section 1 of the Official Secrets Act 1911 made it an offence for anybody to enter any prohibited place 'for any purpose prejudicial to the safety . . . of the state'. This is obviously a national security-related issue, but one dealt with by statute rather than the prerogative. As part of a political campaign against nuclear weapons, Chandler had entered such a prohibited place, a military airfield, and tried to immobilise planes by sitting on the runway. He was subsequently prosecuted under s 1.

His defence to the charge was to argue that his efforts to publicise the cause of disarmament were in fact beneficial to the safety of the state. However the House of Lords declined to be drawn into this argument. The Lords held that the question of evaluating threats to national security was not a justiciable issue. National security was an issue that could only be gauged by the government of the day.

This was not quite a judicial retreat back to the *Ship Money* situation. At least technically, the court seemed to follow the precedent set in the *Zamora* case by requiring some evidence that the protestors' activities had jeopardised national security. That requirement did not seem to be very demanding however – the court was satisfied by an affidavit from an Air Commodore simply saying that the air strip was an important defence installation, and that any intrusion into it was 'prejudicial to the safety of the state'.

This result is obviously very similar to the one reached twenty years later in *GCHQ*. In theory, the government is subjected to a burden of proof to demonstrate that it was indeed motivated by national security considerations. But in practice, that requirement is merely a formality; it is discharged by the most flimsy evidence. So one must beware of falling into the trap of assuming that simply putting prerogative powers on a statutory basis will make them subject to the full rigour of judicial review. National security, whether invoked under a statute or under the prerogative, seems likely always to be a non-justiciable issue.

There may perhaps come a point where there seems to be no justification for claiming that national security issues arise. One

15 [1964] AC 763, HL.

might speculate for example how the Court of Appeal would have responded in *Laker* to a DoT claim that it was indeed entitled to issue 'directions' under s 4(3) – a power which arose only in respect of national security or diplomatic concerns – because in the minister's considered opinion Laker's service did indeed have adverse national security implications. However this theory has not as yet been put to the test.

CONCLUSION

It is obvious that the courts supervise the government's use of prerogative powers much more closely now than they did in the pre-revolutionary era. It is also quite clear that there has been some increase in the *theoretical* reach of the courts' power of review since the 1967 decision in *Lain*. (Quite why this should have occurred is a question to which, in combination with other issues yet to be discussed, we will return in chapter 14). We can also conclude that adminstrative law now seems to treat prerogative and statutory powers in the same way.

The more difficult issue is to decide if the concept of non-justiciability is too widely defined? Are the courts allowing too much government action to take place free from the control of judicial review? We might recall that after *Liversidge v Anderson*, Stable J had written to Lord Atkin suggesting that the House of Lords' decision meant that the judges were not so much 'lions under the throne' as 'mice squeaking under a chair in the Home Office'. We cannot apply such emotive language to the *GCHQ* or *Northumbria* judgments. But what we should remember is that the courts' control of the common law concept of judicial review gives the judges considerable power. By extending the scope of justiciability, the courts can place tighter controls on government's ability to behave in ways that seem inconsistent with traditional understandings of the rule of law. That looks very much like a 'red light' interpretation of the judicial function, and is a desirable result if one is suspicious of government, and fears that government powers might be used for unmeritorious ends. Alternatively, if one favours a 'green light' judicial role, believing that it is important for government to have great freedom to pursue policies which it thinks advance the national interest, one might prefer that the courts decide that more and more types of government action are non-justiciable. At present, the common law's power to extend review to currently non-justiciable issues clearly exists, but it is not clear under what circumstances, if any, it will be used.

We should however remember that resort to the courts is not the only means to regulate the government's use of the prerogative, nor of its deployment of powers granted by statute. In addition to having analysed the legal mechanism of judicial review, we must also assess *political* methods of control. This is a consideration which is as pertinent to the question of parliamentary sovereignty as it is to control of the prerogative. As we shall see in subsequent chapters, political controls take various forms. In chapters 5 and 6, we turn our attention to two of those forms – the House of Commons and the House of Lords.

CHAPTER FIVE

The House of Commons

This chapter does not offer a comprehensive picture of the historical development and modern role of the House of Commons:
such an enquiry would merit a substantial book to itself.[1] Its more
modest objective is to sketch certain aspects of the relationship
between the government and the legislature, in order to develop
more fully arguments concerning the doctrines of parliamentary
sovereignty and the separation of powers within the contemporary
constitution. Much of what follows is rather more descriptive in
tone than both preceding and subsequent chapters largely because
this book takes the view that analysis of particular aspects of the
Commons' past and present significance is better undertaken in
the context of specific events, which are examined in later chapters, than in an ahistorical way.

Crown and Commons – the original intent and the subsequent rise of 'party' politics[2]

The necessarily fragmentary and unreliable historical records of
mediaeval England make it impossible to state with any certainty
when a body which might be regarded as the predecessor of the

1 There are several such volumes available. For an introduction see Silk P (1992)
How Parliament Works (London: Longman); Adonis A (1990) *Parliament Today*
(Manchester: Manchester University Press); Walkland S and Ryle M (eds) (1977)
The Commons in the Seventies (London: Martin Robertson): Ryle M and Richards
P (1988) *The Commons under Scrutiny* (London: Routledge).
2 This section presents a very superficial overview. For a more extensive discussion
see Norton P (1985) *The Commons in Perspective* chs 1–2 (London: Martin
Robertson); (2nd edn, 1991) *The British Polity* chs 8 and 11 (London: Longman).

Commons first emerged.[3] By 1270, several national assemblies, whose members included 'commoners' as well as aristocrats, had met under the King's authority to assist in devising solutions to current political or fiscal difficulties.[4] It would seem that the consolidation of the Commons, Lords and Monarch as the 'three estates of the realm' occurred by 1300. Members of the Lords were individually summoned to attend by the Monarch; the members of the Commons comprised representatives of each county and borough.[5] Nevertheless it was to be another another 100 years before the Commons became a routine component of England's government structure.

The early period of the Commons' history, while intrinsically of great historical interest, need not be dwelt on at length here, although certain episodes are considered in subsequent chapters. For analytical purposes, however, if we accept 1688 as the birth date of the modern constitution, it is helpful to focus briefly on then prevailing perceptions of the Commons' 'correct' constitutional functions, and, relatedly, the political and moral source of its authority within the law-making and governmental processes.

The Commons initially appeared to perform two distinct formal legislative roles. The first, inherent in its status as the embodiment of one estate of the realm, was to safeguard the interests of non-aristocratic élite groups in society against the possible incursions of the Lords and/or the Crown.[6] As such, it provided a very weakly representative base to the governmental process. As will be explained in chapter 7, 'the people' from which the Commons was drawn prior to 1832 was a very narrowly-defined concept; but the notion that legitimate government demanded their consent rather than merely their submission – that they be persuaded rather than coerced to respect the laws of the land – was by then an accepted (if flexible) principle of constitutional

---

3 The Commons shares a site in central London with the House of Lords in the Palace of Westminster. The site was the Monarch's main residence until the mid-1500s, after which time it was increasingly reserved for the sole use of the two houses. The current building was built in the 1840s; Silk *op cit* ch 1.
4 Plucknett (1960) *op cit* pp 130–140.
5 The development of the electoral system through which members of the Commons are chosen is discussed in chapter 7. The Commons is often referred to as the 'lower house' or 'lower chamber' of Parliament; the Lords as the 'upper house' or 'upper chamber'. The three labels for each house are used interchangeably in this book.
6 As we shall see in chapter 7, this is a rather crude oversimplification of the political reality.

morality.[7] The second was to provide a voice for local interests within the national legislature. Its members were 'elected' on a geographical basis, and were expected to act as vigorous advocates for the areas they represented: in some senses, the Commons was as much an aggregation of localities as a 'national' forum.

The MP – representative or delegate?

By 1688, the 'national' dimension of the Commons' role was becoming dominant.[8] This is illustrated at least in part by subsequently accepted perceptions of the nature of the relationship between an MP and the local electors who had chosen him, a perception most famously articulated by Edmund Burke in his 1774 *Address to the electors of Bristol:*

> 'It ought to be the happiness and glory of a representative to live in the strictest union, the closest correspondence, and the most unreserved communication with his constitutents. It is his duty to sacrifice his repose, his pleasures, his satisfaction to theirs; . . . and in all cases to prefer their interest to his own. But his unbiased opinion, his mature judgement, his enlightened conscience, he ought not to sacrifice . . . to any set of men living. . . . Your representative owes you, not his industry only, but his judgement: and he betrays, instead of serving you, if he sacrifices it to your opinion.'

One clearly sees echoes of Burke's thesis in Madison's notion of representative government.[9] Legislators were not to be the mere delegates or mouthpieces of their electors. Madison's words would fit unproblematically into Burke's rationale; as representatives, MPs' legislative task would be to 'refine and enlarge the public view', to 'discern the true interest of their country' and to resist pressure from their electors to sacrifice that interest to 'temporary or partial considerations'. Electors who concluded that their MP had succumbed to such pressures, or, alternatively, who continued to adhere to 'temporary and partial considerations' which their representative did not indulge in the house, might choose a different MP at a subsequent election. But what Parliament had thus far never done was pass legislation which empowered disgruntled electors to recall or dismiss an MP who failed to follow their instructions.

Burke offers an idealised picture of the Commons at work: a

---

7 As subsequent chapters will suggest, the large question then becomes how that extremely flexible (perhaps almost vacuous) principle is to be expressed in practice.
8 Plucknett (1960) *op cit* pp 618–619.
9 See pp 11–12 above.

vision of a legislative chamber in which several hundred independently-minded MPs each address every question before them in a mature, enlightened and impartial manner, free from the fetters both of blinkered parochialism and factional allegiances. In such circumstances, one might plausibly assume that the decisions the house reached would indeed best represent the 'national interest'. Whether such a governmental idyll ever did (or ever could) exist within the British constitution (or indeed any other) is a moot point; what is more certain is that the practicalities of political life in the Parliaments in which Burke sat contained the seeds of a countervailing trend, which by 1900 had hardened into a rigid (if not entirely unbreakable) orthodoxy. In formal, legal terms the Burkean position still exists today. MPs are not under any legal obligation to structure their voting behaviour or the contents of their speeches in the Commons in accordance with anybody else's wishes. Yet in practice, the contemporary MP can defensibly be portrayed as a delegate; a delegate not of her constituents, but of her party.

The fusion of powers, the rise of the party system and Cabinet dominance of the Commons

The concept of the 'independent' MP would seem to fit very comfortably with idealised versions of the separation of powers, in which the legislature and the executive were entirely discrete bodies. Yet a pure separation of powers has always been a myth within the English (and later British) constitution. It is readily apparent that the 1688 constitutional settlement did not effect an extreme separation of powers. The Monarch, who was then the formal and functional core of the executive branch of government, was also a distinct part of the legislature. Similarly, many of his/her advisers and ministers were members of the House of Lords: the holding of ministerial office did not preclude (and nor did it require) fully active membership of either house. The Monarch's advisers were collectively known as the Privy Council,[10] a large and somewhat unwieldy body (with as many as fifty members), many of whom were members of the House of Lords or of the Commons. To an appreciable extent, therefore, two of

10 The term seems to have been in common usage by 1540; Plucknett (1960) *op cit* p 255. The Privy Council still exists, but it has little practical relevance other than on those occasions when (staffed by Law Lords) it sits as a final Court of Appeal for some Commonwealth countries (cf *Trethowan* at p 48 above).

the three branches of government were from the very outset of the post-revolutionary era 'fused' rather than separated.

Yet it would be too simplistic to assume that an overlap of personnel necessarily precluded an effective divergence, if not quite separation, of powers between the Commons and the executive in the immediate post-revolutionary period. Given the turbulence of seventeenth-century political history, so much of which was shaped by antagonism and conflict between the King and the lower house, it is readily apparent that many members of the Commons would continue to regard the Monarch with suspicion, even though his/her law-making powers were now evidently to be inferior to those of Parliament.

The emergence of the parliamentary sovereignty doctrine ostensibly produced a substantial redefinition of contemporary constitutional understandings. Yet as was noted in discussing the royal prerogative, it is clear that certain pre-revolutionary principles continued to structure judicial perceptions of the relationships between the other two branches of government. Such continuities had a political as well as a legal dimension.[11]

Charles II may be credited with introducing the first recognisably modern 'cabinet' within the executive, when in 1671 he effectively marginalised the Privy Council and chose to formulate government policy with a so-called 'Cabal' of just five ministers. Charles' initiative attracted considerable criticism; the Cabal was seen as a factional vehicle, rather than, as was the much larger Privy Council, a source of diverse and (ideally) disinterested counsel.

Yet despite the revolution's apparent distrust of factional government, the more centralised Cabinet rather than the Privy Council formed the core of the executive in the immediate post-revolutionary era. Furthermore, the nature of the relationship between the Monarch and his/her ministers within the core also began to shift. Neither George I nor George II took much interest in the affairs of government (in part because of their poor command of English). By 1740, practical control of the Cabinet rested with the occupant of the newly emergent office of 'Prime Minister'. Sir Robert Walpole is generally regarded as the first holder of the post, but his position had no legal basis, and it was not until the early 1800s that the label came into common usage. George III took much closer control of the government process, but since he suffered periodic bouts of (what contemporary medical

11 I am much indebted in the following pages to Plucknett (1960) *op cit* pp 610–647.

opinion labelled) insanity,[12] his ability to reverse the drift towards prime ministerial pre-eminence within the government was severely limited.

The eighteenth-century Monarchs' disinclination and/or inability to lead 'their' Cabinets coincided with the emergence of a sophisticated system of party political organisation. Outside the House of Commons, the rise of the national political party was facilitated by advances in technology. Improved transport facilities and cheaper printing meant that for the first time, like-minded citizens throughout the country could constantly plan and act in concert on a wide range of political issues.

The perception of the two houses containing 'a government' and 'an opposition' is again associated with Walpole, who from 1717 led a group of MPs which for first time saw its raison d'être as to 'oppose' the government of the day, although it is not until 1826 that the label 'The Opposition' (meaning the second largest grouping of MPs in the house) became commonplace.[13] By this time, the Cabinet, comprised now almost exclusively of members of the Commons and/or Lords, was generally formed from the leading members of the party commanding majority support in the lower house.

As chapters 6 and 7 suggest, the Commons had in practice become the dominant chamber within Parliament by the 1830s. Equally clearly, the Commons was beginning to be dominated by a majority party pursuing a relatively coherent set of policy objectives, within which the Cabinet and especially the Prime Minister exercised an appreciable and increasing degree of control.

For modern observers, the perception that the Commons is little more than an arena within which the Labour and Conservative parties alternately form the government and the opposition is undoubtedly a strong one. It is given considerable force simply by the physical layout of the Commons' main chamber. The 'floor of the house' places government and opposition members directly opposite each other on several rows of benches. Government ministers and their opposition 'shadows' occupy the front benches on each side, with the rest of their party members sitting behind

12 The Monarch's standing qua the head of the government was not aided by George III's disastrous handling of relationships with the American colonies in the 1760s and 1770s; see Bailyn *op cit* pp 145–146, 152–153.
13 Norton P (1988) 'Opposition to government' p 100, in Ryle and Richards *op cit*. The position of Leader of the Opposition is now a salaried public office, over and above that of simply being an MP. At present, the salary is some £64,000 per year.

them.[14] That the lower house is now in practice a body in which party factions are clearly demarcated and constantly jostle for advantage cannot seriously be disputed. Equally clearly, that contemporary reality bears little relation to the Commons' initial role in the post-revolutionary constitution. The desirability or otherwise of this situation is a point to which we shall frequently return. For the moment however, our concern is with the ways in which party discipline in the lower house is maintained.

Party discipline in the Commons: the whips and the appointment of ministers

MPs are not subject to any legal obligation to support their party within the house. Parties are in effect voluntary organisations, within which the maintenance of co-operation between members is an entirely internal matter. Within the Commons, the larger parties have developed a relatively sophisticated control mechanism known as the 'whipping system'.[15] Several MPs in each of the main parties serve as party whips. They function in effect as the party's personnel managers, their task being to ensure that their party's MPs are deployed in whichever ways maximise achievement of party objectives.

'The whip' is also used to refer to the weekly timetable of Commons business produced by each party for its MPs. This alerts MPs to the significance which their party's leadership attaches to particular issues. Specific items of business will be marked with 'one line', 'two line' and 'three line' whips; the higher the number, the more important it is presumed to be that MPs be present to participate in the business in hand and/or to cast their votes in support of their party's preferred policy.[16] Not all of the house's business is whipped in this way. On issues in respect of which a party's leadership has no particular view, it may permit a 'free vote' in which its MPs follow whichever course of action they consider appropriate.

Party whips are often portrayed as a purely coercive force, whose role is to persuade, cajole or threaten MPs to support party policy

14 Hence ministers and shadow ministers are often referred to as 'front- benchers'. Members who do not hold governmental office or shadow positions are referred to as 'backbenchers'.
15 See particularly Norton P (1979) 'The organisation of parliamentary parties', in Walkland S (ed) *The House of Commons in the Twentieth Century* (Oxford: Clarendon Press).
16 Votes in the house are often referred to as 'divisions', as members register their vote by dividing into two lines and physically walking into different parts of an area of the house known as 'the division lobby'.

on pain of all manner of unpleasant political retribution. That is indeed a role they frequently perform; but they also serve as a channel for the exchange of information between the front and backbenches, and government whips will occasionally be concerned more with convincing the Cabinet that its plans will not attract sufficient backbench support than with compelling backbenchers to support every item on the party agenda. Party whips also oversee their MPs' 'pairing' arrangements, whereby two MPs of opposing parties who would expect to vote in different ways agree with each other not to vote on particular occasions, thereby freeing themselves to undertake activities outside the chamber. As with most aspects of Commons procedures, 'pairing' is not a legally enforceable concept, and pairs have on occasion been broken in close votes.

MPs who consistently flout party policy may have the whip withdrawn from them.[17] This can have immediate adverse consequences for the MP, insofar as the member will be deprived of the information sources that her party machine can supply. The longer-term consequences may be more severe. Since an MP is, in legal terms, the representative of her constituency rather than her party, losing the party whip has no impact on her presence in the Commons. However, as we shall see in chapter 7, election to the Commons is now determined primarily by a candidate's party allegiance. A member who is not adopted as her party's candidate at the next general election is unlikely to retain her seat.

If the whipping system can be perceived as in some senses the stick with which parties seek to discipline their MPs' behaviour, the granting of governmental or shadow office may be seen as the carrot. The power to appoint people to ministerial office nominally rests with the Monarch through her prerogative powers – the government is technically 'Her Majesty's Government', just as the largest opposition party is 'Her Majesty's Opposition'. In effect, the appointment, promotion, transfer, demotion and dismissal of ministers are matters for the Prime Minister. An MP's progress up (or down) what is disaparagingly referred to as 'the greasy pole' is contingent on many factors, relating both to the qualities of the individual concerned and the wider political situation prevailing at any given time. But one may fairly safely conclude that MPs who diverge from party policy on a regular basis are unlikely to enter ministerial or shadow ministerial ranks,

17 For examples see Cross J (1967) 'Withdrawal of the Conservative party whip' *Parliamentary Affairs* 169–175. For a more recent episode see pp 557–558 below.

still less to rise within them. Not all MPs have ambitions to hold ministerial office, and many will have returned to the backbenches after having previously served in the government. For such members, the influence of the lure of office on their loyalty to their party is likely to be limited. For the careerist MP, however, the prospect of promotion is a powerful incentive for tailoring her own political cloth to the pattern drawn up by the party leadership.

There are no formal degrees of seniority or status within the Cabinet,[18] but there is undoubtedly an informal hierarchy. Cabinet members are generally 'Secretaries of State' of particular government departments.[19] The three most important (often referred to as the 'great offices of state') are Home Secretary, Foreign Secretary, and Chancellor of the Exchequer. The relative status of departments within the government is constantly shifting. At present one might plausibly suggest that the Leader of the House of Commons (of whom more is said below), and the Secretaries of State for Defence, Trade and Industry, Environment, Scotland, Health and Education occupy the middle ranks, while the incumbents at Energy, Employment, Wales and Northern Ireland are the junior members.

There is no fixed limit to the number of ministers who may serve in the Cabinet (although at present no more than 21 Cabinet members may hold paid posts as Secretaries of State).[20] The number has risen over the past hundred years, from barely a dozen in the 1870s to as many as two dozen in the recent past. Nor is there any legal requirement that Cabinet ministers be members of either house, although it is now virtually unheard of for a minister not to be a member of Parliament.

'Ministers of State',[1] several of whom are appointed for each department, occupy a lower rung of the ministerial ladder, and are rarely members of the Cabinet. They may nevertheless wield very substantial executive responsibilities, and if their particular Secretary of State is a member of the Lords rather than the Commons, they will bear primary responsibility for representing their department in the lower house. At a lower level still, are

---

18 This issue is explored further at pp 356–362.
19 Although Cabinet ministers need not have any departmental responsibilities at all. Such members are known as 'Ministers without Portfolio'.
20 Ministerial and Other Salaries Act 1975 s1. Secretaries of State are currently paid £42,000 per year: Ministers of State £29,000. Ministers who are members of the Commons also receive a reduced MP's salary of some £25,000 per year. The Lord Chancellor, a Cabinet minister who always sits in the Lords, receives some £80,000 per year.
1 Of whom there are currently around two dozen.

junior ministers known as 'Parliamentary Under Secretaries'. At the bottom of the ministerial hierarchy are 'Parliamentary Private Secretaries' (PPSs), who are often rather perjoratively referred to as Ministerial 'bag carriers'. The PPS is not a salaried position. Occupants are nevertheless assumed to be part of the government, rather than simply, as are backbenchers, members of the governing party.

The House of Commons Disqualification Act 1975 currently precludes the government from having more than 95 ministers drawn from the Commons. The maximum number is not a sacrosanct moral principle; it has been periodically increased throughout the twentieth century. This may be attributed in part to the post-war era's growing acceptance of green light theories of the state; since twentieth-century governments have assumed greater responsibilities than their predecessors, it is unsurprising that they feel a need for more ministers. However it has also been suggested that the increase may be explained by successive governments' wishes to exercise more control over its party members in the Commons.[2] This argument does have the force of numbers behind it; since a party needs only 340 MPs to enjoy a comfortable Commons majority, the presence of nearly 100 members in the government itself clearly points to a significant merging of the executive and legislative branches.

Sections II and III of this chapter below offer some preliminary observations on the extent to which this merging might defensibly be presented as an executive takeover of the lower house by assessing the Commons' roles as a contributor to the legislative process, and as a mechanism to scrutinise government behaviour. But before reaching those specific issues, it is necessary to add a little more detail to our picture of the principles and the people which influence the way in which the lower house actually works.

I. SETTING THE CONTEXT

This section focuses on three key elements of the Commons' constitutional identity. The first concerns the roots (legal or otherwise) of its procedural rules; the second addresses the role of 'the Speaker'; while the third considers the resources to which MPs have access in carrying out their duties.

2 deSmith *op cit* pp 264–265.

The sources of the Commons' procedural rules

This book does not assess the intricacies of parliamentary procedure. Several aspects of the Commons' operating practices are analysed in later chapters in relation to specific episodes in constitutional history. The following pages outline some of the more important features of the ways the Commons performs its various tasks.

Parliament has passed little legislation controlling the Commons' proceedings. Nor has there been any significant judicial intervention through the common law in this area. As noted in chapter 2, the courts have generally considered that each house enjoys unfettered control over its own affairs as a concomitant aspect of Parliament's sovereignty.[3]

Such questions have been left primarily as a matter for the house itself. Its rules currently derive from three main sources, traditional customs or 'ancient usage'; various 'standing orders' passed by the house; and Speakers' rulings. In the absence of legislation, the house may amend any of its procedures in any way and at any time by a simple majority vote.[4]

Significant changes are rarely introduced in so peremptory a fashion. The notion that the house's procedures should rest on the basis of consensual reciprocity has generally been a strongly held moral principle among most MPs. Major reforms are generally instigated at the recommendation of the Commons Procedure Committee.[5] This committee has no permanent status, but is established whenever the house considers aspects of its procedures may require examination and reform.

The leading source of guidance (for both commentators and MPs themselves) on Commons' procedure is *Erskine May's Treatise on the Law, Privileges, Proceedings and Usage of Parliament*.[6] But it would be misleading to consider such guidance, or indeed the procedures themselves, as analogous to 'laws'. Perhaps the most important element of the house's working practices is the phenomenon known as 'the usual channels'. The label refers to the various informal agreements and negotiations made between the government and opposition parties as to the way in which the Commons' time should be allocated. Managing the usual channels

---

3 See pp 41–42 above. The issue is examined in more depth in chapter 8.

4 Although as chapter 8 suggests, there are instances when the house has apparently successfully defied legislative regulation of its behaviour.

5 Griffith J and Ryle M (1989) *Parliament* pp 174–175 (London: Sweet and Maxwell).

6 References to *Erskine May* in the following pages are to the 21st edition, edited by Boulton C (1989) (London: Butterworths).

is a task allocated primarily to the Leader of the House (a senior member of the Cabinet) and the government chief whip, together with their opposition counterparts.

The house's procedural rules might plausibly be regarded as a series of presumptions to which members voluntarily acquiesce: in part because they consider the rules intrinsically correct; in part because they feel the wishes of a majority of members should be respected; and in part because they would hope that should they form part of the Commons majority in future, the then minority would be similarly co-operative. The presumptions are not, however, irrebuttable, in either the formal or informal senses.

The dominant presumption is that government business should take priority in each parliamentary session. This presumption is currently given force in a standing order – but that merely reflects rather than creates the government's ability to control the house's proceedings. The crucial informants of the way the Commons conducts its business are the willingness of its members to respect traditional practices, and, in the event of that respect breaking down, the government's capacity to marshall majority support for its preferences.

The Commons generally sits for between 150 and 200 days per session; sessions usually begin in the autumn and run for around eleven months. Each session begins with 'the Queen's Speech', in which the Monarch outlines the government's legislative programme for the coming year. There is no rigid rule as to how precisely the available time will be divided between the different aspects of the Commons' various functions. In recent years, 30–35% of time spent on the floor of the house has been devoted to government Bills; 15–17% has been used for motions (general debates) and ministerial statements on subjects of the government's choosing; 7–8% has been granted to Opposition motions; 8–10% has been for backbenchers' bills and motions, and similar amounts have been devoted to questions to ministers, and passing delegated legislation.[7]

There is invariably great scope for inter-party disagreement as to the propriety of government efforts to manage the house's work flow. Since the Commons' procedural rules are not legal phenomena (in the sense of being subject to judicial oversight), some other form of arbiter is required to resolve disputes. That function is one of several performed by the Speaker.

7 For more detailed breakdowns see Adonis (1990) *op cit* p 87 for 1987–1988; Borthwick R (1988) 'The floor of the house', in Ryle and Richards *op cit* for 1984–1985 and 1985–1986.

The Speaker

The role of the Speaker, an office which can be traced back as far as 1376,[8] is of considerable significance. It is the Speaker's task to interpret and apply the various customs and standing orders structuring the house's proceedings. To some extent, therefore, her role is that of judge or umpire whenever disputes arise as to how parliamentary business should be managed; when, for example, the usual channels cannot produce government/opposition agreement, or when backbenchers feel that the government and opposition front benches are paying insufficient attention to backbench concerns. Her jurisdiction is consequently both extensive and multi-faceted. It embraces such diverse issues as deciding which amendments are to be debated (and for how long) at the report and third reading stages of a Bill's passage; choosing which members may speak during debates or question time; and disciplining members whose behaviour in the house breaches accepted standards.[9]

Before 1688, the Speaker often appeared to function largely as an emissary of the Crown. Given the then fairly effective separation of powers between the Commons and the government, the office could be uncomfortable in times of acute antagonism between the Commons and the Monarch.[10] For Speakers who felt their first loyalty lay to the house rather than the Monarch that discomfort might occasionally grow into quite severe personal danger.[11] It was not until the mid-eighteenth century (by which time the fusion rather than separation of the executive and legislature was becoming apparent) that the Speaker had clearly become a defender of the Commons' interests against the wishes of the government.[12]

---

8 See Plucknett *op cit* pp 207–211.
9 See pp 153–156 below. For an overview see Borthwick (1988) *op cit*; Adonis A (1990) *op cit* ch 4; Silk *op cit* pp 71–76. A helpful source is Laundy P (1979) 'The Speaker and his office in the twentieth century', in Walkland *op cit*.
10 Plucknett observes: 'Sir Peter de la Mare was imprisoned, but worse befell some of his successors . . . Bussy, William Tresham, Thorpe, Wenlock, Catesby, Empson, Dudley, Sir Thomas More – all came to violent ends on the scaffold, in civil war, or by assassination'; (1960) *op cit* pp 210–211.
11 This explains the bizarre ritual, still maintained in the contemporary Commons, during which a newly-elected Speaker is dragged apparently unwillingly by other members to assume her office. For one of the earliest examples of a Speaker overtly defying the King in defence of the Commons see the discussion of the *Case of the Five Members* at pp 290–291.
12 We examine this issue further in chapter 8.

The Speaker is elected by members of the house. It is now accepted that the office is a non-party political post. The Speaker resigns from her political party on election. She nevertheless remains an MP, and continues to act on behalf of her constituents. She must also seek re-election to the Commons at subsequent elections, in which she stands as 'the Speaker' rather than as a party member. She does not vote in divisions within the house except when there is a tie; in such circumstances, tradition requires her to vote for the status quo. In the modern era, Speakers have generally been members of the majority party. However, the present incumbent at the time of writing, Betty Boothroyd, was a Labour MP prior to her assumption of the office in 1992, even though the Commons then contained a majority of Conservative MPs. In such circumstances, Ms Boothroyd could not have won the election without the approval of many Conservative members. That they offered their support is a forceful indicator of the extent to which the Speaker is now perceived, in functional as well as formal terms, to be above and beyond the partisanship of party politics.

The Speaker is not always in the chair when the Commons is in session. Her presence is generally reserved only for the most important parts of the Commons' timetable. On other occasions, her role in the Chamber is taken by one of three deputy speakers, first among whom is the 'Chairman of Ways and Means'. Similarly, when the house is in the 'standing committee' stage of the legislative process, the chair is taken by one of a dozen or so senior backbench MPs who sit on the 'Committee of Chairmen'. When the house meets as a 'committee of the whole' the chair is taken by the Chairman of Ways and Means.[13] In both cases, the respective chairmen/women possess broadly the same powers as the Speaker herself to regulate the conduct of proceedings.

It would be inaccurate to characterise the Speaker as exercising coercive powers. Insofar as a Speaker effectively controls the house in times of dispute, she does so because members voluntarily submit to her authority, even when it might appear that their immediate party political interests would be better served by defiance.[14] As such, the Speaker performs the important (if largely symbolic) task of stressing that the Commons should function as something more than a vehicle for dogmatic pursuit of short-term factional advantage. The Speaker's role will be touched·upon several times in later pages. Before turning to consider the

13 See pp 152–159 below.
14 For a powerful example see pp 302–303 below.

Commons' work more closely, one further contextual point must be addressed – namely the resources on which MPs may draw to assist them in fulfilling their formal constitutional role.

Resources

It is perhaps an exaggeration to classify MPs as poor relations of their legislative contemporaries in other modern democracies. Yet when compared to members of the US Congress, MPs receive little assistance in carrying out their tasks.[15] In the USA, members of Congress enjoy substantial research and administrative staffs, and the office space and facilities for those staff to be effective. The rationale underpinning such expansive provision is clearly rooted in the notion of informed consent to government. Legislators are unlikely to make effective contributions to the legislative process, nor searchingly evaluate the merits of government behaviour, if they lack ready access to expert analysis of relevant information.[16]

Yet in the mid-1980s, the Commons offered only 350 offices to its 650 members. Many MPs were consequently forced to share office space (and not always with members of their own party). Many offices were extremely small – few could accommodate secretarial and research staff as well as the MP herself. We might however observe that MPs are not richly endowed with supporting staff. Members presently receive an allowance of some £40,000 per year for these purposes. This is perhaps sufficient to employ a competent secretary and a junior researcher: it is nowhere near adequate to enable an MP to establish and maintain an extensive information base.

The Commons has what might initially seem a substantial library. The library employs some 150 staff, many of whom devote all their time to researching MPs' queries. The Commons library is however a modest affair compared to the US Library of Congress, and its researchers are constantly and severely overworked. The library's shortcomings typify a more pervasive inadequacy of the Commons' personnel: the Commons employs fewer than 700

---

15 See generally Bennet P and Pullinger S (1991) *Making the Commons work* (London: Institute for Public Policy Research).
16 For a more expansive account of the issues touched upon here see Lock G (1988) 'Information for Parliament' in Ryle and Richards *op cit* Griffith J (1974) *Parliamentary Scrutiny of Government Bills* ch 8 (London: George Allen & Unwin).

staff to service its 650 MPs; the slightly smaller number of legislators in the US Congress have some 20,000 employees.[17]

It is difficult to accept that successive governments' unwillingness to afford MPs more substantial logistical support is motivated by financial considerations: facilities comparable to those provided in the USA would add only an infinitesimally small amount to overall public expenditure. Adequate resourcing would indeed impose a 'cost' upon a government (of whatever party), but the cost would be political rather than financial in nature. A comment from a recent edition of *The Economist* offers a cynical, if realistic, explanation of the current situation:

> 'the government of the day has little to gain by giving Parliaments [sic] their own source of knowledge and advice. Why spend money providing information for backbenchers, when ignorance keeps them so much more malleable?'[18]

Until the late 1970s, the management of office accommodation, services and support staff available to members of the Commons was controlled by senior employees of the house. This somewhat archaic system was reformed (and, unusually, reformed by statute) in 1978. The House of Commons Administration Act 1978 created the House of Commons Commission. The Commission comprises the Speaker, the Leader of the House, a government party MP, and three opposition party members. The Commission is now formally responsible for determining the amount spent on facilities and services. In practice, any substantial increase in expenditure would require the support of a majority of MPs, which is in turn unlikely to be forthcoming without government approval.[19] This suggests that the Commission's effective power is limited to juggling existing resources rather than insisting on new ones.

The Commons also has a Services Committee of 20 MPs which represents the views of backbench members to the Speaker in respect of the facilities available to them. By the mid-1990s, the repeated expressions of backbench dissatisfaction with Commons' working conditions had apparently borne a little fruit; the government had by then accepted that sufficient resources should be provided to ensure that every MP at least had her own office within the Palace of Westminster.

17 Adonis (1990) *op cit* p 62.
18 Cited in Lock *op cit* at p 52.
19 Griffith and Ryle *op cit* pp 160–162.

Nor are MPs' salaries particularly high.[20] They are currently some £34,000 per year, which obviously would not permit the member to finance the research and secretarial assistance she might consider appropriate.[1] This sum considerably exceeds the average earnings of the population as a whole, but compares poorly with the renumeration paid to senior members of the professions. However, being elected to the Commons is not in the legal sense a 'full-time job': many backbench MPs continue to derive income from other forms of employment, such as journalism, practice at the bar, or as solicitors, accountants or doctors, directors of companies, or 'consultants' for commercial organisations. Such practices have latterly caused appreciable controversy, in part on the grounds that dependence on non-Parliamentary income may present a further threat to an MP's 'independence'. We will examine this issue in chapter 8.

The involvement of many MPs in paid extra-parliamentary activities also has some bearing on the Commons' ostensibly bizarre working hours; activity on the floor of the house generally does not begin until 2.30 pm and frequently does not end until the early hours of the morning. Mornings are thus free for other activities. This is very convenient if an MP is maintaining a practice at the Bar or is serving as a director or consultant for commercial interests.[2] There are some MPs who regard membership of the Commons as a full-time occupation. When not in the chamber, they will be found attending to matters arising in their respective constituencies, or participating in the work of the Commons' various committees.[3]

Such backbenchers would now appear to be something of a minority however. This may be because some members now see election to the Commons as a means to other professional or financial ends, rather than as an end in itself. But it may also be,

20 MPs were not paid at all until the early twentieth century. Their present low level perhaps provides members with a financial incentive for seeking ministerial office.

1 This is supplemented by travel expenses, and for MPs who live outside London, an allowance to finance a London home. MPs who have substantial personal wealth, and who choose to spend some of it on assistance in carrying out their political duties, have a distinct advantage over their less affluent counterparts.

2 Modest timetable reforms were introduced in 1994. The reforms introduced a limited number of morning sittings in the chamber, abolished some Friday sittings and proposed an earlier end to business on Thursdays. It is too soon to conclude if this heralds a more far-reaching normalisation of MPs' working hours. See White M (1994) 'MPs vote to reform working hours' *The Guardian* 20 December.

3 Of which more is said below.

as sections two and three of this chapter suggest, because realistic backbench MPs doubt that their individual and collective presence in the house will often have a significant impact, either on the content of legislation or the behaviour of the government.

Financial support for the opposition

In addition to the salaries paid to the Leader of the Opposition, the opposition chief whip, and the shadow Leader of the House, some financial support is now provided to the opposition parties to assist them in carrying out their activities.[4] This is colloquially referred to as 'Short money', after Edward Short, the Leader of the House in the Labour government in power when the scheme was introduced in 1975. Parties with at least two MPs receive approximately £3,000 per year for each member, and some 3p for each vote won at the previous general election. For the main opposition party the sum is a useful addition to its resources (the Labour party received around one million pounds per year in the early 1990s), but is hardly sufficient to finance extensive political activities in a country as large as modern Britain. 'Short money' is paid to party leaders, to spend at their discretion, rather than shared equally among the party's MPs. One need not be overly cynical to wonder if the leadership might find good reasons for concentrating the bulk of that support on activities (and personnel) which were not likely to undermine its preferred policies. A Committee of Inquiry chaired by Lord Houghton was established by the Labour government in the mid-1970s to consider whether far more substantial financial assistance, on a statutory footing, should be made available to all the major political parties. The committee made recommendations to that effect.[5] As yet no government has promoted legislation putting those sentiments into practice.

What has been said so far might suggest that the balance of power between the government and the Commons is weighted heavily in the government's favour. That this should be so is hardly surprising given the fused nature of the government/Commons relationship: in that context, the notion of a meaningful separation between the house and the executive is a misleading dichotomy. Sections two and three consider whether the dichotomy currently has any merit at all.

4 Griffith and Ryle *op cit* pp 117–118. The scheme does not have an explicit statutory basis.
5 (1976) *Report of the Committee on financial aid to political parties* (Cmnd 6601 – London: HMSO).

II. THE PASSAGE OF LEGISLATION

Commentators now seem to agree that the modern House of Commons is only rarely a law *making* body in any meaningful sense. Norton suggests, for example:

> 'Although some writers continue to list "legislation" as one of the functions of the House of Commons, it is a function which for all intents and purposes has not been exercised by the house in the twentieth century.'[6]

Gavin Drewry expresses a similar scepticism:

> '[S]ome would question whether in reality the Westminster Parliament, dominated as it is by a powerful executive, able in most circumstances to mobilise majority support in the division lobbies, can properly be called a "legislature" at all.'[7]

John Griffith, author of a comprehensive study of the Commons in the 1967–1971 sessions, concluded that:

> '[T]he direct impact of the House on Government proposals for legislation was unimpressive. . . . On no occasion was the government either defeated or forced to make a tactical retreat . . . [T]he visible result of a great deal of Opposition and Government backbench activity was very small indeed.'[8]

The broad thrust of such critiques contends that the content of legislation is effectively determined in Cabinet. Governments formulate policies which they expect to command the support of their party's members in the Commons, and it is only rarely that their preferences will be rejected or significantly amended during a Bill's passage through the house. Thus one might sensibly suggest that in seeking to assess the significance of the Commons' legislative role, one should direct attention to considering its efficacy in influencing or pressurising the government to refine, modify or withdraw its proposals.

The various stages a Bill must undergo to complete its passage through the Commons seem now to possess a sacrosanct constitutional status. The process begins with the 'first reading': a purely formal step, in which the measure is introduced to the house. Consideration of the main principles underlying the Bill occurs during its 'second reading', a major set piece debate which takes place on the floor of the house. The second reading debate is

---

6 Norton (1985) *op cit* p 81.
7 Drewry (1988) 'Legislation' p 122 in Ryle and Richards *op cit.*
8 (1974) *op cit* p 206.

followed by a vote. If the Bill is approved,[9] its detailed provisions are then addressed in a 'standing committee', which is empowered to amend the original text. On leaving the standing committee, the Bill returns to the floor for its 'report stage', when any committee amendments (or new ones proposed by the government) are considered by the whole house. On completing its report stage, the Bill (as amended) enters its third reading. If approved by the house, it is then sent to the House of Lords.[10]

This complex process has no legal basis. Nor is it rooted in the house's own standing orders. It is a matter purely of custom and tradition within the house. The various stages are designed to fulfil different functions, and, as suggested below, the process' broad outlines have become encrusted with a bulky layer of detailed provisions.

There are no rigid rules concerning the time taken for a Bill to pass through the legislative process, although a government or private member's Bill must complete all its stages in a single parliamentary session. In emergency situations, especially if the government and opposition are agreed, a Bill may be passed in days or even hours. In such circumstances, the measure is unlikely to have been the subject of mature reflection. On the other hand, it is not uncommon for controversial Bills on major issues to spend six months or more in the Commons.[11]

But even Bills in the latter category are not debated or scrutinised until all members are satisfied that the house has been apprised of all relevant viewpoints. In the 1870s and 1880s, Irish MPs dissatisfied with government policy towards 'Home Rule' for Ireland engaged in a protracted campaign of 'filibustering' – continuing debate until the Commons ran out of time – with the result that Bills were simply talked out.[12] To prevent a minority of MPs sabotaging the government's legislative programme in this way, the house introduced (and subsequently refined and added to) several time management initiatives. The standing committee system, which dates from the 1870s and was firmly established as

---

9 At all stages of the legislative process, a bare majority of members voting in favour amounts to approval.

10 A Bill may originate in the Lords, in which case it would be sent for the Royal Assent after the Commons' third reading. For an informative and detailed study of the passage of a relatively recent and highly controversial measure see Rose H (1973) 'The Immigration Act 1971: a case study in the work of Parliament' *Parliamentary Affairs* 69–91.

11 For an illustration of the progress of such Bills in recent years see Adonis (1990) *op cit* ch 5; Silk *op cit* pp 138–139.

12 Adonis (1990) *op cit* p 70; deSmith (1985) *op cit* pp 282–283.

an integral part of the legislative process by 1910,[13] is one such device which has (as noted below) become entirely uncontroversial. Two other techniques, 'the guillotine' and 'the closure' have proved rather more problematic.

The guillotine

A government with majority support in the house may at any stage of a Bill's passage subject it to what is formally known as an 'allocation of time order', colloquially referred to as the 'guillotine'.[14] The guillotine specifies in advance precisely how long shall be allocated to discussion of a Bill's provisions. Once that time expires, debate ends, irrespective of how much of a Bill remains undiscussed. The guillotine is generally used to regulate proceedings in committee. Standing orders currently require that guillotine motions be debated on the floor.

Allocation of time orders raise sensitive issues. They may from one perspective be viewed as elevating governmental expediency above the principle that proposed legislation should receive rigorous and exhaustive Commons discussion. Alternatively, they can be seen as an entirely legitimate means for the government to overcome perverse obstructionism by minority parties. Before 1980 governments were most reluctant to deploy the guillotine, evidently for fear of the adverse publicity such a move might generate.[15] In recent years, however, successive Conservative governments have had fewer qualms about the constitutional propriety of doing so.[16] Feelings in the house over this issue were sufficiently inflamed in 1994 for the Labour party to withdraw from the usual channels and commit itself to being as obstructive as possible to the conduct of government business.[17]

The 'closure'

A less draconian, but more frequently invoked (especially at the report stage) time-management device is the closure. Standing orders provide that any member may propose, at any time, that 'the question now be put'. If a majority of MPs present (of whom there must be at least 100 in total) support the motion, debate on the question is ended, and the house moves to its next item

---

13 Norton (1985) *op cit* pp 89–90: Adonis *op cit* p 102.
14 See *Erskine May* pp 409–416: Griffith and Ryle *op cit* pp 225–228.
15 For the 1974–1988 period see the helpful table in Griffith and Ryle *op cit* p 303.
16 Adonis (1990) *op cit* p 70.
17 See White M (1994) 'Low acts of attrition' *The Guardian* 17 February.

of business. The Speaker has a discretion to reject the proposal if she considers it to be 'an abuse of the rules of the House, or an infringement of the rights of the minority'. There are no legal rules controlling the exercise of this discretion. Griffith and Ryle suggest that the Speaker would take into account such matters as how many (and which) members have already spoken on the issue and its substantive importance; it seems unlikely that a closure would be permitted on a significant question before two or three hours of debate had been conducted.[18]

The second reading

Second reading debates on government Bills are opened and closed by speeches from the Bill's sponsoring ministers, each of whom is followed by her opposition counterpart. During the central period of the debate, the Speaker controls the order in which MPs are called to speak, although tradition demands that she alternately chooses members of the government and opposition parties. In major debates, demand to speak is intense. This demand has been met to some extent since 1988, when a standing order was introduced which permitted the Speaker to limit individual speeches to a maximum of ten minutes.[19] This goes some way towards ensuring that the house is exposed to a wide range of views on the merits of the government's proposed policy.

It is however unlikely that a contribution by an individual MP, or even a series of like-minded speeches, will persuade members to vote other than on party lines. To some degree, labelling the second reading stage as a 'debate' is misleading. Proceedings are rarely characterised by the cut and thrust of attack and immediate defence. Many members merely recite prepared speeches which outline a particular element of party policy. This is not to say second reading debates are worthless – but rather that they have little immediate impact on the contents of a Bill. Their value lies in other areas.[20]

There is little doubt that the rapidity of a member's entry to (and subsequent rise up) the ranks of ministerial or shadow ministerial office is significantly affected by her oral performance

---

18 *Op cit* pp 222–227. See also Griffith (1974) *op cit* pp 20–24: *Erskine May* pp 405–408.
19 Silk *op cit* p 92.
20 Ministerial speeches have latterly assumed a significant legal status; see the discussion of *Pepper v Hart* at pp 314–320 below.

on the floor of the house. Impressive performances, especially when debating controversial Bills, will mark out a backbencher as a ministerial prospect. Conversely, ministers who cannot command the respect of the house during debate will find their governmental careers either grinding to a halt or slipping into gradual decline.[1]

Second readings are also valuable simply because of their visibility to the wider public. Debates on major Bills are widely reported in the press, and excerpts broadcast on radio and television. Such coverage does not, admittedly, alert voters to the details and nuances of government and opposition arguments, but the aggregated effect of the constant glare of publicity would seem to be an important (if unquantifiable) incentive for both government and opposition to ensure that their policies do not markedly diverge from the wishes of the people.[2]

Standing Committees

It is readily apparent that the Commons' ability to pass a significant number of Bills would be much reduced if their details, as well as their principles, had to be debated on the floor of the house. Thus, while measures of major constitutional significance[3] may undergo their committee stage on the floor of the house, most Bills are sent 'upstairs' to be examined by a standing committee of between 16 and 50 MPs. As many as eight standing committees may be sitting at one time.

The membership of standing committees reflects the party balance in the whole house. Thus a government with a comfortable majority is assured of a proportionate advantage at the committee stage. Standing committees on government Bills always include the sponsoring minister and her shadow. Other members are formally chosen by the house's own Committee of Selection, which is required to take into account a member's fields of expertise when making its choice. It is however clear that selection is in practice controlled by the party whips, and it is most·unlikely that the whips would support inclusion of an MP whose expertise might lead her to reject party policy.

That said, ministers do face far more rigorous questioning in

---

1 See Griffith (1974) *op cit* pp 232–234.
2 As we shall see in chapter 7, there may in practice be rather less to this point than initially meets the eye.
3 This is not a legally defined categorisation.

committee than on the floor. This is due in part to the nature of the committee's task: effective scrutiny of detail demands expertise and intellectual precision, rather than the rhetorical skills that may suffice on the floor of the house. In addition, committee proceedings generally attract much less media attention than second reading debates. Insofar as MPs are playing to an audience when in committee, it is to an audience solely of their colleagues, who are most likely to be impressed by an incisive and knowledgeable dissection of the Bill's provisions.

At the committee stage (unless a guillotine has been imposed), the allocation of time to particular clauses of the Bill is determined by the Chairman. The Chairman also decides which amendments to the Bill may be moved. It is generally accepted that amendments may not contradict the main principles of the Bill as approved at second reading, but should instead be directed at questions of detail.[4] In practice, it appears that the great majority of committee amendments are introduced at the behest of the government itself, either to tidy up the Bill, to correct unnoticed errors, or to respond to what the government regards as acceptable concerns expressed by MPs or other interest groups.[5]

There must however be considerable doubt as to the efficacy even of the standing committee's more searching and informed deliberations when it is dealing with a government dogmatically attached to the details as well as the broad principles of its legislative programme. This point is forcefully made by Adonis' discussion of the passage of the Thatcher government's Bills to privatise the water and electricity services.[6] The electricity Bill consumed over 100 hours of committee time. It was in fact amended 114 times. But 113 of these amendments were moved by the government itself. The other amendment was one (of 22) moved by a Conservative backbencher. None of the 227 amendments proposed by the opposition was carried.

Report and third reading

Since the mid-1960s, the report stage of government Bills has consumed some 10% of time spent on the floor of the house.[7]

---

4 Although as we shall see in later chapters, so-called 'wrecking amendments' are occasionally introduced at other stages of the legislative process.
5 See especially Griffith (1974) *op cit* ch 3: Norton P (1985) *op cit* ch 5.
6 (1990) *op cit* pp 103–104.
7 Griffith and Ryle *op cit* p 237: Silk *op cit* p 135.

This gives some indication of its potential importance within the legislative process. The report stage enables the house to consider a Bill in its entirety as amended in committee. It also offers the opportunity for further amendments to be moved. Controversial Bills may require several full days of the house's time. Procedure is regulated by complex rules concerning the type of amendments admissible and which amendments are debated. The choice of which members may participate in debate is again controlled by the Speaker.

For most Bills which successfully complete the report stage, the third reading is a mere formality. A further debate may be held if six members request one. It is entirely possible for a government Bill to be rejected at the conclusion of the third reading debate, but it is difficult to conceive of circumstances (other than those where a government has only a minority of MPs in the house) when this might occur.

Conclusion

It has become something of a cliché to suggest that the Common's role in respect of government Bills is now one of 'legitimation rather than legislation'. The inference seems to be that because the Commons is an elected body, the wishes of the majority of its members necessarily ensure that its decisions have a 'democratic' basis. As chapter 7 will suggest, that assumption is itself rather problematic: as was noted in chapter 1, legitimacy and democracy may demand rather more than simple majoritarianism.

Yet, seemingly paradoxically, there now also appears to be an academic consensus that backbench MPs have become more assertive in the past thirty years in resisting government policies of which they disapprove.[8] An MP's capacity to do this effectively depends in part on the size of the government's majority, and in part on the number of like-minded colleagues who will rally to her cause. The first Wilson government (1964–1966), which had a majority of only three, found its plans to bring the steel industry into public ownership were blocked by the refusal of two Labour MPs to vote with the government.[9] One may also point to several

---

8 For statistical information see Griffith and Ryle *op cit* pp 118–130. More generally see Johnson N (1988) 'Departmental select committees', in Ryle and Richards *op cit*; Norton P (1980) *Dissension in the House of Commons 1974–1979* (London: Macmillan).

9 See Pimlott B (1992) *Harold Wilson* pp 357–359 (London: Harper Collins).

instances in the mid-1980s when the Thatcher government, which had substantial Commons majorities, misread the mood of its backbenchers and found itself obliged to abandon Bills. The most spectacular example was provided by the Shops Bill 1986, a measure designed to liberalise Sunday trading laws. The government had correctly anticipated that Labour MPs would oppose the measure because of its potentially adverse impact on shopworkers. What the government had not expected was that many backbench Conservatives would support a campaign orchestrated by religious groups to 'Keep Sunday Special'. Squeezed from both sides by this unlikely alliance, the Bill was defeated on second reading.[10]

We will examine several more examples of such behaviour over significant policy issues (by both Labour and Conservative MPs) in subsequent chapters. Such episodes may defensibly be regarded however as exceptions to a more general rule; namely that the passage of government Bills through the Commons is dependent not so much on the intrinsic merit of the ideas which they contain, nor on the skill which ministers display in defending them on the floor or in committee, but on the size and cohesiveness of the governing party's majority. But government measures are not the only Bills which the Commons considers. In respect of 'private members' Bills', rather different considerations seem to apply.

Private members' Bills

A small number of Bills is introduced every session by backbench members. Twelve Friday sittings per session are currently allocated for dealing with such measures. There is in theory no limit to the number of Bills that an MP can introduce. Many Bills are presented to the house simply because the sponsoring MP may wish to draw attention to herself or to a particular issue. But if the Bill is to have any realistic prospect of becoming an Act, it must be initiated through one of two mechanisms.

The most significant is the annual ballot under SO 13. Any backbencher may enter the ballot, and the great majority generally do so. Twenty 'winners' are drawn. The first six are allocated top place in the order of business on a given Friday for a second reading. These six then assume priority on subsequent Fridays for

10 Three other Bills were withdrawn during that Parliament, for less dramatic reasons and in less dramatic circumstances. None of the four could seriously be regarded as of great importance. See Drewry (1988) *op cit* pp 134–136.

their report and third reading over the second readings of the other fourteen Bills. If a Bill is to pass, it is vital that it completes its second reading on the first day. Thus if a Bill is opposed, its sponsor must be able to force a closure to ensure it is not talked out. This may not be easy – it is often difficult to ensure that the 100 sympathetic members needed are present in the house late on Friday afternoon, when many will wish to return to their constituencies.

The popularity of the ballot procedure is due in part to the high profile that a full second reading debate can give to an issue and its sponsor. But the attractiveness is not solely a matter of publicity. Almost 200 Bills introduced through this method were enacted between 1974 and 1989.[11] It thus offers some MPs a good opportunity to make a legislative mark.

The private member's Bill has on occasion introduced quite important legislative reforms in areas which generate considerable moral controversy, but in respect of which opinion does not divide along traditional party lines. The most obvious (and oft-quoted) example of such legislation is the Abortion Act 1967 (which was sponsored by David Steel MP).[12] The process is also frequently deployed to rationalise archaic legislation, or to introduce a regulatory framework around newly emergent social or legal problems.[13]

There is little immediate point in backbenchers launching initiatives to which the government is opposed. The carrot and stick modes of intra-party discipline wielded by the Prime Minister and the whips do not suddenly disappear just because a Bill emanates from a backbencher. The government is under no obligation to allow free votes on such Bills, although there is perhaps some moral pressure for it do so. However, allowing a free vote may sometimes suit a government's purposes very well. An obvious benefit of so doing is to foster the impression that the government respects the independence of MPs as individuals, and of the Commons as a collectivity. On issues about which the government has no strong policy preferences, such action is a substantively painless way of rebutting suggestions that the executive wields an unhealthy degree of control over all aspects of the legislative process. Equally,

11 Silk op cit p 117.
12 For an illuminating discussion of both the background to and passage of the bill see Richards P (1970) *Parliament and Conscience* ch 5 (London: Allen and Unwin).
13 Especially, of late, in the area of intellectual property and information technology. For a list of examples see Silk op cit pp 117–118: Griffith and Ryle op cit pp 386–390.

a government may conclude that facilitating the passage of a private member's Bill in respect of a policy which it supports, but which might be unpopular among some of its MPs or a significant portion of the electorate, is a useful way of achieving preferred outcomes without having to take responsibility for having done so.

The backbencher's need for government support also has a more mundane dimension. Pressures on the Commons' legislative timetable make it most unlikely that Bills other than the first three or four in the ballot could be passed if the government does not allocate some of its own time for their passage. For a government with time to spare, making a little available to backbench initiatives is a painless way to curry favour with the house. The Labour governments of 1964–1970 offered time to over 20 backbench bills.[14] In contrast, during the 1980s, successive Conservative governments did not appear very concerned to facilitate such expression of backbench opinion: the Thatcher administrations were far more reluctant than their predecessors to devote government time to private members' Bills.[15]

Conversely, the private member's Bill can also offer governments with over-full legislative programmes a means to grab an even-greater share of the Commons' time. A backbencher promoting a Bill with which the government is broadly in sympathy, but which does not rate highly on its list of legislative priorities, may find herself invited to modify her measure in accordance with ministerial preferences in return for assistance in finding the necessary Commons time to push it through.[16]

In contrast, there have been instances of governments covertly deploying backbench MPs to block a private member's bill. An egregious example occurred in 1994. The government had not initially indicated that it opposed the Civil Rights (Disabled Persons) Bill, which was intended to prohibit discrimination in terms of employment and access to public facilities against disabled people. It was however widely thought that the government considered the Bill too expansive. Suspicions as to the government's true preferences were roused when several Conservative backbenchers suddenly tabled 70 amendments. The amendments generated sufficient debate to ensure the Bill was talked out at

14 Norton (1985) *op cit* p 102.
15 Griffith and Ryle *op cit* p 398.
16 For example the Chronically Sick and Disabled Persons Act 1970 and Sexual Offences (Amendment) Act 1976; see Griffith and Ryle *op cit* pp 392–393 and Silk *op cit* pp 116–117. See also my discussion of the passage of the 1977 Housing (Homeless Persons) Act; (1995) *Housing Homeless Persons: Administrative Law and Practice* ch 3 (Oxford: OUP).

second reading. The most prominent of the obstructive MPs was Olga Maitland. Maitland informed the house that the amendments were of her own devising. It later transpired they had been provided by the government, which wanted the Bill to fail but feared the public criticism that would result if it achieve its objectives by ordering Conservative MPs to vote against the second reading.

Such furtive tactics on the government's part clearly betoken a disrespect both for the Commons and for the general public. The behaviour of the compliant backbenchers is perhaps even more reprehensible. As we shall see in chapter 8, the house seemingly retains quite draconian powers to punish MPs who it believes have abused it in some way. Maitland perhaps escaped rather lightly – she was compelled to apologise to the house for her deceit. The minister who orchestrated the affair, Nicholas Scott, was subsequently sacked, but it is not clear if the sacking was because he had misled the house, or because he had been found out!

In addition to the ballot, backbenchers may try to initiate legislation though the 'ten-minute rule Bill' process provided by SO 19. One such Bill may be introduced each Tuesday and Wednesday. Its sponsoring member is permitted time to make a brief (hence 'ten-minute' rule) statement to the house outlining its objectives; an equal time is given to a member wishing to oppose the measure.

The procedure is very popular with MPs, primarily because it offers them a public platform when the house is often packed. But it would be misleading to characterise ten-minute rule Bills as a serious component of the legislative process. While most are formally allowed to proceed by the house, there is minimal chance that they will be enacted as there is so little time available for them. It is not unusual for periods of several years to pass without a single ten-minute rule Bill reaching the statute book. Their function might more sensibly be seen as affording an MP a high profile public forum in which to raise an issue of current concern, perhaps in the hope that either a government department or another MP who tops the private member's ballot will be persuaded to introduce a like measure at some future date. There are, as always, exceptions to the general rule. The Sexual Offences Act 1967, which repealed legislation criminalising homosexual acts between consenting adults, emerged from the ten-minute rule. It is however clear that its passage was largely dependent on the government's willingness to find sufficent time for it to be enacted.[17]

17 Richards (1970) *op cit* ch 4.

It would be quite incorrect to assume that private member's Bills are an unimportant part of the Commons' workload. Quantitatively, they are clearly insignificant when compared to government Bills. Equally, many of them address somewhat trivial issues. Nevertheless they do occasionally effect major changes on matters of considerable substance. What they manifestly do not do is provide a vehicle through which the 'independence' of the Commons is promoted over and above party loyalties on any substantial and systematic scale.

Private Bills

'Private' Bills are an entirely different form of legislative creature from private member's Bills, which (notwithstanding their ostensibly confusing nomenclature) are technically regarded, like government Bills, as 'public' measures. Private Bills are intended to confer certain benefits or obligations on a narrowly-defined class of persons or companies, or to authorise specific works or activities in a particular area.[18]

The Bills are introduced to the Commons not by a government department or an MP, but by the interested parties themselves. The parties are represented in the house by lawyers styled as 'parliamentary agents'. As chapter 2 suggested when discussing the *Wauchope* litigation, the house's standing orders impose rigorous requirements which oblige the promoters to notify any affected third parties of the Bill's intentions.

Private Bill procedures are quite cumbersome. By signalling her opposition to the Bill at first reading, a single MP may force a full debate on its merits at every stage of its enactment. This degree of obstruction could well be fatal to a Bill that does not have enthusiastic government support. Furthermore, after its second reading, a private Bill is sent to a special committee of four members which examines it in great detail. It is at this stage that the significance of the need to notify affected parties becomes apparent. The committee sits in a neo-judicial capacity, insofar as it may summon and cross-examine the Bill's promoters and those who object to it, before deciding whether or not to recommend that the Bill be allowed to proceed. Clearly, if affected persons have not been notified of the Bill's passage, they will be unable

18 As noted in chapter 2, the device was often used in respect of the construction and management of railways.

to present their point of view to the Committee, which will thus be proceeding on the basis of incomplete information.

The very different process used to enact private statutes, and the generally sectional interests which they serve, perhaps lend some force to Lord Denning's suggestion in *Pickin*[19] that the courts should reconsider their traditional refusal to assess the procedural propriety of the legislative process. The mechanism was subject to an intensive investigation by a joint Lords/Commons select committee in the late 1980s, but as yet no significant reforms have been introduced.

Private Bills comprised a quantitatively far more significant proportion of the Commons workload 150 years ago than they do now. In the past, they were frequently promoted by local authorities to enable them to carry out specific tasks, or by private companies involved in the construction of various kinds of transport infrastructure. In the modern era, such activities have tended to be subsumed within the government's own legislative programme, and are thus dealt with through public Bills.

Hybrid Bills[20]

A hybrid Bill, as its name suggests, is a government measure which affects a particular individual or organisation in a different manner to other individuals or companies in the same class; it thus bears some resemblance to a private Bill. There are no definitive rules for determining if a Bill is hybrid in substance; the decision is entrusted, via the Speaker, to a House of Commons official designated as the 'Examiners of petitions for Private Bills'.[21] It is thus quite possible that a government may unexpectedly find itself promoting a private measure, with potentially severe consequences for its legislative timetable.

Hybrid bills broadly follow the public Bill procedure. However they must go through a further stage before a select committee in both the Commons and the Lords before undergoing their standing committee stage. These select committees[1] are empowered to hear petitions from opponents of the Bill, and thus can slow down or obstruct the passage of legislation.[2] Neverthless, a

---

19 See pp 41–42 above.
20 See generally *Erskine May* pp 519–524.
21 On the origins of the post see *Erskine May* pp 811–812.
  1 Again the terminology is unfortunately confusing, since, as we shall see below most of the Commons' 'select committees' do not have any legislative role.
  2 See Griffith and Ryle *op cit* pp 227; Silk *op cit* pp 158–160.

government wishing to dispense with this additional procedure may do so if it can muster a Commons majority on a motion to that effect.

Delegated legislation

It would, in 1996, be quite inaccurate to suggest that the bulk of the laws under which the British people live have been subject to searching Commons scrutiny. This state of affairs is due only in part to the logistical and party political constraints operating on the house's analysis of Bills. Its major cause is the government's increasing tendency to promote Bills which delegate secondary law-making power to ministers through the mechanism of 'regulations' or 'statutory instruments' (SIs).[3] Under this form of law-making, the 'parent' Act merely sketches the broad confines of the power conferred upon the government, leaving the minister to fill in the details in SIs produced in her department. The mechanism represents something of a half-way house in procedural terms between purely legislative and purely executive law-making.

SIs spare ministers the time-consuming and potentially problematic task of putting their policy preferences into a Bill and trying to pilot it through the Commons. SIs have been favoured by governments of both parties in the modern era, largely because the growing scope of government intervention in social and economic life means that the house would not have the time to deal with all matters through primary legislation. In recent years, the government's resort to SIs has continued apace: since 1980 over 1,000 per year have been passed on average. It is not possible to form any general conclusion on the significance of such measures. Some are exceedingly trivial – a favourite example being the Baking and Sausage Making (Christmas and New Year) Regulations 1985.[4] Others have profound constitutional implications; the law under which Mr Liversidge was imprisoned was an SI, and as chapter 11 suggests, delegated legislation can afford ministers sweeping powers in very important areas of governmental activity.

A political party's protests (when in opposition) against SIs should consequently be regarded sceptically – it seems likely that any 'principles' which underlie them would be quietly forgotten

---

3 This somewhat over-simplifies the terminology; see Griffith and Ryle *op cit* p 245: Erskine May pp 539–541.
4 See Silk *op cit* pp 148–149.

when that party next formed a government. For constitutional lawyers, however, the issues of principle have more force, since they bear directly on the questions of the sovereignty of 'Parliament' and the separation of powers, and thereby also bear indirectly on the question of what type of 'democracy' the constitution currently upholds. To explore these issues one must ask how closely do MPs oversee the creation of statutory instruments? Are they in effect a sub-stratum of the legislative process, or would it be more realistic to regard them as to all intents and purposes 'law-making by the executive'?

Contemporary principles and practice

The use of delegated legislation assumed considerable prominence in the late 1920s, following the publication of a book called *The New Despotism* by Lord Chief Justice Hewart.[5] Hewart, in a somewhat Diceyan vein, deplored Parliament's practice of affording ministers what he regarded as arbitrary and uncontrolled bureaucratic powers. The critique was hyperbolic, but is helpful in focusing attention on the distinction between substantive and procedural conceptions of the rule of law. A parent Act does not (and indeed cannot) bestow an unfettered power upon a minister: she does not thereby become in any sense a 'sovereign legislature'. Rather her powers are confined by the terms of the 'parent' legislation. Consequently, the terms of statutory instruments are subject to judicial review to ensure that they do not exceed the competence Parliament has granted.[6] But neither does the process require that the Commons consider every detail of each SI enacted.

Hewart might plausibly be seen as concerned entirely with matters of process; it is not what government does that is the problem, but how government does it. Its intervention would be acceptable if only it had exposed its plans to the rigorous scrutiny attaching to the passage of primary legislation. An obvious response to such an argument would be to highlight the Commons' limited role even in respect of most statutes.

That dichotomy is somewhat misleading. It is readily apparent that issues of process and substance are necessarily linked. It is simply not possible to govern a highly interventionist unitary state

5 See Harlow and Rawlings *op cit* pp 119–130.
6 See *Chester v Bateson* [1920] 1 KB 829.

solely through primary legislation.[7] To reject altogether the process of delegated legislation is to reject the substance of social
democratic government.[8] Hewart's attack prompted the government to establish the Donoughmore Committee,[9] which
responded to Hewart much as Harry Jones later critiqued Hayek's
minimalist notion of the rule of law.[10] Delegated legislation was a
necessity in modern society. The issue therefore became one of
how best to ensure that this unavoidable fact of political life
departed as little as possible from orthodox constitutional understandings of the legislative/executive relationship.

To a considerable extent, MPs' capacity to involve themselves
in the production of delegated legislation lay in their own hands.
As such, it was prey to all the party political and logistical pressures
affecting the passage of primary legislation. Donoughmore recommended that a Standing Committee on delegated legislation be
created in both the Lords and the Commons. Such committees
would examine the technicalities and vires of proposed SIs. Their
purpose would not be to question the merits of government policy
per se, but to 'supply the private member with knowledge which
he lacks at present and thus enable him to exercise an informed
discretion whether to object or criticise himself'.[11]

Neither Parliament as a whole, not the Commons itself made
an immediate, far-reaching response to the Donoughmore report.
A Commons Committee on Statutory Instruments was established
in 1944, and the procedures through which SIs were to pass were
to some extent rationalised by the Statutory Instruments Act 1946.
The Act sketches out what may be termed 'presumptions' as to
the processes to be followed, since subsequent parent Acts may
opt out of the 1946 Act if the enacting Parliament so wishes, and
(somewhat ironically) ss 8–9 allow the legislation's scope to be
limited, modified, or expanded by subsequent delegated legislation. A further step supposedly intended to enhance MPs' awareness of and control over the contents of SIs was made in 1972,
when a Joint Commons/Lords Committee on Statutory Instruments (the 'scrutiny committee') was established.

7 The problem of 'legislative overload' is less acute in a federal state; its scale
  varying in inverse proportion to the scope of the powers afforded to the central
  legislature.
8 Which is not to say, as we shall see below, that a government opposed to existing
  social democratic legislation cannot invoke SIs to remove it.
9 Donoughmore, Lord (1932) *Report of the Committee on Ministers' Powers* (Cmnd
  4060) (London: HMSO).
10 See pp 76–77 above.
11 At pp 63–64; quoted in Himsworth C (1995) 'The delegated powers scrutiny
   committee' *Public Law* 34–44 at p 37.

A small percentage of SIs are not subject to any consideration by the house at all. The great majority are however dealt with by either the 'affirmative' or 'negative' resolution procedure specified in the 1946 Act.[12] The affirmative procedure prevents the passage of an SI into law unless it is approved by a majority vote on the floor of the house. The initiative thus rests with the government (within 40 days) both to defend the measure in debate, and to ensure its supporters are present in sufficient numbers to vote it through. Debates on affirmative resolutions on the floor of the house are infrequent in number and short (generally up to 90 minutes) in duration. Most examination is undertaken 'upstairs' in the Standing Committee on Statutory Instruments. Governments seemingly prefer the latter option, although the support of 20 members is sufficient to compel the minister to schedule debate for the floor of the house. Committee debates rarely exceed 90 minutes per SI. The committee's role is merely that of consideration. It cannot amend the SI in any way: nor does it exercise delegated power to pass the measure; the subsequent vote is still taken by the whole house. In practice, it is accepted that the more important SIs should be subject to the affirmative procedure, although this is not a legally enforceable provision, and there is obvious scope for disagreement between government and opposition on how to gauge an SI's importance. During the 1980s, some 20% of SIs were subject to affirmative resolutions.[13]

The 'negative resolution' procedure passes the initiative to the opposition parties, who may table 'a prayer' inviting the house to vote against the instrument's passage into law, again within a 40 day period. Debate on a prayer may be taken either on the floor of the house (generally late at night) or in standing committee. Once again, access to both fora is controlled by the government. Little time is allocated for prayers before the whole house: Silk notes for example that the 9,500 SIs subject to the negative resolution procedure between 1974 and 1985 attracted in total barely 200 hours of debate.[14] One might therefore be forgiven for thinking that the process serves no useful purpose other than to enable a determined opposition to make life uncomfortable for a government with a small majority by disrupting its parliamentary timetable.[15] Drewry is perhaps not being overly cynical in observing that' 'Few prayers are debated, and the government has

12 *Erskine May* pp 545–548.   13 Silk *op cit* p 151.
14 *Op cit* p 152. See also Griffith and Ryle *op cit* pp 345–350.
15 See Punnet R (1968) *British Government and Politics* p 333 (London: Heinnemann).

no difficulty fending off the feeble threat posed by those that are.'[16]

The Joint Committee on Statutory Instruments (the 'scrutiny committee') plays, at least in quantitative terms, a more significant role. It is generally chaired by an opposition MP, which lends it at least an aura of independence. Its members are supposed to eschew party political issues, and to refrain from questioning the merits of a given SI's policy, and to focus instead on the narrower (and essentially legal) question of the SI's compatibility with its parent Act. In the event of any apparent inconsistency, the committee will draw the SI to the house's attention, which may then proceed as it wishes. The committee performs in effect a pre-emptive judicial role, albeit not one with binding legal effect, since neither the government nor the house is obliged to accept its opinions. Nor would a court subsequently be precluded from holding an SI ultra vires the parent Act simply because the committee had concluded its contents lay within the minister's powers.

The vast quantity of SIs approved by the house each year, and the obvious limitations which attach to MPs' scrutiny of such measures, are forceful illustrations of the extent to which the government effectively controls the legislative process. They are not however the most draconian example of the constitution's seeming capacity to reconcile the de jure sovereignty of 'Parliament' with the de facto supremacy of the executive.

'Henry VIII clauses'

The Donoughmore Committee had expressed grave reservations about the growing (but still quantitatively insignificant) parliamentary practice of enacting 'Henry VIII' clauses in primary legislation. Such provisions empower a government minister to use SIs to amend or even repeal existing Acts of Parliament.[17] The label stems from the Statute of Proclamations 1539. Henry VIII, presumably having doubts about the constitutional status of his prerogative powers vis-à-vis legislation and other common law rules, prevailed upon an unwilling Commons and Lords to pass a Bill confirming that the Monarch's proclamations were equal in force to Acts. Once enacted, this legislation would, by virtue of the lex posterior rule, enable the King to repeal or alter existing statutes

---

16 Drewry (1988) *op cit* p 139.
17 See Turpin C (2nd edn, 1990) *British Government and the Constitution* p 382 (London: Weidenfeld and Nicolson).

without further recourse to Parliament; to – as Plucknett put it – 'play the despot by the co-operation of Parliament'.[18]

Applying the Henry VIII nomenclature to contemporary manifestations of this practice has the unfortunate tendency of belittling their constitutional significance. As noted in chapter 4, the relative superiority of statute to the prerogative was not established in the sixteenth century; the King might plausibly have achieved the same result through direct exercise of his proclamatory power. Furthermore, the Statute of Proclamations itself was hedged about with restrictions which substantially compromised its utility.[19] And, most importantly, neither Henry VIII, nor Tudor Parliaments, had any need to justify their behaviour in terms of 'democratic' principle.

There is of course no legal impediment to Parliament granting what is formally a 'circumscribed portion of legislative competence to a subordinate minister'[20]. The power may at any time be withdrawn, and subsequent Parliaments may if they wish undo whatever 'legislative' work the designated minister has done. Rather different issues arise if one asks if the practice is politically legitimate in modern society.

Until very recently, the dubious moral basis of Henry VIII clauses seems to have led Parliament to enact them on a sparing basis. The authors of the 1985 edition of *deSmith's Constitutional and Administrative Law* felt able to conclude that:

> 'This formulation is not widely used, and it is normally innocuous if the grant of power is confined to a limited period for the purpose of enabling draftsmen to make consequential adaptations to miscellaneous enactments that may have been overlooked when the principal Act was passed.'[1]

This view of Henry VIII clauses sees them essentially as time-saving devices through which to remedy unintended omissions or errors in the primary legislation. As such they would be only mildly objectionable, insofar as they spare the government the consequences of its own incompetence. In the past few years, however, the government has seemingly adopted the view that Henry VIII clauses are a perfectly acceptable means to implement sweeping policy programmes. This disturbing trend appeared to scale new

18 Plucknett (1960) *op cit* p 233.
19 *Ibid*, pp 233–234. For detailed analysis see Elton G (1960) 'Henry VIII's Act of Proclamations' *English Historical Review* 208–222: Bush M (1983) 'The Act of Proclamations: a reinterpretation' *American Journal of Legal History* 33–53.
20 Turpin (1990) *op cit* p 369.
1 *Op cit* p 352.

heights of executive law-making in the Deregulation and Contracting Out Act 1994 introduced by the Major government.[2] The Act empowers the Secretary of State for Trade and Industry to make regulations to suspend any existing legislation which he/she considers imposes a burden on any economic activity, and also to transfer many government functions allocated by statute to a minister to any private sector organisation.

Substantively, the 1994 Act adheres to an extreme form of Hayekian minimalism. In a procedural sense, it suggests that the Major government regarded the legislative process as an unwelcome obstacle which it is quite entitled to circumvent whenever convenient. The Act effectively makes the Secretary of State an alternative legislature on matters of economic regulation; as such it marks a significant departure from orthodox understandings of the relationship between the government and the Commons within the legislative process. Whether that departure is construed as a welcome development depends presumably on the observer's party affiliation; and that is in itself perhaps a telling indictment of the extent to which the Commons is prone, even on the most significant issues, to operate simply and solely as a vehicle for promoting the wishes of whichever faction currently forms a majority of its members.

Conclusion

From a legislative perspective therefore, a House of Commons 'independent' of the executive is likely to occur only when the government cannot command a reliable majority. Yet it would seem likely that such circumstances will promote paralysis rather than consensus in the house. The implications that the Commons' essentially factional, antagonistic approach to the legislative process has for the democratic basis of the constitution cannot fully be appreciated until we explore the relationship between the Commons and the Lords, and between the Commons and the people. We return to these questions in chapters 6 and 7. In the remainder of this chapter, we address another dimension of the relationship between the Commons and the government, which (as a convenient shorthand) we might term 'scrutiny of the executive'.

---

2 See Freedland M (1995) 'Privatising *Carltona*: Part II of the Deregulation and Contracting Out Act 1994' *Public Law* 21–27.

III. CONTROLLING THE EXECUTIVE

Although a government's legislative programme is understandably often viewed as its primary raison d'être, much government activity does not require any legislative initiative. As noted in chapter 4, ministers retain substantial legal powers under the royal prerogative, through which (within the boundaries set by judicial review) important policy decisions may be taken. Similarly, ministers may also deploy existing statutory powers, which, if cast in sufficiently loose terms, may permit the government lawfully to pursue quite different objectives from those favoured by its predecessors. In neither case is the government legally dependent on maintaining majority support in the Commons in order to exercise its authority.[3] It is nevertheless clear that the house may play an important constitutional role by monitoring the government's implementation of its preferred policies. This section examines several mechanisms, of varying degrees of formality, via which this task is carried out.

Motions on the floor of the house[4]

Approximately 20 days per session are devoted to general debates on topics chosen by the opposition parties. These occasions are directed towards a critical attack on particular aspects of government policy. Governments with a reliable majority have no difficulty in defeating such motions, but the outcome of the vote is of little significance. The main purpose of 'Opposition days' is to provide a very visible forum in which to display the essentially adversarial character of the British political system. Leading speeches are made by the ministers within whose remit the chosen topic falls and by senior opposition frontbenchers. Backbenchers are dependent on 'catching the Speaker's eye' if they wish to contribute.

Once again, one might doubt if 'debate' is the correct label to apply to such proceedings. Observers are more frequently presented with the recitation of a collection of opposing views rather than an intimately interactive argument. Nevertheless, the process serves certain tangential purposes. A series of impressive (or poor)

3 As chapter 9 suggests, there are occasions when it is so dependent in practical terms.
4 See generally Norton (1985) *op cit* ch 6: Irwin H (1988) 'Opportunities for backbenchers', in Ryle and Richards *op cit.*

speeches can further (or undermine) an MP's prospects of government or shadow front bench office. Additionally, the high profile such debates attract offers the wider public some opportunity to form opinions about the merits of government and opposition policies.

The house has also latterly devoted some 6% of its time to motions on topics chosen by the government. The format of these proceedings is the same as for opposition motions, although the government will select only those topics in respect of which if feels that so public a discussion is likely to enhance rather than undermine its reputation.

Motions on subjects chosen by backbenchers have recently occupied around 10 days per session, all on Fridays. The slots are allocated by ballot. Three motions may be scheduled for each day, although it is in practice rare for more than one debate to be intitiated.[5] The subject of such motions tends to vary according to the party of the mover.[6] Government whips generally prefer their backbenchers to move uncontroversial motions which will not provoke a division, since this frees other government MPs to return to their constituencies or attend to other interests. This concern has rather less force for opposition MPs, for whom debate on a contentious issue offers the opportunity either to threaten the government with an embarrassing defeat, or at least to force recalcitrant government backbenchers to wait around the house until a division is called.

Emergency debates and adjournment debates

Any member may at the start of business on Monday to Thursday request that an 'emergency adjournment debate' be granted on a topic of current importance. The Speaker has a largely unconfined discretion in deciding whether to permit such a debate. Furthermore, if the request is opposed by any other MP, its proposer requires the support of 40 colleagues. Very few emergency debates are permitted, primarily because they would have an extremely disruptive effect on the Commons' timetable.[7]

If granted, the debate is held at 3pm on the next working

5 Irwin (1988) *op cit.*
6 For a much fuller account of the points alluded to in this paragraph see Griffith and Ryle *op cit* pp 400–403.
7 There have on average been two per year since 1974; Griffith and Ryle *op cit* p 350.

day, or (exceptionally) at 7pm on the day the request is made. Emergency debates are obviously concerned with matters of intense public controversy. That substantive characteristic, combined with their timing at a high profile period in the Commons' working day, ensures that the speakers enjoy considerable publicity. As such, they offer a useful tool for the Opposition to embarrass the government on an important issue.

'Adjournment debates' are, in contrast, a regular occurrence. They run for 30 minutes at the close of business on each working day. The Monday to Thursday slots are allocated by ballot; the Speaker chooses a member to speak on Fridays. Adjournment debates generally entail a 15 minute speech by a backbench member, and a similar reply by a (junior) minister. They usually concern aspects of government policy which impact with particular intensity on a member's constituency. Given their timing, adjournment debates rarely attract a sizeable audience in the house, nor much press coverage. They nevertheless offer an opportunity for the government to dwell on the details of its policies, and for a member to demonstrate her assiduity in defence of local interests to her constituency party.

Questions to ministers

The adversarial, almost gladatorial, character of party politics in modern Britain is perhaps best illustrated by oral questions to Ministers put by backbenchers and shadow ministers. The procedure was an established feature of the Commons' working practices by the mid-nineteenth century, and by 1900 the government was fielding an average of 5000 questions each year on the floor of the house.[8] At that time, questions were taken as the first item of business, and 'question time' continued until all had been answered. This meant that other business was frequently not reached until the early evening.

While this state of affairs emphasised (literally as well as metaphorically) the principle that the government should be answerable to the Commons, it offered great opportunities for opposition MPs to upset the government's timetable; the timetabling of innumerable questions was another tactic favoured by Irish nationalist MPs to disrupt government business.[9]

Proposals for reform were introduced by Sir Arthur Balfour,

8 Chester N (1977) 'Questions in the house', in Walkland and Ryle *op cit.*
9 *Ibid.*

Leader of the House in the 1901 Conservative government.[10] Balfour's plans were the subject of considerable controversy and debate in the house, which eventually accepted that question time would in future be held before the commencement of public business, but for a limited time of between 45 and 55 minutes. Questions which were not reached on the floor would receive a prompt written answer. In addition, individual MPs were limited to a maximum of eight questions per day.[11]

Questions are now taken at the beginning of business on Mondays to Thursdays, for around 45 minutes. Ministers answer in rotation, so that the conduct of each government department is open to question at three to four week intervals. At present, as many as 150 questions may be tabled for answer every sitting day. It is unlikely that many more than two dozen will be dealt with in the short time available. Those questions not reached on the floor are responded to in writing. The oral proceedings attract considerable attention, both from MPs and the media. Members are thus extremely keen to ensure that their particular question is one of the few delivered and answered on the floor. To have any chance of securing this objective, members must submit questions ten days in advance to the 'Table Office', which numbers them at random. Ministers thus have the opportunity to arrange for their officials to provide them with detailed answers to the specific questions raised, and also to anticipate follow-up questions ('supplementaries') which might be put immediately after the minister gives her reply.

Both the content and the style of questions to ministers are subject to extremely convoluted rules, interpretation of which is entrusted to the Speaker.[12] The Speaker exercises virtually unconfined discretion over the number of supplementary questions which may be put to the minister, both by the mover of the question and other MPs. The Speaker also chooses which members will speak. Successive Speakers have adhered to rather different policies on this issue, with some favouring more expansive

---

10 Balfour, when Secretary of State for Ireland in the late 1880s, had experienced this tactic at first hand: Chester N and Bowring M (1962) *Questions in Parliament* p 58 (London: OUP).

11 The daily maximum is now two per member per day, and no more than eight may be tabled in any ten sitting days.

12 Griffith and Ryle *op cit* pp 254–258. In practice, the Speaker delegates this role to clerks in the Table Office. The most important rule is that the question's subject matter must fall within the particular minister's sphere of departmental responsibility.

exploration of a small number of questions, and others preferring to maximise the number of members called upon to speak.[13]

It is not possible to offer authoritative generalisations as to the nature of questions asked. *Erskine May* tells us that; 'the purpose of a question is to obtain information or press for action'.[14] However one might sensibly doubt whether such sentiments underlie many of the questions currently tabled. Griffith and Ryle suggest that in the past 30 years questions have become considerably less specific. Rather than request that a minister comment upon a particular detailed issue, often affecting the member's constituency, contemporary questions and the associated supplementaries are increasingly likely to be couched at a general level.[15] One might now be forgiven for thinking that the primary purpose of questions moved by opposition MPs is to use a supplementary to expose a minister's inability to think on her feet, while government backbenchers offer ministers the opportunity to engage in self-congratulation.

Despite the evidently increasing frequency of sycophantic questions from government backbenchers,[16] it would be a gross oversimplification to suggest that party loyalties create an absolute rule, rather than merely a strong presumption, of deference between a government's backbench MPs and its ministers during questions. Small handfuls of MPs, generally acting in collective defence of their individual constituency interests, can on occasion deploy the high public profile that question time provides severely to undermine a minister's standing both in the house and in the Cabinet. A forceful recent example is provided by the furore which met the announcement in April 1995 by the then Health Secretary (Virginia Bottomley) that several London hospitals were to be closed to curb rising public expenditure. The policy was substantively unpalatable to Conservative MPs whose constituencies contained such hospitals. MPs were however further aggrieved by the procedures used for the announcement – a written answer in Hansard rather than orally in the house. Peter Brooke MP (a former Cabinet colleague of Bottomley) accused her in the house of 'lacking moral courage' by failing to make a personal statement on the issue. The insult ensured that the episode gained considerable publicity, to the extent that rumours

13 Griffith and Ryle *op cit* pp 369–70: Laundy *op cit.*
14 *Op cit* at p 337.
15 *Op cit* pp 254–258.
16 See for example Hattersley R (1992) 'The beggaring of PM's question time' *The Guardian* January 28.

circulated suggesting Bottomley would be sacked by the Prime Minister. No such consequences immediately ensued, but it was widely assumed that Bottomley's chances of reaching higher office had been fundamentally damaged by her humiliation in the house.

Vigorous defence of isolated constituency interests has always been a hallmark of backbench behaviour, and serves as a constant reminder that the localist origins of the Commons' representative system has not been entirely subsumed beneath the demands of party politics. Government whips are likely to take a benevolent view of individual members who defy party policy in order to be seen to support their consituents' concerns, especially when such a 'rebellion' raises no prospect of defeat for the government.[17] It would take an unusual combination of circumstances for this aspect of the MP's role to present a serious threat even to an individual minister, still less to the government as a whole. The Bottomley incident was noteworthy because the government then had a Commons majority of barely a dozen, and had announced hospital closures in the constituencies of several of its backbench MPs, some of whom[18] were already distinctly disenchanted with government policy in other fields.

Unsurprisingly, the Opposition took advantage of this dissension in government ranks by tabling a motion on its next opposition day criticising government policy. The motion was phrased in fairly unconfrontational terms, in the hope that several Conservative backbenchers could be persuaded to support it. In the event, the government mustered a majority of 12 to defeat the motion. The episode is however useful, insofar as it reveals that the efficacy of the Commons as a supervisor of government behaviour is often only apparent when various procedural devices are considered in combination, rather than as discrete phenomena.

Private notice questions

This mechanism allows members to raise a question for oral answer by the relevant minister on matters of urgency and importance. The Speaker decides whether the question is worthy of oral answer. In the 1980s, an average of 30 to 40 PNQs were permitted per session. Exchanges on the issues raised lasted for an average of some 20 minutes, which is appreciably more than the Commons

---

17 Not least, of course, because an MP who proves herself indifferent to constituency interests when they are inconvenient for party political purposes may jeopardise her chances of subsequent re-election.
18 For reasons discussed below at pp 551–558.

devotes to individual questions raised at question time.[19] In the past 20 years, 30–40% of PNQs accepted by the Speaker have been tabled by the opposition front bench, with most of the remainder coming from opposition rather than government backbenchers.[20]

Prime ministerial accountability on the floor of the house

The Prime Minister now takes questions on the floor for 15 minute periods on Tuesday and Thursday afternoons. This now traditional practice began in the early 1960s, following a recommendation of the Select Committee on Procedure. Prior to that date, questions to the Prime Minister enjoyed no special priority over and above questions to other ministers, which meant that on many days the Prime Minister was never called upon to give oral answers.[1]

Proceedings are now generally dominated by a ritualised clash between the Prime Minister and the Leader of the Opposition. The Leader of the Opposition is generally permitted to put as many as three questions consecutively to the Prime Minister. The (admittedly) stunted opportunity this offers for immediate argument is perhaps as close as the house ever gets to witnessing a debate in the cut and thrust sense of the word. The exchanges are perhaps most significant for the impact they have on MPs' perceptions of their respective leader's abilities. In the factionalised arena the house offers, a Prime Minister who continually bests the Leader of the Opposition is unlikely to find her ascendancy in her party under threat, while opposition MPs may be tempted to conclude that their prospects of future electoral success are much hampered by their Leader's evident inadequacies on the floor.[2] It certainly seems that all recent Prime Ministers have devoted considerable amounts of time and effort to preparing themselves for this brief exposure to the house.[3]

For opposition MPs, the opportunity to speak is little more than a chance to attract a good deal of publicity by indulging in splenetic rhetoric designed to demonstrate their ideological purity either to their party leaders or their local constituency activists.

---

19 See Griffith and Ryle *op cit* pp 374–376.
20 Griffith and Ryle *op cit* pp 357 and 375 respectively.
1 See Jones G (1973) 'The Prime Minister and parliamentary questions' *Parliamentary Affairs* 260–272.
2 See Watkins A (1994) 'Why young Tony should keep his winning smile' *The Independent on Sunday* June 19.
3 See Jones (1973) *op cit* for a detailed explanation of the mechanics of prime ministerial preparation.

Government backbenchers, in contrast, are likely to produce questions which enable the Prime Minister to lavish praise on particular aspects of government policy.

The copious media attention which Prime Minister's Question Time attracts both in the house and in the media may create a rather misleading impression. A recent study reveals that since 1945 Prime Ministers have contributed far less frequently to life on the floor of the house than their predecessors.[4] James Callaghan, Labour Prime Minister from 1976–1979, and Margaret Thatcher were particularly reluctant to participate in general debates, whether on government or opposition motions or during the passage of legislation. The study suggests that both Prime Ministers (but especially Thatcher) saw their role predominantly as that of running the executive rather than making themselves answerable to the Commons. If this view is correct, it identifies a thus far overlooked but nevertheless highly significant aspect of the executive's contemporary dominance of the Commons.

Early day motions

'Early day motions' provide what is in effect a noticeboard on which MPs can register their concern about particular issues.[5] The mechanism enables a member to table a motion to which supportive MPs may append their signature. There are no limits either on the number of such motions that an individual MP may propose, nor on their contents. The number of motions tabled has risen precipitately since 1945, from fewer than 100 per year to over 1,500 by the late 1980s.[6]

EDMs are very rarely debated in the house.[7] Their primary purpose tends to be as an initial step in a campaign to generate publicity within the house, often in the hope that the issue concerned will subsequently be picked up by the government, the opposition, or a private member who has won a slot for an adjournment debate or private member's Bill, and thereby receive relatively extensive discussion. The device is a particularly helpful way for government backbenchers to demonstrate their strength of

4 Dunleavy P, Jones G, and O'Leary B (1990) 'Prime Ministers and the Commons: patterns of behaviour 1868–1987' *Public Administration* 123–140.
5 See generally Irwin *op cit.*
6 Griffith and Ryle *op cit* pp 380–381.
7 Almost all that are are 'prayers' against statutory instruments; see pp 168–169 above.

feeling on particular matters, and thereby occasionally 'persuade' Ministers to reverse significant policy decisions.[8]

Questions for written answer[9]

For MPs whose main concern is with eliciting information from the government rather than simply confronting a minister, the 'question for written answer' may prove a more effective tool than seeking an oral answer. There is no limit on the number of such questions that MPs may table. In recent years, as many as 40,000 have been raised in a single session. Questions for written answer are to an extent shorn of the partisan baggage attaching to proceedings on the floor. They thus tend to be rather more precisely targeted and more fully answered than their oral counterparts. As such, they represent a valuable resource for backbenchers, since in effect they force the government to undertake research which neither the member herself nor the Commons' library may have the capacity to carry out.[10]

Informal processes

It may be that the most important vehicle for backbench influence on government behaviour is one that defies any straightforward calibration – namely the informal (and often invisible) processes of consultation and lobbying of ministers by individual members on matters of constituency or general concern. Quite often, such influence will be entirely pre-emptive in nature – potential conflicts between frontbench policy and backbench opinion are filtered out by modification to government policies before they make even an initial appearance. Party whips play an important part in this process, by acting as a conduit of backbench sentiment, both to the Cabinet and to individual ministers.

One can only speculate on the extent to which such pressure is effectively applied through channels that are hidden from public

8 For a pertinent recent example see Drewry G (1983) 'The National Audit Act – half a loaf' *Public Law* 531–537. See also Norton (1985) *op cit* ch 6.
9 For a useful guide to the emergence, growth and current utility of written questions see Borthwick R (1979) 'Questions and debates', in Walkland *op cit.*
10 Although the government does on occasion decline to answer questions for written answer on the grounds that the cost of doing so would be prohibitive; see Griffith and Ryle *op cit* pp 373–374.

view.[11] Equally, there is no reliable way of knowing whether governments simply engage in self-censorship of some of their prefered policy objectives simply because they doubt their proposals would find favour in the house.

Thus far, this section has been concerned with the role MPs play in an individual capacity, or as members of ad hoc alliances over specific policy issues. But the Commons' efforts to oversee and influence executive behaviour are also expressed in a more formal, collective manner through the mechanisms of 'select committees'.

The departmental select committee system

The 'domestic committees' of the Commons, which are concerned primarily with regulating the house's internal proceedings, will be considered in chapter 8. This section considers the role played by those Commons select committees[12] which supposedly facilitate MPs' scrutiny of government behaviour.

The so-called 'select committees' have enjoyed a distinctly potted Parliamentary history. Their modern origins derive from an ad hoc committee established in 1855 to examine the government's conduct of the Crimean War, when the army frequently found itself lacking basic supplies. The initiative came from John Roebuck, a radical MP, and was staunchly resisted by the government which considered it incompatible with orthodox understandings of the separation of powers. Gladstone, in seeking to persuade the house not to establish the committee, condemned it as an unprecedented and unconstitutional intrusion into the sphere of executive responsibility. On being overwhelmingly defeated in the subsequent vote, the government resigned, expecting that the committee's inquiry would reveal grave errors in its policies.[13]

The Crimea committee was a single issue body of limited duration. The Public Accounts Committee (PAC), created in 1861, has in contrast been a permanent feature of the Commons' organisational landscape. The PAC scrutinises the implementation of the government's expenditure plans. It is chaired by an opposition MP, frequently one who was formerly a Treasury Minister. It has

---

11 For an indication see Norton P (1982) ' "Dear Minister" . . . The importance of MP to minister correspondence' *Parliamentary Affairs* 59–72.

12 Select Committees are quite different creatures from standing committees, in terms both of their composition and their role.

13 See Magnus P (1963) *Gladstone* pp 118–119 (London: John Murray).

extensive investigatory powers and substantial resources to carry out its tasks. Its reports invariably attract a prompt and considered Treasury reply, and many of its recommendations have influenced subsequent government practice. In consequence, the PAC has gradually acquired a formidable reputation, and is widely regarded as an effective tool for the Commons to raise concerns about government expenditure.[14] But as we shall below, it might justly be regarded as something of an exception to the general trend.

Given Gladstone's hostility to the Crimea committee, it might seem puzzling that he himself, when Chancellor, was a prime mover in establishing the PAC. This evident paradox however serves the useful function of highlighting the possibility that select committees may on occasion help rather than hinder the goverment's plans. Gladstone appeared to see the PAC as an extremely useful tool for pressurising his Cabinet colleagues to accept his preference for placing tight limits on any increase in public expenditure, and thereby (indirectly) to curb British involvement in foreign wars.[15] The PAC has now firmly established itself as an independent actor on the constitutional stage, but its origins indicate that one might often have cause to be wary about the purposes that newly created bodies will serve.

The Crossman reforms

It would be inaccurate to suggest that there was a select committee *system* until the 1960s. Prior to that date, most such committees were ad hoc bodies, established to deal with specific problems and dissolved immediately after delivering their reports. In 1965, the Labour Prime Minister Harold Wilson supported proposals formulated by one of his ministers, Richard Crossman, that the house should create two permanent select committees, which would scrutinise government policy in the areas of science and agriculture. Crossman presented his initiative as in part a means of enhancing government performance. He envisaged committees of a dozen or so backbench members, who would gain some expertise in a particular policy field. The committees would have

---

14 See Bates St J (1988) 'Scrutiny of administration'; and Robinson R (1988) 'The House of Commons and public money', both in Ryle and Richards *op cit*; McEldowney J (1988) 'The contingencies fund and the Parliamentary scrutiny of public finance' *Public Law* 232–245; Drewry G (1985a) 'Select committees and backbench power' in Jowell J and Oliver D (eds) *The Changing Constitution* (Oxford: OUP).

15 Shannon R (1982) *Gladstone* Vol 1 pp 446–447 (London: Hamish Hamilton); Matthew C (1986) *Gladstone 1809–1874* (Oxford: Clarendon Press).

a functional rather than departmental remit, and could conceivably find themselves examining the behaviour of several ministries. Their membership would reflect the party balance in the house, but it was intended that the backbenchers who served on them would put aside party loyalties and advance the collective interest of the Commons overall. Thus constituted, the committees 'could provide an astringent stimulus to . . . our Departments by ventilating issues and exploring corners which had been covered up in the past.'[16]

Crossman was seemingly concerned to redress what he saw as an undesirable imbalance of power between the Commons and the Cabinet:

'Ministers aren't bothered by Parliament, indeed they're hardly ever there . . . The amount of time a Minister spends on the front bench is very small. The Executive reigns supreme in Britain and has minimum trouble from the legislature.'[17]

The policy had been strongly opposed by some ministers. The Treasury feared that Committees would act as lobbyists for additional departmental expenditure, while others resented in principle the notion that their departments' workings should be exposed to constant Commons scrutiny.[18]

It is not clear if Crossman and Wilson were sincere about enhancing the Commons' role vis-à-vis the Cabinet. Wilson's biographer records that they saw the committees as: 'a means for keeping bored backbenchers out of mischief, rather than as a rod for their own backs.'[19] If this is so, the Crossman committees might sensibly be seen as a governmental exercise in what has been termed 'symbolic reassurance'.[20] The idea denotes a process through which decision-makers defend a status quo which they find expedient, but which outside observers consider illegitimate,

---

16 *Diaries* pp 200–201.
17 *Ibid*, p 275.
18 Crossman records the First Secretary to the Treasury, Michael Stewart, as arguing in Cabinet that: 'A backbench MP has a perfectly satisfactory job to do and there is no reason to create work for him to keep him happy. Indeed, our backbenchers should be thankful that . . . we want to keep the Executive strong, not to strengthen Parliamentary control. Michael's remarks had been applauded by many people around the table': *ibid*, p 275.
19 Pimlott *op cit* p 518. Note also the extract from Crossman's *Diaries* with which Griffith and Ryle preface their book on Parliament: 'The government has had its summer recess – a delicious time for any Government. Now we have got to settle down to the dreary nagging strain of Parliament'.
20 See Edelman M (1964) *The Symbolic Uses of Politics* (Urbana: University of Illinois Press).

by initiating 'reforms' which radically alter the outward form of a law or institution and so defuse external criticism, but which are not intended to produce any significant impact.

This thesis is perhaps contradicted by the fact that Crossman's initiative expanded somewhat in the final years of the second Wilson government – four further committees were established.[1] But the government quickly displayed little tolerance for committee activities which effectively questioned the merits of government policy. The chief casualty of Wilson's rapid disenchantment was the Agriculture Committee, which was disbanded after displaying considerable investigative and analytical independence on the issue of the impact that British accession to the EEC would have on the domestic farming industry.[2]

One might therefore crudely (but defensibly) conclude that the Crossman committees did sometimes prove effective as a vehicle for enhancing MPs' knowledge on issues which cut across the party divide. What they seemingly did not do was convince MPs that their primary loyalty lay to their country, their constituents, or the Commons, rather than to their party.

The 1979 reforms

It is perhaps no coincidence that the Crossman reforms were promoted by a government with (initially) a very small Commons majority. The 1974–1979 Labour government which accepted far more systematic proposals from the Commons' Procedure Committee had similarly precarious support. This might suggest that governments are more likely to accommodate the supposed independence of the Commons when they cannot invariably rely on a working majority.[3] However, the proposals were adopted by the subsequent Conservative government (which did enjoy a sizeable majority),[4] and were implemented (if only in part) under the tutelage of the then Leader of the House, Norman St John Stevas.

---

1 Dealing respectively with education and science, race relations and immigration, Scottish affairs and overseas aid.

2 Technically, of course, the government could neither create nor disband a Commons committee. That is a matter for the house itself. It seems however quite clear that when the house did indeed vote to abolish the committee the Labour majority in favour was responding more to pressure from government whips rather than to a considered review of the merits of the case.

3 Although the then Labour chief whip, Michael Cocks, had little empathy with the proposals: 'I didn't want any bloody select committee examining what we were up to!'; quoted by White M and Norton-Taylor R (1995) 'Commons watchdogs lack full set of teeth' *The Guardian* 22 March.

4 For the figures see Table 7.5.

The reform's supposed objective (according both to St John Stevas and his Labour predecessor Michael Foot) was to reverse a perception that the Commons was becoming increasingly impotent in the face of government majorities in the house; the Procedure Committee had argued in 1978 that: 'the day to day working of the Constitution is now weighted in favour of the government to a degree which arouses widepread anxiety.'[5]

The method adopted to address this supposed problem was to create a dozen or so select committees, each having 11 to 13 members, which would closely scrutinise the work of particular departments.[6] Membership was to be fixed for the life of a Parliament, so that MPs could develop specialised knowledge of particular issues. Members were to be chosen by a special Committee of Selection rather than by party whips. A principle nevertheless emerged to the effect that a government with a majority in the house would retain a majority on each committee. It also appears that both government and opposition whips have in practice succeeded in gaining de facto control of the appointment process.[7] Ministers could not serve on committees, and there was a hope, if not an expectation, that members would approach their task in an independent and fair-minded spirit. Their activities were to be overseen and co-ordinated by a Liaison Committee comprising the chairpersons of the individual committees.

The new select committees have been in operation for some 15 years now, which is long enough to form tentative impressions about their impact on the government/Commons relationship. There is no easy way to answer this question precisely; the subject demands close, continuous and long term scrutiny of the various committees' operations and the government's responses thereto.[8] A largely impressionistic sense of their efficacy can however be formed by noting several issues of general applicability and by focusing on some of the more significant episodes in their thus far brief history.

The committees have undoubtedly been prolific in terms of the

---

5 Quoted in Drewry (1985a) *op cit* p 136. See Baines P (1985) 'The history and rationale of the 1979 reforms', in Drewry G (ed) *The New Select Committees* (Oxford: Clarendon Press); Johnson *op cit.*
6 The Committees being Agriculture, Defence, Education, Employment, Energy, Environment, Foreign Affairs, Home Affairs, Scottish Affairs, Social Services, Trade and Industry, Transport, Treasury and Civil Service, and Welsh Affairs.
7 See Griffith and Ryle *op cit* pp 417–420.
8 For examples see Nixon J and Nixon N (1983) 'The social services committee' *Journal of Social Policy* 331–355; Hawes D (1992) 'Parliamentary select committees: some case studies in contingent influence' *Policy and Politics* 227–235; Turpin (1985) *op cit* pp 387–390. More generally see Drewry (ed) (1985) *op cit.*

number and diversity of reports which they have produced. On a few occasions, these reports seem to have led directly to shifts in government policy. Others are intended either to filter in the longer term into the general process of governmental policy-making, or merely to draw attention to issues whose complexities have thus far remained unappreciated.[9] This gradual accumulation of expert knowledge on a wide variety of issues is perhaps the most successful area of committee activity thus far. In other respects, their impact has been far more limited.

Unlike the PAC, the departmental select committees are not well-resourced in terms of accommodation in the house and research and administrative support.[10] The committees do not control any resources of their own; their expenditure is determined by the House of Commons Commission. In this respect, they fare very poorly in comparison with the legislative committee system of the US Congress, which enjoys considerable power and prestige within the US government process.[11] The two systems are not of course directly comparable, since the US constitution adheres to a far more rigid separation of powers than its British counterpart, and often finds itself accommodating an executive and legislature controlled by different political parties. Nevertheless, one cannot doubt that the select committees' paucity of resources undermines their capacity to be fully informed on relevant aspects of government policy.

A further significant constraint on the committees' efficacy derives from their (practically) limited powers to extract information from unwilling government departments. St John Stevas announced to the house in 1979 that:

> 'I give the House the pledge on the part of the government that every Minister from the most senior Cabinet Minister to the most junior Under-Secretary will do all in his or her power to co-operate with the new system of Committees and make it a success.'[12]

One cannot know if such a promise was made in good faith. Nor can one know if committee members exercise their power 'to send for persons, papers and records' in fearless disregard of ministerial sensibilities. But it is evident that a minister may simply refuse to attend a committee inquiry. Or she may decline to answer questions on particular subjects. It may be politically embarrassing

---

9 See generally Griffith and Ryle *op cit* pp 423–428. For an important example of a report in the last catgeory see pp 379–380 below.
10 See Grififth and Ryle *op cit* pp 422–423.
11 See McKay D (1989) *American Politics and Society* ch 8 (Oxford: Basil Blackwell).
12 *HCD*, June 25 1979 c 45; quoted in Turpin (1985) *op cit* p 384.

for a minister to behave in this way, and may expose her to both parliamentary and public criticism. But one must surely assume that she is non-cooperative because a candid discussion would reveal information of an even more embarrassing or damaging nature.

It is also clear that ministers are frequently reluctant to permit senior civil servants to contribute to committee inquiries. The Employment Committee's inquiry into the GCHQ affair[13] was severely hindered by the government's refusal to allow the Director of GCHQ to give evidence. Similarly, the controversy engendered by the so-called Westland Affair[14] prompted inquiries by both the Defence Committee and the Treasury and Civil Service Committee, both of which were severely hampered by the government's decision not to allow particular civil servants to appear.[15]

A further indication of the government's somewhat restrictive interpretation of 'full co-operation' was provided by a 1980 *Memorandum of Guidance* which indicated that certain types of documentary evidence would not be available. The text of the *Memorandum* lent itself to extremely broad interpretation. The forbidden territory included, for example, 'Questions in the field of political controversy'; 'advice given to ministers by their departments'; the 'discussions of Cabinet committees';[16] and 'inter-departmental exchanges on policy issues'.

The list suggests that the Thatcher government was no more willing than previous administrations to open its activities up to searching Commons' scrutiny. It is technically within the power of the house to insist that persons attend committee hearings, or that documents be produced. Defying an order would amount to contempt, which, as we shall see in chapter 8, may still lead to imprisonment. It is however difficult to envisage any circumstances in which a government would find itself unable to persuade its MPs to vote against any such action. Thus while the power may be significant in respect of private individuals, it is largely illusory in the context of government/Commons relations.

Most commentators seem to suggest that while the committees have become accepted as a legitimate part of the Parliamentary landscape, it is only the PAC which exercises a continuously sig-

---

13 See p 121–123 above.
14 We will revisit Westland in subsequent chapters; see p 339 below.
15 See Hennessy P (1986) 'Helicopter crashes into Cabinet: Prime Minister and constitution hurt' *Journal of Law and Society* 423–432.
16 On which see pp 357–360 below.

nificant influence over government behaviour:[17] the reform clearly does not merit the label of a 'revolution' in the workings of government with which St John Stevas initially cloaked it.[18] The suggestion that governments would tolerate select committees only for so long as they did not prove a constant thorn in the executive's side was reinforced after the 1992 general election. Prior to the election, the Health Committee was chaired by Nicholas Winterton MP, an independently minded Conservative who had been a voluble and effective critic of government health policy. The government seemingly wished to remove him from this post, but did not wish to be candid as to its motives. Conservative whips thus formulated a rule that Conservative MPs could not serve for more than twelve years on the same committee. Not, one assumes, by coincidence, it transpired that Winterton fell into this category.[19] His initial reaction was one of blustering indignation, couched in the rhetoric of constitutional impropriety:

> 'What we have now is government by whips' dictat. They are now saying free speech and an independent mind can have no role in Parliament. . . . They [the Cabinet] are being seen as dictators who will not brook any dissent.'[20]

Yet Mr Winterton did not feel compelled to demonstrate his commitment to 'free speech and independence' by resigning from the Conservative party. Nor was his outrage shared by a sufficient number of his colleagues for the Conservative whips to doubt that a Commons majority would support their new policy. The episode may indeed have been, as one anonymous Conservative MP complained, 'a gross interference with the work of Parliament'.[1] Yet in formal terms, the government has no power to determine the rules controlling committee membership; that is a matter for

17 See particularly Hencke D (1994) 'Ministers face reprimand over wasteful projects' *The Guardian* 7 July.

18 See Johnson *op cit*; Drewry (1985a) *op cit*; Griffith and Ryle *op cit* pp 430–434. It is interesting to note that some of the most enthusiastic endorsers of the efficacy of the new system are backbenchers who were formerly members of a Thatcher cabinet; cf Michael Jopling MP in 1995: 'The most important development in Parliamentary procedure in my 30 years in the House. Select Committees are giving backbenchers teeth with which to challenge the executive'' quoted in White and Norton-Taylor *op cit.*

19 Although the government's effort to be 'objective' caught several hitherto 'loyal' Conservative MPs, one of whom, after a long and lacklustre backbench career suddenly found himself elevated to a junior ministerial post.

20 McGhie J (1992) 'Tory backbenchers to ask Speaker to spare them from their whips' *The Observer* 12 July; Knewstub N (1992) 'Ousted Tory MP lambasts government arrogance' *The Guardian* 14 July.

1 McGhie *op cit.*

the house itself. That the whips' gambit was successful reveals the true significance of the Winterton 'sacking' – namely that so very few current Conservative members regarded maintaining the independence of their house as a higher loyalty than pandering to the convenience of their party.

The 1979 reforms have thus far operated only under a Conservative government. It remains a matter for speculation whether Labour members would be similarly quiescent if faced by like demands from a Labour government. It may well be that ministerial unwillingness to accept that the great power they wield is in itself sufficient reason to subject their behaviour to rigorous, inconvenient examination by an informed and relatively autonomous Commons is not the exclusive preserve of the modern Conservative party.

CONCLUSION

It is clear that the contemporary House of Commons is a body in which party politics is the dominant determinant both in the legislative process and in respect of executive accountability. The house is manifestly now a factional rather than national assembly for most purposes. But it would as yet be premature to conclude that the constitution therefore permits factional concerns to determine both the content of legislation and the parliamentary accountability of government behaviour. To answer that question, our analysis must consider several further issues. Firstly, the constitutional role played by the House of Lords – the second limb of our tripartite Parliament. Secondly, the nature of the relationship between factional Commons majorities and 'the people'. And thirdly, the uses to which factional governments put whatever power is at their disposal. This last question is perhaps the most important of all. For even if one accepts that a factional constitution is undesirable in a modern democracy, it does not necessarily follow that such a constitution will lead to the production of factional laws, nor, in the event that it does, that the laws concerned do not attract the 'consent' of the governed.

CHAPTER SIX

The House of Lords

In chapter 5, we began to explore how accurately Parliament's current role reflects the original intentions of the 1688 settlement: those intentions being firstly to secure that a monopoly on law-making power was wielded by élite groups, and secondly to ensure that no one or two factions within that élite could seize legislative power to pursue majoritarian or minoritiarian ends. Chapter 5 suggested there has been a significant change in the role of the Commons since 1688, from a body providing the voice of one distinct segment of society, counterposed to those of the Lords and the Monarch, to a forum in which the divergent political philosophies of the entire population are given expression. The rise of nationwide party politics, and the fusion rather than separation of powers between the legislature and the government, create the danger of a majoritarian lower chamber, in which pursuing factional party advantage rather than safeguarding national interests could be legislators' main occupation. Chapter 7 will consider how development of the parliamentary electoral system has affected this trend. This chapter asks whether the upper chamber plays an effective anti-majoritarian legislative role. We will also ask if its present function is an important one; and if so, could it be more effectively achieved by substantially reforming the Lords.

Bicameral legislatures: a functionalist justification

Most modern democracies have two houses in their central legis-lature.[1] They are referred to as having a bicameral Parliament: countries with only one legislative assembly have unicameral Par-liaments. For example, the United States' Congress comprises the House of Representatives and the Senate. Before returning to

1 New Zealand and Israel being the obvious exceptions.

the institutional mechanics of the United Kingdom's Parliament however, it is helpful to pause to consider once again why the USA adopted this bicameral system.[2]

The American framers' division of their central legislature was in part a continuation of the theme of the separation of powers. By requiring that federal legislation attracted the consent of more than one body, Madison and Jefferson hoped to reduce still further the likelihood that Congress could enact tyrannical laws. In addition, the two houses of the United States Congress fulfil different representative functions. The Senate has two senators from each State, irrespective of the size of the State's population. Senators represent State interests within the national legislature, thereby stressing the constitution's federal nature. In contrast, the members of the House of Representatives are chosen on a population basis; the number from each State reflects that State's share of the national population. This emphasises that the United States' federal legislature was responsible to individual citizens as well as to the States. Bicameralism is therefore intended to maximise the chances that Congress, acting within the legislative competence granted by the Constitution, produces laws that strike an acceptable balance between the interests of the States and of individual citizens.

Most countries with bicameral legislatures consider the composition and powers of both houses as part of their fundamental laws. This is clearly evident in the USA, where the structure of Congress is delineated in the text of the Constitution. Similarly, if we recall *Trethowan*,[3] we see that the New South Wales constitution used procedural entrenchment to safeguard the upper house's existence. Bicameralism was a 'higher' law within that constitutional settlement.

For practical purposes, the two parts of the United Kingdom's legislature are the House of Commons and the House of Lords. In theory, Parliament has a third part – the Monarch. And, again as a matter of legal theory, the Monarch retains the power to veto proposed legislation by withholding the Royal Assent. However, as a matter of practical politics, this particular monarchical power is no longer used. In respect of the Royal Assent, the legal theory and political practice of the constitution no longer coincide.[4]

---

2 For an analysis of the reasoning behind several other countries' choice of this institutional framework see Shell D (1992) *The House of Lords* ch 1 (London: Harvester Wheatsheaf).
3 See pp 48–50 above.
4 We will assess the changing nature of the Monarch's power in chapter 9.

Appreciating the distinction between *theory and practice*, or between what is sometimes referred to as *law and convention*, is essential to forming an understanding of the constitutional status and function of the House of Lords. Indeed, by pursuing this 'gap' between theory and practice at this point, we address ideas which later chapters will show to be absolutely central to understanding how and why the constitution functions as it does. This book does not follow the traditional path of fully discussing 'constitutional conventions' at this early stage. The law/convention distinction is, again, an issue where Dicey's legacy provides us with an important starting point; we will examine his ideas, as well as (once again) Jennings' criticism of his analysis, more fully in chapter 9. For present purposes, we might distinguish law and convention in the following simple way. Both are vehicles through which political power is exercised in an effective and legitimate manner. However, while laws may be enforced by an action before the courts, conventions do not have any actionable legal basis. Rather, they control the exercise of political power because the wielders of that power either believe that conventional restraints are morally correct, or they fear the *political* consequences of departing from conventional understandings.[5]

In applying this analysis to the Lords, the first two sections of this chapter sketch the historical background to the current composition and powers of the Lords by looking at several major episodes from the mid-nineteenth century onwards in which its legal and conventional roles underwent radical redefinition.[6] The third section discusses briefly the various functions that the Lords performs today, and offers some evaluation of how well it does those particular jobs.

I. THE HISTORICAL BACKGROUND

The origins of the House of Lords may be traced to the 'Great Council' of the mediaeval period, a body which gradually assumed a recognisably modern shape in the fifteenth and sixteenth centuries.[7] In the pre-revolutionary era, the Lords was regarded as a

---

5 From this functionalist perspective, we might therefore expect the procedural rules by which the Commons and Lords regulate their internal proceedings to be 'conventions' of the constitution. But as we shall see in chapter 8, that label would be erroneous.

6 The passage of the Great Reform Act 1832 is discussed in chapter 7.

7 See Adonis (1993) *op cit* p 193. For a detailed description see Weston C (1965) *English Constitutional Theory and the House of Lords* ch 1 (London: RKP).

'fundamental' element of the English constitution.[8] In 1688, the Lords and Commons were, in terms of their legal powers, *co-equal partners* in the legislative process. The 1688 revolution established the legal supremacy of *Parliament*, not of the House of Commons. So if the House of Lords disapproved of a Commons Bill, that Bill could not go any further. We have already noted the theory of the 'balanced' constitution.[9] For present purposes, we might relabel that balance as one demanding compromise between monarchical (the Queen/King), aristocratic (the Lords), and 'democratic' (the Commons) forms of government.[10]

Co-equality extended to the formation of the government as well as the passage of legislation. Until the late-nineteenth century, the Cabinet was as likely to contain a majority of members from the Lords as from the Commons: only one member of Lord Grey's 1830 Cabinet was not either a peer or the son of a peer: Roy Jenkins notes that Gladstone assembled a cabinet of 12 in 1880: one was a duke, one a marquess, and five were earls.[11] And it was not until well into the twentieth century that the conventional practice had arisen that the Prime Minister should be a member of the lower house. Furthermore, as we shall see in chapter 7, senior members of the Lords exercised appreciable control over the identity and voting behaviour of MPs until the mid-nineteenth century.

In 1688, the peers who sat in the Lords were either hereditary peers or bishops. The Lords was a combination of the church and the land-owning aristocracy: it was not a democratic chamber in the modern sense. But neither was the Commons, whose members were then 'elected' (the word is used guardedly) by a tiny minority of the (male) population.[12] Co-equality was a co-equality of élites, not of the mass of the population. Such élitism was readily understandable from a functionalist perspective. The constitutional morality of that era discerned a clear and vital

---

8 England had only a unicameral legislature between 1649 and 1657, when Cromwell's revolutionary House of Commons purported to abolish the Lords. Charles II, on being restored to his throne in 1660, recalled the Lords, accepting that the Upper House should again enjoy 'that authority and jurisdiction which hath always belonged to you by your birth, and the fundamental law of the land'; see Smith E (1992) *The House of Lords in British Politics and Society 1815–1911* p 1 (London: Longman).
9 Pp 37–38 above.
10 See Weston *op cit* ch 1.
11 (1968) *Mr Balfour's Poodle* p 27 (London: Heinneman). See also Turbeville A (1958) *The House of Lords in the Age of Reform* p 256 (London: Faber and Faber). For a longer list see Smith E *op cit* p 64.
12 Changes in the electoral process are examined in detail in chapter 7.

purpose for an aristocratic veto within the legislative process. In the wider political sense, that function was conservative – to preserve existing patterns of political and economic power.

As we shall discuss in chapter 7, the impact of the industrial revolution on both the nature and distribution of wealth was immense, and led, in time, to equally significant realignments in the bases of political influence. However even as late as 1800, ownership of land was the predominant form of economic power: and members of the House of Lords were the predominant class of landowners. The concentration of landed wealth among the aristocracy was, to modern eyes, quite startling. In 1876, almost half of the country's 30 million acres was owned by barely 500 peers,[13] many of whom were also deriving substantial incomes from industrial, commercial, and residential development in addition to the more traditional vehicle of agriculture.[14] One should beware of drawing simplistic conclusions about the relationship between economic and political power; but neither should we overlook the possibility that a constitution which has developed in an evolutionary rather than revolutionary fashion over 300 years is likely to have done so in a manner that has accommodated the interests of society's economic élites.

Co-equality to complementarity: a conventional change

The situation of equal status between the two houses within both the legislative process and the formation of the government continued in *legal terms* until the twentieth century. But it very quickly began to undergo a *political change*. From the very outset of the post-revolutionary period, both houses appeared to accept that the House of Lords should not exercise its veto powers in respect of legislation dealing with the raising of government revenue. The original sources of this conventional understanding are obscure,[15] but its scope was clearly delineated in a 1678 Commons resolution:[16]

> '[A]ll Bills for granting such Aids and Supplies ought to begin with the Commons: And that it is the undoubted and sole right of the

13 Turbeville (1958) *op cit* p 408.
14 *Ibid.* See also Smith E *op cit* pp 52–54.
15 Smith E *op cit* p 34.
16 We will address the legal status of resolutions in chapter 8. At this point we need only note that since they are the product of only *one* limb of Parliament, they should not be equated with statutes.

Commons to direct limit and appoint in such Bills the Ends, Purposes, Considerations, Conditions. Limitations, and Qualifications of such Grants: which ought not to be changed or altered by the House of Lords.'

Quite how effective this principle, or indeed any other conventional understandings, have proven in regulating the legislative process is the question to which we now turn. The answer is perhaps best illustrated by example.

The Treaty of Utrecht

A major conflict between the post-revolution Lords and Commons arose in the early eighteenth century. The immediate cause was a disagreement between the government, which commanded a majority in the Commons, and the majority of peers in the Lords over whether the government should accept the terms of the Treaty of Utrecht, although that dispute was indicative of a more pervasive tension. The government was obviously unable to have any of its proposed legislation enacted in such circumstances. The stalemate was resolved by a mix of conventional understandings and prerogative power. The Prime Minister relied on the convention that the Monarch should act on the advice of her ministers to ask the Queen to use her prerogative powers to create enough new peers who supported the government to ensure that it also had a reliable majority in the Lords. The Queen accepted that she should follow the Prime Minister's advice, and created 12 new peers.[17]

The Utrecht episode demonstrated that the Lords' theoretical co-equality could be undermined in practice if the Monarch supported a Prime Minsister who enjoyed majority Commons support. As such, it is of some constitutional significance, for it shows that there was a pro-majoritarian legal loophole sewn into the fabric of the 1688 settlement. For a Prime Minister and Monarch to collude in this way would perhaps undermine the anti-majoritarian sentiment informing the original understanding of parliamentary sovereignty, but it would not be *illegal* in any sense.

A more important focus for constitutional change was provided by the Great Reform Act of 1832. The passage of this legislation is examined in detail in chapter 7. Here we might simply note that the Act was vigorously opposed by many Tory peers, who feared it undermined the traditional 'balance' of the constitution

---

17 Plucknett (1960) *op cit* pp 540–542: Turbeville A (1927) *The House of Lords in the Eighteenth Century* pp 111–118 (Oxford: Clarendon Press).

and thereby threatened the distribution of economic power on which they assumed the stability and security of the nation to rest. The reasons behind the Lords' eventual acquiescence to the Bill are also discussed in the following chapter. That acquiescence meant however that from 1832 onwards one can begin to see a democratic justification for regarding the House of Lords as constitutionally subordinate to the Commons. The Commons was increasingly becoming a body which could plausibly claim to derive its authority from the consent of the governed. As chapter 7 will indicate, the 1832 reform made only very limited progress towards universal adult suffrage, and was indeed intended by its framers to frustrate rather than facilitate the introduction of a democratically elected legislature. Consequently, it would be misleading to suggest that the 1833 Parliament was a truly representative body. But after 1832, the constitution was heading in that direction, and following the further Reform Act introduced by Disraeli in 1867, it was doing so at a fairly rapid pace.

The doctrine of the mandate

The more 'democratic' basis of the post-Reform Act House of Commons had significant implications for the power that a non-elected Lords could realistically expect to wield. By the 1880s the two houses were in legal theory still equal legislative partners, but in practice their relationship had changed profoundly. By 1900 a fairly clear convention had emerged that the Lords would not block Bills that had gone through the Commons unless it seemed that the Commons itself was trying to introduce legislation that could not command popular support. The legitimate limits to the Lords' intransigence were described by Lord Lyndhurst in 1858:

> 'I never understood, nor could such a principle be acted upon, that we were to make a firm, determined and persevering stand against the opinion of the other House of Parliament when that opinion is backed by the opinion of the people.'[18]

Lord Lyndhurst viewed the Lords' capacity to block legislation as a *power*, which it might deploy when it thought the Commons was pursuing policies which lacked electoral support.

In contrast, Lord Salisbury, then leader of the Tory peers, suggested in 1872 that the veto was a constitutional *duty*. The upper house was *obliged* to defy the Commons on major issues unless 'the judgement of the nation has been challenged at the polls and

---

18 Cited in Jenkins R (1968) *op cit* p 28.

decidedly expressed'.[19] This so-called 'doctrine of the mandate' or 'referendal theory' became established in the late 1860s, when the Lords vetoed a government Bill to reform the Irish Church. Lord Salisbury justified the Lords' position on the grounds that the policy was not part of the manifesto on which the Liberal government had fought the last general election, and that another general election was shortly to be held.[20]

The defensibility of this position rested largely on the hardening of party allegiances in both the Commons and the country at large which had occurred by this time.[1] Party membership was all-pervasive in the Lords in 1880: E A Smith notes that '280 peers described themselves as Conservative and 203 as Liberal, against only thirteen of no party'.[2] Party discipline was then (as now) less rigidly enforced in the Lords than in the Commons,[3] but was nevertheless generally sufficiently effective to assure the Conservatives of a majority whenever required.[4] Perhaps unsurprisingly, Tory governments experienced fewer problems in piloting legislation through the Lords than their Liberal counterparts. The administrations led by Sir Robert Peel in the 1840s and Lord Derby and Disraeli in the 1860s and 1870s generally secured majorities in both houses for modest programmes of social, economic and political reform, although even Peel found his policies rejected by the upper house on occasion.[5]

Whether power or duty, the doctrine of the mandate presents a paradox – a body composed primarily of the landed gentry[6] saw one of its crucial constitutional roles as upholding 'democratic' principles against the elected chamber. The Lords perhaps saw itself as the 'watchdog of the constitution', able if need be to 'overreach' the House of Commons and seek the views of the

---

19 *Ibid* at p 31.
20 See Smith E *op cit* pp 166–168: Shell (1992) *op cit* pp 9–10: Jenkins R (1968) *op cit* pp 28–31.
1 Smith E *op cit* pp 94–95.
2 *Ibid* p 157
3 See below at pp 219–220.
4 Smith E *op cit* ch 5: Large D (1963) 'The decline of the "Party of the Crown" and the rise of parties in the House of Lords, 1783–1837' *English Historical Review* 669–695. See also Brock M (1973) *The Great Reform Act* pp 216–217 (London: Hutchinson).
5 See Turbeville (1958) *op cit* pp 347–351, 397–399, 411–416.
6 From the mid-nineteenth century onwards newly created peers had a slightly more meritocratic profile – outstanding service in the law, armed forces or government service were seen as legitimate ladders up which commoners could climb to the lower ranks of the aristocracy; see Turbeville (1958) *op cit* pp 369–370.

people by insisting that a government with radical proposals test its popularity in a general election.

Cynical observers might wonder if the upper house's defence of public opinion would be staunch only when public sentiment coincided with that of the majority of Tory peers. Salisbury was certainly prepared to amend his formula when the original version did not meet his needs. The Lords rejected the Liberal government's Irish Home Rule Bill on the basis that it had been approved by the Commons only with the support of Irish MPs. The majority of MPs from England, which was the 'predominant partner' in Parliament, had in contrast opposed the measure, which Salisbury considered sufficient justification to force the Liberals to put the issue to the electorate once more.[7] This 'predominant partner' principle is of more than historical significance, for it emphasises the more general point that the substance of a convention may be unilaterally altered by the individuals or groups who have considered themselves bound to it.

Such 'overreaching' was sporadically deployed in the late 1800s. The Lords and Commons clashed on several issues during the late Victorian era – especially policy towards Ireland[8] – but disputes were always defused before reaching a constitutional crisis. Yet one must emphasise that the Lords' deference was purely a question of political self-regulation. The Lords exercised self-restraint and *chose* not to frustrate the wishes of the Commons. This choice may have been influenced by the fear that the government might ask the Monarch to swamp the upper chamber with new peers if the Lords rejected a Commons Bill. But there was no *legal* impediment to the Lords simply blocking government policy.

One might suggest there is an inverse correlation between the conventional power of the Lords and the breadth of the Parliamentary franchise; as more people obtained the right to vote for members of the Commons, so it became more difficult for the Lords to find a 'democratic' justification for obstructing the majority party in the lower house. By 1900 almost all adult men were entitled to vote in elections for members of the House of Commons, and at the same time, the Lords' political role was shifting from *co-equality to complementarity*.

The Lords complemented the Commons by acting as a scrutiniser of Bills, as a forum for debate on issues of general importance, and as an alternative vehicle to bring important questions to the nation's attention. As *The Times* had predicted in 1831, the

7 Smith E *op cit* pp 168–169.
8 *Ibid* ch 9.

Lords' political role was drifting towards one in which it might persuade, but not compel the Commons to forgo factional legislative programmes:

'Among the uses of an Upper Chamber ought to be accounted that of . . . subjecting that which may be but a light or transient caprice, to the test of calm, laborious, and reiterated deliberation.'[9]

Between 1909 and 1911 however, the Lords appeared to reject its new conventional role of complementarity in favour of its traditional legal status of co-equality. And as a result, a constitutional crisis did arise.

Lloyd George and the 'People's Budget'

We have suggested already that a convention cannot be legally enforced. It is effective only for as long as the people supposedly bound by it agree to be bound. By 1909, the Lords was no longer accepting conventional constraints on its formal legal power to veto Bills passed in the Commons. The long-term cause of this problem was the consolidation of the party system within national politics, in which substantial blocs of opinion had developed apparently irreconcilable views around several major issues. An acute political fault line appeared over matters of social and economic policy, which, put simplistically, offers an early example of the dichotomy between green light and red light theories of the state in modern British political history.[10]

In 1906, the House of Commons had 671 members. In the 1906 general election, the Liberals and the smaller parties supporting them won 514 seats. The opposition Conservative and Unionist parties had 157 seats. This gave the government an effective majority of 357. Between 1906 and 1909 the Liberal government tried to introduce a series of quite radical social policy programmes.[11] The Finance Bill of 1909, popularly known as Lloyd George's 'People's Budget', planned to raise taxes to (from a 1909 perspective) quite high levels to pay for a greatly expanded welfare state and enlargement of the navy. From a modern viewpoint, Lloyd George's tax plans seem very modest; for even the wealthiest

9 October 3 1831; quoted in Smith E *op cit* p 118. One could find few better examples of a recipe to counter Madisonian fear of faction in the British context.
10 See chapter 3 above.
11 See generally Hay J (1975) *The Origins of the Liberal Welfare Reforms 1906–1914* (London: MacMillan).

people, income tax would be levied at only 9 pence in the pound. Nevertheless, as Roy Jenkins records, the plans provoked furious Tory opposition:

'It "means the beginning of the end of all rights of property" said Sir Edward Carson. "It is a monument of reckless and improvident finance," said Lord Lansdowne [leader of the Conservative peers]. "It is inquisitorial, tyrannical and socialistic," said Lord Roseberry.'[12]

The opposing views of the 1909 budget neatly encapsulate one difficulty inherent in applying Jeffersonian constitutional principles to the problems of modern government. Sir Edward Carson might, for example, be seen as espousing the wealthy's 'inalienable right' not to have their property taken away by taxation. Lloyd George, in contrast, might plausibly have argued that the substantial Commons majority which the Liberals had won in 1906 made it clear that 'the people' had now consented to a more egalitarian route in their 'pursuit of happiness'.

Given the size of the Liberal majority, one might have thought that convention (as expressed in the Commons' 1678 resolution) demanded that the Lords should not obstruct the Finance Bill. However, the Conservative majority in the Lords persistently refused to pass the Bill. The Lords claimed that its provisions had not been clearly put to the electorate in 1906, and that it was therefore justified by the doctrine of the mandate in requiring the government to call a general election to decide if the citizenry supported Lloyd George's People's Budget.

The Liberal government requested the King to create enough Liberal peers for the government to push the Finance Bill through the Lords. Edward VII was reluctant to do this, and he was supported by Arthur Balfour, the leader of the Conservatives in the Commons. Balfour had urged the Lords' Conservative majority to block the government's Bill. This led Lloyd George to suggest that the Lords was not the 'watchdog of the constitution', but 'Mr Balfour's poodle. It fetches and carries for him. It barks for him. It bites anybody that he sets it on to'.[13] Balfour's position was that it did not matter if the Conservatives could not win a Commons majority, because they could rely on the Lords' veto to prevent the Liberals introducing radical legislation. The Conservatives' upper house majority was almost as substantial as that of the Liberals in the Commons. 354 peers took the Conservative whip,

12 (1968) *op cit* at p 76.
13 Quoted in Butler D and Sloman A (1975) *British Political Facts* p 223 (London: Macmillan).

Table 6.1
House of Lords: historical shifts in party allegiance

	1880	1906	1930	1955	1975	1992
Conservative	280	354	489	507	507	475
Labour			17	55	149	119
Liberal	203	98	79	42	30	58
Crossbench	13	43	140	251	281	263

Sources: Compiled from data in Shell (1992) *op cit* p 67; Adonis (1993) *op cit* p 205; Butler and Sloman (1975) *op cit* p 175.

while fewer than 100 were Liberals, and only 43 claimed to have no party allegiance (the so-called 'cross-benchers').[14]

One might here pause to consider which party was acting 'unconstitutionally'. From a contemporary perspective, we might readily accuse the Conservatives, since the Liberals had won the 1906 general election. The Liberals, we might think, had democracy on their side. But to suggest that the Liberal government and its small party allies represented the mass of the people is misleading. We have already referred to the limited franchise which then existed; over half of the adult population were not allowed to choose their law-makers in 1906. Moreover, as we can see in Table 6.2, only 55% of those voting supported the Liberal bloc; 45% of voters preferred an opposition party. The Liberal position was therefore democratic only in the narrow sense of commanding majority support among a 'people' which was in itself only a minority of the population.

It is plausible to argue (as did Professor Dicey)[15] that it was the Conservative peers who remained true to the traditional constitution. The tripartite, sovereign Parliament was created to preclude enactment of factional legislation. The factionalist label could clearly be attached to the People's Budget. In vetoing a Bill of which a substantial minority of the people apparently disapproved, the Lords was presumably upholding the spirit of the 1688 settlement. The Liberal government proceeded on the assumption that electoral majoritarianism was the constitution's 'ultimate political fact'. For Lloyd George, the peers' intransigence was tantamount to revolution. In a public speech he asked: 'Should 500 men . . . override the judgement – the deliberate judgement – of millions of people who are engaged in the industry which

14 Smith E *op cit* p 157: Jenkins R (1968) *op cit* pp 24–25.
15 *Ibid* p 96.

Table 6.2
The 1906 and 1910 general elections

	Seats (% vote) 1906	Seats (% vote) 1910(1)	Seats (% vote) 1910(2)
Liberal	400 (49.0%)	275 (43.2%)	272 (43.9%)
Labour *	30 (5.9%)	78 (7.6%)	56 (7.1%)
Irish Nat *	83 (0.6%)	82 (1.9%)	84 (2.5%)
Conservative	157 (43.6)	273 (46.9%)	272 (46.3%)
Turnout	82.6%	86.6%	81.1%
Electorate	7,264,608	7,694,741	7,709,981

* Aligned with the Liberals

Source: Extracted from Butler D and Sloman A (1975) *British Political Facts 1900–1975* pp 182–183.

makes the wealth of the country.'[16] Accusing the Lords of 'a breach of the Constitution' in blocking the Finance Bill, Prime Minister Asquith requested a dissolution of Parliament in December 1909.

The general election of January 1910 was fought primarily on the issue of the upper house's power to block measures such as the People's Budget. The Liberals achieved a substantial (albeit reduced) effective majority, and proposed a Parliament Bill greatly reducing the Lords' veto powers. While the Lords subsequently accepted the Finance Bill, it refused to approve a Bill reducing its own legal powers. King Edward VII also appeared hostile to the latter Bill, and equivocated about whether or not he would create the hundreds of new peers needed to outvote the Conservative majority. His successor (as of 6 May 1910) George V seemed equally reluctant to follow the Treaty of Utrecht precedent. The Utrecht affair remained an isolated episode in constitutional history. Its authority as a guide to future events was uncertain. As Jennings subsequently remarked; 'A precedent so old is no precedent'.[17]

Facing such uncertainty, Asquith continued to seek a negotiated settlement with the Lords. A cross-party conference was established to find a solution, but failed to do so. Asquith called another general election for December 1910, squarely on the issue of constitutional reform to curb the power of the Lords. The Liberals won this election as well. In the aftermath of this it seemed that

16 Quoted in Jenkins R (1968) *op cit* p 94.
17 (3rd edn 1959a) *Cabinet Government* p 395 (Cambridge: CUP).

the King had agreed to create enough new peers to force the Bill through both houses.

A moderate grouping of Tory peers had proposed that *the composition, rather than the powers* of the upper house should be reformed.[18] Lord Lansdowne, Tory leader in the Lords, introduced a Bill in May 1911. The Bill proposed an upper house of some 350 members. One-third were to be elected by MPs and one third appointed by the government in proportion to parties' strength in the Commons. The final third was to comprise so-called 'Lords of Parliament', hereditary peers who had previously held important public office. The Bill did not envisage any reduction in the Lords' powers. Lansdowne's initiative was designed to reinforce the Lords' legitimacy as a chamber co-equal to the Commons by reducing the obviously unrepresentative character of its members, and simultaneously increasing their apparent expertise and suitability for a legislative task. The Lords would become a meritocratic rather than an aristocratic assembly, designed to restrain the potentially impetuous wishes of a Commons majority enjoying only factional public support by embodying a national interest owing more to sagacity and public service than wealth and geneology.

The reform proposal was cursorily rebuffed by the government, which maintained that its plans to reduce the Lords' power would remain unchanged irrespective of the upper house's composition. Asquith recognised that Lansdowne's new house would still contain an in-built Conservative majority. Had the Cabinet supported the Bill, it would have run the risk of creating a chamber no less powerful and potentially no less obstructive to Liberal policy than the existing house, but better positioned to defend any such obstruction by pointing to its reformed composition. At this point, a substantial number of moderate peers decided that further resistance to government policy was futile, and the Parliament Bill 1911 was passed in the upper house, albeit by only 17 votes.[19]

The Parliament Act 1911

Asquith had been accused of 'treason' by one of the more intemperate Tory peers for promoting the Parliament Bill.[20] While the

18 Jenkins R (1968) *op cit* pp 139–144, 200–205.
19 This greatly oversimplifies the complexity of the inter- and intra-party manoeuvrings over this issue. Perhaps the most accessible and informative guide is provided by Jenkins R (1968) *op cit*
20 Per Lord Hugh Cecil; see Jenkins R (1968) *op cit* p 251.

1911 Act did indeed introduce several important alterations to the Lords' legal status within the legislative process, such accusations now appear quite hysterical.

The Act introduced three major reforms. The first was that the Lords retained a power of co-equality, or absolute veto, over only delegated legislation and a limited range of Bills: the most important of these being Bills to extend the lifetime of a Parliament.[1] Secondly, the Act also effectively eliminated any Lords' control over 'money bills'. These are basically measures concerned with revenue raising. Whether something is a money Bill is simply resolved – the Speaker issues a certificate for any Bill he thinks concerns a money matter.[2] The third significant change was that the Lords could now only delay all other public Bills for a maximum of two Parliamentary sessions. So the Upper House could slow the Commons down, but it could not stop it entirely. These three changes suggest the Parliament Act 1911 was intended to give legal force both to the 1678 Commons resolution on taxation matters, and to the previous conventional shift during the nineteenth century in the Lords' status from co-equality with the Commons towards complementarity on most other subjects.

We might also note that the preamble to the Act announced that it was intended as an interim measure only, pending more thorough-going reform. This was not forthcoming. The World War I coalition government established the Bryce Commission to explore the question of reform. Its recommendations were not acted upon, but its analysis of the functions a second chamber should perform has attracted widespread support.[3] Bryce identified four main tasks for the Lords: examining and revising Commons Bills; initiating Bills on non-party political subjects; offering a forum for untrammelled debate on major issues; and, more controversially, delaying Bills for sufficient time to allow public sentiment to be made clear.[4] We will shortly assess the degree of success with which the Lords has performed these functions. But before doing so we should focus briefly on a theoretical argument thrown up by the 1911 Act concerning the doctrine of parliamentary sovereignty.

1 The 1911 Act fixed the maximum timespan between elections at five years.
2 Ironically, the first Speaker to perform this task suggested that the Finance Bill 1909 would not have satisfied these criteria; Jenkins R (1968) *op cit* p 272.
3 Shell (1992) *op cit* pp 11–13.
4 *Ibid*; Jenkins R (1968) *op cit* pp 80–282.

A limit on parliamentary sovereignty?

The question is whether the 1911 Act reveals a legal means to bypass parliamentary sovereignty. Could one plausibly suggest that a Bill passed under the Parliament Act procedure would not be a true Act of Parliament – but only delegated legislation, because it has been enacted by an 'inferior' or 'subordinate' Parliament?[5] Before the 1911 Act, Parliament had three constituent parts – the Commons, the Lords, and the Monarch. The Parliament Act creates some situations in which legislation can be produced by a body with only two parts – the Commons and the Monarch. Must a court be automatically obedient to legislation passed under the Parliament Act procedure? Such a statute would not have received the approval of 'Parliament' in the 1688 sense. It would perhaps be analogous to the legislation at issue in *Trethowan* or *Harris*. However, the 1911 Act procedure has rarely been used;[6] we have not yet had anyone going to court asking the judges to disallow any of these Acts. So one can only speculate as to how the courts would respond to such an argument.

The difficulty facing this contention is that unlike the 'higher laws' in *Trethowan* (the Colonial Laws Validity Act 1865) and *Harris* (the South Africa Act 1909), the Parliament Act 1911 has no obviously justiciable substantive or procedural criteria against which to evaluate the legality of legislation produced under its authority, beyond the provision in s 4(1) that the text of any such Act must acknowledge that it was passed under the truncated procedures. It might thus be suggested that the two-limb 'Parliament' (as long as it complies with s 4(1)) is, like its three-limbed creator, a body of unlimited legal competence. We might therefore instinctively say that any legal challenge to legislation passed under the Parliament Act procedures would be successfully countered by the enrolled Bill rule. But this proposition seems logically flawed – can one have two sovereign legislatures within a single state? Any resolution of this particular difficulty would, one assumes, lie in the realm of 'political fact'; but we shall return to the question later in this chapter.

The Salisbury doctrine and the Parliament Act 1949

By 1945, the Lords faced renewed difficulties in reconciling its legal powers with newly dominant values of constitutional morality.

5 See the discussion in Wade (1955) *op cit.*
6 The Welsh Church Disestablishment Act 1915, the Parliament Act 1949 and the War Crimes Act 1991 being the only measures enacted in this way.

The 1945 general election returned a Labour government with a very large Commons majority and a commitment to introduce a comprehensive welfare state and nationalise many private sector industries such as coal, transport and electricity. It was not however clear that the Lords, whose members remained overwhelmingly Conservative, would pass the necessary legislation. The prospect therefore arose that the Lords would exercise its powers under the 1911 Act to delay such Bills for two Parliamentary sessions.

This stance would have been quite legal. Moreover, the Labour party's massive Commons majority had been achieved with only 48% of the popular vote. So one could see, as in 1906, some basis for arguing that the Labour government's radically green light plans did not enjoy universal support. However, from 1930 onwards, the parliamentary electorate had embraced virtually all adult men and women; thus the Commons could plausibly be portrayed as the representative of 'the people' in a comprehensive sense. The upper house, which remained, in contrast, almost entirely an hereditary body, appeared an increasingly anachronistic institution for a 'democratic' society to maintain. This trend was lent added weight during the 1930s and early 1940s by the existence of cross-party coalition governments: the evident convergence of policy objectives for Conservative, Liberal and (most) Labour MPs necessarily meant that there was no obvious opposition faction for Conservative peers to represent, and little scope for the Lords to claim it represented the national interest against a partisan Commons. In one commentator's view, the Lords in 1945 was 'a wasted and powerless assembly. It had long ceased to play any remotely significant role in government'.[7]

In recognition of these changed political circumstances, Conservative peers adopted a new convention concerning their powers under the 1911 Act. The convention, known as the *Salisbury doctrine* (after the fifth Marquess of Salisbury, then leader of the Conservative peers and a descendant of the Lord Salisbury mentioned above),[8] was that the Lords would not even delay any measure in the government's 1945 manifesto.

The inverse correlation between the degree of 'democracy' shaping the composition of the Commons and the conventional extent of the Lords' powers again seems to explain this change. However, one must stress that the Salisbury doctrine structured the Lords' legislative role only while the majority of peers accepted its principles. For the 1945–50 Labour government, the doctrine

7 Adonis (1993) *op cit* p 230.
8 See Shell (1992) *op cit* p 13.

had two flaws. The first was that a Lords' majority for self-restraint could not always be relied upon. The second was a question of time. Because the Lords retained a two session suspensory power, the government could only be sure of getting its legislation through both houses if it began more than two sessions before the end of Parliament's five-year term.

The Labour government found this unacceptably restrictive, so used the 1911 Act procedure to introduce the Parliament Act 1949. This second Parliament Act reduced the Lords' delaying power to only one session. There were some suggestions that this was an 'unconstitutional' piece of legislation, in that the 1911 Act had not been intended to curb the Lords' powers any further. That is certainly an arguable point, but not an obviously strong one in the legal sense.[9]

The 1949 Act concided with a cross-party initiative to produce agreement on reforms to the composition and powers of the Lords. The Bryce recommendations as to the functions of a second chamber were broadly approved; agreement was reached on the principles that this body should be a reformed House of Lords rather than a new institution, and that its composition 'should be such as to secure as far as practicable that a permanent majority is not secured for any one political party'.[10] No significant changes were made, and in the immediate aftermath of the 1949 Parliament Act it appeared that the House of Lords would just fade away. In the mid-1950s, attendance averaged around sixty members. It seemed the upper house would become a quaint and curious historical relic; a tourist attraction without any significant constitutional power. However things did not turn out like that.

II. THE HOUSE OF LORDS IN THE MODERN ERA

A book of this nature cannot paint a comprehensive picture of the organisation and work of the contemporary House of Lords. The upper house has lately been a somewhat neglected field of academic study, but readers seeking a deeper insight might usefully consult Donald Shell's *The House of Lords*. This section examines four episodes in the Lords' recent history: the introduction of life peerages; the proposed 1968 reforms; the Lords' role in the 1974–1979 Parliament; and some aspects of the relationship between the upper house and the Thatcher governments.

9 The foremost proponent of the argument being Wade (1955) *op cit.*
10 Jenkins R (1968) *op cit* pp 281–282.

Life peerages

In the late 1800s, the distinguished constitutional theorist Walter Bagehot had observed that 'with a perfect Lower House it is certain that an Upper House would scarcely be of any value. But... beside the actual House [of Commons] a revising and leisured legislature is extremely useful.'[11] By the mid-1950s it was becoming clear that the House of Commons was getting ever more overloaded, both as a legislator and as a scrutiniser of the executive. We saw in chapter 5 that successive governments have promoted various changes to the Commons' internal workings to try to address this problem. In the 1950s, rather than radically reform the lower house, the Conservative government looked to the Lords to lighten the Commons' burden.

The 1958 Life Peerages Act introduced a new category of member to the second chamber. 'Life peers' were appointed by the Monarch on the advice of the Prime Minister. They were entitled to sit, speak and vote in the upper house, but could not pass on their titles when they died. Life Peers have generally been people who made distinguished contributions to public life. Many are former MPs, but one also has trade unionists, military personnel, businessmen and women, and a smaller number from the arts or universities.[12] The new class of peer meant that the upper chamber was better equipped to perform its complementary function. The infusion of life peers with broad expertise and experience enabled the Lords to counter criticism that it was just peopled by elderly landowners who could not make an informed contribution to the legislative and governmental process. It would not be accurate to suggest that the characteristics of life peers mirror those of the general population – but neither of course do those of MPs,[13] and it cannot be denied that a life peerage does offer some prospect of legislative or governmental influence to citizens for whom party politics have been only a peripheral concern.

Proposals to create life peers from the ranks of eminent commoners had been made periodically from the mid-nineteenth century. Queen Victoria and her husband, Prince Albert, allegedly favoured a continental style 'Assembly of Notables' of distin-

11 Quoted in Griffith and Ryle *op cit* p 455.
12 Shell notes that of 601 life peers created between 1958 and 1991 204 were formerly MPs, 86 businessmen/women, 26 trade unionists, 65 academics, 35 local councillors, 19 civil servants, 9 military personnel, 30 lawyers, 11 doctors, 15 journalists, and 50 other types of public servant (1992) *op cit* p 40.
13 On which point see Adonis (1993) *op cit* ch 3; Silk *op cit* ch 2.

guished public servants, artists, scientists, and philosophers as well as hereditary peers.[14] A life peer, Baron Wensleydale, had been created in 1855, but this had provoked substantial upper house opposition, and the peerage was promptly turned into an hereditary title.[15] In part, such opposition rested on a simple fear of a dilution of aristocratic influence; its more principled ground was a concern that the Monarch could be more easily persuaded to create large numbers of non-hereditary peers, thereby affording radical governments the opportunity to swamp the upper house. Some inroads were made into this principle by the Appellate Jurisdiction Act 1876, which gave life peerages to some senior judges (the 'Law Lords').

The shift by 1911 in the Lords' role from co-equality with the Commons to complementarity weakened such arguments. As expertise and ability became increasingly important requirements for the second chamber, so the intellectual shortcomings of hereditary peers caused greater dissatisfaction, and the pressure for adding appointed members intensified. Such pressures were not sufficiently acute to merit an immediate response, but had become so by the late 1950s. The 1958 Act enjoyed some cross-party support, and was designed to strengthen the Lords' complementary relationship with the Commons. Complementarity was not viewed solely as a matter of doing some of the Commons' work. Viscount Samuel, 87 years old and a minister in Asquith's 1911 government, attributed the need for reform to the entrenchment of party politics in the Commons. While regarding parties as a necessity, he feared that the rigidity of party discipline had produced: 'a considerable crushing of the independent mind' thereby excluding from the legislature 'men and women who might be of the greatest value to the community, but who have not the time or the temperament . . . to face the turmoil and the preoccupations of strenuous Parliamentary life'.[16]

There is some irony in the fact that it was the acceptance by successive Labour and Conservative post-war governments of the need for extensive state intervention in social and economic affairs – which necessarily required greater amounts of legislative attention both in formulating policies and scrutinising their implementation – which offered an important role for a mildly reformed

14 Smith *op cit* pp 30–33; Turbeville *op cit* p 366.
15 See Anderson O (1967) 'The Wensleydale peerage case and the position of the House of Lords in the mid-nineteenth century' *English Historical Review* 486–502.
16 Quoted in Weare V (1964) 'The House of Lords – prophecy and fulfilment' *Parliamentary Affairs* 422–433.

second chamber, for it was just such a green light ethos against which the Lords had so vigorously campaigned between 1909 and 1911.

Quite how effective life peers have been in equipping the Lords to perform its complementary functions is considered below. We might conclude this section by making a simple party political point. Many life peers have relatively modest financial means, and so have reduced the average wealth of the upper house. Nevertheless, in 1990, 44 peers featured in the list of Britain's two hundred wealthiest residents, over 300 members were directors of several companies, and 136 held senior positions in the financial services industries.[17] Moreover, life peers remain very much in the minority within the Lords. Even by 1990 they comprised barely one-third of the upper chamber's membership.[18] Consequently, they have made only a limited impact on the Conservative majority, given the Conservative predispositions of most hereditary members. As we see in Table 6.3, Labour Prime Ministers have made substantial efforts to increase non-Conservative representation, but among Conservative governments, only the Macmillan and Home administrations have followed suit. Barely a quarter of the peers created by the Thatcher governments took either the Labour or Liberal whip,[19] and since cross-benchers vote predominantly for Conservative policies,[20] it is difficult to avoid the conclusion that the introduction of life peers has led the Lords some way towards the situation advocated by Lord Lansdowne, and feared by Asquith, in 1911 – namely a Conservative house which may invoke its more expert members as at least a partial justification for obstructing Labour government policy. Appointment of peers remains a non-justiciable issue, although a 'political honours committee', currently comprising three privy councillors, plays a limited role in ensuring that the Prime Minister's nominees are not entirely unsuitable.[1]

The 1968 reforms

The policies pursued by Harold Wilson's 1966–1970 Labour government were intended to 'modernise' the economic, social

---

17 Shell (1992) *op cit* p 45.
18 In July 1992, the house had 1205 members. 26 were clerics, 20 were Law Lords, 382 were life peers. 777 were hereditary peers: see Adonis (1993) *op cit* p 194.
19 Adonis (1993) *op cit* pp 232–233.
20 Shell (1992) *op cit* pp 91–92.
  1 *Ibid* p 39.

Table 6.3
Party allegiance of Life Peers created between 1958 and 1991

Prime Minister	Period	C	L	Lib	CB	Total	Hereditary Peers *
Macmillan and Home	1958–64	17	29	1	18	65	870
Wilson	1964–70	11	78	6	46	141	850
Heath	1970–74	23	5	3	15	46	820
Wilson and Callaghan	1974–79	17	82	6	34	139	805
Thatcher	1979–90	99	45	10	45	199	780
Major	1990	6	5	1	1	13	777

Key: C = Conservative: L = Labour: Lib = Liberal/SDP: CB = Cross-bench. Figures for hereditary peers are approximate only.

Source: Compiled from data in Shell (1992) *op cit* table 2.2: Griffiths and Ryle *op cit* p 457: Adonis (1993) *op cit* p 194.

and political fabric of British society. Such modernisation was often expressed in institutional reform, such as the creation of the Law Commission in 1965, the introduction of comprehensive schooling and the substantial expansion in university provision, the reorganisation of local government in London, and the emergence of the National Economic Development Council to encourage co-operation between government, trade unions and employers.[2] Wilson's initiatives were less successful in respect of Parliament itself. As we saw in chapter 5, an attempt was made to establish Commons select committees, but Richard Crossman's efforts made little impact. Reform of the Lords promised to be a more fruitful endeavour.

Shortly before the 1964 general election, Wilson warned the upper house that if it delayed government Bills 'we shall seek a mandate to amend the Parliament Act so as to end the Lords' power to block Commons legislation.'[3] We have already seen that the Tory peers had adopted a convention which made such obstruction unlikely. However, shortly after the 1964 election, the Lords initially offered strenuous resistance to the War Damage Act, which, as noted in chapter 4, retrospectively reversed the *Burmah Oil* judgment on the extent of the Crown's war-time

2 For a brief overview of this period see Gamble A (1981) *Britain in Decline* ch 4 (London: Papermac).
3 Quoted in Weare *op cit* p 432.

prerogative power to destroy a citizen's property. A Lords' amendment removed the Bill's retrospective element, but this was promptly reversed by the Commons, whereupon the Marquess of Salisbury, defending the convention bearing his name, persuaded peers to allow the Bill to proceed.[4] The Act provides an interesting example of a dispute between the Lords and Commons which did not have a simple party political basis, since the Bill enjoyed cross-party Commons support. Given the Act's incompatibility with most perceptions of the rule of law, the Lords' stance might be thought consistent with the role of 'watchdog of the constitution'. Equally important, however, is the indication the controversy gives of the Lords' impotence when opposing policies supported by Conservatives in the Commons.

The episode may have strengthened the government's resolve to maintain a bipartisan approach to reform, for it established an All Party Committee to consider the future of the upper house. The committee's main innovation was to recommend dividing the members of the Lords into two categories – voting and non-voting peers. Only life peers would be entitled to vote. The monarch could bestow life peerages on hereditary Lords, but they would have to give up their titles to vote in the new house.

The bipartisan approach collapsed in June 1967, when the Lords used for the first time the power left to them by the 1949 Parliament Act to veto delegated legislation.[5] In November 1967 the Labour government produced a White Paper, *House of Lords Reform*. The continuity in this area of constitutional development is well illustrated by the close correspondence between the White Paper's view of the Lords' appropriate legislative role, and that of the Bryce Commission 50 years earlier. The second chamber should serve as a forum for public debate; as a reviser of Bills introduced in the Commons; as an initiator of Bills on less party politicised issues; and as a scrutiniser of the executive and of delegated legislation.

The White Paper's proposals closely resembled the ideas of the All Party Committee, and were enthusiatically endorsed by the Lords. However the Bill introducing the proposals encountered substantial Commons opposition. Right wing Conservatives attacked it for going too far, while Labour's left wing thought that it did not go far enough.[6] The government subsequently withdrew

4 See Jackson P (1965) 'War Damage Act 1965' *Modern Law Review* 574–576.
5 The issue being an Order in Council imposing economic sanctions against Rhodesia. A second order was approved shortly thereafter.
6 Shell (1992) *op cit* pp 21–23.

the Bill in 1969. Since then there have not been any attempts to pass legislation to alter the upper house's powers or composition. This should not lead us to conclude, however, that Lords has not been the cause of appreciable constitutional controversy since that time. In this regard, the 1974–1979 period is illuminating.

The 1974–1979 Parliament

Between 1974 and 1979, Britain had a Labour government which never had a majority of more than four in the Commons. Consequently, the government found it very difficult even to get Bills through the lower house. It faced even more difficulties in the Lords. As Table 6.4 shows, these Labour governments enjoyed only minoritarian support in terms of the share of the vote they won at the two general elections of that year. Furthermore, the government suffered a series of by-election defeats and defections in the course of the Parliament, which temporarily left it in a Commons minority.

For a brief period after 1977, the Labour and Liberal parties formed a 'pact', in which the Liberals guaranteed their support in return for some policy concessions. This might be argued to have enhanced the government's legitimacy (in a crude majoritarian sense), insofar as the parties' combined share of the vote at the last general election exceeded 50%. However the pact had not been part of either party's manifesto, and there is no way of knowing how any such proposal might have affected voter behaviour. Despite its rather weak parliamentary and electoral position, the 1974–1979 government was committed to pursuing radical economic policies. This combination of a clearly factional legislative programme by a government with a precarious Commons majority and limited popular support presented the upper

Table 6.4
The 1974 general elections – seats won and share of vote

	February	October
Labour	301 (37.1%)	319 (39.2%)
Liberal	14 (19.3%)	13 (18.3%)
Conservative	297 (37.9%)	277 (35.8%)
Others	23 (5.7%)	26 (6.7%)

Source: Extracted from Butler and Sloman *op cit* p 186.

Table 6.5
Government defeats in the Lords 1964–1986*

Period	Governing party	Number of defeats
1964–70	Labour	116
1970–74	Conservative	26
1974–79	Labour	355
1979–1986	Conservative	100

Source: Brazier R (1990) *Constitutional Texts* p 527 (Oxford: OUP).
*Reproduced with the permission of OUP.

house with several difficult questions as to its 'correct' constitutional role.

During the 1959–1964 Parliament, when the Conservatives were in government, there were 299 votes or divisions in the Lords. The government was defeated on 11 occasions – 3.7% of the time. Between 1974 and 1979, the Lords had 445 divisions. The Labour government was defeated on 355 occasions – 80% of the time.

Such bald statistics obviously support arguments that the Lords effectively continued to be a Conservative chamber. However we ought to qualify those figures a little. In almost all cases between 1974 and 1979 the Lords gave way if the Commons sent the Bill back. So the government's policies were not being vetoed (a power which the Lords no longer possessed), nor even being delayed for the full period permitted by the 1949 Act. Nevertheless, they were being obstructed. Passing legislation is a protracted process, and as noted in chapter 5, the Commons only has limited time for this task. By constantly refusing to approve the government's measures, and requiring the Commons to discuss and vote on issues again, the Lords was able to impede government policy to a significant extent. Whether or not it was constitutionally acceptable for the Lords to do so raises a difficult question, which we might try to answer by briefly considering two of the measures on which the upper and lower houses were unable to agree.

The Trade Union and Labour Relations (Amendment) Bill and the Aircraft and Shipbuilding Industries Bill[7]

The first of these two Bills was intended to amend the Trade Union and Labour Relations Act 1974, which, because of the government's weak Commons position, had been subjected to

---

7 For a concise but detailed study see Burton I and Drewry G (1978) 'Public legislation: a survey of the sessions of 1975/76 and 1976/77' *Parliamentary Affairs* 140–162.

several opposition amendments. The Act had been primarily concerned with regulating compulsory trade union membership (the
'closed shop') in the workplace; the amending Bill was intended
to restrict the circumstances in which employees could legitimately
refuse to join a union without risking dismissal from their jobs.

The substantive issue seized upon by Conservative and cross-
bench peers was their wish to provide additional safeguards for
newspaper editors whose freedom of expression was thought to
be jeopardised if they had to be members of a trade union. The
government proposed a 'Charter' safeguarding editorial independence, but declined to give it legal force. A Lords' amendment
to make the Charter enforceable in the courts was passed, reversed
in the Commons, but then insisted upon by the Lords. Amid
government threats both of a mass creation of peers and of resort
to the Parliament Acts, the government's position was eventually
accepted by a Lords' majority of 37.

The controversy over the Aircraft and Shipbuilding Industries
Bill, intended to bring these industries into public ownership, was
equally intense. The substantive merits of nationalising private
companies were then an acute source of disagreement between
the Conservative and Labour parties. In respect of this measure,
that substantive controversy was exacerbated by procedural factors.
The Bill's Commons passage, where it was substantially amended,
provoked furious controversy. Opposition MPs suggested the Bill
was hybrid. The government made frequent resort to the guillotine to curtail debate on this and other questions, and on one
occasion a government whip was accused of deliberately breaking
a pairing agreement in a division which the government won on
the Speaker's casting vote.[8] Conservative peers, joined by cross-
benchers and some Labour members, insisted upon several wrecking amendments. The government then initiated the Parliament
Act procedures, but following consultation with the opposition, a
much amended Bill was passed some months later.

The constitutionality of the Lords' behaviour on these occasions
is debatable. Both measures had been included in the Labour
party's 1974 election manifesto, and so were nominally within the
ambit of the Salisbury convention. Yet both were highly contentious matters, for which there were only the barest of Commons
majorities, which had passed the lower house amidst widespread
accusations of procedural impropriety and a collapse of the usual

8 This being the celebrated occasion when Michael Heseltine is reputed, inaccur-
ately, to have seized the Speaker's Mace and advanced, in a threatening manner,
towards the government benches.

channels. Lord Carrington, then leader of the Conservative peers, saw no legal shortcomings in the Lords' position. The Lords was invoking its powers: 'for the purpose for which they were given to us – that is as an opportunity for further consultation, for second thoughts.'[9]

Again, however, we are drawn to the impact of convention in undermining the legitimacy of an undoubtedly legal course of action. Donald Shell has suggested that the Lords committed a serious tactical blunder in the 30 years following World War II by adopting the conventional practice of appearing unwilling to use its delaying powers except in respect of government Bills whose contents had not been put to the electorate. Shell argues that this lent an unwarranted degree of constitutional significance to the delaying power, which had been envisaged by the framers of the 1911 and 1949 Parliaments as a routine, rather than wholly exceptional part of the legislative process. It was precisely because this power had become *delegitimised through disuse* that the events of 1976 and 1977 provoked such a constitutional furore.[10]

Given the great intensity of the political divide between the Labour and Conservative parties in the late 1970s, it is not surprising that the experience of the 1974–79 Parliament led the Labour party to pledge to abolish the House of Lords altogether if it managed to win a general election. It did not succeed at the polls however, and subsequent Conservative governments have displayed no inclination formally to amend the status quo. Yet one would be mistaken in assuming that the relationship between the upper house and the Thatcher governments was unproblematic.

The House of Lords and the Thatcher governments[11]

As we shall see in chapter 9, the Thatcher governments of 1979–1990 assumed office, as did Asquith's Liberals in 1906, and Attlee's Labour party in 1945, committed to implementing a radical policy agenda which would overturn many existing understandings of the appropriate role of government in contemporary society. Furthermore, just like Asquith's and Attlee's adminis-

9 Quoted in Adonis (1993) *op cit* p 227.
10 Shell (1992) *op cit* pp 246–253.
11 See particularly Shell D (1985) 'The House of Lords and the Thatcher government' *Parliamentary Affairs* 16–32; Adonis A (1988) 'The House of Lords in the 1980s' *Parliamentary Affairs* 380–401.

Table 6.6
The 1979, 1983 and 1987 elections – seats won and share of vote

	1979	1983	1987
Conservative	339 (43.1)	397 (42.4)	376 (42.3)
Labour	269 (36.9)	209 (27.6)	292 (30.8)
Liberal *	11 (13.8)	23 (25.4)	22 (22.6)

* 1983 and 1987 includes the SDP.

Source: Extracted from data in Norton P (1991) *The British Polity* pp 97–99 (London: Longman).

trations, the Thatcher governments enjoyed substantial Commons majorities gained with less than 50% electoral support.

Shell records that the Thatcher administrations were defeated 155 times in the Lords between 1979 and 1990. Some 63 of these were accepted by the government, and on 30 occasions a compromise was reached; the remaining defeats were reversed in the Commons.[12] As the decade progressed, the government became increasingly unwilling to accommodate their Lordships' opinions, with the result that Conservative MPs experienced (to a minor degree) the inconveniences engendered by the need to be present in the Commons to vote to reverse Lords amendments.

The reasons for the ostensibly surprising frequency of conflict between the Lords and Commons in this era are difficult to quantify precisely. One contributory explanation may be that Conservatives in the Commons had become significantly more right wing in their political beliefs than the Conservative peers; such differences of opinion were clearly evident in respect of criminal justice legislation in the early 1980s. Another factor may have been the profound disarray among the Labour, Liberal and Social Democrat parties in the Commons, which perhaps convinced some peers that they were the only people capable of providing any effective Parliamentary opposition to Thatcherite policies. In addition, the Thatcher government apparently took some time to realise that many Conservative peers were not as susceptible to unquestioning party obedience as their Commons counterparts; their loyalty and approval had to be won in rather more subtle ways.

The most acute cause of tension between the Thatcher government and the Lords arose over differences in opinion as to the appropriate constitutional role of local government. We will con-

12 See generally Shell (1992) *op cit* ch 7.

sider the philosophical roots of this disagreement in detail in chapter 11; here we might just briefly note its practical impact within the legislative process. The government suffered temporary defeats on several minor issues, such as an attempt to abolish free bus passes for schoolchildren in rural areas, and a clause in the 1985 Housing Bill which sought to force local authorities and housing associations to sell special sheltered accommodation for the elderly to the sitting tenants. Of far greater significance were the reversals the Lords inflicted on government plans to reform the structure of local government in 1985, and the system of local taxation in 1987 and 1988.[13]

Backwoodsmen – the voting house and the working house

The government's eventual success on the latter issues required it to draw on the so-called 'backwoodsmen' within the Lords. Backwoodsmen are hereditary Tory peers who take no real part in the life of the house – they very rarely attend and almost never contribute to debates. They are however occasionally prepared to turn up at the house to vote when it seems likely a Conservative government would be defeated on a major issue. No such resource is ever available to a Labour government, but backwoodsmen are a weapon of last resort even for a Conservative government in serious parliamentary difficulties. Because these peers are so disinterested in the day-to-day responsibilities of legislative activity, they are not very responsive to the government whip. Two or three calls in any Parliamentary session would seem the most that a Conservative government could rely on.

For many observers, even one call is one too many. Since the Lords' continued legitimacy has depended upon its members gaining a reputation for independent thought and expert abilities, the rapid influx of peers who have never demonstrated any legislative skills, and who are clearly acting under party orders, does little to enhance either the dignity or the authority of the house.

The problem of backwoodsmen has led to the suggestion that we can draw a distinction between the 'working house' and the 'voting house'.[14] In the 1980s, the working house – those peers who attend regularly and contribute to debate – was fairly evenly divided between government and the opposition. This can create the impression that the Lords could be as powerful an obstacle

13 See generally Welfare D (1992) 'The Lords in defence of local government' *Parliamentary Affairs* 205–219 and chapter 11 below.
14 Adonis (1988) *op cit*; (1993) *op cit* pp 198–199; Griffith and Ryle *op cit.* pp 465–466.

to a Conservative government as to a Labour administration. However the voting house, which includes the backwoodsmen, is so heavily Conservative that government policies were not seriously threatened.[15] This can lead to the apparently unsatisfactory circumstance in which Lords' debates suggest that majority sentiment opposes the government, only for the non-working Lords to appear and toe the party line when the vote is held.

The backwoodsmen problem would have disappeared had the 1968 reforms been enacted. It would no doubt be a simple matter for a determined goverment with a reliable Commons majority to push through a third Parliament Act to achieve that objective. A rather more difficult question, to which the final section of this chapter is directed, is how effectively the 'working house' does the work which has been assigned it:

III. THE WORK OF THE HOUSE OF LORDS TODAY

Most commentators agree that the Lords has become a more important element of the government process in the past 20 years. Adonis speaks of a 'remarkable revival'; Shell of a 'much better attended and a partly professional House'.[16] As Table 6.7 indicates, the amount of time which the Lords devotes to its tasks has increased markedly since 1950. The House has climbed out of the legislative gutter into which it had sunk by the mid-1950s. In assessing how high it has since climbed, this final section centres on four areas in which the Lords might play an obviously complementary role to the Commons, areas canvassed in the Bryce Report and/or the 1967 White Paper: deliberation on matters of public concern; revision and initiation of legislation; consideration of delegated legislation; and scrutiny of the executive.

At the outset, we might note several characteristics of the Lords which distinguish it from the Commons. Perhaps most significant is its less structured party discipline. In part this results from the non-elected nature of peers, which frees them from any need to cater to the prejudices of their local constituency association. It also accrues from their age and backgrounds; for peers at the end of their careers or with substantial extra-parliamentary interests 'the bait of Ministerial office dangled so effectively in the Com-

---

15 See particularly Adonis' demolition of the claim made by Lord Denham, government chief whip, that 'However you calculate it, the Conservative party has no overall majority in your Lordship's House'; (1988) *op cit* pp 381–382.
16 (1993) *op cit* p 226; (1992) *op cit* p 28.

Table 6.7
House of Lords: sitting hours and attendance 1950–1985

Session	Sitting days	Sitting hours	Average Attendance
1950–1951	96	292	86
1959–1960	113	450	136
1970–1971	153	966	265
1981–1982	147	930	284
1989–1990	147	1072	318

Source: Compiled from data in Griffith and Ryle *op cit* p 472; Shell (1992) *op cit* p 125; Silk *op cit* p 18.

mons is missing'.[17] The major parties maintain formal organisations within the house, for which they receive limited public funds, and also have a whipping system, albeit of an exhortatory rather than, as in the Commons, directory nature. A peer's behaviour must be quite egregious before he/she suffers withdrawal of the whip.[18]

The Lords has also preserved a more negotiatory approach to timetabling its business than the Commons. Government business has no formal priority; that it enjoys that status de facto is the result of the maintenance of conciliatory relations between the parties and cross-benchers through the upper house's variant of the 'usual channels'.

The more loosely disciplined nature of the Lords is further evidenced by the absence of a Speaker with coercive powers over procedure. The Lord Chancellor presides over the House in a formal sense, but regulation of peers' behaviour is a matter for the peers themselves. The chamber is 'guided' on such matters by the Leader of the House. The Lords has on several occasions considered the desirability of creating a Speaker, but has always rejected it, relying instead on members' good manners to maintain decorous standards. The upper house has thus avoided the need for the radical procedural reform adopted by the Commons in the late nineteenth century in response to the disruptive tactics of Irish MPs. The consensual conduct of Lords' business is exemplified by the fact that although the Leader of the House is also the Leader of the government in the Lords, it has never seriously been suggested that he/she has compromised the house's interests to further party political objectives.

17 Griffith and Ryle *op cit* p 510.
18 For examples see Shell (1992) *op cit* pp 93–94.

Deliberation

It is often said that debates on matters of general public concern in the Lords are of a higher quality than in the Commons. This is partly because many members have considerable expertise in particular areas, and partly because party loyalty is not as unswerving as in the Commons. As Griffith and Ryle suggest: 'such subjective judgements are impossible either to prove or to refute'.[19] One can undoubtedly point to debates on major issues where the speakers have brought a formidable body of knowledge and experience to bear on the issue concerned; reform of the legal profession, the administration of justice, and foreign and commonwealth relations are areas where the upper house possesses considerable expertise.[20]

The quality of debate, in the sense of its capacity fully to explore the substance of the issue in question, rather than simply advance a partisan response, is aided by the more muted nature of party politics and the more relaxed procedural régime. However, if one construes the 'quality' of debate in terms of its influence on subsequent policy, the Lords' success is far more difficult to quantify. Somewhat bluntly, Adonis concludes that Lords' debates 'rarely have an impact on policy which is more than minor and indirect'; while Shell maintains that: 'Almost everyone involved with the House acknowledges that a great deal of what is said there is worthless'.[1]

Less cynically, one might suggest that as a deliberative chamber the Lords is intended to function more as a sounding board than as crucial contributor to the formation of policy over the full range of government activities. Debate in the upper house seems to have significant influence only in areas where the Lords combines expertise with personal interests in matters which are fairly non-contentious in the party political sense, such as legal reform, issues concerning the elderly, and policies affecting agriculture and the countryside. The percentage of the Lords' (admittedly growing) overall workload devoted to deliberative activities has also declined markedly in the past 15 years. While over 30% of their Lordships' time was spent on general debate in 1979, barely 14% was so used in 1988.[2] This could be construed as an indication that Parliament has become less enamoured of its reflective role

19 *Op cit* p 497.
20 Shell (1992) *op cit* pp 188–194: Adonis (1993) *op cit* p 194.
 1 Adonis (1993) *op cit* p 216; Shell (1992) *op cit* p 198.
 2 Griffith and Ryle *op cit* p 473.

in recent years, but it may also be due to rather more practical pressures.

Revision of legislation

The reduction in the percentage of Lords' time spent on general debate has been more than matched by an increase in attention devoted to its purely legislative role. By the late 1980s, some 60% of the house's sitting hours were consumed by the revision of legislation, the overwhelming majority of which originated in the Commons.[3] We have already considered the (now limited) circumstances in which the Lords might either reject a Bill or pass a wrecking amendment. In quantitative terms, however, the Lords' revisionary role is primarily concerned with constructive rather than destructive amendment.

The lower profile of party loyalty and greater procedural flexibility in the Lords supposedly enables the upper house to do a better job of revising proposed legislation than the Commons. Peers are assumed to be less firmly wedded to party ideology, and so more willing to accept that Bills may contain technical flaws or practical problems. The presence of a substantial number of cross-bench peers reinforces this assumption. Relatedly, the growing breadth of experience and expertise among life peers makes it most unlikely that the upper house will be unable to muster an informed audience for even the most esoteric of government legislative proposals.

Superficially, a Bill's passage through the Lords mirrors that in the Commons. There are however certain important differences. In the absence of a Speaker, for example, it is for the house itself to decide whether proposed amendments will be discussed. Neither does the house have a guillotine procedure: rather it relies (apparently with considerable success) on individual peers themselves to ensure that their spoken contributions are pertinent and concise.

Perhaps more importantly, the Lords lacks a standing committee structure: the committee stage is taken on the floor of the house and is presided over by the Chairman of Committees, a salaried post, to which a peer is appointed by the house at the beginning of each parliamentary session. During this period, the Chairman must detach her/himself from any party politial activities.

The committee stage has latterly accounted for almost half of

3 *Ibid*, p 473.

the time the upper chamber has given to its legislative functions.[4] The Lords has conducted sporadic experiments with standing committees in the past 30 years, but none have been regarded as a success.[5] In 1993/94, the Lords made a further effort in this regard, by considering five relatively uncontroversial Bills under the so-called 'Jellicoe procedure'. As yet, one cannot predict how successful this strategy might be. The pressure on time is further increased, almost comically, by the physical process of walking through division lobbies whenever a vote on an amendment is taken: 40 hours were spent simply on voting in the 1985–1986 session.[6]

Whether the house can maintain this structure in the longer term is questionable, for it seems at present that the Lords' amending role is continuing to increase. Table 6.7 charts the apparently substantial growth in the Lords' activities. One should beware of reading too much into workload statistics, for crude figures often conceal vast variations in the complexity or importance of nominally equivalent subject matter. Many amendments, for example, may be introduced at the government's request, to remedy defects which escaped the Commons' attention. While this may frequently be a valuable function for the upper house to fulfil, it does raise the danger of the Lords becoming a convenient dumping ground for dealing with the minutiae of the legislative process which the Commons is unwilling to address.[7] A related problem is the government's recurring failure to spread the Lords' legislative load evenly through the Parliamentary session, with the result that the upper house faces impossibly onerous tasks which cannot be discharged in any meaningful way.[8]

Given the Conservative majority in the Lords, it is safe to conclude that many of the amendments carried against government wishes during the 1980s were not motivated by simple party political bias. Yet as Adonis observes: 'On not a single occasion since 1979 has the Lords insisted on one of its amendments once overturned by the Commons'.[9] A Lords' amendment against the government may be significant when the government has only a small Commons majority, for the reasoning behind the Lords'

---

4 Griffith and Ryle *op cit* p 483.
5 Shell (1992) *op cit* pp 140–142; Borthwick R (1973) 'Public Bill Committees in the House of Lords' *Parliamentary Affairs* 440–453.
6 Adonis (1993) *op cit* p 241.
7 Adonis (1993) *op cit* pp 240–242.
8 The problem has been posed by governments of both parties; see Shell (1992) *op cit* pp 139–141; Burton and Drewry *op cit.*
9 (1993) *op cit* p 237.

Table 6.8
Lords Amendments to Government Bills 1970–1990*

Period	Bills	Bills amended	Total amendments
1970–1973	79	31	2366
1974–1977	68	49	1859
1979–1982	82	39	2231
1983–1986	69	43	4137
1987–1990	61	38	5181

Source: Shell D (1992) *The House of Lords* p 144 (Hemel Hempstead: Harvester Wheatsheaf).
*Reproduced with the permission of Harvester Wheatsheaf.

decision might persuade wavering backbench MPs not to follow the party line. But when faced with a cohesive Conservative majority in the lower house, the Lords currently resembles a constitutional watchdog which has long been deprived of any significant bite, and is only rarely willing to bark.

The one notable recent exception to this trend was the Lords' refusal to pass the War Crimes Bill. This Bill was intended to impose retrospective criminal liability for war crimes committed in World War II by foreign nationals who had subsequently become British citizens. The Bill received clear cross-party support in the Commons. However a similarly cross-party consensus in the Lords rejected it for what would appear to be, *pace* the War Damage Act, 'rule of law' type reasons – namely opposition in principle to retrospective legislation, and a belief that in practice it would be impossible to provide a fair trial to the accused.[10]

The Lords' behaviour prompted even some Conservative MPs to question the undesirability of a non-elected chamber frustrating the elected house, but predictions of a constitutional crisis when the government used the Parliament Acts procedure to send the Bill for the Royal Assent proved unfounded. It may be that anyone who is prosecuted will present the courts with the interesting constitutional question we considered earlier; namely whether all 'Acts' passed by the two-part Parliament are merely delegated legislation, and that this particular measure is ultra vires the powers that the three-part Parliament granted in 1911.

The upper house also inflicted a series of defeats on the Major government's Criminal Justice Bill in 1994, relating to matters of sentencing policy and the conduct of criminal trials. Most of the defeats were subsequently reversed in the Commons, but the

10 See Richardson (1995) *op cit.*

government made several concessions to the upper house.[11] The Bill had been announced as a major plank of government policy by Home Secretary Michael Howard at the 1993 Conservative Party Conference. The Lords' intransigence might thus be seen either as an unacceptable barrier to the wishes of an elected government, or, alternatively, as an entirely prudent means to ensure that important legislation was not unduly influenced by unacceptably partisan objectives.

The Lords' greater procedural flexibility also extends to the introduction of private member's Bills, although any such Bill successfully introduced in the upper house is to some extent at the mercy of the government, since passage through the Commons may depend on the allocation of government time in the lower house. In contrast, Bills which successfully proceed through the Commons are invariably (and rapidly) approved in the Lords.[12] Bills introduced in the Lords frequently perform a 'pathfinding' or 'trail-blazing' role, in which proposals for reform in controversial (but largely non-party political) matters are aired, with a view both to testing and perhaps moulding public opinion, in the hope that an initial failure will nevertheless weaken resistance to future reform. Issues such as the decriminalisation of homosexuality, the liberalisation of laws controlling abortion, and a tightening of the statutory framework regulating animal experimentation provide good examples of this episodic, incremental approach to social policy.[13]

Control of delegated legislation

The Lords retains co-equal status with the Commons in respect of private Bills, although this is perhaps insufficiently important a topic to merit attention here. A far more significant issue is the Lords' continued co-equality in respect of statutory instruments. Given the much greater resort made to such measures by modern governments, and the obvious shortcomings of the Commons in monitoring their use, one might have expected this to be an area in which the upper house might function as a meaningful curb on government excesses. The formal parity between the two houses is emphasised by their equality of representation on the joint select

11 Travis A (1994) 'Howard package left limping by Lords onslaught' *The Guardian* 19 July.
12 See Shell (1992) *op cit* pp 151–156.
13 *Ibid.*

committee which examines the technical propriety of such measures.

In respect of the substantive policy merits of delegated legislation, however, we can once again discern a large gap between the Lords' legal and conventional authority. The Lords has only once vetoed an order, that being the aforementioned sanctions order against Rhodesia in 1967. By the mid-1980s, it appeared widely accepted that a repeat of such behaviour would breach convention.[14] It may be that the Lords' reticence springs from a fear that exercising its veto would simply lead to a third Parliament Act removing their legal co-equality, but quite what purpose is served by possessing a legal power one will never use is unclear. Shell points to the 1967 Labour government's decision not to present an instrument designating Stansted as London's third major airport as a response to obvious opposition in the Lords as an example of an upper house 'pre-emptive strike', but it is hard to place any precedential value on such an event. This is perhaps another situation in which the Lords' legal powers have been delegitimised through disuse.

The house has fashioned several devices through which it can express disapproval of government proposals without rejecting them. Motions signalling disagreement with or regret at an instrument may be moved and voted upon. Such devices may prove an embarrassment to the government, especially if they attract press publicity, but their value would appear to be more a symbolic affirmation of the Lords' independence than a practical constraint on executive action.

Scrutiny of the executive

As Bagehot observed, there would be little need for upper house scrutiny of executive behaviour if the Commons adequately performed that task itself. But as we saw in chapter 5, the intensity of party discipline and paucity of investigatory resources in the lower house places stringent restrictions on the effectiveness of MPs' supervisory capacities. Consequently, there is appreciable scope for the Lords to complement and reinforce the Commons in this respect.

Like the Commons, however, the Lords' scrutinising role is subject to resource constraints. These arise not simply, as in the Commons, from the limited office space and research assistance

14 Shell (1992) *op cit* p 219.

financed by the government, but also from more structural institutional sources. While it was commonplace for as many ministers to sit in the Lords as in the Commons in the nineteenth century, almost all ministers are now members of the lower house. Although modern Conservative governments have included a handful of senior ministers from the Lords, it is likely (especially for a Labour government) that the Lord Chancellor and Leader of the house will be the Lords' only two Cabinet ministers. This poses obvious problems of accountability, simply because the politician responsible for the activities of most government departments is never present in the chamber. Occasional suggestions have been floated that all senior ministers should be entitled to speak in either house, but none has been adopted.

The government's limited representation in the house also poses problems of competence. The practice which has consequently evolved is for politicians of sometimes limited experience to assume quite substantial and wide-ranging departmental responsibilities, at a very early stage of their careers. Use is also made of 'Lords in Waiting', junior peers who are given responsibility as government spokesmen, often for several departments, without formally holding ministerial office. Such posts may be a useful testing ground for able peers, but if awarded to members of limited ability their primary consequence is to place further limits on the efficiency with which the house can scrutinise government activity. The Labour party has suffered particular problems in finding sufficient front-bench spokespersons, particularly in opposition. Almost all Labour members are life peers, and as well as being older than many of their hereditary Conservative counterparts, they are also ending rather than beginning their political careers – a junior ministerial or shadow post is therefore not an attractive proposition.

With the exception of a limited number of ministerial posts, Leader of the Opposition, and Opposition Chief Whip, and the non-party political offices of Chairman and Principal Deputy Chairman of Committees, membership of the Lords is not salaried. While peers may claim quite generous expense allowances (over £120 per day) for days on which they attend the house, those lacking independent means cannot afford to be full-time politicians, a factor which necessarily reduces the time and energy peers can devote to examination of government activities.

Within these constraints, the Lords has developed various mechanisms to monitor executive behaviour. Members may ask up to four 'starred questions' on two afternoons per week, when they are taken first in the order of businesses. They are intended to elicit information from the government, and while peers may place a supplementary, the exchange is not supposed to turn into a debate. Sessions may last for half an hour, and are a popular, well-attended part of the house's activities. 'Unstarred questions', in contrast, trigger a debate in which the appropriate minister delivers the final speech. Griffith and Ryle suggest they are the Lords' equivalent of Commons' adjournment debates.[15] They are always the final item on the business agenda, and despite the late hour at which they are often taken, are regarded as a useful forum by the more active of the working peers.

'Private notice questions' offer an emergency procedure to discuss issues which are too urgent to have been scheduled on the order paper. The house itself, advised by the Leader, decides whether to admit such questions. They are infrequently accepted; fewer than three per year were taken during the 1980s. 'Questions for written answer' have expanded substantially in recent years. 283 were placed in 1970, while over 1,400 were posed in 1988. 'Motions for debate' and 'take note' motions are scheduled for one day per week to examine the merits of general or specific aspects of government policy. They are often limited to two and a half hours' duration, generally conducted in a non-contentious fashion, and usually withdrawn by their mover without a division being held.

House of Lords' select committees

Lords' select committees are quite different creatures from their Commons counterparts. Most are concerned purely with the house's own domestic and procedural matters.[16] The two permanent Committees which have an explicitly extra-parliamentary outlook are the European Communities Committee and the Science and Technology Committee. Both are more appropriately seen as part of the Lords' deliberative rather than supervisory functions.

The EC Committee dates from 1974. Its main function is to evaluate proposed EC legislation before it is enacted, thereby equipping the British government with a wider knowledge base upon which to draw when participating in the EC's legislative process. The house has a salaried post, the Principal Deputy Chairman of Committees, primarily concerned with overseeing the EC Committee's activities. The committee is also (in relative terms)

15 *Op cit* pp 474–475.
16 The upper house has also made occasional use since 1972 of ad hoc select committees, established to inquire into matters of current public concern. For a list and brief evaluation see Griffith and Ryle *op cit* pp 494–495.

quite well resourced, having a dozen research and secretarial staff, and being able to appoint paid advisers to offer specific expertise. 24 peers sit on the committee, which may appoint sub-committees to undertake detailed investigations of particular topics. The committee produces a substantial number of reports each year. Most attract a considered government response, but as with most aspects of the Lords' work, their practical impact is hard to discern.

The Science and Technology Committee has also succeeded in becoming a highly regarded investigative forum. The committee was established in 1980, and fills a gap left by the coverage of the Commons departmental select committees. Its 15 members include life peers who are distinguished scientists, and it has sufficient resources to produce a substantial body of detailed reports. Griffith and Ryle neatly capture its character by describing it as 'the non-party political voice of the scientific community.[17]

As noted in chapter 5, a major weakness of the Commons' select committee system is that committee reports are frequently not debated in the house. This is not so in the Lords, where all reports are brought before the house for consideration. As we have already seen however, the impact of any Lords' debate on government policy is generally slight.

CONCLUSION

Both the Labour and Liberal parties fought the 1992 general election on manifestos which included proposals to abolish the upper house and replace it with some form of elected assembly. We will explore these, and other strategies for constitutional reform in chapter 15. At this stage, however, we might briefly consider how one might reform the Lords in ways which enhance its existing complementary role to the Commons.

Effective complementarity would seem to require independence and expertise within the upper house. Both characteristics are themselves determined by questions of composition, resources, and internal organisation. Moreover, they are perhaps more important a feature of the *house as a corporate body* than of its members in their individual capacities. We will return to the question of corporate identity shortly. Firstly, however, we might consider how best to maximise the independence and expertise of individual members.

Many of the Lords' shortcomings derive from its composition.

17 *Op cit* p 494.

There is no defensible basis for an hereditary form of membership in our modern society – expert and independent judgement is not a genetically transmitted trait. The essentially corrupt (because neither meritocratic nor representative) nature of the hereditary system was powerfully illustrated when the Earl of Hardwicke took his seat in 1995. This young man of 24 had been brought up in the West Indies, and according to a profile in *The Times*,[18] supplemented his inherited wealth by 'organising raves' and 'working in public relations'. Hardwicke, who seemingly possessed neither any formidable intellectual powers, nor any substantial record of public service, did not however find taking his seat a daunting experience: 'I had hundreds of cousins in the Lords . . . My cousin Lord Hesketh, the chief whip, was there when I took the oath and he led me to the Tory benches.'[19] He also observed that the Lords was: 'a wonderful place to take friends for lunch – although it should have a snooker table – and you always end up sitting next to someone interesting.'[20]

The indefensibility of this situation arises not just from the significant (and quite unearned) political status which Hardwicke himself acquired, but also from the equally unearned addition which his seat in the Lords makes to the voting power of the Conservative party. But if we accept that the Lords should be both subordinate to the Commons *and* independent of the prevailing patterns of party affiliation in the lower house, there is no evident need for its members to be elected. Indeed, for those purposes an elected second chamber could be quite dysfunctional. If elected on the same basis as the Commons, the Lords might simply reproduce its party alignment, and so lose any plausible claim to independence. If chosen through a different electoral system, the Lords might be construed as a more legitimate expression of the people's wishes, and so pose a threat to the lower house's 'democratically' justified superiority. And whatever form of election was used, there remains the risk that members would be elected because of their appeal to transient popular prejudice, and so produce a chamber intellectually unsuited for its role of bringing to bear a supra-party political influence on legislative and governmental processes.

The life peerage system therefore appears well suited as a selection process for a complementary house. Reform to the Life Peerage Act to place some justiciable limits on the Prime Minister's

18 Thomson A (1995) 'Youngest peer steps into the limelight' *The Times* 5 April.
19 *Ibid.*
20 *Ibid.*

powers to nominate peers might seem desirable, but the greatest weakness in the membership of the Lords that the Act produces would seem to be not one of political bias or limited ability, but of age: a more vigorous house may demand that we have a younger house.

Effecting such reforms is not within the competence of the Lords alone. Nor is the Lords capable of dealing unilaterally with the second existing obstacle that seriously hampers its members' individual effectiveness – namely the paucity of available research and secretarial resources. This weakness is also evident, to a lesser degree, in respect of the house's corporate identity. Its select committees may be well serviced by British standards, but their facilities compare poorly to those available to the legislatures of many other modern western countries.

These are defects which might most sensibly be cured both by substantially expanding the present resources available, but also by substantially reducing the size of the second chamber. One would expect a complementary house to be smaller, not larger than the Commons. The four hundred or so existing life peers would seem a convenient number. There would also seem to be strong grounds for introducing a more expansive system of financial rewards to ensure that those members who regarded their role as a full time occupation received an adequate salary for doing so.

All such initiatives to enhance the calibre of individual members would better equip the house to perform its deliberative functions. Again, however, they are matters for Parliament rather than the Lords alone. But the Lords does control its own internal procedures. As we have seen, these do not seem to make the most of such limited resources as the house possesses. The current voting mechanisms are an obvious absurdity, and the insistence on taking all Bills through a committee of the whole house necessarily places substantial limits on the breadth of vision the house can possess.

There would seem little point in advocating Lords reforms which simply make it more like the Commons; the purpose is to complement not duplicate the lower house. This might suggest that the most effective of reforms to the upper house would be those that minimised its resemblance to the Commons. Given the predominance of the party in modern political life, it would be facile to think one could remove party politics from the Lords. Even if one abolished formal party organisation, it is certain that members' behaviour would continue to be structured by their party loyalties. And indeed, since one of the functions we wish the Lords to perform is scrutiny of the executive, there must be a sufficient number of competent ministers in the house for other peers to question. Consequently, rather than wondering how to abolish party influence, a more pertinent inquiry would be to ask *how much influence* should be accorded to party discipline in respect of each of the house's various functions.

Objections to the Lords' powers to delay or amend government Bills derive not so much from the delay per se, as from its differential party impact. That the Lords indulges in such behaviour far more frequently when a Labour government controls the Commons suggests that their Lordships' stance owes less to a principled belief in the integrity of their position, than to a knee jerk mobilisation of their Conservative majority. There is no justification for according party ideology such scope in a complementary chamber. This suggests the Lords' composition as a corporate entity would have to be based on a quota system which ensured that a government Bill could be delayed or amended only if opposition peers won over a substantial body of cross-bench opinion, and perhaps some governing party peers as well. One would thereby increase the likelihood that any legislative difficulties the government encountered derived from flaws in its policies, rather than simple factional opposition intransigence. Nor should a house of life peers experience any conventional reluctance to use such legal powers – their very purpose would be to cause the government difficulties if it appeared that legislative policy ignored public sentiment.[1]

The Lords' scope as an anti-factional legislative device could be further enhanced by revising the Parliament Acts to provide that government Bills might only be amended or delayed by an enhanced majority of the upper house. A second chamber which could muster only a bare majority against government policy would be reliant entirely on the intellectual merit of its arguments to persuade the government either directly, or indirectly by its impact on public opinion, to modify its objectives. In this context, as with its scrutinising functions, the Lords' role is simply to expose government policy to the oxygen of publicity by alerting the electorate to criticism of the government's position.

Giving legal effect to majoritarian sentiment (within a house lacking a single majority party) is more readily defensible in respect of delegated legislation. Statutory instruments or Orders in Council are far less visible methods than primary legislation for government to, achieve its objectives. A government which felt

---

1 Although of course one might argue as to how effectively 400 life peers are able to reflect and express 'public sentiment'.

sufficently sure of the merits and importance of a given measure might always seek to implement it through primary legislation. Similarly, there is some force in the argument that the Lords should be able to amend or delay private member's Bills by a simple majority. If such Bills are indeed being used to pursue non-party matters possessing a controversial moral or social dimension, it may be that they would actually be better dealt with by a house independent of unthinking party loyalties.

The number of variations on the theme of reforming the Lords are legion, as are the pros and cons of each scheme proposed.[2] But most reform plans present us with a great paradox. The more we ask a second chamber to perform complementary functions to the Commons, then the more we demand of its members that they be (as individuals and as a body) 'expert', 'experienced', 'objective', 'technocratic', and 'non-partisan', and so the more we reveal the crushing dominance of party politics in the lower house, and the incapacity and/or unwillingess of backbench MPs to exert a restraining influence on government activities. This perhaps suggests that the key division within the legislative process is now not Lords versus Commons, nor Labour versus Conservative, but party versus national interest. If that is indeed the case, it is very difficult to identify effective reforming strategies for the Lords without simultaneously considering the merits and drawbacks of 'Parliament' more broadly, in terms both of its legislative powers and its relationship with the 'people'. Discussion of Lords' reform frequently proceeds on the assumption that the upper house's legal and conventional subordination to the Commons is desirable because of what one might intuitively regard as 'democratic' reasons. The Lords may be portrayed as an élitist, unelected body, which has no legitimate power to obstruct the wishes of 'the people', such wishes invariably being accurately expressed by the people's elected representatives in the lower house. Chapter 7 assesses the accuracy of that contention by examining the methods through which members of the Commons are chosen. When we have done so, we may be able to look back over the first 7 chapters and form a preliminary view of the meaning attached to 'democracy' within the contemporary British constitution.

2 See for example Oliver D (1990) *United Kingdom Government and Constitution* ch 3 (Buckingham: Open University Press); Brazier R (1992) *Constitutional Reform* ch 4 (Oxford: OUP); Loveland I (1992) 'Labour and the Constitution: the "right" approach to reform' *Parliamentary Affairs* 173–187.

CHAPTER SEVEN

The electoral system

This book began by suggesting various ways to assess if a society's constitution was 'democratic', in the substantive sense of the content of the country's laws, and the procedural sense of the way laws are made. The first six chapters sketched some characteristics of the version of democracy existing under Britain's constitutional arrangements. We have established that Parliament has traditionally been regarded as sovereign, capable of amending the substance of all laws by the simple majority in both houses plus Royal Assent formula. The Life Peerages Act 1958 shows that Parliament can alter the membership of its component parts. There is no obvious reason[1] why the doctrine of parliamentary sovereignty should not also apply to the Commons' electoral system. The questions we might therefore ask are why Parliament should have exercised its powers in this area in the way that it has; and how far does this choice satisfy democratic requirements?

To begin, we might return to the US Declaration of Independence claim that governments 'derive their just powers from the consent of the governed'. The claim is one most people would consider fundamental to any democratic society – that citizens choose their law-makers. But the concept is fuzzy, demanding sharper focus. How, for example, do citizens choose? How effective is that choice in controlling the legislature's composition? And how do we decide if our choice ensures that the law's substance attracts our consent?

A recent survey of electoral laws in modern societies identified six fundamental characteristics of democratic systems.[2] Firstly, that virtually all adults may vote. Secondly, that elections are held at regular periods. Thirdly that no large group of citizens is prohibited from forming a party and fielding candidates. Fourthly, that almost all places in the legislature are contested. Fifthly, that

1 But as we shall see in chapter 8, there may be some obscure ones.
2 Butler D, Penniman H and Ranney A (1981) *Democracy at the Polls* ch 1 (Washington DC: American Enterprise Institute for Public Policy Research).

election campaigns are conducted fairly and honestly, without physical or economic coercion. And sixthly, that votes are secretly cast and accurately counted.

These criteria address only the way legislators are selected: this notion of 'democracy' is purely procedural. But in a country where effective legal sovereignty is held by whichever political party has a reliable Commons majority, the assumption that democracy is solely about how legislators are chosen is understandable. This chapter asks how well Britain measures up to these yardsticks. Section two reviews the contemporary picture. Section one traces the route Britain has followed in reaching its present system of electoral law and practice, picking up the threads of issues previously encountered but left untied, and weaving a more tightly knit picture of the constitution.

I. THE EVOLUTION OF A 'DEMOCRATIC' ELECTORAL SYSTEM?

As with its discussion of the Commons and Lords, this book offers only a selective examination of electoral history. We focus on four issues: the Great Reform Act 1832; the Chartism movement; the reforms of 1867–1884; and voting rights for women.

The Great Reform Act 1832

The Commons' progress towards becoming a fully representative institution dates from the Great Reform Act 1832. This was not a clean break with the past: the Act intensified existing trends, and retained many features of the earlier electoral law.[3] Nevertheless, its passage provoked an acute constitutional crisis. This arose in part from the House of Lords' decision to wreck a Bill that had majority Commons support, but it also had roots in the Monarch's (William IV) evident unwillingness to exercise his prerogative powers to create new pro-government peers, and in the apparent readiness of middle and working class[4] communities to use violence to secure the Bill's enactment. This complex web of forces makes the Act a useful vehicle for exploring the meaning of 'democracy' in British constitutional history.

---

3 Gash N (1953) *Politics in the Age of Peel* p x (London: Longmans) Mandler P (1990) *Aristocratic Government in the Age of Reform* ch 4 (Oxford: Clarendon Press).
4 'Class' was then a nascent concept, and is used here in the loosest of senses. See Hobsbawm E (1969) *Industry and Empire* ch 4 (Harmondsworth: Penguin); Ward J (1973) *Chartism* pp 46–48 (New York: Harper Row).

By 1830, the nature of élite groups in British society was under-going rapid change. Wealth had moved away from the landed and merchant classes towards manufacturing industry.[5] The techno-logical advance which triggered this trend also facilitated the 'nationalisation of politics'; improved communications and trans-port systems permitted people in different regions to identify common interests transcending 'local concerns'. One can ident-ify 'public opinion' as a distinct political force from 1800.[6] The Commons may still have been a House of Communities; but the nation was increasingly divided by economic class into several large segments, rather than by physical geography into innumer-able cities, towns, and villages.

Dissatisfaction with the electoral system had four principal foci. The first related to the geographical distribution of seats. The second concerned the qualifications needed to vote. The third centred on candidate selection. The fourth arose from the con-duct of election campaigns.

The constituency system

At present, the Commons has 650 members, each representing a given geographical area, or constituency. This geographical div-ision was a firmly embedded principle by 1688. Constitutional theory then accepted that the Commons existed as much to pro-tect local interests as to define national issues. In 1830, 658 MPs sat in the Commons. The population was approximately 16 million. Representation was divided broadly between counties and bor-oughs, with most English counties (39) and boroughs (around 200) each returning two members, and each Scots and Welsh county and borough returning one member. Ireland had two member counties (32) and (mostly) one member boroughs (31). Oxford and Cambridge Universities returned two members each; one MP represented Trinity College Dublin. This framework was established in 1675 (prior to the revolution), and had remained broadly unchanged ever since.[7] Seat allocation bore no relation to population patterns; Parliament had not established any systematic mechanism for altering representation to reflect demographic trends. Thus in 1830, large and rapidly growing industrial towns such as Birmingham, Manchester, and Leeds, where over 450,000 people lived, had no representatives at all.

5 See Hobsbawm *op cit* chs 2–3.
6 Brock *op cit* p 17. Of the many studies of the 1832 Act, Brock's is the most lucid and engaging, and is heavily drawn upon here.
7 Cannon J (1973) *Parliamentary Reform 1640–1832* p 29 (Cambridge: CUP).

Table 7.1
The size of the electorate

	Population	Electorate	% of adult population enfranchised
1830	13,900,000	435,000	3.2%
1840	15,900,000	700,000	4.4%
1870	22,700,000	1,900,000	8.7%
1900	41,155,000	6,730,935	27.0%
1919	44,599,000	21,755,583	78.0%
1949	50,363,000	34,269,770	98.0%

Sources: Compiled from Seymour C (1970) *Electoral Reform in England and Wales* Appendix 1 (Newton Abbot: David & Charles); Coleman D and Salt J (1992) *The British Population* p 41 (Oxford: Oup); Butler and Sloman *op cit* p 200. Figures prior to 1900 are approximate only and are for England and Wales only. Later dates are for the UK.

In contrast, so-called 'rotten boroughs' such as Old Sarum and Dunwich, could have under 20 voters: over 100 boroughs had fewer than 100 voters. The system also threw up startling anomolies in neighbouring constituencies; Bristol had 5,000 voters, for example, while Bath had 30.[8] Boroughs were created by the Royal Prerogative; the ways in which the Monarch exercised the power was of course not subject to any judicial control.[9]

Qualification for the franchise

Entitlement arose in many ways, most deriving from land ownership. The value of the land required was generally set high enough

Table 7.2
Voting population of two member English boroughs 1830

Number of electors	Number of boroughs
0 – 50	56
51 – 100	21
101 – 300	36
301 – 600	24
601 – 1,000	22
1,001 – 5,000	36
5,000 +	7

Source: adapted from Brock *op cit* p 20.

8 Cannon *op cit* p 31.
9 O'Leary C (1962) *The Elimination of Corrupt Practices in British General Elections 1868–1911* p 6 (Oxford: Clarendon Press).

to exclude most local residents, but in the 14 'potwalloper boroughs' enfranchisement extended to any resident man with a family who had facilities to boil food or water, and in the 38 'scot and lot' boroughs to any man paying poor rates. In the 80 'freeman' boroughs, the franchise accompanied the 'freedom' of the borough, a status bestowed according to local custom. Residence was generally not required, which meant that many so-called 'out-voters' both lived beyond borough boundaries and possessed votes in several places. The English county qualification was more straightforward – freehold ownership of land worth £2 per year (the sum was fixed in 1430). As in the boroughs, residence was not needed.[10]

Defenders of the status quo invoked the theory of 'virtual representation'. This saw no need for most citizens to have a vote, since there would be some MPs whose dominant constituency interest would coincide with those of the disfranchised group (generally defined in occupational terms), thus ensuring that representations would be made on that group's behalf as the Commons defined the national interest.[11] The British government had made this argument to the American colonists in the 1770s when dismissing their demand for seats in Parliament; the colonists considered the theory entirely specious.[12] By 1830, its efficacy in countering purely domestic discontent had also been substantially weakened.

The conduct of election campaigns

Three 'traditional' activities attracted considerable criticism by 1830: bribery, 'treating', and intimidation.[13] Bribery is a self-explanatory term. The explicit purchase of votes for cash had technically been illegal since 1696, but the law was so rarely enforced (guilty candidates were disqualified) that the practice had almost acquired conventional status. Activities such as the offer of employment, public office, or advantageous transfers of interests in land in return for votes were also widespread.

'Treating' was indirect bribery, in which voters were 'persuaded' to support a particular candidate by lavish provision of food, drink and entertainments. Treating was much facilitated by the use of pubs as voting centres. While technically illegal since 1696, treat-

10 This oversimplifies the issue; see Brock *op cit* ch 1.
11 See Rawlings H (1988) *Law and the Electoral Process* ch 1 (London: Sweet and Maxwell).
12 Bailyn *op cit* pp 161–170.
13 See generally O'Leary C *op cit* ch 1.

ing was so routine a part of elections that candidates who could not afford to 'entertain' voters were effectively debarred from entering contested elections, particularly as the 'price' of votes tended to increase in closely fought constituencies. Treating was further encouraged by the fact that many constituencies had only one polling booth. However, voters had many days to register their choice. This was a necessity for outvoters, who needed time to journey to their various electoral homes. Outvoters could also generally expect to have their travel, accommodation and refreshment bills met by their preferred candidate.[14]

The cost of candidacy was further increased by the rule that candidates themselves had to pay all the administrative costs of the election, such as the hire of the polling station and the salaries of returning officers. This particular provision survived until well into the twentieth century.

Intimidation took various forms. Mob violence was common, as was the assault of specific voters by supporters of particular candidates. Somewhat more subtle was economic intimidation, entailing dismissal from employment or eviction from property if the employer/landlord's voting instructions were not followed. 'Spiritual intimidation' was less tangible, but one cannot doubt the occasional efficacy of a tactic which involved impressionable voters being informed by their local clergyman that it would be a mortal sin to vote for anyone other than the priest's favoured candidate.

The impact of all three practices was exacerbated by the lack of a secret ballot. The voter's choice was public knowledge. This was justified on the basis that the right to vote was akin to a trust, and so necessarily open to scrutiny.[15] Reformers regarded this as a guarantor of corruption and intimidation. Candidates who bought votes could check they gained value for money, while landlords or employers could identify and then penalise voters of independent inclinations.

The incentive for candidates to engage in corruption was magnified by the political rather than legal nature of the way corruption was policed. Until 1604, defeated candidates alleging malpractice pursued their case before the courts. From 1604–1770, disputed election petitions were heard by the Commons sitting as a whole house. Since so many MPs owed their seats to corrupt practices, only the most egregious misbehaviour led to disqualification. In 1770, a private member's Bill granted jurisdiction to a 13–member

14 Cannon *op cit* p 209.
15 O'Leary C *op cit* p 26.

Commons committee, in the hope that the task could be approached in a less partisan manner.[16]

A corrupt contest was a lesser ground for concern than having no contest at all. Elections with just one candidate per seat were the norm rather than the exception of pre-1832 practice, and frequently resulted from an agreement by groups of candidates of opposing parties to allow each other a clear run in neighbouring constituencies.

Selecting candidates

From 1710, MPs representing county constituencies had to own landed property worth at least £600; for borough members the sum was £300. This statutory selection criterion clearly excluded most of the population, including most of the emergent middle classes, from the electoral contest, and indicates the *formal* influence of landed wealth on the Commons' composition. More noteworthy was the *informal* influence exercised by members of the Lords. The lack of contestation in many seats, the exorbitant cost of the campaign in seats where a contest occurred, the small size of many electorates and the open nature of the voting process, combined to enhance local aristocrats' control of voters' behaviour; although long established patterns of deference, or calculations of economic self-interest, predisposed many voters to concur with their particular Lordship's preferences.

There would have been little point in peers controlling voter behaviour if they could not subsequently control the MP's behaviour. For many local magnates, 'their' MP was as much a part of their property as their land or their livestock. In 'nomination' or 'pocket' boroughs, voters were economically dependent on the local aristocrat, and the candidates were often his sons. In such instances, familial feeling ensured a co-incidence of political opinion between the members of the lower and upper house. Similarly, candidates were frequently protéges of members of the Lords. They were selected to do their patron's bidding, and although they were in legal terms answerable to no-one for their opinions or voting record until the next election, they could not hope to win that election without their patron's continued support. In effect, pocket boroughs offered Commons seats by proxy to legislators who already sat in the Lords. In 1830, 270 MPs represented such constituencies. Some senior peers reputedly controlled as many as 12 MPs.[17] And for patrons whose interest in

16 *Ibid*, pp 9–12.
17 Turbeville (1958) *op cit* pp 244–247.

political influence might wane, a pocket borough was a saleable commodity: a village with a seat attached might sell for as much as £180,000 (at 1830 prices).[18]

One would err in assuming that nomination boroughs ensured that the Commons automatically followed the Lords' wishes: the Treaty of Utrecht episode demonstrates that the two houses could adopt irreconcilable positions on major issues. But their existence on such a scale made a mockery of the Commons' supposed role as a balancing force arraigned against the aristocracy and the Monarch.

Perhaps the most extraordinary illustration of the pre-1832 system is an election at Bute where, according to Brock, 'the candidate had proposed and seconded his own nomination, and then voted for himself, he being the only person present...'.[19] Such tales may be apocryphal. That they could be given any currency at all indicates the electoral system's profound inadequacy for a rapidly industrialising and urbanising society.

The original Bill

The Bill presented by Lord Grey's Whig (Liberal) government was regarded as an extraordinarily radical, even revolutionary measure.[20] It sought to shift the formal balance of power in the Commons away from the landowning aristocracy towards the newly emergent manufacturing and professional classes. Grey was not, however, advocating a 'democratic' society. As Brock suggests, the government wished 'to make aristocratic government acceptable by purging away its most corrupt and expensive features'.[1] Grey himself was candid as to his intentions:

> 'A great change has taken place ... in the distribution of property, and unless a corresponding change can be made in the legal mode by which that property can act upon government, revolutions must necessarily follow. This change requires a greater influence to be yielded to the middle classes, who have made wonderful advances both in property and intelligence.'[2]

Grey established a four-member committee to produce a reform plan sufficiently radical to defuse popular discontent, yet sufficiently conservative to ensure the continued dominance of aristo-

---

18 Brock *op cit* ch 1.
19 *Ibid*, p 32.
20 For a concise account see Cannon J *op cit* pp 206–210.
 1 Brock *op cit* p 44.
 2 *Ibid*, p 152.

cratic *ideas* within the lower house. The committee recommended retaining the county and borough constituencies, but proposed significant reapportionment. Large counties should gain two extra MPs; boroughs with fewer than 2,000 inhabitants would lose both members; boroughs with fewer than 4,000 would lose one; unrepresented towns with over 10,000 residents would gain one MP. The committee retained the property qualification, but recommended a uniform £10 freehold threshhold. Outvoting was to be abolished by introducing a residence requirement, and, most radically, voting would be by secret ballot. These plans would produce a substantially increased electorate, voting in constituencies which began to recognise contemporary population patterns, under conditions encouraging independent voting behaviour.

While agreeing to most of these proposals, the Cabinet rejected the ballot. Grey personally opposed secrecy, as did William IV, considering it: 'inconsistent with the manly spirit and free avowal of opinion which distinguish the people of England.'[3]

The Bill's parliamentary passage

We need not dwell on the Bill's intricacies, beyond noting it was slightly less radical than the Committee's proposals. The Cabinet doubted that it would be approved in the Commons. In the event, the Bill passed its second reading by 302 votes to 301. In committee, however, the Tories carried a wrecking amendment. Grey subsequently resigned, and was granted a dissolution by William IV on 22 April. At the ensuing election, fought entirely on the basis of reform, the government gained a majority of around 130 seats. The legislative battle ground subsequently shifted to the Lords.

As chapter 6 suggested, Conservative peers who regarded Liberal policies as revolutionary were not persuaded even in 1911 to defer to a newly elected Commons majority. In 1831, the convention that the Lords should do so had yet to be established. The Commons was asking the Lords to approve a measure which would have greatly reduced the aristocracy's direct control over the lower house's composition. Tory peers lacked Grey's faith that a middle class electorate would vote for aristocratic principles of government, and, as one might expect, remained intransigent.

As noted in chapter 6, one way to view the constitutional function of the Lords' (then) legislative co-equality was as a guarantor

3 Quoted in Cannon J *op cit* p 211.

of traditional distributions of 'property', in the sense not simply of land or wealth, but also of control of political power. The common law had accepted that an entitled voter could maintain a tort action against a government official who unlawfully prevented him from exercising the right.[4] Casting one's vote could therefore be seen as 'property' in the same sense as security in one's home (*Entick*) or one's physical liberty (*Liversidge*).

But for many Tories, the capacity to vote was also regarded as 'property' in a rather different sense, belonging not to the individual voter, but to the aristocrat on whom the voter was economically dependent, as tenant or employee. In 1829, the Duke of Newcastle responded to criticism of his decision to evict tenants who voted against his preferred candidate by saying: 'Is it presumed then that I am not to do what I will with my own.'[5] The point was more clearly put by Lord Eldon when criticising the Bill's plan to abolish pocket boroughs:

> 'Parliament had no more right, Eldon told the Lords in 1832, "to take away the elective franchise from the present holders of it, than . . . to take away from them the property in houses or land which conferred it".'[6]

The idea that voting for one's legislators was a 'right' that all possessed simply by being a citizen, to be freely exercised according to one's conscience, was adhered to only by the radical fringes of early nineteenth century society.

Grey's Bill had no such intentions. The Cabinet nevertheless expected the Lords to reject it. The first weeks after the election were taken up with delicate negotiations between Grey and William IV concerning a mass creation of peers to ensure the Bill would be passed. The Utrecht episode offered some precedent for such action.[7] Queen Anne had however created only 12 peers, and while William awarded some 20 titles to Whig supporters, he was unwilling to grant the 50 needed to ensure a government majority. Grey hoped that the *threat* of a mass creation would persuade Tory peers to drop their opposition. William's reluctance was however leaked, and thus emboldened, the Lords used its co-equal status to reject the Bill by 41 votes at second reading.

The veto was described as 'the whisper of a faction' by Lord John Russell, a leading government reformer, and triggered widespread public protest and occasional violent conflict. Riots in Bristol led

4 *Ashby v White* (1703) 2 Ld Raym 938,92 ER 126. See further pp 294–295 below.
5 Brock *op cit* p 63.
6 *Ibid*, p 36.
7 See p 195 above.

to over 400 deaths, and several Tory peers found themselves and their property under attack.[8] The government was sufficiently alarmed to use its prerogative power to issue a proclamation, stressing the formation of private militia was illegal.[9] Many observers feared violent revolution was at hand.

Modification of the Bill

Rather than resign again, the government produced a modified Bill, designed to mollify their Tory opponents. As in 1909 and 1911, the Tory party split into two factions – the 'waverers' and the 'die-hards'. The former, fearing that a further government defeat would lead either to its resignation and possibly civil war, or to a mass creation of peers, advocated amendment rather than veto. The latter, thinking the Bill tantamount to revolution, favoured resistance, irrespective of the consequences. Initially, the die-hards kept the upper hand.

The amended Bill received a Commons majority of 162, and on second reading a majority of 9 in the Lords. However, on 7 May the Lords approved a wrecking amendment in committee by 151 votes to 116. William continued to refuse a mass creation, whereupon Grey once more resigned. Given the party balance in the Commons, there was no likelihood of a Tory government being formed, although this was William's preferred solution. Sir Robert Peel, the most eminent Tory MP, considered this solution unacceptable, and declined to serve. The King then asked the Tory leader, the Duke of Wellington, to do so, but he could not muster sufficient Commons support. A final effort, led by the Speaker, Manners Sutton, also foundered.

'Public opinion' voiced many protests against a possible Wellington administration. The 'Days of May' embroiled radical reformers in a co-ordinated effort to destabilise the currency by withdrawing gold from the banks (the movement's slogan being 'To Stop the Duke, Go for Gold'), and there is evidence to suggest that reformers in several towns prepared for armed struggle.[10] Grey subsequently agreed to continue in office if the King agreed to create as many peers as necessary to push the Bill through. At that point, the Tory waverers capitulated, and were joined by sufficient 'die-hards' for the Bill to pass.

For Wellington, the Act was 'a revolution by due process of

8 Cannon *op cit* pp 226–228: Brock *op cit* pp 247–259.
9 Cannon *op cit* p 227.
10 Cannon *op cit* pp 236–240.

law'.[11] What Professor Wade later termed the 'ultimate political fact' of parliamentary sovereignty remained unchanged – but Parliament now reflected a changed concept of 'the people' upon whose consent the stability of constitutional government would in future depend.

The 'constitutionality' of civil disobedience? Chartism and the pursuit of a 'democratic' electoral system

Wellington's 'revolution' created only an élitist electorate of the aristocracy and middle class. In much the same way as the Framers of the American Constitution 50 years earlier, the 1832 reformers distinguished carefully between 'the people' and 'the populace'.[12] The former, the emergent professional and commercial classes, could safely be enfranchised; their property and education led them to accept existing socio-economic norms. The 'populace', in contrast, were the urban working class, who would elect a Commons committed to far-reaching redistribution of wealth and political power.[13]

That the 1832 Act fell far short of real 'revolution' is indicated by the disintegration of the radical movement in the 1837 election. The new electorate appeared as conservative as its predecessor. Further reform disappeared from the Parliamentary agenda: 'The reformed electorate was not radical enough to vote for its own enlargement'.[14] It was therefore among the 'populace', and through extra-parliamentary methods, that the next phase of Britain's journey towards a democratic constitutional settlement occurred.

The legality and legitimacy of public protest

The American War of Independence is a dramatic example of the efficacy of revolution as a route to political change. But what to Jefferson was the pursuit of 'life, liberty and happiness', was treason from the British government's perspective. Armed revolution is an extreme way to signify one no longer consents to one's form of government, but civil disobedience can take milder forms, and

11 *Ibid*, p 204.
12 Brock *op cit* pp 143–144.
13 One might reflect here on the contents of the People's Budget, the product of a government returned by an electorate in which virtually all adult men were enfranchised.
14 Brock *op cit* p 317.

be targeted towards less momentous goals. Furthermore, unlawful action taken for radical motives may, with hindsight, appear as a readily understandable, even necessary, phase of historical development. Few contemporary observers would consider the American revolution illegitimate. Similarly, from a 1990s viewpoint, many illegal acts committed during the Days of May can be justified because protestors sought an entitlement we now regard as a necessity.

This leads us towards the difficult question of whether we can or ought to subscribe to a general rule that an illegal action should nevertheless be considered 'constitutional' because it was undertaken to promote reform which was subsequently enacted, especially if the reform sought is the right to vote? This and later chapters will offer opportunities to broach that issue. But before returning to our historical thread, one further thematic concern should be raised.

It is often possible to draw a clear dividing line between *revolution* (which involves defiance of laws with a view to *overthrowing* the existing constitutional order) and *civil disobedience* (which entails defiance of laws with a view to *amending* the existing political order). Similarly, one can readily distinguish civil disobedience from reform movements which seek to amend the existing political order through methods limited to debate in Parliament or litigation before the courts. Far more elusive is the boundary between civil disobedience and *lawful public protest*, whose protagonists seek to amend the law by imploring, persuading, or cajoling the legislature to introduce reform.

We will return to consider the legal intricacies of the citizen's 'right' to engage in public protest in chapter 14. Here we might just, very simplistically, sketch the broad principles governing such activities in the mid-nineteenth century. We noted in chapter 1 that 'liberty' was an essential element of the British constitutional tradition. Such liberty was widely considered to embrace advocacy of political reform through lawful methods. A government commanding a majority in Parliament could in theory have introduced sweeping laws granting it arbitrary powers to prohibit any critical political expression. To have done so, however, would have overturned conventional understandings as to the centrality of 'the rule of law' to constitutional tradition. While successive Parliaments occasionally succumbed to the temptation to legislate against various forms of free expression, the primary legal constraint on political protest was imposed by public order laws. Individuals or groups might lawfully disseminate their views so long as they did not breach 'the Queen's Peace' – that is engage in, or threaten, violent acts towards people or property. The mere size of an assembly did not in itself breach the peace; an activity that was lawful when conducted by one person or a small group did not become unlawful when engaged in by many.[15] Since breach of the peace was a common law concept, the precise scope of lawful protest was a matter determined by the courts, and so necessarily subject to some uncertainty. What was certain, however, was that the constitution afforded substantial latitude for radical reformers to engage in lawful public action. A brief examination of the Chartist movement illuminates both the limits of legality, and the political factors constraining the introduction of radical constitutional amendment.

Chartism: objectives, methods – and failure?

Modern democrats might regard the 'Six Points' of 'The People's Charter' as eminently reasonable. The demand for annual elections may embody too short a time span, but universal adult suffrage, constituencies of equal size, the secret ballot, the payment of MPs, and removing the requirement that MPs be substantial property owners now appear quite modest objectives. But to most parliamentarians in the 1840s, both the objectives themselves, and the methods through which Chartists sought to achieve them, struck at the very roots of constitutional propriety.[16]

Chartism has been variously described as the 'first working class political party' or 'the first organised effort to stir up class consciousness on a national scale'.[17] It was an umbrella movement, with many local variations[18] on a central theme which linked economic redistribution with democratisation of the political process; it owed as much to its members' acute poverty as to abstract notions of democracy.

Chartism was also beset by a tension between 'respectable' and 'revolutionary' factions the former seeking reform through the persuasive and lawful route of 'moral force', the latter prepared if need be to take up arms and usher in the democratic age through 'physical force'. Both factions were united however, in regarding the 1832 Reform Act as a Whig betrayal of 'the people',

---

15 See Mather F (1962) 'The government and the Chartists' pp 377–379 in Briggs A (ed) *Chartist Studies* (London: Macmillan); Feldman D (1993) *Civil Liberties and Human Rights in England and Wales* pp 782–787 (Oxford: Clarendon Press).
16 I am indebted to J T Ward's (1973) *Chartism* (Harper and Row: New York) for the following pages.
17 Ward *op cit* p 7 and p 245.
18 The most illuminating guide is Briggs *op cit*.

designed solely to consolidate the power of the aristocracy and emergent industrial capitalists.

The People's Charter programme can be traced to the deliberations of the highly 'respectable' London Working Men's Association in 1838. The LWMA planned to gather a vast petition supporting the Six Points, hoping that an overwhelming display of public opinion would lead Parliament to introduce radical reform. The London initiative co-existed with a more overtly confrontational movement in the northern industrial towns, led by Feargus O'Connor, a radical Irish squire and former MP. O'Connor initially favoured prompt resort to 'physical force', and proved remarkably effective in attracting followers, both through his oratory and in his recognition of the emerging power of the press as a vehicle for constitutional reform. His newspaper, *The Northern Star*, had the twin benefits of winning many converts to the cause and making him a substantial fortune.

Chartism's many strands coalesced sufficiently for a National Convention (known as 'The People's Parliament'), to meet to formulate detailed demands and present the petition to the Commons. Should it be rejected, a general strike would be called to persuade Parliament to enact the Six Points. The Convention met in February 1839, but its deliberations rapidly exposed the divisions in Chartist ranks. Many delegates resigned as the majority mood swung increasingly towards violent action and evidence emerged that many of O'Connor's supporters had armed themselves in preparation for civil war. O'Connor, perhaps with an eye to the War of Independence, intensifed the division by seeking to legitimise revolution: 'physical force was violence only when it failed: it was glorious freedom when it was successful'.[19]

The Commons debated the Charter only briefly, voting overwhelmingly to give it no further attention. The general strike attracted few supporters. Many leaders (including O'Connor) were gaoled for public order offences, and an abortive 'revolution' in Newport resulted in capital sentences for treason being imposed on some conspirators. Discredited and demoralised, Chartism appeared a spent force.

In 1842, Chartism re-emerged in a distinctly less abrasive form. The National Charter Association dedicated itself to educative and lobbying initiatives, and by April had some 350 branches. O'Connor's release from jail then re-awakened old divisions. The more moderate Chartists departed, and formed the Complete Suffrage Union movement to campaign peacably for a universal

19 Ward *op cit* p 116.

franchise. O'Connor was now formally opposed to violent measures. However the second petition and National Convention were accompanied by widespread strike action in the north.

On this occasion, the Commons refused even to accept the Chartists' petititon. Strikes were met by prompt prosecutions for any breaches of public order, criminal damage or conspiracy laws. Many of the movement's activists diverted their attention to social reform issues such as temperance and child labour laws. In combination with a distinct upturn in the economy, these factors pushed Chartism once more to the margins of the political process.

Chartism's third and final phase began in 1845. The movement enjoyed considerable successes in local government elections in Leeds, and in 1846 O'Connor was returned as a Chartist MP for Nottingham. Much of O'Connor's energy was now devoted to a utopian land reform scheme, but a third petition and National Convention were planned in early 1848. The Convention co-incided with several revolutions in continental Europe. There was widespread fear among aristocrats and parliamentarians that a similar fate would shortly befall the British constitution when the Chartists planned to march en masse to Parliament to demand radical electoral reform. Such fears proved misplaced. Following a substantial mobilisation of military forces, and the enlistment of as many as 150,000 Londoners as special constables, O'Connor bowed to government demands to call off the march, and such crowds as had gathered peaceably dispersed. The subsequent presentation of the petition further undermined the movement. Chartist claims of six million signatures were grossly inflated, and many names were obvious forgeries. A final series of arrests of the movement's leaders co-incided with the economic collapse of the land reform plan, and led to the final eclipse of the movement. O'Connor himself subsequently became insane. He was removed from the Commons after assaulting fellow MPs, and detained in an asylum.

It has been suggested that one can discern a clear distinction between the ways in which Whig and Tory governments dealt with the Chartist agitation.[20] Lord John Russell, the Whig Home Secretary, declined to act against inflammatory speeches, writings or meetings in 1839 unless it appeared they were likely to lead to imminent violence. Russell's choice stemmed largely from his own attachment to liberal values. His Whig successor, Lord Melbourne, was initially similarly reluctant to intervene, although his reticence

20 Mather *op cit.*

owed more to doubts about his legal powers than to abstract sympathies with public protest.

Chartism's second phase occurred under a Tory government, whose ideological sympathies lay more with preserving public order than permitting public protest. The Home Secretary, Graham, regarded Chartism as treason, and took the view that 'all meetings in large numbers in present circumstances have a manifest tendency to create terror and disturb the public peace, that as such they are illegal . . . and ought to be dispersed'.[1] Graham was prepared both to furnish armed reinforcements to magistrates wishing to prevent or break up mass meetings, and to support the arrest and trial of Chartist leaders on charges which had clear political overtones.

It is tempting to view Chartism simply as an isolated historical anachronism, but as Julius West has suggested, that underestimates its constitutional significance:

> 'The movement's failures lay in the direction of securing legislation. . . . Judged by its crop of statutes, Chartism was a failure. Judged by its essential . . . purpose, Chartism was a success. It achieved not the Six Points, but a state of mind.'[2]

States of mind, like principles of constitutional morality, are invariably elusive concepts. Quite how great an influence the Chartist legacy exercised on subsequent electoral reform is impossible to gauge. Yet as a vehicle for demonstrating the importance of class divisions in the evolution of constitutional orthodoxies and heresies, and for emphasising the links between economic and political reform, it has few rivals.

The 1867–1884 reforms: towards a universal 'right' to vote and a 'fair' electoral contest

Minor reforms were enacted in the 35 years following 1832. The requirement that MPs be substantial landowners was modified in 1838 – personal as well as real property would now suffice. The requirement was abolished altogether, without opposition from the Lords, in 1858.[3] Nevertheless, the system remained manifestly undemocratic. In the 1847 election, over 60% of seats had only one candidate; in 1866 one could identify over 1,200 different

1 Mather *op cit* pp 388–389.
2 Quoted in Ward *op cit* p 245.
3 Turbeville (1958) *op cit* p 418.

qualifications for the franchise.[4] Parliament undertook some ad hoc initiatives to remove the most blatant instances of electoral corruption. Legislation passed in 1844 and 1847 disfranchised the boroughs of Sudbury and St Albans respectively; their seats were reallocated to the larger counties.[5] More systematic revision occurred in 1867.

Disraeli's 1867 Reform Bill attracted no substantial opposition in the Lords.[6] Its Commons passage, in contrast, was extraordinarily tortuous. The episode merits attention, both because it highlights changing parliamentary and governmental perceptions of 'the people', but also because of the insight it offers into the occasional importance of standing committees in the legislative process.

Disraeli led a minority Tory party in the Commons in an administration headed by Lord Derby. It assumed office following the resignation of Lord John Russell's Liberal government when a backbench Liberal rebellion defeated Russell's own reform plans; the rebels (known as 'the Cave') thought Russell's proposals too extensive. The 1867 Act introduced a modest redistribution to take some (limited) account of demographic trends. Its main focus, however, was on qualification for the franchise. Over a million voters joined the electoral roll, doubling its size. This was more than twice as many as envisaged by Russell's measure. Yet those very MPs who had voted against Russell subsequently supported Disraeli. Perhaps the most striking feature of the 1867 controversy is that a matter of such great constitutional significance was resolved not according to its substantive merits per se, but according to what Disraeli calculated would best serve his party's short-term survival in government.[7]

Disraeli's great achievement was to produce a Bill supported not only by moderate Conservatives, but also by radical Liberals and reactionary Tories. At this time, the centre ranks of the Tories and Liberals (led in effect by Gladstone) had become so mutually antagonistic that it was inconceivable either would support the other on any reform measure. It was also generally believed (as a legacy of 1832) that the Liberals favoured more far-reaching reform than the Tories.

Disraeli's Bill detached the radicals from the Liberal party by proposing to reduce the county franchise qualification from £50

4 Brock *op cit* pp 326–333.
5 O'Leary C *op cit* p 22.
6 Turbeville (1958) *op cit* pp 422–425.
7 A fascinating study is provided in Cowling M (1967) *1867: Disraeli, Gladstone, and Revolution* (Cambridge: Cambridge University Press). A rather different version of events is offered in Turbeville (1958) *op cit* pp 396–428.

to £15, and to extend the borough franchise to any adult male who paid poor rates. However it simultaneously placated reactionary Tories by creating 'fancy franchises' to give *additional votes* to individuals who had certain property or educational qualifications. Furthermore, borough ratepayers could vote only if they paid their rates personally: those who paid their rates to their landlord as part of their rent ('composited' ratepayers – who were concentrated among the poorer tenants) would not be enfranchised. Initially one might think Disraeli's concessions to the Tory right wing would have alienated radical support. But it seems Disraeli had tacitly agreed with radical MPs to acquiesce if they removed those restrictions in committee, where the government was in a minority. The committee stage modified the Bill in both progressive and reactionary directions. The personal payment and fancy franchise provisions were removed, and the county franchise reduced to £12, but the radicals could not muster majority support for the secret ballot, for voting by written form rather than in person, for government subsidy of election expenses, or for the explicit enfranchisement of women.[8]

Commons manouevrings were accompanied by extensive public agitation. A Reform League of London-based journalists and artisans lent the campaign a strident, working class edge; it gained a more 'respectable' middle class hue from the Reform Union, dominated by radical MPs and the emergent professionals and entrepeneurs of the industrial towns.

It is impossible to gauge the impact of the sober tactics favoured by the Reform Union, but one cannot doubt it was substantial. The public protests favoured by the League had a more visible, if not necessarily more significant effect. John Bright, leader of the radical Liberal MPs, distanced himself from the wilder rhetoric of Reform League activists, but nonetheless suggested that public meetings, rallies and speeches served the entirely constitutional function of alerting government to the need to forestall potential revolution. They were: 'demonstrations of opinion and if you like . . . exhibitions of force [which] if . . . despised and disregarded, may become exhibitions of another kind of force'.

In April 1867, the League announced it would hold a mass rally in Hyde Park on 6 May. The Cabinet initially wished to prohibit the event, but Walpole, the Home Secretary, could find no statutory power for doing so. Shortage of time precluded new legislation, so Walpole invoked the prerogative to issue proclamations warning protestors the meeting was illegal, despite his own lawyers'

8 Cowling *op cit* pp 223–226.

advice that the proclamatory power did not extend to such matters.[9] The protestors ignored the warnings, assuming firstly that their activities would be sufficiently well-marshalled to ensure the Queen's peace was upheld, and secondly that the government, given its weak legal position, would not risk violent confrontation. The meeting passed peacefully, embarrassing the government and setting a potentially important precedent concerning the status of freedom of speech and assembly within Britain's constitutional traditions.

In 1867, neither Disraeli nor Gladstone could be regarded as 'democrats'. Gladstone's Liberalism did not extend to enfranchising 'the poorest, the least instructed and the most dependent members of the community'.[10] Nevertheless, Gladstone was regarded in some quarters, both reactionary and radical, as coming closer to an embrace of 'democracy' than any other leading politician. Democracy remained an unacceptable philosophy for conservative politicians in all parties. For one leading member of the Cave it meant: ' "handing the country over to the Trade Unions" and the "rule of numbers", enabling "the poor" to tax "the rich" and destroying the monopoly exercised by the existing parliamentary regime'.[11] Yet barely 20 years later, Gladstone led Parliament a considerable way along such a path.

The dawning of the democratic age?

Shortly after the passage of the 1867 Act, Disraeli steered the Election Petitions and Corrupt Practices at Elections Act through Parliament. The Act returned jurisdiction over disputed elections to the courts. The judiciary was initially reluctant to resume this role, but eventually did so when provision was made for the appointment of additional judges and enhanced salaries. The measure had both practical and symbolic effects; the former in ensuring that a coherent body of precedent defining unacceptable behaviour would emerge; the latter in suggesting that the electoral process was henceforth subject to orthodox rule of law principles.[12]

The secret ballot was introduced in 1872. The 1868 general election had been attended by substantial corruption and intimi-

9 See the *Case of Proclamations* at p 104 above.
10 Cowling *op cit* p 40.
11 Cowling *op cit* p 51.
12 As discussed in chapter 8, this point was to prove far from settled.

dation.[13] The most blatant examples were the 100 tenants in Cardi-
ganshire evicted for opposing their (Tory) landlord's candidate,
and 40 mill workers in Ashton-under-Lyne sacked for not voting
as their (Liberal) employer demanded.[14] A select committee established in 1869 identified the ballot as the most effective anti-
corruption device. Gladstone's Liberal administration introduced
a Bill in 1871, which was opposed by the Tories in the Commons,
and vetoed by the Lords. Gladstone submitted a similar Bill in
1872, and threatened to request a dissolution if it was rejected.
The Bill was ' grudgingly approved. Equally significant was the
Corrupt Practices Act 1883. This limited the amount of money
that individual candidates could spend on their local campaign,
the amount being based on a (small) per capita sum for each
voter in the constituency.

Both measures indicated a further cultural shift towards a meritocratic rather than aristocratic constitutional morality. The political process itself was increasingly structured by middle class values
of fair competition, in which political power was fought and won
on the basis of rational argument, rather than the unthinking
deference previously accorded to landowning interests.[15] By the
mid-1880s, that rationality had extended to include a substantial
proportion of working class men.

The key element of Gladstone's 1884 reform was a uniform
borough/ county voting qualification, set at the lower borough
level, which would enfranchise some two million additional
voters.[16] The Tories initially opposed the Bill, ostensibly because
they wished extension of the franchise to be considered simultaneously with further redistribution. Although the Liberals had
a reliable Commons majority, they were a minority in the Lords.
Lord Salisbury, leader of the Tory peers, was ready to apply his
'referendal theory' of the veto power,[17] and force a dissolution.

Many Liberal MPs relished the prospect of a veto, seeing an
opportunity to curb the upper chamber's powers.[18] Gladstone
himself described any such veto as 'A precedent against Liberty'.[19]
As in 1832, the Lords' intransigence provoked widespread public

13 For contemporaneous accounts of the era see Rover C (1967) *Women's Suffrage
and Party Politics in Britain 1866–1914* pp 40–41 (London: RKP).
14 O'Leary C *op cit* pp 61–62.
15 Ibid, ch 3.
16 See generally Jones A (1972) *The Politics of Reform 1884* (Cambridge: Cambridge
University Press).
17 See pp 196–197 above.
18 As we saw in chapter 6, that clash was delayed for a further 25 years.
19 Jones A *op cit* p 149.

agitation in support of reform. Gladstone called for lawful protests, although Joseph Chamberlain, a member of the Cabinet, in urging supporters to add 'a little more devil' to the issue, was seen as responsible for a violent Liberal attack on Tories in Birmingham.[20] The Tory peers' position was undermined by inept opposition tactics in the Commons. Tory MPs failed to follow Salisbury's advice to give the Bill 'a good parting kick at third reading'.[1] The Lords was thus unable to point to a clear and irreconcilable split in electoral opinion on the issue. Crisis was avoided by negotiation between a handful of each party's leaders, in which Gladstone offered Salisbury acceptable assurances about a subsequent reapportionment Bill.

The negotiations were conducted without any substantial debate in either house, prompting the leading Liberal newspaper (*The Manchester Guardian*) to describe them as 'a usurpation of the office and powers of Parliament'.[2] This is in marked contrast to the passage of the 1867 Bill, where the Commons committee stage was of paramount importance to the Act's final shape. The statutory label one may attach to both measures conceals substantial differences in the realities of the legislative process. The origins and passage of the Representation of the People Act (RPA) 1918, through which some women first gained the right to vote, took still another form.

Gender discrimination: women's right to vote

In modern Britain, the notion that only male citizens could vote is manifestly absurd. Yet this most basic of 'democratic' beliefs is a recent innovation, dating from 1918.[3] As chapter 2 observed, English and Scots courts in the Victorian era considered it an axiomatic constitutional principle that women did not vote. While Parliament could amend that principle, the political change entailed would be so profound that it could only be achieved through the most explicitly phrased statutory formulae. But *Chorlton v Lings* and *Nairn v St Andrews University* were merely minor parts of a bitter, protracted dispute which ranged over Britain's constitutional landscape from the 1830s, embracing spir-

20 *Ibid*, at p 168.
 1 *Ibid*, at p 148.
 2 *Ibid*, at p 221.
 3 Nor is Britain unique in this respect. The 'men' Jefferson regarded as created equal excluded women: the US consitution permitted gender discrimination in electoral law until 1920.

ited debate in Parliament, determined public protest, and deliberate crimes of violence. There are few better illustrations of the complex nature of 'constitutionality' in British political history than the campaign for women's suffrage.[4]

'Democracy' – a class or gender issue?

The 1832, 1867 and 1884 Reform Acts were contests conducted principally around the dividing lines of class and urbanisation. Women's enfranchisement was decisively rejected in the Commons in 1867 and 1884, and the Chartists had (briefly) entertained, but (promptly) dropped, the women's cause.[5]

One strand of opposition to female suffrage had a 'natural law' basis, expressed most vituperatively by E Wright's 1913 book, *The Unexpurgated Case Against Women's Suffrage*. This contended that women should never be permitted to vote because their relative physical frailty meant they could not fight for their country, and their emotion-laden psyches led them 'to look upon their minds not as an instrument for the pursuit of truth, but as an instrument for providing them with creature comforts in the form of agreeable mental images'.[6]

One might expect such sentiments among the reactionary male fringes of Victorian society. It is more surprising to find them voiced in 1892 by Asquith, who barely 15 years later embroiled his party in radical constitutional battle against the Tory peers. Democracy, for Asquith, demanded legislation to remove only man-made inequalities: 'not those indelible differences of faculty and function by which Nature herself has given diversity and richness to human society'.[7] Women and men were simply created unequal, at least when choosing their law-makers.

Appreciable currency was also accorded to Willes J's argument in *Chorlton* – namely that benevolent male parliamentarians had spared women the arduous duties inherent upon electoral participation. A related belief was that political activities would drain women of the energies needed to bear and raise children. Opponents of female suffrage also invoked virtual representation theory – women did not need a vote because they were adequately represented by their fathers, brothers or husbands.

For Professor Dicey, women's enfranchisement should be

---

4 The most accessible and informative guide continues to be Rover *op cit.*
5 Brock *op cit* p 322, fn 28.
6 At pp 35–36.
7 Quoted in Pugh M (1980) *Women's Suffrage in Britain 1867–1928* p 8 (London: The Historical Association).

resisted because it raised the spectre of Parliament being dominated by majoritarian sentiments. Women, Dicey noted, formed
the majority of the population, and he assumed that they would
vote in an homogeonous bloc in pursuit of gender discriminatory
policies. Such a Parliament would have no automatic claim to
sovereignty:

> 'Is it certain that in such circumstances Englishmen would obey and
> enforce a law that punished as a crime conduct which they in general
> held ought to be treated as an offence, not against law, but against
> morality.'[8]

Supportive arguments were initially championed by John Stuart
Mill. One proposition drew directly on an intensifying philosophical belief in the centrality of the individual as the repository of
rights and obligations. Mill, invoking Diceyan notions of the rule
of law for ends of which Dicey strongly disapproved, suggested it
was arbitrary and capricious to deny women's individuality solely
on the basis of their sex. Women increasingly possessed those
attributes traditionally regarded as necessary for men to acquire
the vote; namely education, ownership of land or commercial
property, and liability for taxation. This last point drew directly
on Jeffersonian principles – 'no taxation without representation'
was as much a rallying cry of the women's suffrage movement as
of the American revolution.

The opposition case was also undermined by institutional factors
– women had been enfranchised on the same basis as men for
local government elections since 1869. Gender equality in this
sphere attracted little controversy as it was assumed that local
government's parochial, social welfare responsibilities coincided
with women's 'natural' role as wives and mothers.[9] Opponents of
enfranchisement blundered rather by enlisting women in their
campaign. These women engaged in public speaking, pamphlet-
eering, and lobbying – thereby creating the absurd situation in
which they could win their argument only by successfully doing
what they argued they could not do. Consolidation of the national
party system also weakened the opposition case. Installing and
maintaining party loyalty among a growing electorate required
many volunteers, ideally possessed of spare time, economic independence and some education. Middle class women were obvious
recruits.

To speak of *the* 'Women's Suffrage Movement' is misleading,

8 Quoted in Rover *op cit* at p 45.
9 See Pugh (1980) *op cit* p 13.

since the pressure for reform came from many quarters, and was motivated by different conditions and concerns. Rover's leading study describes it as 'a political movement run by middle class women',[10] and concentrated largely in London. For many women, the franchise was undoubtedly not a class but a gender issue. They sought enfranchisement only on the same terms as men, which, even after 1884, would have prevented many women from voting. Nevertheless, working class women also devoted considerable time and effort to the reform movement. That they achieved less prominence in subsequent studies may be in part because they left less extensive records of their activities than their middle class contemporaries, and in part because, like their Chartist predecessors, their demand to vote was inextricably linked with economic and social policy issues arising from their unfavourable employment situation.[11]

Much like Chartism, the suffrage movement harboured a divide between activists favouring 'physical force' (the suffrag*ettes*) and those prepared only to employ moral force (the suffrag*ists*). The suffragist movement dates from 1867, its many component parts typified and led by the National Society for Women's Suffrage (NSWS). The NSWS pursued only lawful routes to reform, and indeed initially only the most genteel of those. 'In the 1870s, great store was set on presenting petitions to Parliament',[12] and much energy was expended on educative strategies aimed both at public opinion, and at potentially supportive MPs. In 1886, the NSWS claimed over 300 Commons supporters. Since 1870, sympathetic backbenchers of both parties had introduced appropriate private members' Bills. None attracted government support, and all failed through lack of parliamentary time.

The militant Women's Social and Political Union, associated with the Pankhurst family, was founded in 1903, in response to the perceived failure of 'constitutional' methods. Its own constitution implored members to engage in: 'Vigorous agitation upon lines justified by the position of outlawry to which women are at present condemned'.[13] Such agitation entailed increasingly serious illegality. It began in 1905 with the disruption of public meetings addressed by anti-suffrage MPs, escalated to confrontations with

---

10 *Op cit* p 12.
11 To redress the balance, see Liddington J and Norris J (1979) *One Hand Tied Behind Us* (London: Virago).
12 Rover *op cit* p 60.
13 Reproduced in Rover *op cit* p 76.

the police during public marches from 1907, to stone throwing at shop windows, and after 1913, to arson attacks on public buildings. Activists frequently welcomed arrest and trial as opportunities for publicity. Imprisonment also offered such possibilities. Many convicted women engaged in hunger strikes, which presented the Liberal government with the dilemma of either allowing them to starve to death, and so emerge as martyrs to a political cause, or releasing them and thereby allow them to evade the criminal law. An attempt to solve the dilemma by forced feeding attracted widespread public condemnation. In 1913, the Prisoner's Temporary Discharge for Ill Health Act (colloquially known as the 'Cat and Mouse Act') was rushed through Parliament with all party support. The Act permitted prisoners to be released, to resume their sentences when they had regained their health. It had little practical impact, and, in symbolic terms, emphasised the political rather than criminal basis of the controversy.

Successive Tory and Liberal leaders ostensibly made determined efforts to present enfranchisement as a non-party issue, in which an MP should act according to conscience rather than the dicates of party whips. Women activists generally subscribed to this bipartisan approach until 1912, when the suffragists formally aligned themselves with the Labour party, which was the only party committed to the women's right to vote.[14] Until then, they threw their (non-voting) support at elections behind whichever candidate, irrespective of party, favoured enfranchisement, a tactic which contributed to the defeat of several prominent Liberals.

But this strategy could also hinder the cause. George Lansbury, a radical Labour MP, was so fervent a supporter of female suffrage that he resigned his seat in 1912 to fight (and he assumed win) a by-election that would serve as a mini-referendum on the (male) elctorate's views on the question. Lansbury's predominantly working class male constituents were so antagonised by the upper class suffragettes contributing to his campaign that they returned the anti-suffragist Conservative candidate.

Both the 'constitutional' and militant wings came to share Chartism's contempt for Liberal governments. Gladstone earned considerable opprobrium for opposing a women's suffrage amendment to the 1884 Reform Bill. But Asquith was the bête noire of the suffrage movement. His 1892 sentiments remained in place in 1911. The various supporters of female suffrage coalesced

14 Although this policy had caused much heated debate within the party; see Pugh M (1985) 'Labour and women's suffrage' in Brown K (ed) *The First Labour Party* (London: Croom Helm).

between 1910 and 1912 around a 'Conciliation Bill', which would enfranchise those women already entitled to vote in municipal elections. The Bill was unexpectedly defeated on a free vote in the Commons. Several reasons contributed to the defeat. One is that the Bill was 'torpedoed' by Asquith's announcement that the government would introduce a wide-ranging Reform Bill in 1913, which might be amended to include women's enfranchisement. A second is that Asquith had secretly threatened to resign if the Bill was carried, a threat which prompted many Liberals and Irish members to renege on previous pledges of support. A third is that wavering MPs were tipped against the cause by the WSPU's extremism.

The subsequent government Bill was in turn 'torpedoed' by the Speaker's ruling that the women's suffrage amendment was inadmissible. There is no evidence that Asquith connived in this episode, but he was pleased by the outcome: 'The Speaker's coup d'état has bowled over the Women for this session – a great relief'.[15] Moreover, Asquith hoped that if the amendment had passed in the lower house, the Lords would exercise its new delaying powers for sufficient time for the Commons to change its mind.[16]

At the outbreak of World War One, both suffragists and suffragettes supended their campaigns. The issue thereafter assumed an entirely consensual air. Asquith appointed a 'Speaker's Conference' composed of 32 MPs, which proposed a franchise for men aged over 21, and women aged over 30, based solely on residence, along with further constituency reapportionment. The proposals were enacted in the Representation of the People Act ('RPA') 1918. The war undoubtedly contributed to the timing of enfranchisement, but the movement's eventual success was as much a symptom of the erosion of pervasive gender inequality in the social and economic spheres as of a sudden recognition of a need to restructure the political basis of the constitution.

Conclusion

The Speaker's Conference offered a formal and transparent device through which major constitutional reform could be planned in

15 Quoted in Rover *op cit* p 196.
16 *Ibid*, p 96. This perfectly ilustrates the point that constitutional law covers a sufficiently wide range of issues to permit a politician or judge to combine radicalism on some issues with rigid conservatism on others.

a way that transcended the generally partisan nature of Parliamentary politics. But in 1918, matters of substance were at least as important as those of process. In addition to proposing female suffrage, the conference made several other recommendations, which when enacted in the RPA 1918, ironed out most of the obvious remaining anti-democratic creases in the fabric of Britain's electoral system.[17]

Adult male suffrage was now granted solely on the basis of six months' residence in a constituency.[18] It was still possible for some citizens to have two votes, since the university franchise and a business premises franchise were retained, but the phenomenon of multiple outvoting was eliminated. The Act also acknowledged the desirability of maintaining constituencies with electorates of equal size, although it did not demand exact mathematical equality. Additionally, the RPA 1918 made several significant financial innnovations. Parliament finally accepted that the government, rather than the candidates, should bear the administrative costs of the election. To discourage frivolous candidates, a deposit of £150 (then a substantial sum) was required. This was returned if a candidate attracted more then 12.5% of the vote. To impose further economic equality on candidates, the spending limits introduced by the 1883 Act were almost halved in real terms. The principle that MPs should receive a salary had been accepted in 1912. It was nevertheless not until 1955 that all seats were contested.

This chapter has dwelt at greater length than most constitutional law textbooks on the historical dimension of electoral law and practice. This is in part because the episodes considered illustrate themes which continue to inform constitutional practice, in part to stress that the contemporary constitution is the product of much messy and hard fought political and social development.

Table 7.3
Uncontested seats in general elections

1906	1910*	1918	1924	1929	1931	1935	1945	1951
114	163	107	32	7	67	40	3	4

* Second election.

Source: Adapted from Butler and Sloman *op cit* pp 180–182.

17 For a useful summary see Butler D (1953) *The Electoral System in Britain 1918–1951* ch 1 (Oxford: Clarendon Press).
18 Women under 30 had to wait until 1928.

But longitudinal analysis also reveals the temporal ephemerality of even 'fundamental' constitutional orthodoxies. We would be rash to assume that the present law, to which we now turn, will not in but a few decades appear as anachronistic as do the situations of 1831, 1885 or 1917 to our modern eyes.

II. THE CONTEMPORARY ELECTORAL PROCESS

Despite the evidently 'democratic' credentials of Britain's electoral system, the contemporary political environment contains many voices advocating further electoral reform. Critics have three foci of discontent. The first relates to constituency apportionment. The second concerns the conduct of election campaigns, especially the cost and content of party political advertising. The third, and most significant, is the nature of the counting system through which citizens' choices are transmitted.

Apportionment – drawing constituency boundaries

The Parliamentary Constituencies Act 1986 is a consolidating statute which defines the powers and responsibilities of a body called the Boundary Commission. The commission is responsible for determining the size and shape of parliamentary constituencies in Scotland, Northern Ireland, Wales and England. This is obviously a task which has to be very sensitive to accusations of political bias. It is conceivable that boundaries could intentionally be drawn in ways that bestow a political advantage on one party. To minimise this problem, each country's commission (although nominally chaired by the Speaker) is headed by a High Court judge. She is assisted by two other members. Members are appointed by the government, but, as a matter of convention, are also approved by the opposition parties. A commission taking this form was first established in 1944. Earlier legislation ,had created bodies with less clearly structured apportionment responsibilities, staffed by party politicians, which consequently had great difficulty rebutting accusations that they could not be objective.[19] At 15-year intervals, the commission holds local inquiries, at which it receives representations from interested parties concerning reapportionment proposals. The commission must then present a report to the Home Secretary making recommendations. The Home Secretary must

19 See for example Cowling *op cit* pp 231–232.

then lay the report, with an implementing Order In Council (which may amend the proposals), before the Commons and Lords for approval.

Apportionment criteria – a non-justiciable issue?

In apportionning constituencies, the commission's discretion is structured by 'rules' contained in the House of Commons (Redistribution of Seats) Act 1949 Sch 2 (as amended). The 'rule' label is an unfortunate misnomer, since the legal status of Sch 2 provisions is frequently merely guidance to which the commission must have regard.

Rule 1 specifies (with some precision) the total number of constituencies. Britain must have not substantially more or fewer than 613, of which Scotland has not fewer than 71, and Wales not fewer than 35; Northern Ireland has 16–18. Rule 7 requires the commission to calculate an electoral quota – a figure arrived at by dividing the total number of registered voters by the number of constituencies. In 1990 the quota was approximately 68,000.

Thereafter, the commission must apply rather more discretionary criteria, seemingly ranked in the following order of importance. Rule 4 provides that, 'as far as practicable', constituencies should not cross county or London borough boundaries. Rule 5 then directs the commission, subject to rule 4, to make all constituencies as near to the electoral quota as possible: it may only depart from rule 4 if respecting county or London borough boundaries would produce 'excessive disparity' between a constituency's size and the electoral quota. Rule 6 then permits the Commission to override rules 4 and 5 if 'special considerations, including in particular the size, shape and accessibility of a constituency, appear to render a departure desirable'.

The legislation therefore does not require mathematical equivalence in constituency sizes. The original 1944 Act did make numerical equality the most important apportionment consideration, but this was amended in 1947 in favour of affording top priority to producing constituencies based on traditional local 'communities'.[20] Parliament clearly still viewed the Commons as the 'House of Communities'.

In practice, the Act produces substantial discrepancies in constituency size. Prior to the 1983 reapportionment, Buckingham constituency had 116,000 voters, while Newcastle Central had only 24,000.[1] Despite the 1983 reforms, by 1987 over one hundred

20 See Craig J (1959) 'Parliament and Boundary Commissions' *Public Law* 23–45.
1 Alder J (1994) *Constitutional and Administrative Law* p 161 (London: Macmillan).

seats deviated from the quota by over 20%. At the various extremes were the Orkney and Shetland constituency with barely 31,000 voters, and the Isle of Wight with over 98,000.[2]

Such variations provoke criticisms of anti-democratic practice, on the grounds that the system ignores the principle of 'one vote one value'.[3] This complaint has a collective and individuated dimension. Collectively, the votes of, for example, Orkney residents are 'worth' more than three times as much as those of Isle of Wight residents, since both constituencies return only one MP. More generally, the 'value' of a given constituency's voting power increases/decreases according to the extent by which its electorate is smaller/larger than the electoral quota. All communities are not created equal for electoral purposes.

The effective 'value' of an *individual* vote is more difficult to gauge. If, for example, residents in Newcastle Central and Buckingham voted in 1983 in identical proportions for the Conservative, Labour and Liberal parties, the relative sizes of the constituencies would not affect the parties' overall performance. However, if a party had only 12,001 supporters in the two areas combined (ie 9% of the total electorate), it could nonetheless win one (50%) of the two seats if they all lived and voted in Newcastle Central. This is an extreme illustration of the more general point that a party benefits greatly if its supporters are disproportionately concentrated in small constituencies. Conversely, parties whose supporters reside predominantly in large constituencies are disadvantaged. The Act does not expressly direct the Commission to take account of past voting patterns when designing new boundaries.

The apportionment criteria undoubtedly contain appreciable scope for unintended political bias,[4] and, thus, one might have thought, similarly wide scope for legal challenges to the Commission's recommendations. However Parliament sought to curtail litigation by providing in s 4(7) that any Order in Council *purportedly* made under the Act 'shall not be questioned in any legal proceedings'. The use of 'purports' presumably safeguards the Act against the judicial 'threat' to parliamentary sovereignty posed by *Anisminic*. This suggests that legislators see apportionment as a non-justiciable issue, to which Diceyan notions of the rule of law

2 Norton (1991) *op cit* p 94.
3 See especially Wade (1980) *op cit* ch 2.
4 Some commentators convincingly argue substantial bias is invariably unavoidable; see Taylor P and Gudgin G (1976) 'The myth of non-partisan cartography' *Urban Studies* 13–25.

cannot apply, despite the more general constitutional understanding that delegated legislation derives much of its legitimacy from its susceptibility to judicial review. Thus far the courts appear to agree with that analysis.[5]

The 1969 controversy

The courts' limited supervisory role has contributed to an explicitly partisan mode of dispute settlement within the Commons and Lords as evidenced by events following the breakdown of Harold Wilson's bipartisan initiative to reform the upper house.[6] The commission's 1969 recommendations, reflecting substantial population movement away from the cities, seemed likely to cost the Labour party a dozen seats in the next general election. James Callaghan, the Home Secretary, decided not to place an implementing Order before the two houses. Instead, the government introduced a Bill effecting only some of the commission's proposals, and also removing the Home Secretary's statutory obligation to lay the Order. The government (feebly) defended its strategy on the grounds that constituency reapportionment should be carried out in tandem with the redrawing of local government boundaries expected within the next few years.

The Conservative opposition considered the government was acting for partisan purposes. Consequently, the Lords' Conservative majority passed several wrecking amendments to the Bill, which was then withdrawn. Rather than reintroduce the Bill and invoke the Parliament Act procedures, the government instructed Labour MPs to *vote against* the Orders when Callaghan laid them before the Commons. The boundary changes could therefore not be introduced before the next election. This was perfectly legal; the Act did not require either House to approve the Orders, it merely commanded the Home Secretary to present them.

The cynicism underlying the Labour cabinet's manipulation of Parliamentary procedure is neatly illustrated by an extract from Crossman's *Diaries*:

'We agreed to have all the Orders put to the Commons and the trick would be to put them but not approve them, so that . . . we would negate the lot. [Wilson has won]. We have not been discredited because the ordinary public are convinced that both the Government and the

5 See *Harper v Secretary of State for the Home Department* [1955] Ch 238, CA. For comment see Craig J *op cit*; DeSmith S (1955) 'Boundaries between Parliament and the courts' *Modern Law Review* 281–286.
6 Pp 210–212 above.

Tories are concerned for our own self-interest. . . . We have defeated
the Lords and the Tories and killed the redistribution.'[7]

The 1983 controversy

The 1969 episode does little to reinforce one's faith in the integriy
of political parties' approaches to the apportionment question,
particularly as the effectiveness of intra-Parliamentary blocking
mechanisms is so obviously dependent on party majorities in each
house. There is however no ouster clause preventing litigation
trying to stop the commission presenting its report to the Home
Secretary. Whether such litigation enjoyed any prospects of success
was, until 1983, an open question – to which the courts then
offered a curt answer.

In the early 1980s, the Labour party feared that the commission's
recommendations for the 1983 election would significantly benefit
the Conservative Party. In *R v Boundary Commission for England, ex p
Foot*,[8] the party's leader, Michael Foot, sought a judicial review of
the commission's findings. Mr Foot contended that the Commission had misconstrued its responsibilities by regarding the statutory 'rule' requiring approximate parity in constituency sizes as
subordinate to the 'rule' that constituencies should not straddle
county or London borough boundaries. Mr Foot argued that the
substantial divergences in constituency size envisaged by the proposals 'offend[ed] against the principle of equal representation for
all electors which is required by our modern system of Parliamentary representation'.[9] The applicants sought a court order to prevent the commission from submitting its recommendations to the
Home Secretary. The application was dismissed at first instance and
on appeal.

Given the wording of the 1949 Act, the applicants were advancing an optimistic argument. Whether the constitution recognises
a principle of 'equal representation' in electoral districting which
demands mathematical equality is a moot (and political) point,
but clearly not one expressed unambiguously in the Act. In effect,
Mr Foot was asking the court to attach the same constitutional
significance to the moral principle of 'one vote one value' as it
had attached to the moral principle of the 'rule of law' in *Anisminic*. The court declined to do so. Sir John Donaldson MR categor-
ised the commission's task as a presumptively non-justiciable issue
in the absence of all but the most egregious malfeasance.

7 *Op cit* p 660.
8 [1983] QB 600, CA.
9 *Ibid*, at 617.

The feebleness of Labour's performance at the 1983 and 1987 elections was so profound that loss of a few seats because of reapportionment decisions had no bearing on the overall result. In subsequent years, the party appeared to have accepted the non-justiciabilty of the commission's recommendations. Rather than devote resources to a retrospective court challenge, Labour appointed a small task force to trail the commission around the country and make representations at every inquiry. The tactic appeared successful. Initial predictions that the 1994 recommendations would cost the Labour Party twenty seats proved ill-founded – as few as two or three were ultimately affected.[10] 'One vote one value' is an idea whose time has not yet come within the British constitution. The potential shortcomings of the apportionment process should not however be seen in isolation from other aspects of electoral law, especially the vote counting method discussed below. But before broaching that question, we briefly explore the conduct of election campaigns.

The contents and conduct of election campaigns

This is a potentially broad topic. We will focus on four subjects: the voters, the candidates, and the financing and content of electoral advertising. The following pages do not offer a comprehensive guide to the minutiae of the law,[11] but merely identify some of the more important elements of the electoral process. Jurisdiction over disputed elections is still vested in the High Court, which is empowered to invalidate results and disqualify malfeasors from subsequent elections. Few petitions are now presented, a state of affairs primarily attributable to an apparently pervasive acceptance of the moral propriety of electoral law.

The voters

Constitutional morality now accepts that voting is not a privilege which must be earned through property or educational qualifications, but a right extending to virtually all adult citizens which can only be forfeited through various specified forms of behaviour. The only citizens presumptively excluded from the franchise are the Monarch and members of the Lords, although since these

10 Wood N (1994) 'Tories may lose eight seats in capital boundary changes' *The Times*, 11 August; McKie D (1994) 'Labour triumph in boundary change review' *The Guardian*, 11 August.
11 A task admirably performed by Rawlings H *op cit.*

individuals may give up their titles, they are not barred from participation in the electoral process.[12]

Since the passage of the RPA 1948, all other citizens over 18 years old may vote if their names are entered on the electoral register of the constituency where they reside.[13] The register is compiled annually by local government officials. One may not vote without registering. While there is no legal obligation compelling registered citizens to exercise their vote, failure to respond to registration forms is an offence. Individuals may not vote if they are serving prison sentences, are suffering serious mental incapacity, or have recently been convicted of electoral malpractice. The university and business franchises were abolished in 1948, since when no-one has been entitled to more than one vote.

Registration was first introduced in 1832 as a device to minimise fraudulent voting among the newly extended electorate. The process was initially subjected to considerable abuse, as parties 'soon discovered ways of utilizing the system to [their] best advantage – making claims for apathetic voters, paying their fees,[14] objecting to hostile applicants, and even securing admission to the register on fraudulent grounds'.[15] The RPA 1918 introduced a more rigorous process, in which local authorities assumed responsibiity for ensuring the register's accuracy. In the modern era, there have been few suggestions that the registration process is abused; although in 1994 accusations were levelled that politicians in Westminster council deliberately omitted to send registration documents to likely Labour voters in marginal parliamentary constituencies.

The candidates

There are few collective prohibitions on candidacy. Parties advocating such extremist political philosophies as the National Front and Socialist Workers Party regularly field candidates, albeit never victorious ones. Nor is there any prohibition on parties such as

---

12 Peers have been permitted to do so since the passage of the Peerage Act 1963.
13 'Residence' is a justiciable concept. For details see *Ferris v Wallace* 1936 SC 561; *Fox v Stirk and Bristol Electoral Registration Officer* [1970] 2 QB 463; *Hipperson v Newbury District Electoral Registration Officer* [1985] QB 1060. A citizen may only be resident for voting purposes in one constituency.
14 The registration fee was known as the 'poll tax'. There is at presently no *direct* fee payable for registering to vote. As chapter 11 notes, it has been suggested that the Thatcher governments introduced an indirect way of achieving that effect.
15 O'Leary C *op cit* pp 16–17.

Plaid Cymru, the Scottish Nationalists, or Sinn Fein, whose primary policy objective is to secure their respective country's independence. The entitlement to contest elections does not however extend to certain 'proscribed organisations', designated under the Prevention of Terrorism Acts, these being such terrorist groups as the UVF, the IRA, and the INLA. Merely to belong to such a group is a criminal offence. The justification for this is presumably that the groups concerned have chosen to pursue their political objectives outside the democratic process.

The requirement that MPs be wealthy was, as noted above, abolished in 1872. At present, electoral law retains a modest financial barrier to candidacy itself. All candidates must produce a deposit of £500, which is forfeit if they fail to gain 5% of the vote. The rationale for the election deposit is not that impecunious candidates are per se unsuitable legislators, but that it prevents frivolous candidates from belittling the election process and/or making it harder to administer.

Candidates need not reside in their chosen constituency, but must be nominated by 10 registered voters. Various statutes also disqualify a miscellaneous collection of citizens from candidacy, including those under 21 years old, non-citizens (except Irish nationals), peers, Church of England and Roman Catholic clergymen, bankrupt debtors, and some categories of criminals and the mentally ill. This is overall a residual and quantitatively insignificant restriction, although as chapter 8 suggests, individual exclusions can provoke great controversy.

The legal framework regulating candidacy is directed towards the candidate as an individual. Unlike most other 'democratic countries', Britain has no legislation dealing explicitly with the question of the organisation and management of political parties. Insofar as the parties' internal affairs conform to democratic principles, they do so entirely as a matter of self-regulation.[16] Such issues as the selection of parliamentary candidates, the formation of party policy, and the election of party leaders, are all matters where Parliament has chosen not to interfere directly with party autonomy. Nor is there as yet anything to indicate that the courts consider such matters justiciable. An opportunity to test that assumption arose in 1990, when the Conservative party ignored its rules for electing its leader when John Major succeeded Margaret

---

16 Norton (1991) *op cit* pp 101–103.

Thatcher.[17] No challenge was issued however. Nor do constitutional lawyers appear to consider the question of much importance: intra-party democracy is an issue few legal commentators
have examined.[18]

After the 1992 election, the Labour party attempted to increase
the number of women MPs in the Commons by imposing 'women
only' candidate shortlists in some constituencies. This policy was
declared unlawful by an industrial tribunal in early 1996.[19] This
raises a further dimension of the 'electoral equality' principle:
women and citizens of minority ethnicity are severly under-repre-
sented both as MPs and candidates, and, as candidates, are disproportionately concentrated in unwinnable seats.[20] Legislative
intervention to address this situation at present seems unlikely,
but it is not to fanciful to speculate that this is an issue where
the present law will appear manifestly 'undemocratic' to future
generations.

Financing elections

More attention has been paid to electoral finance.[21] British campaigns are no longer marked by the violence and intimidation
which so concerned the 1832 reformers. Nor do bribery or treating
affect the contemporary process.[1] Similarly, the practice of spiritual intimidation seems to have faded away. Such threats would
technically be caught by the crime of 'undue influence' (now RPA
1983 s 115), but s 115 prosecutions are more likely in respect of
activities such as defacing a candidate's posters or pulling leaflets
from voters' letterboxes.[2]

But there is more to fairness than an absence of physical force
and financial corruption. This becomes apparent when one
observes that the discrepancy between the historically local form
of the electoral system and the nationalisation of political choice
evident in the apportionment process is also apparent in the
laws governing the amounts parties and candidates can spend on
election campaigns.

17 See Alderman R and Smith M (1990) 'Can British Prime Ministers be given the
   push by their parties?' *Parliamentary Affairs* 260–276; Alderman R and Carter N
   (1991) 'A very Tory coup: the ousting of Mrs Thatcher' *Parliamentary Affairs*
   125–139.
18 The notable exception being Dawn Oliver; see her chapter in three successive
   editions (1985, 1989, and 1994) of Jowell and Oliver *op cit.*
19 See Webster P, Wilkinson P and Gibb F (1966) ' "Women only" Labour seats
   ruled illegal' *The Times*, 9 January.
20 Norton *op cit* pp 101–103.
21 See in particular Rawlings *op cit* ch 5; Ewing K (1987) *The Funding of Political
   Parties in Britain* (Oxford: Clarendon Press).
1 See Rawlings H *op cit* pp 146–149.   2 *Roberts v Hogg* 1971 SLT 78.

The reasoning behind the limits on expenditure first introduced by the Corrupt Practices Act 1883 makes obvious democratic sense. The restrictions ensure that the merits of a candidate's arguments, rather than the size of her advertising budget, determine her electoral popularity. The letter of the 1883 law has been retained, with regularly updated financial thresholds, but one might wonder if we still respect its spirit. At present, each candidate is allowed by RPA 1983 s 76 to spend 3,600 + about 3p (boroughs) or 4p (counties) for every registered voter in the constituency. Rich candidates cannot derive an advantage from their wealth by, for example, employing dozens of full-time helpers, or sending out glossy leaflets for weeks on end. Doubts exist as to when the expenditure clock starts ticking. The announcement of the dissolution of Parliament would appear the most likely point. This means of course that a wealthy candidate could spend unlimited amounts of money on publicity prior to the dissolution, but there is no indication that this is done.

Early efforts to enforce expenditure limits were handicapped by the law's limited focus. Only the candidate himself or his agent were covered by the the rule: expenditure by 'independent' individuals or companies was not subject to any ceiling. This provoked ingenious efforts by candidates and their supporters to establish 'independent' financial relationships, and much litigation ensued as defeated opponents sought to disprove the supporter's allegedly autonomous status.[3] This loophole was plugged by RPA 1918 s 34(1) (now RPA 1983 s 75), which prohibited any expenditure intended to promote a candidate unless the promoter received written authorisation from the candidate's agent. Any such expenditure counts towards the candidate's overall limit.[4]

The candidate's agent must compile an election return detailing all expenses. This is a public document, open to inspection by other candidates. Failure to produce the return is also an offence. However there is no mechanism for independent official scrutiny of returns. Any challenge to the legality of a candidate's expenditure is dependent upon the initiative of other candidates or voters.

The limits on spending only apply to *local* campaigns. As Alder observes: 'The kind of campaign envisaged by the law is centred upon knocking on doors and holding meetings in public halls'.[5] As with apportionment, the law does not recognise the concept

3 O'Leary C *op cit* pp 54–55.
4 For the background to the 1918 reform, its precise terms, and an example of its early implementation, see *R v Hailwood and Ackroyd Ltd* [1928] 2 KB 277, CCA.
5 Alder *op cit* p 163.

of a 'general election' for financial purposes; rather it sees 650 individual elections.

This is illustrated by the *Tronoh Mines* case.[6] Shortly before the 1951 general election, the Tronoh Mines company placed an advertisement in *The Times*, part of which read:

> 'The coming general election will give us all the opportunity of saving the country from being reduced, through the policies of the Socialist government, to a bankrupt "Welfare State" . . .'

The advert was clearly disparaging the Labour party, and thus indirectly boosting the Conservatives' prospects. The company and *The Times* were subsequently prosecuted (under what is now RPA 1983 s 75) for making unauthorised expenditure designed to promote the candidacy of the Conservative in the constituency where the paper was printed. McNair J, held that there was no case to answer. He considered that the advert's purpose was 'to advance the prospects of the anti-Socialist cause generally' by influencing public opinion as a whole.[7] The Act, however, addressed only efforts to promote 'a candidate at a particular election, and not candidates at elections generally'.[8] Since the advert played to a national, not constituency audience, it was not prohibited.

Parliament has not overturned this principle. Thus there is no legal limit to the funds a party can spend on its national campaigns. Parties can put as many adverts as they like in national newspapers; or buy as many poster sites as they like all over the country. The only restriction they are under is the depth of their pockets. Rawlings observes that *Tronoh Mines* 'is an excellent illustration of the blindness of our electoral law to the realities of national election campaigning'.[9] This should not be seen as a criticism of McNair J, whose interpretation of the Act was entirely logical. If the current law is unsatisfactory, blame is more appropriately laid at Parliament's feet.

The courts have however concluded that the rules apply to expenditure intended to secure the *defeat* of a particular candidate. This point was first made in *R v Hailwood and Ackroyd Ltd*.[10] The defendant, a disaffected Conservative, distributed leaflets in his constituency which urged voters not to support the Conservative candidate, but which did not expressly advise them to support

6 *R v Tronoh Mines Ltd* [1952] 1 All ER 697, CCA.
7 *Ibid*, at 698.
8 *Ibid*, at 699.
9 *Op cit* p 135.
10 [1928] 2 KB 277, CCA.

any other candidate. The Court of Criminal Appeal upheld the conviction, on the grounds that such activities indirectly improved the chances of all other candidates in the constituency. The principle was confirmed 50 years later by the House of Lords in *DPP v Luft*.[11] Luft had circulated leaflets in a several constituencies which urged voters not to support the National Front candidate, but did not specify a favoured candidate. A unanimous court approved Lord Diplock's conclusion that 'to persuade candidates not to vote for one candidate in order to prevent his being elected must have the effect of improving the collective prospects of success of the other candidates'.[12] Had Messers Hailwood and Luft, like Tronoh Mines, expressed their distate generally via an advert in *The Times*, their expenditure would have been permissible.

In the Britain of 1883, a concept of financial equality limited to local campaigns was perhaps defensible. The party system was clearly well-established by then, but one still had 'independent' candidates, and the relative technological backwardness of the news media and transport infrastructure made local campaigns an important contributor to voter choice. Certainly, national party loyalties had a strong influence on voter behaviour, but they were not obviously the dominant factor.

In the Britain of the 1990s, political realities are very different. Few would dispute that general elections are fought and won and lost in the national arena. Voter choice is motivated far less by the personal characteristics of a candidate than by her party affiliation. Similarly, the information on which that choice is based is more likely to have been gleaned from national sources, such as televison, the radio, or the press, than from localised techniques such as listening to candidate's local speeches, reading her election literature, or questioning her by letter or in person. One might plausibly conclude therefore that the more money a party spends on its national campaign, the more likely it is to persuade people all over the country that they should vote for that party's local candidate. There is no guarantee that spending lots of money will win a party lots more support. Advertising could be counter-productive; voters may be anatagonised by party propoganda. But as Table 7.4 indicates, campaign expenditure has been rising in recent years.

Whether one can establish a correlation between the Conserva-

11 [1977] AC 962. See Munro C (1976) 'Elections and expenditure' *Public Law* 300–304.
12 *Ibid*, at 983.

Table 7.4
Party campaign spending in recent general elections

	1983	1987	1992
Conservative	£3.6m	£9.0m	£11.2m
Labour	£2.2m	£4.2m	£10.2m
Liberal/SDP	£1.9m	£2.0m	£1.8m

Source: Compiled from data in Butler D and Kavanagh D (1988) *The British General Election of 1987* pp 235–236 (London: Macmillan); (1993) *The British General Election of 1992* p 260 (London: Macmillan).

tive party's higher spending and its electoral success is a question offering no easy answer. Deciding whether the constitution should tolerate the possibility of electoral choice being swayed by party wealth would seem more straightforward. The spirit of the 1883 Act was to sever the direct link between financial and political power; the retention merely of its letter in a quite different political context ensures that that objective is no longer achieved.

An equally significant omission is the absence of any legal requirement that parties reveal the sources of their income. This raises the possibility that powerful economic interests may 'buy' legislative influence. Neither are there any limits on the size of contributions that individuals or corporations may make to a political party. Periodic stories appear in the national press alleging that life peerages have in effect been 'bought' by leading industrialists whose companies have made large donations to Conservative party funds. Such allegations are unproven, but if substantiated would clearly further undermine the Lords' legitimacy. A greater concern is that substantial numbers of MPs may be predisposed to favour policies benefiting a substantial donor, irrespective of their intrinsic merits.

Such gaps in the law merely emphasise that the formal structure of this part of the constitution has not kept pace with changing political circumstances. With one exception, the modern political campaigning process exists within a Victorian legal framework. The exception is televison and radio, perhaps the most powerful modern communication media. On this point, the constitution accepts that parties' wealth should have no bearing on their access to the public. Air time was initially allocated by a body called the Committee on Party Political Broadcasting, composed of representatives from television and radio organisations, and members of the main political parties. The committee allocated a small amount of air time to each party, the share being roughly in accordance with the party's portion of the vote at the last general election.

While both the BBC and the IBA are legally obliged to maintain political impartiality in their programming decisions, the committee itself has no explicit legal basis. Nor could the committee be described as a 'conventional' institution in the formal sense. The process in fact broke down in 1987, when decisions were made solely by the broadcasting organisations themselves. In the run up to the 1987 general election, the three main parties had five television broadcasts and the Greens one. It may seem anomalous that so important a part of the electoral process is not regulated by an explicit statutory framework. Yet paradoxically this is one of the few aspects of the system attuned to the realities of contemporary campaigns. There are no technical obstacles preventing Parliament intervening in this area; as yet no government has invited it to do so.[13]

'Decent, honest and truthful'? The content of political advertising

Nor has Parliament yet taken steps to regulate the content of party advertising. Hyperbolic claims and vitriolic abuse now seem a staple ingredient of election campaigns, as are lurid tales of opposing parties' hidden political agendas. The low points of the 1992 general election campaign were the Conservatives' entirely mendacious statement that a Labour government would increase everybody's tax bill by at least £1200 per year, and Labour's unsubstantiated insistence that the Conservatives were intent on privatising the National Health Service,

Criticisms of individual members of other parties may be subject to defamation laws. However it seems unlikely that a *political party* can sue to defend its reputation.[14] Clearly one would not wish voters' choices to be influenced by lies. But 'truth' is an elusive concept, and has little bearing on matters of political opinion such as 'A Labour government would ruin the economy' or 'A Conservative government will produce increased unemployment'. In 1895, a private member's Bill was enacted which forbade the making of a 'false statement of fact' intended to hamper a candidate's prospects of success. Matters such as a circular letter falsely announcing a candidate's withdrawal from the contest, and press accusations of salmon poaching, were offered by MPs as evidence

13 See generally Boyle A (1986) 'Political broadcasting, fairness and administrative law' *Public Law* 562–596.
14 See Loveland I (1994) 'Defamation of government: taking lessons from America?' *Legal Studies* 61–80.

of such unworthy practices. The courts subsequently held that the Act extended only to statements concerning a candidate's personal characteristics, not his political views. A private member's Bill to reverse this decision failed through lack of government support in 1911.[15] The present law, RPA 1983 s 106, maintains the personal/political distinction: falsely calling a candidate a 'communist' or 'fascist' does not contravene the Act.

One might again note that this measure is directed solely at individual candidates. False statements (assuming their falsity could be established) directed at parties are not covered. Publicity deployed in the notorious 'khaki election' of 1900, in which the Conservatives accused the Liberals of supporting the Boers against whom Britain was then conducting a war, was consequently not illegal. The problem is perhaps intensified by the fact that party manifestos have no legal status in respect of subsequent central government policy,[16] although as we have seen they guide the Lords' conventional interpretation of its delaying powers.

One therefore depends on the electorate being sufficiently sophisticated to recognise when parties are making unfounded claims. Whether such an assumption is justified is an open question. But the nature of press coverage in recent elections, and the extravagance of many claims made by the political parties, might suggest that politicians and journalists have a somewhat low opinion of the voters' analytical capacities.[17]

Counting the vote

There is no evidence to suggest that the integrity of modern elections is compromised by irregularities in the physical process of adding up individual votes. Ballot slips are not altered after the voter fills them in, forged papers are not added to the ballot box, and boxes do not go astray. The count is an open process, which all candidates may scrutinise. But the concept of 'counting' votes can also bear a rather wider meaning. The most frequently voiced complaint concerning the present system is the limited correlation between the votes that a party receives and the number of seats it wins. Chapter one adverted to the problems posed in a democratic

15 O'Leary C *op cit* pp 179–181, 216–226.
16 Their legal status in respect of local government policy is considered in chapter 10.
17 See the sections on press coverage in Butler D and Kavanagh D (1984; 1988; 1993) *The British General Election of 1982; 1987; 1992* respectively (London: Macmillan).

Table 7.5
Votes gained and seats won at general elections since 1945

Year	Conservative		Labour		Liberal *		Turnout
	Votes %	Seats	Votes %	Seats	Votes %	Seats	
1945	39.8	213	47.8	393	9.0	12	72.7%
1950	43.5	298	46.1	315	9.1	9	84.0%
1951	48.0	321	48.8	295	2.5	6	82.5%
1955	49.7	344	46.4	277	2.7	6	76.7%
1959	49.4	365	43.8	258	5.9	6	78.8%
1964	43.4	304	44.1	317	11.2	9	77.1%
1966	41.9	253	47.9	363	8.5	12	75.8%
1970	46.4	330	43.0	287	7.5	6	72.0%
1974 [1]	37.9	297	37.1	301	19.3	14	78.7%
1974 [2]	35.8	277	39.2	319	18.3	13	72.8%
1979	43.9	339	36.9	269	13.8	11	76.0%
1983	42.4	397	27.6	209	25.4	23	72.7%
1987	42.3	376	30.8	292	22.6	22	75.3%
1992	41.9	336	34.4	271	17.8	20	77.7%

* 1983 and 1987 votes include the Social Democratic Party

Source: Compiled from data in Norton *op cit* pp 97–99: Butler and Kavanagh (1993) *op cit* p 246.

state by the tyranny of the majority. Table 7.5 reveals that modern Britain has never suffered the problem of majoritarian government, since (except for the dubious exception of the 1977 Lib/Lab pact) it has never had a peacetime government enjoying majority electoral support. No government elected since 1945 has secured over 50% of the vote. The best Conservative performance was 49.7% in 1955. Labour's highest ever share was 48.8% in 1951. However, Labour lost the 1951 election. The Conservatives, who obtained a smaller portion of the vote, gained seven more Commons seats. Moreover, column 5 reveals that by no means everybody chooses to vote. The Thatcher governments elected in 1979, 1983 and 1987 had the positive support of about one-third of the population.

Thus the British electoral system permits *minority rule*, not simply majoritarianism. If one's concern as a constitutional lawyer is to ensure that government derives its powers from the consent of the governed, this may seem unsatisfactory, especially as that government has de facto control of Parliament's unlimited legal competence. Majorities or minorities are not necessarily tyrannical or undemocratic – both tyranny and democracy can be construed as concepts concerned with what government does with power, as well as how government gets and retains it. Equally, one might wonder if merely avoiding tyranny is an adequate ambition for a democratic constitution? These are points to which we shall return. For the present, we might focus on the question of how the seat/vote discrepancy arises.

This situation is an almost inevitable consequence of a country in which most electoral support is closely divided between two main political parties choosing the 'plurality' counting system in single member constituencies. The 'plurality' or 'first past the post' rule means that one wins a constituency simply by polling more votes than any other candidate. In a two party contest, the winner must gain 50%+1 of the votes cast, an outcome which raises the prospect of barely majoritarian government. However, should four candidates compete, the seat could be won with as few as 25%+1 votes. The more candidates that stand, and the more evenly balanced their electoral support, the fewer votes needed to be successful; a particular constituency can be won by a party representing only a small minority of voters.

Supporters of defeated parties in our hypothetical four-candidate constituency have exercised only indirect, negative power over the selection of their MP, insofar as if they did not vote for losing candidates A, B, or C, winning candidate D would need fewer votes to succeed. But these 75%−1 voters have not exercised any direct, positive control over the choice of their legislative representative. This is often referred to as the 'wasted vote' problem. In legal terms, one votes not for one's party on a national basis, but for an individual representative of one's party in an individual constituency. Indeed it was not until 1969 that candidates were even permitted to record their party affiliation on the ballot paper. The 'general election' label is a misnomer; rather one has 650 simultaneous local elections. Supporters of defeated parties cannot pick up their wasted votes and use them to support another of their party's candidates somewhere else.

Within an individual constituency, there will always be a mismatch between votes cast and seats won in contested elections unless every voter supports one candidate, since there is only one seat to win. But the potential shortcomings of the single member plurality system are magnified when one aggregates the results of all 650 constituencies to determine whose representatives gain de facto control of Parliament's unlimited legal sovereignty.

If modern Britain had only two political parties, enjoying approximately equal popular support, a party could theoretically take every seat by winning each constituency with 50%+1 votes: the party which won 50%−1 votes in every constituency would have no MPs at all. In a country with an electorate of over 40 million, a party would need only 650 votes more than its only rival to control every Commons seat.

Such theoretical extremes do not occur in practice. But candidates regularly win constituencies with only 40% of the votes, because the majority of electors have split their vote among several other parties (see Table 7.6). A constituency is rarely won by a candidate who gains more than 65% support. Consequently at least a substantial minority of votes are always 'wasted'.

In a two party system, where each party enjoys approximately equal support, the parties' wasted votes may cancel each other out. If one examines just the Conservative and Labour performances in Table 7.5, one sees that the party with more votes generally (but not always) wins more seats, and that the Commons majority increases as the voting share expands. But Table 7.5 also shows that the percentage of the *total vote* shared between the Labour and Conservative parties has declined sharply since 1945.[18] Other parties have attracted growing electoral support. They have not as a consequence gained growing Parliamentary representation.

The Liberal party has suffered acutely from the vote/seat discrepancy. In 1983 the SDP/Liberal Alliance received 25.4% of the vote but only 23 MPs. In 1987, their 22.6% of the vote produced only 22 MPs. Liberal support is spread relatively evenly throughout Britain. Consequently, Liberals often come second in both Labour and Conservative constituencies. But in a single MP constituency system, there are no direct rewards for coming second. Small parties whose support is geographically concentrated may fare less badly. Scots, Welsh and Northern Irish nationalists, for example,

Table 7.6
Minoritarianism in parliamentary constituency elections

Constituency	Year	Con	Lab	Lib*	Nat
Carlisle	1983	37.3%	37.5%	25.1%	–
Stockton North	1983	33.3%	37.1%	29.6%	–
Brecon and Radnor	1987	34.7%	29.2%	34.8%	1.3%
South Stockton	1987	35.0%	31.3%	33.7%	–
Nairn and Lochaber	1992	22.6%	25.1%	26.0%	24.7%
Renfrew West	1992	32.9%	36.6%	10.0%	20.2%

* Includes SDP.

Source: Compiled from data in Butler and Kavanagh (1983); (1988); (1993) *op cit.*

18 On the reasons for this decline, which appear broadly to reflect a breakdown of traditional working class/middle class divisions, see Norton (1991) *op cit* pp 105–115.

do not contest seats outside their respective countries, and so are less acutely affected by the wasted vote problem.

Alternative voting systems

The plurality model is generally contrasted with a voting mechanism described as 'proportional representation' (PR). PR is an umbrella term, embracing many electoral systems. Insofar as they share a common theme, it is an intention to produce a closer relationship between the votes cast for and seats won by parties attracting substantial national or regional voter support.

PR is not a novel idea in British constitutional theory.[19] John Stuart Mill coupled his advocacy of women's enfranchisement with support for the 'Hare' scheme of PR (named after its inventor).[20] This system was adopted in Tasmania shortly thereafter,[1] and a variant of it is described below. The 1867 Reform Act contained a Lords' amendment which might now be regarded as a form of PR. The 'minority voting' provision created three member constituencies in Liberal dominated areas in which voters were allowed only two choices – the three candidates with the most votes being returned. This virtually guaranteed the return of a Tory member in constituencies where the Tory party could muster 34+% support.

PR generated a particular flurry of parliamentary and extra-parliamentary activity during the passage of the 1884 Reform Act. Many proponents were motivated by a purely sectarian desire to safeguard the representation of the minority protestant community in Ireland. Others, including E C Clark, then Regius Professor of Civil Law at Cambridge, saw PR as a Madisonian guard against factional legislation, which would remove any incentive for parties to offer sensationalist policies in the hope of appealing to the bigotry or ignorance of an 'impulsive' electorate.[2] The Speaker's Conference established during World War I had indeed recommended that the plurality method be replaced by a PR scheme. This was put to a free vote in both houses, where it attracted substantial, if not sufficient, support.[3]

It is not entirely sensible to consider electoral reform in isolation from other constitutional issues; the method one adopts to choose

---

19 See Hart J (1992) *Proportional Representation: Critics of the British Electoral System 1820–1945* (Oxford: Clarendon Press).
20 Hart J *op cit* ch 2.
1 Brown W (1899) 'The Hare system in Tasmania' *LQR* 51–70.
2 Jones A *op cit* pp 99–100.
3 See Butler (1953) *op cit* ch 1.

one's legislature may well be affected by one's choice as to its powers. It is nonetheless helpful to outline the basic features of alternatives to the plurality/single member model.

The party list system

A national list system maximises the correlation between seats cast and votes won; a party gaining x% of the votes wins x% of the seats. There is in effect only one constituency – namely the entire country – under a national list system. Voters choose a party, not an individual candidate. The parties themselves draw up lists of candidates. Parties which gained sufficient votes for 10, 20 or 50 seats respectively would send the first 10, 20 and 50 members on their list to the legislature. Israel operates the purest list system. In its 120-member Knesset, a party will gain a legislative seat with only 1% of the popular vote.

A national list system completely eliminates both the wasted vote problem and the difficulties of apportionment. Whether it is however more 'democratic' is a complex question. Critics of the Israeli system observe that it affords legislative representation to extremist political parties, thereby lending an unwarranted legitimacy to their policies. In the British system, in contrast, given the existence of three mainstream parties, an extremist candidate will need at least 25%+1 support in a given constituency to win its seat. This danger may be countered by having a representation threshold – a party receives no seats at all unless it passes a 5% or 10% or 15% of the vote barrier. The higher the threshold, the more difficult it becomes for extremist parties to gain representation.

The list method also offers opportunities for small parties to enter government by forming coalitions with larger parties. If such coalitions result from post-election negotiation, one may end up with a government for which no-one has actually voted.[4] That objection could be overcome if parties were to announce their prospective coalition partners prior to the poll.

Critics also point out that the list places complete control of candidate selection in the hands of party officials, although this criticism may be met by a legal framework which opens up parties' selection processes to all of their members. Similarly, accusations that the list precludes any identification between a given legislator and particular parts of the country can be reduced (if not eliminated) by compiling lists on a regional rather than national basis.

4 See Stellman H (1985) 'Israel: the 1984 election and after' *Parliamentary Affairs* pp 73–85.

British advocates of the party list mechanism suggest that if the system had operated for the 1983 general elections, the parties' seat tallies would have been Conservative 275, Labour 179, and Liberals/SDP 168, rather than the 397, 209, and 23 produced by the plurality method. This is a misleading claim, for it assumes that voter behaviour takes no account of the voting system. One cannot know which party voters would have chosen had different electoral mechanisms been used. The Liberals may have attracted even more votes under a list system, since many supporters may reluctantly have chosen another party on the assumption that the Liberal could not win that particular seat. Conversely, many Labour or Conservative supporters may have voted Liberal in constituencies where their preferred party was in third place, hoping to defeat the party they liked least.

The single transferable vote

The unpredictability of voting behaviour applies to all forms of PR, so one would be rash to impute particular consequences to projected reforms. The single tranferable vote (STV) method (a development of the Hare system), does however offer the advantage of being tried, tested and evidently approved in Ireland, Malta and Australia.

STV employs multi-member constituencies. Parties field as many candidates as they wish, while voters mark candidates in order of preference. A candidate is successful if she attains first preference votes equivalent to one more than the number of electors divided by the number of candidates + 1. In a four-member constituency this figure would be 20%+1; in a three member constituency 25% +1, and so on. That candidate's second preference votes are then allocated as new first preference votes to the remaining candidates. Any candidates thereby reaching the quota are also elected, and their second preferences are in turn divided among remaining candidates until all seats are filled. If all seats cannot be filled by working from the top down, one begins to redistribute from the bottom up. The candidate with the fewest first preference votes is eliminated, and his second preference allocated to the others. If need be, the process is repeated until all seats are filled.

STV is time-consuming and complex, and also requires large and potentially unwieldy constituencies. Nevertheless, particularly in constituencies returning four or more members, it minimises the wasted vote problem. It also enables voters not wishing to support a straight party line to express a preference between individual candidates as well as between parties.

Absolute majority systems

Absolute majority systems are not strictly concerned with proportionality, but with ensuring that the winning candidate in a single member constituency attracts majority electoral support, thereby reducing but not eliminating the wasted vote problem. This may be achieved through the 'alternative vote' method. Voters list candidates in order of preference. If a candidate secures 50% first preference votes she is elected. If no candidate does so, the least popular is eliminated and his second preference votes are re-allocated to the remaining candidates. This process is repeated until one candidate passes the 50% barrier.

Another route to a similar end is offered by the 'second ballot' method. Should more than two candidates run, the first ballot operates solely to eliminate all but the two most popular. These two candidates then contest a run-off election shortly after the initial contest. This both ensures majority support, and also offers voters the chance to reflect on their final choice.

The German system

Elections to Germany's *Bundestag* employ a mix method of plurality voting in one member constituencies coupled with a regional list.[5] Half of the *Bundestag* seats are allocated to candidates gaining a plurality in their constituencies, half to candidates on the lists. However, voters also have a second vote in which they express a party preference. After the constituency candidates take their seats, each party's representation in the *Bundestag* is increased to that number which equates in percentage terms to its share of the party votes.

The process can usefully be illustrated by returning to the absurd example canvassed above in which Party A gains 50%+1 votes in every constituency, while Party B gains 50%−1. In Britain, Party A wins every seat. In Germany (assuming voters follow a straight party line), Party A wins every constituency seat, but only one party seat, the rest of which go to Party B. Party A thus gains the slimmest of majorities to reflect its tiny lead in the popular vote.

The German method is somewhat complex, but much less so than STV, and it offers the benefits of almost perfect proportionality along with constituency representation. It also addresses the

5 For a detailed descripton and critique see Bogdanor V (1983) *What is Proportional Representation?* ch 4 (Oxford: Martin Robertson); Pulzer P (1983) 'Germany' in Butler D and Bogdanor V (eds) *Democracy and Elections* (Cambridge. CUP).

criticisms made of national list systems that MP selection is utterly dominated by parties, and that legislators have no ties to particular areas.

The benefits of the present system?

One can identify shortcomings as well as benefits in all voting systems. This section has thus far dwelt solely on the drawbacks of our single member plurality system; one ought also, to focus on its claimed merits. One would assume these are considerable, given that since 1945 both Labour- and Conservative-controlled Houses of Commons have chosen to retain an electoral system in which unlimited legal power is bestowed upon the representatives of a minority of the citizenry.[6]

The first is the so-called 'strong government' thesis. This stresses the importance of ensuring that the country always has a stable government, willing and able to implement a clearly defined set of legislative priorities, unencumbered by the need to compromise its beliefs to maintain the support of minority parties. Relatedly, the electorate knows where to attribute responsibility for failure or success, and can react accordingly at the next election. A second argument points to the simplicity and transparency of the present system. It is easy both for voters to understand and for government to administer. A third dwells on the importance of small constituency representation, which ensures both that MPs are not too distanced from the concerns of ordinary voters, and that all candidates are directly exposed to popular, rather than simply party, scrutiny.

Those points may be promptly rebutted. The strong government thesis is unconvincing if one views the project of government as a long- rather than short-term process. It may not be beneficial for a country to march strongly in one direction during the lifetime of one or two Parliaments, and then equally strongly in an altogether different direction for the next five or ten years. Similarly, if alternative systems are deemed too complex for the electorate to understand, the appropriate solution may be more extensive voter education. Thirdly, the necessity or desirability of having members of the national legislature play a substantial role as constituency representatives is contingent on the powers and struc-

6 For the defence see Maude A and Szemerey J (1981) *Why Electoral Reform? The Case for Electoral Reform Examined* (London: Conservative Political Centre). For a demolition of the defence see Oliver D (1982) 'Why electoral reform? The case for electoral reform examined' *Public Law* 236–239.

ture of sub-central elected government, an issue addressed in chapters 10 and 11.

CONCLUSION

Such arguments demonstrate that there is no 'right' answer to the question of electoral reform. In leaving this topic, we might again try to assess the extent to which electoral law ensures that the political party controlling the legislature enjoys the consent of the governed. In chapters 5 to 7, it has been suggested that the sovereignty of Parliament is in effect the sovereignty of the Commons, which is in turn the sovereignty of the majority party in the lower house, which is in turn the sovereignty of the minority of voters supporting that party. The constitution is, in legal terms, a vehicle facilitating factional government.

Yet factionalism in the law-making process need not lead to factionalism in the law's content. We must also consider what objectives factional parties pursue when they control Parliament's sovereign legal authority. If major parties share similar views on those elements of the constitution regarded as 'higher law' in other democracies, majoritarian or minoritarian control of the Commons is less problematic – factional differences will only be given legal expression in respect of non-fundamental issues. Supporters of the losing party may find such policies unpalatable, but not intolerable, and accept defeat because they anticipate that their opponents would do likewise if they lost the next election. Chapter 9 will explore the extent of such similarities between the major parties in the modern era, and ask whether even if one can identify short-term consensus, one should rely on its continued long-term existence. The thorny question of how one identifies a 'fundamental' law is then returned to repeatedly in chapters 10 to 15. But before broaching either of these extra-Parliamentary issues, we turn briefly in chapter 8 to a question of narrower scope – that of the 'privileges of Parliament'.

CHAPTER EIGHT

Parliamentary privilege

The roots of 'parliamentary privilege' were firmly fixed in England's constitutional landscape long before the 1688 revolution. The concept had begun to assume a coherent form by 1450, from which date the Speaker began each session of Parliament with an address to the Monarch claiming 'the ancient rights and privileges of the Commons'. The scope of parliamentary privilege is both multi-faceted and uncertain. In broad terms however, it embraces such issues as the two houses' power to control their own procedures, to admit and expel MPs and regulate their behaviour, and to punish non-members for obstructing the houses' business.

Early analysis of privilege assumed the Commons and Lords[1] were superior 'courts', and thus possessed exclusive, inherent power over all matters within their claimed jurisdiction. The point is best expressed by Coke CJ:

> 'Every court of justice hath rules and customs for its directions . . . It is lex et consuetudo parliamenti that all weighty matters in any Parliament moved concerning the peers of the realm, or commons in parliament assembled, ought to be determined, adjudged, and discussed by the course of the parliament, not by the civil law nor yet by the common laws of this realm used in more inferiour courts.'[2]

Coke's treatise was written in the pre-revolutionary era. It is therefore unsurprising that it offers no clear guidance as to the legal status of the lex et consuetudo parliamenti (law and custom of Parliament) vis-à-vis statute and the common law.[3] This is in part the consequence of a potentially misleading use of terminology. Coke's attention was focused not on 'Parliament', but on two of its component parts – the Commons and Lords – qua independent constitutional actors. But the inexactitude is not merely linguistic.

---

1 A contention which obviously had greater force in respect of the Lords.
2 1 Inst 15; cited in Keir *op cit* p 251.
3 'Common law' is used here in the umbrella sense alluded to at p 80 above.

It also has an historical base in the very blurred origins of 'Parliament' as a law-making body. Unlike the United States Congress, which was established to fulfil an exclusively legislative function within a limited sphere of legal competence, the two English houses had initially been judicial as well as legislative bodies.[4]

It has already been noted that the revolutionary settlement retained many features of the pre-revolutionary legal and political order. The common law's substantive provisions were left largely intact; the courts remained unwilling to examine the exercise of prerogative powers; and Charles II's move towards 'Cabinet' government was adopted by his successors.[5] Similarly, the Commons' and the Lords' historically eclectic 'judicial' powers were not systematically re-evaluated and redefined.[6] The houses entered the post-revolutionary era with their pre-revolutionary privileges apparently intact. Several theoretical questions (with significant practical consequences) were thus left unanswered. How far did the powers of each house extend? Were they residual powers, or could each house create new ones? Were such powers constitutionally superior to Acts of Parliament and/or the common law whenever a clash occurred? And in the event of such a clash, would responsibility for answering the third question rest with the courts or with the house?[7]

In this area of constitutional 'law' (the term is used guardedly), legal theory and political practice rarely coincide. Matters are further complicated by the frequency with which theory and practice are themselves categories riven with internal inconsistencies.

---

4 Perhaps ironically, this point is best illustrated by a decision of the United States Supreme Court, *Kilbourn v Thompson* 103 US 168 (1880). In *Kilbourn*, the House of Representatives attempted to jail a citizen for refusing to give evidence to a house committee. The house had argued that this power to punish 'contempts', long exercised by Parliament, was an inherent power of any legislature. The court declared the house's action unconstitutional as a usurpation of the judicial function. The court observed that Parliament, in contrast, had initially exercised judicial as well as legislative functions, and until such time as those powers were removed, the Commons' and Lords' 'judicial' jurisdictions remained in place. See Wittke C (1970) *The History of English Parliamentary Privilege* pp 182–184 (New York: Da Capo Press).

5 See pp 80, 112–113 and 138 respectively.

6 Thus one finds in Article 13 of the Bill of Rights that Parliament is afforded a role in 'redressing grievances' (a seemingly judicial function) as well as in 'amending the laws' (a legislative function).

7 The Commons generally assigns questions concerning its privileges to its Committee of Privileges in the first instance. The report and opinion of the committee is thereafter considered by the whole house. See generally Griffith and Ryle *op cit* ch 3; Marshall G (1979) 'The House of Commons and its privileges', in Walkland *op cit*.

In conceptual terms, parliamentary privilege is perhaps the most fascinating component of the modern constitution. And while it has in the twentieth century been relegated rather to the status of an historical anachronism, recent events (discussed in section V below) have lent it renewed significance.

There is no scope here to analyse in detail the pre-revolutionary history of the houses' respective privileges. However, the final parts of this introductory section focus briefly on three of the more significant episodes, with a view to identifying issues which subsequently assumed considerable significance after 1688.

Strode's case (1512)

Strode was an MP who had promoted Bills to regulate the tinning industry. His activities antagonised members of the Stannary Courts of Cornwall and Devon. The Stannary Courts were created by Edward I, and had a geographically limited jurisdiction immune from oversight by the common law courts. The courts convicted Stroud of 'vexing and troubling' local tin miners, and imprisoned him, apparently in a dungeon, for three weeks.[8]

The imprisonment triggered a swift response, not simply from the Commons, but from Parliament. Legislation (generally referred to as Strode's Act) was rapidly passed, both condemning the action taken by the Stannary Court and warning other such bodies against pursuing such a course in future:

> 'Sutes, accusments . . . punyshmentes etc, put or had, or hereafter put or had unto . . . the said Richard, and to every other . . . person of this present Parliament, or that of any Parliament hereafter, fo any bill spekying, reasonyng, or declaring of any mater or maters concerning the Parliament, to be communed and treated as utterly void and of no effecte.'

The contemporaneous legal status of 'Strode's Act' is necessarily unclear, given the then prevailing uncertainty as to the relative importance of statute vis-à-vis the many other sources of legal authority then extant. It is also unclear whether Parliament assumed it was creating new law, or, as seems more likely, merely restating what the Commons believed to be one its existing privileges. The Act's significance is perhaps better construed as a symbolic affirmation of the Commons' increasing confidence in its role as a central component of the law-making process, far superior in practical terms to the myriad of geographically and functionally diverse 'judicial' jurisdictions which littered England's

8 Plucknett (1960) *op cit* pp 248–249.

mediaevel landscape.[9] Yet the greatest threat to the Commons' capacity to make unhindered contributions to the legislative process came not from the almost anarchically fragmented structures of sub-central governmental and judicial bodies,[10] but from the Crown.

Peter Wentworth's defence of freedom of discussion in the Commons

The fact that the 1688 revolution was fought against the last incumbent of the Stuart dynasty tends to divert attention from the significant tensions existing between the Crown and the Commons in earlier periods.[11] Elizabeth I fell on several occasions into profound disagreement with both houses over her failure to marry or nominate an heir, and her unwillingness to countenance legislation promoting religious reform.[12] Elizabeth made frequent efforts, both directly and via her supporters in the lower house, to prevent the Commons even discussing such matters.

The tension became particularly acute in 1587, when one Anthony Cope MP introduced a Bill to the Commons advocating radical religious reform. Elizabeth had expressed a wish that the Bill should not even be presented to the house, still less debated. She had an ally in the Speaker, who both attempted to stop the reading of the Bill, and thereafter furnished the Queen with a copy of its text.[13] Elizabeth's interference, and the Speaker's compliance, prompted considerable controversy within the house. A question was placed by Peter Wentworth MP, asking:

'Whether this house be not a place for any member freely and without controlment of any person, or danger of laws, by bill or speech, to alter any of the griefs of the Commonwealth whatsoever touching the service of God, the safety of the Prince and this noble realm?'

Wentworth had by then been committed to prison several times by the Crown under the *Anderson* principle, and found himself once more confined to the Tower of London, this time by a lower house fearing the Queen's likely response to his temerity in

---

9 The Stannary Courts' jurisdiction was transferred to the Court of Appeal by the Supreme Court of Judicature Act 1873; see pp 79–80 above.
10 Of which more is said in chapter 10.
11 The *Resolutions in Anderson* being an obvious and egregious example; see p 106 above.
12 The following paragraphs are drawn from Plucknett (1960) *op cit* pp 312–328 and Wittke *op cit* pp 26–28.
13 This clearly being an era when the perception of the Speaker's role as the Commons' champion against the Crown was not accepted; see pp 146–147 above.

drawing attention to an entitlement which the Commons itself had so staunchly defended in repect of Strode.

Strode's Act was clearly not then regarded as an adequate legal defence against the Monarch's prerogative powers of imprisonment. Wentworth's misfortune also demonstrated that Commons' privileges did not fasten themselves inviolably on all its members, but could seemingly be diluted or waived by the house acting collectively. This indicates that, at least in early its years, the meaning of parliamentary privilege was less a question of legal niceties than of stark political realities. A second episode illustrates that point even more forcefully.

The Case of the Five Members (1641)

Notwithstanding Elizabeth's evident enthusiasm for invoking the *Resolutions in Anderson*, and her similarly pronounced distaste for liberty of discussion in the Commons, neither she nor her Tudor predecessors sought to rule as entirely absolutist Monarchs. Under that form of constitutional arrangement, there would be no legal protection for legislation, for the common law, or for the privileges of each house against the prerogative.

Charles I had ruled between 1629 and 1640 without summoning Parliament. By 1640, his political and fiscal weakness made that course unsustainable. The newly summoned houses rapidly addressed what they perceived as the worst abuses wrought by the King. MPs agreed to the levying of taxation only after securing (reluctant) royal support for the Triennial Act, an Act abolishing ship money (which also committed the judges who had found for the King to prison), and legislation subjecting the Monarch's power of detention under *Anderson* to (limited) judicial scrutiny.[14]

For many MPs however, such measures inadequately expressed what they conceived as the growing significance of Parliament within the constitution (and of the Commons within Parliament). A motion was subsequently moved in the house to present to the King (and publish) the 'Grand Remonstrance' of 1641 which detailed an extensive list of political and religious grievances. The motion seemingly offers an early instance of the house 'dividing' on a vote, rather than presenting a united front behind which its internal divisions were hidden. A narrow majority of members voted in favour of presenting and publishing the Remonstrance. An enraged Charles I demanded of the Commons that the five leaders (including one John Hampden)[15] of this 'opposition' to

14 See pp 109, 105, and 107 respectively.
15 See the discussion of *Ship Money* at p 105 above.

his government be delivered to him and tried for treason. The Commons showed no sign of complying with this request, regarding it as a gross interference with its deliberative autonomy.

As tension mounted, the house prepared to equip itself with an armed guard, fearing that the King would abduct the five members by force. Charles subsequently entered the house, backed up by over 400 armed men, and commanded that the MPs identify the impugned members. No MP would do so. In an act of some personal courage, the then Speaker William Lenthell (in words frequently invoked to demonstrate the Speaker's role as the Commons' defender against executive interference) defied the King's direct command to reveal the five members' whereabouts:

> 'May it please your majesty, I have neither eyes to see, nor tongue to speak in this place but as this House is pleased to direct, whose servant I am here.'

Charles' 'invasion' of the Commons was perhaps the precipitate cause of the civil war. His Stuart successors nevertheless remained reluctant to accept that the constitution forbade such direct monarchical interference with the houses' internal proceedings. As noted in chapter 2, the *Declaration of Right* stressed the constitutional importance of the Commons' 'independence' from interference either from the Crown directly or (since judges were then appointed by the King and dismissable at pleasure) indirectly via the courts.[16] The crucial provision was subsequently expressed in Article 9 of the Bill of Rights.

Article 9 of the Bill of Rights 1689

> 'That the freedom of speech, and debates or proceedings in Parliament ought not to be impeached or questioned in any court or place out of Parliament.'

Quite what status Article 9 was to possess in England's revised constitutional order was (and remains) uncertain. One interpretation would suggest that, by enacting Article 9, Parliament had abolished all the pre-existing privileges enjoyed by the two houses (and perhaps also by the Monarch qua third 'house'), and

---

16 One might also note that the Commons would also wish to deny the courts' jurisdiction over its privileges because the Lords also performed the role of a court in the ordinary sense as well as that of judge of its own privileges. Submitting to the ordinary courts' jurisdiction would thus in effect place the lower house in an inferior constitutional position vis-à-vis the upper chamber.

replaced them with a new statutory formula. The meaning to be attached to 'freedom of speech', 'debates', 'proceedings', 'Parliament', 'impeached' and 'questioned' would then become purely a question of statutory interpretation entrusted to the courts, in respect of which the previous lex et consuetudo parliamenti might serve as a persuasive authority if the judges so wished.

Much academic, judicial and political opinion has until very recently rejected such an interpretation. The preferred view appears to have been that Article 9 was merely 'declaratory' of the legitimacy of the pre-revolutionary situation.[17] Yet such an opinion is conceptually very problematic. The Bill of Rights, like any other post-revolutionary legislation, enjoys an entirely different constitutional status to any pre-revolutionary statute. In respect of Acts passed before 1688 'declaring' the extent of privilege, there is no difficulty in assuming that Parliament was merely bestowing added legitimacy on a political concept which arguably enjoyed equal but separate status to legislation. In the absence of a clear consensus as to the 'sovereignty' of Parliament, such statutes would merely mirror the lex parliamenti. But it takes no great leap of the legal imagination to wonder if legislation passed by the newly sovereign Parliament could no longer be merely declaratory, but necessarily transformed the constitutional status of the issues it addressed?

Any claim by the Commons or Lords that the interpretation of Article 9 was a matter for them alone has no *textual* basis in the Bill of Rights itself. Such a claim would also contradict orthodox understandings of parliamentary sovereignty and the rule of law, which entrust the task of interpreting statutes to the ordinary courts. But one can readily discern a *contextual* basis for the Commons' wish to exclude judicial interpretation of Article 9. This would derive in part from a suspicion that the Crown could interfere indirectly with the Commons' operations through its power

17 Thus one finds in *British Railways Board v Pickin* (p 41 above) Lord Simon denying that the enrolled Bill rule was created by Article 9. Rather, Article 9 'reflected' an existing functional imperative – namely preserving uninhibited discussion in a democratic Parliament. Simon's analysis is historically quite inept. The pre-1689 Parliament was in functional terms nothing like its present day successor; the 1688 revolutionaries had not the least inclination to produce a 'democratic' legislature. Article 9 could not 'reflect' democratic sentiment, because no such sentiment existed. The judgment does however raise important methodological issues, in that it suggests the scope of privilege falls to be determined by judicial (rather than house) perceptions of what is 'necessary' for the conduct of parliamentary business. See further Denham CJ in *Stockdale v Hansard* (p 312 below), and Lord Browne-Wilkinson in *Pepper v Hart* (p 318 below).

to appoint and dismiss the judges. However, that contextual justification would largely have disappeared following the Act of Settlement 1701, which empowered the Commons to veto the dismissal of members of the judiciary.[18] The Act of Settlement displaced rather than extinguished the Commons' understandable fears about losing control of its claimed interpretive power. Despite the then eclectic structure of the English court system, the House of Lords unarguably enjoyed a dual 'judicial' status, exercising jurisdiction over both its own lex parliamenti and most facets of the common law. For the scope of the Commons' privileges to be determinable by the common law would mean in effect that they were controlled by the Lords. As we saw in chapter 7, the Lords exercised sufficient influence over the composition of the Commons to make it inaccurate to suggest that the two houses held invariably antagonistic views on all issues. The tensions were nevertheless sufficient for the lower house consistently to deny the ordinary courts' authority in matters of claimed privilege. It was not until the passage of the Judicature Acts of 1873 and 1875 that one could plausibly argue that the House of Lords qua 'ordinary court' was both formally and functionally independent of the House of Lords qua legislative assembly; although as suggested below, this initiative was not sufficient to induce the Commons to disclaim its purported interpretive authority.

We will revisit the conceptual problems flowing from the uncertain status and meaning of Article 9 on several occasions below. But the issues that Article 9 addresses are not exhaustive of the scope that privilege had formerly enjoyed. The rest of this chapter sweeps broadly over 200 years of the history of parliamentary privilege in five general areas. Firstly, the houses' power to regulate their own composition through the admission, retention and expulsion of their members; secondly, the publication of details of business conducted in the two houses; thirdly, the admissability before the courts of such published material; fourthly, the concept of 'contempt of the house'; and fifthly, the regulation of MPs' ethical standards.

I. THE ADMISSION, RETENTION AND EXPULSION OF MEMBERS

The tortuous development of the Commons' electoral system was traced in chapter 7. However the Acts which gradually extended

---

18 And, of course, the Act of Settlement could not be repealed or amended without the Commons' consent.

the franchise do not provide a thorough picture of the constitutional principles which have determined the lower house's composition. For much of the post-revolutionary era, the relationship between the 'people' and the Commons has also been affected by questions of privilege.

Ashby v White revisited

As noted in chapter 7, the courts had accepted shortly after the revolution that enfranchised citizens enjoyed common law 'rights of property' in their entitlement to vote. Thus the plaintiff in *Ashby v White* could maintain an action in tort against the returning officer in Aylesbury who had prevented him from voting.[19] The judges hearing the litigation had however held sharply divergent views on the issue. As we saw in chapter 7, the Commons enjoyed statutory authority to determine the outcome of disputed election between 1604 and 1868.[20] The result in the Aylesbury election was not in doubt, and thus the Commons had no statutory jurisdiction over Ashby's suit. The point of contention which Ashby raised was whether a freeholder's right to vote was a matter of common law, or a facet of the Commons' power to control its own composition. The question had profound consequences; if the latter claim were accepted, it would effectively empower the Commons alone to determine the allocation of the franchise.

The majority of the judges hearing Ashby's case at first instance accepted that latter viewpoint. His claim bore directly on an established Commons privilege, with which the court was not competent to interfere. For White and Gould JJ, the matter was a question of hierarchy – in these matters, the lex parliamenti overrode the common law. Powys J added a further point (which we would now recognise as one of justiciability): 'We are not acquainted with the learning of elections, and there is a particular cunning in it not known to us.'[21]

Holt CJ dissented. Ashby's claimed right to vote was firmly based in common law. The judges' duty was to uphold that law. The court should thus hear his claim, and if the case was well-founded, decide in his favour. To do otherwise would breach the court's constitutional duty: 'We must not be frighted when a matter of property comes before us, by saying it belongs to the parliament;

19 See p 243 above.
20 P 239 above. And see O'Leary C *op cit* pp 9–12.
21 92 ER 126 at 130.

we must exert the Queen's jurisdiction.'[1] For Holt, the extent of privilege was a question for the courts, not the house to decide.

Paty's case[2]

The House of Lords (qua final court of appeal) supported Holt's dissent, and reversed the judgment. It is tempting to see this as a victory for the 'rule of law' over the arbitrary inclinations of the Commons. For the lower house, it perhaps appeared as an illegitimate intrusion by the upper house (qua legislative body) into its sphere of responsibility. The Commons proved unwilling to accept the Lords' decision in *Ashby*.[3] It immediately passed a resolution denying the courts' authority:

> '[N]either the qualifications of any elector, or the right of any person elected, is cognisable or determinable elsewhere, than before the commons of England. . . . whoever shall presume to commence any action [before] any other jurisdiction . . . except in cases especially provided for by act of parliament . . . are guilty of a high breach of privilege of this house.'[4]

Shortly thereafter, five other voters in Aylesbury who had suffered similar obstructions to Ashby initiated legal actions. To do so, defying the Commons' resolution, was a bold undertaking, for the lower house immediately held them and their counsel to have breached its privileges and gaoled them. The equivocal role adopted by the courts was then illustrated by a majority judgment which declined jurisdiction over writs of habeas corpus issued on the voters' behalf.

Holt again dissented, in terms stressing the subordinacy of privilege to both common law and statute:

> 'Bringing such actions was declared by the house of Commons to be a breach of their privilege; but that declaration will not make that a privilege that was not so before. . . . The privileges of the house of Commons . . . are nothing but the law . . . This privilege of theirs concerns the liberty of the people in a high degree, by subjecting them

---

1 *Ibid*, at 138. Holt also saw more far-reaching reasons for this conclusion: 'To allow this action will make public officers more careful to observe the constitution of cities and boroughs, and not to be so partial as they commonly are in all elections, which is indeed a great and growing mischief' at 137.

2 *R v Paty* (1705) 2 Salk 503, 91 ER 431.

3 Although Holt CJ had demonstrated his 'independence' of the Lords by denying a claim of privilege made by the upper house in *Knollys' Case* (1694) Marcham's Report 464; see Plucknett (1960) *op cit* p 583.

4 Quoted in Plucknett (1960) *op cit* pp 582–583.

to imprisonment, which is what the people cannot be subjected to without an Act of Parliament.'[5]

The Commons then sought to block Paty's appeal to the House of Lords. A clash between the two houses was only averted when Queen Anne prorogued Parliament, which had the effect of releasing the imprisoned men.

In substantive terms, *Ashby* and *Paty*'s case have little contemporary relevance. Conceptually, however, they retain significance because of Holt's forceful assertion of the sovereignty of Parliament and the rule of law (as Dicey would later use that term) as constitutional principles superior to privilege. That argument has yet to be entirely settled, but, as the following pages suggest, Holt's analysis has gradually gained increasing conceptual legitimacy and practical endorsement.

John Wilkes

The grievances which antagonised the American colonists were not all engendered by British legislative and executive action undertaken in the colonies themselves. The Americans' disenchantment with their colonial status was added to by the treatment meted out by the Commons and successive British governments to radical British politicians sympathetic to the Americans' cause. John Wilkes' role as a critic of government policy has already been alluded to;[6] his career now merits further consideration.

Wilkes was not an obvious revolutionary. His early attachment to 'democratic' principles seemed tenuous; in 1757 he bought his way into the Commons by bribing and treating the electors of (ironically) Aylesbury. Wilkes nevertheless moved in radical political circles, and in the early 1760s edited a journal, *The North Briton*, concerned entirely with disseminating vehement criticism of the government. Wilkes reached a pinnacle of dissent in issue No 45, which castigated the measures contained in the King's Speech opening the 1763 Parliamentary session:

'Every friend of this country must lament that a prince of so many great and admirable qualities . . . can be brought to give the sanction of his sacred name to the most odious measures and the most unjustifiable public declarations . . .'

---

5 2 Lord Raymond 1105 at 1107. Holt's method provides an obvious precedent for the reasoning subsequently deployed by Lord Camden in *Entick*; see pp 66–68 above.

6 See pp 67–68 above. Information in the following section is drawn largely from Rude G (1962) *Wilkes and Liberty* (Oxford: Clarendon Press). See also Maier *op cit.*

Given the close control which George III (when sane) exercised over his government,[7] No 45, despite its protestations of loyalty to the King himself, was broadly perceived as an attack upon the Monarch as well as his ministers. Wilkes then published a potentially blasphemous and seditious tract called *An Essay on Women*. The combined effect of the two publications provoked the government to prosecute him for libel and the Commons to expel him. Wilkes meanwhile fled the country, and was declared an outlaw when he did not appear at his trial. On returning to England in June 1768, he was sentenced to two years' imprisonment.

To modern eyes, the events of the next year have a farcical hue, but they were of considerable significance to shaping emergent understandings of the relationship between the Commons, statute, and the electorate. If a member is expelled, the seat becomes vacant and a by-election is held. Wilkes did not contest his Aylesbury seat after his first expulsion. But at that time, Wilke's status as a convicted prisoner was not a legal impediment to standing for election or taking a seat.[8] Thus in 1769, Wilkes determined to stand as a candidate for Middlesex, where many electors endorsed his views. Wilkes was elected to the house on February 16 – and expelled by the Commons on February 17. Wilkes was returned again on March 16 – and expelled once more the next day. In April, he was again chosen as Middlesex's MP. This time however, rather than expel Wilkes and trigger another election, the Commons declared Wilkes' defeated opponent the 'winner', and admitted him to the house.

The Commons' defiance of the electorate's wishes prompted many English constituencies (and some American colonists) to petition both the Commons and the King to have the 'result' of the election reversed. One of Wilkes' supporters tabled a motion inviting the Commons to resolve that: 'no person eligible by law can be incapacitated from election by a vote of the House, but by Act of Parliament alone'. The motion was defeated by 226 to 186. The house carried (by 224 to 180) a government motion that Wilkes' expulsion was 'agreeable to the law of the land'.[9]

That conclusion was not put to a legal test. Wilkes did not challenge his exclusion in the courts. Had he done so, he would

---

7 See pp 138–139 above.
8 See the discussion of *Goodwin and Fortescue's Case* (1604) in Plucknett *op cit* pp 372–374; Keir D (8th edn, 1966) *The Constitutional History of Modern Britain* pp 175–177 (London: Adam and Charles Black).
9 Rude *op cit* pp 119, 133. See also Wittke (1970) *op cit* pp 115–123. One might then question whether this was a decision of 'the house of Commons' or an early example of effective governmental control of the lower house.

have set up a potentially momentous dispute between the 'rights' of the electorate and the 'privileges' of the Commons. One can only speculate as to whether the courts would even have accepted jurisdiction to entertain such proceedings, and, had they done so, as to the decision they would have reached. Instead, Wilkes turned his attention towards becoming Lord Mayor of London, an office to which he was elected in 1774. By then, sentiment in the Commons had swung sufficiently to allow him to take the seat for Middlesex which he won (yet again) in December 1774.

One might initially attribute the house's conduct towards Wilkes to the era's political context. The Commons then made no claim to be 'democratic'; some 60 years had still to pass before the Great Reform Act would set Britain on the long, slow path towards a universal franchise. In formal terms, Wilkes' repeated expulsion was a defensible expression of the Commons' traditional autonomy. From a functional perspective, the house's action could be construed as a collective expression of Burke's portrayal of the MP as representative rather than delegate: MPs were sparing an ill-advised, intemperate electorate from the consequences of its folly. If so, one might then assume that as the franchise became more extensive and the electorate more 'mature', and the legitimacy of the Commons' legislative role rested increasingly firmly on the assumption that it represented 'the people', the house could no longer defensibly invoke its privileges to exclude a member chosen by his constituents. But as the experience of Charles Bradlaugh suggests, any such assumption would be ill-founded.

Charles Bradlaugh

Bradlaugh was a radical journalist and political campaigner, who had achieved considerable notoriety by the 1870s both for founding an atheistic organisation known as the National Secular Society, and for being prosecuted for publishing a book on the subject of birth control.[10] Such notoriety apparently appealed however to the voters of Northampton, for in 1880 they returned Bradlaugh as their MP.

10 Arnstein W (1983) *The Bradlaugh Case* ch 1 (Columbia, Missouri: University of Missouri Press). Arnstein provides an illuminating insight into both the man and his times. For a more legalistic analsis of Bradlaugh's subsequent difficulties with the Commons see Wittke *op cit* pp 160–169; Anson W (5 edn 1922) *The Law and Custom of the Consitution* pp 93–98, 195–196 (Oxford: Clarendon Press).

Bradlaugh's difficulties began when he tried to take his seat. MPs had been placed under a statutory obligation during Elizabeth I's reign to take an oath of allegiance to the Monarch and the protestant faith before assuming their seats.[11] The oath (administered by the Speaker on the floor of the house) was intended to exclude Roman Catholics from the Commons, but also caught protestant non-conformists and Jews. The oath was modified to admit Catholics in 1829; legislation in 1866 introduced an oath acceptable to members of the Jewish faith, and the Promissory Oaths Act 1868 permitted members of dissentient religious sects to 'affirm' their loyalty rather than swear it. The legislation did not actually exclude members from the house if they had not taken the oath or affirmed, but fined them £500 (even in 1880 an enormous sum) for each occasion when they sat and voted without having done so.

On entering the house, Bradlaugh (having previously announced himself an atheist) claimed to be entitled to affirm rather than swear his loyalty. The house, however, mindful of his early avowal of atheism, resolved that he could not do so. Bradlaugh's subsequent attempt to take the oath instead was also blocked by a resolution. On declining to leave the house, Bradlaugh was forcibly ejected.

The Liberal government, and Gladstone in particular, had opposed the house's conclusion. Gladstone himself considered that since there was no explicit statutory provision granting the Commons the jurisdiction to determine whether a given member was eligble to affirm or take the oath, dispute on that question was a matter for the courts to resolve *after* the member had taken his seat. Gladstone thus offered tacit government support for a motion, narrowly carried, permitting Bradlaugh to affirm.

Immediately upon taking his seat, Bradlaugh was subjected to a legal challenge to his presence in the house. In *Clarke v Bradlaugh*, the High Court and subsequently the Court of Appeal[12] held that he was not entitled to rely on the Promissory Oaths Act, and so could not avoid the oath by affirmation. The majority in the Commons then refused to let him take the oath, and thereafter expelled him in April 1881. He was returned at a by-election a week later, at which point the then Speaker had evidently concluded that: 'the house would do well and wisely, according to

---

11 This oversimplifies the issue rather. For a helpful sketch of the history of the oath see Anson *op cit* pp 93–95.
12 (1881) 8 QBD 63 and (1883) 8 App Cas 354 respectively.

the constitution, to admit him without question'.[13] The majority nevertheless expelled him again. Gladstone subsequently introduced a Bill which, if enacted, would settle the question by enabling any member who so chose to affirm; whereupon Conservative MPs availed themselves of the filibustering techniques (deployed so effectively on other questions by Irish members) to block the Bill's passage.

Bradlaugh was subsequently physically ejected by Commons' officials. Undeterred, he re-entered the house and adopted the extraordinary course of administering the oath to himself and then assuming his place on the backbenches. He was once again expelled; and yet again returned at the ensuing by-election.

The Commons' continued refusal to admit Bradlaugh seemingly negated the impact of the Great Reform Act and Disraeli's 1867 franchise legislation in respect of the electors of Northampton. For those voters, the extended franchise was worthless, since their chosen candidate was unable to represent them in the house. For Bradlaugh the legal and moral position was clear. He, and his electors, were the victims of:

> 'the arbitrary and illegal action of the House of Commons. It is a melancholy exhibition of the tyranny of orthodoxy when we see one branch of the legislature taking upon itself to nullify laws which the whole legislature itself has sanctioned.'[14]

Dicey's *Law of the Constitution* had yet to be published. But in apparent anticipation of Diceyan prescriptions concerning the rule of law, Bradlaugh sought to challenge this allegedly 'arbitrary and illegal action' before the ordinary courts.

Bradlaugh v Gossett (1884)

Bradlaugh's action was directed against the Commons Serjeant-at-Arms, who, obeying a Commons resolution, had ejected Bradlaugh from the house and intimated that he would if necessary use further physical violence to prevent Bradlaugh entering in future. Bradlaugh's suit asked the court to issue an injunction preventing the Serjeant-at-Arms from so doing. As Stephen J indicated, the case raised a straightforward clash between the authority of statute and of privilege:

> 'Suppose that the House of Commons forbids one of its members to

13 Arnstein *op cit* p 104.
14 *Ibid,* p 147.

do that which an Act of Parliament requires him to do . . . is such an order one which we can declare to be void and restrain the executive officer of the House from carrying out.'[15]

The answer that Stephen J eventually offered to this evident conundrum appeared to owe as much to questions of geography as of legal theory.

The judgment held that no no statute could impliedly remove or alter the Commons' power to exercise complete control over its *internal* proceedings. Neither was the house's jurisdiction in such matters overridden by the common law. In reaching this conclusion, Stephen J was influenced by a sense of judicial deference to the Commons:

> 'The House of Commons is not a Court of Justice, but the effect of its privilege to regulate its own internal concerns practically invests it with a judicial character when it has to apply to particular cases the provisions of Acts of Parliament. . . . If its determination is not in accordance with the law, this resembles the case of an error by a judge whose decision is not subject to appeal . . . [I]f we were to attempt to erect ourselves into a Court of Appeal from the House of Commons, we should consult neither the public interest, nor the intersts of Parliament and the constitution, nor our own dignity.'[16]

Since swearing or affirming were procedures conducted entirely within the house, the regulation of the process was a matter solely for the house. In contrast, the house would have no authority to interfere with those aspects of the processes which affected its composition which occurred outside its boundaries; such as, for example, a citizen's common law or statutory entitlement to vote in Parliamentary election. This would be consistent with Holt's opinion in *Ashby* and *Paty*'s case, and reiterates the point that the courts claimed the power to identify the extent of privilege, but not to interfere with its exercise within those identified boundaries. But Stephen J seemed decidedly uncertain as to the courts' response if the house chose to exceed its jurisdiction in this way:

> 'I should in any case feel a reluctance almost invincible to declaring a resolution of the House of Commons to be beyond the powers of the house . . . Such a declaration would in every case be unnecessary and disrespectful.'[17]

In effect, this means that the court was abdicating its role as the guardian of the rule of law and allowing the Commons to

15 (1884) 12 QBD 271 at 278.
16 *Ibid*, at 286.
17 *Ibid*, at 282.

determine the meaning of legislation. Given the vituperative cla-
shes between the Commons, Lords and Monarch over the terms
of nineteenth century enfranchisement legislation, which had led
to considerable modification of the initial Bills,[18] it is implausible to assume that Parliament impliedly granted such jurisidiction
to the Commons. The judgment thus entirely subverts orthodox
understandings of parliamentary sovereignty. Stephen J's judgment implied that even if Gladstone's Bill permitting any member
to affirm had been passed, the courts would not have intervened if
a majority in the Commons subsequently resolved that a particular
member could not do so.

Gladstone had in fact been quietly garnering support for Bradlaugh among Liberal MPs and the less conservative members of
the clergy, and spoke enthusiastically in support of a new Affirmation Bill in 1885. Arnstein also records that from 1884 onwards
both the national and provincial press began to take a more
sympathetic view of Bradlaugh's predicament. The saga was eventually ended in the immediate aftermath of the 1885 general
election, in which Bradlaugh was for the seventh time returned
as Northampton's MP. The solution was, from a legal perspective,
perhaps unsatisfactory, for it involved no momentous clash
between court and Commons. Rather the story ended, as it began,
within the house itself. After the election, the house had chosen
a new Speaker, the former Liberal MP Sir Arthur Peel. When
the house assembled, Peel maintained that the house's previous
resolutions preventing Bradlaugh from taking the oath had lapsed.
The Speaker also made it clear that he would not look kindly on
any new motion on the same issue:

> 'I have no right, original or delegated to interfere between an honour-
> able member and his taking of the oath. . . . It is not for me, I respect-
> fully say, it is not for the House, to enter into any inquisition as to
> what may be the opinions of a Member when he comes to the table
> to take the oath.'[19]

When the Commons reconvened, Peel chose to ignore the
efforts of Conservative MPs to block Bradlaugh's attempt to take
the oath, and he was thus able finally to assume his seat. That
Peel ended the controversy in so simple a fashion is a forceful
testament to the disciplinary authority a determined Speaker may
exercise over the house, even when his/her views are not supported by most members. Yet the solution, as much as the contro-

---

18 See chapter 7 above.
19 Quoted in Arnstein *op cit* p 310.

versy itself, also indicates the extent to which both the Commons and the courts considered themselves competent to deny the electors of Northampton the services of their chosen representative. The Bradlaugh episode neatly illustrates the so-called 'dualism' which attaches to the constitutional status of the houses' privileges:

> 'Thus there may be at any given moment two doctrines of privilege, the one held by the courts, the other by either House, the one to be found in the law reports, the other in Hansard, and no way of resolving the real point at issue should conflict arise.'[20]

Whether that proposition is theoretically sound is a point to which we shall return. But as the following sections suggest, the practical problems raised by dualism are not limited solely to the question of the admission of members to their respective house.

Freedom from imprisonment, arrest and molestation

The first recorded instance of the Commons asserting its privilege to force the release of one of its members from imprisonment seems to be *Ferrers'* case in 1543.[1] The privilege has an obvious functional basis in the pre-revolutionary era, namely to ensure that the members summoned by the King to attend were not impeded from travelling to London and thereafter going about their parliamentary business, whether by unlawful interference or by legal proceedings initiated in any of the courts of inferior jurisidiction which then existed. A statute of 1604 'recognised' the privilege as encompassing both a power to set free a member duly imprisoned by a court of law, and the power to punish any person arresting a member.[2] Neither house was obliged to protect its members from detention. Rather the privilege was a power the house might waive when it saw fit.

The privilege was not invoked in respect of criminal charges, even if the impugned conduct had occurred within the Commons or Lords itself. There have been, unsurprisingly, relatively few occasions in the modern era on which MPs have faced criminal charges. Several Irish MPs were imprisoned during the 1880s and again in 1918 for criminal activities arising from the Irish struggle for independence. On none of these occasions did the House

20 Keir (1978) *op cit* p 255.
1 Plucknett (1980) *op cit* pp 249–250. For earlier examples which might fall into this category see Wittke *op cit* pp 33–35.
2 Plucknett (1960) *op cit* pp 333–334.

make any suggestion that it would interfere with the court proceedings.

A more conceptually difficult case concerned Captain A Ramsay MP, a member with alleged fascist sympathies, detained in 1940 under the regulations at issue in *Liversidge v Anderson*.[3] Ramsay's detention was referred to the Committee of Privileges as a potential breach of the arrest privilege. The committee (and subsequently the house when accepting the committee's opinion) was divided on the question, although the majority concluded no breach had occurred. That many MPs doubted the legitimacy of the government's action presumably stemmed from the fact that Ramsay's detention was not the result of a criminal conviction; the only 'crime' he had committed (like Liversidge) was to have aroused the Home Secretary's suspicions as to his loyalty to Britain's war effort. Ramsay remained in detention until 1944, during which time his constituents did not have a representative in the Commons.[4]

The Parliamentary Privilege Act 1770

The arrest privilege nevertheless had considerable practical significance in respect of civil suits, especially while it remained possible to be imprisoned for debt. In the immediate aftermath of the revolution, the houses' growing sense of self-importance led them to claim an ever-greater scope for the arrest privilege, encompassing not just the persons of members, but also their land, their moveable property and their servants. The extended privilege was frequently invoked as an expedient way for MPs and their retinues to evade numerous legal obligations – a practice which provoked considerable public criticism.[5]

Public pressure eventually led Parliament to place statutory curbs on the privilege's scope. In 1700, legislation was enacted entitled 'An Act for preventing any inconveniences that may happen by privilege of Parliament'. Its main provision, as restated in the Parliamentary Privilege Act 1770 s 1, was that:

'Any person may at any time commence and prosecute any action or suit against any Lord of Parliament or any . . . [member] of the House of Commons . . . or any other person intitled to the privilege of Parliament . . . and no such action shall at any time be impeached, stayed or delayed by or under colour or pretence of any privilege of Parliament.'

3 See pp 83–87 above.
4 Simpson *op cit* pp 113–114, 393–395, 404.
5 For examples see Wittke (1970) *op cit* pp 39–43.

If interpreted literally, (ie *any* privilege), s 1 seems to abolish all aspects of privilege insofar as they restricted access to the courts, including Article 9. The Commons and the judiciary appeared to have reached a shared (and much less expansive) understanding of the Act's impact in 1958, when the Commons (without surrendering its claimed jurisdiction to judge the extent of privilege) invited the Privy Council (in its judicial capacity) to interpret the scope of the 1770 Act.[6]

The 'court' applied the mischief rule rather than the literal rule to s 1. The majority considered that the 'mischief' in issue was solely MPs' increasing predilection to invoke privilege as a blanket immunity against all civil actions. It did not extend to MPs' entitlement to unhindered freedom of speech in the house. The Privy Council considered this freedom to have been so central a value in the 1688 settlement that it was inconceivable that Parliament would have curtailed its scope just twelve years after the revolution. The majority thus concluded that the 1700 Act and its successors reached only those legal actions whose origins did not lie in a 'proceeding in Parliament'.

But this opinion left a crucial question unanswered: namely who was to decide if the action concerned had been precipitated by a 'proceeding in Parliament' – the Commons or the courts? It is generally assumed that the constitution confers the responsibility of statutory interpretation on the courts. Determining the meaning of 'proceedings' would thus be a judicial function. This presumption could however be rebutted in two ways. Firstly, one might argue that this privilege (or indeed privilege in general) enjoyed a special constitutional status, which (unlike the prerogative or other common law rules) rendered it immune to implied repeal. The majority opinion seemed to accept this viewpoint, by observing that the free speech privilege was 'solemnly *reasserted* in the Bill of Rights'.[7] The notion of 'reassertion' suggests that the legal status of privilege was such that it co-existed with Article 9 – that the statutory provision was merely declaratory and not transformative of the substantive entitlements the house had hitherto enjoyed. A second argument, which the majority did not entertain, was that the Bill of Rights itself (or indeed any other statute touching upon privilege) impliedly ousted the courts' jurisdiction and bestowed it on the house.

---

6 *Re Parliamentary Privilege Act 1770* [1958] AC 331.
7 *Ibid*, at 350 (emphasis added).

Lord Denning dissented from the majority opinon.[8] He concluded that the clear meaning of the 1770 Act was that the Commons would be acting illegally if it made any attempt to interfere
with a legal action initiated against one of its members. The Act
was a command from Parliament to one of its component parts
not to undertake such action. But this did not mean such a suit
could be argued, still less succeed. For Lord Denning also held
that the courts remained obliged by Article 9 to refuse to entertain
any action which 'questioned' a 'proceeding in Parliament'.

This might initially lead one to conclude that Denning was
merely playing with words, since his judgment seemed to produce
the same substantive result as the majority opinion – namely that
a 'proceeding in Parliament' was not actionable before the courts.
But that conclusion would be mistaken. Denning clearly stressed
that whatever jurisdiction the Commons might have possessed to
determine the extent and meaning of its free speech privilege
before 1689 had been overridden by Parliament when Article 9
was enacted. Article 9 therefore did not 'reassert' the house's
privilege. Rather it extinguished the privilege and created a new
statutory protection for the Commons and its members. Nor did
Article 9 contain any implied grant of interpretive authority to
the Commons. Privilege thus enjoyed no higher status vis-à-vis
statute than did the common law:

> 'This means of course that it is for the courts to say what is a "proceed-
> ing in Parliament" within the Bill of Rights – which is just what the
> House of Commons do not wish to concede.'[9]

From a formalist perspective, Lord Denning's dissenting opinion
seems perfectly consistent with orthodox theories of parliamentary
sovereignty and the rule of law. In a functionalist sense, it has
rather more force in respect of the 1770 Act than the first statute
passed in 1700, since the latter predated the Act of Settlement.
However neither Denning's opinion, nor indeed that of the
majority, offers any conclusive answer to what is, reduced to its
essentials, a question of great constitutional significance – to what
extent are the Commons and Lords beyond the reach of parliamentary authority?

Further judicial support for Denning's analysis was offered by
the oft-quoted remarks of Scarman J in *Stourton v Stourton*, a 1963

---

8 The dissent was neither recorded nor published in the report itself. See Lord
  Denning (1985) '*Re Parliamentary Privilege Act 1770' Public Law* 80–92.
9 *Ibid*, at 85.

case concerning the applicability of the freedom of arrest privilege to peers:

'I do not think however, that I, sitting in the High Court... must necessarily take the law that I have to apply from what would be the practice of the House. I think I have to look to the common law as deduced in judicial decisions in order to determine in the particular case whether the privilege arises, and if so its scope and effect.'[10]

The implication in Scarman J's judgment that privilege should be regarded as in effect a branch of the common law has great significance, and is considered further below. Before doing so, however, we might usefully turn to a second facet of the role played by the Commons' privileges in regulating the relationship between the house and the people.

II. THE PRINCIPLE OF INFORMED CONSENT?

The American revolutionaries attached much importance to the principle that the proceedings of Congress, and especially the speeches and voting behaviour of legislators, should be matters of public record. The presumption that the people should be furnished with the information needed to make informed choices about their preferred representatives was afforded explicit legal protection within the constitution's text.

At that time, neither the Commons nor the Lords were under any statutory or common law obligation to do likewise. Such publicity as was given to the houses' affairs was a matter for the houses themselves to decide; and their preference then seemed to be for limited disclosure. Both the pre- and post-revolutionary Commons had passed resolutions contending that unauthorised publication of any reports of its proceedings was a breach of privilege.[11] In 1762, the house had declared:

'That it is an high Indignity to, and a notorious breach of the Privilege of this House... for any printer or Publisher of any printed Newspaper... to give therein any Account of the Debates or other Proceedings of this House... and this House will proceed with the utmost severity against such offenders.'[12]

The resolution is quite inconsistent with any notion that the

10 [1963] 1 All ER 606 at 608. See also Leopold P (1989) 'The freedom of peers from arrest' *Public Law* 398–406.
11 Wittke (1970) *op cit* p 51.
12 Cited in Marshall (1979) *op cit.*

electoral process rested upon voters' informed consent. As the century wore on, so the legitimacy and the legality of the Commons' stance were increasingly questioned by emergent radical factions; by 1770 several newspapers published regular reports of Commons debates and votes. An acute controversy flared during Wilkes' exclusion from the Commons. Press coverage of the affair made copious and scathing use of MPs' speeches; several editors took what might now be regarded as the eminently 'democratic' view that electors should know which MPs spoke in favour of Wilkes' admission, which members opposed it, and which labelled signatories of petitions supporting Wilkes as 'scum'.

The government majority in the Commons resolved that several editors had breached the house's privileges by publishing such reports without its consent. When the editors defied the house, the Commons authorised its officers to arrest them. This brought the house into conflict with the Lord Mayor of London, who in his capacity as a magistrate held a judicial jurisdiction over criminal acts undertaken within the city's boundaries. On attempting to seize one of the impugned editors, the Commons' officer found himself arrested for assault and summoned to appear before the Lord Mayor. This in turn led the Commons to resolve that the Lord Mayor had breached the house's privilege by interfering with its officer's execution of its resolution, and thereafter to imprison him in the Tower. When presented with a writ for habeas corpus on the Lord Mayor's behalf, the courts declined to examine the merits of a warrant from the Speaker maintaining that the Lord Mayor had been committed for a breach of privileges.

While the house had successfully asserted its formal authority, the episode's practical consequence appeared to be an undermining of its legitimacy, for unauthorised publication of its proceedings continued apace. One would however be mistaken in assuming that this practical victory for the principle of informed consent was thereafter accorded a legal basis. The house formally revoked the motion in 1971, but it remains one of the most extraordinary anachronisms of the British constitutional order that there is still no *legal* requirement that either house publish records of its business.[13] In practical terms, any citizen who wishes to do so may (albeit at some expense) avail herself of televisual, radio or written reports of the each house's proceedings. But it remains the case that such information as is released is a matter entirely for each house itself.

13 Griffith and Ryle *op cit* p 95.

III. THE JUSTICIABILITY OF 'PROCEEDINGS IN PARLIAMENT'

There has as yet been no indication that the courts consider themselves to have any power to force the publication of any aspect of either house's deliberations or other proceedings. However, the question of what use the courts might subsequently make of such records has been (and remains) an issue of appreciable importance and a source of considerable controversy.

Actions in defamation

Speeches made by MPs in either house which defame other citizens clearly raise a potential conflict with the courts. The fear of losing a defamation action could act as a considerable impediment to MPs' freedom of speech, yet the common law has always provided extensive remedies enabling people to protect their 'right' to a good reputation.[14] In such circumstances, the conceptual problem of 'dualism' might be thought particularly acute. In practice however, the courts and the houses appear to have reached a shared understanding of the scope of law and privilege on this question.

The plaintiff in *Dillon v Balfour*[15] was a mid-wife in Ireland. Balfour (whom we have already met)[16] was then a minister in Ireland. During the passage of the Criminal Procedure (Ireland) Bill in 1887 Balfour had made various remarks about Dillon which she felt undermined her professional reputation, in respect of which she sought substantial damages. Balfour had applied to the court for the action to be struck out, on the basis that speeches made in the house could not be the subject of a defamation suit.

The judgment offers a paradigmatic example of the conceptual obfuscation which attends many analyses of the legal status of such speeches. Palles CB began his judgment by turning to Article 9. However he construed Article 9 not as creating a statutory protection, but as merely declaratory of pre-revolutionary privilege. To complicate matters further, he then observed that the privilege was an 'ancient right and liberty of the realm,'[17] which might suggest it had a basis in the common law.

---

14 See Brazier M (9th edn 1993) *Street on Torts* ch 23 (London: Butterworths).
15 (1887) 20 LR Ir 600.
16 See pp 199–202 above.
17 (1887) 20 LR Ir 600 at 612.

The basis of his judgment, which concluded that the plaintiff's action could not be sustained, was equally unclear. Palles CB held that the courts had jurisdiction in a defamation action only to ask if the words in issue were spoken/written as a 'proceeding in Parliament'. Whether this was simply an inherent common law jurisdiction, or was demanded by Article 9, was not made clear. Whatever its source, however, the court's jurisdiction was 'ousted' (though by what he did not explain) if it determined that the words were indeed a 'proceeding in Parliament'. Any such statement enjoyed complete immunity from actions in defamation.[18]

It is unfortunate that the court was not more conceptually precise in identifying the source of the principle it espoused. It may also be thought that the substantive protection afforded by the case gives MPs an unnecessarily expansive legal immunity. There is no doubt force in the argument that MPs should be able to use the privilege to raise matters of public concern which subsequent investigation proves to be well-founded. However, MPs may also shelter behind privilege to raise unfounded allegations. The Conservative MP, Geoffrey Dickens, caused considerable controversy in 1986 when he availed himself of privilege to accuse a clergyman of having sexually abused young children. The person concerned had already been subject to a police investigation, and the police had concluded there was no basis for a prosecution.[19] In such circumstances, an MP's behaviour is no doubt more reprehensible if she knows the allegation to be false, or has taken no care to establish its accuracy, than if she is acting in good faith. The damage to the reputation of the individual or company concerned has nevertheless been done irrespective of the MPs' motive.

Dickens made his allegation in a speech on the floor. There is seemingly no room to doubt this was a 'proceeding in Parliament'. But as suggested in chapter 5, much of the Commons' work takes place outside the chamber, and much takes the form of written rather than oral communication. The question then arises of how far MPs' immunity should stretch – just what is meant by 'proceedings in Parliament'.

---

18 In the same era, the courts had also concluded that such protection extended to newspapers which produced accurate reports of such 'defamatory' proceedings, so long as the report was circulated with the purpose of informing the citizenry of what was happening in Parliament rather than as a malicious attempt to discredit the person criticised; see *Wason v Walter* (1868) LR 4 QB 73.
19 Leopold P (1986) 'Leaks and squeaks in the Palace of Westminster' *Public Law* 368–374.

What are 'proceedings in Parliament'?

The Privy Council had stressed in *Re Parliamentary Privilege Act 1770* that it offered no view on the meaning of 'proceedings in Parliament'. Nor did it address the more contentious question of whether the power to determine that meaning lay within the jusrisdiction of the courts or the respective houses. The Commons' reference to the Privy Council had been triggered by an episode involving Labour MP George Strauss. Strauss had sent a letter to a minister criticising the London Electricity Board (LEB). The minister had then forwarded the letter to the Chairman of the LEB for his attention. The Chairman considered Strauss' comments defamatory, and threatened a libel action if they were not withdrawn. Strauss thereupon referred the matter to the house, claiming the threat was a breach of privilege.

The issue turned on whether the letter was a 'proceeding in Parliament'. There are strong arguments for assuming that it was. Such communications about matters within a minister's competence would be a frequently occurring and important part of the MP's role, both as a party politician and as a constituency representative. The Committee of Privileges concluded that the letter was a 'proceeding', and that a breach had occurred. However the house rejected the committee's conclusion. In contrast, the house had accepted in 1938–1939 that communications between members and ministers which were initiated with a view to placing a question would be 'proceedings'. A fortiori, oral or written questions themselves would also come within the scope of the privilege. Even if we were to accept that the houses are constitutionally competent to give an authoritative definition of the concept, it is clear that they have not done so. Griffith and Ryle's suggestion that there are many 'grey areas' is perhaps a polite understatement.[20]

The Commons Committee of Privileges actually recommended in 1977 that the concept be given a clearer, legislative meaning. However the house chose not to act upon the proposal, presumably because the passage of such legislation would imply that Parliament had removed the houses' claimed competence to interpret the term. 'Proceedings in parliament' thus remains a legally obscure area of the constitution. That obscurity has in the past given rise to acute controversy.

---

20 *Op cit* p 88. For an absurdly extensive interpretation see *R v Graham-Campbell, ex p Herbert* [1935] 1 KB 594.

Stockdale v Hansard (1839)

The constitutional clash between the courts and the Commons which was avoided in respect of Wilkes' admission to the house in the 1760s eventually occurred in the late 1830s. The trigger for the dispute was mundane. A Commons inquiry into prison administration, published on the house's instructions, had made potentially libellous comments about a medical textbook circulating in one of the gaols. Stockdale, the book's author, commenced defamation proceedings against Hansard, the Commons' publisher.[1]

The house instructed Hansard not to contest the case on its merits, but merely to inform the court that it had resolved that the report was a proceeding in Parliament, and as such not subject to judicial jurisidiction.[2] The court, for which Lord Denman CJ gave the leading judgment, rejected the Commons' assertion of privilege, categorising it as:

> 'a claim for an arbitrary power to authorise the commission of any act whatever, on behalf of a body which in the same argument is admitted not to be the supreme power in the state.'[3]

Lord Denman concluded that such a contention was irreconcilable with orthodox understandings of parliamentary sovereignty and the rule of law. The Commons' (or Lords') constitutional competence in matters of privilege stretched only to the application of existing privilege. With that jurisdiction, the ordinary courts would not interfere. But neither house could grant itself new privileges. Furthermore, the power to determine the boundaries of those existing privileges lay not with either house through resolutions, but with the courts through the common law. Parliament might grant either house a jurisdiction which exceeded the existing boundaries, and give the house the power that it claimed in this case, but the Commons could not achieve that result itself:

> 'The House of Commons is not Parliament, but only a co-ordinate and component part of the Parliament. That sovereign power can make and unmake the laws; but the concurrence of the three legislative

---

1 *Stockdale v Hansard* (1839) 9 Ad & El 1. The text that follows presents a much simplified account of a judgment which merits close scrutiny. Hansard has achieved immortality of a sort, insofar as official records of the houses' proceedngs are now generally referred to as '*Hansard*'.
2 The house was evidently not offering an interpretation of Article 9 of the Bill of Rights qua statute, but construing it as declaratory of a continuing privilege with pre-revolutionary origins.
3 (1839) 9 Ad & El 1 at 107–108.

estates is necessary; the resolution of any one of them cannot alter the law. . . .'[4]

Lord Denman's reasoning follows that of Holt CJ in *Ashby v White* and *Paty*'s case. Just as Holt saw the right to vote as a common law entitlement that could only be overridden by Parliament, so Lord Denman viewed the common law right to protect one's reputation against libellous criticism as immune to anything other than statutory regulation. Lord Denman considered that 'proceedings in Parliament' could not form the subject of a defamation action. However he would not accept that the publishers of reports of Commons proceedings subsequently circulated outside the house enjoyed such protection.

Lord Denman adopted what to modern eyes would be a teleological interpretive strategy by suggesting that the protections the houses possessed under Article 9 extended only to matters 'necessary' for them to perform their duties. Since he saw no 'necessity' for the publishers of parliamentary proceedings to be immune from a libel action, Stockdale could proceed with his action and expect the courts to deliver judgment in his favour if his case was well founded.

The case of the Sheriff of Middlesex[5]

Stockdale did succeed in his action. However, the Commons was not prepared to accept the court's conclusion. Acting on the house's instructions, Hansard refused to comply with the judgment against him. The Sheriff of Middlesex, an officer of the court, then sought to enforce the judgment. The Commons continued to refuse to recognise the court's decision, and ordered that the Sheriff be committed to the Tower for having breached the house's privileges. The Commons' stance on this question is obviously hypocritical, given its long history of opposition in the pre-revolutionary era to the Crown's repeated efforts to invoke a similarly arbitrary power to detain anyone who displeased it. The Sheriff had clearly been detained because he was complying with the court's instructions. In crude terms, he had been punished by the Commons for upholding the rule of law. One might therefore have expected that his subsequent habeas corpus action would lead the courts to order his immediate release.

---

4 Ibid, at 108.
5 (1840) 11 Ad & El 273. This account presents a simplified version of events. For a fuller discussion see Wittke (1970) *op cit* pp 152–156; Stockdale E (1989) 'The unnecessary crisis: the background to the Parliamentary Papers Act 1840' *Public Law* 30–49.

The Serjeant at Arms' return to the writ stated simply that the Sheriff had been committed for 'a breach of privilege and contempt'. The court, for which Lord Denman gave the leading judgment, declined to question the adequacy of the return. Lord Denman held that so long as the Commons complied with the mere formality of stating that the committal was for 'contempt', no court was competent to order the prisoner's release. It would be, he suggested, 'unseemly' for a court to doubt the Commons' bona fides in such circumstances.

The decision is closely comparable with the opinion offered by the judges in the *Resolutions in Anderson* some 300 years earlier; the only difference being that the court was now permitting the Commons rather than the Crown to make a mockery of the habeas corpus remedy. The decision also completely undermined *Stockdale*. Lord Denman began his opinion in *Middlesex* by observing that *Stockdale* was 'in all respects correct'. Yet there is little point in a judgment being 'correct' if the same court subsequently permits it to be evaded.

Neither the Commons nor the judiciary emerged with credit from the *Stockdale* controversy. The specific legal problem that the case raised was subsequently resolved by Parliament, which enacted the Parliamentary Papers Act 1840. The Act empowered the Speaker to issue a certificate staying any legal proceedings in respect of documents published by order of either house. But the episode did not provide 'an ultimate political fact' with which to resolve the problem of 'dualism' in the more general sense. It may however be that a recent decision of the House of Lords has opened the way for that particular gap to be filled.

Redefining the relationship between 'parliamentary sovereignty' and 'parliamentary privilege'? *Pepper v Hart*

One of the first rules to which students of British law were traditionally exposed was that judges would not refer to the records of debates in *Hansard* to clarify the meaning of ambiguous or nonsensical legislative terminology. The legal roots of the 'exclusionary rule' are not entirely clear.[6] One viewpoint would

---

6 The exclusionary rule was of late Victorian rather than venerable vintage. One can find both pre- and post-revolutionary cases in which the courts made explicit reference to parliamentary debate as an aid to statutory interpretation; see *Ash v Abdy* (1678) 3 Swan 664; *Millar v Taylor* (1769) 4 Burr 2303; *Re Mew and Thorne*

suggest it is simply a common law rule concerning the admissibility of evidence. An alternative perspective is that the courts were deferring to a statutory command in Article 9 of the Bill of Rights, wherein the notion of 'questioned' was not limited to absolving MPs for actions for defamation or criminal prosecutions arising from parliamentary speeches, but extended also to even considering the content of debate to aid statutory interpretation. A third argument contends that the courts' refusal to consult *Hansard* was an element of privilege, existing alongside the common law but immune to judicial jurisdiction.

The rule's source is of some significance when considering whether and how it might be revised. If it was a common law concept, there would be no constitutional barrier to prevent the House of Lords changing it. The common law may be amended to accommodate changing social and economic circumstances. This presents no theoretical challenge to Parliament's legal sovereignty: if Parliament disapproves of changes in the common law, it may reverse the judges' decision by statute.

In contrast, if the rule derives from Article 9, the courts could not simply overrule it. That would be inconsistent with parliamentary sovereignty. However, as a law-maker in the interpretative sense, the House of Lords can alter its previous definition of Article 9. The concept of 'questioned' could, for example, be narrowed, perhaps so that it embraced only a defence to defamation proceedings. Using *Hansard* as an interpretive aid would thus suddenly become consistent with Article 9.[7]

If the rule was part of privilege, judicial amendment would be constitutionally problematic rather than impossible. If we accept (per *Stockdale*, Denning's dissent in *Re Parliamentary Privilege Act 1770*, and *Stourton*) that the common law sets the boundaries to privilege, the courts might legitimately conclude that they had previously misinterpreted those boundaries and that the correct scope of privilege did not preclude reference to *Hansard*. This could however provoke a conflict between the houses and the courts, since it is unlikely that either house would wish to cede its claimed jurisdiction over such questions.

The rule's purposes are more readily discernible. Four reasons have been advanced in recent cases. Lord Wilberforce in *Beswick*

(1862) 31 LJ Bcy 87. From a separation of powers perspective, the decision in *Ash v Abdy* is notable, since the judge deciding the case had himself introduced the relevant legislation to Parliament.

7 This interpretation appealed to Popplewell J in *Rost v Edwards* [1990] 2 All ER 641. However, he considered himself bound to accept the broad meaning. Reinterpretation would have to await a decision by the House of Lords.

v Beswick[8] fastened on a question of 'constitutional principle'. The task of interpreting legislation rested solely on the courts; for the judiciary to allow their view of the meaning of a statute to be determined by the speech of a minister made during the Bill's passage would in effect delegate their interpretative role to that minister. This would turn parliamentary sovereignty into government sovereignty. This reason is perhaps overstated. Lord Wilberforce's objection loses force if one suggests that *Hansard* should merely be of persuasive not determinative authority.

In the same case, Lord Reid identified 'purely practical reasons' for the rule. Access to *Hansard* would increase the time and expense of litigation, since lawyers would feel compelled to read debates in their entirety in pursuit of statements supporting their clients' cases. This, too, seems a weak justification. The same reasoning might plausibly be applied to law reports; counsel might avidly scrutinise every judgment ever delivered on the point in issue, hoping to uncover some forgotten judicial subtlety buttressing their client's position. Moreover, it seems unlikely that lawyers would not prioritise their use of information cost-effectively. Access to a wider range of materials could lead lawyers to be more discerning in selecting arguments.

Lord Scarman offered a third justification in *Davis v Johnson*.[9] He suggested that *Hansard* was an unreliable guide to a statute's meaning. The content of debate, suffused with the need to score party political points, would be unlikely to convey governmental intent precisely. This objection ostensibly seems convincing, but on reflection is overly simplistic. While many Commons or Lords exchanges may lack the rationality with which one might hope to find laws expressed, *Hansard* also contains calm, deliberate speeches in which ministers precisely describe the objectives they expect a Bill to achieve. Lord Scarman's point might be met by selective resort to debate; total abstinence seems unnecessary.

A fourth reason, noted by Lord Diplock in *Fothergill v Monarch Airlines*,[10] was that 'elementary justice' demanded that all the materials on which the citizen might depend in litigation should be readily accessible. Lord Diplock felt *Hansard* did not meet this criterion. This is also a weak argument. One would doubt that citizens would find *Hansard* any more esoteric or inaccessible than the *All England Law Reports*. Insofar as Lord Diplock's point raises a valid informed consent issue, it amounts to an argument not for

8 [1967] 2 All ER 1197, HL.
9 [1979] AC 264, HL.
10 [1980] 2 All ER 696, HL.

excluding *Hansard* from the courts but for ensuring that its contents are more widely known and more easily available.

Sporadic challenges to the traditional position were made in the 1960s and 1970s. Dissenting in *Warner v Metropolitan Police Comr*, Lord Reid reaffirmed the rule but added: 'there is room for an exception where examining the proceedings in Parliament would almost certainly settle the matter immediately one way or the other.'[11] Lord Denning also appeared reluctant to accept the rule. On some occasions he simply disregarded it altogether; on others, he circumvented it by referring not to *Hansard* itself, but to pertinent extracts from debates reproduced in legal textbooks or periodicals, or by confessing to taking illicit peeks at *Hansard* when not in court.[12]

Perhaps more significantly (from a practical if not 'legal' perspective), the Commons resolved in 1980 that the courts need no longer petition the house for permission to make 'reference' to *Hansard*. The Commons appeared to root the rule solely in Article 9 of the Bill of Rights, though it was not clear if the House was waiving what it perceived to be a statutory protection or an aspect of its privilege.[13] It subsequently became clear that the Commons' interpretation of 'reference' was restricted: the House would regard use of *Hansard* to clarify the meaning of an ambiguous statute as exceeding the concept of 'reference'.[14] The stage nevertheless seemed set for a more general revision of the rule.

Opening Pandora's box?

The controversy leading to *Pepper v Hart*[15] would not seem the stuff of great constitutional principle, being concerned primarily with the taxation levied on a particular fringe benefit. The language of the relevant statute was ambiguous. However, the taxpayers maintained that a minister had made a clear statement during debate which favoured their interpretation of the legis-

---

11 [1969] 2 AC 256 at 279, HL.
12 See his judgment in the Court of Appeal in *Davis v Johnson* [1979] AC 264 at 276–277. Such peeking perhaps explains his ostensibly heretical observation in *Magor* (p 89 above) some 27 years earlier that the judicial function was to make sense of Ministers' words as well as Parliament's.
13 This again returns us to the question of whether Article 9 is declaratory or transformative of pre-revolutionary privilege. See Leopold P (1981) 'References in court to Hansard' *Public Law* 316–321; Miers D (1983) 'Citing Hansard as an aid to interpretation' *Statute LR* 98–102.
14 See the letter from the Clerk of the House to the Attorney General quoted from in *Pepper v Hart* [1993] 1 All ER 42 at 55, HL.
15 [1993] 1 All ER 42, HL.

lation. This argument could not be sustained without recourse to *Hansard*. The taxpayers were therefore asking the court to over-turn the exclusionary rule.

Lord Browne-Wilkinson's leading judgment departed substantially, if cautiously, from previous orthodoxy. His central conclusion was that:

'Reference to parliamentary material should be permitted as an aid to the construction of legislation which is ambiguous or obscure or the literal meaning of which leads to an absurdity . . . where such material clearly discloses . . . the legislative intention lying behind the ambiguous or obscure words.'[16]

The rationale underpinning Lord Browne-Wilkinson's judgment lay in what he referred to as an issue of constitutional principle. His principle, however, appeared at odds with the principle advanced by Lord Wilberforce in *Beswick*. He observed that it was conceivable that legislators might sometimes be genuinely mistaken as to the legal meaning of the statutory formula they enacted. In such circumstances, the courts would be frustrating rather than fulfilling their constitutional subordination to 'Parliament' by not referring to *Hansard*. This analysis requires one to define parliamentary sovereignty not in the formalistic, Diceyan sense of blind obedience to statutory words, but in a much more functionalist vein of giving effect to legislative intent, in which the courts assume responsibility for protecting citizens from legislators' readily ascertainable mistakes.

Lord Browne-Wilkinson attempted to meet Lord Scarman's afore-mentioned concerns about the cut and thrust of debate by limiting the type of speech to which judges may refer to statements by the Minister or member promoting the Bill. He was, however, less accommodating to other previous judicial justifications for the rule.

He observed that New Zealand and Canada had both recently allowed their courts to refer to legislative proceedings: neither jurisdiction had found that the cost or duration of litigation had increased unacceptably as a result. Orders for costs against the offending party should be sufficient deterrent to lawyers who invited the courts to examine irrelevant parliamentary material. Nor did Lord Browne-Wilkinson attach any weight to the argument that *Hansard* was insufficiently accessible to litigants, for such a weakness was equally attributable to legislation:

'It is a fallacy to start from the position that all legislation is available

16 *Ibid*, at 64.

in a readily understandable form in any event: the very large number of statutory instruments made every year are not available in an indexed form for well over a year after they have been passed.'[17]

His Lordship was less than precise about the rule's source, suggesting it could derive from all three sources outlined above. He consequently dealt with each in turn. If the rule was judge made self-regulation, there was no barrier to the House of Lords remaking it in a more contemporarily relevant form. Should the rule have a statutory base, Lord Browne-Wilkinson concluded that Article 9 should be reinterpreted in the narrow sense canvassed in *Rost v Edwards*: Article 9's 'plain meaning' was simply to protect individual MPs from criminal or civil libility for statements made in 'proceedings in Parliament', and to ensure that MPs collectively, rather than the Crown, controlled the topics of parliamentary debate. Finally, perhaps rather disingenuously, his Lordship addressed the question of parliamentary privilege. Referring to the 1980 Commons' resolution, he suggested that the house viewed its privileges as co-extensive with the scope of Article 9. Consequently, given his redefinition of Article 9, recourse to *Hansard* could not impinge upon privilege. One might doubt that the house would accept this reasoning, for it 'confirms' the subordinacy of privilege to the common law.

Whether this last point has now joined the constitution's array of 'ultimate political facts' is at present an unanswerable question, determinable only when the Commons and the courts again adopt contradictory positions over a question of the magnitude of those posed by Wilkes, Stockdale and Bradlaugh. But one may plausibly speculate that *Pepper v Hart* is a decision with significant constitutional implications. This relates in part to its recognition of the political reality of government dominance of the legislative process. But its greater importance lies in the court's implicit claim that it, rather than the two houses, is the only body possessing the constitutional competence to determine the meaning of privilege.[18] This means that the courts are in effect denying that the Commons has any authority to claim immunity from orthodox understandings of parliamentary sovereignty and the rule of law. There may well be many aspects of privilege with which the courts

---

17 *Ibid*, at 66. The point reinforces the criticisms made in chapter 5 concerning recent governments' increasing use of SIs.
18 As Zander (*op cit* pp 153–157) notes, Lord Browne-Wilkinson framed his judgment in very cautious terms. It has however already been extended in subsequent decisions; see *R v Warwickshire County Council, ex p Johnson* [1993] AC 583, [1993] 1 All ER 299, HL.

feel unable to interfere. But that decision would seemingly now be based on the functionalist criterion of the non-justiciable nature of the privilege in question, rather than the formalist consideration of its source. Quite what meanings the courts will attach to the concept of justiciability in respect of privilege remains as yet unclear. But Lord Browne-Wilkinson's judgment has more profound, as yet undeveloped, implications. For, paradoxically, by asserting the supremacy of Parliament over its component parts in all aspects of their respective proceedings, *Pepper v Hart* adds considerable force to arguments which attack the doctrine of parliamentary sovereignty itself. We will return to this argument in chapter 15. But as the following two sections suggest, it might readily be assumed that many MPs would be most reluctant to tolerate further judicial intrusion into the houses' regulation of privilege.

IV. 'CONTEMPT' OF THE HOUSE

In formal terms, the privileges of each house are now supposedly a closed category. Just as the Crown may not create prerogative powers which it did not possess in 1688, neither can the Commons or the Lords create 'new' privileges. But as chapter 4 suggested in discussing the *Northumbria* case, the prerogative's formally 'residual' nature has little meaning if the courts permit the government to discover 'lost' powers. That point would have equal force in respect of privilege even if it were accepted (which it manifestly, at least by the Commons, is not) that the courts possessed sole jurisdiction to define its limits. If the Commons, prone as it now is to be a mere mouthpiece of the majority party, is to be regarded as the legitimate guardian of those boundaries, claims as to the 'residual' character of privilege would be quite misleading.

Furthermore, the Commons has traditionally claimed the power to punish 'contempts' – a power which the house seems to regard as so expansive that it is in effect claiming an unlimited jurisdiction. *Erskine May* defines contempt as:

'... any act or omission which obstructs or impedes either House in the performance of its functions, or which obstructs or impedes any Member or officer of such House in the discharge of his duty, or which has a tendency, directly or indirectly, to produce such results.'[19]

Were this a statutory concept, one would be tempted to assume

19 *Op cit* p 143.

that Parliament had granted the two houses an arbitrary and illegitimate power, an assumption that is reinforced when one realises that the houses also claim that they may punish contempts with fines or imprisonment. Neither sanction has been imposed in the modern era, but the Commons made frequent use of its imprisonment power in the eighteenth and nineteenth centuries.[20]

Contempts may be committed either by MPs themselves or by non-members. Allegations of contempt may be raised by an individual MP with the Speaker, who will then decide if the matter should be referred for investigation to the Committee of Privileges. The Speaker effectively enjoys an unconfined discretion on whether to refer, while the Committee itself enjoys similar discretion in determining how it investigates any matter brought to its attention. Many of the instances in which a contempt complaint has been upheld have related to matters which could conceivably have amounted to criminal offences. One might point for example to citizens who engaged in a riot outside the house in the hope of intimidating MPs, or assaults upon individual members.[1] Others, while not intrinsically criminal, have related to behaviour which clearly and directly hinders the houses' performance of their work. Obvious examples are failure to attend a committee hearing when ordered to do so; refusing to answer questions at such a hearing; offering obstructive or misleading responses to questions posed; or disrupting the proceedings of the house.[2]

The Commons has also had a long tradition of upholding contempt complaints against journalists or political commentators who have criticised either the house itself or its individual members. In 1702, the Commons resolved that publishing any material reflecting upon its proceedings or members was 'a high violation of its right and privileges'.[3] The rationale for this power is evidently that criticism (apparently even if well founded) detracts from the house's dignity and undermines the public respect which the house seemingly assumes it deserves. This category of contempt is not however a mere historical anachronism. In the twentieth century it has been applied to MPs who claimed to have seen

---

20 As we have seen, it was invoked in both the Wilkes and Bradlaugh sagas. For further examples see *Erskine May* ch 9.
1 *Ibid*, pp 119–120. For a more subtle example of more recent vintage see Leopold M (1984) 'Parliamentary privilege and an MP's threats' *Public Law* 547–550.
2 For an interesting selction of recent examples see Marshall (1979) *op cit* pp 217–220.
3 Quoted in *Erskine May* at p 121 n 9.

other MPs drunk in the house, and to journalists who suggested that MPs were getting extra petrol rations in the 1950s.[4]

Perhaps of rather more interest however are the numerous efforts made by individual MPs to have the most trivial of issues investigated. The petrol rationing episode in the 1950s triggered press comment that the house was invoking privilege to stifle freedom of speech. This in turn led some MPs to have the newspapers concerned charged with contempt. Similarly several Labour MPs sought to initiate contempt proceedings against *The Spectator* magazine when it suggested that they were sympathetic to the North Vietnamese communist régime.[5]

The Strauss case is perhaps the most graphic example of the house's apparent capacity to endow its members with an inflated sense of self-importance. Strauss had suggested the mere threat of defamation proceedings against him could constitute a contempt. The suggestion that a citizen should be punished simply for seeking to establish if her common law rights have been infringed is a quite bizarre contention, utterly irreconcilable with any mainstream understanding of the rule of law.

The 1967 report of the Privileges Committee

Commenting on such cases, Geoffrey Marshall suggested that they had done much 'to bring the House's privilege jurisdiction into disrepute'.[6] The house itself appeared to recognise this in the late 1960s. A wide-ranging Privileges Committee report in 1967 concluded that MPs were 'too sensitive to criticism' and unnecessarily resorted to contempt proceedings in respect both of trivial matters and in circumstances where alternative remedies (notably criminal or civil actions before the court) might be available.[7] The house appears to have accepted this advice – the contempt jurisdiction has been invoked with decreasing frequency since 1967.[8]

Yet one might wonder if there is any need at all for the Com-

4 Marshall (1979) *op cit* pp 229–231.
5 For further examples and comment see Seymour-Ure C (1964) 'The misuse of the question of privilege in the 1964–5 session of Parliament' *Parliamentary Affairs* 380–388.
6 (1979) *op cit* pp 229.
7 Sills P (1968) 'Report of the Select Committee on Parliamentary Privilege' 31 *MLR* 435–439; Seymour-Ure C (1970) 'Proposed reforms of parliamentary privilege: an assessment in the light of recent cases' *Parliamentary Affairs* 221–231.
8 For a list of examples see Griffith and Ryle *op cit* pp 98–102.

mons or the Lords to possess such sweeping powers. Contempts which in themselves amount to criminal offences (such as assaulting MPs) can be addressed in the courts. Nor is there any strong justification for either house to have the power to punish criticism of its members or of the institution itself (even if the punishment consists only of the ritual of being called to the house to be scolded and made to offer an apology). It is perhaps unfortunate that those newspaper editors called in recent times to retract their newspapers' criticisms of the Commons have not simply denied the house's jurisdiction and challenged the legality of its contempt proceedings before the courts.[9] For as we approach the twenty-first century, there would seem to be very good reasons for regarding both houses as being themselves intrinsically inadequate institutions. The predominance of hereditary peers in the Lords is an obvious indication of that house's incapacity to satisfy even modest standards of either representativeness or competence, as is, more seriously, the Commons' minimal capacity to control the Cabinet. But both those weaknesses are collective in nature, pointing to defects in the institutional basis of each house. Of greater significance to the question of the legitimacy of maintaining the privileges of the Commons and the Lords is the houses' apparent failure to address the ethical shortcomings of some of their members.

V. THE REGULATION OF MPs' ETHICAL STANDARDS

The summer of 1995 presented the British public with the extraordinary spectacle of a senior backbench Conservative MP, Sir Jerry Wiggin, tabling amendments during the standing committee stage of a Bill's passage in the name of another Conservative, Sebastian Coe, without Coe's permission. Wiggin had a financial interest in the issue; he was a consultant for an organisation which would benefit from the amendment. He had reportedly used Coe's name for fear that the amendment's prospects of success would be compromised if the house knew its mover had been paid by a commercial organisation to promote it.

Press coverage of the episode was hugely critical of Wiggin, and

9 That they have not done so is presumably due primarily to the fact that the house also claims sole jurisdiction to determine which newspapers are granted facilities within the house to report on its proceedings. MPs may thus 'punish' a newspaper's supposed contempt by reducing the number of 'lobby passes' offered to the paper's reporters, or temporarily banning some or all of its reporters from the precincts of the house.

he found few supporters even on the Conservative benches. One might have thought that his action was prima facie a gross contempt, and that even a house in which his party formed a majority would be compelled to sanction his behaviour. However the Speaker declined to refer the matter to the Committee of Privileges; in her opinion Wiggin's misbehaviour merited no greater punishment than that he apologise to the house.[10]

Until 1975, MPs were under no obligation to declare either the sources or amounts of any income they received over and above their MP's salary. Parliament had not enacted legislation on the subject: nor had the house concluded that it should itself require such disclosure. This lacuna had significant implications for the concepts of informed consent, both within the Commons itself and in terms of the relationship between an MP and her electors. One could not be sure, for example, that individual MPs were not supporting or opposing particular pieces of legislation, making speeches in the house, or putting questions to ministers because they had been paid to do so by commercial interests rather than because they honestly believed in the intrinsic rectitude of the course they were following. Similarly, it is quite plausible to conclude that many electors might decline to support a particular candidate if they knew that she was receiving financial benefits from sources of which they disapproved. Relatedly, it seems quite likely that voters would be less likely to support candidates espousing socialist policies if it was known that such candidates were themselves extremely wealthy.

The Register of Members' Interests

A considerable scandal broke in the early 1970s, when a prominent Labour politician, T Dan Smith,[11] was convicted of various offences of corruption. The scandal was exacerbated by the revelation that Edward Short, then Labour Leader of the House, had accepted a 'gift' of £250 from Mr Smith in 1963 'provided it can be kept a confidential matter between the two of us'.[12]

The episode generated extensive press coverage dwelling on the many opportunities for corrupt and sharp practice which

---

10 The Speaker's decision appeared to astonish many seasoned observers, within and outside the house; see Hencke D and Bowcott O (1995) 'MPs' fury as Wiggin escapes' *The Guardian* 23 May.

11 Smith was not an MP, but the leader of Newcastle city council.

12 See Economist (1974) 'On the low road' *The Economist* 4 May.

became available to MPs as a result of their membership of the house. There was never any suggestion that such behaviour was endemic or even widespread within the Commons. However given the effective dominance of the legislative process which the Commons by then possessed, it seems plausible to assume that even one MP who was prepared to engage in improper financial relationships would be one too many. Without an effective mechanism to regulate such matters, the house could not realistically claim to be above suspicion.

Among the more far-reaching proposals aired in the aftermath of the Smith affair was the suggestion that legislation should be introduced requiring MPs to make their income tax returns available for public inspection. The house apparently regarded this as an intolerable intrusion into MPs' private affairs, and opted for a far more modest system of self-regulation. In May 1974 the Commons resolved that:

'. . . in any debate or proceeding of the house . . . or communications which a Member may have with other Members or Ministers or servants of the Crown, he shall disclose any relevant pecuniary interest or benefit of whatever nature, whether direct or indirect, that he may have or may be expecting to have.'[13]

The house also resolved to create a Register of Members' Interests, on which MPs would record certain sources of income. An ad hoc select committee was established to produce detailed proposals. It is perhaps worth recalling that the Labour government at this time had only the barest of majorities in the Commons; there was thus no prospect of the government simply pushing through its own preferences. That the house endorsed such anodyne reforms is perhaps a powerful indication of its members' (irrespective of party) continuing arrogance and self-righteousness.

The house adopted the select committee's recommendations in 1975. The Register would serve:

'. . . to provide information of any pecuniary interest or other material benefit which a Member of Parliament may receive which might be thought to affect his conduct as a member of Parliament or influence his [sic] actions, speeches or votes in Parliament.'[14]

The register covers a wide range of financial interests, including such matters as directorships of companies, income from practice in the professions and paid employment (which includes 'public relations' and 'consultancy' activities), and overseas visits not

13 *Erskine May* p 384.
14 *Erskine May* p 386.

financed from public funds.[15] The names of any employers or clients should also be disclosed whenever the income the member derives from the relationship relates 'in any manner' to her/his membership of the house. However, there was no requirement that members disclose *how much* income they received from each source. The information that the register disclosed was thus of very limited value. The house also created a 'Select Committee on Members' Interests' to consider amendment to the register and hear complaints about alleged breaches of its terms. But it was not clear what sanctions, if any, would be imposed on MPs whose entries in the register were found to be inaccurate.

The initiative thus appeared to be more an exercise in symbolic reassurance than in effective reform. Edward Short, introducing the report to the house, observed that it amounted to no more than 'broad guidelines within which Members should proceed with good sense and responsibility'.[16] Nevertheless, its measures still proved too much for some MPs. Thus the Conservative MP John Stokes, seemingly oblivious to press coverage and public opinion, argued that: 'there is no demand for all this cumbersome machinery to register Members' interests'.[17]

Quite how effective the register has proved is an open question. One MP, Enoch Powell, simply refused to disclose any of his interests. No action was taken against him. Nor does it appear that the register has become more effective with age. Appreciable controversy arose in 1994, when press stories suggested that Conservative MP Neil Hamilton had failed to disclose that he had enjoyed an expensive six-day stay at the Ritz hotel in Paris paid for by a foreign businessman who was then embroiled in a takeover bid being investigated by the Department of Trade and Industry. The Privilege Committee's 'investigation' of the Hamilton episode thoroughly undermined any contention that the house eschewed party political considerations in such matters. Conservative MPs acquiesced in the government's wish to have a whip on the committee. His presence could serve no purpose but to ensure that other Conservative members did nothing to jeopardise party interests. Opposition MPs eventually walked out of the committee, which then reached the extraordinary conclusion that while Hamilton had failed to make a relevant disclosure, this amounted to no more than 'imprudence' and did not merit any punishment.[18]

15 For a full list see *Erskine May* pp 386–387.
16 *HCD*, 12 June 1975 c 737.
17 *Ibid*, at c 749.
18 See Hencke D (1995) 'Fury as Ritz MP avoids penalty' *The Guardian*, 8 June.

This particular case was however merely symptomatic of an apparently wider malaise.

'Cash for questions' and the report of the Nolan Commission

In 1974, the Labour MP Joe Ashton was found to have committed a serious contempt by alleging that members were prepared to raise issues in the house at the behest of commerical organisations in return for payment.[19] Whether Ashton's claim was then ill-founded is a matter for speculation. It is however clear that some 20 years later the house contained at least two Conservative MPs who, for a sizeable fee, were prepared to do just what Ashton alleged.

Acting on rumours about some MPs' rather lax ethical standards, two *Sunday Times* journalists posed as representatives of a foreign company wishing to raise a question in the house and willing to pay £1,000 to the MP who placed it. The journalists approached ten Labour MPs and ten Conservative MPs. The Labour members refused to take money for such purposes, as did seven Conservatives. The eighth Conservative, Bill Walker, agreed to table a question for a fee given to charity. Two Conservatives, Graham Riddick and David Tredinnick (both parliamentary private secretaries) agreed to table a question and accept the fee.

In the ensuing furore, the Speaker granted an emergency debate to discuss the issue, and referred the case to the Privileges Committee. After a lengthy investigation, the Privileges Committee, dominated by a Conservative majority imposed a punishment of ten and 20 days' suspension on the offending MPs. The 'punishment' was laughably lenient. And it is perhaps an indication of the extraordinary values adhered to by many MPs that suggestions were aired that the *Sunday Times* should be charged with contempt of the house for exposing their colleagues' moral frailties.

The 'cash for questions' scandal generated such hostile press coverage that the government established a committee of inquiry, chaired by Nolan LJ, with a wide-ranging remit to inquire into ethical standards in public life. If the government had hoped that the Nolan Committee would serve as an effective exercise in symbolic reassurance,[20] its hopes were soon disappointed. Rumours rapidly began to circulate that the committee would recommend extensive reforms, whereupon Conservative MPs

19 Marshall (1979) *op cit* p 228.
20 See pp 183–184 above.

equally rapidly began to cast aspersions on its impartiality and competence.

Yet the recommendations contained in the committee's first report were rather feeble. Its most significant proposal was that MPs should in future disclose not just the source but also the amount of income they received for the performance of services arising from their membership of the house. Nolan also urged the creation of a body independent of the Commons to investigate MPs' behaviour. The obvious weakness of the recommendation was that the Nolan Comittee had apparently accepted that MPs' ethical standards should remain a matter for the house. Neither proposal was to have a statutory basis; rather they were to be matters for the Commons itself to introduce.

Although the Conservative government initially welcomed the report, many of its backbenchers (those, one assumes, who received substantial 'consultancy' payments) signalled that they would not support its implementation. Rather than carry the proposals into force by relying on opposition votes, the government decided to refer the Nolan Report to a special select committee for further consideration. The committee had a Conservative majority. It divided on party lines on the main question before it. The Conservative members rejected – while all the Opposition members accepted – the Nolan proposal that the house's rules should require MPs to divulge the amount as well as the source of their 'consultancy' payments. The committee's recommendation was subsequently endorsed by the Cabinet. However when the committee's report was put before the house, some 23 Conservative MPs voted with the Opposition in support of requiring disclosure of the amount of income MPs received for these activities.[21]

Quite how effective this new régime will prove is a matter for conjecture. The disclosure requirement is not a 'law' enforceable in the independent arena of the courts; it is merely an internal rule of the house. Its adequacy is entirely dependent on MPs attaching greater importance to financial candour than to party loyalties. The new rule would presumably be most effective if the house were to expel or suspend those members who fail to make accurate disclosures. But one might doubt that MPs in a governing party with a small Commons majority would take such drastic steps should some of their number be found wanting on a question of

---

21 Wintour P (1995) 'Tories rebel on sleaze' *The Guardian*, 2 November; Smithers R (1995) 'Tory Nolan vote "fuelled by self-interest" ' *The Guardian*, 8 November.

financial integrity. The present outcome of the 'cash for questions' scandal is thus something of a damp squib.

In 1975, Enoch Powell MP had opposed the creation of the Register of Interests on the grounds that: 'we degrade ourselves by implying that our honour and traditions are not adequate to maintain proper standards in this house'.[1] Similar sentiments were voiced in 1995 by Conservative MPs who opposed the Nolan recommendations.[2] Yet it is quite clear that MPs' 'honour and tradition' *is* an entirely inadequate guarantor of 'proper standards'. It would seem most unfortunate that the majority of MPs refuse to accept this.

CONCLUSION

Media coverage of the cash for questions scandal and the Nolan report was perhaps most notable for revealing the casual equation frequently made, both by seasoned media commentators and by MPs themselves, of the House of Commons with Parliament, and relatedly of the privileges of the house with legislation.[3] This may perhaps be seen as a realistic interpretation of the contemporary balance of power between Parliament's three constituent parts. As noted in chapter 6, the Commons is now much the more poweful of the two houses, and we shall see in chapter 9 that the Monarch no longer plays a meaningful role in the legislative process.

The equation is however theoretically inept, and in practical terms both dangerous and underdeveloped, because it fails to take the further realistic step of observing that the Commons is generally just a vehicle for the promotion of factional, party interest. The Commons alone (except on those very rare occasions when no party commands a majority) does not in any sense perform the role that the revolution bestowed upon Parliament. As suggested in chapter 5, the notion that the Commons plays a significantly independent role either as an actor within the legislative process or as a monitor of executive behaviour is quite fallacious in the contemporary political context. The house's response to the Nolan inquiry further suggests that one might

1 *HCD*, 12 June 1975 c 743.
2 See Webster P (1995) 'Major faces Tory backlash over Nolan' *The Times*, 19 May; White M (1995) 'Cautious Hunt tests the temperature as "bureaucratic" rules for MPs alarm Tories' *The Guardian*, 19 May.
3 Thus Andrew Marr, a political correspondent with *The Independent*, characterised the Nolan recommendations as an attack on the sovereignty of Parliament when presenting BBC Radio 4's *The week in Westminster* programme on 13 May 1995.

plausibly entertain serious doubts about the integrity of a small number of its members.[4] Indeed, to talk of 'the house's' response is in itself highly misleading, as it obscures the acute inter-party factionalism the issue raised.

It is perhaps an exaggeration to suggest that our examination of the Commons' legislative and supervisory roles, of the electoral system through which its members are chosen, and of the privileges within which MPs wrap themselves, leads to the conclusion that the lower house as presently constituted and regulated can defensibly be described as unrepresentative, incompetent, and corrupt. Such hyperbole perhaps contains more than a grain of truth, but it would as yet be premature to form firm conclusions as to the adequacy of our present parliamentary institutions. The next three chapters take us rather further towards the position from which a firm conclusion might more plausibly be drawn. Chapter 9 addresses a further set of non-legal principles of the constitution which regulate governmental and parliamentary behaviour, while chapters 10 and 11 assess the uses to which the executive's dominance of the legislature has been put in respect of perhaps the most important of constitutional values in a nominally democratic society – namely the extent to which 'the people' can effectively express the political and moral beliefs which they hold.

---

4 It is an indication of the ludicrous nature of our current constitutional structure that such a claim probably amounts to a contempt of the house.

CHAPTER NINE

Constitutional conventions

Thus far we have focused primarily on legal regulation of constitutional behaviour. Such controls may be construed as performing
a political or moral function – to ensure that the constitution is
sensitive to the demands of democracy and the rule of law (even
though these are concepts bearing various meanings). Chapter 6
addressed more clearly the constitutional inter-relationship
between legal principle and political practice by discussing the
changing functions of the House of Lords, especially instances of
tension between the Lords' legal powers and shifting *conventional*
understandings as to the legitimate scope of its legislative role.
This chapter assesses the nature and purpose of constitutional
conventions more systematically.

We might usefully begin by considering several hypothetical
situations. Assume, for example, that the Queen personally
opposes a government's policy to cut old age pensions. She decides
that when the Bill is sent for the Royal Assent she will not sign it.
She justifies her action on the grounds that 'the people' dislike
the policy – (perhaps observing that the government did not win
a majority of votes cast at the last election) – and claims her first
loyalty is to her people, not to the Houses of Parliament or the
government. Alternatively, assume that the Queen no longer wants
John Major as Prime Minister, and concludes that if the Conservatives win the next electon she will invite Margaret Thatcher to
assume that office, even though John Major remains Conservative
party leader.

Giving the Royal Assent and appointing a Prime Minister are
aspects of the residue of prerogative powers still exercised by the
Monarch in person. The courts have never indicated that such
prerogatives are justiciable. Thus, if the Queen chose to adopt
either course, there is no apparent legal obstacle in her way. Nor
does it answer this problem to suggest that Parliament could pass

legislation preventing such behaviour – for such legislation could only emerge if the Queen assented to the relevant Bill.[1]

But it is not just the Queen who wields potentially important yet clearly non-justiciable constitutional powers. Let us suppose, as a third hypothetical scenario, that the Labour party wins the next election with a two-seat Commons majority, but with fewer votes than the Conservatives. John Major claims that the Conservatives have in reality 'won' the election, refuses to resign as Prime Minister, and he and his Cabinet resolve (with the Queen's support) to stay in office as a minority government.

We can, to borrow Lord Camden's methodology in *Entick v Carrington*, look as hard as we like in our law books, be they *Halsbury's Statutes* or the *All England Law Reports*, but we will find neither an Act nor a common law rule indicating that the law of the constitution has been breached in any of those situations. But it seems most unlikely such events could ever occur? Could the Queen veto the wishes of the Commons? Or impose an unwanted Prime Minister on the Commons' majority party? Would a Prime Minister really have to be dragged out of Downing Street after a general election defeat? That such hypotheses belong in the realm of fantasy is a result of their political impracticality – or, in other words, of their 'unconstitutionality'. They indicate that vital pillars of our constitutional structure may be built upon foundations with no obvious legal basis – foundations which we might call constitutional conventions.

The Diceyan perspective – laws and conventions distinguished

Once again, we might find it helpful in understanding both the constitution's traditional approach to conventions and the ways in which that tradition has evolved, to return to Dicey's *Law of the Constitution*. Dicey identified two distinct types of constitutional rule:

> 'The one set of rules are in the strictest sense "laws", since they are rules (... whether enacted by statute or derived from ... the common law) enforced by the courts;....
>
> The other set of rules consists of conventions, understandings, habits or practices which, though they may regulate the conduct of ... officials, are not in reality laws at all since they are not enforced by the courts.'[2]

---

1 As noted in chapter 2, the present Queen's father, George VI, had assented to just such a Bill from the South African legislative assembly.
2 *Op cit* pp 23–24.

Dicey does not distingush laws from conventions because of their importance, or the role they fulfil, but in terms of whether they are enforceable by the courts; something *is not a convention* if its breach is actionable in the courts. The utility of that proposition is discussed below. But before we do so, it may be useful to approach constitutional conventions from another angle. In Jennings' view, a convention was characterised not just by its legal non-enforcability, but also because there was a *reason* for the rule.[3] We might therefore ask what constitutional role conventions supposedly play, a question answered in part by exploring the mechanisms through which they come into existence.

The functions and sources of conventions

A simple, if incomplete, way to characterise conventions' constitutional function is that they *fill in the gaps* within the legal structure of government. However this notion operates at different levels of generality. Very narrowly, conventions provide a moral framework within which government ministers or the Monarch should exercise non-justiciable legal powers. Slightly more broadly, they function as one means of regulating the relationship between ministers within central government. In a wider vein, conventions also regulate the relationship between the different branches of government – especially between the Monarch and the Cabinet, between central government and the House of Commons, and between central government and local goverment. We analyse that final relationship in chapters 10 and 11. This chapter explores the first three. Before turning to their function and substance however, we should give some thought to their source.

The sources of constitutional conventions

As we saw in chapter 6, George V was most reluctant to accede to Asquith's repeated requests for a mass creation of Liberal peers to overcome the Lords' Conservative majority during the 1909–1911 controversies. The King had sought advice from senior Conservative politicians. Asquith, we may recall, described the Lords' intransigence as 'a breach of the constitution'.[4] That breach was of course of a conventional, rather than legal, nature. Asquith took a similar view of George V's recourse to opposition politicians for advice. In a minute to the King, Asquith explained why:

3 Jennings (1959) *op cit* p 136.
4 At p 202 above.

'The part to be played by the Crown, in such a situation as now exists, has happily been settled by the accumulated traditions and unbroken practice of more than 70 years. It is to act upon the advice of the Ministers who for the time being possess the confidence of the House of Commons. . . . It follows that it is not the function of a Constitutional Sovereign to act as arbiter or mediator between rival parties and policies, still less to take advice from the leaders on both sides, with the view to forming a conclusion of his own.'

Asquith assumed that the reason for the convention that the Monarch 'act upon the advice of the Ministers who possess the confidence of the Commons' was to ensure that the preferences of the party with majority Commons support were always given legal effect whenever personal prerogatives were deployed. We can see an obvious 'democratic' (albeit majoritarian) justification for the convention, since the party with a Commons majority usually represents the largest section (if not a majority) of the electorate.

Asquith also suggests three possible sources of conventions: 'tradition', 'unbroken practice', and a lengthy time span, in this case seventy years. We might reasonably assume that if a particular (non-legal) aspect of the government process possesses all three characteristics it can be regarded as a convention. Whether we could so regard a practice having but one or two such features is a more difficult question.

The idea that there are minimum requirements to becoming a convention is reinforced by the argument that there also a set of non-legal constitutional rules which are somehow inferior to conventions. Dicey used such phrases as customs, practices, and usages to describe these lesser rules of behaviour. Jennings agreed with Dicey on this point. He suggested that these informal practices could be divided into those that eventually became conventions and those that did not. Jennings additionally insisted that a convention only arose if there was an important 'reason' for its existence, ie that its provisions had substantial political significance. But what neither author offered was a set of principles with which one could invariably decide in which camp a particular practice lay.

Determining when a practice matures sufficiently to be a convention is still a question defying authoritative answer. Chapter 6 suggested the Salisbury doctrine was a convention. Griffith and Ryle's *Parliament* approves that classification. But another eminent commentator, Colin Turpin, concludes: 'It may be doubted whether these principles have sufficient clarity, or are supported by a sufficient agreement to give them the status of conventions.'[5]

Such disagreement over so important an element of constitutional history implies we may never find analytical tools which tell us when a custom assumes conventional status. This need not cause concern. Conventions are political rather than legal animals. And politics is reputedly 'the art of the posssible'. Since what is impossible in one political situation may be entirely possible in another, we should expect conventions to be elusive creatures.

We might nonetheless proceed by assuming that a crucial test of whether a custom is a convention is whether the rule is respected by the people it supposedly controls. This suggests that convention spotting is more an empirical than a theoretical task. Consequently, the only way to decide how to classify rules of political behaviour is to examine situations where a supposed convention has either been respected or ignored. The rules on which we initially focus are the concepts of collective and individual ministerial responsibility.

I. COLLECTIVE MINISTERIAL RESPONSIBILITY

The Cabinet, like the office of Prime Minister, has no identifiable legal source. It assumed a recognisably modern form after about 1720, when we can also see the first Prime Minister emerging as the 'first amonq equals' within it. Both the office of Prime Minister and the institution of the Cabinet are therefore creatures of convention. As suggested in chapter 5, except in periods when a ruling party has a small Commons majority, and must be acutely sensitive to its MPs' wishes, the Cabinet is the hub of the legislative and executive arms of government: it is there that government policies are formulated and refined. Consequently, for a government with a reliable Commons majority, parliamentary sovereignty is in effect Cabinet sovereignty. Given the Cabinet's obvious importance, it may seem odd that it operates without any appreciable legal structure. But the absence of legal controls on Cabinet behaviour does not mean that there are no principles regulating its activities.

The convention of ministerial responsibility is perhaps the most important non-legal rule within our constitution. Its concern is with regulating the conduct of government (and especially Cabinet) activities, both in respect of ministers' relations with

5 (1990) *op cit* p 491.

each other, and with Parliament. The convention is divided into collective and individual branches. We will consider individual responsibility in section four. Firstly, however, we address collective responsibility. This convention has three sub-divisions: the confidence rule, the unanimity rule, and the confidentiality rule.

Confidence

The confidence rule originally required a government to resign if it could not command majority Commons support – if the House has 'lost confidence' in the government. Initially the rule applied if a government was defeated on a major policy issue.[6] During the mid-nineteenth century such resignations were commonplace: we noted several over electoral reform in chapter 7, and Ivor Jennings records five between 1852 and 1859.[7]

It is difficult to define 'major' issues. Presumably the Shops Bill on which the Thatcher government was defeated in 1986 did not meet that criterion.[8] But this does no more than tell us that an issue is not sufficiently important to require a government's resignation if the government does not resign when it is defeated. That test would be entirely circular. Furthermore, there have been several instances of modern governments enduring Commons defeats on important issues, but continuing in office regardless. The 1974–1979 Labour administration suffered frequent defeats. Its expenditure plans were rejected by the Commons in March 1976. It is difficult to disagree with the then Leader of the Opposition, Margaret Thatcher, that this policy was so fundamental a part of the government's raison d'etre that defeat demanded resignation. The Cabinet declined to do so however. The government also refused to resign when defeated in an attempt to raise income tax levels in 1977, clearly a matter of major importance.

The experiences of the mid-1970s suggest that the convention's initial form no longer binds Cabinet behaviour. If a necessary feature of conventional status is that politicians consider themselves obliged to follow a given course of action, it is clear that the confidence rule of the 1850s is not a conventional feature of the contemporary constitution. But it would be inaccurate to claim the convention has disappeared entirely; rather, it has evolved into a different form.

6 See generally Norton P (1978) 'Government defeats in the House of Commons: myth and reality' *Public Law* 360–378.
7 (1959) *op cit* pp 512–519.
8 P 159 above.

The rule's modern version seems to require the government to resign only if defeated on an explicit no-confidence motion. The function of this shift in conventional understandings is readily discernible. Governments are rarely elected because of their policy on a single issue, but because of the overall package of policies and personalities they offer. A government's failure to command a Commons majority on a particular issue need not mean it cannot do so in all other policy areas. Defeat in an explicit no-confidence motion, in contrast, implies the Commons considers the government incompetent in *all* matters.

As such, the reason behind the new convention is clear. In one, somewhat abstract, sense, it stresses that the executive is accountable to the Commons, and so provides a rather different illustration of the principle of legislative supremacy. More prosaically, in the age of nationalised party politics, it provides an indirect means for the people, via their MPs, to signify withdrawal of their consent to a particular government.[9] However we have only rather barren historical soil in which to root the new convention. There has been just one occasion since 1945 when the convention has been tested. James Callaghan's minority Labour government resigned in 1979 when defeated by one vote on an explicit no-confidence motion. One might doubt that this amounts to a tradition or long-term unbroken practice.

Only one other Prime Minister has resigned in comparable (if not identical) circumstances after such a defeat this century, that one being Stanley Baldwin in 1924. Baldwin led a minority Conservative administration, which failed to gain Commons approval for the legislative programme outlined in the King's speech at the commencement of the parliamentary session. (At the 1923 election the Conservatives won 258 seats, Labour 191, and the Liberals 159.) Ramsay MacDonald subsequently formed a minority Labour administration from within the same Parliament, which survived for barely 11 months. That administration was also defeated on a confidence vote, although that vote led to a dissolution rather than simply a change of government.[10] It thus seems that the contemporary confidence rule, if rarely invoked in practice, is straightforward in principle. The second limb of collective responsibility, the unanimity rule, seems quite the opposite.

9 Although, as noted below, a successful no-confidence motion might lead not to a dissolution, but to the formation of a new administration from within the existing Parliament.

10 See Norton (1978) *op cit*; Jennings (1959) *op cit* pp 28–30.

Unanimity

The unanimity rule requires all Cabinet Ministers to offer whole-hearted public support for all cabinet decisions, even if a minister opposed the policy concerned in Cabinet. Ministers who find a particular policy unacceptable should resign from office. As Lord Salisbury explained in 1878:

> 'For all that passes in Cabinet every member of it who does not resign is absolutely and irretrievably responsible and has no right afterwards to say that he agreed in one case to a compromise, while in another he was persuaded by his colleagues . . .'[11]

The rule also supposes that ministerial differences of opinion have been aired in Cabinet. The convention demands collective loyalty to collective decisions. It could therefore be undermined either by ministers who openly signalled their disagreement with government policy, or by Cabinet decision-making procedures which prevent ministers having any say in policy formation.

The rule originally arose in the seventeenth century to protect ministers from the King's attempts to undermine their power by exposing or encouraging public arguments. Since the Cabinet is no longer in conflict with the Monarch, the rationale for the rule has changed. The contemporary argument suggests the rule is needed to maintain public and business confidence in the unity and purpose of government. It is alleged that public Cabinet divisions would trigger such dire consequences as reduced investment from overseas, a run on the pound, or various other forms of economic or political instability.

There seem to be three ways to test whether the rule has conventional status. The first, and most elusive, would be to identify occasions when a minister strongly opposed a particular policy, made and lost her argument in Cabinet, and then resolutely kept her dissent a secret from outside observers. Unfortunately, it is in the nature of a secret that we do not know that it happened. We may, in retrospect, gain some insight by the eventual release of Cabinet papers (currently embargoed for at least 30 years), or (more promptly) by the memoirs of former ministers, although the latter may present a skewed interpretation of events. The second test would seek instances when irreconcilable disgreement between Cabinet members led to resignations or dismissals of ministers. Such episodes would reinforce the claim that the con-

---

11 Quoted in Ellis D (1980) 'Collective ministerial responsibility and collective solidarity' *Public Law* 367–396.

vention effectively determined government behaviour. The third test, which would seem to disprove the rule's conventional status, would search political history for public intra-Cabinet disputes in which all protagonists stayed in office. It is an indicator of the unfortunate indeterminacy of conventional rules that one readily finds examples to satisfy all three tests.

Michael Hesletine's resignation from Thatcher's second administration in 1985 over the Westland affair offers a powerful illustration of the convention taking effect. Heseltine, then Defence Secretary, was embroiled within Cabinet in an argument as to whether the financially troubled Westland helicopter company should be rescued by American or European firms. Heseltine favoured the European option, but the Cabinet majority prefered the American bid. It is not clear if Heseltine would have resigned solely because of his disagreement with the substance of Cabinet policy. His own account stresses that he left office because the Cabinet did not accept the second limb of the unanimity convention – namely that a minister may argue her case fully before her colleagues. Heseltine alleged that a Cabinet meeting scheduled for him to make his argument had been cancelled by the Prime Minister in order to force through the American takeover, a strategy which he interpreted as confirming that the Cabinet no longer operated in a collective manner.[12]

A similar accusation that Margaret Thatcher rejected collective forms of decision-making was made by Nigel Lawson. Lawson resigned as Chancellor of the Exchequer in 1989, claiming his position had been undermined by the Prime Minister's preference for taking advice on economic policy from her personal adviser, Professor Alan Walters, rather than from her Chancellor.

Lawson's decision to leave office in defence of his preferred economic policy has several obvious Conservative precedents. In 1886, Lord Randolph Churchill, Chancellor in Lord Salisbury's administration, was isolated in Cabinet over his plans to cut military spending. Rather than defer to majority sentiment, Churchill quit the government altogether.[13] A similarly principled stand was taken by Chancellor Peter Thorneycroft and two junior ministers in 1958, who felt the Cabinet was not committed to sufficiently rigorous anti-inflation policies.

Neither the Churchill nor Thorneycroft departures dealt a fatal blow to their respective government's stability. Prime Minister

---

12 The episode repays close attention; see especially Hennessy (1986) *op cit.*
13 For further details see Madgwick P (1966) 'Resignations' *Parliamentary Affairs* 59–76.

Harold Macmillan famously minimised the impact of the 1958 events by refering to them as 'a little local difficulty'. The impact of Lawson's resignation will be considered further below.

Illustrations supportive of the rule are not limited solely to the Conservative party. In 1951, two members of the Labour Cabinet (Nye Bevan and Harold Wilson) and a junior minister resigned from Attlee's government in protest at plans to introduce prescription charges into the newly founded National Health Service. The action was widely construed as revealing a deep ideological split within the party.[14] It pales in comparison, however, with the events of 1931. As Table 9.1 reveals, the 1929–1931 Labour government was a minority administration. Its tenure coincided with the Great Depression, which wrought severe distress on most western economies. A Cabinet committee proposed large cuts in public expenditure to address the crisis. These were welcomed by the Conservative opposition, but opposed by eight Cabinet members. Faced with so profound a split in his government, Prime Minister MacDonald tendered its resignation to the King.

At the Prime Minister's invitation, George VI played a pivotal role in brokering a solution to the crisis. The suggestion for a coalition government headed by MacDonald was made by Sir Herbert Samuel, the leader of the Liberal Party, and enthusiastically pressed on Stanley Baldwin, the Conservative leader, by the King. The Liberals and Conservatives agreed to join a coalition administration, on the understanding that Parliament would be dissolved as soon as emergency legislation enacting the Cabinet committee's recommendation was passed. Only three of the Labour Cabinet's 18 ministers agreed to serve in a 'National' coalition government, in which MacDonald led what he described as 'a Cabinet of Individuals' – most of whom were Conservatives. As Table 9.1 shows, the ensuing general election was fought on somewhat peculiar party political lines. Its outcome was to install MacDonald as the Prime Minister of an overwhelmingly Conservative administration, even though his 'party' had only 8 members in the Commons.

Reactions to Disraeli's proposals for the 1867 Reform Act also illustrate the operation of the unanimity rule. Three members of Lord Derby's Cabinet, all opposing further democratisation, resigned rather than support the Bill.[15] Similarly, Richard Crossman's *Diaries* reveal the 1966–1970 Labour Cabinet was

---

14 Pimlott *op cit* pp 160–165: Hennessy P (1992) *Never again* pp 415–417 (London: Johnathan Cape).
15 Cowling *op cit* pp 163–165. See pp 251–253 above.

Table 9.1
The 1931 General Election

Party	Seats won	Share of vote
Conservative	387	47.8%
National Labour*	8	1.5%
National Liberal**	33	3.7%
Liberal	21	6.7%
Labour	154	38.0%

* National Labour was the party label chosen by MacDonald and the small rump of members of the previous Labour administration who entered a coalition with the Conservatives.

** National Liberal was the rump of former Liberal party members who chose to enter the coalition.

Source: Extracted from data in Craig F (1989) *British Electoral Facts 1832–1987* pp 30–31 (Aldershot: Parlaimentary Research Services).

deeply divided over lowering the voting age to 18.[16] Such disagreement was not made public (at least not until the *Diaries* were published some years later!). Ministers opposed to the reform stifled their dissent; the government could thus present the Bill as a measure enjoying unanimous Cabinet support.

But electoral reform also provides quite contradictory examples, seemingly disproving the convention's existence. In 1883, for example, Joseph Chamberlain campaigned vigorously for continued extension of the franchise, to which the rest of Gladstone's Cabinet was clearly opposed.[17] Similarly, Asquith's various cabinets were openly divided on the issue of women's suffrage, as indeed were previous Liberal and Conservative administrations.[18]

Asquith presented the last example as 'an agreement to differ', suggesting that the convention could be 'suspended', if only for matters crossing party political boundaries. The same argument was invoked by MacDonald's coalition National Government to justify patent Cabinet disagreement over the question of import controls, although we might wonder if we could expect collective solidarity in a 'Cabinet of Individuals'.

This 'suspension' principle has latterly been deployed by both Labour and Conservative Cabinets over government policies towards the European Community.[19] In 1975, the Labour Prime

16 *Op cit* pp 493–494, 500–501.
17 Jones *op cit* p 106. See pp 254–255 above.
18 Rover *op cit* p 102. See pp 255–260 above.
19 At pp 501–502 and 556–557 below.

Minister Harold Wilson allowed Cabinet members to campaign on both sides in the referendum on whether Britain should remain in the EEC. Wilson explained his decision by saying that the split reflected a similar rift within public opinion – whether or not to leave the EEC was so contentious and important an issue that it was vital that voters received all the arguments for and against.[20] Certainly James Callaghan, the last Labour Prime Minister,[1] supported the idea of selectively applied conventions. Callaghan permitted his Cabinet openly to hold differing views in 1979 about the type of electoral system to be used for elections to the EEC Parliament. When accused of acting unconstitutionally, he defended himself by saying that collective responsibility would always apply 'except in cases where I announce that it does not'.[2] More informally, the second Major government was noticeably divided between 'Euro-sceptics' and 'Euro-enthusiasts', a point explored more fully in chapter 12.

As an organising principle, 'suspension' has little merit – a practice cannot be a binding rule if it can be disregarded at the whim of those it purportedly controls. Moreover, such arguments do not explain the 1883 Cabinet's tolerance of Chamberlain's independent line. Rather, his continued presence in office seems attributable to a deep split within the Liberal party on the reform question. The Cabinet portrayed Chamberlain's 1883 dissent as an example of a principle of 'Ministerial freedom of speech', but such a concept is manifestly incompatible with a unanimity convention. Chamberlain's behaviour was accepted because his dismissal or resignation was impractical from a party political perspective; it would have alienated many Liberal voters, with dire electoral results. He could thus defy the supposed convention and advance both his own prospects within the party and the prospects of more radical electoral reform being enacted.

A similar combination of personal ambition and policy preference seems to underlie James Callaghan's very evident dissent, when Home Secretary, from the industrial relations policies of the second (1966–1970) Wilson administration. The government wished to impose legal sanctions on workers who took industrial action without trade union approval. Callaghan clearly aligned himself with trade union opposition to this proposal. Subsequently, he announced, without having sought Cabinet approval,

---

20 This episode is discussed more fully at pp 501–502 below.
1 His elevation to the party leadership when Wilson resigned suggests his breaches of the unanimity principle in the late 1960s bore fruit.
2 *HCD*, 16 June 177 at c 552.

that the government would take no new measures to regulate wage and price inflation. Many Cabinet members apparently considered that Callaghan was seeking to establish himself as the trade unions' preferred successor to Harold Wilson, and demanded he be disciplined for disregarding the unanimity rule.[3] No action was taken, however, since the government, facing an imminent general election, could not risk losing the political and financial support the unions provided.

Clearly, there are occasions when a minister's propensity to succumb to the 'hallucination of indispensibility'[4] is based in fact, not fantasy. But that is not always so. Resignation may unexpectedly end promising ministerial careers. Randolph Churchill perhaps best illustrates the point that even a most eminent politician can find that resignation leads to a permanent political wilderness.

The inference we might draw from these examples is that whatever 'reason' one might adduce for the rule of cabinet unanimity, it is ignored for reasons of party political expediency too frequently for us to conclude that Asquith's threefold test for conventional status is met. One might refine the convention by suggesting it operates differently for Conservative and Labour governments. Writing in 1980,[5] David Ellis argued Labour governments contained a wider range of opinion than Conservative administrations, and their members were less inclined than Conservatives to compromise ideological preferences to preserve party unity. So fractious an atmosphere was inimical to effective functioning of the unanimity rule, especially since, as noted in chapter 7,[6] most Labour governments have had precarious Commons majorities. Ministers representing distinct party factions may see no need to respect the unanimity rule if their faction's continued support is a prerequisite of the government's survival.

Confidentiality

Lawson and Heseltine withheld their explanations of the events leading to their departures from Cabinet until after they had resigned. In so doing, they respected the unwritten letter of the

3 According to Crossman's *Diaries*, *op cit* at pp 497–500. Crossman notes that Callaghan himself protested that there was nothing unconventional about his behaviour.
4 Madwick *op cit* p 59.
5 *Op cit*.
6 Table 7.5.

unanimity rule. It is also however a convention of the constitution that ministers who resign from office are afforded the opportunity to offer reasons and perhaps justifications for their action to the Commons (or, if they are peers, to the Lords). As we shall see in chapter 13, such speeches can have a devastating political effect. This is another manifestation of the confidence rule, since it enables MPs to evaluate the government's performance after having heard both sides of the argument.

Once out of Cabinet, Lawson and Heseltine explained their actions in detail, both in the Commons and in the media. In so doing, they drew attention to another facet of collective responsibility, namely that all ministers owe their cabinet colleagues a duty of confidentiality. Ministers should not reveal for example how colleagues argued or voted in particular disputes: to do so would seriously undermine the unanimity rule and also inhibit ministers from speaking their minds.

To date this rule seems to have been respected, at least formally. However, reports of Cabinet discussions are leaked to the press with sufficient regularity to suggest that in practice some ministers ignore it. A more contentious issue is whether confidentiality should continue after a minister leaves the Cabinet. And if so for how long, and how stringently? The rule's status, and the political and legal consequences which flowed from ignoring it, came before the courts in *A-G v Jonathan Cape Ltd*, popularly known as the *Crossman Diaries* case.[7]

Can conventions become laws? 1: The Crossman Diaries case

Richard Crossman, a member of Wilson's cabinet between 1964 and 1970, wanted to provide a detailed, first-hand account of Cabinet government in operation. Consequently, he kept a comprehensive diary of Cabinet decisions, intending to publish it following his retirement. Unfortunately Crossman died prematurely, but his widow decided to publish the *Diaries*.

After extracts appeared in *The Sunday Times*, the government sought an injunction preventing further publication. It argued that the courts should preserve the confidentiality of three types of ministerial information. Firstly, the views of individual ministers. Secondly, confidential advice to ministers from civil servants. And thirdly, discussions about the appointment or transfer of senior officials. Crossman's publishers argued that the duty of Cabinet

7 [1976] QB 752.

confidentiality had no legal basis; it was merely a moral obligation, respected or ignored according to the minister's conscience. Lord Widgery did not find history a helpful guide: 'I find overwhelming evidence that the doctrine of joint responsibility is generally understood and practised, and equally strong evidence that it is on occasion ignored.'[8] Widgery eventually delivered a puzzling judgment. Firstly, he accepted that Cabinet Ministers owed each other a legally enforceable duty of confidentiality. However, this duty did not derive from the convention turning into a law. It was created by 'stretching' existing common law principles about confidentiality in respect of other types of relationship, particularly marriage and commercial undertakings.[9] But secondly, Widgery held that unless the disclosures threatened national security, the duty would disappear ten years after the relevant events occurred. Consequently publication was permissible.

The government subsequently established a committee of inquiry, headed by Lord Radcliffe, to make recommendations concerning the publication of ministers' diaries or autobiographies.[10] The committee proposed a 15-year delay on publication of sensitive material. The proposal has not been given statutory force: given the rapidity with which retired ministers have subsequently marketed their memoirs, it seems safe to assume that it should not be regarded as a convention.[11]

If analysed formalistically, the judgment does not sweep away Dicey's claim that conventions are not enforceable by the courts. Technically, the case is not an example of a court enforcing a convention, but accepting that a convention was coincidentally underpinned by existing common law rules. That may seem a semantic distinction. In functionalist terms, we might argue that the court enforced a convention by cloaking it with a common law label. There is no legal impediment to the courts doing so. The common law is recognised to be a dynamic, unstable set of legal rules. In cases such as *Burmah Oil*, *Lain*, and *GCHQ*, 'new' common law principles emerged when judges considered that applying traditional ideas would have produced unsatisfactory

8 Ibid, at 770.
9 *Argyll v Argyll* [1967] Ch 302 and *Saltman Engineering Co Ltd v Campbell Engineering Co Ltd* (1948) (1963) 65 RPC 203 respectively.
10 Radcliffe (1976) *Report on Ministerial Memoirs*, Cmnd 6386 (London: HMSO).
11 For example Clark A (1993) *Diaries* (London: Weidenfield and Nicolson) – by far the most revealing of the genre; Fowler N (1988) *Ministers Decide* (London: Chapman); Baker K (1993) *The Turbulent Years* (London: Faber); Lawson N (1992) *The View from No 11* (London: Bantam); Ridley N (1991) *My Style of Government* (London: Fontana).

results. Parliament may restore the former law by legislation reversing a court decision, but (short of passing legislation forbidding the courts from altering common law principles) it has no power to pre-empt judicial innovation. This inter-relationship between convention and common law within the courts is something to which we shall return. For the present, before concluding our discussion of collective responsibility, we must make a detour in our circuitous journey among the constitution's conventional undergrowth to an ostensibly non-justiciable issue – the relationship between the Monarch and her ministers.

II. THE MONARCH

In formal terms, the Monarch retains substantial legal powers. Unlike the House of Lords, she has the legal capacity to veto *any* Bill passed by the Commons. No court has thus far indicated that it is competent to compel the grant of the Royal Assent. The Monarch also seems to have the legal authority to appoint whomsoever she wishes to be Prime Minister, and to appoint and dismiss other ministers at will: she may dismiss an entire government if she wishes. And she may at any time, without fear of legal reversal, dissolve Parliament and thereby force a general election to be held. All such actions are elements of the royal prerogative which are 'peculiar and eccentrical' to the Monarch herself, and which, per *GCHQ*, appear non-justiciable. Nor, of course, could such prerogatives be altered or abolished by statute without the Monarch's consent. As a legal creature, therefore, the monarchy appears to possess (at least) co-equal status with the Commons.

Yet there is no part of the contemporary constitution in which the mismatch between legal principle and political fact is more pronounced than in respect of the personal prerogatives. The notion that a single individual should wield substantial legal powers bestowed solely by accident of birth is entirely antithetical to the particular form of parliamentary democracy on which the legitimacy of the constitution rests. This is not to say, as is suggested below, that one could not invoke alternative conceptions of 'democracy' to justify such powers in some circumstances. But as a matter of political instinct, one might readily infer that there would be very convincing reasons for the presence of constitutional conventions which subjected the exercise of the personal prerogatives to the wishes of the government which enjoyed the confidence of the Commons. A brief survey of the past 150 years suggests that such a convention has indeed emerged.

'On the advice of her Ministers?' The conventional 'democratisation' of the personal prerogatives

As noted in chapter 7, William IV did not acknowledge that the Great Reform Act's tentative push towards constitutional democratisation affected his power to remove a government which displeased him. In 1834, he dismissed Lord Melbourne's Whig administration, which he regarded as unacceptably radical.[12] William invited Sir Robert Peel to lead a minority Conservative administration. Peel was more sensitive to the Act's implications, and requested an immediate dissolution of Parliament, hoping, one assumes, to legitimise both his own position and the King's by winning the subsequent general election. The electorate, however, returned the Whigs and their allies with a workable Commons majority. Peel had considered the King's case 'a bad one', based as it was largely on the ground that Melbourne's government did not command majority support in the Lords. William subsequently deferred to the Commons majority, and did not obstruct the formation of a new Whig administration.

There have been no subsequent examples of such blatant interference by the Monarch. However, Queen Victoria enagaged in secretive manoeuvrings to keep Gladstone out of power in 1886, when it appeared that Lord Salisbury's Conservative government no longer enjoyed the Commons' confidence. Victoria, like many Liberal MPs, opposed Gladstone's policy of granting home rule to Ireland. With Salisbury's approval, she subsequently approached several prominent anti-Gladstonian Liberals to try and ensure that a Gladstone administration could not enact that policy. Her tone was explicitly partisan:

'I appeal to you and to all moderate loyal and patriotic men, who have the safety and well-being of the Empire and the Throne at heart, and who wish to save them from destruction, with which, if the government again fell into the reckless hands of Mr Gladstone, they would be threatened, to rise above party and to be true patriots.'[13]

It is possible to defend the Queen's action by characterising her appeal that politicians should forswear party allegiances in pursuit of greater national interests as echoing a Madisonian fear of faction. As an abstract exercise in democratic theorisation, that view-

---

12 Brock *op cit* pp 315–317; Jennings (1959) *op cit* pp 403–405. Jennings and Brock disagree on whether this was a 'dismissal'. Jennings characterises it as a forced resignation, which is perhaps an unfortunate excursion into legalistic semantics in respect of what is manifestly a political issue. See further pp 391–392 below.
13 Cited in Jennings (1959) *op cit* p 34. Gladstone himself suggested of Victoria that there was 'no greater Tory in the land'; quoted in Arnstein *op cit* p 151.

point has some substantive attractions, although one might doubt that the process through which such a national interest was defined, namely the Monarch's individual preferences, would satisfy even the most diluted notions of democratic process. But in the context of historical trends in the late nineteenth century, Victoria's initiative was undoubtedly 'unconstititutional'.

By 1886, the Monarch's conventional capacity to engage in independent exercise of her legal powers had been substantially undermined by both the gradual extension of the Commons electoral franchise to ever greater numbers of 'the people' – and relatedly, by the increasing ascendancy of the Commons vis-à-vis the Lords within the legislative process. Neither trend formally affected the Monarch's legal powers, but both emphasised that electoral accountability rather than accident of birth should regulate access to governmental power. Victoria was not so intimately identified with factional Conservative interests as the majority in the contemporaneous House of Lords, but insofar as the legitimacy of her constitutional role depended on her maintaining a studied neutrality between those political parties which each enjoyed substantial electoral support, her machinations in 1886 revealed a distinct failure to accept (or perhaps to understand) the constitutional implications of the political and social changes the country was undergoing.

This gradual process of subordinating legal power to political practice is demonstrated by subsequent Monarchs' increasingly tentative interventions in situations of political instability. As we saw in chapter 7, the behaviour of Edward VII and George V in 1909–1911 was less than fully supportive of Asquith's wishes. At that point, the legal context in which the personal prerogatives were to be exercised was virtually the same as in 1886 – the House of Lords remained a co-equal partner to the Commons, and the franchise had not been substantially extended since 1884. Twenty years later, that context had altered significantly. The far more passive role played by George VI in forming the 1931 national government can be explained largely by the virtual completion of the democratisation process: since 1928, Britain had had an almost universal franchise for elections to the Commons, and since 1911 the Lords' inferior status within Parliament had been established as a matter of law, not merely convention. Elizabeth II was admittedly intimately involved in the choice of a Conservative Prime Minister in the mid-1950s, but that was the result of the fact that the Conservative party had no formal arrangements to choose its leader, who traditionally 'emerged' in some mysterious fashion after consultation among the party's senior figures. In the mid-

1960s, the Conservative party introduced a system in which its leader was chosen through a ballot of its MPs. The Labour party already had such a process, and it now seems inconceivable that it would now be legitimate for a Monarch to appoint as Prime Minister someone who was not the leader of her party. The principle is a powerful, further illustration not just of the primacy of party interests over national interests within Parliament, but also of the ascendancy of convention over law at the very heart of Britain's constitutional identity.

Refusing the Royal Assent

If we borrow Jennings' 'reason' test for conventional status, and (mis)apply it to the 1688 settlement, we might assume that the Monarch's formal co-equality with the Commons and the Lords served to protect both the Queen herself from an alliance of the two houses, and the 'people' from a lower and upper house temporarily seized by a desire to enact oppressive legislation. To suggest that the Queen might ever invoke her veto power would however seem utterly to contradict the trend towards democratisation which we employed to explain why the Monarch generally cannot use her personal prerogatives in an independent manner. This leads us yet again to examine the meaning of democracy in the contemporary constitution. If the concept means simply that a political party commanding a reliable Commons majority can pass any law whatsoever, a refusal of the Royal Assent to any Bill would be 'undemocratic'. Yet it is not difficult to imagine scenarios in which we might intuitively regard such action as essential to defend democratic ideals.

Assume, for example, that a government, fearing it will lose the next general election, promotes a Bill to extend the lifetime of a Parliament without opposition party agreement. At present the Lords may veto such legislation, and so, in its anachronistic way, can operate as a democratic safeguard against a dictatorial Commons majority. But the Lords does not (apparently) possess a veto over a third Parliament Act removing that veto power.

What conventional understandings should guide the Queen's decision about granting the Royal Assent in the following situations? Firstly if the Lords also approved the Bill extending the lifetime of the Parliament? Secondly to a new Parliament Bill, introduced against the Lords' wishes under the 1949 procedures, which removed the Lords' veto power on all legislation? And thirdly, if she assented to the second Bill, to a subsequent Bill extending the lifetime of the present Parliament? Alternatively, what course should the Queen follow in respect of a Bill which requires that the next general election be fought on constituency boundaries designed to secure a vast majority for the governing party? Or a Bill disenfranchising many citizens who would have supported opposition parties?

We might suggest all such Bills would be 'unconstitutional', and that the Queen could therefore legitimately withhold her assent. But the argument is a difficult one to sustain. One could contend for instance, that refusing the Royal Assent would be legitimate because any such Bill would be seeking to change the basis of consent to government within the constitution – to effect, as the Duke of Wellington put it, 'a revolution by due process of law'. The flaw in this argument is that it entrenches contemporary understandings of 'consent', and so suggests that we have now arrived at the ultimate form of democratic government. Yet these allegedly 'unconstitutional' Bills may be no more radical from our perspective than were Grey's Reform Bill or Asquith's Parliament Bill in the eyes of contemporaneous conservative opinion. In the absence of a supra-parliamentary constitution, we simply lack an authoritative yardstick against which to measure the substantive legitimacy of radical constitutional reform. The possibility that the 'people' might look to the Queen to defend them against their elected representatives seems a bizarre legal safety valve for a modern democracy to adopt.

It is some answer to the questions posed above to observe that no such Bill is ever likely to be produced. In all reasonably foreseeable circumstances, there appears to be no difficulty in concluding that the Monarch's personal prerogatives are exercised in accordance with the wishes of a Prime Minister whose government enjoys the confidence of the Commons. The reason for that convention is to subject the Queen's legal powers to democratic control – insofar as we consider prime ministerial control democratic. But that reason disappears when a Prime Minister's government does not possess the lower house's confidence. In such situations, the conventional constraints on the Monarch's legal powers are decidedly ambiguous. Two such circumstances have constantly exercised the minds of constitutional analysts. The first relates to the appointment of the Prime Minister following a general election in which no party has won a majority of Commons seats. The second concerns a Prime Minister's request for a dissolution, prior to the expiry of the five-year term fixed by the Parliament Act 1911, when an alternative government might be formed from within the existing lower house.

Choosing a Prime Minister in a hung Parliament[14]

In the February 1974 general election, Edward Heath's outgoing Conservative government failed to win an overall majority. But although Harold Wilson's Labour party had the largest number of seats in the new house, it had no majority either. The balance of power was held by various small parties, which in combination had only 37 seats.

There is no legal requirement that a government resign after a general election defeat. It does so, as a matter of convention, in deference to an electoral sentiment which indicates that another party is the people's preferred choice. That choice was however far from clear in 1974. While the electorate may have signalled displeasure with the Conservatives, it had not shown obvious enthusiasm for Labour. In these circumstances, Heath decided not to resign immediately, but to conduct negotiations with the smaller parties to see if they would offer him support in a coalition government. In the event, none did so. Heath then concluded that the correct course was for him to resign, and advise the Queen to invite Harold Wilson to form a minority administration.

It is possible to argue that Heath should have automatically resigned, and thereby offered Wilson the first attempt to form a minority or coalition administration, on the grounds firstly that Labour had won more seats than the Conservatives, and secondly that the prospect of a Conservative/Liberal coalition had not been put to the electorate. However, there is neither a legal nor a conventional basis for the claim that the leader of the largest single party has any immediate entitlement to a favourable exercise of the personal prerogatives. Heath, and the Queen, faced a somewhat unusual situation, and it would be difficult to describe the sequence of events as constitutionally indefensible.

Granting a dissolution after a tranfer of party loyalty

In the hung Parliament scenario, constitutional theorists do at least possess some recent historical experience on which to base speculation as to the Queen's behaviour. A far more difficult question would arise in circumstances which have not yet occurred in the modern era, but which are not wholly implausible. Let us suppose a party gains a majority of 20 seats at a general election. After one or two years of the Parliament's five-year term, following a bitter dispute over economic policy, 20 of its members cross the floor and join the opposition party. (Since MPs hold their seats

14 See generally Brazier R (1982) 'Choosing a Prime Minister' *Public Law* 395–417.

as individuals, not party representatives, they are under no legal obligation to resign and fight a by-election under their new party colours.) As a result, the Leader of the Opposition, rather than the Prime Minister, possesses the confidence of the lower house, a point confirmed when the opposition successfully moves an explicit no-confidence motion.

The Prime Minister, hoping the electorate would return his party with a new majority, requests a dissolution, even though the Leader of the Opposition could form a viable administration. If the Queen granted a dissolution, she would be defying the Commons majority, which, as we have seen throughout this chapter, appears to be a key informant of conventional principles. This suggests dissolution would be unconstitutional, and that the Queen's correct course would be to invite the Leader of the Opposition to become Prime Minister. But the Queen would have to dismiss the current Prime Minister before she could do so. The Prime Minister, however, will neither resign nor advise the Queen to dismiss him and then appoint the Leader of the Opposition as his successor: he maintains that the realities of electoral politics are that voters are motivated by party loyalties, not the merits of individual candidates, and that the new Commons majority has no electoral mandate.

In such circumstances, the Queen would have no alternative but to fashion a new constitutional convention. Since there is no minister with majority support on whose advice she can act, she would have to choose her own advisers and form her own opinion on the relative merits of dissolution and dismissal. Yet even if we limit our notion of 'democracy' to electoral majoritarianism, the democratic solution to this situation is unclear. In legal terms, the 'majority' is surely the largest grouping of MPs within the Commons, each of whom has been sent there as the representative of her particular constituency. This majority would clearly prefer dismissal to dissolution. However the 'political' majority might readily be seen as the party which won the greatest share of the vote at the last general election. This majority would obviously prefer dissolution to dismissal. Yet it would seem that for the Queen to grant a dissolution would entail her exercising her prerogative powers in accordance with a version of democracy which Parliament itself has never accepted.[15]

---

15 The legalistically minded might then wonder if the courts would accept that a justiciable issue had been raised here. Per *Laker Airways* (pp 113–114 above), the grant of a dissolution might be seen as elevating the prerogative above statute. There is, admittedly, no specific statute in issue here, but it is clear that our

Variations on this theme are as endless as answers are elusive, and neither will be explored at length here.[16] But readers might consider how the Queen should act when one of the 20 defecting MPs in the above example is the Prime Minister, and the Opposition party agree to select her as their new leader, or to serve under her in a coalition government. Alternatively, what should happen if the defectors do not include the Prime Minister, but, for example, the Foreign Secretary, who does not resign his office on switching parties, and who is adopted as Leader by the opposition before the Prime Minister asks the Queen to dismiss him, and then satisfies Asquith's criterion of being the minister for the time being commanding a majority in the house?

It is a source of much hypothesising amongst constitutional theorists, and perhaps considerable relief amongst politicians, that Queen Elizabeth II has not yet faced any such dilemma. Her intervention in such circumstances would inevitably be regarded by the 'losers' as an illegitimate exercise of constitutional power, with, as a recent episode of Australian constitutional history suggests, serious consequences for the Monarch's constitutional role.

The Australian crisis of 1975

Australia's present constitution, which dates from 1901, established a federal system of government with a bicameral central legislature. The Australian Parliament followed the British model in some respects. The lower house, the House of Representatives, corresponds to the House of Commons. However, unlike the House of Lords, the upper house, the Senate, is elected by a form of proportional representation designed to reflect the country's federal nature. The Governor-General (in 1975 Sir John Kerr) exercises certain prerogative powers as the Queen's appointee. These powers include the granting of the Royal Assent, the granting of a dissolution of either or both houses of Parliament, the dismissal of the government and the appointment of a Prime Minister. The text of the Australian constitution (itself a creation of the Westminster Parliament) did not spell out any legal rules to regulate the exercise of these powers, and it was (even in 1975)

electoral law regards MPs as individuals, rather than party representatives. To grant a dissolution on the grounds of the electorate's presumed party allegiances would subvert that statutory scheme.

16 Readers might wonder how the Queen should have responded to Edward Heath in 1974 had he advised her to dissolve Parliament rather than invite Harold Wilson to form a minority administration; see Brazier (1982) *op cit.*

unclear to what extent Australia's constitution adhered to the British convention that personal prerogatives should be exercised only in accordance with the wishes of a Prime Minister commanding a majority in the lower house.

In 1975, Gough Whitlam's Labour government held a majority in the lower house, but was in a minority in the Senate. The government had been racked by successive scandals, and Whitlam had been compelled to dismiss two Cabinet colleagues after it was revealed that they had lied to the lower house about certain financial dealings. The Australian economy was also in parlous health, and the Whitlam administration appeared to attract little public support.

We need not dwell on the precise allocation of constitutional powers between House and Senate. It suffices to note that the Senate appeared to have a legal capacity to prevent the government levying the taxation or raising the loans needed to finance public services. As a matter of convention, that power had never been used, even during periods of quite acute party political conflict. But in 1975, the Liberal opposition (led in the House by Malcom Fraser) resolved to use its greater strength in the Senate to refuse to grant supply in the hope of forcing Whitlam to request a dissolution of the House of Representatives. Their expectation was of course that they would win a lower house majority in the subsequent election.[17]

The Senate's position is resonant of that adopted by the House of Lords towards Lloyd George's 'People's Budget'. It may be overstating the case to describe the Senate as 'Mr Fraser's poodle', but Fraser was clearly deeply involved in the manoeuvrings. Those manoeuvrings culminated in Sir John Kerr dismissing the Whitlam government, and inviting Fraser to form a minority administration on the understanding that he would firstly instruct his party members in the Senate to grant supply, and secondly request an immediate dissolution.

The Governor-General did not act on the advice of the Prime Minister in following this course. Indeed, it seems it would have been impossible for him to do so. Had Whitlam been aware of the Governor-General's intentions, he would surely have asked the Queen to dismiss Sir John Kerr. And since the Queen should by convention act on the advice of her Prime Minister, one assumes she would have complied with any such request.

Sir John Kerr maintained that he was obliged, rather than simply

---

17 This incident may sound a warning to analysts who suggest that the defects of the House of Lords could be cured by making it an elected assembly.

empowered, to dismiss a government that could not maintain a majority in both houses on the supply question. As David Butler has argued, the text of the constitution provides no obvious support for that proposition.[18] Moreover, Butler suggests, the Governor-General's stance may have been politically defensible, if legally contentious in 1901, but the extent to which both the British and Australian constitutions had been democratised since then made his actions untenable. The parallel between the 1975 episode and William IV's dismissal of Derby in 1834 is ostensibly strong: neither 'Monarch' appeared to realise until after he had acted that effective power to appoint a Prime Minister no longer lay in his hands.

The Governor-General, and by implication the Queen, were spared further difficulties by the outcome of the subsequent general election, in which Malcom Fraser's Liberal party won a substantial lower house majority. In the longer term however, the episode triggered a substantial delegitimisation of the Monarch's role within the Australian constitution. It now seems quite anachronistic that a modern western democracy should permit its most acute political problems to be 'solved' by a power which is neither 'democratic' nor domestic. Kerr's actions appear to provide another illustration of the phenomenon of a legal power being conventionally acceptable only while it remains unused. One may therefore wonder if there is any reason for that legal power to be retained. Australia appears to be approaching that conclusion, for subsequent Australian governments have indicated that they will seek to turn the country into a republic by the end of the century, and transfer all of the Queen's powers to an internally selected head of state. This may not provide a 'better' solution to another scenario like that of 1975; but any solution will then be a matter purely of Australian constitutional law and practice.

We revisit the impact of controversies in Commonwealth countries on our domestic constitution in the penultimate section of this chapter. However, we may at this point conclude that as a matter of constitutional practice, albeit not of constitutional law, the Monarch's personal prerogatives are generally exercised by the Prime Minister. This might lead us to wonder if our previous discussion of collective Cabinet responsibility was incomplete, and to ask just how much effective political power is wielded by the Prime Minister alone in our contemporary constitution?

18 Butler D (1976) 'The Australian crisis of 1975' *Parliamentary Affairs* 201–210.

III. COLLECTIVE MINISTERIAL RESPONSIBILITY REVISITED: FROM CABINET TO PRIME MINISTERIAL GOVERNMENT . . .?

It is perhaps an apocryphal tale that when the Duke of Wellington became Prime Minister, after a career spent in the army rather than the Commons, he remarked on his first Cabinet meeting: 'An extraordinary affair. I gave them their orders and they wanted to stay and discuss them.'[19] We might doubt if there ever was a 'golden age' of Cabinet government in which all ministers participated fully and frankly in decision-making. But in the modern era, James Callaghan's aforementioned belief that he could suspend constitutional conventions whenever he saw fit provides lucid support for the argument that Britain's government is controlled by the Prime Minister rather than the Cabinet.

That argument was first aired in the nineteenth century by Walter Bagehot's leading work on the constitution.[20] Bagehot suggested that the Cabinet was becoming a 'dignified' rather than 'efficient' part of the constitution. Its role was increasingly ceremonial or symbolic, while real power was shifting to the Prime Minister and a few of his most trusted colleagues.

Bagehot's ideas were forcefully restated in a new edition of his book by Richard Crossman in the 1960s. Crossman's introduction, written before he became a Cabinet minister, argued that the Prime Minister effectively dominated the Cabinet rather than being just 'first among equals'. Prime Ministers achieved this through three main powers (powers nominally possessed by the Monarch). Firstly, by being able to appoint and dismiss ministers. Secondly, by setting the agenda for Cabinet discussions, which permitted the Prime Minister to avoid challenges over particular issues by leaving them off the agenda altogether. And thirdly, by controlling the remit and membership of Cabinet committees, where particular policies were discussed in more detail.[1]

Crossman argued that collective responsibility had assumed a new meaning by the 1960s. It no longer meant that all Cabinet ministers were involved in making the policy decisions which they were obliged to support, but rather that all ministers were expected to lend unquestioning support to decisions reached by

19 Quoted in Hennessy P (1986a) *Cabinet* p 121 (Oxford: Basil Blackwell).
20 (1867) *The English Constitution* (1963 edn by Crossman R) (London: Fontana).
  1 The first power is a legal one, being technically another of the Monarch's personal prerogatives, which as we have seen are by convention exercised according to the Prime Minister's wish. The second and third are matters purely of convention.

Cabinet committees, or a so-called inner Cabinet of senior ministers, or the Prime Minister. The unanimity rule would thus have undergone a marked shift. If a minister disagreed with Cabinet policy she would still be expected to either stifle her dissent or resign: she should not however expect to be a full participant in a collective decision-making process.

As we saw above, Michael Heseltine felt this trend had become an established, and (to him) unacceptable feature of the Thatcher cabinets. His resignation was premised, we might say, on his refusal to accept the legitimacy of a Cabinet in which collective decision-making had become entirely a 'dignified' rather than 'efficient' part of the constitution.

Harold Wilson did not invent the committee-based form of Cabinet decision-making, but he did use it more systematically than his predecessors. Nevertheless, Wilson himself disputed the prime ministerial government thesis. Writing in 1972, while in opposition, he suggested that 'The Prime Minister's task is to get a consensus of Cabinet or he cannot reasonably ask for loyalty and collective reponsibility.'[2]

There are undoubtedly sound justifications for a drift away from a fully collegiate model of Cabinet decision-making. As the government's workload has grown, so it has become increasingly implausible to expect all members of the Cabinet to have either the time or expertise to comment usefully on all areas of government activity. One is nevertheless left with the problem of deciding how best to enhance governmental efficiency without simultaneously concentrating power in too few ministerial hands. The only satisfactory way to gauge the accuracy of Crossman's thesis would be exhaustively to study the intimacies of Cabinet decision-making over a protracted period. Such a task is beyond the scope of this work:[3] we can however advert briefly to certain important episodes which indicate one can readily find examples which both underpin and undermine Crossman's argument.

There have been perhaps few more important policy decisions made in the post-war era than the 1945–1951 Attlee governments' conclusion that Britain should develop its own atomic weapons capacity. But to talk of this as a decision of the government, or even of the Cabinet, would be quite misleading. Attlee had permitted only a handful of his Cabinet to know of the progress both of scientific research and of negotiations with the Americans concerning access to their more advanced technology. Commentators

2 Quoted in Ellis *op cit* at p 372.
3 The most accessible and informative guide is perhaps Hennessy (1986a) *op cit.*

divide on quite how determined Attlee had been to exclude this question from collective Cabinet discussion.[4] There is however no doubt that he considered himself entitled, indeed even obliged, to consult only a small inner core of Cabinet colleagues. He recalled some years later that: 'I thought some of them [the Cabinet] were not fit to be trusted with secrets of this kind.'[5]

Similarly, James Callaghan preferred to formulate the major strands of economic policy not in Cabinet, but in a small 'Economic Seminar', containing just a handful of ministers. The role of Cabinet was merely to agree to whatever conclusions the 'Seminar' had reached.

Such dismissive prime ministerial treatment of Cabinet colleagues has not been a trait solely of Labour Prime Ministers. One of the most graphic examples of the apparently paradoxical way in which the Prime Minister's use of his great power within Cabinet can actually much weaken his position is provided by the notorious 'night of the long knives' in July 1962. As Prime Minister, the Conservative leader Harold Macmillan had cultivated an air of 'unflappability', typified perhaps by his reaction to Thorneycroft's resignation as Chancellor. The party's electoral appeal was felt to depend largely on public perception that Macmillan could always be relied upon to act in a calm, rational fashion. That perception was shattered in just one day, when Macmillan peremptorily dismissed one-third of his Cabinet.

Macmillan's initial concern had simply been to replace his Chancellor of the Exchequer, Selwyn Lloyd, whom he considered insufficiently interventionist on economic policy issues. However several Conservative defeats in by-elections, coupled with the government's poor standing in public opinion polls, and press rumours of an impending Cabinet reshuffle, led Macmillan to panic rather, and end up sacking seven ministers, apparently hoping that a new look government would be more electorally appealing.

That a Prime Minister can dismiss so large a part of her government in so cursory a fashion cogently illustrates her short-term dominance of the Cabinet. Yet, since that Prime Minister may have appointed those ministers in the first place, their removal casts doubt on the Prime Minister's own competence, for one of her most important tasks is surely to select able colleagues. Macmillan subsequently described the sacked ministers as 'worn out', and

4 Contrast for example Hennessy (1986) *op cit* ch 4 with Mackintosh J (1962) *The British Cabinet* p 496 (London: Stevens and Sons).
5 Quoted in Hennessy (1986a) *op cit* p 123.

did indeed replace them with much younger colleagues, but his strategy did not attract substantial backbench support. Criticism centred as much on the insensitivity with which the sackings were carried out as on their scale. It seems that only two other ministers had been consulted on the changes, both of whom expected preferment as a result. Whether Macmillan could have survived as party leader in the long term after antagonising so large a section of his party, and whether he could have led the Conservatives to victory in another general election, remained unanswered questions, for he resigned as a result of ill health the following year.[6]

There are no legal rules controlling the identity of individuals appointed to ministerial office. Nor does it seem likely that there could be. It seems clear that the Prime Minister's choices are motivated by two factors: maximising her own standing within her party, while simultaneously maximising her party's standing with the electorate. Neither criterion seems even remotely justiciable. We might wonder if the constitution should require a Prime Minister to appoint the most able of her party's members to ministerial office, but it takes little reflection to conclude that 'ability' is a concept which cannot be objectively defined. There would thus seem to be little alternative but to leave evaluation of the Prime Minister's selection and management of her Cabinet to her parliamentary party, and ultimately to the electorate. Both MPs and voters might plausibly be thought to place some pre-emptive limits on the extent to which Prime Ministers can amend conventional understandings of collective responsibility. The difficulty, as Margaret Thatcher's tenure of 10 Downing Street eventually revealed, is predicting where those boundaries lie.

Thatcher was often portrayed as placing little faith in the idea of full Cabinet participation in policymaking. Shortly before the 1979 election, she had announced that she would lead: 'a conviction government. As Prime Minister I could not waste time having any internal arguments.' Her first Cabinet contained many so-called 'wet' ministers, who were not entirely supportive of her preferred economic policies. To some extent, these ministers were simply by-passed. Peter Hennessy observes that the Thatcher Cabinet met far less frequently than its post-war predecessors, and also considered far fewer policy documents.[7] A further tactic which the new Prime Minister deployed to control policy-making more tightly was to have ministers present their initial ideas to her and

6 See generally Horne A (1987) *Macmillan 1957–1986* (London: Macmillan).
7 Hennessey (1986a) *op cit* ch 3.

her personal advisers, rather than to the Cabinet or even to a Cabinet committee. Furthermore, on those occasions when committees were used, Thatcher had no compunction about 'packing' them with ministers who supported her own point of view. This was occasionally to prove problematic. The decision to withdraw union recognition from GCHQ workers was made by only five ministers; wider consultation may have identified the constitutional implications that the decision subsequently proved to have.[8]

After the 1983 election, when the Conservative majority increased to over 140 seats, Thatcher was able to 'purge' her Cabinet in a manner almost as draconian as the night of the long knives, but secure in the knowledge that in so doing she would be antagonising only a limited section of the parliamentary party. There seems little doubt that Margaret Thatcher exercised more personal power than any other post-war Prime Minister, to the extent that by the late 1980s some commentators were suggesting that she had effectively instituted a form of presidential government.[9] And this supposedly fundamental shift in constitutional arrangements had been achieved without any formal legal changes whatsoever.

Writing in 1986, Peter Hennessy concluded his discussion of Thatcher's style of Cabinet government more cautiously:

> 'At worst she has put Cabinet government temporarily on ice. . . . the old model could, and probably will, be restored in the few minutes it takes a new Prime Minister to travel from Buckingham Palace to Downing Street.'[10]

Events were subsequently to prove that the 'old model' had indeed merely been chilled, rather than deep frozen, in the Thatcher years.

. . . and back again?

At the 1987 general election, the Conservative party retained a Commons majority of over 100 seats. In such circumstances, one might have expected Thatcher's control of her third government to have become even more personalised in both style and substance. However, while that may indeed have been the Prime

8 See pp 121–123 above.
9 Doherty M (1988) 'Prime Ministerial power and ministerial responsibility in the Thatcher era' *Parliamentary Affairs* 49–67.
10 (1986a) *op cit* p 122.

Minister's intention, her belief that she could amend still further the conventional notion of collective Cabinet government was to prove misplaced.

Nigel Lawson's resignation as Chancellor, on the grounds that the Prime Minister was simply ignoring his advice, can be bracketed with Heseltine's earlier suggestion that the Prime Minister was crossing conventional constitutional boundaries. Both resignations threatened the Prime Minister's authority within the Conservative party, in that they offered figureheads around which dissident backbench opinion might coalesce. However their true significance was subsequently seen to lie in the individual contribution they made to a growing sense of collective unease within the Parliamentary party. That unease was given an acute focus by the resignation of Sir Geoffrey Howe as Deputy Prime Minister in 1990, an event which had serious and immediate implications, both for Thatcher herself and the prime ministerial government thesis.

Howe resigned because he could no longer accept the Prime Minister's avowedly hostile attitude towards the EC (a matter explored in chapter 12). In his resignation speech to the Commons, Howe maintained that the Prime Minister had consistently and deliberately undermined the collective decisions which the Cabinet assumed it had reached on EC matters. Invoking a cricketing analogy, Howe suggested that the Foreign Secretary and Chancellor had been sent out by the Cabinet to open the innings at EC matches, only to find when they reached the crease that the Prime Minister had broken their bats.

Howe's account reinforced Michael Heseltine's earlier claims that Thatcher held conventional understandings as to the conduct of Cabinet business in some contempt, and the speech precipitated Heseltine's challenge to Thatcher for leadership of the Conservative party. That challenge led rapidly to Thatcher's resignation as party leader (and thence as Prime Minister) and her eventual replacement by John Major. As we shall see in subsequent chapters, factors other than her evident disregard for the conventional understandings of Cabinet decision-making processes contributed to Margaret Thatcher's fall from power. But her fate would suggest that her preference for an increasingly prime ministerial style of government amounted (eventually) to a serious error of political judgement: even the most powerful of Prime Ministers, it seems, must retain the support of senior ministers.

In reviewing Thatcher's resignation, it is difficult to be sure where the effective political power that removed her actually lay.[11] Was it in the combined resignations of Heseltine, Lawson, and Howe? Or with those remaining Cabinet ministers who intimated to Thatcher that they would resign if she did not? If so, we might plausibly conclude that the convention of collective Cabinet government had merely been dormant during the 1980s, and simply required a sudden jolt to re-awaken it. Or did it lie with the many Conservative MPs who did not vote for Thatcher in the first round of the leadership election? If so, we see a further manifestation of the pre-eminence of party politics within the constitution. Or did it lie (indirectly) in the electorate, who had indicated in many opinion polls that a Thatcher government could not hope to win another general election, and thereby frightened Conservative MPs in marginal seats into withdrawing support from their Prime Minister?

What is clear, however, is that Thatcher's successor, John Major, did return to a more collective style of Cabinet government.[12] Michael Heseltine's return to Cabinet was one manifestation of this trend, as was Major's apparent concern to ensure that his ministerial team reflected the various factional groupings within his Parliamentary party. Yet it would be rash to accept that Thatcher's fate demonstrates that conventions are a self-correcting constitutional mechanism, which can be pushed so far, but no further. To reach that conclusion would require consideration of substantially more evidence; evidence which, as sections four and five suggest, undermines such complacent assumptions.

IV. INDIVIDUAL MINISTERIAL RESPONSIBILITY

The second strand of the ministerial responsibility convention is individual ministerial responsibility, which supposedly identifies the situations in which ministers should resign from government office. Its modern form has two parts. The first addresses the minister's political or administrative competence; the second her personal morality.

---

11 For various perspectives see Brazier R (1991) 'The downfall of Margaret Thatcher' 54 *MLR* 471–491; Alderman and Carter *op cit.*
12 Marshall G (1991) 'The end of Prime Ministerial government?' *Public Law* 1–6.

Issues of competence

The competence rule originally held ministers answerable to Parliament for every action undertaken by their departments' civil servants. Ministers took the credit when their officials got things right. Relatedly they took the blame when their staff got things wrong; if the error was sufficiently grave, a minister would be expected to resign. A corollary of this proposition was that individual civil servants would not face parliamentary scrutiny or public criticism for their own failures. This is not to say that incompetent civil servants would find their careers unaffected, but that sanctions attached to failure were a managerial matter resolved within the executive, not, as for a minister, a political matter resolved in Parliament.

In the early 1800s, the idea that a minister should be personally responsible for everything done in his department was perhaps feasible. But the scale of government has grown so much since 1850 that it has become completely impracticable for a minister to know everything that is being done by her department's civil servants. So the initial form of this supposed convention has altered. It now seems necessary that a minister has been personally involved in a particular decision before she must resign.

This redefinition of conventional boundaries began in a series of late nineteenth century cases,[13] and had hardened sufficiently to merit being described as a rule by the mid-1950s. The resignation of Sir Thomas Dugdale as Minister of Agriculture in 1954 following the Crichel Down controversy is a good illustration. Crichel Down involved a government department's failure to resell land to the family from whom it had been compulsorily purchased for military use just before World War II, in evident breach of assurances to that effect. Dugdale resigned when it became clear he had specific knowledge of his civil servants' activities, but had failed to appreciate the problematic nature of the action being undertaken.

Crichel Down's ramifications went beyond the issue of a minister's personal culpability.[14] The episode triggered a crisis of confidence in the green light variant of the rule of law which had increasingly structured the government process in the immediate

13 See Finer S (1956) 'The individual responsibility of Ministers' *Public Administration* 377–396.
14 Hamson C (1954) 'The real lesson of Crichel Down' *Public Administration* 383–400.

post-war era.[15] The response of the then Conservative government was to promote a wide-ranging 'judicialisation' of many aspects of the administrative process, entailing more tightly defined legislative rules for executive bodies to follow, the creation of quasi-judicial appeal tribunals for citizens dissatisfied with certain types of government decision, and somewhat easier access to judicial review. The change in emphasis was encapsulated in the Tribunals and Inquiries Act 1958, whose provisions corresponded closely to the theoretical perceptions of the rule of law advanced by analysts such as Harry Jones. Longer-term efforts were also made to enhance green light mechanisms of political control: Crossman's Select Committee intiative has already been mentioned, and another of his innovations is considered further below.

For present purposes, Crichel Down's significance lies in the clear indication that a minister need not resign in response to the failings of civil servants of which he was not, and could not reasonably be expected to have been aware, irrespective of the gravity of the consequences. This suggests resignation is more likely to be triggered by a failure of policy, rather than implementation, since the former remains more obviously the province of ministers themselves.

James Callaghan's 1967 resignation as Chancellor from Harold Wilson's second Labour government was clearly precipitated by policy failure, even though the failure was determined largely by matters beyond his control. The government had struggled for some years to maintain sterling's dollar exchange rate at $2.80 (this being in an era of fixed rather than floating rates). After repeated rumors of devaluation, followed by repeated government denials of any such intention, sterling was devalued to $2.40. As Chancellor, Callaghan was the chief architect of a manifestly unsuccessful economic strategy. Nevertheless the devaluation arguably owed far more to previous governments' refusal to acknowledge Britain's declining economic status than to Callaghan's errors per se.

A more pertinent, more recent, example is offered by Lord Carrington's resignation as Foreign Secretary following the Argentinian invasion of the Falkland Islands in 1982. Carrington considered he had underestimated the severity of the Argentinian threat, and thought it necessary that somebody accept responsibility for the governmental failure that the invasion betokened.

This redefinition of the convention to require personal knowledge is strengthened by instances when ministers have *not* resigned

15 See pp 77–79 above.

following gross errors by their civil servants. In 1982, for example, a man named Michael Fagan breached security at Buckingham Palace and wandered around unchallenged for a considerable time before having a conversation with the Queen in her bedroom. William Whitelaw, the Home Secretary, was formally 'responsible' for Metropolitan Police, who provided security at the Palace. Fagan's escapade revealed that security precautions were quite inadequate. Whitelaw's initial instinct was to go, but he was evidently talked out of this by the Prime Minister. Her argument was firstly that no harm had befallen the Queen, and secondly the Home Secretary could not be expected personally to supervise the minutiae of the Metropolitan Police's activities.

James Prior, Secretary of State for Northern Ireland, invoked a similar argument when 38 IRA prisoners broke out of the Maze prison in 1983. Prior felt that convention would require his resignation only if the escape had resulted from a policy initiative he had taken – for example if he had given instructions to relax prison security measures. When an inquiry concluded that the escape resulted from management errors made by the prison governor, Prior decided not to resign. He sacked the prison governor instead.

The experience of one of Whitelaw's successors as Home Secretary, Kenneth Baker, suggests a minister need not resign over such errors even when they happen with disquieting frequency. Mr Baker endured an accident-prone tenure at the Home Office. The most serious incident occurred in 1991, when several IRA prisoners escaped from Brixton prison, using a gun which had been smuggled into the gaol. The Chief Inspector of Prisons had reported some months earlier that security at Brixton was inadequate for high-risk prisoners. However the Home Office had neither stopped using Brixton for such detainees, nor improved its security facilities. One might have assumed this was a high level policy matter within the Home Secretary's personal sphere of responsibility. However Mr Baker contended that responsibility lay with the prisoner governor.

Baker subsequently resigned from the government when offered the less important post of Welsh Secretary in 1992. But his failings in office continued to haunt him. In 1993, he achieved the unenviable distinction of being held by the House of Lords in *M v Home Office*[16] to have committed contempt of court by authorising the expulsion of a political refugee in defiance of a court order. We can only speculate as to whether Baker would have seen this as a

---

16 [1994] 1 AC 377. See pp 98–100 above.

resigning matter.[17] It seems possible that he would have argued that he was just following the advice of his departmental lawyers. If so, it becomes difficult to conceive of any decision-making error which would require a minister's resignation.

The competence limb of the convention seems to be in a fluid, or perhaps fragile, state of health as we approach the end of the century. It may however be rash to conclude that the convention has now evolved to the point where only the most calamitous incompetence will necessitate resignation. We should perhaps focus our attention not simply on the scale of the mistake, but also on the strength or weakness of the Minister's position within the governing party. This is a point to which we will return.

Errors of judgment

The sanction of resignation seems to attach more firmly to ministers making severe errors of judgment rather than policy or administrative mistakes. In recent times, the Westland Affair provides a graphic example of this convention. The then Trade Secretary, Leon Brittan, had authorised the leaking of a letter from the Solicitor-General criticising the constitutional propriety of Michael Heseltine's behaviour. This leak breached another convention – that law officers' advice to ministers should remain confidential within the government. Although the Cabinet initially disclaimed knowledge of the leak's source, the Solicitor-General's threat to resign if a leak inquiry was not conducted led to the revelation that Brittan had condoned a decision by his Press Officer to release the letter. Facing such evidence, Brittan had no option but to resign, albeit amid suspicions that his departure was intended to conceal the Prime Minister's reputed approval of the leak.

Westland provided yet another illustration of ministerial responsibilty when the Prime Minister, Margaret Thatcher, was subsequently compelled to defend her own role in the affair before the Commons in an emergency debate. The potential importance of debate in the house as a mechanism to control executive behaviour is revealed by Thatcher's own belief that a poor performance might result in her own resignation that evening. In the event, an inept speech by Neil Kinnock, then Leader of the Opposition, enabled the Prime Minister successfully both to dis-

17 He had declined to do so when held in contempt by the Court of Appeal; see Marshall G (1992) 'Ministerial responsibility, the Home Office, and Mr Baker' *Public Law* 7–12.

tance herself from the Westland intrigues and to downplay their constitutional importance.[18]

Brittan's case also illustrates that resignation even on the grounds of gross personal culpability need not end a minister's political career. Shortly after resigning, Brittan was granted a knighthood and appointed as an EEC Commissioner, a post (as we shall see in chapter 11) of considerable political importance.

Westland is perhaps a uniquely important episode in modern constitutional history. Other recent resignations over errors of judgement have been more mundane. Nicholas Ridley, for example, resigned as Secretary of State for Trade and Industry in 1990 after expressing hostile and xenophobic attitudes towards Germany in a press interview. Ridley's belief that the interview was off the record did not assist his case. Such sentiments were considered quite inappropriate for a minister, given the closeness of Anglo-German relations within both the EEC and NATO. Similarly, in 1988, Edwina Currie, a junior minister, left the government after alleging that almost all UK egg production was infected by salmonella. The statement's accuracy was questionable. Its devastating, if temporary, effect on British egg producers was not. Protracted vilification from the farming industry, and repeated media questioning of her abilities, persuaded Mrs Currie to resign. The episode need not have ended her ministerial career. She was invited to join the second Major administration, but declined to do so.

It is difficult to extract a 'rule' (qua a predictable, binding behavioural code) from these or any other examples of resignation. Finer's celebrated study of the issue suggested party political expediency rather than moral principle was the critical factor in determining both whether a minister should resign and her subsequent fate.[19] It certainly appears that subsequent resignations have been intended to have symbolic rather than practical effects. Callaghan's aforementioned resignation as Chancellor in 1967 was in effect a sideways transfer, for he simply swapped offices with the Home Secretary, Roy Jenkins. One thus gains the impression that the reason for the resignation was an attempt to wipe the government's economic slate clean before the next general election.

Such an interpretation reinforces Finer's suggestion that ministerial errors will not invariably precipitate resignation unless his/

18 See Young H (1991) *One of us* pp 454–457 (London: Pan); Clark *op cit* pp 132–135.
19 (1956) *op cit.*

her conduct has alienated a substantial body of opinion within his own party. Finer noted, for example, the evident irony that Dugdale's behaviour over Crichel Down attracted far more approval from the Labour opposition than from his own MPs, many of whom represented wealthy farming constituencies. The influence of the farming lobby on backbench Conservative opinion was no doubt also a significant factor in Edwina Currie's eventual resignation.

But it is not just professional or political misjudgement that can bring the convention of individual ministerial responsibility into play. Questions as to moral or personal conduct have also been a regular recent source of ministerial resignations. In these circumstances, questions of party solidarity seem rather less important.

Issues of morality

Few ministerial resignations have generated as much public curiosity as John Profumo's in 1963. Profumo, Minister of War in Macmillan's government, had an extra-marital affair with Christine Keeler. The liaison had obvious security implications, since Ms Keeler was simultaneously sleeping with a Russian Naval Attaché. The affair itself may have been enough to have forced Profumo's departure from office. To choose a mistress who was also a lover of an enemy agent would presumably also have amounted to a gross error of judgement. But Profumo's greatest sin was to lie to the Commons when Richard Crossman raised the matter in the house. When the truth was subsequently revealed, Profumo had no choice but to resign. Macmillan himself thought the episode sufficiently grave to threaten the government's continued existence. In the event, it did not directly do so, but it seems likely the episode added further weight to incidents such as 'the little local difficulty' and the 'night of the long knives' which had already undermined the Conservatives' electoral appeal – Harold Wilson's Labour party subsequently won the 1964 general election.

The resignations of Lord Lambton and Earl Jellicoe in 1973 from Edward Heath's government also had salacious and security related overtones. Both peers had been conducting relationships with prostitutes, and Lambton was also reputed to have been using illegal drugs. Neither minister returned to the government. But sexual indiscretion need not always end a ministerial career. Cecil Parkinson resigned from the Cabinet in 1983 when it was disclosed that he had an affair with Sara Keays, who eventually bore his child. Parkinson's behaviour was considered the more reprehensible as he had allegedly promised Keays he would leave his wife, a promise on which he reneged. However after some years on the backbenches, Parkinson re-entered the Cabinet in 1987.

It is too soon to conclude that the morality rule now demands only that ministers interrupt rather than abandon their career, although Parkinson's precedent may soon be reinforced by David Mellor and/or Tim Yeo. Mellor, a married man with several young children, served as Secretary of State for National Heritage in John Major's Cabinet. He attracted voluminous media publicity in 1992 following his affair with a young actress. There was no suggestion, as in Profumo's case, of any threat to national security. The episode did however cast doubt on his fitness for office, in the sense both of his personal integrity (or lack thereof) and allegations that he felt too 'knackered' to devote as much energy as previously to government responsibilities. Tim Yeo, a junior environment minister, suffered similarly extensive and critical publicity over an affair with a young Conservative party worker, by whom he fathered an illegitimate child.[20]

The Mellor and Yeo resignations suggest immediacy in resigning is a fast disappearing element of the convention. Both ministers, evidently with prime ministerial support, clung to office for several months hoping to ride out the media storm which engulfed them. Mellor decided to resign only when his adultery and apparent exhaustion were coupled with the revelation that he had accepted gifts from a prominent associate of the Palestine Liberation Organisation. Yeo did not resign until his local party members made it clear that they wished him to do so.

Most 'moral' resignations are triggered by the sexual 'misbehaviour' of male ministers. The weight of evidence suggests there is a respected convention that such activities should lead to resignation, albeit only temporarily. The reason behind the rule is less clear, given that Britain's contemporary social mores indicate that adultery and the frequenting of prostitutes are activities in which many citizens engage. One suggestion would be that ministers should set a shining moral example, and are unfit for office if they cannot meet such exacting standards. Another argument would be that resignation is a 'punishment' not for sexual immorality per se, but for the hypocrisy of participating in activities of which the government supposedly disapproves. This contention is especially persuasive in respect of Parkinson, Mellor, and Yeo; all

20 See Brazier R (1994) 'It is a constitutional issue: fitness for Ministerial office in the 1990s' *Public Law* 431–451.

broke their marriage vows while members of Conservative administrations which laid great stress on 'traditional' family values.

Whether a minister's personal life compromises his discharge of public duties is a large question. We now know that such great political figures as Gladstone and Lloyd George engaged in somewhat unusual sexual behaviour – but those revelations weigh lightly when balanced against their respective political achievements. An answer is more easily found when one asks if individual ministerial responsibility could assume a legal basis.

Designating behaviour as grossly immoral, or quite immoral, or not really immoral at all, is a highly value-laden decision. One might assume that when opposition MPs express outrage at a minister's misbehaviour they are more concerned with embarrassing the government than protecting the nation's moral fibre. The obvious political delicacy of these questions of ministerial morality provides a strong argument against having this aspect of the government process overseen by legal rules. It would be extremely contentious for a judge to say that a minister was unfit for office because of the way he conducted his personal life.

That point seems equally applicable to questions of ministerial competence or misjudgement. There are no obvious criteria against which a court could measure a minister's incompetence to decide if it was sufficiently grave to merit dismissal. Nor could a judge reach that conclusion without being accused of taking sides in what will almost invariably be a party political dispute. We saw in chapter 7 that the mid-nineteenth century courts were reluctant to assume responsibility for scrutinising contested election results for just that reason. There is little doubt that their contemporary successors would be far more resistant to legislative attempts to subject individual ministerial responsibility to a Diceyan variant of the rule of law.

This might indicate we could begin to construct some definition of conventions in terms of those parts of the constitution with which the courts could not interfere without jeopardising their supposedly impartial political status. This pushes us towards a suggestion that 'non-justiciability' in the practical sense, rather than legal non-enforceability in the formal sense, may be an essential ingredient of conventional status. If a rule is important to the operation of the government process, and can be framed in a justiciable manner, the diluted Diceyan version of the rule of law to which the constitution adheres would suggest it should be given legal form. The role of the courts in promoting that process has been adverted to above in the *Crossman Diaries* case, and we will shortly pursue this argument in greater depth. Before doing so however, we focus once again on the relationship between conventions and Acts of Parliament.

Reforming the executive – 1: the Parliamentary Commissioner for Administration

Crichel Down's institutional fall-out continued well into the 1960s. We have already noted Richard Crossman's unsucccessful select committee initiative. His reform plans bore more immediate fruit in the creation of the Parliamentary Commissioner for Administration, (colloquially known as the 'Ombudsman', but hereafter referred to as the PCA).

The PCA was established by the Parliamentary Commissioner Act 1967. His role can be seen as plugging various holes in the systems of both parliamentary and judicial supervision of government activities. Section 5 empowered the PCA to investigate any activity of (most) government departments about which he had recieved a complaint from a member of the public. To emphasise that the PCA was complementing rather than replacing the Commons' own supervisory role, she was only permitted to investigate matters referred to her by an MP. Similarly, to emphasise that the PCA was complementing rather than replacing the supervisory role of the courts, the Act stressed that the PCA could not generally investigate complaints which could be pursued through legal action. Rather like the Commons (then and now), the PCA operated with limited resources. However unlike individual MPs, and in practice Commons select committees,[1] the PCA was granted (per s 8) extremely extensive powers to examine government documents and require testimony from ministers and civil servants. Unlike the courts, the PCA could not impose a remedy on an erring department, but it was widely assumed that governments would comply voluntarily with his suggestions. The PCA's 'independence' is protected in the same way as that of a High Court judge. While she is appointed by the Prime Minister, she holds office during 'good behaviour'; dismissal can only be effected by addresses from both houses.

The evil to which the PCA's energies were directed was 'maladministration'. This concept has never been precisely defined, either in statute or litigation. The so-called 'Crossman catalogue', offered to the Commons by Richard Crossman during the Bill's passage remains the primary reference point. This embraced 'bias, neglect,

1 See pp 184–189 above.

inattention, delay, incompetence, ineptitude, perversity, turpitude and arbitrariness'. It may be, post-*Pepper v Hart*, that Crossman's catalogue now enjoys rather more authoritative legal status than formerly. But it seems we are still reduced to defining maladministration in negative terms; it reaches those aspects of the administrative process which, while unsatisfactory, are not unlawful, and so cannot be the subject of an action for judicial review or a claim in tort or contract against the government body concerned.

A detailed assessment of the PCA's (evidently successful and expanding) role in the past 30 years is more appropriately undertaken within a study of administrative rather than constitutional law, and is not attempted here. Our primary concern is her impact on traditional understandings of individual ministerial responsibility. Crossman described the PCA as 'a complete constitutional innovation', a point best illustrated by considering one of her earliest invesigations.

Sachsenhausen[2]

The Sachsenhausen controversy arose out of an agreement negotiated between the British and German governments in 1964, under which Germany paid Britain one million pounds to distribute to war-time victims of Nazi persecution. The agreement itself was an exercise of the prerogative. Foreign Office civil servants (rather than a statutory body such as the Foreign Compensation Commission) administered the funds through prerogative powers. In retrospect, the compensation rules appear eminently justiciable. Claimants qualified if they had been detained in 'a concentration camp'; the amount received was a multiple of the time spent in detention. The scheme was however established prior to *Lain*, and there seemed no contemporaneous expectation that decisions would attract full judicial review.

The claims of several servicemen detained in premises adjacent to the Sachsenhausen concentration camp were rejected by Foreign Office officals who decided they had been ordinary prisoners of war, whose maltreatment was not covered by the scheme. Two successive junior Foreign Office ministers reviewed the claims, as did the Foreign Secretary, George Brown. All confirmed the civil servants' decision.

The PCA's subsequent investigation identified serious flaws in the civil servants' decision-making procedures, and suggested

2 Information in the following paragraphs is drawn from Fry G (1970) 'The Sachsenhausen concentration camp case and the convention of ministerial responsibility' *Public Law* 336–357.

that the decision was substantively indefensible, given the evidence in the Foreign Office's possession. It is not entirely clear if ministers personally scrutinised the evidence de novo, or had simply relied on their officials' advice. In either event, their decisions merely reiterated the original maladministration, and the PCA recommended that the servicemen be compensated in accordance with the scheme's criteria. In a subsequent Commons speech, George Brown accepted the PCA's decision, announcing that compensation would be paid. However, he then criticised both the PCA's findings in the Sachsenhausen case itself, and also what he regarded as a more substantial question of constitutional principle:

> 'We will breach a very serious constitutional position if we start holding officials responsible for things that are done wrong. . . . If things are wrongly done, then they are wrongly done by Ministers. . . . It is Ministers who must be attacked, not officials.'[3]

Brown was correct in concluding that the creation of the PCA had forced a redefinition of the convention of individual ministerial responsibility. The PCA's extensive investigatory and reporting powers did raise the possibility that the individual failings of civil servants would be brought into both the parliamentary and public domain, rather than being dealt with as an internal management matter. One might think, as a matter of policy, that this could be undesirable both because 'accused' civil servants could not defend themselves against such attack, and also because it raised the possibility that ministers would evade personal responsibility by hiding behind an impartial report which laid blame at a civil servant's feet.

The constitutional difficulty raised by Brown's speech was that those issues of policy had already been settled. His speech may therefore itself be seen as a breach of the unanimity rule. He had been a member of the Cabinet which presented the 1967 Act to Parliament. Had he respected conventional principles, he would presumably have been compelled either to resign from the Cabinet before publicly criticising its policy, or to keep his disquiet as a matter only for the ears of his Cabinet colleagues. Brown had prefaced his remarks by saying he spoke in a personal rather than Cabinet capacity, but this contention seems even less satisfactory than other manifestations of the 'suspension' principle to which we have already referred. Unanimity cannot be a conventional rule if ministers may opt in and out of it whenever they wish.

3 *HCD* 5 February 1968, c 123.

One cannot trace a direct link between ministers' apparently increasing insulation against resignation as the price for serious error and the expanding role of the PCA. The fact nevertheless remains that the present political climate seemingly makes it acceptable for ministers such as Prior and Baker to maintain that the chain of responsibility for even very grave mistakes ends with a civil servant, not a politician. The PCA, however, was but a minor innovation when compared to the restructuring of the civil service undertaken since the mid-1980s. What impact those changes will ultimately have on the traditional individual ministerial responsibilty doctrine is not yet clear, but as the following section suggests, they may well be profound.

Reforming the executive: 2 – 'Next Steps' and privatisation

The 'Next Steps' reforms initiated by the third Thatcher government have divided some parts of the civil service into separate 'policy formulating' and 'policy implementation' organisations. While policy formulation remains the province of Ministers and civil servants within traditional government departments, implementation has been entrusted to so-called 'executive agencies'. Under the new system, the department drafts a 'framework document' which outlines the policies which the agency should apply. The agency thereafter proposes 'performance targets', subject to ministerial approval, which it will seek to meet each year. Agencies are headed by 'Chief Executives', drawn both from government and private sector organisations. Similar reforms had been proposed by Harold Wilson's government in 1968, but had not been adopted. The third Thatcher government implemented the changes with some speed. Some 50 agencies had been established by 1992, including the Royal Mint, the employment service, and the prisons service.

The agencies' relationship with their supervising department appears to be 'quasi-contractual'.[4] This has considerable implications for traditional concepts of individual ministerial responsibility, for it raises the possibility that ministers may 'contract out' of responsibility for governmental errors which would previously have been made within their departments. The fear that the 'Next Steps' structure would produce a situation in which ministers might disclaim their accountability to Parliament for agency errors

4 Oliver (1991) *op cit* p 65. On the reforms more generally see *ibid* pp 64–70.

was intensified in late 1994 by a series of failures in prison security. An attempted escape by IRA prisoners was rapidly followed by the discovery of live ammunition in one jail, and explosives in another. At the same time, national newspapers ran stories alleging that the government had authorised a marked relaxation of security measures in respect of some IRA and other prisoners. Various calls were made, both in the press and from opposition parties, for the resignation of Michael Howard, the Home Secretary.

These events raised the difficult question of identifying at which managerial point within a Next Steps agency a minister's influence becomes sufficiently acute to make him responsible for the agency's errors. It seems possible that a minister's responsibility would extend to the contents of the framework document, to the objectives of the annual performance agreements, and the choice of the agency's Chief Executive: imposing an absurd framework, setting ludicrous targets, or appointing a manifestly incompetent Chief Executive would presumably be a personal ministerial decision.[5]

There seems little doubt that the Next Steps initiative has further weakened the already enfeebled convention that a minister accepts responsibility for a civil servant's failings. Nor has that decline in political accountability been accompanied by an increase in legal regulation. The Major governments produced various 'Citizen's Charters', which set targets for government agencies to meet, in terms of such matters as the speed, accuracy and courtesy with which they address citizens' enquiries or concerns. The charters might be seen as reinforcing the role of the PCA, insofar as they are directed at various types of maladministration. They are not legislative instruments, however, and there has thus far been no indication that either the government or the courts regard them as creating common law rights.[6]

Nevertheless, despite its significant impact on the relationship between the government and the Commons, the Next Steps initiative has less profound implications for ministerial responsibility than the extensive programme of 'privatisation' of government functions that has been carried out by the Thatcher and Major administrations.

---

5 Although we might note that the Prison Service was then managed by a man who had previously been a television executive, with no experience of the prision service specifically, or of public administration more generally.
6 Drewry G (1993) 'Mr Major's Charter: empowering the consumer' *Public Law* 248–256.

Privatisation

That television executives could be appointed to run the prison service is a fairly cogent indication of the Thatcher and Major administrations' belief that most aspects of the government process are best performed by private sector companies. As chapter 6 observed, the Labour and Conservative parties had adopted irreconcilable positions concerning the desirability of bringing manufacturing industries within government ownership by the mid 1970s.[7] The controversy over the Aircraft and Shipbuilding Industries Bill illustrated a wider divergence between red and green light perceptions of the best way to govern a capitalist economy. The first Thatcher administration subscribed enthusiastically to the model of government advocated by Hayek's *Road to Serfdom*, and just as previous Labour governments had used their de facto control of Parliament's sovereignty to 'nationalise' private industries, so the first Thatcher government used its Commons majority to return them to the private sector. The Thatcher administrations regarded activities such as shipbuilding, and car and aerospace manufacturing as purely economic in nature, and thus no legitimate part of the government's responsibilities. Similarly, it was thought that services such as the telephone system, the railways, and gas, electricity, and water provision were better run as profit-making private businesses rather than some form of public sector social services.

In addition, the Thatcher and Major governments also believed that more overtly 'governmental' services should also be managed by private sector companies. Unlike the Next Steps reforms, privatisation does not dilute Commons control over service management, but removes it altogether. In privatising former public services, the government effectively abolishes ministerial responsibility for matters which may have a significant impact on citizens' lives and welfare. Quite how far this 'abolition' of government will proceed is unclear, but if we regard the constitution as being concerned essentially with structuring both the substance and the processes of the relationship between a country's government and its citizens, it seems that a major part of the constitution has undergone substantial reform in the past 15 years. We will return to a further, more important aspect of institutional constitutional amendment in chapter 11. For the present, to conclude our analysis of conventions, we return to the question of the relationship between convention, statute and the common law –

7 At pp 214–216.

and find that it may be less straightforward than we might have thought.

V. CAN CONVENTIONS BECOME LAWS? 2: PATRIATING THE CANADIAN CONSTITUTION?

One can only speculate whether Kerr's intervention in the Australian controversy would have been regarded as more legitimate if the conventional rules surrounding the Queen's prerogative had been placed on a statutory basis which explicitly authorised their use in circumstances of budgetary deadlock. It is possible that in such a hypothetical situation, domestic disquiet over the 'Queen's' role would have triggered a change in the relevant laws. It is unlikely that merely attaching a legal 'label' to the Governor-General's reasoning could so dilute its politically contentious substance as to make it acceptable to Australian parliamentary and public opinion. The episode suggests Australian 'consent' to the Queen's constitutional role was a fiction – existing only if her powers were not used.

Yet in the longer term, *non-use* of such powers may have the same delegitimising effect. As chapter 7 suggested in discussing the Lords' disinclination to invoke its delaying powers under the Parliament Act 1949, there may be areas of constitutional practice in which conventional reluctance to deploy legal authority eventually leads to the law shedding its political legitimacy. This chapter indicates that conventions might plausibly be seen as a melting pot in which differing concentrations of legal and political ingredients are constantly mixed. If so, we might ask if a diametrically opposite process to delegitimisation could occur? Might it ever be possible for conventions to have been respected for so long, become so precisely defined, and be so important, that they could 'crystallise' into laws?

One obvious way to give conventions legal effect is to enact them as statutes. The Parliament Acts are themselves a clear illustration of that process. A more radical proposition is that the the courts can achieve that effect through the common law. *Crossman Diaries* suggests the courts can *de facto* do so by finding the common law 'coincidentally' mirrors conventional understandings. This is not the same however, either in symbolic or practical terms, as *de jure* acknowledgement of crystallisation. Events in the early 1980s seemingly offered an opportunity for that constitutional development to occur.

Patriating the Canadian constitution

The country of Canada, as a legal entity, was created by the UK Parliament's British North America Act 1867. The Act gave Canada a federal structure, which, reflecting the USA's system, granted some powers to the federal (central) government, and others to the ten provincial governments. However, while the USA's constitution could be amended by its 'people',[8] the British North America Act required Canada to ask Westminster to enact amending legislation. In the 1931 Statute of Westminster, the UK Parliament recognised that several of its former colonies had de facto achieved the status of independent nations. Section 4 provided:

> 'No Act of Parliament of the United Kingdom passed after the commencement of this Act shall extend . . . to a Dominion as part of the law of that Dominion unless it is expressly declared in that Act that that Dominion has requested, and consented, to the enactment thereof.'

Section 4's political consequence seemed to be that Parliament had sought to bind its successors never to legislate on Canadian issues unless requested to do so by Canada. That consequence would of course be a legal impossibility if one adhered to orthodox notions of parliamentary sovereignty.[9] The 1931 Act also permitted Canada to amend most aspects of the Canadian constitution through domestic procedures. But Canada was still obliged to place a Bill before the UK Parliament to amend the balance of power between the federal and provincial governments.

However, the Act did not specify what was meant by 'Canada'. Was this just the federal Parliament, or the federal government, or some or all of the provinces as well, and/or the country's various racial and ethnic sub-groups? Nor did the Act say if there were circumstances in which the British Parliament might refuse to enact a measure passed from 'Canada'. During the next 50 years, two conventions filled these legal gaps in the Canadian and UK constitutions. The first was that the Canadian government would not send a Bill to Britain which altered the federal/provin-

---

8 See pp 20–21 above.

9 As a matter of Canadian constitutional law, however, one may safely assume that Canadian courts would not obey a subsequent British statute purporting to restore Parliament's previous authority. Nor, one assumes, as a matter of international relations, would Parliament ever legislate in such a way. This 'transfer of sovereignty' to Canada was the source of Lord Sankey's oft-quoted dictum in *British Coal Corpn v R* [1935] AC 500 at 520: 'It is doubtless true that the power of the [UK] Parliament to pass on its own initiative any legislation that it thought fit extending to Canada remains in theory unimpaired. . . . But that is theory and bears no relation to realities.'

cial division of power unless it enjoyed the support of all of the provinces. The second was that the British Parliament would always enact Bills sent by the Canadian Federal government. The conventions arose through 'tradition', 'unbroken practice' (several amendments had been effected in this way) and a lengthy passage of time (some 50 years). Their force was further strengthened by codification in a federal government white paper published in the 1960s.

The reasons for the conventions are readily apparent. The first ensures that the federal nature of Canadian government was safeguarded against unilateral amendment by the central legislature, or factional alteration by a majority or even minority of provincial governments: federalism, in other words, sat atop Canada's hierarchy of constitutional principles. The second acknowledges that 'Canada' had achieved sufficient economic and political maturity to wield de facto, if not de jure, control of its own constitutional destiny.

In the late 1970s, Pierre Trudeau's federal government wished to 'patriate' the Canadian constitution – to make all amendments a matter solely of domestic law. The patriation Bill also contained proposals significantly to amend federal/provincial relations. The Bill provoked considerable controversy in Canada; its contents had been supported by only two provincial governments. The Bill's opponents pursued two strategies to prevent its passage. The first attempted to convince the British Houses of Parliament that the Bill had not been sent by 'Canada', and should therefore not be enacted. The second involved litigation before the Canadian Supreme Court to establish firstly that the Canadian constitution recognised a convention that demanded unanimous provincial consent before the Bill could be sent to Westminster; and secondly that the Canadian courts could give that convention legal effect.

The opinion of the British House of Commons

The Canadian crisis presented Mr St John Stevas' newly invigorated Commons select committee system with an opportunity to engage in an entirely non-partisan and vital investigation of constitutional principle and practice. The first Thatcher government had indicated that it had no power to look behind a Bill sent from the Canadian government to examine the basis of consent which the measure had attracted. Any such Bill, would, per the second aforementioned convention, be introduced into Parliament. But as we have already established, there is no legal mechanism through which the three constituent parts of Parliament can be compelled to approve a Bill.[10] The question the select committee addressed was whether the Commons was morally or politically obliged simply to approve any Canadian Bill, or whether it should satisfy itself that the first of the aforementioned conventions (that the Bill enjoyed unanimous provincial support) had been satisfied.

After taking evidence from many expert academic and political sources, the committee produced a report rejecting the Trudeau government's presumption that Parliament should unquestioningly enact any Canadian Bill.[11] The Committee suggested that the Commons was under no conventional obligation to approve a Bill enjoying so little provincial support. But nor need it withhold approval until unanimous support was obtained. Rather, the committee concluded:

> 'all Canadians (and thus the governments of the provinces too) have, and always have had, a right to expect the UK Parliament to exercise its amending powers in a manner consistent with the federal nature of the Canadian constitutional system. . . .'[12]

This expectation could be met if Parliament required Canadian Bills to enjoy a 'substantial' degree of provincial consent. The committee proposed a complex formula, relating to geographical location and population patterns, to determine if substantial consent had been achieved.[13] Without such consent, Parliament could properly refuse to enact a Canadian Bill.

The select committee report nevertheless left several important questions unanswered. For example, if the two houses approved the Bill, would British courts override traditional understandings as to Parliamentary Privilege and Article 9 of the Bill of Rights[14] and prevent the Bill being sent for the Royal Assent? Equally fascinating was the question of whether, if the British courts refused to intervene, the Queen would breach the convention of acting on her ministers' advice and withhold her assent. Or, assuming assent was given, would a British court disregard the enrolled Bill rule and refuse to apply the statute? No doubt to the regret of constitutional lawyers, most of these questions never

10 Although the Lords' objections could (presumably: see p 207 above) be bypassed by use of the Parliament Act 1949.
11 House of Commons Foreign Affairs Committee (1981) *British North America Acts: the role of Parliament* (London: HMSO).
12 *Ibid* at para 103.
13 *Ibid* paras 107–115.
14 Which were discussed in chapter 8 above.

required a concrete answer. The eventual solution to Canada's difficulties was provided by its own Supreme Court.

The Canadian Supreme Court

In *Reference Re Amendment of the Constitution of Canada*[15] the Canadian Supreme Court confirmed that there was a convention, established by years of practice and acknowledged by former federal governments, that the British Parliament should only be sent Bills supported by a substantial number of provinces. Two out of ten was not substantial. Consequently the federal government was breaching this constitutional convention. The reason for the convention was to ensure that 'Canada' retained its distinctively federal system of government. For two dissentient judges, Martland and Ritchie JJ, the principle of federalism was an 'ultimate political fact' which demanded judicial obedience. The requirement of provincial consent to reform was so vital an element of Canada's constitutional order that it had assumed justiciable status – it had crystallised into law. But more than that, it had become a law possessing higher status than federal legislation.

If transposed to the British context, the implications of the dissenting judgments are revolutionary. Even the most imaginative interpretation of *Crossman Diaries* would maintain only that a convention could crystallise into a common law rule. That process presents no threat to parliamentary sovereignty, for common law rules can be reversed by statute. Rather, the Martland/Ritchie argument would lead us to conclude that some conventions might assume *supra-statutory* status: *Dr Bonham's* case would again become a valid constitutional principle, and the extent of Parliament's supremacy would be unclear. That is of course little more than wild speculation. The argument operates at three steps removed from domestic law, since firstly the British constitution is not (as we shall see in chapter 10) a federal structure; secondly, the judgments of another nation's courts have no binding force in British law; and thirdly, the Canadian Supreme Court majority produced a more orthodox decision.

Having recognised a convention of substantial provincial consent, the majority concluded that while a convention could be admissible as evidence in helping judges decide the correct legal response to a particular problem, it could not become a law, no

15 [1981] 1 SCR 753, 125 DLR (3d) 1. For other critiques from a British perspective see Turpin (1990) *op cit* pp 102–115; Allan T (1986) 'Law, convention, prerogative: reflections prompted by the Canadian constitutional case' *Cambridge LJ* 305–320.

matter how long it had been respected and no matter how important a principle it embodied. Conventions were not justiciable, and could not become so. 'Crystallisation' was a figment of overactive legal imaginations. The Supreme Court had no power to stop the Trudeau government sending the Bill to Britain.

But by laying such stress on the importance of the convention of substantial provincial consent, the Supreme Court completely undermined the *legitimacy* of the federal government's efforts to ignore the provinces. It was not possible as a matter of morality or political practicality for the government to go ahead. The initial Bill was therefore withdrawn, and the Trudeau government reopened negotiations with the provinces in order to produce a conventionally legitimate patriation proposal. A Bill was eventually produced which attracted the support of nine provinces. This Bill was subsequently sent to the Westminster Parliament, where it was enacted as the Canada Act 1982.

Manuel v A-G

The amendment saga had not however fully run its course. Thus far, the dispute as to the meaning of 'Canada' had centred on the federal/provincial relationship. The plaintiffs in *Manuel v A-G*[16] were native Canadian Indians, who maintained their respective tribes were as much a part of 'Canada' as the provincial governments, and that therefore any Bill affecting their constitutional status (as the revised Trudeau Bill did) had not been sent by 'Canada' unless the federal government had secured tribal consent. They thus launched an action in the British courts seeking a declaration that the Canada Act 1982 was ultra vires Parliament's legal powers.[17]

In the High Court, Megarry VC (with admirable understatement) characterised the plaintiff's case as 'bold in the extreme', since it patently rejected the enrolled Bill rule confirmed in *Wauchope* and *Pickin*.[18] The plaintiff's counsel suggested the rule applied only to domestic legislation, and not to statutes enacted as a consequence of the political independence granted to British colonies by the Statute of Westminster. In effect, he contended that such statutes were secondary legislation, their vires

16 [1983] Ch 77, CA.
17 The Foreign Affairs Committee concluded it would be improper for the UK Parliament to ask if a Canadian Bill had the consent of Canada's indigenous peoples; *op cit* paras 116–118.
18 See pp 41–43 above.

set by the 1931 Act.[19] Megarry VC saw no scope for constructing any such hierarchy of statutes. The Canada Act 1982 was an Act of Parliament like any other: 'sitting as a judge in an English court I owe full and dutiful obedience to that Act.'[20] The enrolled Bill rule completely answered the plaintiff's claim.

Slade LJ's Court of Appeal judgment was more ingenious, albeit reaching the same end. Slade LJ observed that s 4 of the 1931 Act did not require that Canada consented 'in fact' to a Bill being sent to Westminster, but merely that such consent was explicitly referred to (as indeed it was in the 1982 Act) in any subsequent British legislation. What s 4 meant in Canadian law was a matter for the Canadian judiciary, but the identity of 'Canada' was not a matter for a British court to pursue; its concern was only with the statute's text:

> 'This court would run counter to all principles of statutory interpretation if it were to purport to vary or supplement the terms of this stated condition by reference to some supposed convention, which . . . is not incorporated in the body of the statute.'[1]

The court thereby avoided the key question of whether the 1931 Act could function as a 'higher form of law' than subsequent 'statutes' affecting the law of former Dominions. We can only speculate as to how a British court would have viewed an 'Act' which seemed to alter Canadian law but did not contain any reference to Canadian consent to its terms. The Diceyan view would be that any such reference is unnecessary – for the courts to demand it would amount to recognition of 'manner and form' entrenchment as a valid principle of British constitutional law, and thereby create a new 'ultimate political fact'. The whole basis of the constitution would then be undermined; for if we accept one statute is 'special' because of the political substance of its subject matter, there is no logical barrier to prevent other 'special' statutes emerging, and indeed for different statutes to enjoy different degrees of 'specialness' according to the enacting Parliaments' and interpreting courts' perceptions of their political importance. As a political or moral principle, such a 'revolution' may be no bad thing, and we will further consider its merits in chapter 15: yet as a matter of orthodox legal theory, it would seem unachiev-

---

19 As we saw in chapter 6, such an argument has also been made in respect of 'legislation' passed under the Parliament Acts. Here however one would have a four (Commons, Lords, Monarch and 'Canada') rather than two (Commons and Monarch) part 'Parliament'.

20 [1983] Ch 77 at 87.

1 [1983] Ch 77 at 107.

able. But the question of whether constitutional lawyers should regard legal theory as more important than political practice is one with which we might usefully conclude this chapter.

CONCLUSION – THE CONVENTIONAL BASIS OF PARLIAMENTARY SOVEREIGNTY?

We suggested in chapters 5 to 7 that the sovereignty of Parliament was de facto the sovereignty of whichever political faction controlled majority support in the House of Commons. Much of the argument advanced in this chapter has indicated that the concentration of effective political power is often very intense even within a political party; small groups of senior ministers or even the Prime Minister alone may occasionally be, to all intents and purposes, 'elected dictators'.[2]

One might think that this type of institutional structure would be a recipe for oppressive, if not tyrannical law-making. But while we may question complacent claims that Britain's form of democracy is incapable of further improvement, it is absurd to claim that our constitution has proven profoundly insensitive to its citizens' wishes. Yet this result has seemingly been achieved in spite of, rather than because of, the constitution's legal structure.

This might prompt us to adopt the argument made by Geoffrey Marshall that:

'the most obvious and undisputed convention of the British constitutional system is that Parliament does not use its unlimited sovereign power of legislation in an oppressive or tyrannical way. That is a vague but clearly accepted conventional rule resting on the principle of constitutionalism and the rule of law.'[3]

In the light of the analysis presented in the first nine chapters of this book, we might wish to qualify that assertion somewhat. We might firstly wonder whether the avoidance of tyranny and oppression is a sufficiently ambitious target for a modern constitution to set itself? That a democratic constitution may avoid such gross evils does not mean that there is no scope for further improvement in the structure and powers of its governing process.

The second qualification relates to the nature of 'Parliament'. We have now established that it is frequently the case that legislative sovereignty is effectively wielded by a small faction within a

2 The phrase is Lord Hailsham's.
3 Marshall G (1984) *Constitutional Conventions* p 9 (Oxford: Clarendon Press).

single political party that enjoys only minoritarian electoral support. In that context, we might plausibly conclude that the most important of all constitutional principles is that *governing parties* (and within them, Cabinets and Prime Ministers) resist the temptation to use Parliament's unfettered legal powers to enact policies intolerable to the majority of the electorate, and moreover, that the electoral majority is not predisposed to consent to laws which impinge substantially on the liberty of minority factions.

The American revolutionaries, and the constitutional architects of most other western democracies, did not have so optimistic a view of their legislators' or their citizenries' political culture. Indeed, Madison and Jefferson saw sound reasons for taking a particularly pessimistic view of the political morality of Britain's ruling élites. It was precisely because they considered that conventional constraints on governmental power could not be relied upon that the American framers erected so elaborate a system of procedural entrenchment of basic values to safeguard them against majoritarian intolerance or irrationality. The great paradox of British constitutional development is that its basic principle, the sovereignty of Parliament, was initially premised on a perceived need to protect fundamental values through an even more rigorous form of procedural entrenchment. In 1688, each faction of 'the people' (as then very narrowly defined) could veto legislation of which it disapproved. Yet now 'the people' comprise virtually the entire adult population, and insofar as the people are ridden by factions, their alliances derive from loyalties to a political party. If we transposed the 1688 revolutionaries' 'Three Estates of the Realm' methodology to contemporary British society, the tripartite Parliament in which each limb exercised veto powers would not be the Commons, Monarch and Lords, but the Conservative, Labour, and Liberal Democrat parties. Yet the constitution currently empowers a government to ignore rather than accommodate the wishes of those among the people who support opposition parties.

It would thus seem that the long-term legitimacy of our modern constitutional arrangements rests on the assumption that we have no need for a system of 'higher' or entrenched laws, protecting fundamental constitutional values against the whims of electoral majorities, because government and opposition parties are in broad agreement as to the basic political and moral principles which the constitution should express. In such circumstances, it would not greatly matter if one's preferred party lost a general election, for one could be sure that while the new government would pursue policies with which one disagreed, that disagreement would be of degree rather than kind. A political party might readily be expected to consent to laws that its supporters found unpalatable, but not intolerable. This may be because it accepts the intrinsic legitmacy of majoritarian law-making in respect of non-fundamental issues, and/or (more cynically) because it hopes to win the the next general election and expects that its own consent to defeat would be reciprocated in respect of its own unpalatable laws by supporters of the previous government.

It is not possible in this book to delve in great detail into Britain's post-war political history. But at the risk of gross oversimplification, most commentators agree that the 1945–1975 period was marked by appreciable agreement between Labour and Conservative administrations about both the substance and the style of government.[4] In the era of 'Butskellite' consensus,[5] both parties broadly adhered to the Keynesian school of economic policy, which advocated extensive government interference in the economy to smooth out the peaks and troughs of the economic cycle. Butskellism embraced a commitment to maintaining full employment, to government ownership of public utilities such as rail, telecommunications, gas, water, electricity and coal, to an extensive network of social security benefits for the elderly and unemployed, and to a comprehensive, government controlled national health service.

This is not to suggest that general elections in that era were not keenly fought, nor that the identity of the winning party made no discernible difference to the way the country was governed. Rather it stresses that the constitution did not face the problem of a people bitterly divided over basic issues.

Chapter 6 used the changing historical role of the House of Lords as a vehicle to explore the notion of democracy as a matter of *procedural* politics – the co-equal legislative status of the upper house had become politically unacceptable because of the consolidation of a conventional principle that 'consent' to government demanded legislators be electorally accountable. But we should be wary, especially given the characteristics of our electoral system, of assuming that periodic voting for members of the Commons is a sufficent guarantor of a democratic constitution. Chapters 10 and 11 return to the idea that democracy may also be a matter of *substantive* politics, by focusing not on the inter-relationship of the

---

4 For an introduction see George and Wilding *op cit* chs 3–4; Gamble (1981) *op cit* chs 3–4.
5 See pp 76–77 above.

various parts of central government, but on the institution of local government, in exploring the importance of inter-party consensus to the legitimacy of our constitutional arrangements.

CHAPTER TEN

Local government 1: Conventional pluralism?

We have thus far encountered the issue of federalism, in the sense of political mechanisms dividing governmental power geographically, in several rather different forms. Chapter 1 noted the inter-relationship in the USA between the people, the national government, and the governments of the States. The geographical separation of powers between national and State government was a (perhaps *the*) fundamental political principle underpinning the constitutional settlement, and was afforded explicit *legal* protection in the constitution's text. In chapter 9, we saw how the Canadian constitution developed a similarly profound attachment to a national/provincial division of powers. In contrast to the USA, however, the 'fundamental' status of Canadian federalism emerged in the early 1980s as a matter of constitutional *convention*. During the 1980–1981 repatriation crisis, the national legislature seemingly retained the legal power to amend the constitution as it thought fit, but was prevented from proceeding as it wished by the moral or political illegitimacy of its plans.

Both the Canadian and American models of federalism rest on the moral premiss that the constitutions of large, democratic nations should permit the inevitably varying political sentiments of 'the people' to be given *constant* expression on matters of substantial (if not fundamental), political significance. A unitary state whose legislators are subject to periodic re-election may provide its people with the opportunity to consent in a *sequential* sense, at a national level, to different governmental philosophies. It may have supra-legislative constitutional provisions which ensure that opposition parties have realistic prospects of winning future general elections if they formulate attractive policies. But such societies cannot provide their people with any legally constituent basis for the *simultaneous* co-existence of alternative governmental programmes.

It is also possible, in theory, for a unitary state with a legislature exercising sovereign powers on a bare majority basis to offer its people substantial sequential *and* simultaneous pluralism within the government process. This would require that whichever political faction controlled a central legislative majority regarded political pluralism as a fundamental constitutional convention. Such legislators would fashion and maintain a governmental system facilitating effective expression of divergent political opinion. The fewer the powers that the national legislature gave to the national government, and the more it allocated to locally elected bodies, the less unitary and thence more 'federal' or 'pluralist' the constitution's conventional basis would be. To revisit familiar analytical terminology, a country could be very federalist in functional terms, while formally being entirely unitary.

As noted in chapter 2, post-revolutionary England adopted a constitutional structure recognising a unitary state, whose Parliament possessed total legislative competence. Any geographical division of governmental power within English (and later British) society could not have a constituent legal status; Parliament might at any time introduce a new division of powers. The geographical separation of powers could have only a conventional basis.

The American framers placed no faith in the proposition that geographical political pluralism could satisfactorily be protected by trusting in the self-restraint of national legislators. Convention was viewed as an entirely inadequate guarantor of political diversity. That the American and English revolutionaries adopted (and that their successors subsequently maintained) such divergent approaches to the geographical separation of powers might suggest either or both of two things. Firstly, that British society did not then (and has not since) contained geographically based divisions of political sentiment among its people; and/or, secondly, that it has such divisions, and they have been respected by successive Parliamentary majorities. It is to exploring these issues, in the period up until 1979, that the rest of this chapter is directed.

I. LOCALISM, TRADITION AND THE 'MODERNISATION' OF LOCAL GOVERNMENT

'Localism' was an important element of the political culture of seventeenth century England. By that time, some parts of the country could already claim several hundred years of local self-government. Kingston-upon-Hull was recognised as a unit of local government by a Charter granted in 1299, while the town of Beverley can trace its local government history back to 1129.[1] Much local government activity was based on a fusion rather than separation of powers. Its origins frequently lay in the need to enforce and maintain law and order, with the result that government officials frequently occupied posts which now appear as much judicial as executive in nature.[2] Indeed, the English '*common law*' was subsequently to emerge as the result of an effort by successive monarchs to impose uniform legal principles on the many divergent inferior jurisdictions which had grown up and flourished in England since the Middle Ages.[3]

Just as the 1688 revolutionaries were content to leave the substance of the common law unaltered, so they also forswore systematic redefinition of the existing system of local government. The system's details need not be addressed here, beyond noting its extraordinary diversity,[4] and its vital importance as a tool for aristocratic interests both to control the conduct and outcome of local political controversies, and to influence the composition of the Commons.[5]

The twin socio-economic forces of urbanisation and industrialisation[6] placed increasing demands on government from the mid-eighteenth century onwards, particularly in respect of maintaining public health and law and order in the rapidly growing urban areas, and providing transport infrastructure to facilitate the mobility of workers, raw materials, and manufactured goods. Initially, however, Parliament chose not to respond to these pressures in a systematic way. Rather, it created ad hoc units of local government in response to perceived social needs in particular areas. Often these government bodies had only one responsibility; for poor relief, or sewerage works, or policing, or providing elementary education for example. Some, but by no means all of these office holders were elected (and as we saw in chapter 7, electorates were at that time extremely small and entirely unrepresentative of local populations). The majority were appointed by central government, which had in turn often delegated that responsibility to powerful locally-based politicians. In terms both

---

1 Elcock H (2nd edn, 1986) *Local Government* ch 1 (London: Metheun).

2 See Jennings I (4th edn, 1960) *Principles of Local Government Law* ch 2 (London: University of London Press).

3 Plucknett (1960) *op cit* ch 3.

4 See Russell (1971) *op cit* ch 6.

5 See pp 240–241 above.

6 See Loughlin M (1985) 'Municipal socialism in a unitary state', in McAuslan and McEldowney *op cit*; (1986) *Local Government in the Modern State* ch 1 (London: Sweet and Maxwell).

of the type of powers that its office holders exercised, and the way that they were chosen, local government at this time might more appropriately be described as a form of 'magistracy' rather than a manifestation of representative democracy.

The preponderance of single function authorities obviously produced a very complex governmental structure. As well as presenting difficulties in co-ordinating service provision, the profusion of small single issue bodies prevented local government deriving the advantages of economies of scale, and offered many opportunities for corruption and patronage in the allocation of offices and the performance of public duties. It was not a system well suited to the social, economic and political demands of a country in the throes of the world's first industrial revolution.

The Municipal Corporations Act 1835

Chapter 7 discussed the passage of the Reform Act 1832 in some detail. That legislation may plausibly be seen as the first (very modest) step towards the creation of a representative democratic basis for the government of British society. Following the passage of the 1832 Act, the Whigs, then led by Lord Melbourne, promised further reform of the country's governmental structures, this time at the local level. Such radicalism triggered one of the last exercises of explicitly partisan monarchical interventions in the political process. William IV dismissed Melbourne's government and dissolved Parliament in the hope that an election would produce a Tory majority led by Peel. However the January 1835 election returned the Whigs (with Melbourne as Prime Minister and the radical Lord John Russell as Leader of the Commons) with an adequate Commons majority. Melbourne resumed office only after having extracted a pledge of support from the King,[7] and immediately set his government to the task of promoting a Bill to modernise and rationalise the country's system of sub-central government.

While the Bill's passage through the Commons was relatively uneventful, it met determined opposition in the Lords. This is perhaps surprising, given the obvious 'defeat' that the Lords had suffered over the Reform Act 1832.[8] It seems more readily understandable, however, when one considers the Act's impact on aristo-

---

7 Brock *op cit* p 317.
8 See pp 241–245 above.

cratic control over the country's governance. To some contemporary commentators, it was the stuff of revolution:

> 'There never was such a coup as this Bill. . . . It marshalls all the middle classes in all the towns . . . in the ranks of reform: aye, and gives them monstrous power too. I consider it a much greater blow to Toryism than the Reform Bill itself.'[9]

While the 1832 Act had cut a swathe through the foliage of the landed classes' political influence, the 1835 legislation promised to initiate a trend that would attack that influence at its roots. The Act signified that the twin economic forces of urbanisation and industrialisation had been joined by the political catalyst of increased pressure for the democratisation of the country's constitutional arrangements. The functionally-haphazard, aristocratically dominated structure of sub-central government which then existed offended the emergent middle classes' attachment to the principles of both efficiency and representativeness in the conduct of public affairs.

The Tories in the Lords launched a vigorous campaign against the Bill.[10] The 'ultras' were led by the Duke of Newcastle, who, as in 1832, presented this further dose of electoral and governmental reform as an assault upon the property rights of existing holders of local political power. The Lords proposed and passed numerous wrecking amendments. The government offered no resistance to this process, seemingly believing that if given enough legislative rope the Tory peers would succeed in hanging themselves from the scaffold of reformist, middle class public opinion. Lord Greville suggested that the government was:

> 'content to exhibit its paltry numbers in the House of Lords in order that the world may see how essentially it is a Tory body, that it hardly fulfils the conditions of a great independent legislative assembly, but presents the appearance of a dominant party faction.'[11]

As in 1832, the intransigence of reactionary Tory peers finally foundered on Peel's refusal to condone their obstruction of an elected government's policy. Shorn of lower house support, Tory peers subsequently contented themselves with fashioning amendments which the Whig government was willing to accept.

The 1835 legislation reformed only urban areas – the system of rural local government remained intact. Nor did the Act effect a significant transfer of powers to the new borough councils from

9 See Turbeville (1958) *op cit* p 351: Brock *op cit* p 317.
10 See generally Turbeville (1958) *op cit* pp 351–358.
11 Quoted in Turbeville (1958) *op cit* at p 354.

existing single function bodies. Its importance lay rather in its recognition that councillors should hold office on the basis of periodic elections, and that their continued occupancy of that office should depend on their winning the consent of a local electorate whose right to vote was defined by a uniform, national franchise based on low levels of property ownership.[12] The seeds of democratic government had been planted in the soil of local as well as national government.

Parliament nevertheless continued to create single issue bodies, which remained under the close supervision of central government, to address new social and economic problems at a local level. The 1834 Poor Law had vested responsibility for the administration of poor relief in local Boards of Guardians, rather than granting it to the soon-to-be reformed boroughs. Similarly, following acute public anxiety in the 1850s over the spread of cholera, Parliament created local boards of health, rather than bestow such powers on the boroughs. It was not until the 1870s that the legislature was ultimately convinced of the desirability of allocating this task to the boroughs.[13]

By the 1880s, the boroughs' 'multi-functional'[14] nature was firmly established. In addition to their public health powers, they had also begun to assume increasingly extensive responsibilities in the areas of housing provision and town planning. Relatedly, Parliament had in 1871 created a central government department, originally titled the Local Government Board, to co-ordinate and oversee local authority activities.[15]

The system of rural local government was not rationalised in the sense of becoming multi-functional and elected according to a uniform franchise until enactment of the Local Government Act 1888. A county council for London was created in 1899. The 1902 Education Act further reinforced councils' multi-functional importance by transferring responsibility for state elementary schooling from the specialist school boards established in 1870 to the county councils and the larger boroughs.

---

12 The local electoral franchise was more expansive than its Parliamentary counterpart. This was not only a class matter; as noted in chapter 7, women were enfranchised at the local level some years before being permitted to vote for members of the Commons.

13 Jennings (1960) *op cit* pp 55–57.

14 See Loughlin M (1994) 'The restructuring of central-local government relations', in Jowell and Oliver *op cit.*

15 This role successively passed to the Ministry of Health, the Ministry of Housing and Local Government, and, from the 1970s onwards, the Department of the Environment (DoE).

During the next two decades, Parliament made further significant extensions to local government's responsibilities for administering the newly emergent welfare state.[16] There were at this time
some 1,500 units of elected, multi-functional local government.
They were divided on the basis of powers as well as geography.
Many authorities existed within a two-tier structure, in which different types of authority had different responsibilities.[17] Thus a
county council, which provided education and social services
throughout its area, might contain within its boundaries several
borough councils, each controlling such issues as housing and
town planning.[18] The picture was further complicated by some
areas which had only a single-tier structure; larger boroughs might
be granted 'county borough status', and thereby take over the
county's responsibilities within the borough's boundaries.

Given their profusion, there was obviously no scope for local
councils to exercise powers on a scale comparable to those possessed by the state governments of the USA, or the Canadian
provinces. But this does not mean that their powers were politically
insignificant. In a welfare state, citizens will be intimately and
acutely affected by governmental decisions in such fields as education, housing, social services and town planning. Moreover, the
combined impact of these services would be sufficient to enable
electors to express appreciably divergent opinions as to the precise
content and conduct of citizen–government relations in their
respective areas.

By 1920, the democratisation of British society was firmly established. Parliament had introduced a near universal franchise, and
the legal reduction in the Lords' powers effected by the Parliament
Act 1911 stressed the elected chamber's dominance in the legislative process. It was also the case, as the results of the 1906–1910
general elections made clear, that the 'people's' political
allegiance was almost equally divided between the Conservative
and the Liberal/Labour parties.[19] A powerful local government
sector, enjoying appreciable independence from central control,
would thus offer defeated voters the opportunity to see their

16 Which became firmly established following the eventual passage of Lloyd
   George's 'People's Budget' (see pp 199–203 above). For details of local government's role in this period see Hampson W (2nd edn, 1991) *Local Government
   and Urban Politics* ch 2 (London: Longman).
17 This presents a much over-simplified picture. For more detail see Hampson *op
   cit* pp 17–20.
18 And which might of course be controlled by a party other than the one with
   majority support on the county council.
19 See Table 6.2 above.

preferred policies given some effect. If our concept of democracy rests on reasonably sophisticated notions of popular consent to government, it is therefore of crucial importance to consider, as a matter both of law and of convention, the constitutional principles which structured the relationship between central government, local authorities, and the national and local electorates from the 1920s onwards.

II. LOCAL GOVERNMENT'S CONSTITUTIONAL STATUS IN THE EARLY TWENTIETH CENTURY – LAW AND CONVENTION

A sophisticated understanding of consent might provide us with (per Jennings)[20] a 'reason' for parliamentary self-restraint in respect of local political pluralism. From this perspective, it makes little sense to begin a search for conventional understandings of central/local relations prior to 1918. That date does offer, from a contemporary vantage point, the advantage of giving us (to borrow from Asquith) a sufficiently lengthy time span to scrutinise in order to see if any clear 'traditions and settled practices' have emerged.[21]

Several strong presumptions as to the 'correct' allocation of power between central and local government were apparently consolidated among politicians of all parties during World War II, when Britain was governed by a Conservative–Labour–Liberal coalition. The parliamentary roots of the Butskellite consensus are highly significant for consent-based theories of constitutional law, since Churchill's war-time administration is the only modern government which can plausibly be portrayed as commanding the level of popular support which, in democracies such as the USA, would be sufficient to redefine 'fundamental' constitutional values.

The election campaigns of 1945, 1950 and 1951 featured hyperbolic denunciations by both parties of their opponent's policies.[1] But the depth of the consensus between mainstream Conservative and Labour policies is well-illustrated by Churchill's first Commons speech following his return as Prime Minister in 1951:

'What the nation needs is several years of quiet, steady administration,

20 P 333 above.
21 See p 334 above.
1 Cf Churchill's ludicrous claim in a June 1945 election broadcast that Labour's economic policies could not be implemented without the creation of a *Gestapo*; see Butler and Sloman *op cit* p 227.

if only to allow the socialist [ie Labour government's] legislation to reach its full fruition.'[2]

The 'socialist legislation' to which Churchill referred had entailed some significant transfer of formerly local responsibilities to newly created national bodies, especially in the fields of health care and the management of gas, water, and electricity supplies. In terms of the *multiplicity* of its functions, local government in the Butskellite era was thus less important than it had been immediately before the war. It was also subject to more central oversight, insofar as legislation increasingly contained explicit powers which would enable ministers to interfere with or override council decisions in certain circumstances.[3]

However in terms of the *scale* of its activities, local government had become more important than ever before. Local responsibilities lay primarily in the fields of housing, education, land use planning, social work and consumer protection services. Given the substantive importance of such functions in a modern welfare state, their reservation to elected local government could be seen as a guarantor of political pluralism within the government process. Should the Labour, Liberal or Conservative parties win control of councils endowed by Parliament with such significant responsibilities, they might reasonably assume that their respective political preferences would be implemented in some parts of the country, irrespective of the outcome of general elections. This is not to suggest that it was ever envisaged that local councils would enjoy complete independence in these spheres of activity, but rather that they would possess sufficient autonomy to exceed or modify centrally determined standards.[4]

There was a readily discernible party split along regional lines in general elections during the post-war era.[5] Crudely stated, a greater percentage of the electorate in London, Wales, Scotland and Northern England consistently voted Labour rather than Conservative, and that tendency was reversed in the rest of Southern England. Powerful and autonomous local councils would ensure that this geographically based divergence of opinion was con-

---

2 *HCD*, 4 November 1951; quoted in Jenkins R (1994) 'Churchill: the government of 1951–1955' at p 497, in Blake R and Louis W (eds) *Churchill* (Oxford: Clarendon Press).

3 Hampson *op cit* ch 10: Buxton R (2nd edn, 1973) *Local Government* ch 5 (Harmondsworth: Penguin).

4 See especially Griffith J (1966) *Central Departments and Local Authorities* ch 1 (London: Allen and Unwin).

5 See Butler D and Butler S (1986) *British Political Facts* pp 230–232 (London: Macmillan). For a detailed breakdown of the past four elections see Table 11.1 below.

stantly accommodated within the country's overall government structure. It seems entirely plausible to assume that 'the people' in these regions would more readily consent to defeat at the national level if they could be sure that their respective political preferences could influence the government process on a significant, if limited, scale in their particular areas.

The Butskellite view of government also acknowledged reasons of a less profoundly 'constitutional' nature for preserving a powerful and vibrant local government sector.[6] The first might be called the 'local knowledge' factor. This argument assumes that one will improve the efficiency of service provision if it is entrusted to an organisation that has an intimate and long-standing knowledge of relevant social and economic conditions in a particular area. This advantage is reinforced when one is dealing with a package of services, and where trade-offs need to be made between the amount of resources that each is allocated.

A second justification falls under the heading of political education. Councils can serve as training grounds for politicians before they move on to central government. In another sense, local government's role as a political educator draws more people into the government process, thereby making them aware of their rights and responsibilities as citizens. This can be achieved not only through the route of becoming a councillor. Involvement with local pressure groups, or even individual lobbying over such issues as school closures or housing repairs also give citizens the opportunity to participate in the government process.

A third justification sees local government as a vehicle for experimental social policies. The sheer diversity of political opinion to which local councils might offer expression makes it likely that some authorities will dream up ideas which may never have occurred to central government. Relatedly, the small geographical scope of any such authority's jurisdiction offers a guarantee of damage limitation if experimental policies prove unsuccessful in practice.

Broadly stated, this Butskellite perception of local government suggests that there is much more to the concept of 'democracy' in a modern multi-party state than simply a five yearly stroll to the ballot box to express a preference concerning the party composition of national government. Rather, it indicates that democracy in post-war Britain was widely perceived as a *perpetual and multi-faceted process*, within which various sub-groups of 'the people' would push and pull 'government' at all levels in contradictory

6 See Sharpe J (1970) 'Theories and value of local government' *Political Studies* 153–174.

directions, and to which a geographical separation of powers could make a vital contribution.

The remaining sections of this chapter attempt to gauge the nature of the geographical separation of powers within the British constitution in the Butskellite era by focusing on four elements of central/local relations: the question of councils' fiscal autonomy, the provision of public housing, the management of state schools, and, pervading all areas, the regulatory role played by administrative law. Before turning to this task however, we must briefly address the question of geographical boundaries.

The physical boundaries of local authorities

In terms of their physical boundaries, no less than in respect of their precise powers, local authorities have not enjoyed a sacrosanct, permanent, coventional status in the modern era. The Macmillan government had persuaded Parliament to create a Local Government Boundary Commission in 1958, which was to exercise powers analogous to those of its parliamentary namesake.[7] Boundary redrawing had previously been undertaken on an ad hoc basis, a process clearly vulnerable to accusations of political bias. Macmillan's initiative appeared to lend the issue a distinctly less partisan appearance, imbuing it with a consensual rather than factional character.[8]

However, the Commission was abolished during Harold Wilson's first administration. Wilson established a Royal Commission (the Redcliffe-Maud Commission) to conduct a thorough review of the structure of local government in England. Richard Crossman (whose zeal for 'modernising' government institutions we encountered in respect of the Commons in chapter 5) was then the Minister of Local Government, and was largely responsible for determining the commission's personnel and terms of reference.[9]

After several years of extensive investigations, Redcliffe-Maud recommended radical reforms. It proposed as a first principle that England should contain just 58 local councils, each exercising all

---

7 Local Government Act 1958. See Jennings (1960) *op cit* pp 88–94.

8 Although this lofty ideal did not always commend itself to the responsible Minister; see Crossman's *Diaries* at pp 44–46.

9 Crossman's *Diaries* suggest that his zeal for 'modernisation' in this process did not always override his concern with party political electoral advantage; *op cit* at p 201.

the powers formerly divided between counties, county boroughs, and boroughs. A two-tier system would be retained only in London and several other large conurbations. The commission also advocated the creation of eight 'provinces', whose governments (indirectly elected from the other local authorities) would exercise broad, strategic economic planning powers.

Redcliffe-Maud suggested that this package of reforms would eliminate conflict and confusion between different types of authorities with geographically overlapping responsibilities, heighten people's awareness of which government body was responsible for local service provision, and by enhancing both the geographical size and range of powers each council wielded, significantly increase the political importance of the local electoral process. Had they been implemented, the proposals would have lent the overall structure of English government a distinctly more 'federal' character than it had previously possessed.

The Labour and Conservative parties were divided on the merits of the Redcliffe-Maud proposals, although both rejected the proposal for provincial government. Labour's initial Bill watered down the proposals quite significantly, although it did not reject in principle the extension of single-tier local government. However the Wilson government lost office in the 1970 general election before its measures could be enacted. The Heath government, in contrast, while accepting that England contained too many small authorities, remained attached to the multi-tier principle. The Local Government Act 1972 (which came into force in 1974) abolished many of the 1,500 or so small councils which then existed, and merged them into larger units. The 'larger units' were still however numerous and therefore often quite small. In 1974 there were 47 county councils in England and Wales, 36 metropolitan district councils, and 333 district councils.[10] Only the metropolitan districts were single-tier authorities in the sense envisaged by Redcliffe-Maud and apparently preferred by the Labour party. The Bill had been appreciably amended, at least in matters of detail, during its parliamentary passage, when the government accepted that its original proposals should be adjusted to accommodate local sensitivities.[11] The Bill was never-

10 For a helpful explanation (and even more helpful maps) of the eventual structure see Hampson *op cit* ch 2.
11 See Burton I and Drewry G (1972) 'Public legislation: a survey of the session 1971–1972' *Parliamentary Affairs* 145–185.

theless opposed at second reading by both the Labour and Liberal parties.

The size and range of powers exercised by local councils has obvious implications for the sector's efficacy as a representative of divergent political opinion. The larger a council, and the more extensive the services for which it is responsible, the greater the scope it possesses to act as a meaningful 'alternative' to central government for a local electorate which opposes the party commanding a Commons majority. It is clear that neither the Conservative nor Labour parties during the Butskellite era saw any merit in creating a conventionally federal model (in the US or Canadian sense) of central/local relations; councils remained too small, too numerous and too functionally heterogeneous for that argument to have any force. But this is not to say either that local authorities therefore lacked a significant degree of political autonomy, or that the British constitution was insensitive to the pluralist nature of its people's political beliefs. Before introducing its Bill, the Heath government had stated that:

'A vigorous local democracy means that authorities must be given real functions – with powers of decision and the ability to take action without being subjected to excessive regulation by central government through financial or other controls . . . [A]bove all else, a genuine local democracy implies that decisions should be taken – and should be seen to be taken – as locally as possible.'[12]

The following pages address the extent to which such rhetoric reflected the realities of central/local relations.

III. TAXATION AND REPRESENTATION: THE FISCAL AUTONOMY OF LOCAL GOVERNMENT

It is a cliché that the American revolutionaries fought the War of Independence on the basis of the slogan 'No Taxation Without Representation'. As chapter 1 suggested, their grievances were far more widely based. The slogan nevertheless conveys the intimacy of the nexus between fiscal and political autonomy within the 'government' process. The notion of 'government' carries within it the idea that elected representatives have the power to raise sufficient revenue to put the policies preferred by their electorate

12 DoE (1971) *Local Government in England* p 6 (London: HMSO Cmnd 4584).

into practice: such limits as were imposed on this power would be a purely political matter regulated by the electoral process. An elected body whose revenue and expenditure was determined entirely by another government organisation would not in any meaningful sense be a 'government' at all, but would be merely an administering agency doing the bidding of its fiscal master. These are extreme positions, but they serve to illustrate a proposition of general applicability to the British constitution in the modern era; namely that the more fiscal autonomy the council sector possessed, the greater its capacity to express pluralist political sentiment, and hence the more 'governmental' and less 'administrative' its constitutional role.

The multi-functional, elected local authorities with which Britain entered the modern democratic age traditionally derived their funding from three sources. The first source was grants from central government. The second was income from various trading operations, especially rents from council houses. The third source was a locally levied property tax, colloquially known as 'the rates', which was paid both by local businesses and householders. In 1950, these three sources of income were of approximately equal importance across the local government sector as a whole. However, the Butskellite era produced a marked shift in this state of affairs.

As Table 10.1 suggests, the trend in the 30 years following 1945 was for an increasingly larger part of local government's income

Table 10.1
Sources of local authority income 1945–1974

Year*	Total income (£m)	% Rates	% Grants	% Trading operations
1950	966	34	34	32
1955	1415	33	36	31
1960	2182	33	37	30
1966	3767	33	38	29
1970	5511	31	40	29
1974	9764	28	45	27

* Financial year, ending in the year specified.

Source: Extracted from data in Layfield/DoE (1976) *Local Government Finance* Table 21 (Cmnd 6453. London: HMSO).

to be central government grant. In the mid-1970s almost half of a council's income came from grants; barely a quarter derived from the rates.

One reason for this heavy financial input from central government lay in the need to avoid massive inequality in service provision between various councils. Local authorities obviously cover very different areas. There can be significant discrepancies both in their wealth and their needs for welfare services. In general, poorer areas will need more services but have less capacity to pay for them through local taxes than more affluent regions. Central grants were allocated according to various complex formulae which tried to take these factors into account – in effect the process involved a transfer of wealth from richer to poorer areas to enable all councils to meet minimum standards of service provision.

But while greater central funding may enhance equality, it also poses the threat of undermining local authorities' political independence from central government. As suggested above, a key characteristic of a 'government' is that it has the power to raise sufficient revenue to put its political plans into effect. If a local authority could levy and spend only that amount of money which central government was prepared to provide, the local electoral process would be a mere charade; the constitution might just as well provide for a local office of a central government department to administer whatever services central government wished to offer, and abolish local elections altogether.

Several steps were taken to reduce this risk. From the 1950s onwards,[13] central grants were paid in a single 'block', rather than being earmarked for specific services. This afforded councils some scope to prioritise expenditure on different activities according to their particular political preferences. Perhaps of more significance was the apparent existence of a conventional rule that central government would not use statute to place limits on the amount of revenue that local authorities raised through the rates. The question of local taxation levels was presumed to be a matter for a council and its electors. If rates were too high, the appropriate means to reduce them was for local electors to vote the party controlling the council out of office, and replace it with a party committed to lower levels of expenditure on local services. Central government might request an authority to keep its rates within certain limits; it might negotiate about total spending plans and the amounts allocated to particular services; it might even

13 Loughlin (1994) *op cit.*

threaten to reduce the grants it provided; but it did not ask Parliament to place legal limits on councils' tax levying 'independence'.

The significance of Parliament's conventional self-restraint on the question of local taxation to the maintenance of a politically pluralist geographical separation of powers was forcefully stressed by Jennings in 1960:

> 'Local authorities are elected by the people of the area not to carry out as agents of the central government the policy of that government, but to carry out the policy of the electors of the area. The furtherance of that policy needs expenditure, and for the expenditure and the means of meeting it the local authority is again responsible, not to the central government... but to the electors.... The importance of this principle cannot be overestimated.... so long as the rating power is independent of [central government] control, local government as a whole must be, to a large extent, independent.'[14]

One must beware of exaggerating this degree of 'independence'. Indeed, independence is perhaps an inappropriate word to use here, if (unlike Humpty-Dumpty)[15] we assume our language can bear only a limited range of meanings, and that these meanings must be shaped by shared understandings of the broader context in which they are used. 'Autonomy' is perhaps a better term than 'independence' to describe local government's constitutional relationship vis à vis central government, given that so substantial a proportion of its financial resources derived from central grants.

But 'autonomy' is a complicated concept. Its extent may depend as much on precisely how a council is permitted to spend its resources as on the amount of revenue itself. To explore this issue, we must examine the legal framework regulating council behaviour in rather more detail.

IV. THE ROLE OF THE JUDICIARY

Since all councils are statutory creations, their legal competence is necessarily confined within the limits that Parliament has set. Consequently, their actions are susceptible to judicial review to ensure that the boundaries that Parliament has defined are not exceeded. However the absence of explicit legal limits on a council's rate levying power typified a general trend in legislation

14 (1960) *op cit* pp 184–186.
15 See p 86 above.

defining local government's powers prior to 1980. Many local government statutes were drafted in very loose language, reflecting the fact that Parliament accepted both the need for local variation in service provision, *and* the competence of elected councillors to reach those exact decisions.

Consequently, we can find several important cases which suggest that the courts might be reluctant to apply the ultra vires doctrine to local authorities acting under loosely drafted statutes. In *Kruse v Johnson*,[16] for example, the local authority had passed a bye-law[17] making it an offence to play an instrument on the highway within 50 yards of a dwelling house if asked to stop by an occupant or constable. The bye-law apparently expressed the wish of local electors to maintain rigorous standards of peace and quiet in their neighbourhoods. Kruse was charged with the offence, but raised in his defence the assertion that the bye-law was invalid because it was 'unreasonable'. In addressing this question, the court held that because councils were elected bodies accountable to their voters, bye-laws should be 'benevolently' interpreted. While a bye-law would be ultra vires if unreasonable, unreasonable bore a special meaning in this context. The substance of a decision would only be ultra vires if it was: 'manifestly unjust'; or contained elements of 'bad faith' or fraud; or involved 'gratuitous and oppressive interference' with citizens rights.[18]

This expansive concept of substantive reasonableness in relation to local authority discretion was reiterated in the 1948 decision in *Associated Provincial Picture Houses Ltd v Wednesbury Corpn*, a case briefly noted in chapter 3.[19] In *Wednesbury*, the Court of Appeal refused to interfere with a council decision to use its statutory power to license cinemas to prohibit children from attending shows on Sunday mornings. The court considered the policy was well within the range of opinions that reasonable people might hold. The courts should only invalidate the substance of such a decision if it was so grossly unreasonable that no reasonable person could have thought it within the powers conferred by the Act.

These two cases both seemed to accept that the courts should be very slow to question the merits of council policy decisions. Their rationale appears to be that Parliament has entrusted these

---

16 [1898] 2 QB 91.
17 In effect a piece of delegated legislation whose geographical reach was confined within the council's boundaries.
18 [1898] 2 QB 91 at 99.
19 See pp 81–82 above.

democratically elected bodies to *govern* their particular areas in certain fields. This process necessarily involves the making of value judgements about political issues, a task which, in accordance with traditional notions of the separation of powers, one might reasonably assume that politicians are better equipped to make than judges. But *Kruse* and *Wednesbury* co-existed with another line of cases in which judges had placed far more restrictive limits on a council's power to pursue its preferred policies. The best known of these is *Roberts v Hopwood*, a case which reached the House of Lords in 1925.[20]

Roberts v Hopwood: the 'fiduciary duty'

Poplar Council, a small inner-London authority, was controlled by a radical faction of the Labour Party (led by George Lansbury) in the 1920s. The councillors had an uneasy relationship with central government over their social policies. This conflict came to a head when the council decided to mitigate the effects of the economic recession by paying all its employees a flat rate wage much higher than offered for similar private sector jobs.[1]

The councillors presumed that they were entitled to do this. Section 62 of the Metropolitan Management Act 1855 empowered the council to pay its employees 'such wages as it thought fit'. The council assumed this meant either that there were no limits on its discretion, or at most, that its policy in this area should be 'benevolently' interpreted per *Kruse*. This was the view taken by the Court of Appeal in *Roberts*.

However the House of Lords reached a different conclusion. Their Lordships decided that the council's apparently unfettered statutory power to pay 'such wages as it thinks fit' was subject to a common law 'fiduciary duty' to local ratepayers. The council owed a duty of financial prudence to ratepayers just as a limited company owes a duty to shareholders, or trustees owe a duty to the trust's beneficiaries. The doctrine apparently required that local authorities be construed as businesses, operating on a profit and loss basis, rather than as governments which can redistribute wealth in whatever way attracts electoral support.

The House of Lords characterised Poplar's policy as the pursuit of 'eccentric principles of socialist philanthropy'. Such principles had no legitimate place in a council's decision-making process. Councillors should not allow their personal political or philosophi-

---

20 [1925] AC 578.
1 For background to the case see Keith-Lucas B (1962) 'Poplarism' *Public Law* 52–80; Jones G (1973) 'Herbert Morrison and Poplarism' *Public Law* 11–31.

cal preferences to influence their policy choices. Such a view seems entirely to ignore the argument that giving effect to local partisan political preferences is one of the main justifications for having elected sub-central government in a democratic unitary state. The decision attracted a stinging, contemporaneous rebuke from Harold Laski, then a Professor at the LSE and subsequently a member of Attlee's 1945–1950 Cabinet:

> 'The council's theory of what is "reasonable" in the exercise of discretion is, even though affirmed by its constituents, seemingly inadmissable if it does not square with the economic precon-ceptions of the House of Lords; it is, it appears, a function of the courts to protect the electorate from the consequences of its own ideas.'[2]

Several Poplar councillors were jailed for contempt of court after refusing to amend their policies.[3] However central govern-ment (then Conservative-controlled) considered this an extreme sanction, and introduced legislation enabling councillors who approved unlawful expenditure to be personally surcharged and disqualified from office for five years.[4]

Conclusion

It is obviously rash to draw general conclusions from so limited a survey of the case law, but one might perhaps safely suggest that judicial supervision of council policy-making in the first half of the twentieth century displayed both very expansive and extraordinarily stunted[5] perceptions of local govern-ment's role in a modern, 'democratic' state. The next two sections add rather more historical flesh to this analytical skeleton by examining how central government and judicial control of local authorities was exercised in the Butskellite era in respect of two important areas of council activity: housing and education.

---

2 Laski H (1926) 'Judicial review of social policy in England' *Harvard LR* 832–848 at p 844. For a retrospective view see Fennel P (1986) '*Roberts v Hopwood*: the rule against socialism' *JLS* 401–422.

3 See Branson N (1979) *Poplarism* (London: Lawence and Wishart).

4 Board of Guardians (Default) Act 1926; Audit (Local Authorities) Act 1927. For comment see Keith-Lucas *op cit*.

5 This is perhaps best illustrated by Lord Sumner's comment in *Roberts* that the limits of a council's discretion was reached in such matters as deciding 'the necessity for a urinal, and the choice of its position': [1925] AC 578 at 605.

V. COUNCIL HOUSING

By 1974, the council sector contained over six million properties and housed 17 million people.[6] Council housing performed several governmental functions in the Butskellite era in addition to the obvious concern of providing reasonable quality, low cost accommodation for individual families. The 1945 Labour government regarded an expanding council sector as a useful tool for wealth redistribution.[7] Conservative administrations were less attached to this principle, but shared enthusiasm for public housing's role in shaping the environment. And both parties found the labour-intensive nature of house building a useful tool to regulate overall demand in the economy.

The public sector's style and scope varied considerably across the country. Local discretion over such macro-issues as stock size and design was not formally structured by tightly defined legislative rules;[8] decisions on such matters were largely determined by local election results. The absence of a precise legal framework might appear peculiar given council housing's important role in central government economic and land development policy. Legal compulsion was however largely unnecessary; councils formulated policies in close consultation with ministers and civil servants at the Ministry of Housing and Local Government (MHLG) and (subsequently) the Department of the Environment (DoE), in a process which typified the generally consensual, negotiatory ethos informing central-local government relations between 1945–1970.

However, the national–local government system'[9] which dominated housing policy did not offer tenants any significant legal or political control over the management of their homes. Parliament's allocation of power to local authorities in this area was

6 For an overview of public sector development see Bowley M (1985) *Housing and the State 1919–1945* ch 1 (London: Allen & Unwin); Merret S (1979) *State Housing in Britain* (London: RKP); Malpass P and Murie A (1987) *Housing Policy and Practice* ch 2 (London: Macmillan); Forrest R and Murie A (1988) *Selling the Welfare State* ch 2 (London: Routledge).

7 Forrest and Murie *op cit* pp 22–24.

8 Although in the 1960s central government 'encouraged' councils to build particular types of dwelling, and to meet minimum (and, subsequently, maximum) standards of space and amenity provision, by variations in the financial support it offered; see Cullingworth J (1979) *Essays on Housing Policy* ch 1 (London: Allen & Unwin); Malpass and Murie *op cit* pp 78–81.

9 See Loughlin (1985a) 'The restructuring of central-local government legal relations' *Local Government Studies* 59–73; Hampson *op cit* ch 9; and more exhaustively Rhodes R (1986) *The National World of Local Government* (London: Allen and Unwin).

a paradigmatic example of green light theory, which afforded individual citizens few legal 'rights'. The Housing Act 1936 had simply placed the 'general management, regulation and control' of public housing within the discretion of the local authority with no discernible substantive or procedural constraints. With respect both to macro-issues such as the number and types of dwellings built, and to such micro-questions as allocation mechanisms, rent levels, maintenance standards, tenancy conditions, and management styles, council discretion was not closely regulated by statute.

Nor were the courts eager to subject local authorities' housing powers to the *Wednesbury* principles of substantive and procedural ultra vires. In *Shelley v LCC*,[10] the plaintiff was a tenant summarily served with an eviction notice. Shelley had no opportunity to argue against eviction, nor was evidence offered of any breach of the tenancy agreement. The council's decision would thus seem both procedurally and substantively ultra vires. The House of Lords however declined to intervene, asserting that housing authorities could 'pick and choose their tenants at will',[11] and evict them in similar fashion. Thirty years later, the judgments in *Bristol District Council v Clark* (1975) and *Cannock Chase District Council v Kelly*[12] (1978) confirmed the *Shelley* rationale; tenants had no recognisable rights in their housing.

Both Parliament and the courts adopted a similarly non-directive role over the issue of the rents that councils charged. Section 83 of the Housing Act 1936 required that rents be 'reasonable'. This did not make it clear to what extent councils might 'subsidise' rents by increasing the rates paid by all local householders and businesses. In *Belcher v Reading Corpn*,[13] the court held that 'reasonableness' required councils to balance tenants' interests (the presumed beneficiaries of public subsidy), with those of ratepayers (the supposed financiers of the subsidy). Romer J held that rent levels would be unreasonably high only if significantly more costly than similar private sector dwellings.[14] Tenants thus had no legal right to subsidised rents. *Belcher* nevertheless upheld local authorities' politically accepted role to use rent policies to *ameliorate* market forces – council house rents would be unreasonably low, and thus breach the council's fiduciary duty, only if *significantly* less expensive than comparable private dwellings. The decision

10 [1948] 2 All ER 898.
11 *Ibid* at 900.
12 [1975] 1 WLR 1443, CA and [1978] 1 All ER 152, CA.
13 [1950] Ch 380. See also *Summerfield v Hampstead Borough Council* [1957] 1 All ER 221; *Luby v Newcastle under-Lyme Corpn* [1965] 1 QB 214, CA.
14 [1950] Ch 380 at 392.

thus seemed to take a more 'benevolent' view of local fiscal autonomy than *Roberts v Hopwood*.

Belcher suggests that litigation over council tenancies presented the courts both with a question of administrative law between an authority and its tenants, and a question of constitutional convention concerning local autonomy from central control. The 'hands-off' approach adopted by both Parliament and the courts towards public housing administration reflected the wider norms regulating central–local government relations between 1945–1975. Tightly drafted statutes or interventionist case law would have overridden the traditional expectation that councils should *govern* their local areas, rather than simply administer centrally defined services on an agency basis. The inference one might draw from this is that legalisation of council/tenant relations might have to await a redefinition of the constitutional relationship between central and local government. Such a redefinition appeared to occur in 1972.

The Housing Finance Act 1972

Notwithstanding its evident commitment to principles of local fiscal autonomy prior to introducing the Local Government Bill 1972 to the Commons,[15] the Heath government adopted a considerably more directive policy towards rental levels in the Housing Finance Act 1972. This legislation sought to raise council house rents to levels analogous to those in the private rented sector, while simultaneously providing rent rebates to poorer tenants. For many councils, this required a substantial rent increase. The government had anticipated that many councils might not wish to implement this legislation; consequently, the Act also gave the DoE stringent enforcement powers against obstructive authorities.[16]

Following the passage of the Act, several Labour-controlled councils threatened not to apply it. Only one authority eventually refused to do so. Clay Cross council in Derbyshire, whose 11 councillors were all members of the Labour Party, resolutely refused to raise rents.[17] DoE attempts to persuade the councillors to implement the Act failed, and they were subsequently surcharged and disqualified. At the subsequent election, local voters

15 See p 400 above.
16 With which the courts proved reluctant to interfere: see *Asher v Secretary of State for the Environment* [1974] Ch 208, CA.
17 Mitchell A (1974) 'Clay Cross' 45 *Political Quarterly* 165; Sklair L (1975), 'The Struggle Against the Housing Finance Act', in Miliband R and Smith J (eds) *Socialist Register* (London: Merlin).

returned 11 new Labour councillors, all committed to maintaining their predecessors' unlawful policy. The conflict was eventually resolved indirectly, in that Clay Cross was one of the many authorities merged into larger councils when the Local Government Act 1972 came into force in 1974.

The Clay Cross episode raises interesting questions both about the relationship between law and convention, and about the nature of the central/local government partnership convention itself. There is no doubt that the Clay Cross councillors broke the law. If we are concerned solely with issues of law, it is obvious that the council's behaviour was unconstitutional. If however we approach the issue in terms of convention, the picture is decidedly less clear.

The traditional approach to housing policy had been that local authorities should have considerable freedom to set rent levels. Thus the Clay Cross councillors considered the Housing Finance Act to be conventionally 'unconstitutional'. Relatedly, they regarded their own illegal refusal to implement the Act as entirely legitimate. The practical difficulty which this stance presented for them was of course that they could not draw on the Heath government's alleged breach of convention as a defence in legal actions arising from their own breach of the law.

Nor was it entirely clear that convention was on the council's side. There is no great weight of historical practice which supported the notion that councils might legitimately defy the law so flagrantly. Convention seemed to require that councillors kept their political preferences within the legal limits set by legislation. From this perspective, the 'constitutional' course of action for the council to have followed would have been (reluctantly) to have enforced the Act and hope that the Heath government's breach of convention would lead voters to turn it out of office at the next general election.

The objection to such a strategy is that it suggests the disputed policy is tolerable to the factions which oppose it, and thereby dilutes or diffuses popular antagonism to central government's preferences. One then faces the argument that had the American revolutionaries, or the 1832 electoral reformers during the Days of May, or the Suffragettes adopted similarly quiescent tactics, they would not have achieved (at least so quickly) the results we would from our more sophisticated democratic vantage point regard as entirely justified. It may of course be argued that the issue of local electoral control of council house rents in 1972 is qualitatively distinct from the enfranchisement struggles of the 1770s, 1830s, and 1900s: we might assume that 'democracy' within the British constitution is a concept that reached its fullest expression in 1930, when all adults became entitled to vote in Parliamentary elections. From that perspective, there would be no justification for any defiance of any statute, as long as people remained free to argue and campaign for its repeal. This is a question we have already broached, and to which we will return in more detail in chapter 14. For the present, however, our attention moves from council housing to perhaps the most important of local government functions – the management of our children's education.

VI. EDUCATION

A major expansion of the education service was effected by the Education Act 1944. The Act placed a vaguely defined responsibility on both central and local government to provide schooling for all children up to the age of 15. The Act did not specify precisely how this should be done. However there was near universal agreement among central and local government and education professionals that children could and should be segregated according to academic ability. Consequently a tripartite system of secondary education developed all over the country. Children would attend a common elementary or primary school between the ages of 8 and 11. They would then sit an examination and be placed in one of three types of schools according to their supposed academic abilities. The 'cleverest' children would attend grammar schools; the remainder were sent to either secondary modern schools, or, if they were thought to have technical aptitude, to technical high schools.[18] In practice, few technical highs were created, with the result that the system was effectively bipartisan; children who passed the 'eleven plus' went to grammar schools; those who 'failed' to secondary moderns.

The selective system had no explicit legal basis, although it was given an official seal of governmental approval in successive reports and circulars.[19] This legal lacuna is the most graphic example of the extent to which the governance of post-war British society was dependent upon conventional understandings between different tiers of government. As in the field of housing,

18 See Pedley R (1966) *The Comprehensive School* pp 38–49 (Harmondsworth: Penguin).
19 A circular being an official statement of government 'advice' as to its preferred interpretation of particular statutory powers. Circulars have no binding legal force, but are something to which decisionmakers should have regard when exercising the statutory powers concerned.

state education policy and practice was shaped by a 'national-local government system', which embroiled central government ministers and civil servants, local authority councillors and officials, and the leadership of the teaching profession in a complex, inter-active and overwhelmingly consensual relationship.[20]

This does not mean that a bland uniformity of opinion prevailed in all quarters, but rather that local departures from orthodox practice were insufficiently frequent, and insufficiently radical, to merit a legalistic and coercive central government response. The West Riding of Yorkshire County Council, for example, had firmly rejected the selective principle on which national policy was based:

> '[Our councillors] have been unable to accept certain suggestions . . . made in Ministerial circulars. They cannot for instance agree that at the age of eleven children can be classified into three recognised mental types and allocated to grammar, modern and technical schools accordingly.'[1]

In reliance on its beliefs, the West Riding provided a single mixed ability secondary school system (colloquially referred to as 'comprehensive') for its children. A few other councils followed suit. Such action amounted to an important assertion of local autonomy. What is significant for our purposes is that both Labour and Conservative governments appeared in the main content to allow such diversity to occur.[2]

Once again, however, just as the administration of council housing had accorded little legal or direct political influence to tenants, so the politicians' and professionals' dominance of education policy gave little obvious scope for the wishes of parents and students to influence the schooling process, other than through the rather indirect mechanism of local elections. Section 76 of the 1944 Act provided that:

> 'in the exercise and performance of all powers and duties conferred and imposed upon them by this Act, the Minister and local education authorities shall have regard to the general principle that, so far as is compatible with the provision of efficient instruction and training and the avoidance of unreasonable public expenditure, pupils are to be educated in accordance with the wishes of their parents.'

A literal interpretation of s 76 might suggest that parental wishes

---

20 See Buxton R (2nd edn, 1973) *Local Government* ch 8 (Harmondsworth: Penguin); Ranson S (1988) 'From 1944–1988: education, citizenship and democracy' *Local Government Studies* 1–19; see also the references at p 407, fn 9 above.

1 Quoted in Pedley (1966) *op cit* p 43.

2 Pedley (1966) *op cit* pp 47–49; (1958) 'Lord Hailsham's legacy' *Journal of Education* (January) 4–5.

occupied a rather lowly status in the administrative scheme of things. This was confirmed by the Court of Appeal in *Watt v Kesteven County Council*.[3] Lord Denning held that parental wishes were merely one factor to which councils should have regard: 'this leaves it open to the county council to have regard to other things as well, and also to make exceptions to the general principle if it thinks fit to do so.'[4]

Watt again exemplifies a green light approach to the government process. Denning LJ's opinion suggests that Parliament had not intended to empower individual parents, nor small groups of parents within a particular local authority, to frustrate the policy choices made by elected councillors. In contrast to the sentiments displayed in *Roberts*, there is no indication here that parents needed to be 'protected' from the outcome of the local electoral process.

Moreover, although the Act made no express effort to oust the courts' jurisdiction to supervise ministerial or council behaviour,[5] its terms implied that disputes should be resolved without ready recourse to the courts. Section 99, for example, permitted parents to make representations to the Secretary of State if they were dissatisfied with their council's policies or practice. The Secretary of State was also empowered under s 68 to issue 'directions' to local authorities which she considered were acting 'unreasonably' in discharging their functions under the Act. Section 68 was apparently envisaged very much as a power of last resort by the 1944 Parliament, to be invoked only in exceptional circumstances.[6] By the mid-1960s, however, both the depth and breadth of consensus within the education branch of the national–local government system began to change.

The emergence of comprehensive education

By the late 1950s, some authorities, primarily but not exclusively Labour-controlled, had embraced the concept of comprehensive secondary schooling. The comprehensive/selective debate was keenly contested, and cut across party lines. Many Labour-controlled councils (and a smaller number of their Conservative counterparts) were attracted by the more egalitarian ethos of the

---

3 [1955] 1 QB 408.
4 *Ibid*, at 424.
5 On ouster clauses see pp 92–96 above.
6 See Harlow and Rawlings *op cit* pp 333–334.

comprehensive system. Other authorities, particularly those with small and scattered populations, favoured it for financial reasons. In contrast, many Conservative (and some Labour) councils wished to retain the tripartite structure.

Harold Wilson's first Labour government, elected in 1964, also supported the comprehensive approach. However, this significant policy shift was not given an explicit legislative base. Instead the government issued Circular 10/65, a document whose legal status was purely advisory, in which the Department of Education and Science (DES) expressed the hope that local authorities would follow central government's preferences.

The circular made no suggestion that the government would legislate to force compliance with its preferences. The DES 'requested' councils to submit plans for re-organising their selective systems along comprehensive lines. The circular did not specify a preferred model of reform, but outlined several different options. It also stressed that:

> 'The proper processes of local government must leave initiative on matters of principle and the ultimate responsibility for decisions with the elected representatives of the community.'[7]

Such sentiments may suggest that the Labour government was prepared to allow appreciable divergence from its preferred aims. By introducing the new policy in a circular rather than an Act, the government was not equipping itself with the legal powers to enforce its preferred policy. This may have been because the Wilson government was committed to the principle of local democracy in education matters. Or it may have been because Labour then had a Commons majority of only four, and could not have pushed so radical a Bill through the house. Pimlott provides some support for the latter view. He records the then Secretary of State, Tony Crosland, as pronouncing (in a private letter): 'If it's the last thing I do, I'm going to destroy every fucking grammar school in England. And Wales.'[8]

Crosland's sentiments were not then a matter of public record. But other sources suggested that compliance with central policy was perhaps not to be entirely voluntary. Para 44 of the circular hinted that the DES would only fund new secondary schools if they were comprehensive rather than selective. This was of course an informal enforcement mechanism that the government did not have to pilot through the Commons. If that was indeed the

7 Circular 10/65 para 41.
8 *Op cit* p 512.

threat underlying para 44, it was one that many councils did not take seriously. The circular had given local authorities two-and-a-half years to submit their reorganisation plans. Some 20% of councils failed to meet that deadline, seemingly more as a result of their rejection of the legitimacy of the policy than simple inefficiency. The government's plans received a further setback in the local elections of 1967 and 1968, in which the Conservative party enjoyed considerable success,[9] and which produced a substantial increase in the number of councils hostile to the comprehensive system.

The attitude adopted by the courts continued to be one of leaving outcomes to be determined by the political process. In *Wood v Ealing London Borough Council*,[10] the High Court rejected an attempt by a group of pro-selection parents to overturn their council's reorganisation plans. Goff J confirmed that parents had no right to insist upon the retention of grammar schools:

'It has to be observed that the Act nowhere provides for grammar school education, or secondary modern education as distinct from grammar, and in my judgment . . . all that the local education authority has to provide is schools adequate in number, character and equipment for providing a full range of secondary education suitable for the number and kind of pupils for which it has to cater.'[11]

A group of parents achieved rather greater success in *Bradbury v London Borough of Enfield*,[12] when they succeeded in convincing the courts to quash both a local council's reorganisation plans and the Secretary of State's subsequent efforts to provide the council with a way round this legal obstacle. Their victory was based however only on the grounds of procedural impropriety, since both the council and the Secretary of State had displayed a complete disregard for the procedures specified by the Act. The case could in no way be seen as a judicial pronouncement on the merits of selective education.[13]

The Conservatives' local electoral successes in 1967–1968 were followed by victory at the 1970 general election. The 1970–1974 Heath government immediately withdrew Circular 10/65. Margaret Thatcher, then Secretary of State for Education,

---

9 See Butler and Sloman *op cit* pp 338–340: Gyford J *The Politics of Local Socialism* pp 24–29 (London: Allen & Unwin).

10 [1967] Ch 364.

11 Ibid, at 384. See also the comments of Donaldson J in *Lee v Secretary of State for Education and Science* (1967) 66 LGR 211 at 215: '[T]he court is not concerned with the merits of what is proposed but solely with its legality.'

12 [1967] 1 WLR 1311, CA.

13 See Buxton *op cit* pp 214–223.

explained that she disapproved of the circular, apparently because she adhered to the conventional constitutional principle which left such matters to the local electoral process. She considered that the circular had imposed an unwarranted degree of 'compulsion on democratically elected authorities'.[14] It seems unlikely that any councils were in fact coerced, and indeed the essentially bipartisan commitment to the introduction of comprehensive schooling was demonstrated by the 1970–1974 Heath government's decision to continue to approve local authority reorganisation plans.[15] Margaret Thatcher 'destroyed' rather more grammar schools than did Tony Crosland. It was not until the subsequent election of a Labour government in 1974 that the comprehensive question once again assumed a highly controversial political (and legal) status.

Tameside

The case of *Secretary of State for Education and Science v Tameside Metropolitan Borough Council*[16] arose after the Conservatives won control of Tameside council in the May 1975 elections. The Conservatives had pledged in their manifesto that they would scrap the previous Labour council's plan to switch to comprehensive schools in September 1975, and instead retain the authority's existing selective system. This policy ran counter to the preferences of the third Wilson government, which, in DES Circular 4/74, had forcefully restated its desire to see all councils adopt a selective system.

The Labour government subsequently tried to block the new council's plans, and hence de facto achieve its Circular 4/74 policy, by resorting to s 68 of the 1944 Act. The Secretary of State concluded that Tameside was acting 'unreasonably', and directed the now Conservative council to reinstate the plans formulated by its Labour predecessor. As noted above, Parliament had intended that s 68 be invoked only in exceptional circumstances. This indicates that the term 'unreasonable' was deployed in the (subsequently formulated) *Wednesbury* sense – was the decision so peculiar that it seems the decision-maker must have taken leave of her senses?

Given the acute division of opinion within both political and educational circles over the merits of comprehensive education, there would have been little scope for the DES to argue that

14 *HCD* 8 July 1970, c 688.
15 Pimlott *op cit* p 512.   16 [1977] AC 1014.

Tameside's preference for a selective system was per se 'unreason-able'. Rather the government argued this criterion was met because the main teaching unions had refused to co-operate with the new council's plans. The DES contended this would make it impossible to set up an accurate selection procedure in the two months remaining before the new school year.

The House of Lords rejected this argument. While it might be difficult for the new council to put its plans into effect, it would not have been impossible. Consequently it was not grossly unreasonable of the council to pursue this policy. Therefore the criterion set out in s 68 of the Act which empowered the Secretary of State to intervene had not arisen.

In coming to this decision, the House of Lords attached great importance to the election result. Electoral support for the Con-servative policy was considered 'vital' in establishing that the policy itself was not unreasonable. If one's starting point is a concern that local government is accountable to its voters, the House of Lords' invocation of electoral approval as a means to establish the legality of the council's plans has considerable force. However it does not seem to fit very easily with the House of Lords' earlier decision in *Roberts v Hopwood*, in which, we may recall, electoral support for Poplar's high wage policy was considered irrelevant.[17]

The obvious conclusion to be drawn from *Tameside* is that the Labour Government was acting unlawfully in trying to impose its preferences on the council. But its action would also appear to have been contrary to the long accepted principle that until such time as Parliament made a definite choice between the selective and comprehensive systems, local authorities should remain free to provide schooling in their respective areas in accordance with the wishes of the local electoral majority.

Whether or not the House of Lords was drawing upon this conventional consideration in deciding its response to the legal issue before it is difficult to decide. As we saw when we looked at the Canadian controversy in 1980, the courts have thus far held that there are no circumstances in which even the most important convention can assume legal status. Of course that does not mean that judges do not allow conventional values to tip the legal bal-ance in difficult cases. *Tameside* may be a good example of that process.[18] Whether we would regard such judicial innovation as legitimate, and against what criteria we might seek to measure its

17 We return to this issue in chapter 11.
18 As, one assumes, is *A-G v Jonathan Cape Ltd*; pp 344–345 above.

legitimacy, are much larger questions – to which we will return in chapter 11.

The Wilson government seemed unwilling to accept the pluralist implications of *Tameside's* interpretation of the 1944 Act. The Education Bill introduced to the Commons in 1976 was intended, in Wilson's words, to 'abolish selection in state education'.[19] At second reading, the then Secretary of State (Fred Mulley) suggested that the negotiatory, consensual orthodoxies of the 'national–local government system' had broken down. Seven Conservative controlled councils had bluntly refused to implement Circular 4/74:

> 'I should have preferred to deal with this by agreement rather than by legislation. But we face an impasse. We can progress no further by discussion and agreement towards our declared policy of comprehensive secondary education for all. . . . The Bill . . . will, I hope lead to a determined effort by all local education authorities . . . to bring their reorganisation to a speedy and as efficient a conclusion as possible.'[20]

Section 1 of the proposed Act would provide that councils shall:

> 'in the exercise . . . of their powers and duties relating to secondary education, have regard to the general principle that such education is to be provided only in schools where arrangements for the admission of pupils are not based (wholly or partly) on selection by reference to ability or aptitude.'

It is not clear that s 1 would have had the legal effect of abolishing selection; the notion of a 'general' rather than 'universal' principle necessarily implies the existence of exceptions to the mainstream trend. That was nevertheless how most MPs interpreted the formula at second reading.[21] The debate split on party lines. Conservative MPs expressed opposition both to the comprehensive principle per se, and to the erosion of local autonomy that the Act would seemingly impose. The latter point was perhaps best put by Paul Channon MP, who subsequently served in several of Margaret Thatcher's Cabinets:

> 'I had always understood that education was a matter for local people to decide in the light of local interests. Is [Mr Mulley] saying that the

19 Wilson H *op cit* p 189.
20 *HCD*, 4 February 1976, c 1219–1220.
21 For an exception see Norman St John Stevas, at *HCD* 4 February 1976, c 1241–1242.

Government intend to introduce the Bill to flout the democratically-expressed wishes of the parents involved?'[1]

The government won the second reading debate with a majority of 40, and the Bill became law in November 1976. The DES did not anticipate that the Act would immediately bring about a complete end to selection, nor would it impose a uniform model of non-selective education on the local authorities. Quite how much diversity would have remained is a matter for speculation. By 1977 the Labour government was in some disarray, and enforcing the Act slid down its list of priorities. As the next section suggests, it was becoming embroiled in a controversy over the geographical separation of powers in a rather different form, a controversy which eventually led to the fall of James Callaghan's Labour government.

VII. SCOTS AND WELSH DEVOLUTION

The *MacCormick v Lord Advocate*[2] litigation in the 1950s indicated that at least some of the Scots people rejected the orthodox view of the Treaty of Union that Scots MPs were simply absorbed into the English Parliament.[3] Since Scotland's population was far smaller than England's, the principle of approximate parity of constituency sizes adopted in respect of parliamentary elections since 1948 necessarily meant that Scotland sent only a small minority of MPs to the Commons.[4] Scotland's 'separateness' was to some extent recognised by the creation of a Secretary of State for Scotland in 1926, and by the existence of a Scots 'Grand Committee' in the Commons,[5] yet neither afforded Scotland any constituent political autonomy. Its Secretary was merely one member of the Cabinet; the Grand Committee merely a small fraction of MPs.

But Scots discontent was not limited solely to questions of parlia-

---

1 *HCD*, 4 February 1976, c 1222. Mr Channon apparently had a rather selective notion of local democracy. As Mr Mulley pointed out in reply, Channon had been a minister responsible for pushing the Housing Finance Act 1972 through Parliament.

2 See pp 58–59 above.

3 Dicey was perhaps the prime example of this theory. As Vernon Bogdanor notes, Dicey's analysis of Anglo-Scots relations spoke always of the *Act* (rather than the *Acts*) of Union, a linguistic sleight of hand which implicity rejects the merger theory of union; see Bogdanor V (1979) 'The English constitution and devolution' *Political Quarterly* 36–49.

4 Some 11% of MPs represent Scots constituencies.

5 See Turpin (1990) *op cit* pp 183–188.

mentary representation. Rather it expressed in an acute form a more general perception that Scotland's historical status as a 'nation', and its contemporary status as a discrete area of the United Kingdom whose people had a distinctive political and cultural identity, had been unacceptably submerged beneath a legislative and governmental structure pervasively and perpetually dominated by 'English' concerns.

Such sentiments appeared to be gaining wider support from the early 1960s onwards, when Scots (and Welsh) nationalist parties began to attract substantially increased electoral support. In response to this pressure, both the Conservative and Labour parties had indicated in the late 1960s that they would be prepared to introduce legislation creating distinctively Scots and Welsh 'national' governments. The second Wilson government established a Royal Commission (the Kilbrandon Commission) to address the question of the relationship between the various countries of the United Kingdom. Its report, published in 1973, recommended that Parliament enact potentially far-reaching schemes of 'devolution'.[6]

Neither Conservative nor Labour governments in the 1970s ever suggested that Wales or Scotland should become independent sovereign states, nor even that the United Kingdom should become a federal country like the USA. Any such proposal would of course run into the legal difficulty of the sovereignty of Parliament. In terms of strict legal theory, any grant of 'independence' that Parliament might make to Wales or Scotland (or indeed England), or any legislation that sought to reconstruct the UK's unitary state on a federal basis, would lack constituent legal status; a subsequent Parliament could at any time restore the previous arrangements. As we saw in respect of Canada, such legal niceties are frequently swept aside by the brute force of new political facts. But the political realities which shaped the Kilbrandon report offered no obvious, immediate threat to the legal structure of the constitution. They did, however, point to a significant redefinition of conventional understandings.

Kilbrandon's concept of 'devolution' was an idea quite distinct from either federalism or independence in the formal, legal sense of those terms. The idea suggests that Parliament is delegating or lending legal competence in certain areas of government activity. But it is not giving its sovereignty away, for it reserves the power

6 For a useful summary of the Commission's investigations, the varying views of its members, and its conclusions see Mackintosh J (1974) 'The report of the Royal Commission on the Constitution 1969–1973' *Parliamentary Affairs* 115–123.

to revoke or redefine the nature of the delegation at any future date. Scotland was to have an elected Assembly (often colloquially referred to as the Scottish Parliament), whose members were to be chosen through a process analgous to that used for the Commons. In technical terms, however, it would be quite inaccurate to describe a body implementing devolved powers as a legislature, or to label its 'laws' as legislation. The Scots Assembly would be an executive body, just like a local council, empowered to produce bye-laws in certain specified fields. It might indeed prove, as a matter of practical politics, to be a tier of local government unlike any other the British constitution had ever contained; but it would nevertheless depend (at least until political realities dictated otherwise) for its continued legal existence on the whim of Parliament.

The schemes of devolution ultimately enacted[7] in the Scotland Act 1978 and Wales Act 1978 were presented to the Commons by the then Prime Miniser James Callaghan as:

> 'a great constitutional change ... There will be a new settlement among the nations that constitute the United Kingdom. We shall be moving away from the highly centralised State that has characterised our system for over two and a half centuries.'[8]

Whether the Acts would mark a first step in a longer march towards significant constitutional change was an open question. But there was little in the Scotland Act itself to merit such hyperbolic language.[9] Although the government firmly rejected any suggestion that enacting its Bills would 'federalise' the constitution, it would nevertheless be the case that the more powers that the Scots and Welsh Assemblies possessed, the more defensibly one might describe the UK's new system of government (if only in the conventional sense) as federal in nature.

It is difficult to determine from the Act's text how substantial a devolution of power it would effect.[10] The powers which were clearly not devolved included all of the major issues reserved to the federal government in the United States (foreign policy, the control of military forces, the issuance of currency), but also many others which in America would be regarded as primarily state

---

7 The Bill was resolutely opposed by the Conservative party. Its Commons passage was secured because the Labour government, by then in a Commons minority, had the support of the Liberals and the Scots and Welsh nationalist parties.

8 *HCD*, 13 December 1976, c 993.

9 The Wales Act was even less radical. The discussion that follows focuses solely on the Scots legislation.

10 What follows is a much simplified and selective description of the Act.

rather than national government responsibilities (such as the electoral system, industrial strategy and aspects of labour relations and land development). Perhaps most importantly, the Assembly was not granted any tax raising powers at all, nor was it permitted to raise loans. All of its income would derive from a block grant provided by the Westminster Parliament (although the Assembly could divide that grant as it wished among the services it was responsible for providing). In one very significant sense, therefore, the Assembly would (in functional as well as formalist terms) be an 'administrative' rather than a 'governmental' body.

The scope of the Assembly's 'administrative' powers initially seemed quite extensive, but close examination of the Act reveals a very tortuous legal position. One commentator was moved to suggest that: 'The allocation of powers to the Assembly . . . is the most complex part of the Act, and one unlikely to be understood by most Assembly members and the public.'[11]

The Act's method was to outline in Part I of Schedule 10 a series of 'groups' of powers over which the Assembly would enjoy complete autonomy. These seemed very far-reaching. For example, group 2 embraced 'social welfare'; group 3 covered 'education'; group 6 encompassed 'land use and development'; and group 7 dealt with 'pollution'. However Part II of Schedule 10 then listed a great many specific functions within each group which were *not* devolved. Thus all matters relating to Universities were excluded from the education group. Similarly, all social security benefits were excluded from the social welfare group. Furthermore, Part III of Schedule 10 contained a lengthy list of powers within particular statutes which were not to be devolved. In combination, these specific exceptions could effectively negate the delegation apparently made in Part I. Thus Part III reserved so many detailed land use and development powers (group 6) to central government that it was a nonsense to suggest that the Assembly exercised such responsibilities in any meaningful form. In contrast, however, the Assembly would have virtually unfettered control of the structure and revenue raising capacity of Scots local government.

The Scotland Act came closest to an American form of federalism in the provision it made for the resolution of disputes between the Assembly and Parliament on the question of whether a Scots Bill intruded into the sphere of competence retained by the UK Parliament. Per s 19, such questions were to be referred to the

11 *Current Law Statutes Annotated 1978*, ch 51 – General Comments para d (London: Sweet and Maxwell).

Privy Council (in its judicial capacity). If the Law Lords considered the Bill ultra vires the 1978 Act, it would not be enacted into law. It need hardly be added that should central government ever have found itself in disagreement with a judicial decision on such a question, it could have invited Parliament to amend the Scotland Act to overrule the Privy Council's opinion. The retention of so many powers by Parliament (including the 'ultimate political fact' of its legal sovereignty) suggests that the Scots Assembly would initially have been little more than a glorified local authority, albeit one with 'national' geographical boundaries. The extent of its 'autonomy', would, as with local government more generally, be contingent entirely on parliamentary self-restraint. Quite how willing national government would be to tolerate (and more importantly to fund) the preferred policies of a Scots Assembly controlled by a different political party was a matter of conjecture.

No answer was ever given to that question, however, since the provisions of the Act never came into force. The Labour government had broken to some extent with the tradition of 'parliamentary government' by including in both the Scotland and Wales Act a provision that required the proposed changes to be approved by a referendum conducted among the Scots and Welsh electorates respectively before they could be implemented. (As we shall see in chapter 12, the use of referendums to ascertain the people's views on issues of constitutional significance then enjoyed a brief and controversial history.) The Acts required not simply that a majority of those voting supported devolution, but also that any such majority comprised at least 40% of the eligible electorate. The government was empowered to repeal the Act if its terms were not approved by the electorates. In Wales, on a mere 59% turn-out, 80% of voters rejected the devolution proposals. In Scotland, 55% of voters approved the change. However, since the turnout was only 64%, the 40% threshhold was not reached.[12]

The outcome of the referendums suggests that there was no great enthusiasm among the Scots or Welsh for the Labour government's proposals. Scots Nationalist MPs nevertheless saw the election result as sufficient reason to vote against the Labour government in a subsequent vote of confidence, with the result that the government resigned, Parliament was dissolved, and the first Thatcher administration was returned at the ensuing general election. The Thatcher and Major governments deployed their

---

12 See Balsom D and McAllister I (1979) 'The Scottish and Welsh devolution referenda of 1979: constitutional change and popular choice' *Parliamentary Affairs* 394–409.

majorities in the Commons and Lords to repeal the Scotland and Wales Acts, and saw no need to introduce devolution Bills of any sort, notwithstanding the fact that their share of the Scots vote in successive general elections was so small that barely a dozen of Scotland's 72 MPs were Conservatives (Table 10.2 below).

Table 10.2
General election results in Scotland 1979–1992

	1979 seats/vote	1983 seats/vote	1987 seats/vote	1992 seats/vote
Conservative	22/ 31.4%	21/ 28.4%	10/ 24.0%	11/ 25.7%
Labour	44/ 41.5%	41/ 35.1%	50/ 42.4%	49/ 39.0%
Liberal	3/ 9.0%	8/ 24.5%	9/ 19.2%	9/ 13.1%
Nationalist	2/ 18.1%	2/ 11.8%	3/ 14.0%	3/ 21.5%

Source: Butler D and Kavanagh D (1980; 1984; 1988; 1993) *The British General Election of 1979; 1983; 1987; 1992* respectively (London: Macmillan).

Throughout the 1980s, therefore, Scotland was governed by a party pursuing policies which enjoyed the support of only a small minority of the Scots people. In the 1995 local government elections, the Conservatives were unable to win a majority of seats on any Scots local authority. By this time, the Scots Nationalists were stridently committed to the creation of an independent Scots state, while the Labour and Liberal parties advocated a more extensive form of devolution (including the crucial power to levy taxation) than that proposed in the Scotland Act. The status quo was preferred only by a party which had attracted little more than 40% of the popular vote in general elections since 1979; but as we have already seen on many occasions, such minoritarian support is quite sufficient to control every level of the law-making process under the British constitution's particular form of democratic government.

CONCLUSION

It is difficult to draw firm conclusions about the constitutional position of local government in the period up to 1980. It is tempting simply to categorise central–local relations in the post-war era as a 'partnership' model,[13] in which governments of both parties adhered to a principle of constitutional morality which accepted

13 See Loughlin (1985a) *op cit.*

that elected local authorities should enjoy appreciable political freedom, and should be persuaded rather than legally compelled to follow central government preferences on those occasions when central government regarded uniformity as desirable. From this viewpoint, we might plausibly conclude that the constitution did indeed by 1975 contain a convention to the effect that legislative majorities should generally tolerate a significant, geographically defined separation of powers – that parliamentary self-restraint in deference to the preservation of political pluralism had, as a matter of 'tradition and settled practice', become a matter of fundamental moral significance.

We should however recall that there was considerable consensus between the main political parties on major issues in this period. It is not politically intolerable from central government's perspective for Parliament to maintain a legal structure which allows local councils to pursue their own preferred policies over such important issues as housing and education if those policies diverge only mildly from central preferences. But in situations where that divergence was significant, such as Clay Cross or Tameside, it is clear that central government would try to invoke its formal legal powers in an attempt to force councils to comply with its wishes. Clay Cross and Tameside were however isolated examples, and we might perhaps regard them as the legalistic exceptions which prove the partnership rule. But this conclusion is largely impressionistic, and speaks of general trends rather than absolute truths. Anthony Crosland, having returned to the opposition benches after the Wilson government's defeat at the 1970 general election, offered a more cynical explanation of ministers' attitudes towards local autonomy:

> 'On the one hand, they genuinely believe the ringing phrases they use about how local government should have more power and freedom. . . . On the other hand a Labour government hates it when Tory councils pursue education or housing policies of which it disapproves, and exactly the same is true of a Tory government with a Labour council. This ambivalence exists in everybody I know who is concerned with relations between central and local government.'[14]

In chapter 11, we will examine the constitutional role that Parliament has allocated to local government since 1980; from that time it seems that both the legal and conventional rules regulating central/local relations have undergone a profound change, in which 'ambivalence' no longer plays a major role.

14 Quoted in Bogdanor V (1976) 'Freedom in education' *Political Quarterly* 149–159 at 156.

CHAPTER ELEVEN

Local government 2: Legal authoritarianism?

The first Thatcher administration was not the first modern government to pursue monetarist economic policies fundamentally concerned with reducing public expenditure. The Heath government had done so between 1970 and 1972, as did Wilson and Callaghan's Labour administrations between 1974 and 1979 in response to an economic crisis.[1] Most areas of public expenditure, including local government spending, were cut back. The Labour governments sought to control council expenditure through the negotiatory model of central/local relations. Authorities were requested, or cajoled, or threatened to reduce their spending, but were not legally obliged to do so. Relatedly, the amount of tax revenue that a council raised was an issue left to be determined at local elections.

Nevertheless, the 'ambivalence' adverted to by Crosland swung markedly in favour of greater central control in the mid-1970s. Wilson's government had established a Committee of Inquiry (the Layfield Committee) to investigate the question of local government finance. Layfield suggested that the issue raised profound questions about the nature of democracy in modern Britain. To maintain close control over total public spending, central government would require legislation placing tight limits on local fiscal autonomy. But Parliament would thereby necessarily curtail local political pluralism. Close central control over finance and meaningful political diversity could not co-exist. A choice as to which was the more important moral value would have to be made. Layfield's preference was clear: '[T]he only way to sustain a vital local democracy is to enlarge the share of local taxation in total local revenue.'[2]

---

1 See Gamble *op cit* ch 4.
2 DoE (1976) *Report of the Committee of Inquiry into Local Government Finance* p 300 (London: HMSO; Cmnd 6453).

The Labour government appeared unwilling to accept the pluralist argument. The resulting 1977 DoE policy paper, *Local government finance*, analysed local government's role in a way which relegated localised forms of democracy almost to an afterthought.[3] One cannot know if such sentiments would have been given legislative effect had Labour won the 1979 general election. The Conservative government elected in 1979 also wished to reduce local authority spending, but for the Thatcher government tight control of local government's tax raising and expenditure plans was but one part of a more systematic attempt to restructure the constitution's conventional basis.

'Authoritarian populism' – the ideological agenda of the Thatcher governments.[4]

The first Thatcher administration rejected the Keynesian approach to economic management and extensive welfare provision favoured by previous Labour and Conservative administrations. It adhered instead to a Hayekian philosophy stressing a much reduced social and economic role for state institutions. This philosophy entailed substantial reductions in public expenditure on welfare services, in respect of many of which (as noted in chapter 10) local authorities exercised significant responsibilities and enjoyed appreciable discretion. Moreover the fiscal reductionism adopted by the Thatcher administration co-existed with a fervent belief in the moral superiority of its political ideas, and a determination to impose those moral principles on all levels of government.

This authoritarian outlook did not fit easily with the hitherto pluralist model of central/local relations. Nor did it reflect the wishes of even a small majority of the electorate. As noted at the end of chapter 10, the Thatcher governments mustered barely 30% of the popular vote in Scotland, and were clearly 'the losing party' in Wales and many parts of England.

The geographical fragmentation of support for Thatcherism was reinforced by the fact that many local authorities continued to be controlled by opposition parties which had no sympathy at all with central government's preferred policies: the Conservatives suffered further considerable losses in the local government elec-

3 See para 2.3 (London: HMSO).
4 See particularly Hall S (1983) 'The great moving right show', in Hall and Jacques *op cit.*

Table 11.1
General election results (% of vote and [seats]) by region
1979–1992

1979	Conservative	Labour	Liberal	Nationalist
Scotland	31.4 [22]	41.6 [44]	9.0 [3]	17.3 [2]
Wales	32.2 [11]	48.6 [22]	10.6 [1]	8.1 [2]
South East	51.5 [146]	31.7 [46]	15.3 [1]	———
South West	51.3 [37]	24.8 [5]	22.7 [1]	———
North West	43.7 [31]	42.6 [45]	13.0 [2]	———
West Midlands	47.1 [31]	40.1 [25]	———	———

1983	Conservative	Labour	Liberal*	Nationalist
Scotland	28.4 [21]	35.1 [41]	24.5 [8]	11.8 [2]
Wales	31.1 [14]	37.5 [20]	23.2 [2]	7.8 [2]
South East	50.4 [162]	21.2 [27]	27.3 [3]	———
South West	51.4 [44]	14.7 [1]	33.2 [3]	———
North West	40.0 [36]	36.0 [35]	23.4 [2]	———
West Midlands	45.0 [36]	31.2 [22]	23.4 ——	———

1987	Conservative	Labour	Liberal*	Nationalist
Scotland	24.0 [10]	42.4 [5]	19.3 [9]	14.0 [3]
Wales	29.5 [8]	45.1 [24]	17.9 [3]	7.3 [3]
South East	52.2 [165]	22.3 [24]	25.0 [3]	———
South West	50.6 [44]	15.9 [1]	33.0 [3]	———
North West	38.0 [34]	41.2 [36]	20.6 [3]	———
West Midlands	45.5 [36]	33.3 [22]	20.8 ——	———

1992	Conservative	Labour	Liberal	Nationalist
Scotland	25.7 [11]	39.0 [49]	13.1 [9]	21.5 [3]
Wales	28.6 [6]	49.5 [27]	12.4 [1]	8.8 [4]
South East	51.2 [154]	26.6 [38]	20.4 [1]	———
South West	47.6 [38]	19.2 [4]	31.4 [6]	———
North West	37.8 [27]	44.9 [44]	15.8 [2]	———
West Midlands	44.8 [29]	38.8 [29]	15.0 ——	———

* Includes SDP

Source: Compiled from data in Butler D and Kavanagh D (1980; 1983; 1988; 1992) *The British General Election of 1979; 1983; 1987; 1992* appendix 1 (London: Macmillan).

tions of 1980 and 1981.[5] But the limited nature of the 'consent' which 'Thatcherism' enjoyed did not persuade the government that it should moderate its wish to impose its policies on the entire

5 See Butler D, Adonis A and Travers T (1994) *Failure in British Government: the Politics of the Poll Tax* p 29 (Oxford: OUP).

Table 11.2
Local election turnout 1945–1985

Year	England	Wales	Scotland
1945	45.5%	57.7%	50.9%
1950	46.6%	51.3%	44.2%
1955	41.0%	56.0%	43.7%
1960	37.8%	44.6%	39.8%
1965	38.7%	44.5%	40.2%
1970	36.3%	48.5%	44.1%
1975	32.7%	–%	–%
1979	76.0%	76.9%	–%
1986	41.9%	40.0%	53.2%

Source: Figures extracted from Craig F *op cit* p 134.

country. For local government, this absence of governmental self-restraint had profound consequences.

The legitimacy of the Thatcher government's plans to impose its own ideological preferences on all local electorates lay partly in the argument that local authorities were not in any meaningful sense 'democratic' institutions. Turnout for local elections since 1945 was very low: it rarely rose above 50%, and in 1975 it fell to below 33% in England (Table 11.2). The atypical figures for 1979 arose because the local and general elections were held on the same day. This limited participation compares unfavourably with turnout in general elections, which averaged 70%-80% since 1945.[6]

The Thatcher administrations suggested these figures revealed a 'silent majority' of local electors who needed to be 'saved' by national government from the unrepresentative and possibly extremist views of the small minority of political activists controlling local councils.[7] Given that the Thatcher governments had themselves attracted the support of barely one-third of the national electorate, such arguments might not appear to withstand close scrutiny. One might also assume that if turnout in local elections was indeed unacceptably low, the appropriate response for central government to adopt would have been to promote measures encouraging greater participation – an obvious example being an increase in local government's powers in order to stress its political importance. However the Thatcher administrations

6 See Table 7.5.
7 See Jenkins J (1987) 'The green sheep in Colonel Gadaffi Drive' *New Society*, 9 January 1987.

rejected such arguments; instead, they chose to 'protect' local people from elected councils by substantially reducing the powers that authorities could wield.

I. FINANCIAL 'REFORM' 1: GRANT PENALTIES AND RATECAPPING

The period from 1976 onwards reversed the twentieth century trend for an increasing proportion of local government finance to come from central government grant. As Table 11.3 shows, rates became a more important source of council income during the 1980s: it is also clear that total spending by local authorities increased markedly after 1980. This trend might suggest that the Thatcher governments embraced Layfield's recommendations, and that local authorities were beginning to enjoy even greater freedom from central control, and that local electorates thus exercised even greater choice over the social and economic policies which their respective councils pursued. Initial impressions can however be misleading; a different picture emerges when we place this particular trend in a rather wider political context.

Grant penalties

The first statute to regulate central/local relations in the Thatcher era was the Local Government Planning and Land Act 1980. The

Table 11.3
Sources of local authority income (%) 1979–1989

Year	Rates	Grant	Service
1979	24.1	47.2	29.7
1980	24.5	46.7	28.8
1981	25.8	45.4	28.8
1982	27.8	41.3	31.9
1983	30.2	40.3	29.5
1984	29.4	43.5	27.1
1985	30.0	43.7	26.3
1986	36.1	43.0	20.9
1987	35.0	44.5	20.5
1988	35.3	43.9	20.8
1989	37.0	42.4	20.6

Financial years ending in the year specified.

Source: *Annual Abstract of Statistics* (1991) Table 16.18 (London: HMSO).

Act's key component was the notion of 'grant penalties'. The DoE calculated a total spending plan for each authority, apportioned between grant income, local tax through the rates, and trading services. Local councils were not legally obliged to respect the DoE's spending target. However the Act introduced a financial disincentive against non-compliance. If a council's spending exceeded the DoE's expenditure target, the DoE withdraw a specified amount of grant. This meant that ratepayers had to finance both 100% of extra expenditure *and* the resultant loss of grant.

Many councils nevertheless continued to spend at higher levels than the DoE wished. Consequently, the Local Government Finance Act 1982 increased the rate of grant withdrawal. From the government's perspective, this measure was little more successful than its predecessor. Some councils simply imposed ever-higher rates on local voters, and so received ever-lower central government grants, yet still attracted electoral approval.

Some penalised authorities also initiated judicial review proceedings to challenge expenditure targets. This strategy met with mixed results. In *R v Secretary of State for the Environment, ex p Hackney London Borough Council*,[8] the council argued that expenditure targets should be attainable; if the reductions could not be achieved without large cuts in services, surely the target must be substantively ultra vires? The court refused to be drawn into what it saw as essentially a political dispute between central and local government; this was evidently another non-justiciable issue.

However both the 1980 and 1982 legislation was poorly drafted. The Acts contained various technical loopholes which some authorities hoped to exploit. Several councils initiated successful judicial review proceedings to have particular DoE expenditure targets declared ultra vires. The Court of Appeal upheld such a claim in *Nottinghamshire County Council v Secretary of State for the Environment*, although the decision was rapidly reversed by the House of Lords.[9] In addition to finding against the council in that particular case, their Lordships indicated that they had no wish to enter this political controversy. Lord Templeman observed that judicial review was not 'just a move in an interminable game of chess'; rather than commence litigation against unfavourable DoE decisions, councils should 'bite on the bullet' and govern their

8 (1985) Times 84 LGR 32, CA.
9 [1986] AC 240.

areas within whatever financial constraints the DoE thought appropriate.[10]

Nothwithstanding the courts' evident reluctance to participate in this dispute, the DoE rapidly concluded that the grant penalties system was not very effective either in curbing council expenditure or in 'persuading' local electorates not to vote for high spending parties. Some councils overcame the threat of penalties by raising rates to such high levels that they no longer received any government grant at all. That situation presumably enhances a council's accountability to its local electorate, given that local ratepayers would pay almost the entire cost of the services their council provided. It would also seem to insulate a council from central government control; threats to withdraw grant will not work if councils receive no grant anyway. Thus the government introduced more direct methods to curb council expenditure.

Ratecapping

As suggested in chapter 10, the post-revolutionary constitution seems always to have harboured a conventional principle that Parliament would not use its sovereign legal authority to impose direct legal limits on a council's power to raise revenue through the rates. The grant penalties legislation undermined that understanding, but did not overturn it altogether. In the Rates Act 1984, the Thatcher government cast this principle aside.

The 1984 Act introduced the practice of 'ratecapping'. This simply permitted the DoE to impose a ceiling on the amount of rates revenue a council could raise. The new control was placed on income rather than expenditure. Twenty authorities were originally targeted for capping; 18 were Labour controlled.

The 'democratic' implications of ratecapping were profound; local voters wishing to choose a council providing extensive services simply could not do so, even if they wished such services to be financed through increased local taxation. They might vote for any party they chose, but their chosen councillors could raise

---

10 It should be noted that some judges displayed a similar reluctance in litigation claiming that a council's own spending plans were too high. See *R v Greater London Council, ex p Kensington and Chelsea Royal Borough* (1982) Times, 7 April: *Barrs v Bethell* [1982] Ch 294.

only that amount of revenue which central government deemed appropriate.[11]

The government had some difficulty in pushing the 1984 Act through Parliament. A few Conservative MPs, and rather more Conservative peers, felt the Act would take too much power away from local authorities and their voters. They shared the sentiments of opposition parties that local government's conventional status as an independent political organ was being too severely undermined. But with a Commons majority of 140, the government's problems in the lower house were only minor, particularly as ready resort was made to the guillotine to stifle debate.[12]

As noted in chapter 6, the Thatcher governments faced some problems in forcing their local government Bills through the Lords. Opposition, cross-bench and some Conservative peers were sufficiently alarmed by the 1984 Bill's anti-pluralist implications to mount a determined amendment campaign, which on occasion reduced the government's majority to single figures.[13] The Bill nevertheless emerged virtually unscathed from the Lords. The focus of political opposition then shifted to its implementation.

Resistance to ratecapping – legal and illegal strategies

As was the case with the Housing Finance Act 1972, some Labour councils attacked the Rates Act as constitutionally illegitimate, and resolved to refuse to apply it. They hoped that widespread defiance would trigger a constitutional crisis which would force the government to return to the conventional, fiscally pluralist model of central/local relations. As the deadline for compliance approached however, support for illegal defiance melted away. Only two councils eventually refused to abide by the Act's provisions – the latterday equivalents to Clay Cross being the London Borough of Lambeth and Liverpool city council.[14] Many Lambeth and Liverpool councillors were eventually surcharged and disqualified from office as a result of their non-compliance.

One reason for councils' flirtation with illegal resistance to

11 On the immediate background to the Bill, and for a detailed description of its mechanics, see Jackman R (1984) 'The Rates Bill: a measure of desperation' *Political Quarterly* 161–170. For a more 'economic' analysis see Wilson T (1988) 'Local freedom and central control – a question of balance', in Bailey S and Paddison R (eds) *The Reform of Local Government Finance in Britain* (London: Routledge).

12 The Thatcher administrations deployed the guillotine frequently on local government Bills; see Loughlin (1994) *op cit* at n 49.

13 See Welfare *op cit.*

14 Butler, Adonis and Travers *op cit* p 65.

ratecapping was that the Rates Act was more tightly drafted than the grant penalties legislation: there was less scope successfully to challenge DoE actions via judicial review. There was however *some* scope. And given the utter inconsistency of the ratecapping principle with conventional understandings of local government's constitutional role, it is understandable that several authorities declined to take Lord Templeman's earlier advice to 'bite the bullet' of government decisions which denied their electorates the power to vote for local services to be administered as they preferred.

Both Birmingham and Greenwich councils initiated successful judicial review proceedings against ratecapping in 1986.[15] But these proved short-lived successes. The government had by now tired of defending its policies in the courts; judicial review was a time-consuming process, in which favourable outcomes could apparently not be guaranteed. Consequently, the government began to respond to defeats in the courts by introducing retrospective legislation.

The highly unconventional constitutional character of retrospective legislation has already been adverted to on several occasions. Both the War Damage Act 1965 and the War Crimes Act 1991 provoked appreciable public controversy, and met fierce opposition during their parliamentary passage, as their terms could not be reconciled with traditional notions of the rule of law.[16] The Thatcher government saw no impediment to using retrospective legislation to curb local government's financial independence; what had previously been regarded as a presumptively 'unconstitutional' exercise of Parliament's sovereign power, to be invoked on a cross-party basis in response to extraordinary situations, had evidently become a routinised and partisan feature of government policy.[17]

Grant penalties and ratecapping comprised the first two phases of the Thatcher government's efforts to redefine conventional constitutional understandings about central/local financial relations. We address the third phase of that process below. Before doing so however, we devote some further attention to the courts'

---

15 *R v Secretary of State for the Environment, ex p Birmingham City Council* (15 April 1986); *R v Secretary of State for the Environment, ex p Greenwich London Borough Council* (17 December 1986). Neither case is reported, but both are noted in Loughlin (1994) *op cit.*

16 See pp 96–98, 211–212 and 224 respectively.

17 In much the same way, it seems, as the use of Henry VIII clauses; see pp 169–171 above.

role in determining the limits of local authorities' political and economic autonomy.

II. COLLECTIVE POLITICS AND INDIVIDUAL RIGHTS: THE JUDICIAL ROLE

A notable consequence of the grant penalty and ratecapping policies was that it became accepted as a normal aspect of central/local relations for councils to challenge the legality of government action. Between 1945 and 1980 it was rare for disagreements between central and local government to be resolved in this way.[18] Disputes were generally settled through negotiations which eventually produced acceptable compromise. After 1980, such compromises proved unattainable; and it fell to the courts to provide solutions. But the so-called 'juridification'[19] of the financial relationship between central and local government was not the only issue relating to local democracy in which the courts were embroiled.

'Fares Fair': *Bromley London Borough Council v Greater London Council* (1983)[20]

While most of the country had waited until the Local Government Act 1972 for its Victorian local government structures to be modernised, local government in London was overhauled in the mid-1960s. Many small London councils were abolished, and new larger authorities created. The London County Council was also replaced by a strategic council with limited functions for the entire capital. The 'Greater London Council' (GLC) assumed responsibility for, among other things, public transport systems, waste collection, major planning proposals and housing provision. An elected 'Inner London Education Authority' (ILEA) was also created, with wide-ranging education functions. The GLC's creation was the result of a prolonged process of negotiation, initiated by the establishment of a Royal Commission in 1957 to investigate the whole question of the capital's government. The Commission's proposals were subsequently introduced as a Bill,

18 Loughlin (1985) *op cit*; (1994) *op cit.*
19 The term is Martin Loughlin's; see (1985) *op cit.*
20 [1983] 1 AC 768, HL.

and, following substantial amendment in response to the wishes of the opposition and various local authorities, enacted in 1965.[21]

The GLC's most noteworthy policy in the 1980s attempted to shift the burden of transport provision in London away from cars towards greater use of buses, tubes, and trains. The GLC's transport role was set out in the London (Transport) Act 1969, a statute introduced by Wilson's second Labour government. Section 1 required the GLC to provide an 'economic, efficient and integrated' transport system for Greater London. The Act did not give the GLC direct control of London's bus and underground networks; rather it created a body called the London Transport Executive (LTE) to co-ordinate and manage services. Following the green light philosophy then prevailing in parliamentary circles, the 1969 Act did not specify precisely how the LTE should go about the management process; but s 7 indicated that the LTE should as far as practicable avoid making a financial loss in successive years. The Act envisaged that the LTE and the GLC would work closely together, and in particular s 3 empowered the GLC to make grants to the LTE for 'any purpose'.

At this point we might ask what 'purposes' the 1969 Parliament intended London Transport to serve. From a social democratic perspective, the system might be seen as a social service, with operating losses met through a subsidy from the ratepayer or the taxpayer. This approach could have several advantages. By encouraging people to use trains and buses rather than cars one presumably reduces traffic congestion and air pollution, speeds up journey times, reduces overcrowding on trains, and makes public transport a more pleasant and reliable way to travel to work and to leisure activities. An alternative, Hayekian view would see London Transport as a business like any other, providing a system that made an overall profit. If the LTE or GLC wanted to run loss-making routes, they would have to subsidise them through profits on other routes, not by taking subsidies from ratepayers.

Scrutiny of the Act, and of Hansard, indicates that Wilson's government was unclear about its preferences. When introducing the Bill, the minister had said that:

> 'The GLC might wish . . . the LTE to run services at a loss for social or planning reasons. It might wish to keep fares down at a time when costs are rising and there is no scope for economies. It is free to do so. But it has to bear the costs.'[1]

21 See Hampson *op cit* pp 23–26.
1 *HCD*, 17 December 1968, c 1247–1248.

But the minister also stressed that the LTE should attempt to break even. Consequently, one could find neither a legislative nor governmental answer to the crucial question of whether the GLC could use s 3 to cancel out successive deficits the LTE might incur if it ran London Transport as a 'social service' rather than as a 'business'.

In its manifesto for the 1981 GLC elections, Labour put forward a programme (called 'Fares Fair') to increase bus and tube services, and simultaneously cut fares by 25%. 'Fares Fair' would cost £120 million per year; a sum comprised of a simple £69 million operating deficit, and a £50 million loss in central government grant because the programme took the GLC over its expenditure target. The Labour group planned to raise this money by levying a special rate on all the London boroughs – all householders and businesses in Greater London would share the cost.

Labour won a majority in the GLC elections, and prepared to apply the new transport policy. However a legal challenge to Fares Fair was immediately launched by the Conservative controlled Bromley Council, a suburban London borough liable to pay the supplementary rate. The issue before the court was straightforward: what had Parliament meant when it ordered the GLC to maintain 'economic, efficient and integrated' transport services? Was London Transport a social service, heavily subsidised by London ratepayers? Or a business, whose primary concern should be to avoid operating losses? Or was there a mid-point between these extremes?

The House of Lords decided unanimously against the GLC. The majority held that s 1's reference to an 'economic' service required the GLC to ensure that the LTE ran on a break even basis. The GLC could use s 3 to provide a subsidy to make up for unforeseen losses, or to compensate for exceptional circumstances, but it was not 'economic' deliberately to adopt a s 3 subsidy policy which underwrote a long-term operating deficit. Lord Diplock adopted a slightly different argument. He considered that the argument over the first component of the policy's cost, the £69 million rating loss, was finely balanced. However he did not feel obliged to resolve this question, for the second element of the cost, the loss of £50 million of government grant, clearly breached the council's fiduciary duty to its ratepayers.

The judgments obviously owe much to the *Roberts v Hopwood* fiduciary duty doctrine. Like Poplar's councillors, the GLC Labour councillors had perhaps been guided by 'eccentric principles of socialist philanthropy' in formulating the Fares Fair policy. As in *Roberts*, the House of Lords did not consider that electoral approval had any bearing on the policy's legality. This initially seems difficult to reconcile with the *Tameside* decision. In *Tameside*, Lord Wilberforce had concluded that electoral approval for the council's selective education policy was 'vital' in establishing that the policy was not ultra vires. Yet in *Bromley*, Lord Wilberforce held that voter support 'could not confer validity' on Fares Fair.

It is difficult to see why the same judge seems to have adopted such different positions in cases which apparently present similar problems. The decisions can be distinguished in a rather formalistic way (premised on a particular reading of the separation of powers doctrine), if one assumes that the GLC's action was ultra vires because of its alleged 'illegality' rather than (as in *Tameside*) its alleged 'irrationality'. Since irrationality is a concept concerned with bizarre departures from accepted moral standards, it is difficult (but not impossible) to sustain the argument that a local electoral majority can be irrational: a widely shared opinion is unlikely to be morally outrageous. Illegality, in contrast, is a technical question, which only judges, not lay people, are competent to decide. Electoral majorities may form entirely rational opinions as to desired policy outcomes premised on a misunderstanding of the correct legal position; in such circumstances, the electorate's view is irrelevant.

While superficially attractive, that distinction may not withstand close scrutiny. As Lord Greene MR suggested in *Wednesbury*, the various grounds of review run into each other – it is quite possible for a particular action to contravene all of the *Wednesbury* principles. This raises the suspicion that a judge might classify the question before her as one of irrationality if she wished the electorate's view to prevail, and as one of illegality if she did not.[2]

There is a temptation to explain the divergent outcomes of *Tameside* and *Bromley* simply in terms of judicial bias; Tameside won because a conservative House of Lords approved of grammar schools; the GLC lost because the still conservative House of Lords did not approve of cheap bus fares. This rather simplistic political reductionism (which in effect alleges that the courts are constantly engaged in an anti-Labour conspiracy which subverts the sovereignty of Parliament, the separation of powers, and conventional models of central–local relations), has attracted some support

2 For an incisive analysis see Himsworth C (1991) 'Poll tax capping and judicial review' *Public Law* 76–92.

from authoritative commentators.[3] The argument is however difficult to sustain. Its weakness in respect of *Tameside* has already been adverted to.[4] In respect of *Bromley*, one cannot avoid the conclusion that Wilson's government presented Parliament with an ambiguous Bill, which neither house succeeded in clarifying. The Act's text lent itself to two irreconcilable interpretations; it could hardly be a source of surprise that the judiciary ultimately favoured the more fiscally conservative meaning.[5]

Nevertheless, the re-emergence of the fiduciary duty doctrine intensified the juridification process. The high profile it was afforded by *Bromley* led many councils routinely to seek counsel's opinions on the legality of their expenditure plans.[6] Yet it was not simply questions of fiscal autonomy that led local authorities to the courts in the mid-1980s.

Wheeler v Leicester City Council (1985)[7]

From 1979, the 'new urban left' grouping of Labour controlled councils[8] undertook many experimental social and economic policy initiatives directed towards reducing racial discrimination. Section 71 of the Race Relations Act 1976[9] required local authorities to promote good race relations when discharging their functions. Labour councils invoked s 71 to justify such diverse strategies as promoting ethnic minority cultural and political associations, and requiring contractors to use workforces reflecting the local population's ethnic balance.[10] Councils of all parties also took

3 See Griffith J (1985) 'Judicial decisionmaking in public law' *Public Law* 564 582; Pannick D (1984) 'The Law Lords and the needs of contemporary society' *Political Quarterly* 318–328: McAuslan P (1983) 'Administrative law, collective consumption and judicial policy' *MLR* 1–21.

4 See p 417 above.

5 This being 'conservative' with a small 'c'.

6 Bridges L et al (1987) *Legality and Local Politics* (Aldershot: Avebury).

7 [1985] AC 1054.

8 On its origins, composition and policy objectives see Gyford J (1985) *The Politics of Local Socialism* (London: George Allen and Unwin).

9 A measure introduced by a Labour government with the broad support of the then Conservative opposition.

10 See Ousley H (1984) 'Local authority race initiatives', in Boddy M and Fudge C (eds) *Local Socialism* (London: Macmillan); Hall W (1986) 'Contracts compliance at the GLC' *Local Government Studies* 17–24.

related initiatives in discharging their education functions, by developing multi-cultural and anti-racist school curricula.[11]

Notwithstanding the fact that the councils pursuing these policies had been elected by local citizens, such activities were described as 'loony leftism' by sections of the national media. Such stories were frequently entirely innaccurate; but Margaret Thatcher evidently saw them as identifying another evil against which local people required protection, insofar as she accused the ILEA of subjecting its pupils to political 'indoctrination'.[12] However one particular allegation levied at Leicester City Council did have a factual basis, and attracted the attention of the courts as well as the mass media.

During the 1970s and 1980s, political parties and pressure groups in many Commonwealth countries conducted campaigns to discourage sporting links with South Africa, which then still maintained the apartheid régime introduced in 1948.[13] That movement culminated in the 1977 Gleneagles Agreement, in which the Commonwealth member states pledged to take 'every practical step' to discourage national teams from playing South African opposition. In Britain, neither Labour nor Conservative governments considered the Agreement an appropriate instrument to incorporate into British law. In 1984, the English Rugby Football Union (ERFU) accepted (despite government disapproval) an invitation to tour South Africa. ERFU denied that it approved of apartheid, and advanced the widely held argument that the best way to hasten reform in South Africa was to maximise its people's exposure to the representatives of democratic nations.

The question of 'representatives' much concerned Leicester city council. Several members of the touring party played their club rugby for Leicester RFC. Councillors feared these players' participation might indicate that Leicester's citizens approved of apartheid. The council's ruling Labour group consequently requested the club to condemn the tour and urge its players not to partici-

---

11 On the rise and fall of curricula reform see especially Ball W, Gulam W and Troyna B (1990) 'Pragmatism or retreat? Funding policy, local government and the marginalisation of anti-racist education', in Ball W and Solomos J (eds) *Race and Local Politics* (London: Macmillan).

12 Haringey council reportedly refused to buy black dustbin bags because associating the colour black with garbage might offend people of African-Caribbean ethnicity. Similarly, Hackney Council allegedly ordered its nursery schools to sing 'Baa Baa Green Sheep' rather than 'Baa Baa Black Sheep'. Subsequent investigation suggested these stories had no sustainable base; see Jenkins (1987) *op cit.* For a full account of press coverage see Gordon P (1990) 'A dirty war: the new right and local authority anti-racism', in Ball and Solomos *op cit.*

13 See pp 50–53 above.

pate. The club stressed that it deplored apartheid, but noted that since its members were under no legal compulsion not to tour South Africa, it felt unable to act.

The council was dissatisfied with the club's response, and explored ways to register its disapproval. The club had for many years leased a council playing field. Councillors decided to terminate the club's use of the ground, even though advised by their officers that this might be unlawful since: 'the council has taken an unreasonable action against the club in response to personal decisions of members of its team over which it had no control.'[14]

The council justified its behaviour through s 71:

'The council considers it appropriate, to encourage racial harmony, to be seen publicly to distance itself from bodies who occupy an important position in the city, which may be seen to be representing the city and which do not actively discourage or condemn sporting contacts with the South African regime which discriminates and oppresses people of the same ethnic origin as a substantial proportion of Leicester's population.'[15]

The club's action to have the council's decision quashed as irrational failed at first instance. In the Court of Appeal, Ackner LJ considered that as the council's action accorded with the Gleneagles Agreement:

'It would be quite wrong to categorise as perverse the council's decision to give an outward and visible manifestation of the club's failure, indeed refusal, "to take every practical step to discourage" the tour, and in particular the participation of its members.'[16]

Supporting the appeal, Browne-Wilkinson LJ felt the case presented a conflict between 'two basic principles of a democratic society'; the council's right to conduct its operations according to its own views was counterposed to the individual's right to freedom of speech and conscience. Browne-Wilkinson LJ considered that the councillors were *'punishing'* the club for not supporting the council's views. The question therefore was whether s 71 permitted such punishment.

Browne-Wilkinson LJ rejected assertions that Leicester's wish to disassociate itself from sporting bodies linked to South Africa was *Wednesbury* unreasonable under s 71. The ban on the club was

---

14 Quoted by Lord Templeman in *Wheeler v Leicester City Council* [1985] 14 AC 1054 at 1081.
15 Affidavit evidence of the council's Chief Executive, quoted by Ackner LJ in the Court of Appeal, *ibid* at 1059.
16 *Ibid* at 1061.

nevertheless unlawful. Browne-Wilkinson LJ elaborated a tripartite hierarchy of legal authority. Since common law 'rights' were not of a positive nature, 'but an immunity from interference by others',[17] they could be modified or removed by statute. Thus far the argument conforms to orthodox interpretations of parliamentary sovereignty. However Browne-Wilkinson LJ then drew a distinction between the subordination of common law rights to 'express' and 'general' statutory control. Some common law rights were evidently sufficiently 'fundamental' to be immune from abolition through 'general' legislation. Although he did not enumerate these rights, he held that:

> 'Each individual has the right to hold and express his own views. . . . I do not consider that general words in an act of Parliament can be taken as authorising interference with these basic immunities which are the foundations of our freedom. Parliament . . . cannot be taken to have conferred such a right on others save by express words.'[18]

Promoting good race relations was merely a general power, impliedly subordinate to the individual's 'fundamental' common law 'rights'. Consequently the council's action was unlawful.

Sir George Waller found the council's action lawful through the same direct route as Ackner LJ; Browne-Wilkinson LJ had unnecessarily complicated the issue:

> 'The argument based on fundamental rights fails. Nobody is interfering with the right to express an opinion. The discouraging of rugby football players from going to play rugby in South Africa is not an interference with such a right.'[19]

The majority afforded local authorities considerable power to pursue political preferences whose effective expression depended upon winning public office. In refusing to quash the council's decision, they defined the issue as one of *political legitimacy*, to be resolved through the local electoral process. The House of Lords, in contrast, proceeded from a different premiss and held unanimously in the club's favour.

Lord Roskill found several reasons for declaring the council's action unlawful. The first was substantive unreasonableness:

> 'I greatly hesitate to differ from four learned judges on the *Wednesbury* issue, but for myself I would have been disposed respectfully to do this

---

17 *Ibid* at 1065. We return to this issue in chapter 14.
18 *Ibid* at 1063.
19 *Ibid* at 1067.

and to say that the actions of the council were unreasonable in the *Wednesbury* sense.'[20]

Lord Roskill accepted that the council would not act *Wednesbury* unreasonably if it sought to 'persuade' the club to accept its views:

'But in a field where other views can equally legitimately be held, persuasion, however powerful, must not be allowed to cross that line where it moves into the field of illegitimate pressure coupled with the threat of sanctions.'[21]

This sentiment echoed Browne-Wilkinson LJ's 'punishment' analysis. But rather than pursuing this line of thought, Lord Roskill immediately turned his attention to condemning the council's 'request' to the club as too imprecise to permit an affirmative response. He regarded this imprecision as a 'procedural impropriety' which invalidated the council's substantive decision; it was on this ground that he eventually decided the case.

Lord Templeman based his decision on wider grounds:

'My Lords, the laws of this country are not like the laws of Nazi Germany. A private individual or a private organisation cannot be obliged to display zeal in the pursuit of an object sought by a public authority and cannot be obliged to publish views dictated by a public authority.'[1]

The casual equation of the council's behaviour with that of the Hitler government is a ludicrous analogy, and does much to undermine the credibility of Templeman's opinion. In a less absurd vein, Lord Templeman accepted that the council was not bound to allow its property to be used by an organisation which contravened the spirit of the Race Relations Act 1976. He did not explain what the spirit of the 1976 Act might entail, but some further judicial guidance was promptly forthcoming.

R v Lewisham London Borough Council, ex p Shell UK Ltd (1988)

The issue before the High Court in *R v Lewisham London Borough Council, ex p Shell UK Ltd*[2] was whether s 71 empowered a council to boycott products manufactured by a company with extensive South African interests. Lewisham had sought assurances from Shell UK that the company would sever these links. When such

20 *Ibid* at 1079.
21 *Ibid* at 1078.
 1 *Ibid* at 1080.
 2 [1988] 1 All ER 938.

assurances were not given, the council decided to boycott Shell products.

Unlike Leicester, Lewisham took pains to establish that its actions were legally defensible. Councillors were apprised by their solicitors of the fiduciary duty doctrine. The council decided that the boycott would extend only so far as was financially 'feasible'. It established that alternative suppliers were available, and that the boycott's total cost would not exceed £2,000 per year. The council also sought counsel's opinion before implementing the policy. This emphasised the limits imposed by *Wheeler*, and also advised that if the council sought to justify the boycott per s 71, councillors:

> 'must be guided, not by their abhorrence of the Apartheid system in itself, but their judgement as to the effect on race relations in their Borough of taking or not taking action . . .'[3]

Given that advice, it is surprising that the letter to Shell UK in which the council announced its boycott not only stressed its wish to promote good race relations but also observed that the authority was 'keen to ensure that we are not inadvertently contributing to Apartheid via our pension fund investments and purchase of goods.'[4]

Like the rugby club in *Wheeler*, Shell responded by reiterating its abhorrence of apartheid. It also observed that disinvestment was merely one of several competing views on how to hasten South Africa's progress towards democracy. Shell subsequently sought a declaration that the boycott was ultra vires. The council's decision was variously alleged to be *Wednesbury* unreasonable; to have breached the council's fiduciary duty; to have been reached without investigation as to whether it reflected the views of local electors; and to have been motivated by a wish to punish the company and induce a change of policy.

On the *Wednesbury* issue, Neill LJ felt that the council's decision was 'very near the line', but had not crossed it; the boycott was a plausible way to promote good race relations. Nor need the council adduce evidence confirming electoral support for the decision; this was a conclusion the authority might lawfully reach 'on the basis of its own experience and perception.'[5]

In finding for Shell, Neill LJ followed *Wheeler*. He observed: 'though the scope of s 71 of the 1976 Act is wide and embraces

3 *Ibid* at 945.
4 *Ibid.*
5 *Ibid* at 952.

all the activities of the council, a council cannot use it . . . to punish a body or person who had done nothing contrary to English law'.[6] The remaining issue was therefore to determine if the boycott was a bona fide attempt to promote good race relations or a 'punishment'.

The court thus turned to the council's reasons for its decision. Neill LJ accepted that the motives underlying government action could be complex and multi-faceted. Some might be lawful, others unlawful. However the applicable legal principle was clear:

> 'W]hen . . . two reasons or purposes cannot be disentangled and one of them is bad or where, even though the reasons or purposes can be disentangled, the bad reason or purpose demonstrably exerted a substantial influence on the relevant decison the court can intefere to quash the decision.'[7]

Given the council's evidently mixed motives, Neill LJ felt bound to conclude that Lewisham's 'wish to change the Shell policy towards South Africa was inextricably mixed up with any wish to improve race relations . . . and this extraneous and impermissible purpose has the effect of vitiating the decision as a whole.'[8]

Both *Lewisham* and *Wheeler* exposed the courts to accusations of interfering with an arguably non-justiciable problem more appropriately addressed and resolved in Parliament. On this occasion, the government appeared to agree.

Section 17 of the Local Government Act 1988

The Local Government Act 1988 s 17 addressed the contract compliance initiatives at issue in *Lewisham*. Local authorities were now obliged to exercise their contractual powers 'without reference to . . . non-commercial matters . . .'. These included, *inter alia*:

'(5) (c) any involvement of . . . contractors with irrelevant fields of government policy;

...

(e) the country or territory of . . . supplies to, or the location in any country or territory of the business activities or interests of contractors;

(f) any political, industrial or sectarian affiliations or interests of contractors . . .'

Nicholas Ridley, the Environment Secretary, regarded s 17 as a necessary response to Labour councils' 'loony left' excesses:

6 *Ibid* at 951.
7 *Ibid.*
8 *Ibid* at 952.

'Although as yet only a small minority of councils go in for such posturing, the disease is spreading. Already more than 40 local authorities impose contract conditions relating to links with South Africa. Too many councilllors seem to find it more fun to play at national politics at their ratepayers' expense than to deal with the real local challenges and problems.'[9]

Ridley attached little consequence to arguments that a council's electoral accountability ensured that council activities attracted popular approval: 'ratepayers do not elect the councils; in . . . many . . . areas a very small minority of the electorate pays full rates'.[10]

III. INSTITUTIONAL AND IDEOLOGICAL REFORM

In the context of Britain's existing constitutional order, one cannot question the legality of the s 17 restrictions. Nevertheless, they add further force to the argument that the Thatcher governments had little sympathy with the pluralist, tolerant, view of local government's constitutional role. But it was by no means the most extreme example of authoritarian legislation passed in that era. That label might plausibly be attached to the Local Government Act 1985.

The abolition of the GLC and the metropolitan counties

The Local Government Act 1985 was a straightforward measure to abolish the GLC. The commitment to do this was apparently slipped into the Conservative party's 1983 election manifesto at the last moment by the Prime Minister.[11] The governmental investigations preceding the creation of the GLC had spanned several years and comprised several thousand pages of investigation and

9 Mr Ridley was convinced that 'electors did not want the council's views and posturing on national policy issues to be a surcharge on the rates, through the imposition of conditions in contracts for the provision of services'; *HCD*, 6 July 1987, cols 83–84.

10 *Ibid*, col 84. Ridley's apparent suggestion that effective voting rights should depend on an ability to pay is obviously reminiscent of the political philosophy underpinning the 1832 Reform Act, but seems inconsistent with modern notions that make voting rights contingent merely on being an adult, mentally competent citizen. As we shall see below, the idea that a citizen should have to 'pay' for the right to vote was by that time exercising considerable influence on central government.

11 Butler, Adonis and Travers *op cit* pp 37–39.

proposals. The DoE report recommending abolition, *Streamlining the cities*,[12] took two months to produce, spanned 31 pages, and involved no significant consultation with opposition parties, local authorities, or the people of London. Its recommendation was that the council should be abolished and their functions given to the London Boroughs or boards appointed by central government. The GLC was simply presumed to be an unnecessary tier of government, which added to bureaucracy without producing any worthwhile benefits.[13]

The GLC campaigned skilfully against abolition. The council hired an advertising agency to produce newspaper and billboard adverts and to conduct constant lobbying of MPs and the House of Lords. The campaign questioned the constitutional legitimacy of simply doing away with an elected local authority which represented over five million people, and on the technical efficiency of scrapping an authority which provided co-ordinated strategic services for one of the world's most important cities.

The GLC attracted considerable public support. It also seemed that some Conservative MPs and many Conservative peers would vote against the government on this issue, as they had over ratecapping. The government's abolition timetable had two parts. The Local Government (Interim Provisions) Bill 1984 proposed that the GLC elections scheduled for May 1985 would be scrapped. Arrangements for transferring the GLC's powers to new bodies would not be effective until April 1986, and would be introduced in a subsequent Bill early in 1985. Parliament was thus being asked to approve the details of abolition before debating the merits of the central question. Many peers found this offensive to their perception of the separation of powers, regarding it as a particularly stark illustration of executive dominance of the legislative process.

This procedural objection was compounded by the Bill's substantive effect. During the 11-month gap between May 1985 and April 1986, the GLC's powers would be wielded by 'interim councils' based on the various London Boroughs, which in effect would give the Conservative party majority control of powers which the GLC's electorate had bestowed on the Labour party.

The Lords inflicted a substantial defeat (191 votes to 143) on

12 (1983) Cmnd 9063 (London: HMSO).
13 For an analysis of the motives behind abolition see O'Leary B (1987) 'Why was the GLC abolished? *International Journal of Urban and Regional Research* 192–217; (1987) 'British farce, French drama and tales of two cities' *Public Administration* 369–389.

the government in committee. The government then conceded that the existing GLC councillors could remain in office until the abolition in 1986.[14] The government did not however concede on the cancellation of the 1985 elections, presumably because it feared that London's voters might use it to signify massive popular disapproval of the abolition proposal. The Lords' stance on this question did much to enhance its resurgent reputation as a valuable limb of the legislature; *The Times* hailed the government's defeat as 'a triumph for the principles of constitutionalism' and specifically for the principle of a bicameral Parliament.[15]

Upper house opposition continued when the abolition Bill itself was debated. After several narrow defeats on successive reasoned amendments, opposition peers almost 'ambushed' the Bill on Ascot Gold Cup day, when they expected many Conservative peers to be at the racecourse rather than in the House. An amendment creating an elected 'co-ordinating authority' to supervise all of the GLC's former powers was lost by only 17 votes. One commentator paints a picture of pro-government peers filibustering to delay the vote, while government whips desperately ferried backwoodsmen back from Ascot to cast their vote.[16] The episode has a comic dimension. But, in a serious vein, it wholly negated the positive image the Lords had created for itself the previous year by instead emphasising its negative capacity to provide inexpert, unthinking, partisan approval for Conservative government policy.

That the Bill was ultimately enacted virtually unscathed illustrates the fragility of conventional constitutional principles when they are opposed by a determined central government with a large Commons majority and a posse of Lords' Backwoodsmen available for crucial votes. The geographical boundaries of local government have been restructured many times before. But in the modern era, the process has not been conducted in so peremptory a way, nor on the basis of substantive terms prompting so much party political dispute and public opposition, and not without the creation of a new elected body to assume the powers of the abolished authorities.

The abolition of the capital city's elected council is perhaps the most graphic example of local government's declining constitutional significance since 1980. But it is merely one part of a more complex tapestry. The GLC abolition Bill, seen in conjunction with the previous reforms to local government finance, was described

14 See Welfare *op cit*; Shell (1992) *op cit* pp 168–173.
15 30 June 1984; quoted in Shell (1992) *op cit* p 169.
16 Welfare *op cit*.

in 1984 as the 'most determined assault on local government autonomy in recent history'.[17] It is overly simplistic to suggest that this assault was 'anti-democratic' in nature. Rather it represented the triumph of a highly centralised, authoritarian perception of minoritarian democracy over a decentralised, consensual perception of pluralist democracy. This trend raises large questions as to the adequacy of Britain's contemporary constitutional arrangements, but before turning to that issue it is appropriate to examine several other legislative innovations enacted from the mid 1980s onwards.

'Propaganda on the rates'

From the perspective of a Madisonian view of democracy, the success of the GLC's anti-abolition campaign in raising awareness both among the public and within the House of Lords as to the constitutional implications of the 1984 Bill might be seen as an example of creating 'informed consent' among the citizenry to legislative policies. However central government did not perceive the campaign in that way. Rather it was regarded as 'propaganda on the rates' – another example of extremist ideology against which local electors required central government protection.

The Local Government Act 1972 s 142 allowed local authorities to provide local people with 'information as to local government matters affecting the area'. In 1983, ILEA (then Labour controlled) had campaigned against being ratecapped with such slogans as 'Education cuts never heal' and 'What do you get if you subtract £75 million from London's education budget?'.[18] The acutely partisan nature of the issue was revealed when Conservative-controlled Westminster council challenged the legality of the publicity. In *R v Inner London Education Authority, ex p Westminster City Council*,[19] Glidewell J held that the campaign was unlawful, insofar as it was designed not simply to 'inform', but to 'persuade'.[20]

---

17 Jackman *op cit* p 161.
18 See Thompson H and Game C (1985) 'Section 137: propaganda on the rates?' *Local Government Studies* 11–18.
19 [1986] 1 All ER 19.
20 This seems a particularly stunted judicial perception of local democracy. As noted above, the House of Lords in *Wheeler* accepted that s 71 of the Race Relations Act 1976 could be deployed to 'persuade' electors to accept a council's preferences. Quite how one draws the line between informing and persuading one's audience is unclear.

Subsequently, some authorities concluded that s 137 of the Act allowed councils to spend a small proportion of their revenue on the very loosely defined concept of a cause 'which in their opinion is in the interests of their area'. Authorities which invoked s 137 to finance public opposition to government policy subsequently found themselves denounced by the then Environment Secretary for 'squandering millions on virulent propaganda campaigns'.[1]

The Local Government Bill 1985 sought to prevent councils producing any publicity 'which can reasonably be regarded as likely to affect' support for a particular political party. The Bill anticipated that the DoE would subsequently produce binding regulations spelling out the details of the prohibition. The measure amounted in effect to a denial that local authorities had any legitimate political autonomy at all. The Bill was watered down in the Lords, before being enacted as the Local Government Act 1986. Only material 'designed' to affect party political support would be forbidden, and the DoE's role would be limited to 'advising' councils of the meaning of the Act.[2]

Local government as business or politics? The Widdicombe Report.[3]

The 1986 Act was the first governmental response to the report of the Widdicombe Committee of Inquiry into the *Conduct of Local Authority Business*,[4] which the DoE had established in 1985 following the GLC abolition imbroglio. The committee's title perhaps hints at the kind of recommendations the government was hoping the report would produce – the concern apparently being more with 'business' than with 'government'. If so, the government was disappointed both by the committee's investigations and its conclusions. Widdicombe identified an important role for party politics in the local government sector, and produced a package of recommendations which would seemingly have strengthened councils' capacities to pursue distinctive political agendas.[5]

The legislation which followed the report, the Local Govern-

1 Quoted in Thompson and Game *op cit* at p 13.
2 Shell (1992) *op cit* p 170.
3 The sub-title is borrowed from McAuslan P (1987) 'The Widdicombe Report: local government business or politics' *Public Law* 154–162.
4 (1986) (London: HMSO, Cmnd 9797).
5 See Leach S (1989) 'Strengthening local democracy? the government's response to Widdicombe', in Stewart J and Stoker G (eds) *The Future of Local Government* (London: Macmillan).

ment and Housing Act 1989,[6] was however highly selective in the principles it accepted. The DoE policy statement which preceded the Act announced that the reforms were intended 'to ensure that local democracy and local accountability are substantially strengthened.'[7] Once again, however, the government chose to define 'democracy' in terms which increased the likelihood that the outcome of locally based decision-making procedures would accord with central government preferences.

Thus the Act responded to the fact that many Labour councillors were the employees of other councils by prohibiting such 'twin-tracking',[8] but refusing to accept that councillors should be paid for the tasks they performed. Relatedly, the Act created so-called 'politically restricted' posts in local authorities. Citizens employed in such jobs were not permitted to engage in such political activities as holding office in a political party, canvassing at elections, or speaking or writing in public in a way that might affect support for a political party. The Act made several other significant intrusions into local authorities' internal management processes, often by simply making provision for the DoE to issue regulations to control particular aspects of council behaviour. The Act exemplifies, as McAuslan suggests, a perception of democracy in a unitary state in which: 'insofar as local government has a role in the governance of the United Kingdom . . . it is to carry out and obey central government policies in the manner required by central government.'[9]

IV. PRIVATISING LOCAL GOVERNMENT

Forcing local government, either indirectly through ratecapping, or directly via such legislation as the LGA 1988 s 17, to conduct its activities along business lines is one method by which a government with a legislative majority can ensure that local electorates which prefer social democratic forms of government cannot vote for councils which can implement those principles. It is not however the only method. Rather than force elected councils to act like businesses, central government might simply decide to remove certain powers from the council sector altogether, and give them

6 Ganz G (1990) 'The depoliticisation of local authorities: the Local Government and Housing Act 1989, Part I' *Public Law* 224–242.
7 DoE (1988) *The Conduct of Local Authority Business* p v (London: HMSO, Cmnd 433).
8 Except in respect of teachers.
9 (1988) *op cit* pp 157–158.

to individuals or bodies who might be more likely to share central government's political predispositions. This section examines two major areas of local government activity which have been 'privatised' in this way.

Housing – individuated and collective privatisation

A corollary of councils' traditional autonomy in the area of housing mangement was that neither Parliament nor the courts granted tenants legally enforceable rights against their landlords over the way that their homes were managed. Many councils evidently thought that tenants' 'rights' were unnecessary, considering councils' 'democratic accountability . . . a sufficient safeguard against any abuses'.[10] But by 1975, it was widely accepted that council house management could often justifiably be accused of inefficiency and insensitivity to tenants' wishes.[11]

The Callaghan government's 1979 Housing Bill included a 'Tenant's Charter'.[12] The Charter limited councils' eviction powers, forbade certain restrictive tenancy conditions, and would have required authorities to establish a Tenants' Committee which was to be consulted on all aspects of housing management, including allocation policies and rent levels. The Bill fell with the Labour government in 1979.

The Tenant's Charter enacted in the Thatcher government's Housing Act 1980 superficially resembled Labour's Bill. The new legislation added a 'right to buy' for existing tenants, and replaced Tenants' Committees with a more diffuse, locally determined consultation mechanism over a limited range of issues, which excluded rents. The 1980 Act nevertheless fundamentally recast the legal basis of a council's relationship with its tenants. In granting tenants legally enforceable rights, the Thatcher government necessarily curtailed local authority autonomy, at least at the formal level. From a functionalist perspective, however, the change did not appear to have either an immediate or a substantial effect.

The Tenant's Charter in practice

A wide-ranging study of the Charter's implementation was carried out between 1980 and 1983 by the City University Housing

---

10 Cited in Lafffin M (1986) *Professionalism and Policy* p 194, n6 (Aldershot: Gower).
11 See for example Cullingworth, *op cit* pp 38–47; Merret *op cit* ch 8.
12 DoE (1977) *Housing Policy: a Consultative Document* ch 11 (London: HMSO).

Research Group (CUHRG).[13] The Tenant's Charter was introduced with several other major housing initiatives. All authorities faced the prospect of having to allocate considerable administrative resources to handling 'right to buy' sales; councils in London had the additional task of inheriting former GLC properties; and the entire local government sector was adjusting to the new financial régime created by the Local Government, Planning and Land Act. These various demands led councils to prioritise their housing management resources: CUHRG reported that many housing managers were concerned more with 'coping with these other priorities and keeping their basic activities going, than with introducing the tenants' rights.'[14]

CUHRG also criticised councils' efforts to publicise the Act. 30% of authorities simply failed to meet the October 1982 deadline for informing tenants of their new legal entitlements. However, the survey's 'most striking' result was that many authorities did not realise that the Act's provisons were part of the tenancy agreement; only 56% of authorities had incorporated the Act's security of tenure requirements into their leases.[15]

The report doubted that the Tenant's Charter had revolutionised landlord-tenant relations; '[T]he 1980 rights have had only a limited impact and in general . . . have not been widely exercised. . . . In our opinion, poor implementation by local authorities has been a major factor in this disappointing result.'[16] But in respect of the 'right to buy', a different picture emerged.

The right to buy

The Housing Act 1980's 'right to buy' entitled council tenants of three years' standing to buy their homes at a discount of 33% on their market value, with an extra 1% for each year of additional occupancy, to a 50% maximum.[17] Over a million units were sold during the 1980s.

The right to buy was a controversial policy in 1980. Some Labour councils decided they did not want to apply it: several decided to make it difficult for tenants to become owner-occupiers.[18] Antici-

13 Kay A, Legg C and Foot J (1985) *The 1980 Tenant's Rights in Practice* (London: City University).
14 *Ibid*, p 18 and p 22.
15 *Ibid*, Table 3.1.
16 *Ibid*, p 231.
17 This was subsequently increased to 70% for tenants living in flats.
18 For examples see Ascher K (1983) 'The politics of administrative opposition – council house sales and the right to buy' *Local Government Studies* 12–20.

pating Labour councils' resistance to the policy, the 1980 Act gave the DoE sweeping interventionist powers against authorities suspected of obstructing sales. Section 23 provided that where it appears to the minister that the tenants are experiencing difficulty in buying their houses, the minister may send in centrally-appointed housing commissioners to take over the sales process.[19]

Following complaints from tenants in Norwich, the minister invoked s 23 against the council. The council challenged the use of this power, arguing that it had deployed staff on other responsibilities which it was obliged to undertake and so there was nothing 'unreasonable' about the delays that tenants experienced. In *R v Secretary of State for the Environment, ex p Norwich City Council*,[20] the Court of Appeal characterised s 23 as 'draconian . . . without precedent in legislation of this nature'.[1] But whether the council's action was reasonable was not relevant. The person whose conduct was in question was the minister – was his intervention so grossly unreasonable that no reasonable minister would have acted in that way? Given that no sales at all had been completed in the first seven months it would seem difficult to categorise the minister's action in that way. His intervention was clearly a 'legal' exercise of executive power. Whether s 23 was itself a 'legitimate' exercise of legislative power is an altogether different, and more difficult question.

The right to buy has enabled many less wealthy householders to become owners, and therefore to benefit from long-term increases in property values and to escape from a paternalistic or restrictive landlord-tenant relationship. The policy's full impact on local government's role as a housing provider is however only evident when one also considers central government policies towards the building of new council housing. The Thatcher administrations placed significant restrictions on new construction. Proceeds from the right to buy exceeded nine billion pounds by 1986. But councils were permitted to spend only a fraction of those receipts on new housing. Fewer council houses were built in the 1980s than in any decade since 1920. While over one million units were sold, only 330,000 were built.[2]

---

19 An anlysis of the power and subsequent case law is provided in Loughlin (1986) *op cit* pp 104–110, n 44.

20 [1982] QB 808, [1982] 1 All ER 737. For a description and analysis of events see Malpass and Murie *op cit* pp 233–240.

1 *Ibid*, per Kerr LJ at 748.

2 I have explored this issue in greater depth in (1992a) 'Square pegs, round holes: the 'right' to council housing in the post-war era' *Journal of Law and Society* 339–364.

'Opting out' and Housing Action Trusts

Nevertheless, over 20% of the population still lived in council houses in 1988. Few of these tenants could afford to buy their homes; many lived in properties with no resale value. Consequently the DoE sought other methods further to reduce the local authority's landlord role. The Housing Act 1988 empowered tenants to 'opt out' of local authority control and 'vote' for a new, government-approved landlord.[3] Early votes indicated little tenant support for wholesale privatisation. This perhaps suggests that tenants, if not central government, continued to see councils as legitimate and desirable providers of subsidised housing.

Part III of the 1988 Act also introduced the 'Housing Action Trust' (HAT). HATs are government appointed boards which assume control of public housing and land use planning in government designated inner-city areas. HATs were to act as temporary landlords, responsible for upgrading the housing and thereafter selling it, either to current occupants or new private sector landlords. Such 'improvements' may involve demolition of existing dwellings and their replacement with retail or commercial developments. HATs attracted little support from council tenants initially. Seven estates were originally targeted for HAT schemes. By late 1990, none had voted to leave council control. Several estates subsequently chose HAT status in 1991. This was perhaps not an entirely 'free' choice, insofar as prospective HATs were offered funds for refurbishment and redevelopment not available to local authorities.[4]

'Ring-fencing' housing revenue accounts

The exclusion of rent levels from the Tenant's Charter consultation provisions means that tenants have little influence over the cost of their housing. But legislative initiatives have also reduced local authorities' traditionally loosely confined discretion. Significant reductions in DoE rent subsidies since 1980[5] compelled many councils to raise rents well above prevailing inflation rates. Tenants have been shielded from the full cost of meeting higher rents by increased housing benefit expenditure, but since housing benefit

3 Abstaining tenants are counted as *supporting* privatisation. This is a rather unusual interpretation of democratic procedure.
4 See Fast Facts (1990) 'Housing Action Trusts: an End of Term Report' *ROOF* 12 (November/December); Owens R (1991) 'If the HAT Fits' *ROOF* 17 (November/ December); Woodward R (1991) 'Mobilising opposition: the campaign against housing action trusts in Tower Hamlets' *Housing Studies* 44–56.
5 Loughlin (1985) *op cit* p 104: Malpass and Murie *op cit* pp 110–113.

is primarily a centrally determined system, the redirection of DoE subsidy has limited local authorities' previous control over rents. Councils' scope to subsidise rents from their general revenue was obviously also curbed by general DoE expenditure constraints during the 1980s.

The Local Government and Housing Act 1989 reinforced this indirect pressure by 'ring fencing' councils' housing budgets. Local authorities may no longer use their general revenue for housing purposes; council stock must run on a break even basis. This requirement far exceeds the 'balance' required in *Belcher.* Ring fencing provoked vigorous criticism from Labour and Conservative authorities. Many considered it an unwarranted, further limitation on council autonomy and a severe financial blow to tenants: 20 authorities increased rents by over 30% in 1990, with Conservative controlled Canterbury DC and South Buckinghamshire DC levying 54% and 53% rises respectively.[6]

When 'ring-fencing' is combined with compulsory sales, little new building, and the opting out proposals, it becomes clear that the constitutional legitimacy of council housing has been increasingly undermined by central government since 1980. What has traditionally been an important vehicle for councils to apply the benefits of local knowledge, political education, political pluralism, and policy innovation to the government of their respective areas has been appreciably weakened since 1980. But housing is by no means the only area of local authority responsibility to be reformed in such a way.

The Education Reform Acts

In 1947, Quentin Hogg MP (who as Lord Hailsham subsequently sat in several Thatcher Cabinets) stressed the need for cross-party consensus on education policy:

> 'Education is a matter which must be handled by statesmen on pragmatical and objective lines ... not the least valuable feature of the 1944 Education Act is that it has placed the general framework of our educational system beyond the range of party politics.'[7]

Hogg seemed to suggest that education policy was too important to be left to a political process in which outcomes may be shaped

6 See Ward M (1988) 'Priced out' *Housing* 9 (October); Warburton M and Malpass P (1991) 'Riding the rent rocket' *ROOF* 27 July/August; Fast Facts (1990) 'The top twenty percentage council rent increases 1990/91' *ROOF* 16 (July/August).
7 (1947) *The Case for Conservatism* pp 143–144 (Penguin: West Drayton).

by the transient, populist desires of a faction of 'the people'. His concern was largely allayed by the pervasively bipartisan character of British party politics in the Butskellite era. But it is a necessary feature of a consensual, negotiatory approach to policy-making that governments permit critical views to emerge. By the mid-1960s, a forceful critique of the educational consensus coalesced around a group of educators and politicians associated with the Conservative party's right wing. This ideological standpoint had three primary foci: firstly, it favoured the selective system and vehemently opposed comprehensive education: secondly, it feared that the 'traditional' concern of equipping children with adequate literacy abilities, numeracy skills and knowledge of 'British' history and culture had been sacrificed to the 'trendy' ideas of the teaching profession and DES policy-makers; and thirdly, it contended that the (allegedly always sensible) wishes of parents were being subverted by the extremist preferences of local politicians.[8]

Under Edward Heath's leadership of the Conservative party, such sentiments enjoyed little influence, even though his Education Secretary during the 1970–1974 government, Margaret Thatcher, was a right-wing sympathiser.[9] However Thatcher's emergence as party leader in 1975, and the Conservatives' general election victory in 1979, raised the prospect, in respect of local government's role in education, of a significant redefinition of conventional constitutional understandings.

The changes initiated by the first and second Thatcher governments were couched in terms of enhancing 'parental choice' within the education process. Two strands of these early reforms merit mention here; the first concerned the powers of parents to determine which school their child would attend; the second the powers of school governors.

Parental choice of school[10]

As noted in chapter 10, s 76 of the 1944 Act did not entitle parents to insist that their child attend a particular school; individual parental preferences were clearly subordinated to the council's

8 See especially Dale R (1983) 'Thatcherism and education', in Ahier J and Flude M (eds) *Contemporary Education Policy* (London: Croom Helm); 'Centre for Contemporary Cultural Studies' (1981) *Unpopular Education* pp 201–207 (London: Hutchinson).

9 For an account of Thatcher's tenure at the DES see Young *op cit* ch 6.

10 The following paragraphs draw heavily on Harris N (1993) *Law and Education: Regulation, Consumerism and the Education System* ch 5 (London: Sweet and Maxwell).

judgments as to its area's overall requirements. That emphasis was altered by the Education Act 1980, which the DES presented as a device granting parents enhanced 'rights of choice'. Section 6 provided that:

> (1) 'Every local education authority shall make arrangements for enabling the parent of a child in the area of the authority to express a preference as to the school at which he wishes education to be provided for his child . . .'.
> (2) 'It shall be the duty of a local education authority . . . to comply with any preference expressed in accordance with the arrangements.'

Section 6(3) then provided that an LEA need not comply with parental preference when to do so would 'prejudice the provision of efficient education or the efficient use of resources'.

Parents could appeal to a special tribunal (composed of LEA nominees) if the LEA did not grant their preference.[11] In the procedural sense, the admissions process was thus reconsituted on a distinctly more juridified basis. The substantive change however was perhaps less significant. The courts generally construed s 6(3) as granting LEAs substantial latitude to determine questions of efficiency.[12] Furthermore, the Act did not remove the LEA's power to decide when a school was 'full'. Thus if an LEA wished to restrict pupil numbers at particular schools to ensure that other schools still attracted sufficiently large student populations, it was free to do so.

An LEA could not however refuse to accommodate a parent's wishes because they rested on an objectionable moral basis. In *R v Cleveland County Council, ex p Commission for Racial Equality*, the Court of Appeal confirmed that s 6 obliged councils to defer to parental wishes even if the parent's motive was to place her child in an all-white school because she harboured a racist dislike of ethnic minorities.[13] The government had anticipated such segregation might occur, but did not regard it as a problem. During the Act's passage, Baroness Hooper, government spokeswoman in the Lords, commented: 'If we are offering freedom of choice

---

11 See Bull D (1980) 'School admissions: a new appeals procedure' *Journal of Social Welfare Law* 209–233.

12 *R v Greenwich London Borough Council Shadow Education Committee, ex p John Ball Primary School* (1990) 88 LGR 589, CA; *R v Governors of Bishop Challenor Roman Catholic Comprehensive Girls' School* [1992] 2 AC 182, [1992] 3 All ER 277, HL.

13 [1993] 1 FCR 597, 91 LGR 129. For analysis see Loveland I (1993) 'Racial segregation in state schools: the parent's right to choose?' *Journal of Law and Society* 341–355.

to parents, we must allow that choice to operate. If it ends up with a segregated system, then so be it.'[14]

Section 6 altered the balance of power within the school admissions process, but it did so in only a modest fashion; its impact was perhaps more symbolic than practical, inasmuch as it paved the way for more intrusive legislation. The same analysis might plausibly be made of the Act's second main innovation.

Governing bodies[15]

The Education Act 1902 had required local authorities to establish boards of 'managers' to assume responsibility for routine management decisions in schools. Councils had virtually unfettered discretion in regard to appointing managers under these provisions, which were retained in 1944. By the early 1970s, in a manner mirroring the growth of tenant discontent with the management of council housing, considerable dissatisfaction had arisen with the often remote and insensitive way in which councillors controlled school administration.

The Labour government established an inquiry to explore the question. The ensuing Taylor report[16] had recommended radical reforms to the manager system, foremost of which was a proposal that parents, teachers, pupils (in secondary schools) and the LEA should each have equal representation on management boards. Just as the first Thatcher government borrowed selectively from its Labour predecessor in adopting the 'Tenant's Charter', so it introduced a diluted version of the Taylor recommendations. The Education Act 1980 ss 1–5 renamed managers as 'Governors' and limited the LEA's appointment powers. Each governing body would henceforth be required to have two parent governors (elected by parents with children at the school) and a teacher governor.

Initial research on the new system suggested that councils and teachers rather than parents were continuing to exercise the greatest influence on governing bodies.[17] The Education (No 2) Act 1986 thus increased the level of parental representation, and also required LEAs to seek co-opted governors from the local business community. The Act dictated the relative weight which each 'interest' should have on the governing body, and ensured that

14 Quoted in the *Times Educational Supplement*, 4 December 1987.
15 Harris *op cit* pp 65–77.
16 Taylor/DES (1977) *A New Partnership for our Schools* (London: HMSO).
17 For an overview see Golby M (1993) 'Parents as school governors', in Munn P (ed) *Parents and Schools* (London: Routledge).

parents and co-opted governors would form a majority. What the Act could not of course do was ensure that parental or co-opted governors would not hold the same opinions as the local authority-appointed governors with whom they shared the school's management powers. It came as a disappointment to central government to learn that the newly structured governing bodies did not in the main see any need to reject the prevalent basic understandings about good school practice. The provisions of the 1986 Act did not come into force until 1988, but by then the government had apparently already decided that its efforts to persuade parents to accept DES orthodoxies would prove unsuccessful. More coercive measures were therefore introduced after the 1987 general election.

The Education Reform Act 1988

Margaret Thatcher's speech at the 1987 Conservative party conference returned to the hyperbolic concept of 'indoctrination' with which she had previously attacked the ILEA. This time however, it was not just the 'silent majority' of voters who needed protection from the local democratic process, but also their children:

> 'Too often our children don't get the education they need . . . that opportunity is all too often snatched fom them by hard-left education authorities and extremist teachers. Children who need to be able to count and multiply are learning anti-racist mathematics – whatever that may be. Children who need to be able to express themselves in clear English are being taught political slogans.'[18]

The empirical foundations of such beliefs were never made clear. Nevertheless, Thatcher's concerns were acted upon in several ways by the Education Reform Act 1988.[19] The Act attacked local authority autonomy in three ways: firstly by creating a new central government body, the National Curriculum Council, which exercised virtually unfettered control over the curriculum that children were taught; secondly by forcing councils to delegate the financial management of schools to schools themselves; and thirdly by enabling schools to 'opt out' altogether from local authority control.

18 Quoted in Coulby D (1989) 'From educational partnership to central control', in Bash L and Coulby D (eds) *The Education Reform Act: Competition and Control* (London: Cassell).
19 See particularly Ransom S and Thomas H (1989) 'Education reform: consumer democracy or social democracy', in Stewart and Stoker *op cit*; Raab C (1993) 'Parents and schools: what role for education authorities?', in Munn *op cit*.

The national curriculum—Section 23 of the 1944 Act had formally left the question of the curriculum that schools should teach to the discretion of the LEA. In practical terms, curriculum development and delivery exemplified the pluralist, multi-institutional approach to policy-making which characterised central–local relations in the Butskellite era. The DES exercised appreciable advisory influence on local authority behaviour, as did the universities and teacher training colleges. Relatedly, this particular facet of the 'national–local' government system left considerable leeway for individual councils to experiment with newly emergent pedagogic techniques. The DES might invoke s 68 in extreme circumstances, but, as Harris suggests, this was not regarded as a routine feature of the governmental process:

> 'central government viewed its powers to intervene in respect of deficiencies in curricular provisions by LEAs to be dangerously punitive and a matter of last resort.'[20]

It would also seem unlikely, given the court's interpretation of s 68, that the DES could have used it to exercise close control over curriculum content even if it had wished to.[1]

The Education Reform Act 1988 radically altered this position. As originally conceived, the legislation would give the Secretary of State the power to prescribe through delegated legislation the detailed contents of lessons which would fill some 90% of the school timetable.[2] Ten 'foundation' subjects were identified, within which English, mathematics and combined sciences were to serve as a core. The National Curriculum Council would draw up extremely detailed 'programmes of study' which all LEA schools would be obliged to follow. The Secretary of State would be required to refer his/her orders specifying the programmes of study to 'Curriculum Councils' for further scrutiny. These are not however 'independent' bodies, given that (per s 14) all their members are appointed by the Secretary of State. Nor (per ss 20–21), in the unlikely event of the Curriculum Councils disagreeing with the Secretary of State's proposals, is he obliged to accept any recommendations they might make.[3]

In the face of massive professional, parental and local authority opposition, the original proposals were diluted. The programmes

---

20 Harris *op cit* p 200. See also Pedley (1966) *op cit* pp 97–103.
1 See pp 414–418 above.
2 See generally Simon B (1988) *Bending the rules* ch 4 (London: Lawrence and Wishart).
3 The Councils have made several recommendations of which the Secretary of State disapproved – and which he overruled; see Harris *op cit* pp 204–205.

of study were less directive, and the precise amount of time to be devoted to foundation and core subjects was not identified. The version of the national curriculum specified in the Act neverthe-less represents a substantial centralisation of power; the legislation contains no provisions to ensure that centralised decision-making procedures take account of, still less accommodate, divergent opinions.

The government faced similar difficulties with the second limb of its curriculum reform plans – namely the introduction of mass testing of children. Test results were to be published in a form which would rank schools in so-called 'league tables'. The DES defended the initiative on the grounds that it would enable parents to make informed choices about how successfully a school was performing. Opponents of the tests suggested they were overly-simplistic, insofar as they simply measured children's abilities at a given time, without considering the abilities they possessed on entry; the results would therefore not measure the extent of children's progress during their time at the school. The advent of testing suggested that the government had concluded that schooling was no longer a service in respect of which local authori-ties would plan and implement integrated policies designed for their respective areas as a whole, but rather one which encouraged 'competition' between individual schools. As one might therefore expect, the 1988 Act contained mechanisms to ensure that 'suc-cessful' schools flourished, while those that 'failed' would wither and die.

'Open enrolment' and local management of schools[4]—The atomisation of the education service triggered by league tables was intensified by provisions in the 1988 Act which transferred former LEA func-tions, including such significant matters as the employment and dismissal of teachers, to individual schools. The extent to which the DES had embraced a 'business' ethos is neatly illustrated by the fact that the preliminary investigations on which the so-called 'local management of schools' (LMS) reforms were based were conducted not by a Royal Commission, nor by central or local government bodies, but by Coopers and Lybrand, a firm of management consultants.[5]

The Act subsequently required that decision-making powers over how to spend some 90% of the school's budget (which would

4 Harris *op cit* pp 78–82.
5 Coopers and Lybrand (1988) *Local Management of Schools* (London: Coopers and Lybrand).

necessarily include the appointment and dismissal of teachers) should be delegated to governing bodies. This significantly reduced LEA control of the school management process. The notion that it enhanced parental control is however somewhat illusory, since the governors' obligations to implement the national curriculum placed tight limits on their discretion. In effect, therefore, local management of schools amounts, indirectly, to DES management of schools. In other parts of the Act, the DES's wish to oust local authorities from school management was more clearly expressed.

'Open enrolment' coupled the parental choice provisions of the 1980 Act with the removal of the LEA's power to determine the size of each school's population. Parents would be entitled to send their child to a given school as long as it was not physically 'full'. A school was defined as 'full' only if its pupil numbers exceeded those it had in 1979 (historically a year of very high enrolment). This provision essentially removed a council's power to plan its overall admissions policies in order to achieve an acceptable balance in its overall provision.

'Opting out'—The Act also made provision for the creation of a small number of 'City Technology Colleges' (CTCs). These would be new schools, funded directly by central government (at levels which were apparently significantly higher than provided for LEA schools),[6] entirely free from any local authority control, able to select their pupils on the basis of ability, and not required to follow the national curriculum. Opponents of the measure suggested CTCs would have an indirect delegitimising effect on nearby council schools, insofar as they would 'cream off' the most able pupils and thereby depress the LEA schools' league table performance. There is so far little evidence to suggest that CTCs are having this effect. Barely a dozen had been created by 1995, which indicates that this is another initiative which has thus far had primarily symbolic rather than practical effect.

The Act's provisions on 'opting out', which mirror those available to council tenants under the Housing Act 1988, are more significant. The governors (or 20% of parents) may call for a ballot on the question of whether the school should be removed entirely from local authority control and thereafter operate as a 'Grant Maintained' (GM) school receiving its funding direct from

6 The government initially appeared to believe that CTCs would attract the bulk of their funding from private businesses. That presumption proved quite ill-founded.

central government. A simple majority of parents participating in the ballot is sufficient to trigger the change. The DES offered significant financial inducements to schools which opted out, yet by 1992 fewer than 2% had chosen to do so.[7] Despite its small size in absolute terms, the GM sector can cause severe disruption to LEA efforts to plan its overall school provision. As yet, it is unclear if the government intends to promote legislation which will force LEA schools to assume GM status. It nevertheless seems clear that the DES will continue to 'encourage' them to do so, in a process which will further undermine the legitimacy of the LEAs' role as a provider of a vitally important government service.

Conclusion—The tone of the shift in central–local relations was vividly illustrated by an episode in 1993. John Patten, the then Secretary of State for Education, made what he evidently thought was to be an unreported speech at a conference, in which he described Tim Brighouse, the Director of Birmingham's education service and a fierce critic of government policy,[8] as 'a nutter' who was not fit to be in charge of any child's schooling. Unbeknown to Patten, his comments were recorded by a parent attending the meeting, who released the tape to the national press. Brighouse subsequently sued Patten for defamation. Facing near-certain defeat in the courts, Patten settled the action for a substantial sum.

Patten was subsequently sacked from the Cabinet, but his dismissal was not accompanied by any significant shift in policy, although his successor, Gillian Shepherd, adopted a more conciliatory tone towards both local authorities and the teaching profession.[9] The Major government found itself in early 1995 facing considerable pressure and criticism from both LEAs and many governing bodies over continuing cutbacks in school funding. The focus of that discontent on the question of finance forcefully demonstrates the largely illusory nature of the 'choice' which the successive education Acts passed since 1980 have created. For neither parents, nor schools, nor local authorities possess the legal competence to provide education services whose overall costs exceed the sum which central government deems appropriate. The Thatcher and Major reforms to the education system have been concerned with curtailing ideological as well as fiscal plural-

7 For details of the process see Harris *op cit* pp 48–61, 110–112.
8 See Simon *op cit* ch 5.
9 For an outline of post-1988 developments see Harris *op cit.*

ism in the local authority sector, but it is frequently difficult to disentangle the two issues. The final section of this chapter consequently returns to questions of local government finance, but, in discussing the rise and fall of the 'poll tax', does so on the assumption that this particular episode of British constitutional history might more sensibly be seen less as an attempt to intiate reform, and more as an effort to complete an already well advanced 'revolution'.

V. FINANCIAL REFORM 2: THE COMMUNITY CHARGE[10]

By 1980, the rates had long been seen by all political parties as having several defects. Since they were levied on householders, many citizens were not legally obliged to pay them. Consequently many people were presumed to be immune from the financial consequences of voting for increased local authority spending. And since business ratepayers had no vote at all, their only way to register disapproval of council policies was to relocate – an often impractical option. A second flaw was that there was no direct link between the size of a rates bill and the services provided. Since rates were based primarily on property values, the amount a householder or business paid could depend more on the value of her house or shop than her council's spending plans. Thirdly, rates were not sensitively related to ability to pay. People could live in an expensive house but have only a limited income: the apocryphal little old lady living in her family home on a widow's pension is the obvious example. On the positive side, rates were easy to administer, and, since they were levied on properties not people, were difficult to evade.

Successive governments had sporadically tried to create an alternative local taxation system. Such measures as a local income tax or a 'head tax' on individuals had been suggested and rejected; the rates were the least of several evils. Rates reform was thus a popular but impractical political slogan. When Leader of the Opposition, Thatcher had promised her first administration would abolish the rates; that pledge was quietly forgotten.[11] Indeed, the Thatcher government concluded in 1983 that: 'rates should

---

10 I am much indebted in this section to Butler D, Adonis A and Travers T (1994) *Failure in British Government: the Politics of the Poll Tax* (Oxford: OUP). The book merits close attention, not just for its analysis of the poll tax itself, but also for the light it casts on the mechanics of the policy-making process more generally.
11 *Ibid*, p 22.

remain for the foreseeable future the main source of local revenue for local government'.[12]

But reform reappeared on the political agenda in 1986, when a DoE report, *Paying for Local Government*, recommended replacing the rates with a 'community charge' or 'poll tax'. It has been suggested that the community charge's immediate origins stem from a 1985 pamphlet (*Revising the Rating System*) published by the Adam Smith Institute, a right wing think tank.[13] However, the Thatcher Cabinet had seemingly by then become attracted to a 'poll tax'.[14] *Revising the Rating System* at most lent added impetus to an already maturing reform.

The government's volte face seems to have been triggered by the evident failure of grant penalties and rate-capping to curb the spending of Labour-controlled local authorities. The poll tax would be levied on a flat rate basis on everyone resident in a local authority area, and would thus require councils to compile a residence register. Some groups would be exempt, and there would be a limited rebate scheme for people on extremely low incomes. Local councils would set the community charge for their respective voters; central government would set a uniform rate for businesses. Under the rates, councils had set both figures. The government assumed that a flat rate, universal tax would convey to voters the true cost of electing a council providing expansive (and expensive) services. What is less clear is whether the government intended that such transparency would ensure that local electoral choices would be made on the basis of fully informed consent (in which case they would presumably have to be respected as meaningful exercises in democratic practice), or whether it hoped that opposition parties would be 'priced out' of office.

As originally conceived, the community charge would not be subject to capping. This suggests that the government was willing to give local electorates unimpeded freedom to determine their council's expenditure. However when it became apparent that many councils still proposed to finance high spending through very high community charge levels, the government introduced capping powers into the Bill.[15] Charge capping seems completely inconsistent with the principle of increased political accountability

12 DoE (1983) *Rates* p 14 (London: HMSO, Cmnd 9008).
13 Mason D (1985) *Revising the Rating System* (London: Adam Smith Institute). See Himsworth (1991) *op cit.*
14 Butler, Adonis and Travers *op cit* pp 70–72.
15 See Himsworth (1991) *op cit* for a helpful explanation.

between a council and its electorate. If a council is capped, voters who want lots of services and are prepared to pay for them cannot do so.

Furthermore, the poll tax's very nature suggests the latter objective was predominant. A flat rate tax is necessarily highly regressive – it falls with disproportionate severity on taxpayers with low incomes. One might thus expect that less affluent voters would be deterred from devoting substantial proportions of their income to council services. An income tax, in contrast, in which the percentage of tax levied rises as the taxpayer's income increases, has a progressive character, being closely corrrelated with ability to pay. As noted above, the rates were crudely progressive – one might plausibly assume that the value of one's property (generally) reflects the size of one's income.

The community charge's regressive nature seems to have led some Cabinet ministers, foremost among them Nigel Lawson, to regard it as an ill-advised venture. Leon Brittan (then Home Secretary) also voiced doubts, on the basis that compulsory registration for the tax might lead some people to 'disappear' from the electoral register to evade payment: the charge might thus be portrayed as a tax on voting. But in accordance with the unanimity limb of the convention of collective ministerial responsibility, neither Lawson nor Brittan resigned over the issue; their dissent was kept secret until they published their memoirs.

The Bill which eventually became the Local Government Finance Act 1988 met sustained opposition in the Commons and the Lords. In the Commons, the government's greatest difficulties were caused by one of its own backbenchers, Michael Mates, who moved an amendment relating the amount of poll tax levied to the individual's ability to pay. Government whips exerted considerable pressure on Mates to withdraw his amendment. When he declined to do so, they turned their attention (with more success) to Conservative MPs expressing support for it. Notwithstanding such efforts at 'persuasion', 38 Conservative MPs voted with Mates, while 13 abstained. The government, which had feared defeat on the issue, found its notional majority of 100 reduced to only 25.[16] In the Lords, a similar amendment was defeated by mobilising the backwoodsmen. While the government had a majority of 134 on the crucial vote, 140 of their supporters were non-working peers.[17] On several less significant amendments, which exempted various groups from payment, the backwoodsman could not be

16 Butler, Adonis and Travers *op cit* pp 118–121.
17 Welfare *op cit.*

relied upon, and the Lords inflicted several defeats on the government.

Local authority efforts to challenge the Act's implementation in the courts were unsuccessful.[18] However a more broadly-based political campaign against the poll tax proved considerably more effective.

A step too far? The demise of the poll tax

Many local authorities had opposed the poll tax because of its regressive nature and the threat that it posed to their political autonomy. This disquiet straddled party boundaries; Conservative councillors were among the fiercest of critics, some resigning the party whip in protest.[19] Concern among councils increased markedly when they faced the prospect of collecting the tax.

A 1987 report by the Institute of Revenues, Rating and Valuation (IRRV – the local authority finance officers' professional body) had predicted the poll tax would be twice as expensive to collect as the rates because of the difficulties of maintaining an accurate register and the ease of evasion. Non-payment rates of 20–30% were forecast for some areas.

The legislation subjected householders to fines, initially of £50, and thereafter £10 per day, for not providing details of people living in their properties. If registered individuals refused to pay the tax, a local authority could seek a 'liability order' from the magistrate's court. This allowed councils to use various enforcement measures, including attachment of earnings, deductions from welfare benefits, and distress – an archaic remedy which enables private bailiffs to seize and sell a debtor's property. Refusal to pay the poll tax could (and did) ultimately lead to imprisonment.[20] Moreover, since the legislation made a designated individual liable for his/her spouse/cohabitee's payment, it was also possible to be jailed for someone else's non-payment.[1]

---

18 See *R v Secretary of State for the Environment, ex p Hammersmith and Fulham London Borough Council* [1991] 1 AC 521, [1990] 3 All ER 589; and more generally Himsworth (1991) *op cit.*

19 'Tory councillors resign on poll tax' *The Guardian*, 21 March 1990: 'Tory poll tax feud hits the hustings' *The Guardian*, 17 April 1990: 'Tory council heads for poll tax capping' *The Guardian*, 20 December 1990.

20 See Luba J (1991) 'Legal eye' *ROOF* (January/February); Dickman J (1989) 'Debt and the poll tax' *Municipal Review* (May). In relation to the distress and the poll tax see Murdie A (1990) 'Bailiffs, Henry III, the community charge and all that' *Municipal Journal* 17–23 August. On imprisonment see 'Grantham man first to be jailed over poll tax' *The Guardian*, 17 December 1990.

1 'Husband jailed for wife's poll tax protest', *The Guardian*, 5 June 1991.

The Labour party had pledged to repeal the legislation if it won the next general election, but did not advocate non-payment. This reflected a legalistic interpretation of appropriate constitutional behaviour; how could the party present itself as an alternative government if it set a precedent for ignoring legislation, a precedent which might be used against future Labour administrations? Unofficially, however, many Labour party members (including several MPs and many councillors) supported non-payment.

Opposition to the tax was magnified by a loose-knit group called the *All Britain Anti-Poll Tax Federation.*[2] Its leaders had links to far-left parties, but the membership appeared to cross party lines and included people who had not previously been politically active. The federation's techniques included encouragement of non-payment, marches and demonstrations, offering legal assistance to individuals facing court action, and a practice called 'scum-busting', in which members formed a human barrier around the houses of people issued with liability orders, thereby preventing bailiffs from seizing goods.

Due in part to the success of the Federation's activities, the IRRV's predictions about the expense of administering the tax were borne out by data on collection costs. An Institute of Fiscal Studies report confirmed that non-payment rates reached 50% in some areas (Table 11.4 below).[3] There was initially appreciable variation in the enthusiasm with which local authorities approached the collection process. As Table 11.4 indicates, there was no obvious correlation between the number of non-payers and the number of court actions initiated. However, when faced with the income shortfall caused by mass non-payment, even some of the more radical Labour councils began to make full resort to all collection processes.[4]

The Anti-Poll Tax Federation also promoted legalistic techniques to frustrate administration of the community charge. The federation assumed that the magistrates' courts would only be able to process large numbers of poll tax cases if people did not turn up to contest them. The Federation reasoned that if citizens resisted liability orders, if only by insisting that technical require-

2 For a description of the federation's objectives by its organisers see Nally S and Dear J (1990) 'No surrender' *Municipal Journal*, 12–18 October.

3 Institute of Fiscal Studies (1990) *Local Government Finance: the 1990 Reforms* (London: IFS).

4 'Cash crisis looms after anti-poll tax campaign' *The Independent*, 14 November 1989. For an account of the London Borough of Hackney's approach see Hill D (1991) 'A job to do' *New Statesman and Society*, 8 March.

Table 11.4
Community charge collection rate January 1991

Council	Tax level	% non-payment	liability orders
Liverpool (Lab)	£449	34.0	111
Hackney (Lab)	£499	44.0	32,600
Medina (Con)	£321	0.7	1,527
Nottingham (Lab)	£390	24.0	38,225
Cardiff (Lab)	£253	6.0	14,000
Trafford (Con)	£298	6.2	9,000
Pool (Con)	£325	5.6	6,000
Wandsworth (Con)	£148	8.0	6,300

* At October 31 1990

Source: Figures extracted from data in *The Guardian*, 28 January 1991.

ments be satisfied, the courts would be overloaded, making enforcement impossible. The strategy had some successes. The Conservative-controlled Medina council tried to push 2,000 cases through the courts on 2 and 3 June 1990. But after several liability orders had been made, one defendant noticed that the council had not allowed enough time between sending its final demand for payment and commencing legal proceedings. The remaining 1,950 summonses were withdrawn. Similarly chaotic scenes occurred elsewhere.

In the abstract, such outcomes are demanded by the Diceyan principle of the rule of law. Executive bodies should not be permitted to impose losses on individuals without lawful authority. In practice, some magistrates' courts were equivocal about their role as the guardian of individual rights. On 5 July 1990, Wandsworth Council sought 200 liability orders. The first case, which was contested, lasted 90 minutes. The other 199, not contested, took ten minutes – three seconds each. Given the Act's technical complexities, it seems likely that some summonses were issued without legal authority.

The non-payment campaign continued on a grand scale, which in turn obliged local authorities to make frequent resort to the courts. The Audit Commission, a central government watchdog of local authority finance, predicted that as many as four million people might have to be taken to court in 1991 and 1992 to collect poll tax arrears.[5]

5 The Audit Commission (1990) *The Administration of the Community Charge* (London: HMSO).

Conclusion

If the story ended here, it would be difficult not to regard the poll tax policy as revealing major deficiencies in Britain's constitutional structure. One might point to minority electoral approval for the principle; to rebellions within the parliamentary Conservative party when the tax was enacted; to clear public opposition to the policy in opinion polls; to the display of more overt dissatisfaction through widespread non-payment; to very limited enthusiasm on the part of the local politicians and professional officers responsible for the tax's collection; and to a breakdown of basic legal principles in the enforcement process. Despite all this, the poll tax's legality remained beyond challenge. As previous chapters have already suggested, however, the operation of the British constitution is shaped as much, if not more, by issues concerning the legitimacy of government behaviour than questions over its legality. And from the perspective of legitimacy, the poll tax proved to have significant defects.

As chapter 13 reveals, Thatcher's fall from power in 1990 was caused in part by her attitude towards the European Community. But her association with the poll tax also made her an electoral liability for many Conservative MPs, who feared that they would lose their seats at the next general election if the tax was not removed. Unsurprisingly, therefore, Michael Heseltine's challenge to Thatcher for the party leadership in 1990 was coupled with an announcement that he would, if elected, institute a thorough review of the community charge. John Major made a similar commitment when announcing his candidacy for the leadership. His government subsequently introduced a Bill replacing the poll tax with a so-called 'council tax', based primarily on property values. While less regressive and easier to collect than its predecessor, the council tax does not indicate any resurgence of pre-Thatcherite conventions concerning local authority fiscal autonomy: the DoE retains the power to 'cap' council tax levels. Nor, as suggested above, has there as yet been any indication that the Major governments wish to restore local autonomy in such areas as housing and education policy. Notwithstanding the demise of the comunity charge, the 'partnership', pluralist model of central-local relations was by 1995 becoming evermore clearly a feature of past constitutional history rather than current constitutional practice.

CONCLUSION – FROM AMBIVALENCE TO INTOLERANCE?

It was suggested in chapter 9 that legislative self-restraint in deference to 'traditionally fundamental' political and moral principles might be the most important of Britain's constitutional conventions. There is room to dispute the precise conventional understanding of central/local relations in the modern era, but the preponderance of evidence suggests that prior to 1980 governments of both parties considered maintaining some significant simultaneous political pluralism within the overall structure of government to be an important constitutional principle.

We might argue whether that principle should be regarded as a 'convention' in the orthodox sense, but there is little scope for disagreement as to its importance in the context of modern British society. The recent history of local government suggests that the pluralist principle was ignored by the Conservative administrations which enjoyed a Commons majority from 1979 onwards. The Thatcher and Major governments' defiance of accepted conventional norms was not limited exclusively to the question of the geographical separation of powers; their ready resort to the guillotine in Commons debates,[6] Ministers' increased disinclination to accept personal responsibility for departmental failings,[7] and the creation of Next Steps Agencies within central government in respect of which ministers do not accept accountability to the Commons, also indicate a political readiness (married with a legal capacity) to flout long-established moral values.

But it is in the area of local government that (to borrow from the Duke of Wellington) 'the revolution through due process of law' wrought on the constitution since 1979 is most evident. The paradox, of course, is that the 'revolution' to which Wellington referred was intended to introduce a more sophisticated notion of popular consent to government in British society; the Thatcher and Major administrations' incremental local government revolution appears to seek quite the opposite result.

As noted in chapter 10, some contemporary commentators regarded the Municipal Corporations Act 1835 as having a more radical impact on the allocation of political power than the Great Reform Act 1832. The reasons underpinning this interpretation are not difficult to discern. Elected, multi-functional and fiscally autonomous local authorities would permit differences in political opinion to be given constant expression. Once rooted at some

6 See p 154 above.
7 See pp 365–366 and 374–376 above.

(albeit modest) point in the governmental structure, political ideologies which reject central government orthodoxies may gain a familiarity and hence legitimacy which might lead more and more of 'the people' to evaluate the merits of divergent policies and exercise their power to vote accordingly, whether at the local or national level. If the ideas which had controlled the government process were to hold sway in post-1835 society, they would do so because of their intrinsic merits, not because Parliament had granted their proponents monopolistic control over the allocation of government power. Simply put, such commentators recognised (and feared) that a powerful local government sector would prove a vital vehicle for cultivating and maintaining the informed consent of the people in a large modern democracy.

Those principles are no less valid in the context of late twentieth-century British society. Consequently, it is quite misleading to suggest that the restructuring of central-local relations enacted since 1980 has left the constitution's democratic basis unchanged simply because the electorate has remained free to return a Labour or Liberal government at successive general elections. The notion that political powers may become delegitimised through prolonged disuse has already been raised in respect of the House of Lords and the personal prerogatives of the Monarch.[8] The idea has equal force with respect to local government. In the Butskellite era, the local electoral process functioned as a perpetual 'market place of ideas',[9] within which competing political philosophies were formulated by politicians, selected by voters, tried and tested in practice, and thereafter reaffirmed or rejected according to the success they had achieved. The post-1979 reforms have reduced the scope for alternative ideas to be put into practice, thereby denying the voters power to make informed choices about party policy and ultimately undermining the process of popular consent to the government process.

The Thatcher and Major governments' efforts to deligitimise social democratic policies by preventing their implementation at the local level should, moreover, be seen in conjunction with the increase in the number of 'governmental' functions, formerly exercised by local authorities, which are now controlled by single issue, (often) non-elected bodies, whose members are frequently

8 See pp 216 and 377 above.
9 The concept is borrowed from Holmes J (of the US Supreme Court) in *Abrams v United States* 250 US 616 (1919).

appointed by government ministers.[10] It is inherent in the nature of such 'quangos'[11] that their policies are dictated by central government, not determined by local electors. The trend has led one commentator to identify 'a new magistracy' occupying more and more positions of political power.[12] The label, recalling the nature of Britain's pre-1830 local government structure, starkly conveys the highly antiquated notion of democracy which Parliament has latterly pursued.

Yet it is a profound paradox of constitutional history that just as the Thatcher and Major governments so successfully deployed their Commons' and Lords' majorities to dismantle the country's internal structures of post-war pluralism and eradicate the influence of Butskellite philosophy on the government process, so they faced increasingly formidable opposition to their ideological agenda from two hitherto unexpected quarters. Chapter 14 considers the courts' role in developing a common law doctrine of 'fundamental' rights. But firstly, chapters 12 and 13 address the more significant question of the impact on traditional constitutional understandings of Britain's membership of the European Community.

10 The National Curriculum Council, HATs, grant maintained schools and CTCs are obvious examples, as are the newly created National Health Service 'Trusts'. For further comment see McAuslan (1988) *op cit.* The Nolan Commission (see pp 327–329 above) recommended that appointments to quangos be overseen by a non-partisan body, a proposal which found little favour with Conservative MPs.

11 The acronym originally stood for 'quasi-non-governmental organisations'. A new acronym, quacgos, would perhaps be more appropriate – 'quasi-*central* government organisations'.

12 Stewart J (1993) *Defending Public Accountability* (London: Demos). See also Davies H and Stewart J (1994) *The Growth of Government by Appointment: Implications for Democracy* (Local Government Management Board: Birmingham); (1994a) 'A new agenda for local governance' *Public Money and Management* 29–36, October.

CHAPTER TWELVE

The European Economic Community 1957–1986

As chapter 2 suggested, the UK's accession to the European Economic Community[1] has markedly affected traditional constitutional understandings, especially, but not exclusively, in respect of parliamentary sovereignty. This chapter and the next will not examine developments in the EEC's institutional structure in great detail.[2] It is nevertheless essential broadly to understand the EEC's history to appreciate its importance to modern British constitutional theory and practice.

The pervasive historical theme revolves around the meaning of European 'federalism'. Madison's classical account of a federal constitution divides the ordinary structure of government both horizontally and vertically. Each governmental unit has particular powers, into which other units cannot intrude, prescribed by a higher form of law, and alterable only by a cumbersome, super-majoritarian law-making process. Federalism in its pure sense is thus a *legal* rather than *conventional* doctrine. But 'federalism', like democracy or the rule of law, may take many forms: the number and nature of governmental divisions which federal constitutions adopt vary enormously.

Nor need a federal constitution be 'democratic'. Dictatorial governments which respected a formal division of competence within the state could be federal, just as a dictatorial government

---

1 There are technically three communities, the EEC, the ECSC and Euratom, which 'merged' in 1965. These two chapters deal only with the EEC. Since the ratification of the Treaty of Maastricht in 1994, the European Economic Community (EEC) has been formally renamed the European Community (EC), and its member states also established a body known as the European Union (EU). The EC label has been in common usage since the passage of the Single European Act in 1986. This book will refer to the 'EEC' in relation to pre-1986 events, and to the 'EC' thereafter.

2 Jo Shaw's (1993) *EC Law* (London: Macmillan) is probably the best introductory text.

which announced and respected limits to its powers would satisfy a formalistic version of the rule of law. However, as we saw in discussing Madison's views on federalism as a legal rule, the conventional versions of the concept which influenced British central-local government relations between 1945 and 1975, and the Callaghan government's failed attempt to devolve governmental powers to Wales and Scotland, and Canadian provincial-central relations prior to 1982, federalism is usually adopted for a particular 'democratic' purpose; namely to enable large sections of 'the people' whose favoured party does not control the national legislature to have a significant, if subsidiary, influence on how their country is governed.

The challenge thrown up by the EEC was to what extent one could sensibly describe its objectives and structure as federal. Countries had for many years signed treaties with each other, promising to respect particular undertakings. But treaties were traditionally seen as agreements between sovereign states. They could not therefore be 'federal' in the strict sense. For constitutional lawyers, the crucial questions raised by the EEC are: firstly, how is its legal system 'different' from those created by all other treaties; secondly, what impact does this 'difference' have on its member states' constitutions; and thirdly, is that impact sufficient to demand that we now attach a new meaning to the concept of 'federal' government?

I. THE TREATY OF ROME 1: FOUNDING PRINCIPLES

The European Economic Community was created in 1957 by six countries who signed the Treaty of Rome.[3] Its immediate origins can be traced to the foundation by the same six states of the European Coal and Steel Community (ECSC) under the Treaty of Paris in 1951. The most basic concern of the founders of the ECSC was to prevent another war between France, Germany and Italy. Coal and steel were clearly an essential part of a country's war-making capacity: the ECSC was intended to integrate its member countries' coal and steel industries so closely that war between the states would become impossible. The ECSC was

---

3 These being West Germany, Italy, France, Holland, Belgium and Luxembourg. We should note at this point that the European Convention on Human Rights is legally and politically quite distinct from the EC. It has different member states, different substantive law, and its own Commission and court. The convention is discussed in chapter 14.

also motivated by a belief that co-ordinated rebuilding of these basic industries would hasten the member states' economic recovery from the devastation inflicted by World War II. More amorphously, the ECSC offered a means for Italy and Germany to demonstrate that they could function as civilised, democratic societies.

The Treaty of Rome pushed the idea of political co-operation through economic integration several steps further. The treaty's explicit objective (outlined in articles 2 and 3) was to create a 'common market' between the members of the European Economic Community. The common market would eventually require free movement of goods, workers, services, and capital across national boundaries; a common policy on agriculture; uniform rules governing competition law; and community rules regulating imports of goods from non-member states. It seems plausible that the treaty's architects envisaged that increased economic interdependence would slowly lead to some kind of political union. Winston Churchill had previously spoken approvingly of the creation of a 'United States of Europe', as a means to ensure political stability and enhance economic growth within Western Europe. Britain was not a founder member of the EEC, and quite how widely such sentiments were shared within the six original member states is a matter for speculation.

The organisation established by the Treaty of Rome was not a single country, and thus not 'federal' in the orthodox, de jure, sense. However, we have seen in previous chapters that constitutional behaviour may owe more to issues of practical politics than to legal theory. It may therefore be defensible to suggest that 'federalism' may be a de facto construct, and that specific allocations of powers between different organs of government can be of sufficient significance for us to conclude that a federal system has indeed emerged.

We will build up a fuller picture of the EC's substantive role in the next two chapters. At this introductory stage, there are five essentially procedural issues to address. These are: firstly, the various types of EEC law; secondly, the various types of law-making process within the EEC; thirdly, the status of EEC laws compared with the domestic laws of the six member states; fourthly, the ways in which EEC laws are enforced; and fifthly, the relationship between law and politics (or, to use familiar terminology, between legal and conventional rules) within the EEC's constitution.

The types of EEC law and law-making processes

It has been suggested at various points that most modern democratic societies (but not Britain's) accept the principle that their constitutions should recognise a hierarchy of laws. The more important the political value at stake, the more difficult it should be to amend it. That principle is clearly expressed within the Treaty of Rome.

The treaty itself is the original source of EEC law. It is a *constituent document*: the EEC, and all of its institutions, are bodies of limited competence; they can only do those things the treaty permits. There is no doctrine equivalent to parliamentary sovereignty available to any EEC institution. Article 236 provides for the treaty to be amended, but this entails cumbersome procedures, involving an inter-governmental conference between the signatory nations, and their unanimous support for any changes. So there was no possibility of a tyranny of a majority, or even of an overwhelming majority, concerning the basic scope of EEC law. Even tiny Luxemburg had a power of veto on treaty amendment.

The treaty's terms are however quite flexible. It is a 'traité cadre' rather than a 'traité loi': its text contains broadly-framed objectives and basic principles about institutional structures and law-making procedures, rather than precise rules detailing what the Community can do and exactly how it must do it.[4] Consequently, most EEC law is made without the need for treaty amendment. But within the treaty, there is a clear hierarchy (or perhaps more accurately, heterogeneity) of laws. Most EEC laws are made by the *Council of Ministers*, where each member state has one representative, generally the minister whose domestic responsibilities coincide with the issue the Council is addressing.[5] The Council was empowered (per *art 148*) to make laws through three types of voting system. In some areas of EEC activity, the treaty required *unanimous member state approval*. In other fields, the Council may proceed by a *qualified majority*, in which each member state's voting power is (crudely) adjusted according to its population size.

---

4 See Shaw *op cit* ch 1.

5 This would obviously mean that the personnel on the Council would constantly be changing. To enable the member states to maintain a 'permanent' presence on the Council, art 151 allowed the Council to create a Committee of Representatives to perform whatever tasks the Council thought appropriate. The body established is known by the acronym COREPER. Each state's delegation to COREPER is staffed by domestic civil servants and headed by each country's ambassador to the Community.

Thirdly, the treaty also permits some laws to be made by a *simple majority system*, which gives all member states equal weight.

These differential voting systems illustrate a theme pervading the EEC's institutional structure: namely a tension between *inter-nationalism* and *supra-nationalism*. A purely inter-national Community, in which every action required the consent of all member states, would permit short-term national interests (or temporary political pressures within a particular country) to frustrate achievement of Community policy. In contrast, too strong an emphasis on supra-national objectives and law-making processes might have dissuaded some countries from joining the EEC at all, or alternatively have convinced member states that they could not adequately protect their national interests within the Community, and would therefore have to leave it.

In crude terms, we might conclude that the more important an issue was to the national interests of member states, the more likely it was that the treaty would require unanimous voting – the most inter-national law-making process. Qualified majority voting originally weighted the member states' votes according to the following formula: Germany 4; France 4; Italy 4; Luxembourg 1; Netherlands 2; Belgium 2. Twelve votes were required to pass the law. This is a more supra-national process than unanimity, but nevertheless permitted one big state plus one other to invoke shared national interests to block integrationist legislation. Simple majority voting is clearly the most supra-national of the three processes – perhaps unsurprisingly it was rarely provided for in the EEC's initial development.

But the treaty did not envisage that the inter/supra-national balance within the Council's voting process would be static. Its framers presumed that as the EEC became more firmly established as an essential part of each member state's constitutional structures, national suspicion of supra-national sentiment would diminish, in turn permitting a gradual move from the unanimous voting system towards qualified majority and ultimately simple majority voting. Consequently, the treaty set out several phases in the Community's development (transition periods) by which certain EEC objectives were to be achieved. At the expiry of these periods, unanimous voting would be replaced with either the qualified or simple majority system. This provided an incentive for member states to reach unanimous agreement – a failure to legislate might mean a less desirable law would subsequently be imposed on a recalcitrant member. However, the complex balance of inter-national and supra-national forces within the law-making processes sketched by the treaty extends far beyond the Council's voting mechanisms. To appreciate this point, we must consider the roles of two of the Community's three other main[6] institutions; the Commission, and the Parliament.

The Commission and the Parliament

Unlike the Council, the Commission was intended to be an avowedly supra-national body. It had nine members, not more than two of whom could be nationals of the same member state. Per art 158, Commissioners were appointed for four-year terms by the common accord of the member states. One Commissioner, selected by the common accord of the member states, would serve as President of the Commission. A 'convention' emerged that member states would approve each other's nominees. The treaty did not specify how the nominations should be made. However, per art 157, Commissioners were to be 'chosen for their general competence and of indisputable independence'. This independence was presumably to be from national pressures – whether directly, or indirectly from the Council – for art 157(2) provided that Commissioners 'shall not seek or accept instructions from any Government or other body'. Per art 163, the Commission would act by a simple majority. It also adopted a principle of collective responsibility – arguments among Commissioners were not made public.[7]

Article 155 charged the Commission with various powers of promoting, implementing and monitoring measures 'with a view to ensuring the functioning and development of the Common Market'. It was also the Commission's task to introduce much of the legislation on which the Council would vote: the Council had very few powers of legislative innovation. Thus the supra/international complexities of the Council's various voting systems would be applied to measures which had themselves passed through the supra-national filter of the Commission's collective decision-making process.

The Parliament was composed of delegates chosen by each member state from their own legislatures in (crude) proportion to their population size.[8] It had very few powers. Some parts of the treaty specified that the Council had to consult the Parliament before enacting legislation, but the treaty did not compel the

---

6 Since these chapters deal with the EEC only in broad terms, its minor institutions are not examined here.

7 The 'reason' presumably being to stop the Council or member states exploiting divisions among the Commissioners.

8 Germany 36; France 36; Italy 36; Netherlands 14; Belgium 14; Luxembourg 6.

Council to take any notice of the Assembly's opinions. The Parliament also had to be consulted by the Council over the Community's budgetary process, but again, its views did not bind the Council's eventual decisions.[9]

Under art 144, the Assembly could sack the entire Commission if two-thirds of the members present so voted.[10] It could not, however, dismiss individual Commissioners, which further strengthens the presumption that the framers anticipated that the Commission should act as a collective body. The dismissal power was so crude an instrument that it was unlikely ever to be used.

The forms of EEC 'law': art 189

The treaty's sensitivity to supra and inter-national tensions is further evidenced in art 189, which empowers the EEC to produce various types of secondary legislation to fill in the gaps left by the Treaty's nature as a traité cadre. Article 189's text identified five types of 'law'. *Regulations* were to be 'binding in their entirety'. They were to have 'general application', binding not just national governments, but also citizens and companies in EEC countries. Regulations were also 'directly applicable', a concept initially taken to mean both that they assumed legal force as soon as they emerged from the EEC's law-making process, and that member states need take no steps to incorporate them into domestic law. These legal characteristics of 'universality' and 'completeness' suggest that regulations would be the most supra-national *form* of EEC legislation.

The form of *directives* made more concessions to inter-national sentiment. Article 189 provided directives would not be generally applicable, but could be addressed only to member states. Directives would bind member states, but only as to the *result* the EEC sought; the means of achieving that result would be left to each member state's discretion. Article 189 does not expressly say that directives could be directly applicable. This suggests that the Treaty would permit member states either simply to incorporate a directive verbatim into domestic law, or to 'translate' it through their own law-making processes.

---

9 Article 200 initially required the following contributions from the member states to the EC budget: Germany 28%; France 28%; Italy 28%; Belgium 7.9%; Netherlands 7.9%; Luxembourg 0.2%. It was expected that the Community would eventually be self-financing from the taxes placed on imported foreign goods; but initially, the Budget was an area of potentially significant inter-state disagreement. Perhaps anticipating this problem, art 203 provided that the Budget could be approved by a qualified majority.

10 And this comprised an absolute majority.

Decisions were to be more supra-national in character than directives. They were to bind their addressee, and were unlikely to give member states any discretion in implementation. However unlike regulations, decisions would not be generally applicable: they would bind only the individual, company, or member state to which they were addressed.[11]

The treaty's individual articles specified the type of legislation to be used for particular EEC objectives. If one links this heterogeneity with the Council's tripartite voting system and with the Commission's initiatory role and the Parliament's consultative powers, it is clear that the EEC's constitution created a very elaborate lawmaking structure, with innumerable checks and balances curbing the powers of the EEC's own institutions and of its member states.

Since that elaborate structure could be amended only by the cumbersome art 236 procedure, the EEC established a very complex separation of powers within its constitutional structure. But this separation does not comfortably correspond to orthodox British understandings of that concept. No part of the EEC was directly elected by its citizens, which clearly raises some questions as to the community's democratic base. Such electoral control as citizens exercised on EEC law-making would pass through the indirect filter of their respective government's representative on the Council of Ministers, and their governments' nominees to the Commission and Assembly. But we should resist the temptation of adopting an over-simplistic definition of democracy. For in another sense, the EEC could be seen as bolstering democratic principles, by creating the possibility that citizens of a member state who did not vote for their own government would find that other governments on the Council would more accurately reflect their own preferences on matters within the EEC's competence, and thereby block or dilute a national government's majoritarian or minoritarian preferences.

In British terms, the Commission appears to serve as the executive branch of the Community's government, but one should qualify this in several ways. It has, for example, a (very) few legislative powers, which it may exercise independently of the Council. More significantly, the Commission was (and remains) a small organisation, and consequently could not realistically be involved in the

11 Article 189 also identified two 'legislative' measures, recommendations and opinions, which, according to the text of the Treaty, were not to have binding effect.

detailed implementation of Community law. For that task, the EEC was to rely primarily on member state governments.

The EEC Parliament was obviously not comparable to Parliament in the British sense. That it was not an elected body would seem of little import, given that it had no significant powers. But this perhaps raised the longer-term question of whether the EEC should contain a powerful, directly elected legislative branch. Quite where the Parliament would stand on the supra/international axis was initially unclear. Its members' status as governmental appointees, rather than directly elected representatives, suggested it might simply reproduce inter-national tensions on the Council. But there was also the possibility that its members would form alliances according to political ideology rather than national origin, and thus gradually emerge as a truly pan-European forum. Article 138(3) required the Parliament to draw up proposals for an electoral system to choose its members. The proposals had to be approved unanimously by the Council, which seemed in no hurry to do so.[12] This is perhaps unsurprising, since endowing the Parliament with elected status may have enhanced its legitimacy in democratic terms, and thereby strengthened the case for increasing its powers, and so shifting the institutional balance within the Community firmly in a supra-national direction. In microcosm, that question in turn presented the broader issue of whether the EEC was simply another treaty among member states, or whether its laws would reach beyond intergovernmental boundaries, and attach themselves directly to 'its' citizens.

The role of the Court of Justice (ECJ)

As stressed above, the treaty is a constituent document: it was thus necessary to devise some mechanism to ensure firstly that the substance of the laws made via art 189 and the processes by which those laws were made respected the limits imposed by the treaty; and secondly that all the other activities of the EEC's institutions had a defensible legal base, either in the treaty's text, or in secondary legislation passed under its authority.

Under art 164, the ECJ was to ensure that 'in the interpretation and application of this Treaty the law is observed'. The ECJ initially had seven judges. They were (like Commissioners) to be people whose 'independence is beyond doubt', and who would be eligible

---

12 Lasok D and Bridge J (1991) *Law and Institutions of the European Communities* pp 246–253 (London: Butterworths).

for high judicial office in their own countries or were eminent legal scholars. They were appointed by common accord of the member states for six-year terms.

The treaty gave the ECJ several specific powers. Under art 173, it can review the legality of acts of the Council or Commission at the instigation of the Council, Commission or a member state. Article 173 also specified the grounds of illegality. Per art 174, the ECJ could declare illegal acts void. Articles 169–170 empowered the ECJ, if requested by the Commission or a member state respectively, to determine if a member state had breached its treaty obligations. Such a power would in itself appear rather confrontational. The potential for conflict was softened by requiring the Commission to seek a negotiated settlement before passing the matter to the ECJ, and by the absence of any measure forcing an errant state to comply with a judgment against it.

Neither is there any treaty provision empowering the ECJ to quash domestic legislation or executive action; nor, conversely, any mechanism equipping national courts to declare EEC measures contrary to the treaty. The treaty's framers envisaged that the ECJ and the domestic courts should operate as partners within the EEC legal system, performing vital but distinctive roles. The link between the ECJ and domestic courts was forged by art 177. This enabled the ECJ to give a 'preliminary ruling' on the effect of a treaty provision or secondary legislation when requested to do so by a national court hearing an action in which judgment would depend on the meaning of EEC law. Any court *might* make such a reference; reference *had* to be made by a court 'from whose decision no appeal lies under national law'. Article 177 is not an appeal procedure, whereby the ECJ overrules national courts. Such a process would have had unacceptably supra-nationalist implications. Rather art 177 interrupts domestic legal proceedings, gives national courts an authoritative interpretation of EEC law, and returns the case to the domestic arena. What neither art 177 nor any other treaty provision revealed was what should happen if the 'preliminary ruling' suggested EEC law was incompatible with domestic law.

Article 5 did however place the following duty of 'loyalty' on the member states;

'Member States shall take all . . . measures which are appropriate for ensuring the carrying out of the obligations arising out of this Treaty or resulting from the acts of the institutions of the Community. They shall facilitate the achievement of the Community's aims. . . . They shall abstain from any measures likely to jeopardise the attainment of the objectives of this Treaty.'

Such phraseology exemplifies the Treaty's nature as 'cadre' rather than 'loi'. The practical implications of art 5's grand principles could only be guessed at in 1957. By 1964, they had assumed a clearer shape.

The supremacy of EEC law: *Costa v ENEL*

The 'common market' principle demanded that EEC law have uniform impact throughout the community – there should be a 'level playing field'. If a member state could 'opt out' of EEC law and maintain its own laws in areas where the treaty gave powers to the EEC, the level playing field would be undermined. And if one member state could do this, presumably all the others could as well. This suggested that treaty provisions and EEC secondary legislation would have to take priority over inconsistent domestic laws. However, the treaty text does not expressly state that EEC measures are superior to domestic law. The doctrine of the 'supremacy' of EEC law was created by the ECJ in 1964.

Costa v ENEL[13]

Signor Costa was an Italian citizen who objected to a charge of about £1 added to his electricty bill by an Italian law. That measure seemed to conflict with EEC law. Signor Costa refused to pay the charge, claiming that EEC law overruled inconsistent domestic laws. In an oft-quoted passage, the ECJ concluded:

"The transfer by the States from their domestic legal systems to the Community legal system of rights and obligations arising under the Treaty carries with it a permanent limitation of their sovereign rights, against which a subsequent unilateral act incompatible with the concept of the community cannot prevail'.[14]

The judgment suggests that EEC membership required member states to surrender, or at least lend, some of their sovereignty to the EEC: they could no longer apply domestic laws in areas where the treaty gives powers to the EEC. This bears some resemblance to a federal system, insofar as the ECJ identified a *legal* barrier to unilateral state action in 'common market' matters. The ECJ's reference to 'permanency' is more problematic. It perhaps meant that the limitation applies while the country remained in

---

13 Case 6/64: [1964] ECR 585. (*ENEL* is an acronym for the Italian state electricity company.)
14 *Ibid*, at 593.

the EEC, not that a member state must stay in the EEC for ever. The treaty made no explicit arrangements for a country to leave the Community. That result could have been 'legally' achieved through the art 236 amendment process. But there is little doubt that the 'ultimate political fact' was that a member state could leave unilaterally if it wished. In consequence, the Treaty could not establish a truly federal system. But *Costa* stepped in that direction, as did the earlier ECJ decision in *Van Gend en Loos*.

The direct effect of EEC law 1: treaty articles

Costa seemingly answered the theoretical question of the relationship between EEC law and domestic law. But this still leaves the practical question of how supremacy was to be enforced. Articles 169–170 were an obvious mechanism. However, there would be several disadvantages to making that the only way to challenge domestic laws.[15] The first, logistical, problem is that there was only one ECJ, so it could handle only a very limited workload. Secondly, arts 169–170 only permit actions by the Commission or another member state; they do not allow litigation by individual citizens or private companies. Since the Commission and member states would constantly be co-operating with each other in the EEC's legislative process, it would be plausible to suggest that some breaches of EEC law would be 'overlooked' in order to maintain harmonious political relations. Articles 169–170 clearly do not satisfy a red light, Diceyan model of the rule of law, in which citizens may challenge the legality of government action before the 'ordinary courts of the land', nor even Jones' greenishly tinged 'meaningful day in court'. Rather, they suggest the EEC was simply an agreement between member states – a contract whose breach was actionable only by its signatories and the special agencies they created.

The ECJ rejected this interpretation. The court's initial response to the problem of enforcing EEC law was to conclude that parts of the treaty possessed a status termed 'direct effect'. Like supremacy, direct effect does not feature explicitly in the treaty: it is an ECJ creation. 'Direct effect' means that a citizen or a company in a member state can enforce her EEC rights by an action in her own country's courts. The ECJ first deployed the principle in 1962.

15 See the extremely incisive article by Paul Craig (1992) 'Once upon a time in the west: direct effect and the federalisation of EEC law' *Oxford Journal of Legal Studies* 453–479.

Van Gend en Loos[16]

Article 12 forbade member states to increase customs duties on goods imported from other EEC countries. The Netherlands subsequently redesignated certain chemicals into an already existing band, attracting a higher duty. Van Gend challenged the legality of this tax before a Dutch court, asking that the court refuse to apply the Dutch law because it amounted to a new tax contravening art 12. The Dutch court invoked art 177 to refer two questions to the ECJ. The first concerned the substantive issue of the Netherlands' government's claim that the reclassification was not a tax increase. Unsurprisingly, the ECJ decided against the Netherlands on that point.

The second, more significant issue, was the procedural question of whether the Dutch court could entertain the action at all. The Dutch government, supported by France, argued that the only way to challenge the compatibility of domestic legislation with EEC law was via art 169 and 170. This argument of course assumes that the EEC was simply an orthodox exercise in treaty-making – an agreement between member states.

The ECJ rejected this reasoning. Its brief judgment contained several radical conclusions. The Court stressed that the EEC was '*more than an agreement* which merely creates mutual obligations *between the contracting states*'. Rather, it was '*a new legal order* of international law for the benefit of which the states have limited their sovereign rights, and the subjects of which comprise not only the Member States but also their nationals'.[17] This new legal order demanded new legal procedures to protect the new legal benefits it created. To restrict legal challenges against member states art 169–170 'would remove all direct legal protection of the individual rights of [EEC] nationals'.[18] If EEC law was to be effectively enforced, the national courts would have to serve as fora where the conformity of a member state's laws with the treaty could be gauged at the instigation of individuals; only domestic courts were sufficiently numerous and proximate and familiar to citizens. As well as acting in defence of their own EEC entitlements, citizens invoking direct effect would be 'private Attorneys-General', policing member states' compliance with EEC law.

The treaty has no obvious textual basis to support the principle. The ECJ 'found' it in the treaty's 'spirit, scheme, and general wording'. *Van Gend* and *Costa* typify what is known as the 'teleologi-

16 Case 26/62: [1963] ECR 1.
17 *Ibid*, at 12.
18 *Ibid*, at para 13.

cal' or 'schematic' approach to legislative or treaty interpretation. This means that the ECJ's primary concern is with the 'effet utile' of EEC law – namely how best to ensure that the Treaty's art 3 objectives are realised. To achieve this, it will interpret EEC law in imaginative ways, and not allow itself to be bound by the treaty text.[19]

As we saw in chapter 3, such an interpretive strategy was quite foreign to then accepted principles of statutory interpretation within Britain's constitutional tradition. The closest one can come to finding a textual justification for supremacy and direct effect is art 164's command that the ECJ's constitutional role is to uphold 'the law'. The meaning of 'the law' is not further defined. One might argue that 'effet utile' is an implied term of arts 2, 3 and 5 of the treaty, and therefore part of 'the law'; but, at least to British eyes, that would have seemed a somewhat strained justification. Quite how strained, and thence how legitimate, we shall consider below.

But while *Van Gend* established a radical principle, that principle initially seemed to have limited scope. The case concerned a treaty article, rather than legislation, so one might assume that direct effect would only apply to the treaty itself, and not to art 189 measures. In addition, the ECJ stressed that a treaty article would only be directly effective if it was 'clear and unconditional'. This seemed to mean that the EEC law concerned did not require any implementing measures by the EEC itself or the member state.[20] This resembles a justiciability test – a concept we met in the British context in *GCHQ*. As noted in chapter 4, 'justiciablity' is a vague term; it would have been rash in 1962 to predict how the ECJ would use it. At its nub, of course, is the question of the location of the dividing line between law and politics. One might plausibly assume politicians and judges would draw that line in different places. As, indeed, might politicians of different countries.

Laws, conventions and 'ultimate political facts': the 'empty chair crisis' and the Luxembourg Accords

The doctrines of supremacy and direct effect evidently surprised several member state governments. *Van Gend* and *Costa* also appeared just as the supra-national acceleration built into the

---

19 See generally Brown L and Kennedy T (1994) *The Court of Justice of the European Communities* ch 14 (London: Sweet and Maxwell).
20 Ie those parts of the treaty which were 'loi' rather than 'cadre'.

treaty, in the form of a move towards greater use of majority voting in the Council's legislative process, became an imminent rather than distant reality.

For the French government, this supra-national shift represented an unacceptable surrender of national autonomy. In 1965, in what has since become known as 'the empty chair crisis', the French government simply withdrew from the Council, and declined to take part in the Community's legislative process. The French government's wish was that even in respect of issues where the treaty provided for the replacement of unanimous voting by majority processes, the Council should act only on the basis of unanimity in matters where a member state's 'vital interests' were at stake.

France's absence from the Council obviously prevented the passage of any EEC legislation requiring unanimous approval.[1] As a matter of law, the other member states could have continued to pass legislation which required only qualified majority or simple majority support. There would however have been little political point in doing so if the French government was unwilling to apply that law in France. It also seems that France's withdrawal breached art 5, which could in turn have led to an art 169 or 170 action. Again, however, this would not have been a practical course to pursue: its likely consequence would have been France's departure from the Community.

The crisis was resolved in 1966 by the so-called 'Luxembourg Accords'. These 'reforms' to the Council's voting system were not introduced via a treaty amendment per art 236. Rather they were agreed by the member states entirely outside the treaty's legal structure, and were quite inconsistent with its terms. The nub of the Accords was an agreement that the Council would not invoke qualified or simple majority procedures on matters affecting a member state's vital interests, but would delay adoption of any Commission recommendation until such time as unanimity could be achieved. The Accords did not clearly define what a 'vital' interest was; nor specify a time scale in which unanimity had to be achieved.[2]

It is tempting to see the Accords as a 'convention' in the British

---

1 Article 148(3) provides that an abstention by a member state which is actually represented in the Council does not prevent unanimity. Abstention through absence presumably does so.
2 See Nicol W (1984) 'The Luxembourg compromise' *Journal of Common Market Studies* 35–43.

sense.[3] Whether one can unproblematically apply such terminology is questionable. Yet they clearly amounted to a fundamentally important, but non-legal rule within the EEC's constitutional structure. Equally clearly, they refute the argument that the treaty initially functioned as a de facto federal construct. France's action indicated that, contrary to the ECJ's statement in *Costa*, it had not 'surrendered' its sovereignty in any meaningful sense. It also suggested that 'sovereignty' might more sensibly be regarded as a political, rather than legal concept.

Direct effect 2 – nature rather than source

The empty chair crisis did not seem to have any immediate impact on the ECJ's evidently supra-national perception of its constitutional role. We may recall that in *GCHQ* the House of Lords concluded that the amenability of a government power to full judicial review should depend on its *nature*, not on its *source*.[4] We can see a similar rationale in the ECJ's subsequent expansion of the reach of direct effect. In cases decided in the late 1960s and early 1970s, the ECJ suggested that if a provision of EEC law was 'clear and unconditional' in its nature, then its source was irrelevant to the question of its direct effect.

In *Politi*,[5] the ECJ held that if *regulations* created clearly defined individual rights, a citizen could invoke such rights before her own country's courts. The ECJ did not rely on the 'effet utile' doctrine, or any other aspect of the controversial teleological interpretive strategy. Rather it simply pointed to the text of art 189. This provided that regulations were to be 'directly applicable' in the member states. One might wonder if 'direct applicability' means the same as 'direct effect'. This is a complex legal point, but it need not detain us here, since most courts (including the ECJ) and commentators use the concepts interchangeably.[6] Notwithstanding this technical question, one can readily see why the ECJ might invoke a literalist approach to treaty interpretation: it is less controversial, from an orthodox separation of powers perspective, for the court to give a meaning to the treaty's precise

---

3 The 'reason' for it presumably being that without it France would leave the EEC, and the Community would collapse if it lost such an important member.
4 See pp 122–123 above.
5 Case 43/71: [1971] ECR 1039.
6 See Winter J (1972) 'Direct applicability and direct effect: two distinct and different concepts in Community law' *Common Market Law Review* 425–438; Pescatore P (1983) 'The doctrine of direct effect: an infant disease of Community law' *European Law Review* 155–177.

words than to conjure a legal principle from its 'spirit, scheme, and general wording'.

The treaty text was less helpful in respect of *decisions*, which are not identifed as 'directly applicable'. Nevertheless, in *Grad*, the ECJ held a decision could be directly effective. The key point the court made was that:

> 'It would be incompatible with the binding effect attributed to decisions by Article 189 to exclude in principle the possibility that persons affected may invoke that obligation [in a national court].'[7]

Nor do article 189's bare words support the proposition that *directives* have direct effect. Article 189 expressly provides that member states would have discretion in choosing how to achieve the directive's intended result, which implied that *Van Gend's* criteria of negativity, precision, and unconditionality could not apply to this type of law. Yet in *SpA SACE*,[8] the ECJ answered the question before it in distinctly teleological terms. In deciding if a directive could be directly effective: 'it is necessary to consider not only the form of the measure at issue, but also its substance and its function in the system of the Treaty'.[9] The directive at issue in *SpA SACE* identified a date by which certain (clear and unconditional) Treaty obligations had to be fulfilled. The court held that once that time limit expired, the directive's 'result' element became binding on the member states to which it was addressed. If that result met the criteria of unconditionality and certainty, it could be directly effective. It did not matter that its source was a directive rather than a regulation or a treaty article.

Cases like *Grad* and *SpA SACE* further illustrate the ECJ's teleological approach to its task. As well as confirming the 'nature not source' test, *SpA SACE* demonstrated the 'nature' a law must have to be directly effective was not fixed, since the 'result to be achieved' there required *positive* action by the member states (ie abolishing all customs duties) rather than simply as in *Van Gend*, the *negative* restraint of not introducing new customs duties.

The overall thrust of the ECJ's early decisions on the constitutional impact of EEC membership suggested that if a member state found its own constitution incompatible with its EEC obligations, the only 'legal' remedies available were to have new EEC legislation enacted or have the treaty itself amended. Such sentiments are obviously consistent with the ECJ's concern to enhance

---

7 Case 9/70: [1970] ECR 825.
8 Case 33/70: [1970] ECR 1213.
9 *Ibid*, at 1233.

community law's effet utile; but for Germany's Constitutional Court, they seemed too radical a step.

Domestic disquiet 1: *Internationale Handelsgesellschaft*

The treaty's text contained few references to human rights issues. Nor, unlike its member states, was the EEC a signatory to the European Convention on Human Rights. Article 119 prohibited gender discrimination in employment, while art 7 prohibited discrimination based on national origins. However such 'fundamental rights' as freedom of speech, freedom of assembly, or the prohibition of racial discrimination did not feature in the treaty's text. Given the EEC's initially limited 'common market' focus, the omission is unsurprising: the Community was not (initially) competent in 'political' matters. For countries whose constitutions safeguarded basic political values from their own legislatures or governments, this was a worrisome lacuna, as some EEC powers might cut across their own 'fundamental rights'. *Costa* implied that even the lowliest EC law enjoyed a higher legal status than a member state's fundamental constitutional laws whenever those two laws were inconsistent. The matter came to a head in the 1970 *Internationale Handelsgesellschaft* litigation.

The case threw up a conflict between an EEC regulation controlling flour exports, and individual rights protected in Germany's 'Basic Law'. A Frankfurt court refused to enforce the regulations because it considered them 'unconstitutional' under German law. In an art 177 reference, the Frankfurt court asked if it could do so.[10] The ECJ's response was forthright:

> 'The validity of a Community measure or its effect within a Member State cannot be affected by allegations that it runs counter to either fundamental rights as formulated by the Constitution of that State or the principle of a national constitutional structure'.[11]

The ECJ softened its judgment by observing that 'the law' it was charged to uphold by Article 164 included respect for fundamental human rights, implying it would invalidate per art 173 any EEC measure transgressing such principles. This in itself is an innovative conclusion. It has an obvious *political* basis; member states would be unlikely to remain in a Community in which other members could require them (through majority voting) to enforce

10 [1972] CMLR 177.
11 [1970] ECR 1125 para 3.

laws violating their basic constitutional values. As such, it was an essential part of the effet utile strategy. But its legal roots are obscure; and even assuming the ECJ maintained this commitment, it was not clear against what criteria the EEC's own 'fundamental human rights' would be measured.

When the case returned to Germany, it was argued before the Federal Constitutional Court.[12] That court accepted the ECJ's opinion that the regulations did not in fact offend against Germany's Basic Law. But, more importantly, it refused to accept the ECJ's conclusion that any EEC law automatically took precedence over any domestic law. The Constitutional Court claimed it retained the power to evaluate EEC laws against Germany's Basic Law, clearly implying it would not allow inferior German courts to give automatic priority to EEC laws until the 'fundamental human rights' principle was firmly established within the EEC's own constitutional order.

By the early 1970s, therefore, it seemed that innovations contained in the treaty's text, though significant in themselves, only partially revealed the impact of EEC membership on the member states' own constitutional systems. The Luxembourg Accords and *Internationale Handelsgesellschaft* indicated that the treaty's legal rules might on occasion give way to a member state's governmental or judicial intransigence, while the ECJ's teleological dynamism indicated that new legal rules would always be emerging without any need for treaty amendment. The EEC's constitution was, in many senses, an unstable and unpredictable legal construct. How fully this point was understood by domestic proponents of British membership is far from clear.

II. UNITED KINGDOM ACCESSION

Britain tried to join the EEC twice during the 1960s. However new states could only be admitted with the consent of all the existing members, and on both occasions the French government vetoed British entry. Harold Macmillan regarded membership as a central element of his government's foreign and economic policy, and had assigned Edward Heath the task of negotiating acceptable terms of entry. Macmillan and Heath were however thwarted by de Gaulle's firm belief that British entry would lead to Anglo-American domination of the Community.[13] The Labour party at

12 [1974] 2 CMLR 540.
13 See Horne *op cit* pp 444–451.

that time opposed entry; its then leader, Hugh Gaitskell, suggested membership would mean 'the end of a thousand years of history' of Britain as a sovereign state. Gaitskell's historical sense was obviously somewhat bizarre, but although a significant minority of Labour MPs favoured accession, most (including the next leader, Harold Wilson) then shared his sentiments.[14] Wilson subsequently changed his mind, and his government (supported by many Conservative MPs and opposed by 35 Labour backbenchers) applied for entry in 1967. This too was vetoed by de Gaulle.

British opponents drew on two substantial political arguments against accession. The first related to Britain's world role. Opponents of EEC entry felt that Britain should align itself with the Commonwealth countries and the USA, linking those nations to the EEC, rather than risk merging into a 'European super-state'. The second argument focused on 'sovereignty'. The principles of supremacy and direct effect alarmed many British politicians. This faction feared that some of Parliament's powers would be irretrievably lost to Community institutions. Opponents of entry argued that such a transfer of political power was undesirable. But they also argued that it was constitutionally impossible for Britain to honour the obligations EEC membership entailed. We need here to recall two key elements of Diceyan theory: that Parliament cannot bind itself or its successors; and that no British court is competent to say that a statute is unconstitutional.

If we translate *Costa* into orthodox British constitutional language, we seem to say that Parliament could no longer pass legislation inconsistent with EEC law: that any Parliament which incorporated the treaty into British law would bind itself and its successors not to breach EEC law in the future. Direct effect is equally problematic. If Parliament enacted a statute which contradicted a directly effective EEC provision, but which did not also withdraw Britain from the Community, a British court would have to refuse to apply that statute. Thus, the courts, via the medium of EEC law, would have a higher constitutional status than Parliament on EEC matters. Furthermore, the ECJ's teleological approach to treaty and legislative interpretation was incompatible with British courts' more literalist tradition; EEC membership would thus demand that the constitution abandon its traditional approach to the separation of powers.

14 Pimlott *op cit* pp 245–248; Jenkins R (1991) *A Life at the Centre* pp 144–146 (London: Pan).

EEC membership and parliamentary sovereignty: the legislators' views – and their votes

With the benefit of hindsight, the earliest efforts of British commentators to analyse the potential impact of EEC membership on the British constitution appear woefully inadequate.[15] By the late 1960s, such analyses were becoming more sophisticated. Professor deSmith produced a prescient article in 1971,[16] identifying the EEC as 'an inchoate functional federation', which while not initially a federal state, was likely to evolve in a direction demanding the 'pooling' of sovereignty.[17] deSmith suggested national sovereignty need not be abandoned if the UK acceded to the treaty, since it might always withdraw from the Community. Nevertheless, he also presumed (in terms reminiscent of Wade's seminal analysis of parliamentary sovereignty) that 'full recognition of the hierarchical superiority of Community law would entail a revolution in legal thought'.[18] deSmith expected that a 'reformulation' of traditional understandings would be sufficient to deal with the likely eventuality of unintended conflicts between EEC and domestic law, and that such reformulation might be achieved by the simple expedient of the domestic courts presuming that Parliament never intended to legislate in breach of EEC law and interpreting domestic legislation accordingly.

The courts' traditional approach to international law would be an inadequate device for these purposes. We saw in chapter 2 that unincorporated treaties have no binding force in domestic law. However, that does not mean they are entirely without legal effect. British courts will assume that Parliament does not intend accidentally to legislate in breach of the government's treaty obligations. Thus in circumstances where a statute's phraseology could bear more than one meaning, the courts will choose whichever meaning best corresponds to the international obligations. Similarly, if a treaty has been incorporated into domestic law, subsequent statutes will be construed, insofar as their language is ambiguous, in a manner consistent with the obligations enacted in the incorporating statute. This interpretive technique would be of no assistance when a later statute expressly repealed or was impliedly

---

15 For example Keenan P (1962) 'Some legal consequences of Britain's entry into the European Common Market' *Public Law* 327–343.

16 deSmith S (1971) 'The constitution and the Common Market: a tentative appraisal' 34 *MLR* 21 597–614. Interestingly, the article made no reference at all to *Van Gend.*

17 *Ibid*, at pp 597 and 614.

18 *Ibid*, at p 613.

irreconcilable with the incorporating legislation. It would also seem incompatible with the ECJ's characterisation of the treaty as a 'new legal order', quite unlike other international law.

Professor Wade recommended more radical steps. He suggested either that a standard clause be inserted into every domestic statute enacted after accession, providing that the legislation took effect subject to the supremacy of EEC law. Alternatively, Parliament might annually enact (with retrospective effect) a statute reaffirming the supremacy principle.[19]

Successive governments remained unconvinced of the need for such measures. Harold Wilson's 1966–1970 Labour government had made the extraordinary suggestion that all EEC measures would take effect in the United Kingdom as delegated legislation,[20] an analysis which betokens the subordinacy rather than supremacy of Community law. Edward Heath's 1970–1974 administration, which eventually secured the UK's accession, seemed similarly confused. The government boldly stated that while it would introduce a Bill to incorporate the treaty into domestic law, 'there is no question of any erosion of essential national sovereignty'.[1] The distinction between 'essential' and (presumably) 'non-essential' sovereignty is a novel one, and was replaced when the aforesaid Bill was before the Commons by a different but equally legally nonsensical proposition. MPs were informed by a government spokesman that while the Bill would ensure that directly applicable EEC law: 'ought to prevail over future Acts of Parliament insofar as they might be inconsistent with them. . . . nothing in this Bill abridges the ultimate sovereignty of Parliament'. What might happen to Parliament's penultimate or ante-penultimate sovereignty (whatever those strange creatures might be) was unclear! Neither of the main parties seemed willing to accept that it was either desirable or possible to entrench the supremacy principle. The 1967 government had indeed seemed to accept the inevitability of the orthodox Diceyan perspective, observing that if the UK was to honour its EEC obligations: 'Parliament would have to refrain from passing fresh legislation inconsistent with [Community] law.[2]

---

19 (1972) 'Sovereignty and the European Communities' 88 *LQR* 1–5. For a survey of other contemporaneous suggestions see Trinadade F (1972) 'Parliamentary Sovereignty and the primacy of community law' 35 *MLR* 375–402.
20 (1967) *Legal and Constitutional Implications of United Kingdom Membership of the European Communities* para 22 (London: HMSO Cmnd 3301).
1 (1971) *The United Kingdom and the European Communities* para 29 (London: HMSO Cmnd 4715).
2 Quoted in Wade (1972) *op cit* at p 2–3.

That is however not a legal solution. It may be that politicians of both parties adopted such equivocal positions because they feared that candid recognition of the *Costa* and *Van Gend* principles would further harden internal opposition to accession, which, as we see below, already presented a threat to the government's European ambitions.

The European Communities Act 1972 – the passage

The political question as to the desirability of EEC membership exposed some unusual divisions in the by then firmly established split between the Labour and Conservative parties. Both the Labour left and Conservative right wings opposed the idea. Both factions disliked the partial 'loss' of sovereignty they assumed accession would entail, since that would reduce their capacity (should they ever form a Commons majority) to promote legislation favouring their respective (very different) political ideologies. The support for membership of some more centrist MPs in both parties depended on the entry terms (especially Britain's budget contribution) that the government negotiated. We will return to these divisions on several occasions, but we might gain an initial appreciation of the EEC's capacity to cut across party lines by examining the Commons' vote on the 1971 Bill.

Accession would have two domestic phases; a Commons vote on whether to accept the entry terms, which, if successful, would be followed by the Bill incorporating the treaty into domestic law. At the 1970 election the Conservatives had won 330 seats, Labour 287, and the small parties 13. A rebellion by 21 anti-EEC Conservatives would have deprived the Heath government of a majority. Heath himself was passionately pro-accession: the great majority of Conservative MPs supported him, but 40 announced they would not approve the terms.

Labour was more deeply split. As Prime Minister in the late 1960s, Wilson had supported EEC membership, reversing his previous opposition. In 1971, he and most of his Shadow Cabinet again opposed it. The 1971 Labour Party Conference voted overwhelmingly against membership, and Wilson authorised a three line whip instructing Labour MPs to vote against the terms. Sixty-nine Labour MPs, led by the Shadow Chancellor Roy Jenkins, defied the whip and voted with the government; a further 20 abstained. The government majority was 112. Had the whip been respected, the terms would have been rejected. This would probably not have been regarded as a resigning issue, as Heath had allowed Conservative MPs a free vote.

But while many Labour MPs approved the terms, they would not defy the whip on votes during the Bill's passage, in part because Heath had announced that he would treat the second reading as a confidence issue.[3] Only a few (Jenkins foremost among them) elevated what they saw as Britain's national interest in joining the EEC above questions of party loyalty. On the Bill's third reading, the government's majority was just 17. For the moment, at least, the UK had entered the EEC. What now fell to be determined was the constitutional adequacy of the legislation enacted.

The European Communities Act 1972 – the terms

As we saw in *Mortensen v Peters* and *Cheney v Conn*, a government cannot change British law by using its prerogative powers to sign a treaty. If a treaty's terms are to be effective in British law, they must be incorporated by statute. The Treaty of Rome was incorporated by the European Communities Act 1972 (ECA 1972). Four sections merit attention here, in terms of their consistency both with orthodox British constitutional theory and the ECJ's principles of supremacy and direct effect.

Section 1 listed the various treaties to which the Act would apply. It also provided that the government might add new treaties to the list by using Orders in Council. This could be seen as a form of Henry VIII clause, insofar as it effectively allowed the government (via its prerogative powers) to incorporate new treaties into domestic law which, by virtue of the supremacy principle, would override existing legislation. No new legislation would be needed, nor need the House of Commons be consulted.

Section 2(1) seems to provide that all directly effective EEC law will be immediately enforceable in domestic courts:

> 'All such rights, powers, liabilities, obligations and restrictions from time to time arising by or under the Treaties, as in accordance with the Treaties are without further enactment to be given legal effect . . . in the United Kingdom shall be recognised and available in law, and be enforced, allowed and followed accordingly . . .'

Section 2(2)(a) empowers the government either through Orders in Council or statutory instruments to 'translate' any non-directly effective EEC law into domestic law. Section 2(4) then provides that '. . . any enactment passed or to be passed. . . . shall be construed and have effect subject to the foregoing provisions of this section'. Section 3(1) then states that:

3 Norton (1978) *op cit* pp 363–364.

'For the purpose of all legal proceedings any question as to the meaning or effect of any of the Treaties, or as to the validity meaning or effect of any Community instrument shall be . . . [determined] in accordance with the principles laid down by and any relevant decision of the European Court.'

There are several principles of startling constitutional significance in the ECA's few words. There is no constitutional difficulty in the ECA 1972 telling a court to give effect to EEC obligations even if there is a contradictory domestic law if that domestic law predated the ECA 1972. The ECA, as the later statute, would prevail. But what would happen if the inconsistent British statute was passed after 1972?

The 'from time to time' formula of s 2(1) and the 'passed or to be passed' formula of s 2(4) seem to instruct the courts that any such Act would not have domestic legal effect. As we saw in chapter 2, Parliament had produced such forward-looking legislation before. The Treaty of Union was incorporated by an Act which said some of its provisions would endure forever.[4] But those provisons have been repealed. Similarly, the courts held that s 7(1) of the Acquisition of Land Act was repealed by an inconsistent later Act. Why should the ECA 1972 be any different? Indeed, how could it be any different? To recognise it as a 'special' statute would undermine the entire basis of the parliamentary sovereignty doctrine.[5]

Section 3 seemed equally problematic: in ordering the British courts to apply ECJ case law, it again set up a potential conflict between EEC law and subsequent domestic legislation. Until such time as the ECJ reversed its decisions as to supremacy and direct effect, s 3 appeared to attempt to bind the courts to disobey as yet unenacted UK statutes which might breach treaty requirements.

How the courts would respond to these novel instructions was a matter for speculation. Writing in an academic journal, prior to the ECA 1972 coming into force, Lord Diplock had argued:

'It is a consequence of the doctrine of [parliamentary sovereignty] that if a subsequent Act . . . were passed that was in conflict with any provision of the Treaty which is of direct application . . . the courts of the United Kingdom would be bound to give effect to the Act . . . notwithstanding any conflict'.[6]

For Lord Diplock, it seemed, there could be nothing 'special'

---

4 This is of course to take a Diceyan view of the treaty's status, rather than to see it as a 'constituent' document establishing the British state; see pp 57–59 above.
5 See pp 42–43 above.
6 (1972) 'The Common Market and the common law' *Law Teacher* 3–12.

about the ECA 1972. Lord Denning was initially rather more equivocal.

Parliamentary sovereignty: a non-justiciable concept?

Opponents of accession had lost the political argument. In a last effort to prevent entry, they tried a legal approach. In *Blackburn v A-G*,[7] Mr Blackburn asked the Court of Appeal to declare that it would be unconstitutional for the government to sign the Treaty of Rome, because to do so would amount to an irreversible surrender of parliamentary sovereignty. This was an outlandish contention. For the government to sign the treaty would require an exercise of the prerogative. In 1971, long before *GCHQ*, hardly any prerogative powers were subject to full judicial review. Even after *GCHQ*, treaty ratification is a non-justiciable prerogative power, within Lord Roskill's 'excluded categories'. Consequently, the Court of Appeal told Mr Blackburn that it could not intervene, even if it had wanted to.

Lord Denning did however make some interesting comments about the impact EEC membership would have on parliamentary sovereignty:

> 'We have all been brought up to believe that, in legal theory, one Parliament cannot bind another and that no Act is irreversible. But legal theory does not always march alongside political reality'.[8]

Lord Denning referred approvingly to Professor Wade's 1955 article on parliamentary sovereignty: the root of the principle lay in ultimate political facts. But what is not clear from *Blackburn* is whether Denning thought that accession entailed the surrender of sovereignty or merely the lending of it. The Court of Appeal assumed that Parliament would never legislate contrary to its EEC obligations. If it did so, what would the courts decide? Lord Denning was non-committal: 'We will consider that event when it happens'.[9] As one might expect, 'it' seemed to happen rather quickly. But in the interim, the ECJ had been continuing its teleological approach to EEC law (as we shall see in section III), and the UK's political argument about membership had reawakened.

---

7 [1971] 2 All ER 1380.
8 *Ibid*, at 1382.
9 *Ibid*, at 1383.

The 1975 referendum

Labour's two narrow election victories in 1974 brought into power a party deeply split over the desirability of EEC membership. Labour's 1974 election manifestos had promised that the electorate would be given the opportunity to vote on continued membership, either by another general election or by a referendum. A third general election was not a plausible option, so a referendum seemed inevitable. The question which then arose was how the referendum was to be conducted. Having renegotiated the UK's terms of membership, Prime Minister Wilson set off down a political path along which several constitutional principles fell by the wayside. The first casualty was the convention of Cabinet unanimity. Wilson decided to 'suspend' the convention for the referendum campaign. His justification was that the question transcended party politics, although most commentators suggest his real motivation for both the referendum itself and the suspension was his assumption that there was no other way to keep his party together. The party's National Executive Committee had voted against remaining in the Community.[10] It was then announced that seven (identified) members of Wilson's Cabinet opposed continued membership, as did many backbench Labour MPs and the leaders of the largest trade unions. A Commons motion approving the new terms was carried by a majority of 226; but only 137 of the 315 Labour MPs voted in favour.[11] The success of government policy was entirely dependent on Conservative support.

The second casualty was the Burkean notion of the MP as a representative law-maker rather than the delegate of her voters. Parliament had in effect chosen to divest itself of its sovereignty on membership, by allowing the people the unusual opportunity of expressing an opinion on a single matter, rather than, as in general elections, on a whole package of issues. Neither the government nor Parliament was legally bound to respect the outcome of the referendum, although one imagines it would have been impossible, as a matter of practical politics, for them to do otherwise.

---

10 Irving R (1975) 'The United Kingdom referendum, June 1975' *European Law Review* 3–12; Pimlott *op cit* pp 654–660. Pimlott suggests that Wilson's real fear was that, in a repeat of 1931, Roy Jenkins would play the MacDonald role and emerge as the Leader of a predominantly Conservative coalition government: *ibid*, p 657. Jenkins (as one might expect) makes no allusion to any such ambition; (1991) *op cit* pp 399–418.
11 Wilson H *op cit* pp 103–105.

The EEC thus brought to the forefront of British politics the fundamental question of the desirability of leaving every political issue within the legal competence of a bare parliamentary majority. Some commentators suggested the EEC referendum might have a 'ripple effect', in convincing Parliament that there might be other issues on which the direct wishes of the people should be ascertained. The Scots and Welsh devolution campaigns might be seen as an example of this,[12] but there was no obvious enthusiasm in either of the main parties for referendums to become a routine part of the law-making process. In the 1890s, Dicey had written approvingly of referendums, seeing them as devices for 'the people' to express authoritative opinions on matters of great constitutional significance. This suggests that Dicey doubted the political wisdom of maintaining a constitution in which Parliament enjoyed legal sovereignty, although given his stunted perception of 'the people', it would be rash to see this approval as espousing an avowedly 'democratic' position.[13]

Such a conclusion is perhaps more justifiable in respect of the 1975 referendum. The campaign was not fought along traditional party lines, but might crudely be described as a contest in which right wing Conservatives and the left of the Labour party again united in opposing membership, while the Labour centre-right and Conservative centre-left supported it. Both sides received substantial funds from the government to publicise their arguments. The question was very simple: 'Do you think that the United Kingdom should stay in the European Community (the Common Market)?' The result was a resounding victory for the pro-EEC lobby; 67.2% to 32.8% on a 65% turnout.

Thereafter, constitutional orthodoxies rapidly reasserted themselves. The anti-EEC members of Wilson's Cabinet re-embraced the unanimity convention, and traditional inter-party rivalries rapidly reappeared.[14] Nevertheless, the mere fact that a referendum was held, the peculiar political divisions which it exposed, and the overwhelming support it revealed for EEC membership, suggested that the Treaty of Rome was undoubtedly a 'special' ingredient in Britain's constitutional recipe. Yet while British politicians and British voters again raked over the old ground of even belonging to the Community, the ECJ was continuing to indulge its attachment to a federalist schemata of treaty interpretation.

---

12 See pp 419–424 above.
13 For a discussion of Dicey's views see Irving *op cit*
14 Lent a sharper edge by Thatcher's election as leader of the Conservative party.

III. THE TREATY OF ROME 2: SUPREMACY AND DIRECT EFFECT REVISITED

We have seen several examples of innovative common law decisions in earlier chapters. But judicial dynamism is not a trait exclusive to the common law; it was also eagerly embraced by the ECJ. And in the mid-1970s the court took the opportunity to root the twin trunks of its jurisprudence, direct effect and supremacy, evermore firmly in the Community's legal soil.

Immediate supremacy: *Simmenthal*[15]

The 1977 case of *Simmenthal* concerned the compatibility of certain Italian laws regulating meat imports with EEC law. The Italian court hearing Simmenthal's claim referred two questions to the ECJ. The first related simply to the domestic law's substantive compatibility with the EEC regulations, and need not concern us here. The more important question concerned the consistency with EEC law of the Italian constitution's requirement that Italian laws which breached international obligations could only be disapplied by the Italian Constitutional Court, not by an inferior court such as the one hearing Simmenthal's claim. This would be a time-consuming process, during which the Italian law would remain in force. The ECJ held that it was not enough that a member state accept the supremacy of EEC law eventually – it had to do so immediately. It was the duty of *any* national court to 'disregard forthwith' any national law conflicting with EEC law: 'without waiting until those measures have been eliminated by action on the part of the national legislature concerned . . . or of other constitutional authorities'.[16] Furthermore, supremacy applied as much to national laws passed after the relevant EEC law as to those predating the EEC measure.

The conclusion reaffirmed the *Internationale Handelsgesellschaft* decision that even the fundamental constitutional principles of member states are inferior to inconsistent provisions of EEC

15 Case 106/77: *Amministrazione delle Finanze dello Stato v Simmenthal SpA (Simmenthal II)* [1978] ECR 629.
16 *Ibid*, para 7.

law.[17] The ECJ thus reinforced its conclusion that EEC law is unlike traditional international law, the enforcement of which depends on the mutual agreement of signatory states. Rather, EEC law had a distinct existence of its own, with enforcement mechanisms existing independently of the member states.

The direct effect of directives – again

As noted in chapter 4, the logical inference of *GCHQ's* decision to assess the reviewability of prerogative powers according to their nature rather than source was that some statutory powers would escape full review. In *Politi, Grad,* and *SpA SACE* the ECJ adopted a similar approach to direct effect. Nevertheless, several member states maintained that directives, irrespective of their substance, could *never* have direct effect. They presumed that since that directives reserved discretion to the member states they could not be 'clear and unconditional' per *Van Gend.* However, in 1974, the ECJ confirmed *SpA SACE* in forceful terms.

Van Duyn v Home Office[18]

The legislation at issue, Directive 64/221, contained measures implementing art 48, the provision establishing free movement of workers within the EEC. Article 48 is not framed in 'unconditional terms'; member states may per art 48(3) derogate from it for reasons of public policy, public health or public security. Article 56 required the EEC to issue directives regulating member states' use of the art 48(3) derogations. Directive 64/221 art 3 demanded that any such derogation be based solely on the 'personal conduct' of the individuals concerned.

The Home Office wanted to prevent Ms Van Duyn, a Dutch citizen, entering the country to work for the Church of Scientology, a cultish religion of which the government disapproved. She claimed that this infringed art 48, and challenged the Home Secretary's action before the British courts. In an art 177 refer-

---

17 In 1975, Scots fishermen angered by the EEC's fishing policies argued that Parliament was not competent (via the ECA 1972) to incorporate EC law which infringed provisions of the Treaty of Union. As in *MacCormick,* (p 58 above), the Scots court hearing the case did not categorically dismiss the 'Treaty of Union as fundamental law' argument, but considered it inapplicable to the instant case: *Gibson v Lord Advocate* (1975) SLT 134. Even had the court done so, one assumes that *Simmenthal* would prevail over any such 'fundamental law'.
18 Case 41/74: [1974] ECR 1337. The case was the first involving the British government following the UK's accession.

ence, the Court of Appeal asked the ECJ firstly if art 3 of Directive 64/221 was directly effective, and secondly if membership of the Scientologists could be 'personal conduct'?

The ECJ held art 3 directly effective because it confined the discretion accorded to the member states by art 48(3) with sufficient precision to make it justiciable: a national court could easily ensure that decisions a member state made on this question were indeed based on the individual's personal conduct. In language reminiscent of *Van Gend*, the ECJ confirmed that there was no principled reason to exclude the possibility that directives (wholly or in part) could be directly effective:

> 'It is necessary to examine, in every case, whether the nature, scheme and general wording of the provision in question are capable of having direct effects on the relations between Member States and individuals.'[19]

But while the British government's arguments were rejected on this point, the ECJ also decided membership of the Scientologists could be 'personal conduct'. The British court could thus hold that Van Duyn's exclusion did not breach EEC law.

The ECJ's decision might be thought as much an exercise in diplomacy as law-making.[20] Judgment was delivered just before the UK's 1975 referendum. By permitting the Home Secretary to exclude Ms Van Duyn while simultaneously upholding *SpA SACE*, the court reaffirmed a principle of long-term significance to efforts to enhance EEC law's 'effet utile', while handing British supporters of EEC membership a precedent to refute opponents' claims that remaining in the Community required surrendering control over such basic issues as excluding undesirable foreign citizens. One cannot gauge if *Van Duyn* did influence voting behaviour in the referendum, or ascertain if the ECJ was consciously (if covertly) pursuing an avowedly political agenda, but it would be rash to exclude either possibility.

The justiciability test reaffirmed – *Defrenne v SABENA*

Just as the form EEC legislation took could not preclude enforcement by national courts, neither did it assure that end. We saw in *Chandler v DPP* that putting a prerogative power into statutory

---

19 At para 12.
20 For a searching analysis see Weiler J (1986) 'Eurocracy and mistrust . . .' *Washington Law Review* 1103–1142.

form did not necessarily make it justiciable.[1] In *Defrenne v Sabena*[2], the ECJ drew a similar conclusion regarding direct effect.

Article 119 requires member states to 'ensure and maintain the principle that men and women should receive equal pay for equal work.' Ms Defrenne worked for SABENA, a Belgian airline, as an air hostess. SABENA paid its air hostesses less than its male stewards, even though both jobs entailed exactly the same duties. While admitting discrimination, SABENA claimed art 119 was not directly effective. SABENA contended that art 119's principle was too complex an economic concept to be justiciable before national courts; more detailed legislation explaining the meaning of equal pay and equal work would be needed before art 119's principle became 'unconditional'.

The ECJ was only partly convinced by this argument. It held that gender discrimination could take two forms; 'direct and overt' or 'indirect and disguised'. Direct discrimination arose where (as for Ms Defrenne) differing wages were paid for exactly the same job, or where discrimination was specifically permitted in legislation or collective labour agreements. Such inequality could be detected by 'purely legal analysis . . . the court is in a position to establish all the facts which enable it to decide whether a woman is receiving lower pay than a male worker'.[3] However, indirect discrimination, involving inequality between different jobs or even different industries, could only be established against more detailed legislative criteria. Not until such legislation had been enacted could the prohibition on indirect discrimination become directly effective. Once again, the ECJ is stressing that it is the nature, not the source of the EEC law that determines its enforceability in domestic courts.

An equally important element of *Defrenne* was the ECJ's conclusion that art 119's justiciable terms were enforceable in national courts not simply against member states, but against any employer; they would be directly effective not just 'vertically' (ie upwards from citizen to state) but also 'horizontally' (ie between citizens):

> '[S]ince Article 119 is mandatory in nature, the prohibition on discrimination between men and women applies not only to the action of public authorities, but also extends to all agreements which are intended to regulate paid labour collectively, as well as to contracts between individuals'.[4]

---

1 Pages 130–132 above.
2 Case 43/75: [1976] ECR 455.
3 *Ibid*, paras 22–23.
4 *Ibid*, para 39.

This seems a logical extension of *Van Gend's* principle that the treaty bestowed rights on individuals. If effective realisation of those rights depended on other individuals respecting reciprocal obligations, it seemed obvious that those individuals should resolve disputes as to the meaning of EEC law in their national courts. Directly effective regulations would also be horizontally as well as vertically enforceable, given that art 189 specified that they were of general application. As we will subsequently see, the horizonal direct effect of directives proved a more contentious issue. But before that question was broached, the ECJ once again faced domestic resistance to *SpA SACE* and *Van Gend*. According to France's highest constitutional court, the Conseil d'Etat, a directive could not be directly effective at all.

Domestic disquiet 2: *Cohn-Bendit*

France endured its own 'Days of May'[5] in May 1968, when student-led protests against the French government threatened the overthrow of the existing constitution. One of the leaders of the protest was Herr Daniel Cohn-Bendit, a German national studying in Paris. 'Danny the Red', as he was popularly known, was subsequently deported and banned from re-entering France, on the obvious ground that he posed a threat to public order.

Ten years later, Cohn-Bendit's revolutionary fervour had dimmed, and he was offered a job in France. The entry ban was still however in place. He claimed before the French courts that the ban infringed his rights under art 48, unless it was justified under the art 48(3) derogations. As we saw in *Van Duyn*, art 3 of Directive 64/221 allowed those derogations to be invoked only if the threat to public order, public safety or public health arose from the individual's personal conduct. Cohn-Bendit was in effect asking the French court to conclude that his personal conduct no longer threatened public order, and thence overturn the banning order.

The French court hearing the case tried to make a reference to the ECJ concerning the direct effect of Directive 64/221, but was forbidden to do so by the the Conseil d'Etat. The French government had in the interim revoked the order, but it invited the Conseil d'Etat to rule whether, as a matter of French constitutional law, Directive 64/221 could be directly effective. The Conseil d'Etat simply concluded that directives could not have

5 See p 244 above.

direct effect. The treaty's framers had stated in art 189 that a regulation would be directly applicable and binding in its entirety; it could therefore be directly effective. That they had not said so about directives, but had specifically granted member states discretion in implementing the law, must mean that they envisaged that directives would not have direct effect.

The Conseil d'Etat restricted its search for the meaning of EEC law solely to the treaty's text, rejecting the ECJ's teleological approach to interpretation. From a narrowly legalistic perspective, the Conseil's conclusion has some merit, but it is utterly inconsistent with both the *Costa* and *Van Gend* principles. One commentator describes *Cohn-Bendit* as 'a clear and deliberate act of defiance . . . a blow at the foundations of the community'.[6] It is impossible to gauge to what extent the Conseil d'Etat was simply following a nationalistic political agenda, and how far it was motivated by a genuine belief in the legal integrity of its conclusion. Much the same ambiguity seemingly pervades the UK courts' initial efforts to address the constitutional implications of accesion.

IV. EEC LAW, PARLIAMENTARY SOVEREIGNTY AND THE UK COURTS: PHASE ONE

The UK judiciary's earliest encounters with EEC law suggested that the radical principles of *Van Gend* and *Costa*, and Parliament's evident attempt to enact those principles in the ECA 1972, would meet a trenchant restatement of orthodox Diceyan theory. Lord Denning's non-committal attitude in *Blackburn* was soon followed with a somewhat firmer view in *Felixstowe Dock and Rly Co v British Transport Docks Board*.[7] The case raised the possibility that the provisions of a Bill shortly to be enacted would contravene art 86's rules on competition law. However Lord Denning did not think that possibility raised a difficult constitutional issue:

'It seems to me that once the Bill is passed by Parliament and becomes a Statute, that will dispose of all this discussion about the Treaty. These courts will have to abide by the Statute without regard to the Treaty at all'.

It is not clear if Lord Denning felt that the ECA 1972 *had not* limited Parliament's sovereignty, or whether it simply *could not* do

---

6 Hartley T (1988) *The Foundations of European Community Law* p 232 (Oxford: Clarendon Press). Chapter 8 of Hartley's book offers an interesting discussion of the various member states' responses to the supremacy and direct effect issues.
7 [1976] 2 CMLR 655.

so. Nevertheless, in his view, the ECJ's 'new legal order' had apparently not taken root in British constitutional soil.

Lord Denning seemed to adopt a different approach in respect of the ECJ's adherence to teleological methods of treaty and legislative interpretation. In *HP Bulmer Ltd v J Bollinger SA*,[8] he suggested British judges would have to forgo their traditional, literalist techniques, and:

'follow the European pattern. No longer must they examine the words in meticulous detail. No longer must they argue about the precise grammatical sense. They must look to the purpose or intent. . . . They must divine the spirit of the Treaty and gain inspiration from it. If they find a gap, they must fill it as best they can.'

Lord Denning's advice[9] extended however only to the treaty and to EEC legislation, not to British statutes. Domestic legislation, it seemed, even if dealing with EC matters, would still be interpreted according to orthodox principles. It came therefore as a surprise when Lord Denning himself advocated a radical break with constitutional tradition some two years later.

The end of the doctrine of implied repeal? *MacCarthys Ltd v Smith*

Macarthys Ltd v Smith arose from an art 119 dispute. Mrs Smith was employed at a lower wage by Macarthys than the man who previously did her job. She claimed this breached Article 119. Macarthys contended that the British courts should apply the relevant British legislation (the Equal Pay Act 1970 as amended by the Sex Discrimination Act 1975), which forbade discrimination only between men and women doing the same job for the same employer *at the same time*. If Macarthys' interpretation of the domestic legislation was correct, the British courts faced a difficulty. For British purposes, art 119 came into force in 1973. The Sex Discrimination Act was passed two years later. Should the later Act prevail, as Dicey's theory would suggest? Or should EEC law, per *Costa*, be regarded as the superior legal authority?

In the Court of Appeal, Lord Denning thought that a literal reading of the British legislation supported Macarthys' claim. However, following his own advice in *Bulmer*, he rejected a literalist approach. Rather, the Act should be construed subject to the 'overriding force' of the treaty 'for that takes priority even over

8 [1974] 3 WLR 202 at 216 CA.
9 Reiterated, reinforced and also applied to other Treaties in *James Buchanan Co Ltd v Babco Forwarding and Shipping (UK) Ltd* [1977] QB 208, CA.

our own statute'. Denning's own view of art 119 was that its prohibition on unequal pay extended beyond 'same time' situations to successive employment.[10] Construing the treaty and the 1975 legislation 'as a harmonious whole . . . intended to eliminate discrimination against women', Denning found in Mrs Smith's favour.

Denning suggested he was obliged to adopt this expansive interpretive strategy because of the ECA 1972 s 2. That would in itself give the ECA a somewhat 'special' status, but Denning's argument went beyond technical questions of interpretation. He also concluded that s 2 had abolished the doctrine of implied repeal for British statutes affecting EEC matters. Domestic courts should assume that if ever a British statute was impliedly inconsistent with an EEC obligation the inconsistency arose because Parliament had erred in the language chosen: legislators could not have have intended to achieve such a result, so the courts would save them from the consequences of their mistake by according supremacy to EEC law.

This radical contention endows the ECA with a very 'special' constitutional status.[11] In effect, Denning's judgment in *Macarthys* recognised a weak 'manner and form' entrenchment of the supremacy and direct effect of EEC law. These values were not however substantively entrenched, for:

> 'If the time should come when Parliament deliberately passes an Act with the intention of repudiating the Treaty or any provision of it . . . and says so in express terms then I should have thought it would be the duty of our Courts to follow the statute of our Parliament. I do not envisage any such situation. . . . Unless there is such an intentional and express repudiation of the Treaty, it is our duty to give priority to the Treaty'.[12]

Denning did not explain how the 1972 Parliament had managed to bind itself and its successors in this (limited) way. There is, as we have repeatedly suggested, no obvious legal principle supporting such a conclusion. One must therefore conclude that Denning was recognising a new 'ultimate political fact' – that accession to the EEC 'revolutionised' orthodox constitutional understandings.

---

10 Denning was in a minority on this point. The majority (Cumming-Bruce and Lawton LJJ) were uncertain as to art 119's scope, and referred the question to the ECJ. They seemed to agree however with Denning's approach to the constitutional issue.
11 An excellent analysis is offered in Allan T (1983) 'Parliamentary sovereignty: Lord Denning's dexterous revolution' *OJLS* 22–33.
12 [1979] 3 All ER 325 at 329.

This argument rests on the presumption that the political, economic and foreign policy implications of acceding to the treaty were so profound that the courts had to assume a new, protective role. This operates on two levels. The first, itself controversial, is that Parliament should be protected from the adverse political consequences of unintended breaches of its EEC obligations. The second, more controversial still, is that UK citizens should be protected from underhand or deceptive parliamentary efforts to renege on the UK's EEC commitments. We might think that, as an exercise in constitution building, such protective devices would be desirable. But they are constituent rather than interpretive values, and as such, beyond conventional understandings of the judicial role. One might discern some legal precedent for Denning's innovation in *Chorlton v Lings* and *Nairn v St Andrews University*, where the courts refused to accept that Parliament could depart from fundamental constitutional understandings through 'furtive' legislation.[13] As statements of legal principle, these cases do not carry great authority. And from a political perspective, we might wonder if nineteenth century views on women's enfranchisement and late twentieth century understandings about the EEC can readily be equated? Certainly Denning himself made no reference to them. Yet nor did he advert explicitly to the ECJ's 'new legal order' arguments to justify his decision.

Despite its obscure roots, Denning's judgment staked out new constitutional ground. We have already seen, in *Gouriet*, one of Lord Denning's innovative constitutional judgments being rapidly reversed by the House of Lords.[14] His judgment in *Macarthys* would seem an even more radical step, but the Lords showed itself reluctant to disapprove it.

A matter of interpretation? *Garland v British Rail Engineering Ltd*[15]

The issue before their Lordships in *Garland* was whether the Sex Discrimination Act 1975 prohibited gender discrimination in relation to concessionary travel facilities extended to BR's retired employees. Such discrimination seemed as though it might contravene art 119, so the prospect again arose of a conflict between EEC law and a subsequent domestic statute.

Somewhat peculiarly, Lord Diplock (for a unanimous

13 See pp 59–61 above.
14 See pp 118–120 above.
15 [1983] 2 AC 751.

House) made an extensive reference to how he would approach the question if the EEC was an ordinary international law treaty:

> 'It is a principle of construction of United Kingdom statutes ... that the words of a statute passed after the Treaty has been signed and dealing with the subject matter of the international obligation of the United Kingdom are to be construed, if ... reasonably capable of bearing such a meaning, as intended to carry out the obligation and not to be inconsistent with it.'[16]

This technique would be incompatible with *Van Gend's* 'new legal order' principle, and would thus breach the ECA 1972 s 3. It would be not 'irrelevant',[17] but legally indefensible.

Lord Diplock perhaps made this point to highlight the innovative nature of EEC law, for he did not decide the case on that basis. Rather he suggested that the ECA 1972 s 2 introduced a *new rule of statutory interpretation*. A UK court should construe all domestic legislation in a manner respecting EEC obligations; 'however wide a departure from the prima facie meaning of the language of the provision might be needed in order to achieve consistency'.[18] In this case, the 1975 Act could be interpreted as compatible with EEC law 'without any undue straining of the ordinary meaning of the language used'.[19] In that respect, Diplock shared Denning's sentiment in *Macarthys*. He also agreed with Denning that UK courts must obey a statute breaching EEC law in 'express positive terms'. He was more circumspect about the doctrine of implied repeal: this was not an appropriate case to decide that question.

Barely ten years after accession, Lords Diplock and Denning had both moved considerably from their previously Diceyan position concerning the EEC's constitutional impact. One might wonder if they had gone far enough to satisfy *Van Gend* and *Costa*, but their dynamism is undeniable. Yet while British courts struggled to accommodate long-established principles of EEC law, the ECJ was facing jurisprudential difficulties of its own.

---

16 *Ibid*, at 394–395.
17 Hood-Phillips O (1982) 'A Garland for the Lords: Parliament and community law again' *LQR* 524–526.
18 *Ibid*, at 935.
19 *Ibid*

V. THE TREATY OF ROME 3: DIRECT EFFECT – THE SAGA CONTINUES

As noted earlier, the ECJ had concluded that treaty articles and regulations could be both vertically and horizontally directly effective. This characteristic of 'universal enforceability' of aspects of EEC law is an important part of the effet utile doctrine. But art 189's text seemingly precludes the horizontal direct effect of directives; it states they are binding only on the addressee member state. As we have seen, the ECJ had not generally allowed textual considerations to constrain its articulation of 'the law'. We might therefore initially find its judgment in *Marshall* somewhat surprising.

The horizontal and vertical direct effect of directives? *Marshall v Southampton and South West Hampshire Area Health Authority*[20]

Marshall returned to the adequacy of the UK's attempts to implement art 119. Mrs Marshall's employer operated a discriminatory retirement age policy: men could work until 65, women had to retire at 60. This was lawful under the UK's sex discrimination legislation, but seemed incompatible with Directive 76/207.[1] The Court of Appeal asked the ECJ if the directive precluded discriminatory retirement ages, and, if so, whether Mrs Marshall could enforce the directive against her employer in the national courts.

The ECJ answered both questions affirmatively. However it then made a more general point: directives could only be directly effective against 'public authorities' (ie vertically); they could not be enforced in national courts against private sector organisations or individual citizens (ie horizontally). Mrs Marshall's employer was a public or governmental body for these purposes: had she worked for a private hospital, she could not have claimed her EEC entitlements until Parliament had implemented the directive by amending the domestic legislation.

Quite how to distinguish between private and public bodies more generally was unclear, particularly as the responsibilities assumed by government varied appreciably between the member states. This posed a threat to the 'level playing field concept', and also raised the possibility that public employees would have

---

20 Case 152/84: [1986] ECR 723.
  1 A piece of secondary legislation in which the EEC addressed some aspect of the 'indirect and disguised' discrimination adverted to in *Defrenne*.

easier access to EEC benefits than private sector workers.² It may be that the ECJ was more concerned with offering reassurance to national courts concerned about the legal basis of *SpA SACE* and *Van Duyn* by laying clear limits to the reach of the direct effect doctrine. But that concern is not present in the judgment's text, and is manifestly a 'political' rather than legal consideration.

Normative and decisional supra-nationalism

The interplay of law and politics was clearly a pervasive feature of the EEC's early constitutional development. In an influential critique published in 1981, Joseph Weiler suggested that this process was best understood in terms of a distinction between what he termed 'normative' and 'decisional' supra-nationalism.³

Normative supra-nationalism concerned the formal status of EEC law vis-à-vis the domestic law of the member states. In decisions such as *Van Gend*, *Costa* and *Simmenthal*, the ECJ had fashioned principles which indicated that: 'the relationship between the legal order of the Community and that of the Member States has come to resemble increasingly a fully fledged (USA type) federal system'.⁴ Yet Weiler suggested that just the opposite trend was evident in respect of decisional supra-nationalism, which concerned the characteristics of the practical reality of institutional relations within the Community's legislative and administrative processes. In this sphere, the EEC had become increasingly inter-governmental in nature. The Luxembourg Accords were a cogent illustration of this trend, as was the emergence of a body known as the 'European Council', a forum for regular summit meetings of heads of government of the member states, which (like the Luxembourg Accords) existed entirely outside the treaty's legal structure, but manifestly had an important influence on the conduct of Community business in the Council of Ministers. Weiler also suggested that a similar, albeit not obviously 'unconstitutional', result was produced by the growing influence of CORE-PER⁵ on the Commission's task of initiating legislation. The

2 See Curtin D (1990) 'The province of government: delimiting the direct effect of directives in the common law context' *European Law Review* 195–223; Arnull A (1987) 'The incoming tide: responding to *Marshall*' *Public Law* 383–399.
3 (1981) 'The Community system: the dual character of supra-nationalism' *Yearbook of European Law* 267–306.
4 *Ibid*, at p 273.
5 See fn 5, p 478 above.

combined effect of these developments was that the Council had become a forum for individual countries to engage in 'package deal decision-making' and 'high powered political horse- trading'.[6] Moreover, the Commission and Parliament were ill-equipped to counter this trend, in part at least because of the Community's so-called 'democracy deficit'. Without an electoral mandate from 'the people' of the EEC, neither institution could forcefully assert an integrationist agenda against the nationalist wishes of (elected) member state governments.

Although this normative/decisional divergence presented an apparent paradox, in that the EEC was in one sense increasingly coming to resemble a pure form of federal constitutionalism, while in another it seemed no more than a loose association of entirely autonomous sovereign states, Weiler suggested that, on further consideration, the EEC could not, in the short term, have survived in any other way. By pulling in opposite directions, these forces had created:

> 'An equilibrium which explains a seemingly irreconcilable equation: a large . . . and effective measure of transnational integration, coupled at the same time with the preservation of strong, unthreatened, national Member States.'[7]

Weiler's argument is a contentious one, and since it lies in the realm of constitutional and political theory, cannot be 'correct' in any definitive sense. But for our purposes, it is more important for the questions it raises than any answer it might provide. For if the EEC was by then established as a unique form of governmental authority, if it was indeed unlike anything with which Britain's three hundred year old constitution had previously had to deal, one might plausibly wonder if the stage had not been set for Professor Wade's legal revolution to make its long-awaited appearance? That is a question to which chapter 12 will turn.

The reduction of the 'democratic deficit' and the emergence of human rights as general principles of EEC law

Some tentative steps had been taken to address the Community's 'democratic deficit' in the 1970s, primarily by altering the powers and composition of the Parliament. A treaty amendment which became effective in 1975 greatly enhanced the Parliament's role

6 *Ibid*, at 288.
7 *Ibid*, at 292.

in the budgetary process.[8] Perhaps more significantly, from 1979 onwards, the Parliament was to be composed of members directly elected by each nation's electorate, thereby providing it with a 'democratic' basis from which to argue that its powers within the Community's law-making process should be increased.[9]

In the same period, the ECJ also sought to reassure domestic courts as to the substantive legitimacy of EEC law through a more enthusiastic and explicit embrace of an implied doctrine of human rights protection within the treaty, fleshing out the skeletal jurisprudence adverted to in *Internationale Handelsgesellschaft*. In *Nold*,[10] the ECJ suggested it would annul EEC laws contravening fundamental constitutional principles (styled as 'general principles of law') common to the member states, and also indicated it would draw on international human rights treaties for guidance as to what those principles might be. Subsequently, in *Hauer v Land Rheinland-Pfalz*,[11] the ECJ explicitly referred to the European Convention on Human Rights in gauging the 'constitutionality' of EEC secondary legislation. The ECJ did not go so far as announcing the convention's de facto incorporation into EEC law, yet that seemed an implicit consequence of its judgment. That implication did appear to satisfy Germany's Federal Constitutional Court. That court had never in fact exercised its self-proclaimed power to prevent domestic enforcement of EEC measures which contravened the Basic Law, but in *Re Wunsche-Handelsgesellschaft Application*,[12] it also abandoned its theoretical entitlement to do so.[13]

---

8 Ehlermann C (1975) 'Applying the new budgetary procedure for the first time' *Common Market Law Review* 325–343; Lasok and Bridge *op cit* pp 258–264.

9 British Labour MPs opposed to any such increase 'persuaded' the Callaghan government in 1978 to introduce a Bill providing that any treaty enhancing the EP's powers could not be ratified by the government unless approved by an Act of Parliament. This measure, enacted as s 6 of the European Parliamentary Elections Act 1978, had two effects. The first was to qualify the government's power to incorporate new treaties into domestic law via Orders in Council. The second, more generally, was to place a clear statutory limit on the government's foreign policy prerogatives. It was not however clear then, some seven years before *GCHQ*, if this statutory limit would prove justiciable: (nor is it clear now; see further pp 554–557 below).

10 Case 4/73: [1974] ECR 491.

11 Case 44/79 [1979] ECR 3727.

12 [1987] 3 CMLR 225.

13 For an overview see Pescatore P (1972) 'The protection of human rights in the European Communities' *CMLRev* 73–79: Dauses M (1985) 'The protection of fundamental rights in the Community legal order' *ELRev* 398–417.

CONCLUSION

The combined effects of the preliminary 'democratisation' of the Community's institutional structure and the ECJ's continued attachment to the effet utile strategy were not in themselves sufficient, as Weiler had predicted, to maintain the Community's integrationist momentum. The European Parliament had promoted a Draft Treaty on European Union (DTEU) in 1984, which advocated a radical overhaul of Community institutions and (unsurprisingly) a substantial extension of its own powers. The initiative, which seemed to entail significant political as well as economic integration, was not embraced by the member states. By the mid-1980s, it had become evident that even the pervasive economic integration envisaged by the treaty's framers had yet to be achieved. The Commission consequently sought to re-energise the Community, proposing a wide range of measures (both normative and decisional in nature) which eventually led to the first major amendment to the Treaty of Rome, some 30 years after its birth, in the shape of the Single European Act, by which time the Community had grown in size to contain 12 member states.[14]

14 The additional members being the UK, Ireland, Spain, Portugal, Greece and Denmark.

CHAPTER THIRTEEN

The European Community after the Single European Act

Chapter 12 traced the history of the EEC, and its impact on the UK's constitutional structure, as far as the mid-1980s. This chapter covers the period between 1986 and 1994. It begins by analysing the origins and objectives of the Single European Act (SEA). We then examine the ways in which the ECJ has continued to develop principles to facilitate the enforcement of EC law in the member states, and consider to what extent our domestic courts have been prepared to apply such ideas. After examining the controversy engendered by the Maastricht Treaty, the chapter concludes by assessing in what senses, if any, continued membership of the EC will entail a loss of the United Kingdom's 'sovereignty' to a federal European constitution.

I. THE SINGLE EUROPEAN ACT – THE TERMS

The SEA's roots lay in a growing perception within the Commission that the Community's original objectives were being achieved at a painfully slow rate. If one accepts that the Treaty of Rome was intended to foster political convergence through the medium of economic integration, it is clear that by the early 1980s the realisation of a 'United States of Europe' remained a distant vision. But there were also considerable shortfalls in the ostensibly less controversial sphere of economic convergence.

The Treaty of Rome had envisaged that the four fundamental freedoms of movement for goods, capital, persons and services upon which the Community was to be based would be achieved by 1970. But even by 1984, this objective remained unfulfilled in various respects: the national laws of the member states still contained many effective barriers to free movement, and thus prevented the creation of a truly 'common market'. That such barriers remained in place is a cogent illustration both of the limits of the

ECJ's supra-nationalist competence and the continued vitality of nationalist, protectionist sentiment in the more inter-national arena of the Community's legislative process. The Commission's eventual response to this apparent impasse was to seek new means to realise the treaty's original ends.

In the 1960s and 1970s, the Commission had sought to create the 'common market' by embarking on a huge programme of harmonisation through detailed Community legislation. These so called 'Euronorms' were intended to impose a complex, uniform regulatory structure on each of the member states. The celebrated 'level playing field' would require all member states to apply identical legal rules, precisely defined by the EEC itself, to all areas of domestic activity which fell within the EEC's sphere of competence.

By the early 1980s the 'Euronorm' approach was regarded as inappropriate for several reasons. Firstly, the Commission's small size limited the amount of legislation it could initiate. Secondly, several member states were sceptical about the need to homogen-ise regulatory structures, suggesting that a 'common market' need not be a *uniform* market, but could happily accommodate appreci-able geographical divergences in both the substance and appli-cation of EEC law principles.[1] The third reason, flowing in part from the second, was that it frequently proved impossible to achieve all the member states' agreement on the intricacies of proposed Euronorm legislation.

The regenerative programme first outlined in the Commission's 1985 White Paper consequently represented a move away from what has been described as the Commission's 'almost theological dogmatism'[2] in pursuit of uniformity. The White Paper attempted to reinvigorate a stalled programme of economic integration through the twin devices of reforming both the methods and substance of the Community's law-making process. The heart of the 'Internal Market' strategy was to be a new art 8A within the Treaty of Rome.

The proposed art 8A announced the intention to create an 'internal market' by 1 January 1993. The shift from an emphasis on the 'common market' to the heralding of an 'internal market' was not simply a question of semantic relabelling. The internal

1 This is perhaps an obvious conclusion for countries where sub-central units of government have appreciable legislative competence in the economic sphere; a key ingredient of federal systems of government is of course that the constitution affords effective legal protection to such diversity.
2 Edward D (1987) 'The impact of the Single European Act on the institutions' *CMLRev* 19–30 at p 26.

market proposed that the Community seek enhanced economic integration by rejecting the Euronorms methodology, and relying instead on a process of 'mutual recognition' and home country certification of acceptable standards. As Forwood and Clough note, the internal market strategy was based on a 'minimalist approach to economic regulation' in which the notion of 'equivalence' is the key.[3] Crudely stated, the internal market would operate on the assumption that goods and services lawfully marketed in one member state should be saleable throughout the community.

However, the White Paper's original integrationist thrust was much diluted when exposed to the nationalistically motivated scrutiny of the successive Inter-Governmental Conferences required by the treaty's art 236 amendment process.[4] That these negotiations were protracted and keenly contested by the member states is sometimes portrayed as a weakness in the Community's decision-making structure. But the tortuous process might equally plausibly be seen as perfectly compatible with that view of democracy which contends that alterations to a constitution's fundamental principles should not be easy to effect.

It is perhaps therefore not surprising that the amendments introduced by the SEA present an even more complex balancing of inter-national and supra-national forces than provided by the original treaty.[5] In the supra-national sphere, one can point to an appreciable extension of the Community's substantive competence into the fields of environmental protection, regional development, research and technical innovation, and some aspects of social policy.[6]

In contrast, the Community's continuing inter-national dynamic was expressed by various member states during the amendment negotiations with sufficient vigour to recast the Commission's initial internal market strategy in a more circumscribed form. Thus for example the Commission's original intention that art 8A should announce the 'complete removal of all physical, technical and fiscal barriers within the community' eventually emerged with the caveat that the internal market was to be pursued 'without

---

3 (1987) 'The Single European Act and free movement' *ELRev* 383–408.
4 Corbett R (1985) 'The 1985 intergovernmental conference and the Single European Act', in Pryce R (ed) *The Dynamics of European Union* (London: Croom Helm).
5 Constraints of space permit only a very selective analysis of the SEA's provisions here. For further details see Shaw *op cit* pp 37–42, 78–95 and ch 15; Ehlermann C (1987) 'The internal market following the Single European Act' *CMLRev* 361–409.
6 See Ehlermann (1987) *op cit.*

prejudice to the other articles in the Treaty'.[7] This is well illustrated by the progressive dilution of the mutual recognition reforms. The Commission had initially proposed simply to remove arts 36 and 56,[8] thereby simply sweeping away national powers to obstruct free movement. This step was however too radical a reform for all of the member states to approve. The subsequent acceptance in art 100B that the Council of ministers should retain the power to decide the extent of equivalence required by EC law provides a graphic example of the resolution of questions of economic sovereignty by the evident subordination of supra-national legal principle to inter-national political pragmatism. Furthermore, the bulk of the internal market programme would be implemented through directives, a form of EC law which, as noted in chapter 11, has a less supra-national flavour than regulations.

But such concessions to inter-national sensitivity were in turn subject to supra-national checks and balances. A specific (albeit apparently not legally binding)[9] date (31 December 1992) was set for achievement of the internal market programme. Relatedly, the 'equivalence' standards underpinning the mutual recognition principle were to be based on 'high standards', and while the new art 100A para 4 formally permitted member states to derogate somewhat from the free movement principle in defence of major 'needs', their invocation of this power was subjected to close Commission control.[10]

The SEA also enhanced the Community's supra-national profile by extending the use of qualified majority rather than unanimous voting within the law-making process. In particular, art 100A provided that all measures taken in pursuit of the art 8A internal market programme could be enacted in this way. Such reforms offer an obvious antidote to the frustration of EC objectives by a single member state. However some commentators (no doubt with the 'Empty Chair' crisis in mind) questioned whether imposing such legal compulsion on reluctant states was the best way forward: unanimity may be difficult to achieve, and delay the implementation of integrationist policies, but may well produce

---

7 Ibid at p 364.
8 We have seen the application of art 56 in the *Van Duyn* and *Cohn-Bendit* cases at pp 504–505 and 507–508 above. Article 36 makes analogous provisions in respect of the free movement of goods.
9 See Edward *op cit.*
10 The new provision might be seen as a device simultaneously 'legalising' and diluting the sentiments underlying the Luxembourg Accords.

substantive outcomes from which member states will be less likely to resile.[11]

The SEA acknowledged that many areas of government activity could not sensibly be brought within the EC's legal competence. Perhaps the best example of this is the Declaration attached to the SEA to the effect that the reforms to the treaty should not be construed as derogating from the member states' powers to take such measures as they considered necessary regarding immigration control for regulating the movements of non-EC nationals, combating crime, and preventing terrorism.[12]

It is more difficult to decide whether to locate two other substantial innovations introduced by the SEA on the Community's supranational or inter-national axis. Title I of the SEA gives a formal legal status to the meetings of the European Council, while Title III formalises the hitherto entirely informal process of 'European Political Co-operation', primarily in the area of foreign policy. But while 'recognised' by the SEA, these two aspects of Community action were not incorporated into the body of EC law; rather they were to exist outside the treaty in the sphere of traditional international law agreements. From a federalist perspective, their greatest significance perhaps lay in their long-term potential to 'normalise' joint member state action in explicitly non-justiciable areas, and thereby pave the way at a future date for the Community's legal competence to extend into avowedly 'political' fields.

Reducing the democratic deficit – treaty amendment

That the EEC had failed to produce a truly common market by 1986 is perhaps unsurprising given the cultural heterogeneity, linguistic pluralism, and economic nationalism of the various member states. However, the difficulty might be thought to be exacerbated by the institutional balance of power in the Community legislative process. As suggested in chapter 11, the original treaty cast that balance firmly in favour of the inter-nationally constructed Council at the expense of the more supra-national Commission and Parliament. An increase in the powers of the

---

11 See for example Ehlermann's analysis (1987, *op cit*) of the harmonisation of indirect taxation laws within the Community.

12 The legal status of Declarations is unclear. But as Toth points out, the more expansive scope and pro-nationalist sentiment of the SEA declaration suggests the member states hoped that it would temper the ECJ's integrationist inclinations; (1986) 'The legal status of Declarations attached to the SEA' *CMLRev* 803–812.

Commission would have offered one route to achieving a more communitaire balance of legislative power. But any such reform would also have intensified accusations as to the EEC's so-called 'democratic deficit'. The SEA consequently sought a modest rebalancing of the supra/inter-national axis by enhancing the legal status of the European Parliament. Such a reform could plausibly be construed as encouraging pan-European sentiment within the Community while simultaneously defusing criticism that Community decision-making processes are too far removed from electoral influence.

The SEA's amendments fell far short of the proposals aired by the Parliament itself in the DTEU,[13] but were nevertheless an advance on the Treaty of Rome's original institutional balance.[14] The most important initiative was the creation of a Parliamentary power of 'co-operation' in the legislative process in respect of some areas of Community competence, foremost among them internal market measures per art 100A, some aspects of free movement of workers, workplace health and safety regulation, environmental protection and the common transport policy. The Council cannot simply ignore the Parliament's views when the co-operation procedure is being employed:[15] the initiative thus gave the Parliament an audible voice in important areas of Community activity. Its significance should not however be exaggerated. An early assessment concluded that the Parliament: 'is still some way from becoming an equal chamber with the Council in a fully bi-cameral system, but some progress has been made in this direction'.[16] One might plausibly add to that statement that the progress was initially both slight and stilted.[17]

Moreover, the SEA left one of the Parliament's basic weaknessses untouched – namely its lack of a single geographical site. The Parliament has always operated in 'bits and pieces', partly in Lux-

13 To the intense disappointement of some member states. See for example the Luxembourg position in European Council (1986) *Speeches and Statements Made on the Occasion of the Signing of the Single European Act* at pp 16–18 (Brussels: EC).
14 For analysis of post-1986 developments see Boyce B (1993) 'The democratic deficit of the European Community' *Parliamentary Affairs* 458–477.
15 The complexities of the procedure are helpfully explained in Shaw *op cit* at pp 79–82.
16 Corbett R (1989) 'Testing the new procedures; the European Parliament's first experiences with its new "Single Act" powers' 7 *Journal of Common Market Studies* 362–372 at p 364.
17 The increase in the EP's powers did however necessitate explicit statutory approval of the SEA Treaty by the UK Parliament in accordance with s 6 of the EPEA 1978, rather than the process of 'incorporation' via Order in Council provided for in the ECA 1972 s 1; see pp 498–500 above.

embourg, in Strasbourg and in Brussels. Such fragmentation both undermines the efficiency with which it can operate, and deprives it of a coherent physical identity with which to convey its significance within the Community's structure. While the Parliament has repeatedly sought a single site,[18] the power to grant that request lies with the Council, which has thus far failed to respond.

On a more grandiose plane, the SEA's preamble announced that the member states were:

> 'DETERMINED to work together to promote democracy on the basis of the fundamental rights recognised in the constitutions and laws of the member states, in the Convention for the Protection of Human Rights and Fundamental Freedoms and the European Social Charter, notably freedom, equality and social justice' (original emphasis).

Despite this statement of intent, the SEA did not introduce any substantial scheme of human rights protection into the treaty's text, nor take the seemingly obvious step of expressly incorporating the provisions of the European Convention on Human Rights into Community law. Nevertheless, the preamble may be seen as tacit member state acceptance of the ECJ's by then evident fondness for concluding that the EC's constitutional order contained implied terms analogous to the ECHR's provisions.

The preamble encapsulates a recurrent feature of Community law-making; namely member states' acceptance of the abstract legitimacy of political values to which they are not prepared to give explicit legal status. For some commentators, such legal lacunae in the SEA's formal structure were a cause of great regret. Ehlerman, for example, seemed to assume the necessity of an almost messianic role for formalistic legal change as a mechanism for effective Community integration in concluding that: 'the SEA not only fails to live up to the Commission's expectations, but also leaves much to be desired in its wording'.[19] In contrast, Edward advances a rather more pragmatic view, describing the SEA as a 'political manifesto . . . a moral and political commitment'.[20]

It is perhaps surprising that seasoned EC commentators should place much emphasis on the 'wording' of the SEA. For one could not accurately predict in 1986 what interpretation the ECJ would subsequently give to the amended version of the treaty. In the first 30 years of the Community's existence, the ECJ had propounded and (eventually) won member state acceptance of a series of integrationist legal principles which do not feature in the treaty's

18 See Case 230/81: *Luxembourg v European Parliament* [1983] ECR 255.
19 (1987) *op cit* p 404.
20 (1987) *op cit* p 20.

text. It would seem entirely plausible to assume that the ECJ would subsequently bring such an ethos to bear on the terms of the SEA. But for at least one national government, the fear of the EC's 'creeping competence' was triggered not by the ECJ's jurisprudence, but by the integrationist enthusiasm of the President of the Commission.

Domestic disquiet: Margaret Thatcher's Bruges speech

The driving force behind the the SEA reforms had been the then Commission President, Jacques Delors, a Frenchman who had served as a minister in François Mitterand's socialist government. Delors was committed to the incrementalist ideal of furthering political union between the member states, and suggested in a speech in 1988 that the EC would evolve into a federal government akin to that of the United States in the forseeable future.

Such sentiments alarmed the then British Prime Minister Margaret Thatcher, who promptly publicised her own view of the Community's future development in a speech delivered at the College of Europe, Bruges, on 20 September 1988.[1] Thatcher premised her view of Europe's development on what she regarded as the essential issue of preserving British 'sovereignty':

'Willing and active co-operation between independent sovereign states is the best way to build a successful European Community . . . It would be folly to try to fit [the member states] into some sort of identikit European personality.'

It would be somewhat misleading to describe this view as defending 'national' sovereignty. Rather it entailed undiluted retention of the UK Parliament's omnicompetent legal authority so that successive Thatcher governments could continue (unhindered by either domestic or EC dissent) to impose their preferred ideological agenda on the people of the United Kingdom:

'We have not successfully rolled back the frontiers of the state in Britain only to see them re-imposed at a European level with a European superstate exercising a new dominance from Brussels. . . . The lesson of the economic history of Europe in the 1970s and 1980s is that

---

1 The speech is thoroughly reported in *The Times*, 21 September 1988.

central planning and detailed control don't work, and that personal endeavour and initiative do. . . .'

Given the UK's poor economic performance during the 1980s relative to other member states, Thatcher's lauding of Hayekian theory may seem ill-founded, especially since the economically most successful state, Germany, had a highly interventionist government and advocated still closer EC integration. But the speech's main significance was that it suggested that the Thatcher government would adopt a sceptical, obstructionist approach to all integrationist EC initiatives; that the UK would be a grudging, ill-tempered member of the Community club.

The Commission described the Bruges speech as 'unrelentingly naive'. Its contents had not been cleared with the then Foreign Secretary, Sir Geoffrey Howe, who evidently viewed its style and content with 'weary horror'.[2] The speech lent a sharper edge to the fundamental divisions over European policy which had riven the Conservative party ever since the 1972 accession rebellion. It was enthusiastically received in the Eurosceptic wing of the party,[3] but was met with dismay by several senior Cabinet members and a substantial number of Euro-enthusiast backbenchers.[4] As we shall see below, Thatcher's perception of both the nature and location of what we might term the 'ultimate political fact' of the UK's EC membership was in the longer term to prove seriously flawed.

In the shorter term, however, it had a significant effect. In 1989, eleven of the member states had adopted a *Community Charter of Fundamental Social Rights of Workers*. The so-called '*Social Charter*' advocated a significant extension of Community competence in social policy matters, to encompass workers' rights to fair remuneration and adequate protection against unfair dismissal, redundancy, and unsafe working conditions. The British government opposed such measures, seeing them as a re-expansion of the 'frontiers of the state'. The Charter was merely a Declaration, not a binding part of EC law. Even in this form however, it was unacceptable to the Thatcher government, which refused to sign the Declaration.[5] As noted below, the Social Charter was to return to haunt Margaret Thatcher's successor as Prime minister. For the present, however, our analysis of the Community's impact on

---

2 Young (1991) *op cit* p 550.
3 Clark *op cit* pp 225–227.
4 See Young *op cit* ch 23.
5 See generally Shaw *op cit* ch 16.

the United Kingdom's constitution takes us once again to the case law of the ECJ.

II. NORMATIVE SUPRA-NATIONALISM – THE ECJ CONTINUES

The passage of the SEA presented the ECJ with continuing as well as new challenges. We will focus on two issues in the following section. The first concerns the domestic legal impact of unincorporated or incorrectly incorporated directives; the second, the nature of 'democracy' within the EC's law-making process.

The 'indirect effect of directives'

As we saw in chapter 11, the ECJ had concluded (for one assumes 'diplomatic' reasons) in *Marshall* that directives could have only vertical direct effect; they were enforceable in national courts only against 'government' bodies. This created two substantial problems for the effet utile of community law, insofar as it undermined the level playing field as between those member states which accurately implemented directives into national law and those which did not, and also raised the possibility that public sector employees working in dilatory member states would enjoy greater protection under EC law than those working for private sector organisations. The problem threatened to become more acute in the aftermath of the SEA, since much more EC legislation would subsequently appear in the form of directives rather than regulations. The ECJ did not long delay its search for a new legal principle which could solve this difficulty without at the same time running the risk of antagonising the domestic courts.

The roots of so-called 'indirect direct effect' were actually laid a year prior to *Marshall*, in the combined cases of *Von Colson* and *Harz*.[6] The cases presented the ECJ with blatant examples of gender discrimination, in *Von Colson* by a government employer, and in *Harz* by a private company. The ECJ suggested that the the literal meaning of the German law passed to implement the relevant EC Directive (No 76/207) did not give adequate effect to the EC law's intentions. Ms Von Colson could of course have invoked the direct effect of the directive itself; Ms Harz, however, could not. Rather than approve so patently discriminatory an

6 Case 14/83: [1984] ECR 1891; and Case 79/83: [1984] ECR 1921.

outcome in the two cases, the ECJ opted for a strategy which allowed both claimants to enforce their EC rights in the same way.

The nub of the ECJ's judgment was that the German courts hearing the *Von Colson* and *Harz* cases were obliged by EC law to interpret domestic law in a manner that facilitated the achievement of EC objectives. The duty of loyalty imposed by art 5 bound not just national legislatures and governments, but embraced:

> 'all the authorities of the member states including . . . the courts. It follows that, in applying the national law and in particular the provisions of a national law introduced in order to implement Directive 76/207, national courts are required to interpret their national law in the light of the wording and purpose of the directive in order to achieve the result referred to in the third paragraph of Article 189 . . . in so far as they are given discretion to do so under national law.'[7]

The above extract typifies the rather ambiguous nature of the ECJ's *Von Colson* judgment. Read superficially, *Von Colson* seems to suggest no more than the uncontroversial proposition that a domestic court interpret ambiguous domestic legislation in a manner that accords with its country's international law obligations. But once the judgment is placed in the context of the EC as a 'new legal order', several rather thorny questions arise.

For example, is 'discretion under national law' to include the supremacy principle espoused by the ECJ itself in *Costa* and *Simmenthal*, or is it to be restricted to 'purely' domestic legal principles? Similarly, is the 'interpretive' technique to be adopted by the national court one which mirrors the ECJ's own teleological, integrationist position, or one that remains loyal to less adventurous domestic principles?

Relatedly, is the 'national law' to be interpreted as a concept entirely at large within the domestic legal system, or one limited solely to legislation introduced specifically to implement a directive? If the former view was taken, national courts could presumably scour all domestic laws for a suitable legal peg on which to hang the EC law, or even, in some legal systems, fashion a new remedy themselves with which to achieve the result sought by the directive. If the latter view prevailed, *Von Colson* would not assist citizens in member states which had either assumed that domestic legislation predating the directive in question adequately fulfilled the EC's objectives, or had declined to introduce any implementing legislation at all.

While providing a route round *Marshall* in some instances, *Von*

7 *Ibid*, at paras 26 and 28.

Colson perhaps raised more questions than it solved. Yet in one sense it was an extraordinarily clever exercise in supra-national judicial constitution making, in so far as the ECJ managed to recast the problem of unimplemented directives from being a dispute between the Member State and the ECJ to a dispute between the member state and its own courts. The ECJ further emphasised this point in *Johnston v Chief Constable of the Royal Ulster Constabulary*, when it held that a domestic court should invoke the direct effect of a directive against a government body only if it was unable to achieve the same result through creative interpretation of national law.[8] Quite how that dispute was conducted in the UK is explored below. But before we turn to that question we should focus briefly on the second major case in the indirect direct effect saga.

Some six years after *Von Colson*, in *Marleasing*,[9] the ECJ resolved the temporal ambiguity created by *Von Colson*. After referring to its *Von Colson* judgment, the ECJ continued:

> 'it follows that, in applying national law, *whether the provisions in question were adopted before or after the directive*, the national court called upon to interpret is required to do so, as far as possible, in the light of the wording and purpose of the directive in order to achieve the result pursued by the latter . . .' (emphasis added).[10]

We will shortly consider the impact of both cases in the UK's domestic law. Firstly, however, we turn to ECJ innovations in the regulation of the Community's own law-making process.

Reducing the democratic deficit: judicial initiatives

The treaty has always required that EC institutions identify the 'legal base' of their legislative actions. This would seem a logical demand in respect of any legislative body which has only limited competence. Prior to 1986, the ECJ was called upon on several occasions via art 173 proceedings to decide if the acts of a particular institution had any defensible legal base at all within the treaty.[11]

---

8 Case 222/84: [1986] ECR 1651 at paras 53–54.
9 Case C-106/89: [1990] ECR I 4135.
10 *Ibid*, at para 8.
11 *Stölting* Case 138/78: [1979] ECR 713; *France, Italy and UK v EC Commission* Case 188/80: [1982] ECR 2545; Case 281/85: *Germany v EC Commission* (*Migrant policy*) [1987] ECR 3203. See generally Biebr R (1984) 'The settlement of institutional conflicts on the basis of Article 4 of the Treaty' *CMLRev* 505–523.

However the super-imposition of new community competences in the SEA on to the existing Treaty raised the prospect that it would theoretically be possible for the Community to achieve particular objectives through more than one type of law-making process. In such circumstances, the treaty itself did not specify which process was to be accorded priority. The question was not simply an abstract one; it had substantial implications for both the 'institutional balance' and the supra/inter-national balance within the Community's legislative machinery. It was clear, for example, that the Parliament's relative importance vis-à-vis the Council would be enhanced if an Act's legal base required the co-operation procedure rather than the consultation process. Similarly, supra-national forces would enjoy greater influence at the expense of inter-national sentiment if legislation could be adopted via qualified majority or simple majority voting rather than unanimity. In either case, the base chosen would be likely to influence the substantive content of the legislation enacted. One might plausibly assume that the enacting institutions should opt for whichever base was most likely to facilitate achievement of Community objectives. However the SEA offered no precise criteria against which to assess that question. This was a legal lacuna which the ECJ rapidly took the opportunity to fill.

The issue before the ECJ in *EC Commission v EC Council (Generalised Tariff Preferences)*[12] concerned the legal basis of a Council Regulation fixing the tariff régime for certain imported goods. The Council had adopted the measure via art 235, which required unanimous voting and consultation of the Parliament. The Commission maintained that the measure should have been adopted via art 113, which demanded qualified majority voting (but had no role for the Parliament). In upholding the Commission's claim, the ECJ offered a broad statement of principle in respect of legal base questions:

> 'It must be observed that in the context of the organisation of the powers of the Community the choice of the legal basis for a measure may not depend simply on an institution's conviction as to the objective pursued but must be based on objective factors which are amenable to judicial review.'[13]

Quite what was meant by 'objective factors' was not entirely

12 Case 45/86: [1987] ECR 1493, [1988] 2 CMLR 131.
13 *Ibid*, at para 11. Readers seeking a domestic analogy might refer to the *De Keyser Royal Hotel* case (pp 112–113 above).

clear from this particular case. However in subsequent litigation,[14] the ECJ conflated this notion of 'objectivity' with the requirement that the Community must always choose the most 'democratic' and integrationist legislative method when a choice is available. Thus a simple majority vote is to be preferred to qualified majority procedures, which are themselves preferable to unanimity. Similarly, processes which demand the co-operation of the Parliament are to be chosen in preference to those requiring merely consultation.

To label such criteria 'objective' is something of a judicial sleight of hand, for it assumes that supra-nationalism and minimising the democratic deficit are in some sense 'natural' or uncontested values.[15] In the context of the ECJ's jurisprudential tradition, those assumptions are readily understandable, but that is to ignore questions as to the legitimacy of the tradition itself. As we have repeatedly seen, that larger question remains distinctly controversial in the eyes of some domestic political and judicial audiences. We return to the issues of institutional balance and democratic deficit in considering the terms of the Maastricht Treaty. Before doing so, however, we address the reception afforded by the UK courts to the principles espoused by the ECJ in *Von Colson* and *Marleasing*.

III. EC LAW, PARLIAMENTARY SOVEREIGNTY AND THE UK COURTS: PHASE TWO

We saw in chapter 12 that the British judiciary took some time to come to terms with the constitutional implications of the supremacy and direct effect principles. *Von Colson* and *Marleasing* presented a challenge of a rather different kind, since they seemed to require national courts to adopt avowedly teleological or purposive interpretive techniques in respect of domestic legislation, and, insofar as the 'national law' was a concept broadly construed,

---

14 Case C-300/89: *EC Commission v EC Council* (*Titanium dioxide*) [1991] ECR I-2867; Case C-295/90: *European Parliament v EC Council* (*Student residence rights*) [1992] 3 CMLR 281. For an overview see Bradley K (1987) 'Maintaining the balance: the role of the Court of Justice in defining the institutional position of the European Parliament' *CMLRev* 41–64; Crosby S (1991) 'The single market and the rule of law' *ELRev* 451–465.

15 The ECJ's predisposition to enhance the Parliament's status within the Community's institutional balance has also been displayed in decisions which, in apparent contradiction of the terms of the treaty, afforded the Parliament the capacity to challenge the legality of Acts of the Commission and Council before the court. See Case C-70/88: *European Parliament v EC Council* (*Chernobyl*) [1992] 1 CMLR 91.

to create new common law principles to give practical effect to EC directives. British courts could plausibly point to the ECA 1972 s 2 as a parliamentary command for them to accept the supremacy and direct effect principles. However the literal interpretation of s 2 was that it *reached only directly effective EC law*; it would thus not apply to any attempt to enforce the provisions of a directive against a non-governmental body.[16] Consequently, if British courts felt that they required a domestic, statutory basis for applying the *Von Colson* and *Marleasing* principles, they would have to turn to the ECA 1972 s 3. Alternatively, it was conceivable that British courts could simply amend common law principles of statutory interpretation to achieve the same end. Both techniques would have unorthodox constitutional connotations. But after a hesitant start, the House of Lords responded to the challenge with some alacrity.

Duke v GEC Reliance

Like Mrs Marshall, Mrs Duke, the plaintiff in *Duke v GEC Reliance Ltd*[17] worked for an employer who required women to retire at 60, but permitted men to work until they were 65. Such discrimination, Mrs Duke assumed, contravened the Equal Treatment Directive. We may recall that in *Marshall*, the ECJ held that Directive 76/207 (and indeed all other directives) did not have horizontal direct effect. Mrs Marshall could rely on the directive because the Area Health Authority was a government body for direct effect purposes; but since GEC was a private company, Mrs Duke could not do so. She was forced instead to rely on either the *Von Colson* principle – namely that art 5 required UK courts to interpret the Sex Discrimination Act 'in so far as it is given discretion to do so under national law' to give effect to the directive's intentions – and/or that the ECA 1972 s 2(4) in itself directed the courts to interpret the SDA 1975 in such a way.

The House of Lords rejected both arguments. Section 2(4) could only have the effect Mrs Duke wished in respect of directly effective EC provisions. As noted above, that conclusion is unavoidable if s 2 is interpreted in a literalist fashion. However, the court also declined to apply *Von Colson*, not because it considered the ECJ's principle unsound, but because the principle was not relevant to Mrs Duke's factual situation. *Von Colson*, Lord Templeman concluded, did not require national courts to invent new domestic

16 See p 498 above.
17 [1988] 1 All ER 626, HL.

laws empowering them to 'distort' domestic statues in order to give effect to *all* non-directly effective EC directives. Such 'distortion' would be permissible only in respect of domestic legislation passed in order to give effect to pre-existing EC law. In respect of UK statutes which predated the relevant EC directive, the court could do no more than invoke the traditional interpretive theory applied to international law obligations: namely that in the event of ambiguity, a statute should given whichever meaning best satisfied the UK's international obligations. Unfortunately for Mrs Duke, Lord Templeman considered that the SDA 1975 s 6(4) unambiguously permitted discriminatory retirement ages; it could not plausibly be interpreted in any other way.

The difference between 'interpretation' (which Lord Templeman thought acceptable) and 'distortion' (which he considered illegitimate) is less than entirely clear. Critics of *Duke* suggested that it would not have been impossible for the House of Lords to have found for the plaintiff.[18] Indeed, its failure to do so created several anomalies, both between the UK and those member states where the directive was fully implemented, and within the UK between women working for public and private sector companies. The judgment suggests that the House of Lords was unwilling to accept that the ECA 1972 s 3 had empowered it to disobey or 'distort' domestic legislation to give effect to non-directly effective EC rights: in such litigation, a statute's clear words remained the judiciary's rule of recognition. Nevertheless, *Duke* did indicate that domestic legislation which had been introduced in order to implement an EC directive, but whose words failed to produce a result consistent with EC law, would be open to judicial 'distortion'. The opportunity to test that hypothesis soon arose.

Pickstone v Freemans plc

The plaintiff in *Pickstone v Freemans plc*[19] contended that she and other women colleagues working as 'warehouse operatives' were being paid less than male 'warehouse checker operatives' whose work was of equal value to their own. The Equal Pay Act 1970 (EPA) had initially provided that comparative studies of the 'value' of different jobs could be conducted only with the employer's consent:

---

18 Fitzpatrick B (1989) 'The significance of EEC Directives in UK sex discrimination law' *Oxford Journal of Legal Studies* 336–355; Szyszczak E (1990) 'Sovereignty: crisis, compliance, confusion, complacency' *ELRev* 480–488.
19 [1989] AC 66, HL.

an obstructive employer could therefore prevent women employees establishing that discrimination had occurred. The Commission regarded this 'employer's veto' as in breach of EC law, insofar as it prevented individuals enforcing their EC entitlements. In a subsequent art 169 action, the ECJ upheld the Commission's claim, holding that EC law required that employers could not be permitted to deny employees access to job evaluation mechanisms.[20]

The UK government (acting under the ECA 1972 s 2(2)) subsequently introduced regulations which, according to the speech of the sponsoring minister in the Commons, were intended to implement the ECJ's judgment. This was done by empowering Industrial Tribunals to order job evaluation studies in certain circumstances. However, *Pickstone* revealed a flaw in the regulations' text. On their face, they seemed to preclude an action before a tribunal when a man was employed in exactly the same job at the same pay as the woman complainant. If this was correct, an employer could evade evaluation of different jobs by employing one 'token' male amongst a predominantly female workforce (as Freemans had allegedly done). The UK would therefore have failed to comply with its EC obligations.

A unanimous House refused to reach this conclusion. Lord Keith felt that: 'Parliament cannot possibly have intended such a failure'.[1] Consequently he thought it appropriate to go beyond the bare words of the regulation, and to construe it 'purposively' by examining *Hansard* to confirm that 'Parliament's' intention was to comply with the Directive. Thus construed, the regulation was consistent with EC law. This technique was in itself a quite radical innovation.[2] But Lord Templeman went a step further. His examination of *Hansard* led him to conclude that: 'In my opinion there must be implied in paragraph (c) . . . the words "as between the woman and the man with whom she claims equality".'[3]

Litster v Forth Dry Dock and Engineering Co Ltd [4]

Litster raised a dispute over Directive 77/187, which the EC enacted to 'provide for the protection of employees in the event

---

20 Case 61/81: *EC Commission v UK* [1982] ICR 578.

1 *Ibid*, at 112.

2 This case of course pre-dated *Pepper v Hart*, and provided part of the justification for the overturning of the traditonal rule in the latter case. We will return to the inter-relationship of the two cases below.

3 At 120.

4 [1990] 1 AC 546, HL.

of a change of employer, in particular to ensure that their rights are safeguarded'. Art 4(1) specifically provided that: 'The transfer of an undertaking, business or part of a business shall not in itself constitute grounds for dismissal by the transferor or the transferee'. The rationale behind the directive was to ensure that employers could not evade unfair dismissal or redundancy payment legislation through the simple expedient of transfering their business to someone else.

The UK tried to incoporate Directive 77/187 through the Transfer of Undertakings (Protection of Employment) Regulations 1981. Regulation 5(1) provided that any transfer did not extinguish the employee's contractual rights, but made them enforceable against the new employer. The problem in *Litster* arose because reg 5(3) then provided that the rule in reg 5(1) applies only to employees employed by the transferor 'immediately' before the transfer. The employees in *Litster* were sacked at 3.30pm on the day of the transfer. The transfer itself happened at 4.30 pm. The new company then claimed that this one hour gap meant that the workers were not employed by the transferor 'immediately' before the transfer, and so could not enforce their contractual rights against the new owner.

The ECJ had recently held that workers should be regarded as still employed by the transferor if the only reason for their dismissal was the projected transfer.[5] It was accepted on the facts that this was indeed the reason for the dismissal in *Litster*, but the employer argued that the British courts were bound to apply the UK legislation in its literal sense; literally construed, a gap of one hour could not amount to immediacy.

The House of Lords accepted that a literal interpretation of 'immediately' supported the transferee's argument. A unanimous House nevertheless found in the employees' favour, albeit through slightly different reasoning. Lord Templeman accepted that *Von Colson* required domestic courts to adopt a purposive approach to domestic law 'issued for the purpose of complying with directives'.[6] However, in contrast to his decision in *Duke*, he saw no need to read words into the domestic legislation. Rather, he preferred to construe reg 5(3):

'on the footing that it applies to a person employed immediately before the transfer or who would have been so employed if he had not been

---

5 Case 101/87: *P Bork International A/S v Foreningen af Arbejdsledere i Danmark* [1989] IRLR 41.
6 *Ibid*, at 558.

unfairly dismissed before the transfer for a reason connected with the transfer.'[7]

Lord Oliver referred back to *Pickstone* to justify purposive construction of domestic law introduced to give effect to EEC law: 'even though it may involve some departure from the strict and literal application of the words which the legislature has elected to use.'[8] He regarded the employer's strategy as a transparent device to evade the spirit of the regulations. Invoking Lord Templeman's methodology in *Duke*, Lord Oliver considered it beholden upon the courts to counter such evasion by implying words into the domestic legislation:

> 'In effect this involves reading reg 5(3) as if there were inserted after the words "immediately before the transfer" the words "or would have been so employed if he had not been unfairly dismissed in the circumstances described in reg 8(1)".'[9]

Pickstone and Litster – usurping the legislative function?

By adding words to legislation, Lord Templeman in *Pickstone* and Lord Oliver in *Litster* seemed to embrace the position adopted 40 years earlier by Lord Denning in *Magor*,[10] a position promptly dismissed by Lord Simonds as a 'naked usurpation of the legislative function'. There would seem to be two possible ways to explain this development. Both imply there is something 'special' in the constitutional sense about EC membership, but neither presents a direct threat to orthodox theories of parliamentary sovereignty.

Firstly, Lords Templeman and Oliver could clothe their constitutional nudity beneath the cloak of the ECA 1972 s 3, which might be construed as ordering the UK courts to adopt whichever interpretive technique the ECJ currently required of them. The ECA 1972 would thus be unorthodox (indeed perhaps even 'unconstitutional') from a conventional perspective, insofar as it seeks to give the courts pervasive commands about interpretive techniques, a matter which, as stressed in chapter 3, has traditionally been regarded as a question of common law. Such an Act (while obviously not 'illegal'), could plausibly be seen as incompatible with traditional understandings of the rule of law and the separation of powers.

The second amounting to no more than a judicial recognition that EC membership has triggered such a profound change in

---

7 *Ibid.*
9 *Ibid*, at 577.

8 *Ibid*, at 559.
10 See pp 89–90 above.

social and economic conditions that it is time for the common law to recognise the legitimacy of a new interpretive strategy in order to protect EC law entitlements. That conclusion need have no root in the ECA 1972, nor indeed in any other statute. And until such time as the courts' new presumption is negated or amended by statute, it presents no theoretical threat to Parliament's sovereignty.

Yet while *Litster* and *Pickstone* can be reconciled with Diceyan orthodoxies, they did not meet the ECJ's requirements in *Marleasing*. The reasoning deployed by the House of Lords in *Litster* gives full effect to the narrow interpretation of *Von Colson*. The House appeared to say that it was 'given discretion under national law' (per *Von Colson*) to invent a new common law new rule of statutory interpretation in respect of legislation passed specifically to implement pre-existing EC law (or to find such a command in the ECA 1972), but such 'discretion' did not extend (as required by *Marleasing* or the broad interpretation of *Von Colson*) to applying similar rules to domestic legislation predating the relevant EC measure.

It is difficult to discern any functional basis in domestic legal theory for such a chronological distinction.[11] Stripped to its bones, the judicial methodology employed in *Duke* and *Litster* is to ask: 'What would Parliament have done if it had realised that the literal meaning of the words it wished to use was incompatible with a new EC law?' The answer, of course, is that 'Parliament would have used the words which we are now implying into the Act'. The methodology required by *Marleasing* is just the same – namely to ask 'What would Parliament have done if it had realised that it needed to alter the literal meaning of the words in an existing statute in order to avoid incompatibility with a new EC law?' The answer, of course, is that 'Parliament would have enacted amending legislation containing the words which we are now implying into the original Act'. In both circumstances, the court is putting words into Parliament's mouth. It is no less a radical innovation for a court to do so when Parliament has spoken in error than when it has, again in error, failed to speak at all. The House of Lords appeared to recognise this illogicality shortly afterwards, and in *Webb v EMO Air Cargo (UK) Ltd*[12] it adopted the temporal aspect of *Marleasing*.

---

11 See the critical comment by Szyszczak (1990) *op cit.* For an attempt to do so see Steiner J (1990) 'Coming to terms with EC directives' 106 *LQR* 144–159.

12 [1992] 4 All ER 929, HL. For comment see Szyszczak E (1993) 'Interpretation of Community law in the courts' *ELRev* 214–225.

IV. THE END OF PARLIAMENTARY SOVEREIGNTY: OR ITS REAPPEARANCE?

Despite their radical practical implications, *Duke* and *Litster* could be portrayed in theory simply as an innovation in judicial interpretation of statutes. They did not involve a blunt challenge to legislation which could be reconciled with EC law only by affording the concept of 'interpretation' a meaning that paid no heed at all to linguistic limitations and encompassed the presumably distinct concept of defiance. That challenge, however, was not long in coming.

The demise of the legal doctrine – *Factortame?*

The *Factortame* litigation arose from a dispute over fishing rights in British waters. The Merchant Shipping Act 1894 had allowed foreign owned vessels to register as 'British', and thereby gain the right to fish in British waters. By the late 1980s, some 95 boats owned by Spanish companies had done so. The British government, alarmed by the impact this 'foreign' fleet was having on fishing stocks, asked Parliament to enact the Merchant Shipping Act 1988 (MSA 1988). The 1988 Act altered the registration rules to require a far higher level of 'Britishness' in a ship's owners or managers.[13] None of the 95 Spanish ships could meet this test. Factortame, one of the affected companies, subsequently launched an action in the British courts claiming that the 1988 Act was substantively incompatible with EC law.

The High Court referred the substantive question to the ECJ. It was likely that 18–20 months would elapse before the ECJ issued its judgment. The High Court therefore granted Factortame an interim injunction 'disapplying' the Act and ordering the Secretary of State not to enforce it against any ship that met the previous registration criteria.[14] The Court of Appeal set aside the order for interim injunction, on which point Factortame appealed to the House of Lords.

Lord Bridge gave the sole judgment. He accepted that not issuing an interim injunction would cause irreparable damage,

---

13 Including, inter alia, requirements that individual owners had to be British citizens or residents, and that corporate owners had to be incorporated in Britain, with 75% of their shares owned by British citizens/residents.
14 See Gravells N (1989) 'Disapplying an Act of Parliament pending a preliminary ruling: constitutional enormity or common law right' *Public Law* 568–586.

perhaps even bankruptcy to Factortame, since the company had no immediate prospect of using its boats elsewhere. He also accepted that the House of Lords would accord supremacy to EC law if the ECJ eventually ruled that the Merchant Shipping Act was inconsistent with EC law. This apparently clear acceptance of the supremacy doctrine goes considerably further than the formulae advanced in *Macarthys* or *Garland*. Lord Bridge suggested that the 1972 Parliament had passed legislation in the form of the ECA 1972 s 2 which in some mysterious manner was incorporated into every subsequent UK Act which affects a directly effective EC right. The inference thus appeared to be that the courts would no longer obey an Act of Parliament which breached directly effective EC law even if the Act expressly stated it was intended to achieve that result.

But that conclusion was not germane to the present appeal, the nub of which was that a British court should refuse to allow the government to apply an Act of Parliament because of the *possibility* the Act might subsequently prove incompatible with EC law. This request:

> 'unlike any order for interim relief known to the law, would irreversibly determine in the applicant's favour for a period of some two years rights which are necessarily uncertain until the preliminary ruling of the ECJ has been given. If the applicants fail to establish the rights they claim before the ECJ, the effect of the interim relief granted would be to have conferred upon them rights directly contrary to Parliament's sovereign will. . . . I am clearly of the opinion that, as a matter of English law, the court has no power to make an order which has these consequences.'[15]

Lord Bridge could not find any domestic authority for such a radical proposition. Nor was he ultimately persuaded that there was an overriding principle of Community law requiring the House of Lords to issue the interim injuction. Lord Bridge noted that after hearing the arguments made by Factortame's counsel:

> 'I was strongly inclined to the view that, if English law could provide no effective remedy to secure the interim protection of the rights claimed by the applicants, it was nevertheless our duty under community law to devise such a remedy.'[16]

However, on hearing the arguments of the government's counsel, Lord Bridge was persuaded that any such duty on the domestic courts arose only in respect of substantive rights already clearly

15 *Ibid*, at 142–143.
16 *Ibid*, at 151.

established under EC law. The 'rights' claimed by Factortame had yet to be pronounced upon by the ECJ. Consequently, the House of Lords referred its own question to the ECJ, asking if it should disapply domestic law in order to safeguard as yet unproven EC law rights.

The litigation before the ECJ

Shortly thereafter, the ECJ heard an art 169 action brought by the Commission against the UK which claimed that the Merchant Shipping Act breached the UK's treaty obligations. In *EC Commission v UK*,[17] the Commission asked the ECJ to make an interim order per art 186 ordering the British government not to enforce the 1988 Act.

The ECJ saw some merit in the UK's position, since the 1988 Act might prove a defensible means to pursue the EC's own objective of conserving long-term fish stocks. However the Act's overt discrimination against non-British EC nationals seriously undermined the UK's case. Moreover, there was no doubt that enforcement of the Act would inflict extremely heavy losses on the Spanish shipowners. In those circumstances, the ECJ granted an interim order requiring the UK to 'suspend' the 1988 legislation.

The ECJ subsequently gave judgment on the question referred to it by the House of Lords, in *R v Secretary of State for Transport, ex p Factortame Ltd (No 2)*.[18] After referring explicitly to the *Simmenthal* principle of immediate supremacy, the court observed that national courts, were obliged by the 'principle of co-operation laid down in Article 5' to ensure that domestic legal systems give practical legal effect to directly effective EC rights. Any provision within the national legal system which impairs this effect would be incompatible with EC law. This principle applied as readily to questions of interim as final relief. Consequently, if the sole obstacle to interim relief is 'a rule of national law', the national court must set aside that rule.

Back in the House of Lords . . .

The House of Lords announced that it had held in Factortame's favour, and would disapply the MSA 1988, in June 1988. Its reasons would be given a later date. The announcement provoked apoca-

---

17 C-246/89R: *EC Commission v UK* [1989] ECR 3125.
18 Case C-213/89: [1990] ECR I-2433.

lyptic denunciations from Prime Minister Thatcher[19] about losses of national sovereignty to the Commission. The leading judgment in *R v Secretary of State for Transport, ex p Factortame Ltd (No 2)*[20] was given by Lord Goff. However Lord Bridge took the opportunity to comment on claims (whose source he diplomatically did not name) that the decision 'was a novel and dangerous invasion by a Community institution of the sovereignty of the UK Parliament'.[21] Such criticism was misconceived. Parliament had been quite aware of the supremacy doctrine in 1972, so any 'limitation' of sovereignty that EC membership entailed was 'voluntary'. The ECA 1972 had ordered domestic courts to respect that 'voluntary limitation', so there was nothing novel in this judgment.[1]

As Lord Goff made clear, the ECJ's decision in *Factortame* did not determine the outcome of the domestic litigation. Rather it required the British courts to reject those principles of domestic law (the non-availability of interim injunctions against the Crown and the courts' incapacity to disapply clearly worded statutes) which presented an *absolute* bar to Factortame's claims. Lord Goff made only a passing reference to the ECJ's decision, apparently seeing no need to need to justify or explain it, but accepting it as an uncontentious (if brand new) principle of national law to be integrated into the existing common law rules governing the availability of interim injunctions.

Those rules suggested that interim relief was only available if there was no possibility of the plaintiff eventually gaining damages to cover any loss suffered pending resolution of the main question. No such damages could (at that time)[2] be recovered from the government. The court had then to ask itself if there was a 'strong prima facie case' indicating that the plaintiff would ultimately be successful. Lord Goff considered that the *EC Commission v UK* decision suggested that the substantive issue would be answered by the ECJ in Factortame's favour, which would in itself predispose the court to grant interim relief. However, he also implied that

19 See also Watkins A (1991) 'Mrs Thatcher and the Spanish fishermen' *The Observer*, 30 June.
20 [1991] 1 AC 603.
21 *Ibid*, at 658.
1 Lord Bridge perhaps oversimplified the issue. As we saw in chapter 11, British judges and British governments displayed confusion in the late 1960s and early 1970s as to the nature and implications of *Costa* and *Van Gend*. Moreover, many innovative aspects of the ECJ's own constitutional jurisprudence had appeared after the UK's accession.
2 But see now the discussion of *Francovich* below.

he doubted that the plaintiff needed to show such a high probability of eventual success in this case:

> 'I cannot dismiss from my mind the possibility (no doubt remote) that such a party may suffer such serious and irreparable harm in the event of the law being enforced against him that it may be just or convenient to restrain its enforcement by an interim injunction even though so heavy a burden has not been discharged.'[3]

It seems that *Factortame* has led the House of Lords to a position which suggests that it will allow Parliament to relieve itself from the obligations imposed by directly effective EC law only if the UK leaves the Community altogether. The constitution's basic 'rule of recognition' has undoubtedly undergone a substantial redefinition in recent years. It is perhaps too soon to say if that redefinition amounts to the 'legal revolution' of which Wade wrote in 1955. However it may be that we should ask if a revolution is something that does not require a 'big bang', but can happen incrementally, through a series of radical steps, each of which, ratchet-like, prepares the ground for the next. If so it may indeed be that a revolution in legal theory has occurred. Yet in terms of political practice, it can perhaps be argued that the EC has pushed the constitution in quite the opposite direction, back towards both the anti-factionalist doctrine which underpinned the original formulation of 'parliamentary' sovereignty and towards traditional understandings of Cabinet government as a collective rather than presidential process.

The reappearance of the political doctrine? Monetary union, collective ministerial responsibility and the fall of Margaret Thatcher

Several factors contributed to Conservative MPs' decision to remove Margaret Thatcher as their Leader (and thence as Prime Minister) in November 1990. As chapter 11 suggested, the unpopularity of the community charge led many Conservative MPs to fear defeat in the next general election. Thatcher's close personal identification with the poll tax offered an obvious reason for some Conservative MPs to want a new Leader. Others remained continuingly unhappy with her evident preference for a Presidential style of Cabinet government (a preference which had triggered the resignations of Heseltine in 1985 and Nigel Lawson in 1989).[4]

3 *Ibid*, at 674.
4 See p 339 above.

But the catalytic event was Thatcher's attitude towards the UK's EC membership.

The Treaty of Rome (Title II, Chapter 1) had contained various (seemingly non-justiciable) provisions heralding a co-ordinated approach to macro-economic policy. Member states undertook to maintain the stability of their respective currencies and an approximate equilibrium in their balance of payments. The Commission was empowered to monitor member states' performances in this regard, and to offer financial assistance to member states suffering severe currency or balance of payments crises.

These modest co-ordinatory policies were seen by some observers as a tentative first step towards full blown 'monetary union', which would ultimately require a single EC currency and a central EC bank controlling the Community's money supply and interest rates. This objective has an obvious economic logic in the context of creating a truly 'common' market, insofar as it removes the transaction costs engendered by currency exchanges, and also ensures that businesses in particular member states are not advantaged or disadvantaged vis-à-vis their EC competitors as a result of their own government's monetary policy.

But full monetary union also has profound political implications. A single EC currency and a central EC bank would present a distinct challenge to orthodox notions of national sovereignty. By the late 1960s, it is possible to argue that western economies were sufficiently closely interconnected for it to be practically impossible for any one European country successfully to pursue economic policies entirely independent of those adopted by neighbouring states. Nevertheless, economic and monetary union would remove such practical controls as national governments still possessed, thereby significantly extending the de facto federal nature of the Community and adding further force to arguments for a full political federalisation on the American model.

The EC's first steps towards monetary union had begun in 1969, but rapidly foundered during the recession of the early 1970s. Roy Jenkins, having resigned from the Labour government to become President of the Commission in 1977, put the issue at the top of the Commission's list of priorities, and by 1979 the European Monetary System (EMS) was in place. The EMS existed outside the legal structure of the treaty, and so was not a Community measure in the strict sense. Its central feature was the Exchange Rate Mechanism (ERM), which placed fairly tight limits on fluctuations in currency exchange rates. Member states were not obliged to join the ERM, and successive Labour and Conservative governments chose not to do so, preferring to retain autonomy in exchange rate and interest rate policies.

The SEA itself made scant reference to monetary union, beyond noting the obvious point that giving the EMS and ERM a legal basis within Community law would require further treaty amendment. However in 1988, the European Council instructed Jacques Delors to produce a phased plan for achieving de facto and de jure economic and monetary union. The 1989 Delors *Report on Economic and Monetary Union* envisaged a three-stage process. Firstly, a gradual 'convergence' of the member states' economies in respect of such matters as inflation rates, economic growth, and the balance of payments; secondly, the locking of all member states' currencies into a far tighter ERM, which would tolerate only very small currency fluctuations; and thirdly, the introduction of the single currency.

While many member state governments welcomed the plan, the UK government expressed reservations. The Conservative manifesto for the 1989 EC elections warned that monetary union would 'involve a fundamental transfer of sovereignty. . . . The report, if taken as whole, implies nothing less than the creation of a federal Europe.'[5] Nevertheless, at the Madrid Summit in 1989, the European Council agreed to begin the first stage in 1990, and to initiate the process of treaty amendment to establish a timetable for phases two and three. The British government also agreed that it would enter the ERM at some point in the near future. It seems that the Thatcher government regarded the Madrid summit as a recipe for delay rather than prompt action. However, the other member states took quite the opposite view, with the result that by mid-1990, the Prime Minister and some of her Cabinet colleagues were making distinctly hostile comments about the Delors plan. We noted in chapter 9 that Nicholas Ridley, perhaps the Cabinet member most in sympathy with Thatcher's EC views, had resigned in July 1990 after giving an interview critical of Germany. Some parts of that interview merit further attention here. Ridley had suggested that monetary union was simply: 'a German racket designed to take over the whole of Europe'. He thought that the scheme posed an intolerable threat to British sovereignty: 'You might just as well give it to Adolf Hitler, frankly'.[6]

Ridley's resignation might have been thought to suggest that ministers holding such sentiments should at the least not express them in such terms. But the Cabinet was clearly split on the

---

5 Quoted in Nicol W and Simon T (1994) *Understanding the new European Community* at p 158 (London: Harvester Wheatsheaf).
6 *The Spectator,* 14 July 1990.

monetary union question. The UK finally joined the ERM in October 1990, yet immediately afterwards the Prime Minister herself engaged in a Ridleyesque tirade against the Delors plan. At the European Council's Rome Summit, the other 11 member states expressed their willingness to accelerate plans for further monetary integration. Thatcher resolutely opposed any such initiative, decribing the summit as 'a mess' and her fellow heads of government as living in 'Cloud Cuckoo Land'. On her return to the Commons, Thatcher accused Jaques Delors and the Commission of trying to 'extinguish democracy', and announced she would greet every 'federalist' EC measure with a resounding 'No!'

Thatcher's outburst prompted Geoffrey Howe (the then Deputy Prime Minster) to resign from the Cabinet. His initial explanation that his resignation was over the question of government policy towards the EC was to be expanded upon in a speech to the Commons on 13 November 1990.[7] Howe was never noted as an inspiring orator. He once earned the memorable soubriquet from Dennis Healey that to be criticised by him in debate was 'like being savaged by a dead sheep'. His resignation speech did not contain any stylistic fireworks; but its content had an explosive political effect.

Howe attributed many of the country's economic difficulties to the government's refusal to join the ERM in 1985. He then revealed that the government's eventual commitment to join had been extracted from an unwilling Prime Minister only when he (then Foreign Secretary) and Nigel Lawson (the then Chancellor) had threatened to resign from the Cabinet if it did not do so. Yet Howe suggested that the question of ERM membership was merely a symptom of a more pervasive prime ministerial distaste for the European Community. Echoing Lord Bridge's oblique criticism in *Factortame (No 2)*, Howe asserted that it was a serious error to regard closer European integration, as the Prime Minister appeared to do, as involving the 'surrender of sovereignty'. Making an overt reference to the Bruges speech, Howe argued that such hyperbolic language served only to create:

> 'a bogus dilemma, between one alternative, starkly labelled "co-operation between independent sovereign states", and a second, equally crudely labelled alternative, "centralised federal super-state", as if there were no middle way in between'.[8]

Howe observed that the EC's development was more likely to

---

7 *HCD*, 13 November 1990, c 461–465.
8 *Ibid*, at c 463.

proceed in a direction which coincided with British interests if the government argued its case from the centre of the EC policy-making process, rather than standing on the sidelines and eventually being dragged reluctantly into a reformed Community in which the political agenda had been set to reflect the preferences of its other members.

But Howe's criticism of the Prime Minister did not dwell merely on tactics, it reached also to the question of her basic attitude towards the UK's EC partners. Howe saw no merit in what he termed Thatcher's 'nightmare image' of an EC 'positively teeming with ill-intentioned people, scheming in her words to "extinguish democracy", to "dissolve our national identities" and to lead us "through the back-door into a federal Europe".' Against such Europhobic 'background noise', it was impossible for the Chancellor of the Exchequer to be taken seriously by other member states in any discussion of EC economic policy.

Howe's speech is a graphic example of the Commons' capacity to serve occasionally as a forum for calling the executive to account. The speech revealed not simply a disagreement between a Prime Minister and a senior colleague on a matter of major substantive importance, but also suggested that the country was being governed by a dogmatic Leader who held an ill-mannered contempt for any divergent opinion (be it within Cabinet or from other EC member states), and who utterly rejected traditional principles of Cabinet government. Such criticisms of Thatcher had frequently been made by opposition parties; but they were likely to carry more weight with Conservative MPs when delivered by the man who had served as Chancellor and Foreign Secretary for over ten years in Thatcher's Cabinets.

Thereafter, domestic political events moved with great rapidity. Michael Heseltine, five years after leaving the Cabinet, challenged Thatcher for leadership of the Conservative party. Her failure to win an adequate majority in the subsequent election held among Conservative MPs led to her resignation as party Leader and Prime Minister, and then to John Major's eventual succession.

These events reinforce the presumption that EC membership has wrought significant changes in both orthodox constitutional theory and orthodox constitutional practice. In practical terms, the constitutional history of twentieth-century Britain has been dominated (except during the two world wars) by a straightforward party political division, in which single party governments with relatively distinct and coherent ideological beliefs have deployed a Commons majority to use Parliament's legal sovereignty to pursue their preferred policy programmes. But that picture may now be changing. In part, that is attributable to the courts' recognition of supra-legislative constraints on parliamentary sovereignty on EC matters. It may be fanciful to equate *Costa* and *Factortame* with the pre-revolutionary supra-legislative notion of 'common right and reason', but the analogy is not entirely spurious. Unlike domestic British legislation, most EC laws (those requiring unanimity and qualified majorities in the Council) are the result of consensus and compromise between all the Community's legislators; they cannot be 'factional' in the Madisonian sense. As such, the ECJ and the national courts have assumed the role of anti-majoritarian watchdogs in those areas of government activity where the Community has legislative competence.

But perhaps of greater immediate significance to analysts of the British constitution is the argument that the demise of Margaret Thatcher, seen in conjunction with the extraordinary party political alignments produced in the 1972 accession controversy and the 1975 referendum, indicates that the EC has introduced a profound ideological fault line into the very core of the traditional party political divide. In 1990, it seemed plausible to suggest that neither the Labour nor Conservative party could any longer rely on its MPs to present a unified front on EC questions. Equally, it appeared that EC questions could never be settled in any definitive sense, for Eurosceptics seemed wedded to the belief that only a bare Commons majority would be needed to unravel whatever EC commitments Parliament had previously undertaken. In combination, these factors held out the prospect of a significant weakening of prime ministerial authority vis-à-vis the Cabinet, and of government authority vis-à-vis the House of Commons. We will return to this question in the final section of this chapter. But before doing so, we must make one final journey to the case law of the ECJ.

V. BEYOND DIRECT EFFECT: *FRANCOVICH*

Thatcher's dominance of Britain's political agenda in the 1980s (and thence of much of Britain's constitutional history in that decade), lent her resignation major domestic significance. Yet it was of little moment for the on-going development of the Community's constitutional history. Very rapidly, all eyes turned to the proposals that would eventually feature in the Maastricht Treaty on European Union. But in the interim, the ECJ was continuing its efforts to clarify the relationship between EC law's normative supra-nationalism and the member states' respective constitutional autonomy.

Francovich[9]

The EC Directive at issue in *Francovich* (No 80/987) required member states to institute (by October 1983) a scheme which guaranteed a minimum level of financial protection for workers whose employers became insolvent. The maximum amount of compensation envisaged was modest, being only three months' salary. Nevertheless, Italy chose to ignore the directive. The Commission instituted an art 169 action against Italy in 1987.[10] The ECJ held Italy to be in breach of its treaty obligations, but the Italian government still refused to take steps to implement the directive. Mr Francovich was owed some six million lira by his employer, who had become insolvent in 1985. An Italian court had given judgment in Mr Francovich's favour against the employer under Italian insolvency laws, but since the employer had no resources, it was not possible for that judgment to be enforced. Mr Francovich consequently sued the Italian state in the domestic courts for the compensation he would have received if Directive 80/987 had been correctly incorporated into national law. In an art 177 reference, the ECJ was asked firstly if the directive was directly effective against the Italian state; and secondly, if it was not directly effective, could Mr Francovich nevertheless claim damages against Italy to reimburse him for the loss he had suffered as a result of the directive's non-implementation?

It is conceivable that the ECJ might have found Directive 80/987 directly effective, and thereafter simply applied the supremacy principle to 'instruct' the domestic court to award Mr Francovich the minimum compensation the EC law required. However the court concluded (somewhat unconvincingly)[11] that the measure was not directly effective, since it afforded member states the choice of financing the scheme themselves or requiring it to be underwritten by private sector institutions.

However the ECJ found in Mr Francovich's favour on the second question. The court employed an interpretive methodology very reminiscent of *Van Gend*, suggesting that: 'This problem must be

---

9 Case C-6/90: *Francovich v Italy* [1992] IRLR 84.
10 Case 22/87: *EC Commission v Italy* [1989] ECR 143.
11 Steiner J (1993) 'From direct to *Francovich*: shifting means of enforcement of community law' *ELRev* 3–22.

examined in terms of the general scheme and basic principles of the Treaty.'[12] This purposive approach led the ECJ to hold that: 'the principle of the liability of the State for damage to individuals caused by a breach of Community law for which it is responsible is *inherent in the scheme of the Treaty.*'[13]

Literalists might suggest that 'inherency' is simply a cloak underneath which the ECJ has invented an entirely novel principle of law, which could legitimately be introduced into the EC's constitution only by an amendment to the treaty introduced via art 236. The court did also suggest that this inherent principle also enjoyed some textual basis in art 5 of the treaty, but even that conclusion demands some fairly creative interpretation.

The ECJ continued by identifying three conditions which had to be satisfied before individuals could rely on this newly discovered principle. Firstly, that the relevant EC measure was intended to confer benefits on individuals. Secondly, that the substance of such benefits was clearly defined by the EC legislation. And thirdly, that a causal link existed between the individual's loss and the member state's breach of its treaty obligations. Since all three conditions were met in Mr Francovich's case, he was able to recover damages from the Italian state.

Francovich seemingly opens a new chapter in the history of the domestic impact of EC law. The judgment itself left unanswered many important questions: how tight a causal link would be required between the member state's misfeasance and the loss caused; would liability attach only to egregious and deliberate non-compliance (evidenced by failure to comply with an art 169 judgment) or extend even to unwitting mistakes; would there be a ceiling on the quantum and heads of damages available; on which particular organ of government would liability ultimately fall; and to what extent would the ECJ be prepared to allow the national courts to devise their own answers to these issues?[14]

These remain, at present, matters for speculation. Yet even if *Francovich* is initially to be narrowly construed, the ECJ's gradual extension of the initially narrow concept of direct effect created in *Van Gend* might suggest that *Francovich* will in time grow into an expansive and highly effective tool for citizens to use to enhance the effet utile of EC law. When seen in conjunction with *Marleasing*, the case also reinforces the supposition that the ECJ

12 [1992] IRLR 84 at para 30.
13 [1992] IRLR 84 at para 35 (emphasis added).
14 For initial speculation see Steiner (1993) *op cit*; Craig P (1993) '*Francovich*, remedies and the scope of damages liability' 109 *LQR* 595–621.

is developing its own version of the 'mutual recognition' rather than 'Euronorms' approach to integration which underpinned the Single European Act. Both judgments place responsibility for ensuring the effet utile of Community law firmly in the domestic constitutional arena, with the onus being placed on national courts to pull their respective legislatures into line with EC principles. On a grander scale, this might lead us to suggest that the EC is now lending a further, geographical dimension to traditional British understandings of the separation of powers, in the sense that national judiciaries may be beginning to see themselves as sharing more common ground with their counterparts in the ECJ and the other member states than with their own countries' legislative and judicial branches. It is possible to suggest, for example, that we can identify a 'ripple effect', in which principles espoused by the ECJ and thereafter applied by the domestic courts in respect of EC matters have also begun to influence judicial decision-making on purely domestic issues. We will address this point in greater detail in chapter 14, but two already familiar cases might be adverted to here to illustrate the argument. As noted in chapter 8, in *Pepper v Hart*,[15] the House of Lords departed from the traditional 'exclusionary rule' and concluded that reference might be made to *Hansard* as a guide to statutory interpretation, while in *M v Home Office*[16] the House of Lords rejected traditional assumptions that interim injunctions and the contempt jurisdiction were not available in actions against the Crown. *Pepper* adopted an interpretive rationale very similar to the one the House of Lords had previously applied in *Pickstone* and *Litster. M* seems to elevate the pursuit of effet utile (the 'effet' here being a Diceyan notion of the rule of law) above the constraints of orthodox constructions of statutory régimes.

Neither result was, nor could be, in any sense *required* by EC law. Rather we might suggest that the constitutional principles of the EC have become sufficiently firmly established in the minds of British judges to begin to merge into the courts' constantly evolving conceptions of the contemporary role of the common law. If the hypothesis about a 'ripple effect' is proved accurate, then a further, significant shift towards a purely federalist constitution has slipped, indirectly, and largely unnoticed via the EC's 'new legal order' into the domestic legal system. Other shifts, in contrast, played out in the political rather than judicial arenas, have attracted rather more attention.

15 See pp 314–320 above.
16 See pp 93–100 above.

VI. MAASTRICHT

The substantive reforms to the Community's legal structure introduced by the Maastricht Treaty on European Union (TEU) in 1993 were perhaps less far-reaching than those in the Single European Act. Yet the amendment process proved extremely problematic in several states. The final section of this chapter outlines briefly the substance of the TEU, and then considers the diffculties which attached to its incorporation into UK domestic law.

The terms[17]

The least controversial of the TEU amendments was one of nomenclature; the Community was now formally renamed as the EC rather than the EEC, a measure which formalised popular usage. Questions of labelling retained a symbolic importance throughout the negotiatory process. The British government insisted that any reference to the creation of a 'federal' Europe be deleted from the TEU's text. A somewhat more ambivalent statement of intent was eventually adopted, to the effect that the TEU was intended to be: 'a new stage in the process of creating an ever closer union among the peoples of Europe, in which decisions are taken as closely as possible to the citizen',[18] but which would respect the 'national identities' of the member states.

The TEU introduced several minor extensions in the EC's competence.[19] The Community now has powers in respect of consumer protection, industrial policy, and some education and cultural matters. Perhaps more significantly, a specific timetable was also introduced for commencement of phases two (1 January 1994) and three (1 January 1997 or 1999) of the Delors plan for monetary union.

Further modest efforts were made to reduce the Community's continuing democratic deficit. A new type of law-making process, requiring 'co-decision' between the Parliament and the Council in some areas of Community activity, has increased the influence of the elected chamber. Some effort was also made to strengthen the links between the Community and individual citizens by

---

17 For a brief guide see Hartley T (1993) 'Constitutional and institutional aspects of the Maastricht Agreement' 42 *International and Comparative Law Quarterly* 213–237.
18 TEU art A.
19 An accessible summary is provided by Lane R (1993) 'New Community competences under the Maastricht Treaty' *CMLRev* 939–980.

creating a (thus far largely symbolic) status of EU 'citizenship', and by empowering EC nationals to stand for office and vote in local or European elections anywhere in the Community.[20] The TEU also created a 'Committee of the Regions' within the EC's institutional structure. The committee was intended to give a voice (but, at least initially, little power) in the Community to sub-central units of government within the member states.[1]

The Maastricht negotiations emphasised the plurality of meanings attached to the concept of federalism, both by different member states, and by different political parties within an individual country.[2] The constitutional device eventually adopted to paper over these ideological cracks was the concept of 'subsidiarity'. This in itself is a term bearing a variety of meanings relating to decentralisation of decision-making power.[3] However for the TEU's purposes, this principle was defined thus in what is now art 3b of the EC Treaty:

> 'In areas which do not fall within its exclusive competence, the Community shall take action ... only if and in so far as the objectives of the proposed action cannot be sufficiently achieved by the member states and can therefore, by reason of the scale or effects of the proposed action, be better achieved by the Community.'

Whether subsidiarity would prove a justiciable concept was (and remains) a matter for speculation.[4] It is certainly possible that the concept will provoke 'legal base' litigation before the ECJ. Given the ECJ's commitment to fostering the integration process, it seems unlikely that it will construe subsidiarity as a device to maximise member state autonomy.

The TEU also introduced significant reforms in respect of the

---

20 Raworth P (1994) 'A timid step forwards: Maastricht and the democratisation of the EC' *ELRev* 16–33.

1 In a manner consistent with its dismissive attitude towards local government, the Major administration (uniquely among the member states) proposed that the UK's representatives on the Committee be central government appointees rather than drawn from the elected local authority councillors serving in the areas concerned. The government was defeated on this issue in the Lords. Given the obviously 'anti-democratic' character with which its preference could be painted, the government accepted the defeat, thereby once again enabling the non-elected upper house to don the mantle of guardian of electoral democracy.

2 See Koopmans T (1992) 'Federalism: the wrong debate' *CMLRev* 1047–1052.

3 Peterson J (1994) 'Subsidiarity: a definition to suit any vision' *Parliamentary Affairs* 116–132; Emiliou N (1994) 'Subsidiarity: panacea or fig leaf?', in O'Keeffe D and Twomey P (eds) *Legal Issues of the Maastricht Treaty* (London: Wiley Chancery Law).

4 See Toth A (1994) 'Is subsidiarity justiciable?' *ELRev* 268–285.

Social Charter. Eleven of the 12 member states had wished to place the 1989 Declaration[5] on a legal basis within the Treaty of Rome, thus making it directly effective in all of the member states. The Major government had refused to agree to this reform. This resulted in the rather peculiar legal creature of a Protocol on Social Policy, attached to the TEU, in which the other 11 states agreed to incorporate the Charter into their respective legal systems, and all 12 states agreed that the 11 could use Community institutions (including the ECJ) to administer it.

But for both proponents and opponents of a United States of Europe, other aspects of the TEU may have seemed of greater long-term importance. The TEU provided that the EC itself was now to be seen as merely one 'pillar' of the 'European Union' (EU). The other two pillars would be Common Foreign and Security Policy (CFSP) and Justice and Home Affairs (JHA), which in combination substantially extend the range of the former system of 'European Political Co-operation' introduced by the Single European Act. In formal, legal terms, the CFSP and JHA are not part of the EC, and should perhaps be seen as an exercise in traditional inter-governmental co-operation rather than another 'new legal order' operating in parallel to the Community. However they are serviced by the EC's institutions, and there can be little doubt that many proponents of the Maastricht reform anticipate that all three pillars will in the longer term merge into a single legal order. Such plans may however prove overly optimistic. CFSP and JHA take the member states into far less justiciable territory than that covered by the EC. Nationalist sentiment is likely to be at its most intense over questions of foreign and defence policy: national governments would seem unlikely to wish to cede control over so emotive an issue as involvement in foreign wars, which may dilute EU responses to the point that they are utterly ineffective. Certainly the first test of the EU's ability to operate as an effective player on the foreign policy scene, the war in former Yugoslavia, suggested that the framers of the TEU had severely underestimated the difficulties that would attend joint initiatives in this area.

The inference that Maastricht may have gone too far too fast may also be drawn from consideration of the fate of the plans to achieve monetary union within the EC. The ERM collapsed in spectacular fashion in the autumn of 1993, before the TEU even came into effect. The member states were unable to maintain exchange rate stability in the face of massive speculation on the international money markets against the weaker currencies.

5 See p 526 above.

Consequently several countries, including Britain, left the system. All have expressed a desire to re-enter when economic circumstances permit, but there seems little immediate prospect of that happening. The Major government's withdrawal from the ERM might fancifully be seen as a surrender of sovereignty, not to a political union within which it might wield substantial influence, but to international currency speculators over whom it apparently exercised no control at all. Such an outcome was perhaps a logical consequence of the Thatcher and Major administrations' embrace of Hayekian economic theory – but it betokened a rather larger 'democratic deficit' than had ever afflicted the EC.

The Community's failure to resist these forces undermined its credibility in the eyes of supporters of further integration, and was construed as a sign of more pervasive weakness by its opponents. It is therefore unsurprising that the ratification and incorporation of the Treaty proved so tortuous in several of the member states.

The ratification and incorporation of the treaty

Under the terms of art 236 of the Treaty of Rome, those parts of the TEU which amended the EC Treaty could not come into force until it had been ratified by all the member states in accordance with their own constitutional procedures. The people of Denmark had initially rejected the terms of the treaty in a referendum. Some rapid renegotiation between the member states ensued, whereupon the TEU was approved by a tiny majority in a second Danish referendum. Public opinion was also sharply divided in France, in which the requisite referendum produced a very small majority in favour of the treaty. In Germany, the political argument was clearly won by pro-Maastricht forces, although the German government subsequently faced an (unsuccessful) legal challenge which argued that the TEU was inconsistent with provisions of the Basic Law.

'Ratification' of the TEU presented considerable political difficulties in the UK. The non-EC pillars of the treaty were unproblematic; since there was no need to incorporate their provisions into domestic law, the government could satisfy its international law obligations simply by ratifying the measures through an exercise of the prerogative.

In contrast, the TEU's reforms to the EC would have to be incorporated into national law. Since the TEU increased the powers of the European Parliament, the government was bound by the European Parliamentary Elections Act 1978 s 6 to gain Parliament's approval of the TEU before ratifying it.[6] Given the small size of the government's majority in the Commons at that time (1993),[7] and the continued presence of a dozen or so anti-EC backbenchers within the Conservative ranks, it was not clear that such approval would be forthcoming.

Three possible outcomes to the controversy could be envisaged, none of which seemed to command a majority in the Commons. The first, preferred by the government and loyal backbench Conservatives, was to incorporate the amendments to the EC Treaty and the Social Policy Protocol (including the UK 'opt-out') into domestic law through a simple two clause Act. The second, favoured by the Labour and Liberal parties, was to incorporate a revised treaty in which the UK had 'opted in' to the Social Charter. The third, supported by rebel Conservatives, was to incorporate none of the TEU at all. There then followed an extremely complex series of manoeuvres in the Commons.[8] The government introduced a two clause Bill which stated that the pertinent parts of the TEU were to be added to the list of treaties incorporated by the ECA 1972. The opposition parties succeeded in persuading the Speaker to allow them to table two potentially significant amendments to the Bill.

The first was designed to prevent incorporation of the Social Policy Protocol. If this amendment was carried, the TEU could not be 'ratified' in British law in accordance with art 236. The opposition hoped that in these circumstances the government would feel compelled to seek a renegotiation of the treaty, this time removing the UK's Social Charter opt out, rather than risk losing the entire Maastricht agreement. For Conservative rebels, the allure of the amendment was that a defeat for the government might lead it to reject the TEU in its entirety, thereby forcing the Community to remain at the stage of integration produced by the Single European Act. However, when the amendment was put to the vote, very few Conservative rebels were prepared to take the chance that the government might respond to defeat in the way the opposition parties envisaged. The outcome was a tie, at 317 votes for and against the amendment. The Speaker (to the consternation of Labour MPs, but in accordance with

6 See fn 9, p 516 above.
7 The Conservative majority at the 1992 general election was 21.
8 See Rawlings R (1994) 'Legal politics: the UK and ratification of the Treaty on European Union (part one)' *Public Law* 254–278; Baker D, Gamble A and Ludlum S (1993) 'Whips or Scorpions? The Maastricht vote and Conservative MPs' *Parliamentary Affairs* 147–166.

Commons tradition), used her casting vote in support of the government.

The opposition parties designed the second amendment as an alternative line of attack should their first option be defeated. The amendment provided that the Act would not come into force until the Commons had 'come to resolution' on a government motion considering incorporation of the Social Charter. Given the terms of the EPEA 1978 s 6, approval of this amendment would seemingly prevent the government ratifying the TEU until the lower house had expressly voted in favour of the opt-out.[9] Over 20 Conservative MPs supported this amendment, which was carried by 8 votes.

The Prime Minister thereupon announced that the government's motion on the Social Policy Protocol would be the subject of a vote of confidence the next day, and implied that a defeat would lead to a dissolution. For rebel Conservative MPs, the prospect of a general election in which they might lose their seats, and Labour might win a sufficient Commons majority to incorporate the treaty and the Social Charter, was sufficiently daunting to bring them back into (the party) line. The government's majority in the confidence vote was 40.

But the controversy had not quite run its course. In a manner reminiscent of Mr Blackburn's feeble attempt to prevent the UK's accession to the Community in 1971,[10] right-wing Eurosceptics launched an action in the courts after their cause had been defeated in the Commons.[11] The action was fronted by Lord Rees-Mogg, a crossbench peer and former editor of *The Times*, and funded by Sir James Goldsmith, an ex-patriate financier. Such arguments as Rees-Mogg could muster against ratification and incorporation were peremptorily dismissed by the High Court, whereupon Goldsmith withdrew his financial support and

9 It had initially been thought that the government would have satisfied the terms of the amendment even if it had been defeated on the ensuing motion. It could thus ratify even though it lacked a Commons majority on a central provision of the Treaty. The Commons clerks subsequently suggested the motion would have to be successful to satisfy the amendment; see Rawlings (1994) *op cit* pp 273–275. This raised the spectre of a intense conflict between the courts and the House, in which the courts might assume jurisdiction to determine the meaning of the Act, while the House maintained the issue in question was a 'proceeding in Parliament'. As we shall see, that potential crisis was avoided.
10 See p 500 above.
11 *R v Secretary of State for Foreign and Commonwealth Affairs, ex p Rees-Mogg* [1994] 1 All ER 457. For a detailed analysis of the background to and conduct of the case see Rawlings R (1994a) 'Legal politics: the United Kingdom and ratification of the Treaty on European Union (part two)' *Public Law* 367–391.

the plaintiff declined to seek an appeal. The litigation was a trivial event compared to the extraordinary convolutions that had gripped the Commons and divided the Conservative party in previous months. But if the Major government had assumed the question of the UK's EC and EU membership to be settled, subsequents events proved quite the opposite to be the case.

CONCLUSION

The cliff-hanging events that occurred in the Commons over the incorporation of the Maastricht Treaty were replayed in the autumn of 1994. At the 1992 Edinburgh Summit, the member states had agreed to a modest increase in the Community Budget from 1995 onwards. Only one Eurosceptic Conservative MP had voiced any opposition to this agreement at the time. However, when the Major government introduced legislation in November 1994 to give that obligation legal effect in domestic law, it encountered a substantial rebellion from those backbench Conservative MPs who had opposed the Maastricht reforms. For a government whose majority had fallen to only 14 (plus the equivocal backing of 9 Ulster Unionist MPs), the prospect of a Commons defeat on this question was very real.

The Cabinet consequently took the unusual step (although it had its own Maastricht tactic as a precedent) of agreeing to what became known as a collective 'suicide pact'. The Prime Minister announced that the second reading vote would be a matter of confidence, evidently on the basis that a government that could not honour its international obligations could not continue in office. Should the government be defeated, the entire Cabinet would resign and the Prime Minister would ask the Queen to grant a dissolution.[12] Rebel Conservatives promptly accused the Prime Minister of constitutional sharp practice in elevating a minor financial matter to the status of a confidence issue, and some discussion ensued as to whether the Queen would be conventionally obliged to grant a dissolution in such circumstances.[13] Such speculation ultimately proved of only academic interest. The threat of a general election at a time when the Labour party

12 Technically, of course, Mr Major would have to have asked for the dissolution before resigning.
13 See Budgen N (1994) 'Confidence in crisis' *The Guardian.* 24 November; Castle S (1994) 'Divided they dither and drift' *The Independent on Sunday*, 27 November.

enjoyed a substantial lead in the opinion polls was again sufficient to bring most of the potential rebels back into the government camp. Nevertheless, (in a manner reminscent of Roy Jenkins' elevation of his perception of national interest over party interest in the 1972 Accession votes),[14] eight Conservative MPs abstained on the second reading division. They were subsequently stripped of the party whip, and rumours abounded that their local constituency associations were being pressurised by Conservative Central Office to withdraw their support from the errant MPs at the next general election.

Such events indicate that the EC is now exercising a considerable influence at every level of the domestic political process. We are, perhaps, in an era (if not of permanent revolution) of permanent political and legal instability. EC membership has overturned many orthodox constitutional principles, and cast considerable doubt on many others. The Community is undoubtedly a very 'special' element of the modern constitution.

14 See pp 497–498 above.

CHAPTER FOURTEEN

Civil rights and civil liberties

As chapter 1 suggested, the framers of the US Constitution reached a broad consensus concerning the moral values which should not be left at the mercy of the federal legislature or executive. Madison's assumption that 'the people' could not always rely on the integrity and competence of government institutions was expressed in part by imposing a rigid separation of powers on the national government, and by constituting America as a federal country where States retained extensive powers.

America's third anti-majoritarian/minoritiarian safeguard was the civil liberties entrenched in the Bill of Rights. The Bill of Rights' amendments outlined broad principles, based on ideas which several states had already accepted as fundamental tenets of their own constitutional orders. The Bill of Rights was in no sense a detailed code, but its constitutional purpose was, and remains, clear. One hundred and fifty years after it was framed, the moral values underpinning Madison's creation were powerfully restated by the US Supreme Court:

> 'The very purpose of a Bill of Rights was to withdraw certain subjects from the vicissitudes of political controversy, to place them beyond the reach of majorities and officials and to establish them as legal principles to be applied by the courts. One's right to life, liberty, and property, to free speech, a free press, freedom of worship and assembly, and other fundamental rights may not be submitted to vote; they depend on the outcome of no elections.'[1]

Within the British constitution, it has traditionally been presumed that every social value is constantly prey to 'the vicissitudes of political controversy'; that no moral principles are 'beyond the reach of majorities'; that no constituent concepts enjoy protection from the 'outcome of parliamentary elections'. The UK's EC mem-

---

1 *West Virginia State Board of Education v Barnette* 319 US 624 (1943) per Jackson J.

bership has perhaps imbued EC law with constituent, 'fundamental' status. That question has yet however to be put to a determinative test. (Nor, at least on its face, does the EC Treaty reach the 'political' or 'moral' principles in the US Bill of Rights.)[2] Leaving this question aside for the moment, the organising principle in respect of civil liberties in Britain is that citizens may engage in any activity not prohibited by statute or common law. Relatedly, neither other individuals nor government officials may intefere with an individual's legal entitlements unless they can identify a statutory or common law justification for so doing.

The principle is very clear. Civil liberties are 'residual'. Citizens may do anything which is not legally forbidden. The principle is also, as a practical long-term guide to the substance of citizen–state relations, quite meaningless. This relates in part to the discretion exercised by the courts when interpreting statutes or developing the common law. As we saw in cases such as *Liversidge v Anderson* and *Aninismic*, judges sometimes produce unexpected decisions. More significantly, the principle accommodates the blunt political reality that Parliament can at any time forbid activities hitherto permitted, or conversely, permit activities previously forbidden. Civil liberties in Britain are extremely precarious *legal* concepts.[3] They may enjoy a more assured *conventional* status, insofar as the courts, the executive and the legislature may fear the political or moral consequences of undermining them; but, as we saw in chapters 9, 10 and 11, conventional understandings about constitutional morality may themselves be nebulous creatures.

This chapter does not offer a substantial survey of either the history or current status of civil liberties in Britain; so large a task is quite beyond its scope.[4] Instead, more modestly, it focuses on

---

2 It now seems to be doing so indirectly however. See Phelan D (1992) 'Right to life of the unborn v promotion of trade in services' *MLR* 670–689: Coppell J and O'Neill A (1994) 'The European Court of Justice: taking rights seriously' *Legal Studies* 227–245.

3 One might respond to this by saying that any values contained in the US Constitution are also 'precarious' – the Constitution's text may be changed via the art 5 amendment process. Similarly, the EC Treaties may be altered via the art 236 process. Both mechanisms are however highly cumbersome, time-consuming and also extremely visible. Amendment is difficult to achieve. In contrast, any aspect of the UK constitution could be changed in a day by a government enjoying majority support in the Commons and Lords. (This probably means only a Conservative government could do so. A Labour government would first have to remove the Conservatives' upper house majority.)

4 It has however been admirably undertaken recently by several authors. See particularly Feldman *op cit*; Bailey S, Harris D and Jones B (3rd edn 1991) *Civil Liberties* (London: Butterworths).

several discrete issues raising principles of general applicability. Sections I-III address the regulation of public protest, the protection of personal privacy, and the publication of 'secret' information; section IV then touches upon the supra-national or 'federalising' role of the European Convention on Human Rights; while section V turns to the issue of the separation of powers in an internal and horizontal, rather than as with the ECHR external and vertical, sense, by assessing the argument that the judiciary has recently become far more assertive in its defence of civil liberties.

I. PUBLIC PROTEST AND PUBLIC ORDER

Earlier chapters have discussed several instances in which citizens engaged in formally unlawful behaviour to protest against, and seek to change, legal principles to which they felt unable to consent. The American revolutionaries, the rioters in the 'Days of May', the Chartists and the Suffragettes all broke laws which formally denied them legal rights to which they considered themselves morally entitled. It is not difficult to defend such actions, since all the groups concerned were excluded from the electoral process.

We have also encountered more recent episodes of unlawful protest, when, clearly, the justification of disenfranchisement could not be invoked.[5] It may however be too simplistic to assume that such protests are necessarily 'unconstitutional' simply because they are unlawful. That conclusion would demand that we draw no distinction between the legality and legitimacy of the laws promulgated by Parliament and the courts, and relatedly, that we ascribe to the formalist notion that whatever laws a governing party persuades Parliament to enact are invariably 'democratic' simply because that party won a majority of seats at the previous general election. It may therefore also be similarly simplistic to assume that a universal franchise is in itself an adequate guarantor of what many people might regard as fundamental civil liberties.

The classic dilemma – *Beatty v Gillbanks*

Public meetings or processions may be an extremely effective way for citizens to draw the attention both of law-makers and the

---

5 Mr Cheney's refusal to pay his income taxes, the Clay Cross episode and some of the activities of the Anti-Poll Tax Federation being obvious examples.

wider public to particular causes, and thereby, in the longer term, promote legal reform. The size of a march or meeting can itself be a forceful indicator of an idea's popularity; a crowd of thousands rather than a few dozen may suggest to observers that the protestors' sentiments merit further consideration. Timing and location may also substantially affect a protest's impact on public and political opinion; a protest against a planned school closure is likely to prove more effective in stimulating discussion if held outside the town hall while councillors are discussing their policy than if conducted in a distant park weeks after the closure decision has been taken.

It seems plausible to conclude that citizens must enjoy extensive rights to engage in public, collective displays of their feelings over political or moral questions if the consent of the people to the laws under which they live is to be informed in any expansive sense. It is equally clear that extensive protection of that value will impose certain burdens on other individuals or groups within the community. At a trivial level, marches, processions and rallies entail a degree of noise and obstruction to local highways and other public places. But in a 'democratic' society, such factors will presumably weigh only lightly in the scales when counterbalanced against the principle of free expression. However, there perhaps comes a point when they assume sufficient weight to pose lawmakers, be they legislators or judges, a rather more evenly balanced question.

Beatty v Gillbanks[6] was triggered by the Salvation Army's plans to hold a march in Weston-super-Mare in 1882.[7] An earlier march had been abandoned when the Salvation Army was attacked by a violent mob, calling itself the 'Skeleton Army'. Local magistrates, fearing further violence and disorder, which had obviously alarmed and disturbed local residents, issued a notice forbidding any public assemblies in the town. The Salvation Army ignored the notice, and planned another march, led by Mr Beatty. When the march began, members of the Skeleton Army also appeared. When asked to stop the march by a constable, Mr Beatty refused to do so and was arrested.

The High Court subsequently concluded that the magistrates' notice was unlawful. Field J observed that there was nothing intrinsically illegal about Beatty's behaviour. Nor would it be correct to suggest that he had 'caused' any breach of the peace. That

6 (1882) 9 QBD 308.
7 For discussion of and the backgound to the case see Bailey, Harris and Jones *op cit* pp 217–221.

responsibility lay squarely on the Skeleton Army. The magistrates' reasoning was therefore fundamentally flawed, for it meant in effect that: 'a man may be convicted for doing a lawful act if he knows that his doing it may cause another to do an unlawful act. There is no authority for such a proposition . . .'[8]

The magistrates' decision amounted to approval for what has been subsequently been termed the 'heckler's veto' – that citizens opposing a particular viewpoint could hinder its dissemination by suggesting that they would be provoked to violence if it was advocated at a public meeting or procession. Field J's judgment implies that the correct response for the government to make in such circumstances was not to ban the Salvation Army's intrinsically lawful march, but to arrest and prosecute any member of the Skeleton Army who violently tried to disrupt it. That might prove an expensive and difficult task; but Field J is presumably suggesting that it is a price society must pay.

Even at that time, however, the extent of residual liberty citizens possessed at common law was unclear. The appellant in the 1864 Irish case of *Humphries v Connor*[9] was a Protestant extremist living in Ireland. Humphries had entered a predominantly Catholic area wearing an orange lily, a symbol then grossly offensive to Catholics. Connor, a constable who feared that some Catholic citizens might be provoked to violence by the display, asked Humphries to remove the lily. When Humphries refused to do so, Connor, using only minimal force, removed it himself. Humphries subsequently sued Connor for assault. Connor contended that his action could not be construed as an assault, since qua constable he was subject to an overriding duty to take whatever steps were 'necessary' to preserve the Queen's peace. The court accepted this conclusion as a matter of law. Whether a constable's action in particular circumstances was indeed necessary was a question of fact to be left to the jury. There would seem little doubt that in circumstances such as these, so minimal an intrusion would be considered necessary. One is then left with the difficult question of whether Humphries has been denied freedom of expression by a potentially violent mob, or whether she has merely been prevented from engaging in a course of conduct designed to provoke a riot?

In *O'Kelly v Harvey*, decided the year after *Beatty*, the court appeared to proceed on altogether different principles:

'I have always understood the law to be that any needless assemblage

8 (1882) 9 QBD 308 at 314.
9 (1864) 17 ICLR 1.

of persons in such numbers and manner and under such circumstances as are likely to provoke a breach of the peace, was itself unlawful.'[10]

This rather begs the question of what is meant by 'needless'. Narrowly construed, the concept might encompass only actions required to save life or limb. A wide construction, in contrast, might maintain that a democratic society *always* 'needs' to protect citizens who wish to express their opinion on matters of political controversy against violent opponents.

Beatty and *O'Kelly* seemingly occupy very different points on that interpretive spectrum. One might reasonably assume that the common law was sufficiently ambiguous to require legislative clarification. Yet while a statute might clarify the legal position, it may leave rather broader political questions unresolved. At present, there are many Acts which conceivably regulate public protests.[11] A systematic survey cannot be undertaken here; the following pages focus on just two such measures – the Public Order Acts of 1936 and 1986.

The Public Order Act 1936

The 1936 legislation was enacted as a direct reponse to the public disorder created by Oswald Moseley's fascist party in the 1930s.[12] Its contents were however phrased in general terms, rather than being targeted solely at fascists. Nor was the Act repealed after World War II, by which time Moseley's influence had waned to vanishing point.

Section 3(1) empowered the chief officer of police in a particular area to 'impose such conditions as appear to him necessary to maintain public order' on any public procession which he had reasonable grounds to believe might cause serious public disorder. If the chief officer concluded that a breach of the peace would inevitably occur, s3(3) empowered her, with the Home Secretary's consent, to ban all marches in her area for up to three months.[13]

Section 5 provided that:

10 (1883) 15 Cox CC 435.
11 See for example *Duncan v Jones* [1936] 1 KB 218: *Arrowsmith v Jenkins* [1963] 2 All ER 210; *Papworth v Coventry* [1967] 2 All ER 41. For a radical critique see Ewing K and Gearty C (1990) *Civil Liberties under Thatcher* ch 5 (Oxford: OUP).
12 On the background see Cross C (1961) *The Fascists in Britain* ch 8 (London: Barrie Books); Skidelsky R (1968) 'Great Britain', in Woolf S (ed) *European Fascism* (London: Weidenfeld and Nicolson).
13 For a helpful collection of instances when the power has been invoked see Bailey, Harris and Jones *op cit* pp 182–184.

'Any person who in any public place or at any public meeting – (a) uses threatening, abusive or insulting words or behaviour . . . with intent to provoke a breach of the peace or whereby a breach of the peace is likely to be occasioned, shall be guilty of an offence.'[14]

On its face, s 5 appeared to subject abusive or insulting language to a heckler's veto. This could be construed as a significant intrusion into freedom of expression, since there may be occasions on which an idea's force would be much reduced if it had to be delivered in a polite, respectful manner. An audience which would be provoked to violence by abuse or insults, irrespective of the reasonableness of the views expressed or the intolerance of the audience itself, could seemingly prevent a hitherto lawful protest being made. Similarly, s 3 raised the prospect that the force that an idea might gain by being visibly advocated by large numbers of marchers could be undermined if its opponents threatened violent disruption of the procession. There would of course be no legal obstacle to Parliament choosing to achieve either result, but the political legitimacy of such a departure from 'traditional' (if ambiguous) common law principles would be open to question.

Many difficulties which surround legislative provisions such as s 3 or s 5 arise from the fact that the right to free expression is often claimed by speakers in whose ideas it is difficult to see any substantive merit. This is not to say simply that one views the ideas as odd or ill-advised, as no doubt would many observers of the Salvation Army's evangelism. Nor is it because the speaker is advocating a mainstream political ideology with which one happens to disagree. Rather it assumes that the ideas are so vile and extreme in content, and/or delivered in such a reprehensible fashion, that society could not possibly derive any benefit from their expression.

The obvious problem with this argument is that vileness and extremism are not concepts with an ahistorical, objective meaning. Ideas once broadly perceived as entirely subversive of orthodox constitutional morality may after the passage of (even a relatively short) time be seen as no more than imprudent or even as quite acceptable. A further difficulty arises if the legal principles which regulate such speech or behaviour are cast in loose, potentially expansive terms. This is what has been referred to as 'the slippery slope' argument.[15] The argument suggests (in a manner recalling

14 For a survey of and comment on prosecutions under s 5 see Bailey, Harris and Jones *op cit* pp 202–214.
15 For an account, and rebuttal of the argument see Barendt E. (1987) *Freedom of Speech* ch 3 (Oxford: Clarendon Press).

Dicey's cynical view of governmental predispositions)[16] that the executive is always likely to be tempted to use its power to constrain speech or expression which it finds unpalatable, but which is by no means comparable to the initially egregious problem which prompted Parliament to legislate. In such circumstances, respect for parliamentary sovereignty and a Diceyan perception of the rule of law would require either that a subsequent government did not seek to invoke the statute for purposes that the enacting Parliament had not envisaged, or, if the government sought to do so, that the courts would find its actions ultra vires the powers the Act conferred. The following cases offer some insight into the way such conventional understandings might influence the application and interpretation of legal powers.

Kent v Metropolitan Police Comr (1981)[17]

The Campaign for Nuclear Disarmament (CND) attracted considerable public support in the late 1970s and early 1980s. In 1980, some 70,000 people attended a CND rally in central London. CND subsequently proposed to hold a major march through London in 1981, to protest against the government's decision to allow the American air force to keep cruise missiles on its British bases. These plans were disrupted when the Metropolitan Police Commissioner (per s 3 of the Public Order Act 1936) sought and received the Home Secretary's approval to ban all processions in London for a four-week period. There had been several outbreaks of rioting in Britain in 1980 and 1981 in inner-city areas, notably the Brixton district of London and St Pauls in Bristol. The Commissioner had apparently formed the view that any political protest march in London at that time might lead to further outbreaks of violence.

Bruce Kent, a senior figure in CND, challenged the legality of the ban. Lord Denning's judgment contained some stirring rhetoric about the importance of public protest:

> 'It was in the public interest that individuals should possess and exercise a right to protest and demonstrate on issues of public concern . . . it was often the only way by which grievances could be brought to the knowledge of those in authority.'[18]

Lord Denning also accepted that there was no suggestion that CND itself sought to instigate violence. But his conclusion rather

16 See p 66 above.
17 (1981) Times, 15 May.
18 *Ibid.*

belied his earlier sentiments. He assumed that Parliament had granted the Commissioner a very wide discretion under s 3 in deciding what measures were necessary to preserve public order. Given the prevalence of serious disorder on the streets in recent months, a temporary moratorium on public marches could not be thought to exceed that discretion. Ackner LJ, concurring, seemed to suggest that the ban was for the benefit of CND members, as it protected them from likely violence, observing that: 'it was hooligans the police were trying to control, not members of peaceful marches.'[19]

This might lead one to ask why the court did not require the police to direct their energies towards curbing the obviously illegal actions of the alleged 'hooligans' rather than the apparently lawful activities planned by CND and other marchers. The court may be regarded as having been unduly deferential to the Commissioner's evaluation. It certainly appeared to reject the assumption that s 3 should be interpreted in accordance with the principle articulated in *Beatty v Gillbanks*.

Jordan v Burgoyne (1963)[20]

Jordan was a senior figure in a fascist political party which had organised a rally in Trafalgar Square. Many communists, and members of CND and Jewish organisations were attending the meeting to barrack the fascist speakers. When Jordan heaped fulsome praise on Nazi Germany,[1] his opponents stormed the speakers' platform and a violent melee ensued.

Jordan was subsequently prosecuted under s 5. His first defence, that s 5 per se was 'unconstitutional' because it curtailed the ancient liberty of free expression, was in effect an attack on the doctrine of parliamentary sovereignty. Unsurprisingly, it failed. In a second defence, which seemed to have rather more legal merit Jordan argued that s 5 applied only to language or behaviour which would provoke 'a reasonable man' to breach the peace: the communists and CND supporters who stormed his platform had attended the rally intending to engage in violent opposition to his speech; hence they were not 'reasonable men' and so he had not breached s 5.

19 *Ibid.*
20 [1963] 2 QB 744.
 1 For an account of the application of public order legislation to explicitly fascist and racist speech and behaviour see Wolffe W (1987) 'Values in conflict: incitement to racial hatred and the Public Order Act 1986' *Public Law* 85–95; Loveland I (1995c) 'The criminalisation of racist violence', in Loveland (1995a ed) *op cit.*

As a matter of abstract principle, one might discern some force in this argument, insofar as it draws on the heckler's veto concept. However, the court saw no reason to assume that Parliament had impliedly accommodated this reasoning in the 1936 Act. Lord Parker CJ concluded that the legislation was intended to preserve public order, an issue not affected by the 'reasonableness' or otherwise of the audience:

> 'If words are used which threaten, abuse or insult . . . then that person must take his audience as he finds them, and if those words to that audience . . . are likely to provoke a breach of the peace, then the speaker is guilty of an offence.'[2]

Lord Parker CJ continued by suggesting that s 5 did not restrict free speech in any sense. This is a curious contention, for the Act, as interpreted by the court, clearly did punish certain types of speech. Whether Parliament's intrusion into the realm of free expression was *legitimate* is a difficult (and essentially political) question, with which Lord Parker CJ evidently saw no need to grapple.

Brutus v Cozens (1972)[3]

The subsequent decision in *Brutus* nevertheless suggested that the courts could interpret s 5 quite narrowly by taking such 'political' questions into account. Brutus, an anti-apartheid campaigner, disrupted a singles match at Wimbledon in which a South African was playing. Brutus' action enraged many spectators – some assaulted him as he was escorted away. A breach of the peace had certainly occurred. However the House of Lords concluded that Brutus had not 'insulted, abused or threatened' the spectators. Lord Reid's leading judgment approached the task of interpreting s 5 within a paradigm which afforded considerable importance to the principle of preserving free expression:

> 'Parliament had to solve the difficult question how far freedom of speech or behaviour must be limited in the general public interest. It would have been going much too far to prohibit all speech or conduct likely to occasion a breach of the peace because determined opponents may not shrink from organising or at least threatening a breach of the peace in order to silence a speaker whose view they detest.'[4]

Lord Reid's opinion suggested that an 'insult' had to be targeted

---

2 *Ibid*, at 749.
3 [1972] 2 All ER 1297, HL.
4 *Ibid*, at 1299–1300.

directly at the spectators. Brutus, in contrast, had merely displayed contempt of or indifference to the spectators' right to watch tennis without interference. That might amount to an annoyance or an irritation, but it was not an insult. If Parliament wished to make annoying behaviour a criminal offence, it would have to enact more sweeping legislation.[5]

The Public Order Act 1986

Writing in the late nineteenth century, Dicey concluded his survey of the common law's regulation of public meetings and processions by noting that:

> 'The government has little or no power of preventing meetings which to all appearances are lawful, even though they may turn out when actually convened to be unlawful because of the mode in which they are conducted. This is certainly a singular instance of the way in which adherence to the principle that the proper function of the state is the punishment, not the prevention, of crimes, deprives the executive of discretionary authority.'[6]

What Dicey neglected to add at that juncture however was the equally authoritative constitutional principle that a government that wished to enjoy such discretionary authority need only convince Parliament to pass legislation to that effect. As we have seen, modern governments experience little difficulty in persuading Parliament to enact their preferred policies. The Public Order Act 1936 revealed the impermanence of the common law presumptions to which Dicey referred. The Public Order Act passed some fifty years later impinged more severely on traditional understandings of constitutional morality.[7]

Section 11 of the 1986 Act requires organisers of most public processions to give advance notice of their plans to the police at least six days prior to the march. The notice must specify the time and route of the procession, and identify the organisers. Section

5 Reid's judgment poses an interesting question as to the interpretive technique he was using. His phraseology suggests that he was indulging in strict literalism – what did 'insulting' mean? Yet one might plausibly suggest his reasoning indicated he was applying either the mischief rule, or even the (then still heretical) teleological approach advocated by Denning in *Magor*.
6 Dicey *op cit* p 282.
7 For a caustic critique of the 1986 Act see Scraton P (1985) ' "If you want a riot, change the law": the implications of the 1985 White Paper on public order' *Journal of Law and Society* 385–393: Bonner D and Stone R (1987) 'The Public Order Act 1986: steps in the wrong direction?' *Public Law* 202–230.

11 operates in conjuction with s 12, which empowers the police to impose on the procession whatever conditions they think necessary to preserve public order, or prevent serious damage to property, or avoid 'serious disruption to the life of the community'. Section 12 seems to extend the powers the police exercised under s 3 of the 1936 Act; 'serious disruption' presumably encompasses obstruction of the highway or other public places, and loud noise – inconveniences which do not in themselves amount to a breach of the peace. Section 14 also enhances the police's powers to control public assemblies which are confined to one location; conditions may be attached to such meeetings on the same basis as under s 12. In contrast, the police's power to ban marches altogether continues to be triggered only if the chief police officer in a given area fears that 'serious public disorder' would inevitably result if a march took place.

The 1986 Act also creates a new offence of 'criminal trespass' under s 39. The new provision was seemingly introduced to deal with the problem posed by 'new age travellers', who periodically gathered en masse on privately owned land (especially Stonehenge in mid-summer).[8] Section 5 also creates a new offence, by extending the reach of s 5 of the 1936 Act to insulting, abusive or threatening behaviour which is likely to cause 'harassment, alarm or distress' to anyone nearby. The government suggested that it expected s 5 to be used only to control rowdy, anti-social behaviour, which served no worthwhile political purpose. Yet it seems s 5 has been invoked against clearly political activities, such as wearing a tee-shirt satirising Margaret Thatcher and producing a poster criticising government policy towards Northern Ireland.[9] It thus seems to offer a potent example of the slippery slope problem.

Notwithstanding such use of s 5, it would be an exaggeration to claim that the implementation of the 1986 Act per se has thus far amounted to gross interference with the citizenry's entitlement to engage in political protest and argument. It is however equally clear that the Act does facilitate greater governmental control of free expression. As such it exacerbates rather than counterbalances recent anti-pluralist trends in other areas of the consitutional structure – primarily the increasing limitations of the House of Commons as a forum for meaningful political debate, and the significant constraints imposed on local government's capacity

8 See Vincent-Jones P (1986) 'The hippy convoy and criminal trespass' *Journal of Law and Society* 343–370: Ewing and Gearty *op cit* pp 125–128.
9 Ewing and Gearty *op cit* pp 122–124.

to express and indulge political sentiments with which central government disagrees. The Act's true significance perhaps lies therefore in its addition of several further threads to an increasingly complex tapestry of political orthodoxy with which the Thatcher and Major governments have cloaked the conventially more pluralist features of the constitution.

II. PRIVACY

The actions of the government officials in *Entick v Carrington* clearly amounted to a tortious intrusion against both Mr Entick's home and his possessions. His home was physically invaded, and his belongings were physically removed from his control. The 'invasion' suffered by Mr Malone in the late 1970s, in contrast, took a less tangible form.

Malone v Metropolitan Police Comr (1979)[10]

The Metropolitan Police Commissioner, suspecting Malone was involved in criminal activities, arranged with the Post Office for a tap to be made on Malone's phone calls. The tap did not involve physical interference with Malone's home or property, and so was not a trespass in any traditional sense. The tap was thus not obviously unlawful. However, the Commissioner could not point to any statutory or common law power expressly permitting taps to be made.

Mr Malone subsequently challenged the legality of the Commissioner's action. His argument rested in part on provisions of the European Convention on Human Rights, which we consider below. But he also made contentions based purely on domestic law. In effect, Mr Malone was asking the court to recognise that the common law had (by 1979) developed sufficiently to treat telephone tapping by government bodies with the same opprobrium that Lord Camden had regarded a physical trespass in *Entick* two hundred years earlier: to restrict the concept of trespass to tangible inteference with a person's body or possessions would be to adopt an unduly formalist interpretation of the law.

In considering, and rejecting, Malone's argument, Megarry VC offered a cogent analysis of the common law's innovatory power:

10 [1979] Ch 344.

'I am not unduly troubled by the absence of English authority: there has to be a first time for everything, and if the principles of English law . . . together with the requirements of justice and common sense, pointed firmly to such a right existing, then I think the court should not be deterred from recognising the right.'[11]

However, Megarry VC's perception of 'justice and common sense' did not lead him to accept that the common law now recognised a right to 'privacy' which could be compromised by phone taps only if the listener had explicit legal authority for her intrusion. Since neither Parliament nor the common law had prohibited phone tapping, the practice was not unlawful. And since it was not unlawful, it could not infringe Mr Malone's legal rights.

Megarry VC's opinion was influenced by questions of justiciability. He suggested that the whole question of privacy in telecommunications was so complex that it could only be settled by legislation. No such package of rights could properly 'spring from the head of a judge'.

Megarry's judgment is open to several criticisms.[12] His reasoning on the privacy argument is rather circular. The Commissioner's action was not unlawful because it did not affect Mr Malone's legal entitlements: and Mr Malone's legal entitlements were not affected because the Commissioner's action was not unlawful. Admittedly, a decision in Mr Malone's favour would have been similarly tautological in conceptual terms. The question which then arises however is, in the event of uncertainty, should the courts construe the common law in a manner that facilitates or impedes governmental interference with a citizen's privacy? That Megarry VC chose the former course is perfectly defensible as a matter of narrow legalism; whether his choice shares that characteristic in respect of its political legitimacy is a rather different question.

The justiciability point is also quite specious. Mr Malone was not asking the court to create an elaborate scheme to regulate all interceptions of telecommunications.[13] He sought merely to establish that the tap made in his case was unlawful. It seems entirely plausible that had he succeeded on this point, the govern-

---

11 *Ibid*, at 372.
12 See Bevan V (1981) 'Is anybody there?' *Public Law* 431–453: Ewing and Gearty *op cit* pp 56–61.
13 One might recall here the ECJ's reasoning in *Defrenne*, namely that a court should not tolerate a 'direct and overt' interference with a loosely defined individual entitlement simply because it can also conceive of many other 'indirect and disguised' infringements which could only become justiciable when defined by a legislature; see pp 505–506 above.

ment would have found time in its legislative timetable to introduce the comprehensive statutory scheme which Megarry VC evidently thought desirable. If we (cynically) accept that governments are happiest when their actions escape legal control, it makes little sense merely to *invite* them to promote legislation subjecting unregulated powers to judicial supervision. If the court's purpose was to seek legislative clarification of ambiguous common law principles, it would be more likely to achieve that purpose if it resolved ambiguities in a manner which inconvenienced central government. It is not surprising that the first Thatcher government declined Megarry VC's invitation.

But the existence of statutory authority may not settle the question of the legitimacy of intrusive governmental action; as the following case suggests, it may simply demand that scepticism be directed at Parliament rather than the courts.

R v IRC, ex p Rossminster Ltd[14]

The text of the Taxes Management Act 1970 s 20C seemed to bestow sweeping search and seizure powers on Inland Revenue employees. Section 20C empowered the Inland Revenue to seek a search warrant from a circuit judge. If the judge was satisfied that there were reasonable grounds to assume that evidence of a tax fraud might be found on particular premises, she could issue a warrant authorising a named officer to: 'Seize and remove any things whatsoever found there which he has reasonable cause to believe may be required as evidence ...'. The Act did not explicitly require that the warrant specify the precise offence being investigated, nor identify the suspected perpetrator(s).

Very early one morning, acting under such a warrant, Inland Revenue officials raided Rossminster's premises and, without offering any details of the matter under investigation, seized large quantities of documents. The legal background to the *Rossminster* seizure is clearly distinguishable from the background to the *Entick* case, since it was purportedly rooted in a statutory power. Rossminster nevertheless claimed that Lord Camden's reasoning was relevant to interpretation of s 20C. Rossminster argued that the court should presume that Parliament intended s 20C should be construed in a manner consistent with the common law principles

14 [1980] AC 952, HL.

informing the *Entick* decision – namely that the power would only be used in a precisely targeted way, and would not be invoked by Revenue officials to enable them to embark upon a speculative trawl through all of a company's or an individual's private papers.[15]

Lord Wilberforce, delivering the leading judgment in the House of Lords, saw no point in referring to old cases such as *Entick* to support Rossminster's contention. He concluded that the 'plain words' of s 20C authorised the Inland Revenue to engage in behaviour which could not be justified at common law. Nor could he see any basis for finding an implied term in the statute which required much greater specificity in the terms of the warrant: Parliament's intention had been to override common law principles.[16] Lord Wilberforce's invocation of the 'literal rule' of statutory interpretation is entirely orthodox, and quite consistent with traditional understandings of the separation of powers:

> 'While the courts may look critically at legislation which impairs the rights of citizens and should resolve any doubt of interpretation in their favour, it is no part of their duty, or power, to restrict or impede the working of legislation, even of unpopular legislation; to do so would be to weaken rather than advance the democratic process.'[17]

Lord Wilberforce nevertheless cast some doubt on the political accceptability of the legal rule which the statute had enacted, by observing that: 'I cannot believe that this does not call for a fresh look by Parliament'.[18]

Inviting Parliament to take a 'fresh look' at civil liberties issues may however lead to unanticipated results, especially when the Commons is controlled by a government which seems to see little merit in traditional understandings of the nature of citizen–state relations. We noted above that the provisions of the Public Order Act 1986 placed relatively tight constraints on public protest activities. The following section suggests that a similar trend may be apparent in respect of 'official secrets'.

---

15 That argument had led the Court of Appeal to hold that the search was unlawful as ultra vires the power conferred by s 20C.

16 Lord Wilberforce was led to this conclusion in part by what he perceived as the 'substantial safeguards' the Act introduced to minimise the prospect of the power being used arbitrarily, namely that the warrant could only be sought by two senior officials, and it could only be granted by a circuit judge rather than, as was often the case, by a magistrate.

17 *Ibid*, at 988.

18 *Ibid*, at 999.

III. OFFICIAL SECRECY

The Official Secrets Act 1911 was enacted at the instigation of Asquith's Liberal government. The legislation was prompted by a public panic about the supposed presence of German spies and saboteurs, at a time when war with Germany no longer seemed a distant prospect.[19] The Act passed all of its Commons stages in one hour. This might suggest that it was not subject to searching scrutiny and consideration, an omission which is perhaps all the more surprising when one notes the very wide terms in which it was framed.

As we saw in *Chandler v DPP*,[20] s 1 forbade entry to any 'prohibited place' for 'any purpose prejudicial to the safety or interests of the State'. Section 1 also criminalised the making of any 'note, sketch or plan' for such purposes, or the communication to any other person of any information 'which is calculated to be or might be or is intended to be directly or indirectly useful to an enemy'. Section 2 was drafted in even broader terms; it penalised the passing of *any* official information (irrespective of whether the information compromised national security) to anybody 'other than a person to whom he is authorised to communicate it, or a person to whom it is in the interest of the State his duty to communicate it'. The potential reach of s 2 was subject to frequent criticism; the most oft-quoted being that of Sir Lionel Heald that the Act 'makes it a crime . . . to report the number of cups of tea consumed per week in a government department'.[1]

Legal rules which punish or otherwise restrict the publication of information which arguably compromises the security of the state invariably raise difficult questions.[2] The evident flaw of s 2 however was that it was not restricted to national security questions. Nor did it appear to offer the discloser any opportunity to defend his/her actions on the basis that disclosure was in the public interest.[3] It is not difficult to envisage circumstances in which such disclosure might be desirable; when for example it exposed corruption in the award of arms contracts, or revealed that government officials were misleading ministers, or that ministers were misleading the Commons. On its face, s 2 could, as the

---

19 French D (1978) 'Spy fever in Britain 1900–1915' *Historical Journal* 355–370.
20 See pp 130–132 above.
1 See Bailey, Harris and Jones *op cit* pp 421–422.
2 For a helpful discussion see Marshall G (1986) 'Ministers, civil servants and open government', in Harlow C (ed) *Public law and politics* (London: Sweet and Maxwell).
3 See *R v Fell* [1963] Crim LR 207; *R v Berry* [1979] Crim LR 284.

following cases suggest, be invoked simply to punish the disclosure of information which the government for reasons of either administrative expediency or party political convenience preferred to keep secret.

Sarah Tisdall[4]

In the early 1980s considerable controversy arose over the Thatcher government's decision to allow the United States to keep cruise missiles at its air force bases in Britain. The government had apparently decided to announce the missiles' arrival at the very end of Commons questions to the Defence Secretary, Michael Heseltine. Heseltine would then leave the chamber without giving MPs the chance to question him immediately. A civil servant, Sarah Tisdall, subsequently leaked a memo disclosing this plan to *The Guardian* newspaper. Tisdall evidently believed that Heseltine's planned behaviour was 'immoral', insofar as it denied the Commons the opportunity to question the government on a policy question of major significance.[5]

The government demanded the return of the memo, seemingly because markings on the text would enable the leak's source to be identified. *The Guardian* claimed it was not obliged to return the documents. The Contempt of Court Act 1981 s 10 empowered the courts to order disclosure of the media's sources only if 'necessary in the interests of justice or national security'. The government contended that national security questions did make such disclosure necessary in this case. The information itself posed no such threat, but the government contended that the mere presence of a leaker within the Defence Ministry would so undermine our allies' confidence in the government's defence capabilities that it was vital that she/he be identified.

The High Court, the Court of Appeal and House of Lords (by a 3–2 majority)[6] accepted the government's argument, and ordered *The Guardian* to return the documents. Tisdall was subsequently identified as the leaker, convicted under s 2 and imprisoned for six months. On the next occasion that the government resorted to s 2, however, the outcome was perhaps not what it had expected.

---

4 See Ewing and Gearty *op cit* pp 137–142.
5 See Barker R (1986) 'Obedience, legitimacy and the state', in Harlow (ed) *op cit.*
6 Lord Scarman and Lord Fraser dissented. Neither felt a threat to national security had been established. Scarman seemingly thought that the government's main motive was to spare itself party political embarrassment.

Clive Ponting

Mr Ponting was, in the early 1980s, an apparently high-flying civil servant in the Ministry of Defence, who had been singled out for praise by the Prime Minister. However, after the Falklands War, Ponting formed the conclusion that his Secretary of State, Heseltine, was systematically misleading the Commons over the circumstances surrounding the sinking of the Argentine battleship, the *Belgrano*. Ponting subsequently leaked information which he regarded as accurate to Tam Dalyell, a backbench Labour MP who had been harrying the government on this question. Dalyell passed the information to the Chair of the Commons Foreign Affairs Select Comittee, who (in an act exemplifying the committee's deference to the executive) returned it to Heseltine.[7]

Ponting was subsequently prosecuted under s 2.[8] The government accepted that the information released did not compromise national security. The issue was simply one of enforcing the civil servant's supposed duty of confidentiality to the Crown. Ponting did not deny leaking the information. He claimed however that Mr Dalyell was a person 'to whom it was in the interest of the State' that the information be passed. The nub of Ponting's argument was that Heseltine was deliberately misleading the house, and thereby subverting the doctrine of ministerial responsibility.[9] It could not be in 'the interests of the state' that the Commons (and thence the public) formed conclusions about government behaviour based on information which the government knew was false. Since Mr Dalyell would raise the matter in the house, giving him the information would in fact advance the public interest.

However at Ponting's trial, McCowan J instructed the jury that this argument had no legal basis. Section 2, he maintained, adopted a highly factionalised interpretation of 'the interests of the state'. This was not a matter that concerned 'the people', nor even the Commons. Rather:

'The policies of the State mean the policies laid down by the those recognised organs of government and authority . . . The government and its policies are for the time being the policies of the State.'[10]

In formal terms, therefore, Ponting was guilty. The jury never-

---

7 See Drewry G (1985b) 'Leaking in the public interest' *Public Law* 203–212; Thomas R (1987) 'The British Official Secrets Act 1911–1939 and the Ponting case', in Chapman R and Hunt M (eds) *Open Government* (London: Routledge).

8 *R v Ponting* [1985] Crim LR, 318.

9 For a less benevolent view of Ponting's motives and behaviour see Marshall (1986) *op cit.*

10 *R v Ponting* [1985] Crim LR 318.

theless declined to convict him. British juries are not permitted to disclose their reasoning, but it seems plausible to assume that the jurors hearing Ponting's case concluded that the government was invoking legal means to justify immoral ends and decided it should not be permitted to do so. Parliament has thus far not introduced legislation permitting such legally perverse acquittals to be reversed, presumably because the concept that a citizen should only be tried for serious crimes before a randomly selected jury is too deeply embedded a principle of constitutional morality.[11] The jury nevertheless remains a somewhat unreliable defender of 'just' solutions when faced with clear legal arguments: Tisdall's jurors seemingly took a less robust view of constitutional morality than their counterparts in *Ponting*.

Spycatcher

The Thatcher government was obviously not unique in invoking legal proceedings to restrain publication of information which would enable the Commons and the electorate to make more informed choices about the adequacy of government behaviour. The *Crossman Diaries* case, instigated by a Labour government, served in effect the same purpose as the Tisdall and Ponting trials – namely to deter people with access to sensitive information about government behaviour from making their knowledge available to the general public. But the Thatcher government was perhaps atypical in respect of the patently absurd lengths to which it was prepared to go in order to deter civil servants and the media from revealing 'secret' information.

Peter Wright had been employed in the 1960s and 1970s by MI5, one of the security services.[12] Just exactly what Wright did in that capacity remains unclear. He was however disgruntled with the financial benefits the work provided, and some years after retiring published a book, *Spycatcher*, alleging that MI5 agents had plotted to destabilise Harold Wilson's Labour governments.[13] Rather than ensure that such extraordinary accusations (which amounted if proven to treason), were thoroughly and publicly

---

11 As evidenced by its inclusion in both the US Declaration of Independence and England's earlier Declaration of Right.

12 The exact nature of the security services, their effective powers, and the extent to which they are meaningfully controlled by elected politicians is, as one might expect, a mystery. For an overview see Lustgarten L and Leigh I (1994) *In From the Cold: National Security and Parliamentary Democracy* (Oxford: Clarendon Press).

13 Wilson had long held the view that such plots had been hatched against him; Pimlott *op cit* pp 697–715.

investigated, the Thatcher government devoted its energies to trying to prevent Wright's story being made available to the British public.

The facts of the case raise several rather different issues. One might readily suggest that Mr Wright should not have been permitted to profit financially from any disclosures he made, irrespective of their content. However that presumption is quite separate from the question of whether or not his allegations should have been discussed in the press. If the allegations posed a present threat to national security, one could see strong arguments for prohibiting disclosure. Yet if they exposed illegal or treasonable behaviour, one would presumably favour disclosure in the expectation that public discussion and criticism might prevent a recurrence of such activities. The practical difficulty attending either viewpoint is of course that citizens could not form a view on whether the allegations threatened national security or revealed subversive behaviour until they had been made public. Essentially, therefore, the issue is reduced to a question of whether one can (or should) trust central government to identify and remedy any wrongdoing among the security services. Diceyan or Madisonian orthodoxies might suggest that would be a dangerous assumption to make; especially when the allegations apparently have a party political dimension, and one's government is composed solely of members of one political party.

As noted in earlier chapters, the British courts have tended to adopt a very deferential stance towards government claims that litigation raised 'national security' questions. One can trace an insistent thread of judicial acquiescence from *Ship Money*, through to *The Zamora*, to *Liversidge v Anderson*, to *Chandler v DPP* and on to *GGHQ*.[14] The *Spycatcher* litigation suggested that this tradition still enjoyed appreciable judicial support.[15]

Mr Wright had taken the precaution of going to live in Tasmania before publishing his book. He could thus not be prosecuted under s 2. The government therefore resorted to the civil law to stop publication and discussion of the book. As we saw in the *Crossman Diaries* case, the common law principle of confidentiality was an elastic concept. In the *Spycatcher* litigation, the government suggested that Wright owed his employer (the Crown) a lifelong duty of confidentiality in respect of any official information he acquired during his employment. The government argued that

---

14 At pp 123, 83–86, 130–132 and 121–123 respectively.
15 For an overview see Barendt E (1989) 'Spycatcher and freedom of speech' *Public Law* 204–212; Ewing and Gearty *op cit* pp 152–174.

this duty prevented Wright from publishing any such material, and that if he did so, any profits made would belong to the Crown. But the government also contended that its interest in maintaining confidentiality also prevented *the media* from reporting or commenting on Wright's allegations.

In 1986, both *The Observer* and *The Guardian* ran stories commenting on Wright's claims. The government immediately sought a temporary injunction prohibiting such stories, pending a full trial to determine if such publication could be prevented permanently. This was granted by Millet J. It remained in place for a year, until the newspapers persuaded the High Court to lift it. The judge, Sir Nicolas Browne-Wilkinson, saw no point in retaining the injunction, given that the book had by then been published in the USA and its contents were widely known to British citizens who had access to foreign newspapers or had imported copies from foreign sellers.[16] However both the Court of Appeal and the House of Lords reinstated the constraint on publication.[17]

The Lords' decision in *Spycatcher No 1* upheld the injunctions, albeit only by a 3–2 majority. The majority were strongly influenced by the government's claim that publication would damage the public interest in maintaining efficient security services, because it would undermine officers' morale. Lord Bridge's dissent took a different view of the 'public interest', employing grandiloquent language reminscent of Lord Atkin's speech in *Liversidge*:

> 'Freedom of speech is always the first casualty under a totalitarian régime. . . . The present attempt to insulate the public from information which is freely available elsewhere is a significant step down that very dangerous road. . . . [The government's] wafer thin victory in this litigation has been gained at a price which no government committed to upholding the values of a free society can afford to pay.'[18]

The Thatcher administration seemed however quite ready to pay this price. In *Spycatcher No 2*, the government sought permanent injunctions against *The Guardian* and *The Observer*, and against the *Sunday Times* which intended to publish Wright's book in serial form. At first instance, Scott J discharged the temporary injunction and refused to grant permanent restraints.[19] His decision was upheld by a 2–1 majority in the Court of Appeal, and by a 4–1

---

16 *A-G v Guardian Newspapers Ltd* [1987] 3 All ER 316.
17 *Ibid.*
18 *Ibid*, at 346–347.
19 *A-G v Guardian Newspapers Ltd (No 2)* [1990] 1 AC 109.

majority in the House of Lords.[20] However Lord Keith's leading judgment in the Lords seemingly did not wish to be drawn into consideration of the large constitutional issues which the government's conduct seemed to raise:

> 'I do not base this upon any balancing of public interests nor upon any considerations of freedom of the press, nor upon any possible defences of . . . just cause of excuse, but simply upon the view that all possible damage to the interest of the Crown has already been done by the publication of *Spycatcher* abroad and the ready availability of copies in this country.'[1]

It would thus be misleading to characterise the decision as a forceful judicial assertion of the constitutional right of the British people to be informed of their government's alleged inadequacies. The protection afforded by *Spycatcher No 2* to free expression seems at best oblique, premised on the fact that the laws of other countries had permitted both the publication and export of Wright's allegations.

In the interim, the government had also trailed around the courts of the world in an effort to prevent publication of *Spycatcher* in foreign jurisdictions. The government suffered defeats in Australia and New Zealand, before obtaining the dubious benefit of a victory in Hong Kong – a British colony which then had no elected legislative assembly. There was no point in pursuing such an action in the USA, where publication would clearly have been protected by the First Amendment.

The Official Secrets Act 1989[2]

The combined impact of the *Ponting* and *Spycatcher* embarrassments prompted the third Thatcher government to reform the 1911 Act. The 1989 Act does remove the catch all provisions of s 2 of its 1911 predecessor, but it is difficult to portray the new legislation as an exercise in enhancing the transparency and accountability of the government to its citizens. One commentator has suggested that the Act's:

> 'stated purpose . . . is to reduce the amount of information protected by criminal sanctions to areas where disclosure would be harmful to

20 *Ibid.*
 1 *Ibid*, at 260.
 2 For a helpful summary and critique see Palmer S (1988) 'In the interests of the state' *Public Law* 523–535; (1990) 'Tightening secrecy law: the Offical Secrets Act 1989' *Public Law* 243–256.

the public interest. Yet it is tempting to conclude that the primary rationale behind this reform is to tighten the criminal law of secrecy, with the aim of making convictions more likely.'[3]

Section 1 imposes an absolute and permanent duty of confidentiality on all members and ex-members of the security services. Any disclosure of any official information by any such person under any circumstances is now a crime. Thus, to take an extreme example, it would apparently be illegal for an MI5 or MI6 agent to reveal that her superior officers were planning to assassinate the Prime Minister. At the other extreme, even the most trivial of information may not be disclosed by security service officers. There is no requirement that the prosecution prove the disclosure to have damaged the national interest. Nor may officers argue that their action was designed to defend the public interest. Furthermore, under s 1(1)(b) the government may extend this absolute obligation to any person it wishes.

Other civil servants and government contractors are caught by widely framed provisions which criminalise the disclosure of 'damaging' information in the specific areas of defence (s 2), international relations (s 3) and the investigation of crime (s 4). This is clearly a less expansive prohibition than the one contained in the former s 2. Additionally, accused persons have a defence if they can establish that disclosure would not be 'damaging'. However, the Act does not permit a 'public interest defence' – it is a crime to reveal 'damaging' information even if one believes one thereby exposes government behaviour that would be even more 'damaging'.

As Palmer notes, Lord Keith's judgment in *Spycatcher No 2* approved the principle that:

> 'It is unacceptable in our democratic society that there should be a restraint on the publication of information relating to government when the only vice of that information is that it enables the public to discuss, review and criticise government action.'[4]

The Thatcher government seemed wholly unpersuaded by this principle. The thrust of the 1989 Act appears to be a rejection of the idea that government employees' duty of loyalty lies anywhere other than to the government of the day. That a government should make such an assumption is an entirely logical conse-

---

3 Palmer *op cit* p 243. For similarly critical comment see Ewing and Gearty *op cit* pp 189–208.

4 (1990) *op cit* p 247, citing Lord Keith's approval of the quote by Mason J of the Australian High Court in *Commonwealth of Australia v John Fairfax & Sons Ltd* (1980) 147 CLR 39 at 51–52.

quence of the supposed 'ultimate political fact' of the contemporary constitution – namely that a Commons majority generally enables it to do whatever it wishes. This is, as suggested in earlier chapters, a theme which pervades every aspect (except perhaps issues involving EC law) of our current constitutional arrangements. We turn to the broad question of whether and how this ultimate political fact might be reformed in chapter 15. Before doing so however, we focus briefly on a device through which the government may be persuaded, if not compelled, to deploy its control of the legislature to give legal effect to rather more broadly supported moral principles.

IV. THE EUROPEAN CONVENTION ON HUMAN RIGHTS

The European Convention on Human Rights is an international treaty, whose origins lie, like the EC's, in the reconstruction of Europe's political order following World War II. In 1949, 25 European states formed a body known as the Council of Europe.[5] The Council's broad concern was to foster the growth and entrenchment of democratic government within western Europe. One means of doing so was to persuade its members to become signatories to the convention.

The convention's terms cover a broad sweep of political issues. Art 3 prohibits the use of torture, and the infliction of degrading or inhuman treatment and/or punishment. Articles 5 and 6 are aimed primarily at the conduct of criminal proceedings. Article 7 places strict limits on retrospective criminal laws. Article 8 addresses the right to privacy and family life, while Article 12 concerns the right of adults to marry and found a family. Articles 9 and 10 focus on freedom of thought, conscience, religious belief and expression.[6]

The Council of Europe also established several institutions to enforce and monitor the convention's provisions. The European Commission of Human Rights performs both an investigatory and conciliatory role. Its members are distinguished lawyers, their

5 Which, despite the similarity of its name, should not be confused either with the EC's Council of Ministers or the EU's European Council. On the background to the Council of Europe's formation, and the subsequent production of the convention, see Robertson A and Merrill J (3rd edn 1994) *Human Rights in Europe* ch 1 (Manchester: Manchester UP).

6 The scope of the initial convention has subsequently been expanded by various Protocols, although not all of the original signatory states have acceded to all of these.

number being equal to the number of states which have ratified the convention; no state may have more than one of its nationals sitting on the Commission.[7] The Commission is the body to which complaints of a breach of the convention must initially be notified. The Commission is also empowered to determine if the complaint was admissible. The Commission will not admit complaints which it considers 'manifestly ill-founded'. Furthermore, per article 26, the applicant must have exhausted all effective domestic remedies before the Commission can intervene. Nor can the Commission act if the applicant is raising a question which is 'substantially the same' as one with which it has already dealt. Admissibility has proven a formidable hurdle for applicants to surmount. By 1990, the Commission had entertained over 17,000 applications; fewer than 700 were admitted.[8] It would thus be quite inaccurate to portray the Commission as a body constantly interfering with internal affairs of the convention's signatory states.

Should the Commission conclude that the complaint was justi-fied, it attempts to negotiate a 'friendly settlement' between the parties. If no settlement can be reached, the Commission drafts an 'opinion' detailing its view of the breach, which is sent to the Committee of Ministers (comprising the Foreign Ministers of each signatory state). The Committee may either (by a two-thirds majority) produce its own 'judgment', or may refer the case to the ECHR. The term 'judgment' is used guardedly. The conven-tion does not require the Committee to adopt court-style proce-dures. Its decision-making process is conducted in secret, and the impugned member state can vote on the outcome. This process is obviously unsatisfactory from a narrowly legalistic perspective, but it does alert observers to the important fact that the conven-tion retains a substantial 'inter-national' element.

Approximately 25% of the Commission's opinions have been dealt with in this way. The great majority have in contrast been referred to the ECHR. The court's members are selected by the Committee of Ministers, generally for a nine-year term; the court's total membership may not exceed the number of signatory states, and no state may have more than one of its nationals sitting on the bench. The applicant is not formally a party to the ECHR proceedings, although she may appear and be legally represented. The Commission acts as the 'defender of the public interest', rather than as the applicant's advocate.

The convention provides that the ECHR's judgments 'bind' the

7 See Roberson and Merrill *op cit* ch 7.
8 Bailey, Harris and Jones *op cit* p 757.

signatory states. Responsibility for ensuring compliance is entrusted to the Committee of Ministers. Compliance generally requires the offending state to alter its domestic law in a manner which satisfies the ECHR's judgment. Thus far, such amendments have almost always been forthcoming. Nevertheless, pursuing a complaint all the way to the court has proved a very time-consuming process. Suits are rarely concluded in under two years, and time spans of five years between the first action in a domestic court and the eventual ECHR judgment are not uncommon. The convention's Ninth Protocol has offered individuals the possibility of direct access to the ECHR. But as yet no state has adopted this provision.

The convention has to some extent 'federalised' the constitutional orders of some its signatory nations. Its provisions are the supreme source of legal authority in some states. For those countries whose constitutions provide that treaty obligations automatically become part of domestic law, or have made specific arrangements to accord the convention that status, it is also (to borrow familiar terminology) 'directly effective'; their own courts must apply the ECHR's case law, a situation which greatly speeds their citizens' access to their convention entitlements.

Yet one should not equate this degree of supra-nationalisation of basic moral principles with the imposition of a rigid constitutional orthodoxy on the signatory states. The convention does not impose a uniform coda of detailed legal rules. Its text is itself liberally sprinkled with provisions allowing states to derogate from its formal provisions. Article 15, for example, is a derogation clause of wide application in respect of many convention entitlements. Similarly, the 'rights' protected in specific articles are often immediately qualified by provisions permitting state regulation. Thus, while article 10(1) announces the 'right to freedom of expression', article 10(2) provides that the right:

> 'may be subject to such formalities, conditions, restrictions or penalties as are prescribed by law and are necessary in a democratic society, in the interests of national security, territorial integrity or public safety, for the prevention of disorder or crime . . .'

Much of the ECHR's case law has been concerned with the interpretation and application of such qualificatory provisions. Relatedly, the ECHR has developed a doctrine known as 'the margin of appreciation', which permits significant variations in the precise ways in which states protect the individual rights they have committed themselves to respect.

Furthermore, several countries have chosen not to incorporate the convention into their domestic legal systems. For these states, the convention operates only as international law. Nor does the convention require that states grant their citizens direct access to the Commission and the ECHR. If a country did not give its citizens that entitlement, its laws' conformity with the convention could be challenged only at the instigation of another signatory state.[9] In countries where the convention is neither directly effective, nor actionable by individuals before the Commission, compliance with its terms would be a matter to be resolved through the political rather than the legal process.

Although Attlee's 1945–1950 Labour government was closely involved in drafting and promoting the convention, his Cabinet was bitterly divided on the question of whether this country should be a signatory. Some ministers appeared to display the same arrogant xenophobia that later characterised Gaitskill's hostility to the EC.[10] Attlee's government did eventually accede to the convention. However, it was not until the mid-1960s that a UK government allowed UK citizens the right of direct access to the ECHR. But no post-war government has ever introduced a Bill to incorporate the convention into domestic law. UK citizens are thus apparently unable to enforce its terms before their courts.

The failure to incorporate cannot be explained on party political grounds. Both Labour and Conservative governments have refused to promote the necessary legislation. It is also misleading to suggest that this reluctance stems from a concern to ensure that the wishes of a democratically elected legislature are not frustrated by an unelected judiciary. That argument fails on several counts. The shortcomings in 'Parliament's' democratic credentials have already been alluded to; the Commons' electoral system is crudely minoritarian, and the Lords' composition is entirely indefensible. Moreover, if the convention were to be incorporated (on terms analogous to those used in the ECA 1972), the government and Parliament's subordination would not be to the domestic courts, but to the ECHR, on whose behalf the British courts would act as an agent. Rather, the convention's formal constitutional status as merely international law seems to derive from the traditional unwillingness of either the Labour or Conservative parties to accept that they are not each entitled to make whatever

9 There have been very few such actions; see Bailey, Harris and Jones *op cit* pp 756–757.
10 See p 494 above. On the Attlee government's views see Lester A (1984) 'Fundamental rights: the United Kingdom isolated' *Public Law* 46–72.

use they wish of Parliament's sovereignty whenever their electoral fortunes afford them a Commons majority.

The United Kingdom's record before the court has not been a happy one, although it is overly simplistic to suggest that British law has been found wanting significantly more often than that of the convention's other signatories.[11] Successive governments have generally responded to defeats before the ECHR by introducing Bills to amend domestic law,[12] although if one adds the time needed to pass legislation to the lengthy wait required to bring a claim before the ECHR, it is clear that British citizens do not yet enjoy speedy access to the convention's protection.

We will return to the question of the convention's status in domestic law shortly. Before doing so, however, we consider the judgments that the ECHR eventually reached in respect of two of the controversial English cases discussed above.

Malone v United Kingdom[13]

Having failed to convince Megarry VC in the High Court that the common law did not permit the Metropolitan Police Commissioner to tap his phone, Mr Malone pursued his case before the ECHR. The ECHR saw no difficulty in concluding that telephone conversations were within art 8's concepts of 'private life' and 'correspondence'. The question which then arose was whether the Commissioner's interference with this right had been exercised 'according to law'. This concept is one which the ECHR had been gradually elaborating for some years.[14] It is concerned not simply with legal formality, but with substantive questions as to the predictability and foreseeability of government action. As such, it reflects principles of the rule of law which are firmly embedded in orthodox British constitutional theory.[15] The meaning afforded to it in *Malone* was that the:

> 'law must be sufficiently clear in its terms to give citizens an adequate indication as to the circumstances in which and the conditions on which public authorities are empowered to resort to this secret and

---

11 For a helpful analysis of the statistics see Bradley A (1991) 'The UK before the Strasbourg court', in Finnie W, Himsworth C and Walker N (eds) *Edinburgh Essays in Public Law* (Edinburgh: Edinburgh University Press). For an up-to-date listing of the cases see *HCD*, 17 December 1993 c964.

12 See Bradley A (1991) *op cit*.

13 (1984) 7 EHRR 14.

14 Bailey, Harris and Jones *op cit* pp 819–822: Robertson and Merrills *op cit* pp 196–198.

15 See pp 70–71 above.

potentially dangerous interference with the right to respect for private life . . .'[16]

No such clarity could be found in British law. The Post Office Act 1969 s 80 required the Post Office to pass information to the police when requested to do so. However the Act itself did not specify the circumstances under which such a requirement arose. Furthermore, William Whitelaw (when Home Secretary) had explained to the Commons in 1980 that he considered such guidance as existed regarding use of s 80 unsuited to enactment.[17] These factors led the court to conclude that the tapping power had not been exercised 'according to law'. The court answered the question before it in terms evocative of Diceyan principle:

'It would be contrary to the rule of law for the legal discretion granted to the executive to be expressed in terms of an unfettered power.'[18]

On this occasion, the government appeared willing to amend domestic law accordingly. The Interception of Communications Act 1985 (ICA 1985) introduced a statutory framework to regulate phone tapping. Unauthorised tapping has been made a criminal offence, although the Act grants government bodies extensive discretion to authorise taps in a wide range of circumstances.[19]

Spycatcher

That the ICA 1985 affords the government wide discretion is itself a powerful reminder that compliance with the convention does not impose detailed or uniform standards on its signatory states. That point is reinforced when one considers the reasoning and conclusions of the ECHR when the *Spycatcher* litigation eventually came before it.[20]

The litigation concerned both the temporary and continuing injunctions granted against *The Guardian* and *The Observer* in *Spy-catcher (No 1)* by Millet J and the House of Lords respectively. The ECHR's judgment did not amount to an expansive protection of freedom of expression. The court concluded that the initial injunction did not contravene art 10 provisions on freedom of

---

16 (1985) 7 EHRR 14 at para 67.
17 The ECHR it seems does not feel compelled to respect restrictive interpretations of parliamentary privilege or art 9 of the Bill of Rights concerning the justiciability of proceedings in either house.
18 *Ibid*, at 41.
19 See Ewing and Gearty *op cit* pp 66–81; Leigh I 'A tapper's charter' *Public Law* 8–18.
20 *Observer and Guardian v UK* (1991) 14 EHRR 153.

expression. The court considered it was entirely reasonable for Millet J to have assumed that Wright's book may have contained information that jeopardised national security; in such circumstances, pending a full trial, a temporary restraint could be regarded as (per art 10(2)) 'necessary in a democratic society'. However, the court also held that the House of Lords' continuation of the injunction did breach art 10. Since the book had by then been published in the USA, its contents were common knowledge; the ban on media discussion therefore served no useful purpose.

For advocates of an expansive notion of 'informed consent', the ECHR's judgment is rather unsatisfactory, in that it seemed to hinge (as did the House of Lords' decision in *Spycatcher No 2*), on the fact that the book had been published in the USA. As Ian Leigh has suggested,[21] one might therefore wonder if the convention per se would have permitted the newspapers to discuss *Spycatcher* if not for the more extensive protection of free expression afforded to the book in America under the First Amendment.

Incorporating the convention – de jure

That the British government is so frequently found to have breached the convention by the ECHR is explained in part by the fact that the convention has yet to be incorporated into domestic law. Members of the House of Lords (generally either Law Lords or prominent barristers) have frequently tried to incorporate the convention through private members' Bills.[1] These initiatives invariably trigger brief media interest in the question of fundamental rights, and as such exemplify the Lords' useful role as a forum for debate on issues of public concern. No such Bill, however, has yet come close to being enacted.[2]

In recent years, several High Court and Court of Appeal judges have also advocated incorporation of the convention.[3] The Liberal party has long been committed to incorporation of the convention as one element of a more far-reaching package of constitutional reforms (discussed in chapter 15). It now appears that the Labour party has also accepted the desirability of incorporation, although

---

21 Leigh I (1992) '*Spycatcher* in Strasbourg' *Public Law* 200–208.
1 For the most recent initiative see Lord Scarman (1995) 'Points of common law' *The Guardian* 8 May.
2 See Bailey, Harris and Jones *op cit* pp 19–20.
3 Scarman Lord (1987) 'Human rights in an unwritten constitution' *Denning LJ* 129–136; (1995) *op cit*: Bingham T (1993) 'The European Convention on Human Rights: time to incorporate' *LQR* 390–400. See also the dissenting speech of Lord Bridge in *Spycatcher (No 1)*.

whether it would retain that view should it win a Commons majority is a matter for speculation. The Conservative government, one perhaps need not add, has evinced no such inclination.

Thus far, advocates of incorporation have assumed that it can only be achieved through legislation, whether as an isolated instance of constitutional reform or as part of a broader process of political restructuring. As a matter of strict legal theory, however, there is no impediment to the House of Lords (qua final court of appeal) concluding that the convention should be construed, de jure, as an authoritative source of law, binding on British courts. That contention might be thought nonsensical, but it is not as fanciful as it initially appears.

As suggested in chapters 2 and 4, the formal rule that treaties have no binding force in domestic law until incorporated by legislation had an obvious functional basis in 1688. In the absence of such a rule, the Crown could conceivably have overridden legislation by using its prerogative powers to undertake international obligations. Affording treaties binding legal status would have subverted a revolutionary settlement which supposedly established the supremacy of Parliament vis-à-vis the Crown. That functional basis does not exist in so stark a form in the modern era. The fusion of the executive and legislative branches, coupled with the consolidation of the party system, has meant that in general the government effectively controls the legislature. It is thus oversimplistic to assume that Parliament needs judicial protection against executive law-making in the international law arena.

There is a subsidiary justification for the rule. This derives from the courts' historical deference to the personal prerogatives of the Monarch. The point was clearly expressed in *Rustomjee v R*, by Lord Coleridge CJ, who observed that 'as in making the treaty, so in performing the treaty, [the Queen] is beyond the control of municipal law, and her acts are not to be examined in her own courts'.[4] *Rustomjee* was quoted approvingly by Lord Denning in *Blackburn v A-G*,[5] and identified as the source of the traditional rule.

However, there are obvious flaws, both intrinsic and contextual, in adhering to this reasoning today. In 1864, given Queen Victoria's manifest reluctance to acknowledge the process of democratisation which the constitution was undergoing,[6] it may just have been conceivable to assume that the Monarch played a significant

4 (1876) 2 QBD 69 at 74, CA.
5 See p 500 above.
6 See pp 347–348 above.

personal role in influencing the treaty terms to which her government adheres. To suggest that the present Monarch does so is a nonsense; as Lord Roskill observed in *GCHQ* in response to the argument that the Monarch personally had abrogated her civil servants rights of trade union membership: 'To talk of that act as the act of the sovereign savours of the archaism of past centuries.'[7] Archaism has no greater validity in respect of foreign policy than it does in respect of employment conditions.

The intrinsic flaw lies in the fact that the *Rustomjee* rationale conflates the two quite distinct issues of the government's power to conclude a treaty and that treaty's subsequent impact in domestic law. The first issue is essentially non-justiciable in nature. Whether it is advantageous for this country to accept a particular set of obligations vis-à-vis other countries is a political question in the broadest sense; it is not an issue meet for judicial determination. However, where those obligations are expressed in terms of legal rules, and are purportedly intended to bestow legal rights on individual citizens, they are manifestly justiciable in character.

This elision of discrete phenomena was nevertheless restated by Lord Oliver in 1989 in *Maclaine Watson & Co Ltd v Department of Trade and Industry*:

> 'A treaty is not part of English law until it has been incorporated into the law by legislation. ... [I]t is outside the purview of the court [ie unenforceable] not only because it is made in the conduct of foreign relations, which are a prerogative of the crown, but also because as a source of rights and obligations, it is irrelevant.'[8]

The reasoning in the final clause of Lord Oliver's quotation is of course completely tautological; the court cannot apply a treaty because it is irrelevant to the domestic legal issue before it, and it is irrelevant because the court will not enforce it.

On reflection, irrelevance and unenforceabilty are obviously just different names for the same concept. The pertinent question is surely to ask *why* treaties are irrelevant/unenforceable? Lord Oliver's evident answer to that question – namely that a treaty is an exercise of the 'foreign relations' prerogative – is not convincing in the post-*GCHQ* era. As suggested in *Everett*, 'foreign relations' is a blanket term which covers a wide range of both justiciable and non-justiciable issues. The question of whether a government body has contravened the convention in its dealings

---

7 [1985] AC 374 at 377, HL.
8 Popularly known as *The International Tin Council* case: [1990] 2 AC 418 at 500, HL.

with a citizen is no less justiciable than the question of whether a passport has been withheld on unlawful grounds.

The traditional rule is thus reduced to one based on pure formalism. The convention (or any other treaty) is not enforceable in domestic courts because its *source* lies in an exercise of the prerogative rather than in statute. There is no doubt that the *nature* of the convention (in contrast perhaps to the contents of many other treaties) is eminently justiciable: its meaning is after all found in the judgments of the ECHR. If the traditional rule is no more than a common law presumption, the House of Lords is competent to reverse it, and conclude that courts should now presume that a treaty whose terms are justiciable and intended to bestow rights and obligations upon individual citizens is part of its domestic law until such time as Parliament says it is not.[9]

In conceptual terms, that conclusion would be no more radical than the ones taken in *GCHQ* or *Pepper v Hart*; in all three cases the court is simply giving legal expression to the obvious political fact that the government is generally the dominant actor on the constitutional stage, and as such should expect all its justiciable actions to be subject to the High Court's supervisory jurisdiction unless Parliament ousts that jurisdiction in the most explicit of terms.

Nor would judicial incorporation infringe upon Parliament's legal sovereignty. That challenge would only arise if a government subsequently convinced Parliament to enact legislation which explicitly forbade the domestic courts from applying the convention and the courts refused to obey the statute concerned: in that event, we would indeed be in a 'revolutionary' situation. At present, judicial incorporation de jure of the convention would be unexpected, unorthodox, and even perhaps so unconventional that many observers would consider it unconstitutional. But it is difficult to sustain the argument that it would necessarily be illegal.

. . . and de facto?

It would however seem that a domestic court determined to allow its judgments to be shaped by the law of the convention could often achieve that result, if only episodically, in rather less speculative ways. As noted in chapter 12, the ECJ has embraced the idea that the provisions of the convention are analogous to the 'fundamental human rights' contained in the EC's 'general principles of law'.[10] The member states declined to incorporate the

---

9 Parliament would thus retain the power to prevent a minority government 'legislating' via the prerogative.
10 Page 516 above.

convention into community law de jure at Maastricht. Nevertheless, the TEU's preamble offers explicit support for the ECJ's more circuitous approach to the same end:

> 'The Union shall respect fundamental rights, as guaranteed by the European Convention for the Protection of Human Rights ... and as they result from the constitutional traditions common to the member states, as general principles of Community law.'[11]

This has significant implications for British courts, insofar as it would seem to oblige them (post-*Factortame*) to disapply any domestic statutory or common law provision (in an area within the EC's competence) which could not be construed to comply with the convention.[12] This development does not of course answer the methodological question of how *any* EC law obligation has assumed such 'special' constitutional status within the UK, but its substantive impact seems uncontentious.[13]

A question of greater interest arises when one wonders whether the alleged 'ripple effect' of EC law will carry with it into matters purely of domestic law some or all of the convention's legal principles, or indeed, if the ECHR's jurisprudence possesses its own 'ripple effect'. If this were to happen, it would entail at the least a radical alteration of accepted common law principles and thence of techniques of statutory interpretation, and could, if enthusiastically embraced by the courts, provide a moral launchpad for a considerably more far-reaching redefinition of orthodox constitutional understandings. In the final section of this chapter, we consider whether the foundations of such a 'revolution' have been laid, before turning, in chapter 15, to discuss what form a restructured constitutional settlement might most appropriately take.

CONCLUSION: THE (RE-)EMERGENCE OF FUNDAMENTAL RIGHTS IN ADMINISTRATIVE LAW

The legal education of many law students in Britain in the past 20 years has included exposure to successive editions of Professor John Griffith's celebrated work on *The Politics of the Judiciary.* Griffith promoted considerable controversy in suggesting that the

---

11 Art F(2) TEU.

12 See the development of this argument by Grief N (1991) 'The domestic impact of the ECHR as mediated through Community law' *Public Law* 555–567.

13 See Grief *op cit*; Lord Browne-Wilkinson (1992) 'The infiltration of a Bill of Rights' *Public Law* 397–410.

judiciary's social and educational background predisposed most judges to adopt a highly conservative attitude when faced with contentious political questions. Griffith was not accusing judges of acting in a crudely party political sense:

> 'But it is demonstrable that on every major social issue which has come before the courts during the last 30 years – concerning industrial relations, political protest, race relations, governmental secrecy, police powers, moral behaviour – the judges have supported the conventional, established and settled interests. And they have reacted strongly against challenges to those interests.'[14]

Griffith suggests that such judicial bias may explain the Labour party's historic reluctance to embrace the idea of a supra-legislative constitution. The point is echoed by other commentators. Wallington and McBride observe for example that any enthusiasm the third Wilson government might have had for such reform was snuffed out by the ostensibly pro-Conservative decision in *Tameside*.[15] Yet from any sophisticated view of democratic government, the *Tameside* saga reflects poorly on the Labour government rather than on the courts. *Tameside* was defensibly decided both as a matter of law and of broader constitutional morality. The Labour government's efforts to ignore the clear meaning of the 1944 Education Act (an Act promoted by an all-party coalition government) so that it could impose a particular educational ideology on all parts of the country, irrespective of local preferences, forcefully disproves assertions that only the Thatcher and Major governments succumbed to the minoritarian vice of assuming that having a Commons majority entitles them to do whatever they like to whoever they wish whenever they choose.

The Griffith thesis draws much of its force from its attachment to such a crude notion of 'democracy'. The unelected judiciary's 'conservatism' is undesirable because it obstructs the policies preferred by the 'democratically elected' government of the day. Such assumptions are themselves vulnerable to criticism on the ground that they leave a rather more important question unasked – namely whether it is 'democratic' for a constitution to permit barely majoritiarian or even minoritarian ideologies to exercise ultimate control of the law-making process? In a democracy which had placed its basic moral principles beyond the reach of bare majorities, one would of course expect the judiciary to adopt a

14 *Op cit* pp 239–240.
15 Wallington P and McBride J (1976) *Civil Liberties and a Bill of Rights* pp 28–29 (London: Cobden Trust), cited in Bailey, Harris and Jones *op cit* p 15. On *Tameside*, see pp 416–419 above.

conservative stance in defence of constituent moral values. By doing so, they evince loyalty to a rather broader conception of 'the people' than one is likely to find in a transient electoral majority. This might suggest that insofar as judicial conservatism reveals a 'problem' within the constitution, it is a problem that stems from the doctrine of parliamentary sovereignty rather than from the courts.

Professor Griffith has latterly revised his opinion a little, and suggested that many judges who have risen to senior positions in the past 10 to 15 years have displayed a significant degree of independence from and suspicion of the particular brand of conservatism favoured by the Thatcher and Major administrations.[16] Yet one might plausibly suggest that decisions such as *M*, or *Factortame*, or the *Fire Brigades Union* case are just as anti-democratic from a crude majoritarian perspective as were *Tameside* or *Bromley v GLC*. Judicial decisions do not suddenly become 'correct' simply because they happen to coincide with one's own preferred party political perspective.

Simon Lee has suggested that Professor Griffith's modest revisionism does not go far enough.[17] In a fascinating critique of judicial politics during the Thatcher and Major eras, Lee argues that the courts have effectively donned the mantle of 'the opposition' to the minoritarian preferences of the elected central government. But this is not 'opposition' in a party political sense; the judiciary is not simply plugging the constitutional holes left by the feebleness of the Labour party during the 1980s, or more systemically, by the Commons' pervasive inadequacy as a monitor of and restraint on governmental extremism. Lee is not suggesting that the courts' allegedly more interventionist ideas are intended to compete on equal terms with those of politicians, but rather that they exist above party political dispute, in a kind of constitutional moral stratosphere.

Lee's thesis receives some support from essays and articles written by members of the judiciary. Sir John Laws has recently characterised the judiciary's more interventionist stance in administrative law as an attempt to give legal expression to a series of moral principles 'about whose desirability there can be no serious argument'.[18] Sir John Laws suggests that much of the impetus for this

---

16 Griffith J (1993) *Judicial Politics Since 1920 – a Chronicle* (Oxford: Blackwell).
17 Lee S (1994) 'Law and the constitution', in Kavanagh D and Seldon A (eds) *The Major Effect* (London: Macmillan).
18 Sir John Laws (1993) 'Is the High Court the guardian of fundamental constitutional rights?' *Public Law* 59–79.

development has come from the judiciary's increasing exposure to the constitutional orders of the EC, the European Convention, and the domestic legal systems of EC's and convention's member states.

A perhaps more significant analysis, given its author's current status as a Law Lord, has been offered by Lord Browne-Wilkinson.[19] Lord Browne-Wilkinson also acknowledges that the ECHR and the ECJ have had a significant influence on the judicial consciousness. However he also suggests that British courts have increasingly been returning to a more rigorous (and often overlooked) schemata of statutory interpretation, in which judges should assume that: 'a presumption in favour of individual freedom almost certainly reflects the true intention of Parliament.'[20]

Yet it would be rash to assume either that such sentiments point towards even a dominant trend, still less an inviolable truth, in recent judicial decisions, or that allowing judges to determine the meaning of 'individual freedom' without the benefit of guidance from a supra-parliamentary constitution is politically desirable. To conclude this chapter, we consider two significant judgments which convey the shortcomings of reliance upon judicial innovation as an effective counterweight to an elected government's minoritarian preferences.

Brind v Home Secretary (1991)[1]

The *Brind* litigation was provoked by the government's efforts to address the problem of IRA terrorism. The government formed the opinion that the IRA cause would be hindered if the radio and television media were not permitted to broadcast statements made by members of terrorist organisations or by members of political parties which the government designated as supportive of such groups. The ban extended however only to the speaker's actual voice; her words could be quoted verbatim by reporters, or, as frequently happened, dubbed by actors. Prime Minister Thatcher evidently believed the measure would deprive terrorists of

---

19 Browne-Wilkinson *op cit.*
20 *Ibid*, at p 408. Lord Browne-Wilkinson suggests *R. & W Paul Ltd v Wheat Commission* [1937] AC 139, *National Assistance Board v Wilkinson* [1952] 2 QB 648, and *Raymond v Honey* [1983] 1 AC 1 as examples.
1 [1991] 1 All ER 720, HL.

the 'oxygen of publicity'.[2] In the event, the ban arguably achieved precisely the opposite effect, as litigation challenging its legality trailed all the way through the English court system and on to the Commission on Human Rights, attracting considerable press coverage both in this country and abroad.

The Home Secretary assumed he could impose the ban on the IBA under the powers granted to him by the Broadcasting Act 1981 s 29:

> '. . . the Secretary of State may at any time by notice in writing require the authority to refrain from broadcasting any matter or classes of matter specified in the notice.'[3]

Brind was a journalist who considered that the ban was ultra vires s 29, and thus unlawfully infringed free expression. He based his arguments on several grounds, three of which are appropriately considered here.

Brind firstly contended that the ban was *Wednesbury* unreasonable. The court saw little merit in that argument. Lord Bridge thought it was 'impossible' to reach that conclusion:

> 'In any civilised country the defeat of the terrorist is a public interest of the highest importance. . . . What is perhaps surprising is that the restriction is of such limited scope.'[4]

Similarly, Lord Ackner considered it entirely understandable that the government had concluded that terrorists enhanced their legitimacy by appearing on television and radio. There is little scope for disagreeing with this dismissal of the *Wednesbury* point. The test applies only to ludicrously illogical or morally outrageous decisions. The government's decision in *Brind* seems well within the range of views that reasonable people might hold. The policy may indeed have been ill-advised, and was probably counterproductive, but ineffectiveness and a lack of wisdom do not amount to irrationality.

Mr Brind also deployed two rather more unorthodox arguments, both of which invited the House of Lords to accept that

---

2 Extracts from the speech made by Douglas Hurd, then Home Secretary, when explaining the ban to the Commons are reproduced in Lord Ackner's opinion at 729. Interestingly (since the case preceded *Pepper v Hart*) Lord Ackner did not seem to think that this reference to *Hansard* was precluded by parliamentary privilege or art 9 of the Bill of Rights.

3 In respect of the BBC, the Home Secretary assumed that he could issue the ban under cl 13(4) of the BBC's licensing agreement with the government, which provided that: 'The Secretary of State may from time to time . . . require the Corporation to refrain . . . from sending any matter or matters of any class. . . .'

4 [1991] 1 All ER 720 at 724.

the common law should now recognise additional criteria against which to evaluate the legality of government action. The first suggested ground was 'proportionality'. The proportionality test would require the courts to examine the substantive merits of a government decision more rigorously than they do when applying the irrationality criterion, and to ask in effect if the government has achieved the ends it sought by employing means which impinge too harshly upon the legitimate interests of groups or individuals. Thus construed, proportionality does not amount to a judicially created appellate jurisdiction – the court does not substitute its own preferred outcome for that chosen by the government – but it does assume that the irrationality test affords government bodies too much autonomy.

Much recent interest in proportionality has been prompted by its use by the ECJ, the ECHR and the German courts.[5] Since proportionality is an EC 'general principle of law', British courts must apply it when evaluating government actions in respect of matters with an EC dimension. Its import into issues concerned purely with domestic law might thus be expected as another manifestation of EC law's 'ripple effect'. It would be unduly formalist to assume that English law should adopt ECJ principles simply because they are ECJ principles. But one can readily discern a more functionalist basis for common law recognition of the idea in the modern era. Attaching a more limited meaning to statutory formulae would force governments to be far more precise in the language they choose to use in the Bills they promote. As such, the doctrine would fill in a constitutional hole created by the acknowledged inadequacy of the Commons and Lords as scrutinisers of a government's legislative policy choices. A similarly enhanced degree of precision would be required in respect of actions taken under statutory authority:

> 'Ministers would have to spell out much more carefully than before exactly why they are adopting certain policies and they would have to show that there were no, less draconian, alternatives, which would have worked.'[6]

In *GCHQ,* Lord Diplock had referred explicitly to proportionality as a ground of review which might in future be adopted by

---

5 See particularly Jowell J and Lester A (1988) 'Proportionality: neither novel nor dangerous', in Jowell J and Oliver D (eds) *New Directions in Judicial Review* (London: Stevens and Sons). On the ECJ see Hartley T (3rd edn 1994) *The Foundations of European Community Law* ch 5 (Oxford: Clarendon Press).
6 Lee (1994) *op cit* p 137.

British courts.[7] If Mr Brind had assumed that day had dawned, he was to be disappointed. Lord Roskill's judgment in *Brind* accepted that the principle might some day play a role in domestic law, but it could not appropriately be used on this occasion.[8] Lord Ackner was more dismissive. He evidently saw no distinction between review based on proportionality and appeal based squarely on the merits. Since only Parliament could create an appellate jurisdiction, the courts would in effect be usurping the legislative function by embracing proportionality as a new ground of review.

Lord Ackner's argument is perhaps oversimplistic. The suggestion that there is no judicially occupiable space between *Wednesbury* unreasonableness and appeal on the merits does not withstand close scrutiny if one accepts that the *Wednesbury* test is indeed concerned only with absolutely outrageous decisions. A conclusion which was simply 'outrageous' or 'bizarre' or 'extremely odd' or 'downright silly' should not in principle be quashable on irrationality grounds. But, notwithstanding the elasticity of language, one surely goes too far in equating appeal on the merits with the prohibition of outrageous or bizarre decisions.

Mr Brind's second suggested innovation was that the House of Lords should hold the ban unlawful because it contravened art 10 of the convention. This found no favour with any member of the court. Lord Ackner reiterated the traditional view that the convention could be invoked as a source of persuasive authority only if the domestic legislation was ambiguous or uncertain. He saw no such ambiguity in s 29(3). Nor did he discern any merit in Mr Brind's suggestion that, as matter of domestic law, the court should at least insist that the Home Secretary consider whether or not the ban was consistent with art 10. Lord Ackner suggested that accepting this argument: 'inevitably would result in incorporating the convention into English law by the back door.'[9] That contention is poorly founded. Requiring ministers to pay attention to the convention as part of the government's decision-making process does not in itself empower domestic courts to quash executive decisions which appear in substance to breach the convention.

It would however seem that the government's wishes would not have been in the least compromised if the House of Lords had construed the convention as a binding or even highly persuasive authority. Three years after the *Brind* judgment was delivered, the European Commission on Human Rights held that the application

7 [1985] AC 374 at 410, HL.
8 [1991] 1 All ER 720 at 725.
9 *Ibid*, at 735.

Mr Brind had subsequently made under the convention was inadmissible, seemingly concluding that the government's interference with free expression was too trivial to contravene art 10.[10] This conclusion was perhaps surprising, but it does inject a useful, cautionary note into a sometimes fevered domestic debate, by suggesting that advocates of incorporating the convention overestimate its capacity to forbid government behaviour which impinges upon freedom of expression, while opponents of incorporation have a similarly exaggerated view of the extent to which it would impinge upon the sovereignty of Parliament and the autonomy of the government.

Derbyshire County Council v Times Newspapers Ltd (1992)[11]

The *Derbyshire County Council v Times Newspapers Ltd*[12] litigation was triggered by a *Sunday Times'* story alleging that Derbyshire had been improperly using its pension funds. When sued for libel by the council, the *Sunday Times* argued that local authorities lacked the legal capacity to bring a libel action over criticism of their 'governing reputations'. This contention was initially rejected by Morland J. A unanimous Court of Appeal reversed the decision.[13] All three judges (Balcombe, Ralph Gibson, and Butler Sloss LJJ) thought that the common law position on this question was ambiguous. Consequently, the court felt that it was appropriate to examine the provisions of the European Convention on Human Rights to assist it in finding the 'correct' solution to the problem before it. Indeed, both Balcombe LJ and Butler Sloss LJ, while observing that the convention was not formally part of domestic law, went so far as to say they considered it appropriate to 'apply' the case law of the ECHR in this instance.[14] On examining the ECHR's case law, the Court of Appeal concluded that allowing a local council to launch a libel action was an 'unnecessary' restriction on free expression.

---

10 For a (very persuasive) criticism of this conclusion see Pannick D. (1994) 'No logic behind gagging terrorists' empty rhetoric' *The Times* 2 August.
11 The following section is a much condensed version of an argument I have made elsewhere; see see Loveland I (1994) *op cit.*
12 [1993] 1 All ER 1011.
13 [1992] 3 All ER 65.
14 The court's methodology seems to mirror that used by the ECJ to 'incorporate' the convention into the EC treaties via 'general principles of law'; see p 516 above; Grief *op cit*

Lord Keith delivered the leading judgment in the Lords. Unlike the Court of Appeal, he did not either 'apply' the convention, nor resort to judgments of the ECHR to resolve ambiguities in the common law. Lord Keith considered the common law quite clear:

> [N]ot only is there no public interest favouring the right of organs of government, whether central or local, to sue for libel, but it is contrary to the public interest that they should have it. . . . because to admit such actions would place an undesirable fetter on freedom of speech.[15]

Lord Keith focused on the *function* served by criticism of government in a modern democratic society. He thought this purpose was best described by Lord Bridge in *Hector v A-G of Antigua and Barbuda*:

> [T]hose . . . responsible for public administration must always be open to criticism. Any attempt to stifle or fetter such criticism amounts to political censorship of the most insidious and objectionable kind. . . . [T]he very purpose of criticism . . . is to undermine public confidence in their stewardship and to persuade the electorate that the opponents would make a better job of it than those presently holding office.[16]

Lord Keith found further support for his perception of the requisite 'public policy' concerns in several United States' decisions, primarily that of the Illinois Supreme Court in *City of Chicago v Tribune Co* (1923),[17] and the 1964 Supreme Court judgment in *New York Times v Sullivan*.[18]

Lord Keith's concern was obviously to remove an undesirable fetter on free speech. But by forbidding a council to use a libel action in all circumstances, he perhaps oversimplified the issue, for there is a line between robust, or even vitriolic *criticism*, and premeditated *deceit*. From an American perspective, the legitimacy of government rests, in Jefferson's terms, on the 'consent of the governed'. One purpose of the First Amendment is to maximise the likelihood that consent is 'informed'. In *Sullivan*, the US Supreme Court had held that the common law of libel must be subjected to First Amendment protection of free expression. The

---

15 [1993] 1 All ER 1011 at 1019.
16 [1990] 2 All ER 103 at 106, PC.
17 139 NE 86.
18 376 US 254 (1964). He referred also to South African case law, though quite what relevance one should attach to this is unexplained. If, as Lord Keith says, public policy favours free speech on political matters as a means for the citizenry to call government to account, one assumes that no lessons can usefully be learned from a society in which, even pre-apartheid, the majority of the population had no right to vote.

court formulated an 'actual malice' test, which demands that a plaintiff proves that the defendant either knew that the information was false, or that she entertained serious doubts as to its truth which she did not explore.

'Actual malice' balances competing constitutional evils. Adopting a no-fault or negligence test as the basis for liability for publishing untruths would corrupt the basis of consent to government by rationing the dissemination of 'true' information. Facing such a test, the media or individuals would self-censor themselves, and so suppress possibly true information, for fear of incurring substantial liabilities. The court considered this so-called 'chilling effect' a greater constitutional evil than the certainty that vigorous debate will result in some 'false' information entering the public arena if the knowledge/recklessness test is applied.

But this 'lesser of two evils' argument has no force when the disseminator *knows* her information is untrue. As Brennan J observed in *Garrison v Louisiana*: 'the use of a known lie as a tool is at once at odds with the premises of a democratic government'.[19] From this perspective, Lord Keith's absolute prohibition on councils suing for libel is flawed. The publicity generated by news stories alleging corruption and incompetence does have a substantial (if diffuse) adverse impact on the interests of those many million citizens for whom the political preferences of a council's ruling party represent the most desirable moral code according to which their country should be governed. If critical press coverage of such councils' activities rests on false information, every citizen who supports the ruling party suffers a loss through a probable diminution in their preferred party's electability. And if local failings undermine a party's national reputation, all of its supporters are injured by false accusations.

A complete ban on libel actions would therefore seem defensible only if one takes a simplistic view of the democratic process. This might suggest that there is much merit in the argument that one should permit an elected government body to sustain a libel action on the basis of the *New York Times* test. It is unfortunate that the House of Lords in *Derbyshire* appeared to have misunderstood both the legal rule which the US Supreme Court has developed and the political principle to which the rule gives effect.

19 379 US 64 at 75 (1964).

Conclusion

Judicial pronouncements that the common law and the convention bestow identical levels of civil liberties protection on British citizens are now commonplace. An early example is Lord Goff's comment in *A-G v Guardian Newspapers Ltd (Spycatcher) (No 2)*:

> 'I can see no inconsistency between English law on this subject and art 10. . . . This is scarcely surprising, since we pride ourselves on the fact that freedom of speech has existed in this country perhaps as long as, if not longer than, it has existed in any other country in the world.'[20]

But it is very misleading to argue that the ECHR and the common law confer the same degree of protection for free expression, or indeed, for any other civil or personal liberty. The crucial distinction between the ECHR and the common law is of course that the former is regarded by most of its signatories as a *constituent framework* of political values, which exist beyond the reach of reform or repeal by a simple legislative majority. The protection the ECHR affords has, therefore, some degree of legal longevity. The common law, in contrast, is utterly transient; its substance may be promptly modified by whichever political faction can command even a bare Commons majority.

Lord Keith's reliance on American precedent in *Derbyshire* is open to the same criticism as Lord Goff's comment in *Spycatcher*. If the American cases Lord Keith examined were indeed concerned purely with developing the 'common law' to protect democratic government, their relevance to the British situation is unarguable. But *Sullivan* was not a case which *developed* the common law. Rather it recognised that common law rules had been *overridden* by the supra-legislative moral values which Madison wrote into the First Amendment of the Bill of Rights. It articulated the basic moral principle that, as Madison put it, in the United States: 'the censorial power is in the people over the Government, and not in the Government over the people'.

In claiming to protect a 'fundamental' component of public policy, Lord Keith's judgment deflects attention from the brute political reality that 'Parliament' may at any time reverse or amend the *Derbyshire* judgment in any way it thinks fit. Once made, this observation raises a larger question. It takes little reflection to lead one to ask whether the greatest impediment to freedom of expression (or indeed to any other civil liberty) in modern British society stems from the doctrine of parliamentary sovereignty.

20 [1990] 1 AC 109 at 283.

Crudely put, this argument would contend that a political party with a Commons majority may simply legislate to curb the promulgation of political ideologies with which it disagrees. This supposition is not so far fetched as it might initially sound; the Thatcher governments' efforts to curb 'propaganda on the rates' and restrictions on the political activities of local government employees,[1] are all legislative incursions into the realm of free political discourse. Nor is it difficult to discern an anti-free speech rationale in such statutory initiatives as the rate and poll tax capping of local government, and, conversely, in Parliament's continuing failure to limit the national campaign expenditure of political parties.

Eric Barendt's discussion of *Derbyshire* recognises this concern to some extent. He suggests that a satisfactory long-term resolution of the issues that the case raised requires that Parliament incorporate the convention into British law.[2] But that would be in itself only a transient remedy, unless incorporation was part of a more fundamental constitutional reform which radically restructured the allocation of governmental power in ways which more accurately expressed the essentially pluralist political sentiments of the British people. The concluding chapter of this book thus turns to the question of constitutional reform, and considers both whether such reform is possible, and, if so, what shape a modernised British constitution might take.

---

1 See pp 449–451 above.
2 (1993) 'Libel and freedom of speech in English law' *Public Law* 449–464 at pp 463–464.

CHAPTER FIFTEEN

Reforming the constitution?

The question of constitutional reform is in itself worthy of book-length examination.[1] This final chapter does not offer a detailed prescription of the ways in which the United Kingdom's constitution should be structured. Rather it briefly surveys several proposals which have been aired in recent years, before concluding with some bluntly formulated and rather fanciful suggestions as to the approach to reform that might be taken by a government prepared to restructure the constitution in accordance with a pluralist rather than minoritarian understanding of democratic principle and practice. This is done, it should be stressed, to provide discussion points for students rather than blueprints for politicians. Initially, however, we return to what might be regarded as the two logically precedent questions to any discussion of radical constitutional reform. Firstly, whether it is legally possible to entrench legislation in a manner which safeguards it from repeal by the traditional 'simple majority in Commons and Lords plus royal assent' formula. And secondly, if such a legal device can be found, under what political circumstances might it legitimately be employed?

1. ENTRENCHMENT REVISITED: ISSUES OF LEGALITY AND LEGITIMACY

As suggested in chapter 2, it now seems rather less difficult to construct a legal argument supporting the idea of entrenched

---

1 A short and stimulating example of a modest reform programme is offered by Brazier R (1991) *Constitutional Reform* (Oxford: OUP). For a (C)conservative perspective see Mount F (1992) *The British Constitution Now* (London: Heinemann). For a recent academic critique see McEldowney J (1994) *Public Law* ch 21 (London: Sweet and Maxwell). The ideas recently advanced by the Labour and Liberal parties are outlined in sections two and three below.

legislation than it was in the 1950s, when the *Harris* and *MacCorm-ick* cases triggered a rash of interest in the possibility of finding domestic limitations to Parliament's evidently sovereign legal status. The orthodox Diceyan view, so persuasively restated by Professor Wade in 1955, need not be repeated here. The argument that such orthodoxy need no longer be construed as binding rests on several premises, both formalist and functionalist in nature. Some of these premises were evident but underdeveloped when Wade and indeed Dicey himself outlined the traditionalist view-point; others have emerged far more recently, as a result both of modern political history and contemporary judicial practice.

The first issue we might address is a problem raised by linguistic imprecision, an imprecision that has in turn produced consider-able conceptual confusion. The conceptual confusion may arise if one fails to distinguish between two quite different routes to achieve the same moral/political ends. If one should somehow succeed in legally 'binding' future Parliaments to respect particu-lar values, then one has necessarily succeeded in entrenching[2] those values. But one need not necessarily have to achieve the former result to bring about the latter consequences; it may be that one can now entrench legislation without having to destroy 'Parliament's' legal sovereignty. This argument assumes that entrenchment need not place any limits at all on 'Parliament's' legislative capacities; rather it need only convince the High Court that it has an appropriate role to play in controlling the internal proceedings of the Commons and the Lords and the prerogative powers of the Monarch.

To illustrate this argument, we might begin with a hypothetical entrenching provision, contained in a 'Constitution Act' passed in the ordinary manner. The Constitution Act specifies that a statutory provision (whether enacted prior or subsequent to the Constitution Act) affecting an entrenched value detailed in the Constitution Act (which would include the entrenching provision itself) would have legal force only if the court was satisfied that the following criteria had been met:

1. the Act concerned had begun its parliamentary passage in the Commons;
2. the Commons had voted for it by a two-thirds majority at third reading before sending it to the Lords;

---

2 'Entrenchment' is used here in the sense adverted to at pp 46–47 namely any device protecting a given value against repeal by the simple majority plus Royal Assent formula.

3. the Lords had voted for it by a two-thirds majority at third reading before sending it for the Royal Assent;
4. The Monarch had granted the Royal Assent only after establishing that the requisite majorities had been achieved in both houses.

We may then assume that a subsequent 'Parliament' purports to pass an 'Act' by the traditional simple majority plus royal assent formula which contains terms breaching the provisions of the Constitution Act.

It is tempting to conclude simply that a citizen who asked the court to obey the Constitution Act and disapply a later statute would be asking the judiciary to override the wishes of Parliament, which had seemingly enacted the subsequent provision. However, steps 1–3 of the entrenchment process can be analysed in a rather different way. They could be seen as merely asking the courts to 'question' the proceedings adopted in each house in respect of a Bill. Step 4, in contrast, could be seen as simply requiring the courts to undertake the now uncontentious task of reviewing an exercise of the prerogative.[3]

The argument assumes that 'Parliament' has the legal capacity to regulate the powers of its component parts – that the Commons, the Lords, and the Monarch as parts of Parliament are legally inferior to Parliament itself. If this view is accepted, it seemingly follows that Parliament may enact legislation placing specific limits on the legal competence of either house or of the Monarch. The hypothetical Constitution Act essentially provides that the Commons would be acting ultra vires its powers in sending a Bill which infringed the Constitution Act to the Lords if the Bill had not attracted a two-thirds majority; similarly, the House of Lords would be acting ultra vires in sending that Bill for the Royal Assent if it was not supported by that enhanced majority of peers; while the Monarch would be acting ultra vires if she assented to such a measure without having established that the requisite majorities in each house had been achieved.

There is similarly a need here for precision in describing what the High Court would be doing if it declined to disapply a subsequent statute which infringed the Constitution Act, on the basis of the orthodox theory that no Parliament can bind its successors. In refusing to disapply such a statute, the courts would in effect

---

3 It is perhaps feasible to argue that the granting of the Royal Assent is itself a 'proceeding in Parliament'. This would however seem implausible, given that privilege and art 9 emerged as devices to protect the two houses against the Monarch. But for the purposes of this argument, the legal source of the Royal Assent is irrelevant.

be concluding that the privileges of each house (steps 1–3)[4] and/ or privilege plus the royal prerogative (steps 1–4) and/or the royal prerogative alone (step 4) outrank legislation in the constitution's legal hierarchy.

This rationale would draw us into a rather bizarre series of conclusions. It was suggested in chapter 2 that the orthodox view does indeed recognise one limit on Parliament's sovereign authority – namely that it cannot bind itself and its successors. But the orthodox view seemingly also requires us to accept three further constraints to Parliament's omnipotent legal power – namely that it cannot remove the Commons and Lords' powers to approve a Bill by simple majority vote, nor attach conditions to the Monarch's legal capacity to give the Royal Assent. To accept one limit to a nominally unlimited power might perhaps be accommodated as an inconvenient necessity: to accept four suggests that the integrity of the central argument is seriously flawed.

It is most unfortunate that the common elision in constitutional parlance of Parliament itself and the two houses of Parliament (but particularly the Commons) has so thoroughly pervaded analysis of the question of sovereignty as well as the question of privilege.[5] A perfect example of this is provided by Lord Simon's previously quoted observation in *Pickin*,[6] that the exclusive right of each house to control its own proceedings is a 'concomitant' of the sovereignty of Parliament. That view is however fundamentally misconceived, as a matter both of simple logic and of constitutional history. To allow each house an unfettered and apparently unfetterable power to control its own proceedings is not a concomitant of parliamentary sovereignty, but a blatant denial of it. By suggesting that each house has such an 'exclusive power', Lord Simon is setting privilege above both common law and statute. One thus finds oneself facing the oxymoronic proposition that Parliament possesses its legal sovereignty not because it cannot bind itself and its successors, but because it cannot bind its component (and hence inferior) parts.

The suggestion that one might entrench legislation in Britain by placing limits on the powers of the respective houses of Parliament rather than on those of Parliament itself is not, it should be stressed, a novel idea. Heuston had advanced a very similar thesis

---

4 *Wauchope* and *Pickin* might thus be reclassified as cases which did not concern the sovereignty of Parliament at all, but the non-justiciability of the privileges of the two houses.

5 See pp 329–330 above.

6 At p 42 above.

in 1964.[7] Heuston chose to support his argument with reference to the litigation in Commonwealth countries which we discussed in chapter 2. This might be thought to weaken both the legal and political force of his thesis. As Wade observed in 1955, there is little point in invoking this case law in the British context.[8] The entrenchment formulae in issue in *Trethowan* and *Harris* each enjoyed a certain, unambiguous legal and political status because they were 'created' by a British statute which the 'people' of New South Wales and South Africa had accepted as expressing their preferred constituent moral values.[9] Since the British Parliament has no 'creator' in this sense, we might assume (as traditionalists always have) that the 'manner and form' principle cannot be applied here.

But this involves perhaps too ready a dismissal of the *Trethowan* rationale. Heuston's argument has also been offered more recent support by Paul Craig, in a thesis premised on a discussion of basic, indigenous constitutional principles rather than a speculative importation of inapposite foreign case law.[10] Both authors operated under something of a disadvantage when advancing their ideas. Heuston, writing in the 1960s, laboured under the handicap of courts' adherence to the principle that exercise of the prerogative was not reviewable under any circumstances, a common law rule which would presumably incline the judiciary to consider the Royal Assent beyond legal scrutiny. In the post-*GCHQ* era, that principle no longer presents an obstacle to entrenchment.

Similarly, both Heuston and Craig's critiques were formulated when the courts were seemingly not prepared to examine events that occurred in either house during the passage of a Bill in order to ascertain the meaning of a statute. In the aftermath of *Pepper v Hart*, it seems clear that art 9 of the Bill of Rights (whatever its legal status)[11] is no longer regarded by the courts as an insuperable barrier to questioning either house's proceedings. There is a clear danger here that one simply ends up suggesting that entrenchment is now possible because the courts have embraced an increasingly expansive notion of justiciability, in which the legitimacy of judicial intervention is determined not by the legal identity of the

---

7 Heuston R (2nd edn, 1964) *Essays in Constitutional Law* ch 1 (London: Stevens and Sons).
8 See pp 53–55 above.
9 In the case of South Africa, 'the people' was obviously an extremely narrow concept, which would not be regarded as legitimate in the modern context.
10 Craig P (1991) *op cit*.
11 See pp 314–320 above.

institution whose actions are being impugned, but by the nature of the question the courts assume they are being asked. (In the hypothetical Constitution Act, the terms of the entrenchment procedure itself simply require the courts to perform a simple arithmetic calculation, and are thus obviously justiciable. Care would also have to be taken that the Act's substantive terms were similarly amenable to judicial analysis: we might accept here for the sake of argument that those terms simply embraced the provisions of the European Convention on Human Rights, which are also clearly matters courts can address.) To do so would in effect return us to Jennings' view that the 'rule of recognition' is a common law concept. This would however be no solution at all to the entrenchment conundrum, rather it makes the legal problem even more vexed.

As Jennings suggested, accepting that the rule of recognition is a common law concept implies that it could be redefined by Parliament. But equally (and this is a point on which we did not dwell in chapter 2), it could be redefined by the courts without any parliamentary initiative having been undertaken at all. In formal terms, if the rule of recognition is a purely common law phenomenon, there is no legal barrier to the High Court suddenly deciding that it would not 'recognise' any statute that impinged upon particular moral or political values, or that it would 'recognise' such statutes only if they had been enacted with an enhanced Commons and/or Lords majority. Jennings' thesis, taken to its logical conclusion, suggests that the common law is legally superior to Acts of Parliament, that the courts and not the legislature are the ultimate source of legal authority, and that we might, as a matter of law, find that at any moment the courts had exercised a power explicitly to refuse to apply statutes of which they disapproved. The extravagant interpretation of the principle espoused in *Dr Bonham*'s case would thereby be reasserted, and the 1688 revolution would have taken place in vain.

It is readily apparent that any search for a purely legal solution to the entrenchment question is likely to be severely hampered by the conceptually tangled constitutional undergrowth which has now grown so luxuriantly from the soil of the 1688 settlement. But Craig's critique is also helpful to advocates of entrenchment in that it asks us to consider not what the traditional rule is, but what the traditional rule is *for?* This approach then forces us to consider that entrenchment should not be analysed as a legal issue, but as a moral one.

Craig observes that 'much of the current literature fails to pay attention to the reasons why Parliament should or should not be regarded as sovereign'.[12] This comment applies with particular force to Professor Wade's influential 1955 article. Wade, we may recall, tells us that parliamentary sovereignty is the 'ultimate political fact' of the constitution. But what Professor Wade did not do in 1955 was ask *why* that fact should enjoy ultimate political status?

Craig begins to remedy this omission by recasting the issue in functionalist rather than formalist terms. He suggests that the Diceyan orthodoxy derives from a misunderstanding of political history and a misinterpretation of Blackstone's earlier defence of the parliamentary sovereignty principle. Traditionalists have seized upon particular passages of Blackstone's *Commentaries* to support the orthodox doctrine without adequately examining the political reasoning which underlay the legal conclusion. Craig adverts to 'an oft-quoted passage' in the *Commentaries* where Blackstone seemingly offers unambiguous approval for the theory Dicey later developed, concluding at one point that: 'True it is, that what the Parliament doth, no authority can undo.'[13]

However, in contrast to Wade's 1955 critique, Craig's analysis takes several steps backwards into the *Commentaries* themselves, and, more importantly, into the historical milieu within which the *Commentaries* were written. Craig observes that Blackstone was led to his conclusion about Parliament's sovereign authority by the political theories developed and refined during the seventeenth century which strove to identify the law-making process which was least likely to produce tyrannical laws. Some examples of such theorisation were adverted to in chapter 2.[14] Craig suggests that the doctrine of parliamentary sovereignty emerged in order to preserve what he refers to as a 'balanced' constitution. The doctrine might more appropriately be relabelled as a presumed guarantor of an *anti-factional* constitution. Crudely stated, Blackstone endorsed the principle of parliamentary sovereignty because he could conceive of no more broadly based mechanism for ensuring that laws enjoyed the consent of 'the people'. Parliament was 'sovereign' for political or moral reasons – namely that it minimised the possibility that the English 'people'[15] would be subjected to factionally motivated legislation: the principle which the concept embodied, the principle which commanded the obedience

---

12 *Op cit* p 221.
13 Vol I at p 91. See also the extract quoted at p 40 above.
14 See pp 37–39 above.
15 Narrowly defined of course as the Monarch, the Lords, and the small portion of citizens permitted to participate in electing members of the Commons.

of the judiciary, was not one of law, but of morality; not one of legality, but of legitimacy; not one of coercion, but of consensus.

Questions of legitimacy

Yet while parliamentary sovereignty may have emerged as a very crude mechanism to prevent factional legislation, it is quite clear that by the early twentieth century it had evolved into a constitutional doctrine which would in most circumstances facilitate achievement of entirely the opposite result. The combined impact of the Commons' dominance within Parliament, and of minoritarian governments within the Commons, generally places uninhibited legislative power within the grasp of political factions which represent the preferred political views of only a minority of the population. It is perhaps in this political reality, rather than in tortuous arguments about legal practicality, that the real difficulties posed by entrenchment actually lie. For in such a context, we might plausibly wonder whether even if the entrenchment of particular political values was possible as a matter of law, would it be defensible as a matter of morality if it was triggered simply by a legislative initiative enacted by Parliament?

On reflection, it is quite clear that the entrenching device upheld by the Privy Council in *Trethowan* offers a very poor model for the creation of fundamental, supra-parliamentary values in the British context. The effect of such a provision would be to place the power to entrench laws in the hands of a barely majoritarian or even minoritarian faction. There would seemingly have been no legal impediment to a legislature introducing 'manner and form' legislation which rooted the preferences of the then governing party so deeply that they could not in practice be changed – by insisting for example on 75% or 80% majorities in both houses, or requiring similar levels of support in a referendum.

Transposed to the modern British context, this would have permitted the Thatcher or Major governments to impose their own preferred brand of minoritarian ideology on the substantial majority of the electorate which consistently chose not to support them. Similarly, a future Labour government which took the view that it should attempt to entrench certain social democratic moral values against an extremist right wing administration would be doing so with (on the most optimistic of electoral predictions) 50% of the vote on an 85% turnout.

One would have to embrace a rather peculiar view of democracy to discern any moral legitimacy in a process which allowed minority factions within modern British society to impose entrenched 'fundamental' political values on the entire population. Such 'reform' would be the very antithesis of the supra-majoritarianism required to shape the outlines of the US Constitution and the unanimity needed to fashion and subsequently amend the provisions of the EC Treaty and the European Convention on Human Rights. Its terms would be not consensual but coercive; its rationale would be not pluralist but authoritarian; its effect would be not to empower 'the people' but to oppress them.

Thus even if we assume entrenchment is legally possible, we do not thereby prove that it is constitutionally desirable. As has been stressed throughout this book, constitutional law forms but one ingredient (albeit an important one) of a complex constitutional recipe. Issues of politics and morality as well as mere legality pervade the much larger and and more complex issue of constitutionality.

There would seem to be only two ways in which entrenchment could plausibly claim to have a legitimate constitutional basis. The legitimacy of constituent moral values appears to depend primarily on the breadth of consensus that they attract. The rationale underpinning this principle was perhaps best articulated, as we saw in chapter 1, in Madison's celebrated critique of factionalism: the higher the level of support required to enact a law, the less likely it is that the law concerned will be arbitrary, oppressive or intolerant, because its terms will express a compromise between groups of citizens holding different moral and political views. The Americans chose the 'two-thirds of Congress plus three-quarters of the States' rule to protect the terms of this initial compromise. We have seen that other constitutions have adopted devices which differ in their detailed form – the 'substantial provincial support' formula discovered by the Canadian Supreme Court in 1982, or the two-thirds of both chambers sitting in joint session criterion originally upheld by the South African Supreme Court in *Harris* and *Harris No 2*, or the legislative majority plus referendum approach favoured in New South Wales – but which serve a broadly similar function.

Two-thirds or three-quarters legislative majorities clearly do not eliminate the possibility that a country will produce oppressive laws. Such countries are however less likely to do so than those whose constitutions permit unfettered minoritarian or bare majoritarian law-making. But in the British context, this 'enhanced legislative majority' route to entrenchment could be followed only by a government which enjoyed hitherto unachieved levels of electoral support, in terms both of Commons seats *and* share of the popular vote. There would seem no prospect of a single political party coming remotely close to achieving such levels of popular approval. The position could presumably only be reached if the Labour party won a comfortable Commons majority, attracting perhaps 45% of the vote, but rather than govern as a single party chose to initiate major constitutional reform with the support of a Liberal party which had maintained its recent average electoral support of around 20%. Ideally, such a coalition would also detach at least a handful of MPs from the left-wing of the Conservative party, and attract the support of Scots, Welsh and Irish nationalist members of the Commons. The legitimacy of such reform would be further enhanced if the various governing parties had announced their intentions prior to the general election; the government could then more convincingly argue that the consent of their supporters to a constitutional revolution was informed.

In the absence of such a broad coalition, a minoritarian or barely majoritarian government seeking to entrench certain basic values could only stake a plausible claim to legitimacy by promoting substantive reforms which would both reduce its own share of political power and enhance the political influence wielded by opposition parties. A programme of reform which meets those criteria is outlined in section four below. The claim would however be a weak one, since many observers might genuinely doubt that any political party could ever be motivated by such selfless objectives. In these circumstances, a reformist government would necessarily be embarking on an élitist and ostensibly unrepresentative course of action.

It would nevertheless be rash to assume that a reform of this nature could not be 'democratic'. The moral quandary such a government would face forces us rather to focus again on the intimate linkage between matters of substance and process in the context of constitution-building which were adverted to in chapter 1. One should perhaps add that this observation applies, albeit perhaps with less force, to a context in which reform attracted overwhelming popular support. Even a super-majoritarian coalition government could not defensibly claim much legitimacy for its plans unless it sought to entrench principles which both restricted its own authority and increased the political power exercised by citizens who did not support its 'revolution'.

Several blueprints for constitutional reform were put forward by assorted pressure groups and think-tanks in the late 1980s. A body calling itself Charter 88 managed to attract appreciable media interest in its broadly framed proposals for an extensive overhaul of Britain's constitutional arrangements, while the centre-left Institute for Public Policy Research produced an extremely detailed programme of measures.[16] The initiatives promoted by such organisations merit close attention from an academic perspective, and it is likely that the publicity they generate will mean that at least some of their provisions seep into the minds if not overtly into the policy programmes of the political parties. The final sections of this chapter do not however dwell on the intricacies of such abstract intitiatives; that task has been admirably undertaken elsewhere.[17] Sections two and three are instead directed towards the reform proposals put before the electorate in the 1992 general election by the Labour and Liberal parties respectively, while section four concludes the book by offering some simplistically formulated suggestions as to how a reformist government might restructure our constitution's increasingly factional foundations.

II. THE LABOUR PARTY'S 'CHARTER OF RIGHTS'[18]

The Labour Party entered the 1992 general election campaign advocating a policy which it claimed amounted to 'the most radical change in the British constitution proposed by any political party this century'. The core of Labour's plans was contained in a document entitled *The Charter of Rights*, published in 1991. *The Charter* maintained that the Thatcher governments had 'abused' the constitution, arguing that 'many of the liberties we once enjoyed were inadequately protected against assault by an authoritarian government'.

The constitutional philosophy underlying *The Charter* was outlined by the party's then deputy leader and spokesman on constitutional affairs, Roy Hattersley, in an unpublished speech at a Fabian Conference in January 1990. Hattersley accused the Thatcher governments of having launched 'a sustained assault on these centres of independent power . . . which contributed to the plurality of our political system', and suggested of Thatcher herself that 'No Prime Minister in the modern era has been more impatient with dissent, more intolerant of criticism'. To some

16 IPPR (1991) *A Written Constitution for the UK* (London: IPPR). For a discussion see Oliver D (1992) 'Written constitutions: principles and problems' *Parliamentary Affairs* 135–152.

17 Oliver (1992) *op cit.*

18 The following section presents a condensed version of an argument I have made elsewhere: see Loveland I (1992) 'Labour and the constitution: the "right" approach to reform' *Parliamentary Affairs* 173–187.

extent Labour's thunder in urging the need for reform was stolen by Conservative MPs' decision to remove Mrs Thatcher from office. However, it seems reasonable to assume that proposals for constitutional reform should be built on more substantial foundations than distaste for a former Prime Minister's personality traits. But the degree to which Labour's programme amounted to a positive statement of intrinsically desirable reform was far from clear.

A charter of rights

The Charter's introduction noted that 'many rights have been eroded by government action' since 1980. Its prescription for reform, therefore, was that 'rights' must be both restored and extended. *The Charter* contained proposals for a series of detailed and specific Acts of Parliament intended to realise these objectives. It did not however express any enthusiasm for the idea of incorporating the convention into domestic law.

First among the proposed 'Charter Rights' was a Freedom of Information Act to replace the Official Secrets Act 1989. The new legislation would assume that there would be a general right of access to official information. The general right would, however, be subject to various exceptions. These would include information that would 'seriously impair' Britain's defence or foreign relations interests, impede law enforcement, or reveal policy advice given to individual ministers. A less ambiguous distinction between *The Charter*'s recommendations and the 1989 Act was that the new legislation would have granted leakers of official information a 'public interest' defence. This would make it unlikely that a government would risk initiating a prosecution in a Ponting-like scenario. *The Charter* also proposed a 'prior publication' defence, precluding prosecution of newspaper editors or journalists who published extracts of books like *Spycatcher.*

Hattersley's 1990 speech suggested that 'civil and economic liberty cannot easily be separated . . . the relationship between liberty and purchasing power is undeniable'. In the abstract, *The Charter* embraces this theme, accepting that there is more to rights than the mere promulgation of governmental good intentions: 'We define freedom not simply as the absence of restraint, but as the practical ability to do those things which we may choose to do . . . It is based on what ought to be a self-evident proposition that rights are of no value if they cannot be exercised.'

Consequently, *The Charter* committed the Labour party to legislation designed to promote 'justice' in the workplace. There would (overruling *GCHQ*) apparently have been no exceptions to workers' rights to join a trade union, and a minimum wage would have been introduced. More rigorous legislation to forbid gender or racial discrimination would also be enacted. *The Charter* also laid some stress on issues concerning access to justice in a more legalistic sense, perhaps most notably 'increased rights to legal aid'.

A pluralist constitution?

The individual rights which *The Charter* advocated were directed at reforming the 'what' of government by elevating the rights of individuals to a new level of importance. But *The Charter* also addressed the 'how' of government. It proposed a significant restructuring of state institutions. This was to include a new second chamber within Parliament, the introduction of regional government and a revitalisation of the local government sector.

Scotland and Wales

As suggested in chapter 10, the votes cast for and seats won by Scots Conservative MPs in the past four general elections reveal that Thatcherism was always a most unpopular programme with the Scots electorate. *The Charter* accepted that the contemporary case for some significant degree of Scots self-government was a strong one. It therefore announced that the next Labour government would create a Scottish Assembly during its first year of office.

Quite what form such self-government should take was a question with which the last Labour government grappled with limited success. The ill-fated Scotland Act 1978 envisaged a form of devolution which explicitly rejected federalism, and also retained revenue-raising powers at Westminster. As such, the powers of self-determination which the Scots people would have gained would have been quite limited.[19]

The Charter seemed to envisage that the proposed Scots Assembly would exercise wider powers than its 1978 counterpart, including the crucial issue of revenue raising. However, if the passage of the 1978 Bill provides any sort of precedent, there is every likelihood that a draft Bill and the resultant Act would be significantly different animals. An Assembly with lesser powers, bearing more resem-

19 See pp 419–424 above.

blance to the regional structures discussed below than to the projected Scots institution, was proposed for Wales.

Regional government

The Charter provided little detailed information about the powers and structure of its proposed regional assemblies. However, some of the main themes in this area of reform were incorporated as party policy in *Looking to the Future*, published in 1989. The Labour party's advocacy of regional government was in part based on an appeal to pluralist democratic principles. *Looking to the Future* appeared to accept that those large sections of the electorate which did not vote for the party in power at Westminster should nevertheless have an opportunity of seeing their political preferences given some meaningful effect.

Quite how meaningful that effect would be was not clear. *Looking to the Future* suggested that it was embracing a rather stunted notion of the geographical separation of powers, since it proposed that regional governments would be funded almost entirely by block grant from central government. They would therefore have been entirely dependent on central indulgence if they were to pursue expensive alternative policies. This would clearly have placed significant limits on the right enjoyed by a region's citizens collectively to express effective political preferences which diverged from central government orthodoxy.

In its proposals for regional government, *Looking to the Future* purported to borrow quite heavily from the then nascent EC principle of subsidiarity. It was suggested that regional government would gain powers downwards from central government, not upwards from local authorities. Rather than dealing with such issues as housing or education, the regions would have 'a strategic and coordinating role in economic planning, industrial policy, transport and other areas where a region-wide perspective is essential'. *The Charter* suggested that only the Foreign Office and the Ministry of Defence need remain as highly centralised functions. Regional governments would be controlled by elected assemblies, but *The Charter* itself offered no details of how their members would be chosen.

Local government

Labour's major reform proposals for local authorities were published in the 1987 paper *Local Government Reform in England and Wales*. *Local Government Reform* stressed Labour's perception of local authorities as units of 'government' rather than simply administration. It was therefore fiercely critical of such central government initiatives as grant penalties, ratecapping, abolition of the GLC and metropolitan counties, and the privatisation of council services pushed through Parliament by the Thatcher governments in the 1980s.

Local Government Reform made several recommendations which would ostensibly have enhanced local authorities' powers to diverge from central government orthodoxies. These would have included giving councils a power of general competence to make contracts and spend their revenue, the restoration of local control over new house-building and the re-nationalisation of water supply industry under local authority control. As a general principle, however, *Local Government Reform* proposed that central government would negotiate a series of minimum standards of service provision with local authorities. The financing of services which met these standards would be underwritten by central government grant. Councils would thereafter be free to offer enhanced facilities funded from local taxation if they and their electors so wished. This necessarily means that there would be no place for rate/poll tax capping of local authorities. The degree to which these reforms would have reversed recent trends remains dependent on the efficacy of Labour's proposed 'Fair Rates' system of local finance, a policy about which many uncertainties remained prior to the 1992 election.

Viewed purely at an *abstract* level, the plans outlined in *Local Government Reform* and approved in *The Charter* would arguably have introduced an appreciable degree of institutional pluralism within the overall government structure. But tolerance of significant local diversity obviously has implications for the uniformity of service provision. Quite how far a Labour government's commitment to local pluralism would have extended is unclear: citizens who voted for councils which wished to introduce selective schooling or wholesale privatisations of public housing stock for example might have found they had exceeded the boundaries of acceptability. It may have been rash to assume that the Labour Party had by then purged itself of the 'ambivalent' attitude to central–local relations of which Anthony Crosland had spoken in the 1970s.

Protecting charter rights – the short term

While *The Charter* might have seemed to represent a considerable break with the policies pursued by the Thatcher governments, it frequently used extremely vague language to express important criteria. Its efficacy as a guarantor of individual liberty and political pluralism would therfore have depended in large part on the detailed form of the various Acts in which the charter rights would have been contained, and thereafter on the enthusiasm with which ministers and officials embraced the policy ideals those Acts propounded.

Effective implementation would also presumably have required some form of enforcement process independent of the government itself. *The Charter* was, however, very ambivalent about the role to be played by the courts in its supposedly new constitutional order. The Labour party appeared most unwilling to grant the judiciary a significant constitutional role. *The Charter* suggested that 'judges were no less culpable than ministers in contributing to the erosion of rights in the past decade'. Unfortunately, *The Charter* did not appear to have identified any effective alternative mechanism to uphold the rule of law.

It is difficult to envisage how citizens can safely assume that their government will not overstep its powers and erode individual rights if they have to rely on the goodwill of a government official for that restriction to be respected. Some form of legal control of executive action would seem necessary in any democratic constitution. The need would appear even more pressing if, as *The Charter* recommended, the government was to assume a wider range of responsibilities, some of which would be exercised by executive bodies opposed to central government's policy preferences. *The Charter's* failure to identify a forum independent of government to which citizens may have resort when they feel that executive activities have overstepped legal boundaries seemingly presented a significant barrier to ensuring even that a Labour government which professed support for its values was in practice obliged to respect them. This was in itself a major weakness in *The Charter's* overall programme. However it paled in comparison to the Labour party's failure to address the question of whether and how it might entrench *The Charter's* supposedly 'fundamental' constitutional principles.

Protecting charter rights – the long term

The Labour party appeared to have entirely accepted the orthodox Diceyan notion of parliamentary sovereignty. *The Charter* therefore advocated only a modest and temporary mechanism to protect the values it espoused, a mechanism which purported to amend the composition of the legislature rather than reduce its powers.

The Charter proposed abolition of the House of Lords, suggesting it be replaced by a new, elected second chamber. It seemed that the proposed new chamber was intended further to strengthen the Lords' current role as an institution which could complement the Commons, while simultaneously addressing the question of the unrepresentativeness of its members. But the characteristic of the new chamber on which *The Charter* dwelt was that: 'it will have the power to delay, for the lifetime of that Parliament, change to designated legislation dealing with individual or constitutional rights'. The Labour Party apparently assumed that this device would ensure that its constitutional reforms would be effectively entrenched against immediate repeal by a succeeding government. That conclusion is not however self-evident.

If the rights advocated by *The Charter* merited long-term protection, subject to express electoral rejection, one might have expected the second chamber to have a duty rather than merely a power to delay what it considered to be 'unconstitutional' legislation. Power to delay necessarily co-exists with power to approve. A government that could attract bare majority support in both houses could therefore override 'charter rights' at will.

Speculation about what the second chamber might want to do when faced with an 'unconstitutional' Bill is inextricably bound up with a second issue, namely how its members are chosen. If elected through the same mechanism and at the same time as the Commons, they would simply reproduce the latter's party majority. It would seem unlikely that an upper house of that nature could be relied upon to exercise its delaying power. This would suggest that the second chamber would have to be elected by some form of proportional representation system. *The Charter* however made no such commitment.

The Charter nevertheless lauded the delaying power of the new second chamber, suggesting that 'within our system that is the only way to entrench civil rights legislation'. But to call such a procedure 'entrenchment' amounts almost to a misuse of language. The degree of relative fixity which charter rights would thereby attain is negligible. As suggested above, a government commanding majority support in the reformed upper house could amend them immediately. But even if a governing party found its Bills blocked by the second chamber, it could by winning successive elections with, for example, 40% of the vote on a 70% turnout, overturn all *The Charter's* reforms within five years, or even sooner if it called and won an election on a charter issue. Charter rights, regional government, and revitalised local authorities would therefore all have been vulnerable to the short-term preferences of barely a third of the electorate. In such circumstances, what the Labour party grandly termed 'the most radical change in the British constitution proposed by any political party this century' could rapidly have been consigned to the legislative dustbin.

For *The Charter* made no recommendations whatsoever about reforming the Commons' localised, plurality-based electoral system. The Labour Party's allegedly new constitution would have accepted in its entirety an electoral system that has not on even one occasion in the modern era produced a Commons majority that has come remotely close to attracting the support of even a bare majority of those citizens entitled to vote.

The Charter seemingly suggested that the Thatcher governments had 'abused' the constitution because their policies attracted so little electoral support. In so doing, it also argued that the great majority of British citizens favoured a social democratic, pluralist political culture. The preservation of that culture would presumably demand a package of reforms which were designed to minimise the possibility of another extremist, minoritarian government gaining control of Parliament's legal sovereignty. In the absence of a supra-legislative constitutional settlement (which *The Charter* appeared to consider neither possible nor desirable), it would seem quite impossible to achieve that objective without introducing sweeping changes to the electoral system – changes which ensured that a party's level of electoral support was fully reflected in its strength in the Commons.

By rejecting such reforms, *The Charter* ensured that its proposed changes to the constitution would at most have been ephemeral. Indeed, to label them as 'constitutional' when they made no serious attempt to address fundamental principles of political morality, is in itself very misleading. Their viability was premissed on optimistic views of Labour's long-term electoral appeal, future governments' integrity and the efficacy of informal constitutional restraints such as public opinion and pressure group activity on a single-minded Cabinet. *The Charter* clearly assumed that these restraints proved inadequate during the 1980s as a protection against a legislature controlled by a Thatcherite government. It offered no convincing reason for assuming they would not continue to be equally ineffective in the future.

Conclusion

Labour's claim that *The Charter* comprised a radical programme of constitutional reform does not withstand close examination. The suggestion that one can introduce sweeping constitutional change without either removing the sovereignty of Parliament or radically altering the Commons' electoral system was at best naive, and at worst quite dishonest.

Roy Hattersley had concluded his speech introducing Labour's plans by claiming that the Labour Party had come to embrace 'an ideology which is essentially based on trust in people's wisdom and a willingness to allow an adult electorate to take more and more decisions on its own behalf'. Hattersley used very similar language when speaking of the Labour party's plans to create more autonomous units of regional and local government:

> 'There is, of course, a penalty to be paid from passing out power. It is one which a genuinely democratic government has to accept. Occasionally the regional governments which we create will operate policies of which the Labour Party disapproves. That is the penalty of democracy. The willingness to accept that inevitable conflict is also the test of real democratic credentials.'

That the Labour Party evidently viewed such pluralism as a 'penalty' perhaps suggests that its view of democracy remained rather centralised in the late 1980s; the inference seems to be that the powers of the people should rest on the consent of the government, rather than, as Madison and Jefferson would have it, that the powers of the government should be determined by the consent of the people.

Reduced to essentials, the Labour Party's position in respect of constitutional reform prior to the 1992 general election revealed a continuing fixation with the Commons as the sole source of legitimate political authority in modern British society. The analysis seemed to accept that it is the function of Parliament (qua a Commons majority) to define the rights of the people, rather than for the rights of the people to control the power of Parliament. By presenting its reform package in terms of entitlements which Parliament would bestow on citizens, *The Charter* did not seem to envisage changing the starting point of constitutional analysis. As such, it could not in any real sense be described as a programme for redefining the constituent values of Britain's political and legal order. Voters who sought such a programme would therefore have been better advised to direct their attention to the reforms advocated by Britain's second opposition party.

III. THE LIBERAL DEMOCRATS' REMODELLED CONSTITUTION

The Liberal party offered a relatively detailed vision of a reformed British constitution in a 1990 policy paper, entitled *'We the people . . .'*. As might be surmised from its title, the paper drew heavily on the American constitutional model, in matters both of abstract theory and practical detail. *We the people* outlined a far more radical programme of substantive reform than Labour's *Charter of Rights*, and also devoted considerable attention to planning a reform process which would enhance the legitimacy of the 'fundamental' values it hoped to introduce. The Liberal programme was and remains primarily a focus for discussion; given the low levels of electoral support the party has attracted in recent years, there is little likelihood of it being in a position to achieve its objectives in the foreseeable future.

In its critique of the Thatcher governments, *We the people* shared much common ground with Labour's proposals. However it quite plausibly (given the feebleness of Labour's reform plans) suggested that both major parties were quite content to leave the basic features of the constitution intact, as each harboured ambitions to control the virtually unlimited legal power that the winning of a Commons majority bestowed. It is therefore no surprise that *We the people* dealt squarely with the two basic issues which *The Charter of Rights* declined to address – the Commons' electoral system and the creation of supra-Parliamentary legal principles.

Electoral reform

Electoral reform was described as 'the cornerstone' of the Liberals' reform programme. The discrepancy between votes cast and Commons seats won in general elections was adverted to in chapter 7, and need not be repeated here.[20] *We the people* proposed that the first objective of a Liberal government would be to promote a Bill which introduced a 'single transferable vote in multi-member constituencies' electoral system.[1] This would not produce perfect proportionality in respect of party representation in the Commons, but would obviously come much closer to that goal than does the present system. Multi-member constituencies would also permit voters to distinguish between their preferred candidates

20 See pp 276–280 above.
1 For an explanation of the system see pp 281–282 above.

within a single party, and retain a linkage between an MP and her constituents.

The stress laid on electoral reform was not however focused solely on the process of choosing elected representatives; it was also intended to have a profound influence on the way in which the legislature would behave once it had been elected, and on the legitimacy of any laws which it might subsequently enact. *We the people* assumed that it would be unlikely that a single party would be able to form an administration under the new electoral system. Coalition governments would thus become the norm. It was hoped that this would preclude the pursuit of extremist polices, since parties would have to accommodate the presumably countervailing wishes of other parties in order to maintain a working majority in the house. If a single party should win such a majority, one could at least plausibly argue that its preferred policies were supported by a majority of the electorate. *We the people* also assumed that the probable emergence of coalition governments would weaken the influence of the party whipping system in the house, and thereby promote greater independence of thought among its members.

The central legislature

The Liberals also proposed significant reform of the second chamber. The House of Lords was to be abolished, and replaced by a 'Senate' elected via the STV system. The chances of the Senate's party composition merely mirroring that of the Commons would be minimised by requiring one-third of its seats to be subject to election every two years. The Senate's legislative powers would initially be little changed from those of the House of Lords. It could delay all Bills (with the exception of money Bills) for up to two years.

The Liberals also advocated several reforms to the internal organisation of the Commons. They proposed a substantial increase in the research and administrative resources provided both to individual MPs and to select committees. In a more general vein, *We the people* argued that the failings of the Commons were due in large part to its assumption of too onerous a workload. This problem was however to be addressed not by treating its symptoms, but removing its cause.

Regional and local government

The Liberals proposed that the membership of the Commons should be reduced to around 450 members. It would initially seem difficult to reduce the Commons' workload while simultaneously reducing its membership. But *We the people* managed to square this apparent circle by advocating a substantial transfer of legislative and executive responsibility away from Parliament and central government to a new elected tier of regional government.

The Liberal reforms envisaged that Scotland, Wales and Northern Ireland would gain legislative assemblies, exercising substantial levels of competence within their respective boundaries. Similarly powerful assemblies would also be created in around a dozen English regions. Regional boundaries would be drawn up by a specially created Boundary Commission. *We the people* did not specify precisely which powers would be transferred to the regions, but suggested that defence, foreign policy, macro-economic policy and the substance of the criminal law were the only matters which should be reserved exclusively to central government. In respect of such matters as the administration of justice, public housing, education and health services and land development policies, regional assemblies would assume the powers previously exercised by central government.

Such a broad array of powers indicated that regional government would be an important actor on the political stage. This impression was reinforced by the proposal that regional assemblies should be permitted to levy their own income taxes, at whatever levels their respective electorates were prepared to support. However, in order to ameliorate the fiscal consequences of differences in the various regions' affluence, central government would provide a grant based on 'objective criteria'.

Had these reforms recommended that members of regional assemblies be elected by the first past the post system, the Liberals' programme would presumably have instituted a significant degree of geographically demarcated pluralism within the United Kingdom, within which both the Labour and Conservative parties could each have expected to control particular parts of the country, irrespective of their performance in elections to the Commons. However, *We the people* rather reduced the scope for such a marked form of pluralism by suggesting that regional assemblies, like the Commons, should be elected on the STV system. Coalition governments would thus be likely in all of the regions.

In contrast to its prolonged focus on the merits of regional government, *We the people* devoted very little attention to the issue of local government. It was suggested that the county/district dichotomy should be removed; all local councils should henceforth have the same range of responsibilities. The proposals did not however make any recommendations concerning the extent to which councils' powers would be safeguarded against the preferences of the regional assembly within whose boundaries they lay. The gist of the programme seemed to be that local authorities would in future stand in relation to regional assemblies in precisely the same position as councils currently stand vis-à-vis central government.

The reforms would thus create only around a dozen geographically discrete loci of significant political power. One might wonder if this amounted to an adequate guarantor of diversity in a country of Britain's size. The Liberal proposals point to an obvious dilemma which attends any attempt to 'federalise' the constitution. The more numerous the units of sub-central government one creates, the more difficult it becomes to grant them substantial levels of political power. Yet as one reduces the number of such bodies, so one also reduces the scope for the effective expression of divergent political sentiment. Whether the Liberals' plans struck the right balance is a matter for speculation.

A Bill of Rights and the role of the judiciary

The Liberal agenda also advocated immediate incorporation of the European Convention on Human Rights into domestic law. This would be achieved by a 'Bill of Rights Act', whose terms would also include some additional entitlements over and above those specified in the Convention. The Act would contain a supremacy clause, explicitly confirming that it precluded the use by any central or local government body of any existing statutory or common law powers inconsistent with its substantive provisions. The Act (simply because it was an Act) would also prevent the courts developing the common law in a manner which breached the convention's provisions.

The Bill of Rights Act would also seek to bind future Parliaments, by providing that its provisions could only be breached by subsequent legislation if that breach was expressly acknowledged in the subsequent Act. Quite what the courts would make of that clause is uncertain. The Liberals presumably assumed that the judiciary would regard the Bill of Rights Act in the same manner as they now appear to treat the provisions of the European Communities Act 1972.

In contrast to Labour's *Charter of Rights*, *We the people* expressed considerable confidence in the competence and integrity of the judiciary. The Liberals recognised that their programme would require the courts to engage explicitly in resolving disputes which had an obviously 'political' agenda. However, it was suggested that the judiciary could effectively rebut any accusation that their decisions were shaped by party political bias since they would be rooted in the supposedly supra-party political provisions of the convention.

The Liberals suggested the 'independence' of the judiciary could be further enhanced by entrusting the apppointment of High Court judges to a 'Judicial Services Commission'. The Commission would have some 18 members: six judges, four barristers, four solicitors, and four lay members, each of whom could serve a maximum of one nine-year term. No details were offered concerning the way in which selection would be made.

The Commission's members would be appointed by the government. This was perhaps a surprising conclusion to have reached. One might plausibly reduce the scope for accusations of judicial bias to vanishing point if half of the Commission's members had been appointed by the Leader of the Opposition.

We the people also proposed that the House of Lords qua final court of appeal should be replaced by a Supreme Court. The judges on the court would initially be the Law Lords. Their replacements would be nominated by the Judicial Services Commission, and subject to the approval of the Commons. They could be removed from office only by resolutions of both houses. The Supreme Court would be obliged to 'strike down' legislation which it considered unconstitutional. Affording such power to the court would necessarily require that the provisions of the 'constitution' were in some way entrenched, and it is on this issue that the Liberals' proposals are perhaps most interesting.

Entrenchment

As suggested above, any attempt by a single party government returned under the existing electoral system to entrench constitutional values with any significant degree of fixity would be most unlikely to have a legitimate moral base: the breadth of popular consent such a government attracted would simply be too narrow to justify the imposition of constituent principles. *We the people* clearly recognised this difficulty, and offered an ingenious mechanism to overcome it.

Had the Liberals won a Commons majority at the 1992 general election, its government would not have attempted to implement its entire reform programme during the life of that Parliament. Rather it would have limited itself to promoting Bills to reform the Commons' electoral system, to incorporate the convention into domestic law, to establish home rule for Scotland and Wales, to create a Commission to define the boundaries of regional governments, and to establish a body to be called the 'Constituent Assembly'.

Parliament would then be dissolved, and a general election fought on the basis of the new STV electoral system. The second stage of the reform programme would then be undertaken by the newly-elected Parliament. This would entail legislation during its first session creating the regional assemblies and the Senate. Elections for these new bodies would then be held during the second session of the new Parliament. Once those elections had been held, the third and final phase of the reforms would be instituted by the Constituent Assembly

The Constituent Assembly would be composed of the members of the Commons returned after the first general election fought on the basis of the new STV electoral system. The Assembly would have been empowered by the previous Parliament to adopt (by a two-thirds majority) a new constitutional settlement, within which the Bill of Rights, the STV electoral system, and the powers and boundaries of the Scots, Welsh, Northern Irish and regional governments would all assume supra-parliamentary status. These values would be entrenched in the procedural sense; they could be amended only with the approval of two-thirds of both houses sitting separately.

In legal terms, using the Constitutent Assembly to implement a constitutional revolution might be thought something of a nonsense: Parliament presumably cannot create something more powerful than itself. It would however seem that *We the people* proceeded on the assumption that its proposals were at root designed to achieve a political rather than legal objective. By requiring a two-thirds majority of a body chosen by the STV system to create the new constitution, the Liberal programme ensured that its terms could not be given legal effect unless they enjoyed a very high level of popular support. The proviso that the Commons should in effect wear a different political hat when assessing the merits of fundamental reform would also have served a useful legitimising purpose, insofar as it would focus both MPs and the public's attention on the gravity of the task being undertaken.

Given the Liberals' evident belief that our political system con-

centrates too much power in the Commons and central government, it is odd that the Commons (albeit elected via STV) should
be seen as the most legitimate source of a constitutional revolution. The moral status of the new constitution would presumably
have been further enhanced if the Constituent Assembly included
representatives drawn from the regional, Scots, Welsh and
Northern Ireland Assemblies.[2] It is similarly strange that the proposed entrenchment mechanism affords no role to the assemblies;
so centralised an amendment process sits uneasily with a constitution purportedly resting in large part on the assumed desirability
of a decentralised political culture.

Conclusion

For adherents to a pluralist perception of democracy, the Liberal
party's inability to mobilise greater electoral support is something
of a disappointment. There is no doubt that *We the people* offered
a radical and far-reaching programme to modernise Britain's constitutional arrangements. One might of course suggest that the
Liberals' limited electoral support is in itself indicative of 'the
people's' disinclination to have the constitution reformed in any
meaningful way. The only immediate prospect of the Liberal programme being implemented would be for the party to hold the
balance of power in a hung Commons, and to convince one of
the main parties that pursuing its reforms was an acceptable price
to pay for the benefit of forming a coalition government for one
parliamentary term. It would however seem unlikely that either
the Labour or Conservative parties would accept such reasoning.
Nor would the reforms enjoy much legitimacy if their opponents
could plausibly argue that the major partner in the coalition
had been 'blackmailed' into accepting them. In the longer term,
elements of the Liberal agenda might perhaps seep across the
party political divide and be embraced by the other parties. In
1996, there is little evidence that the leadership of the Labour
party has any such inclination, despite having lost four successive
general elections. To assume that the Conservatives might do so,
after four successive victories, is little short of ludicrous.

2 On this point, see Madison's comments at p 19 above.

IV. A RADICAL CRITIQUE?

As suggested above, the proposals for constitutional reform offered in this section are intended as no more than a starting point for discussion about the broad principles that such political restructuring might entail. Any significant reform programme would demand extensive consideration of a myriad of detail which cannot sensibly be addressed here. Nor is any attempt made to tease out the implications of the initiatives proposed; that is a task which might more appropriately be left to students to undertake in class. The ensuing discussion also proceeds on the assumption that constitution-building should be an essentially *negative* task. Its purpose should be seen not as producing an ideal moral foundation upon which a society's political and legal superstructure can rest. Rather its much more modest – and hence achievable – objective should be to remove and thereafter prevent the recurrence of the most egregious characteristics of the constitutional order under which a society is currently governed.

The reform agenda advanced here rests on the premiss that the constitution should be amended in a manner which introduces a far more fragmented allocation of legal and political powers. The proposals would best be implemented as a distinct 'revolution', consequent upon the Labour/Liberal/wet Conservative coalition government scenario adverted to in section one. In that case, all the values suggested below would be procedurally entrenched in accordance with a variation on the American model. Amendment of the constitution would firstly require a two-thirds majority of each house of the central legislature sitting separately. The second requirement would be the support of at least three-quarters of local authorities (their members voting by simple majority), which is to include a majority of councils in Wales, Scotland and Northern Ireland respectively. This mechanism would attach a very high degree of relative fixity to the constituent political values. However, no amendment altering the boundaries of a local authority could be introduced unless it also received the support of the particular authorities affected (by a two-thirds majority of each authority's councillors).

However, the reforms could also be implemented (albeit with a less firmly fixed legal status) by a government which either did not wish or did not feel able to attack the principle of parliamentary sovereignty. In those circumstances, one would attempt to by-pass the incapacity legally to entrench constituent political values by redefining the Commons and the Lords in a manner which minimised the possibility that a government attracting only minoritarian or barely majoritarian electoral support could ever command majority support in both houses. Quite how this result might be achieved is discussed further below. Our first step, however, is to return to the question of the separation of powers.

Federalisation

The concept of federalism lies at the core of these proposals. Their purpose is to both give intra-national rein to, and place supra-national limits on, the essentially pluralist political sentiments of the electorate. The Redcliffe-Maud proposals for far fewer, more powerful unitary organs of local government would have gone some small way to achieving this objective, albeit only on a conventional rather than legal basis.[3] The introduction of effective and meaningful political pluralism into the soil of the constitution would demand rather more draconian ploughing of the geo-political landscape.

As suggested in chapter 1, countries which have adopted a federal constitution have in effect concluded that the separation of powers is a principle that should be expressed in both the vertical and horizontal senses.[4] The creation of a significant geographical separation of powers in modern Britain would demand far fewer local authorities, all wielding substantial decision-making capacities. Voters should be able to conclude that the electoral choices they make at a local level will have a significant impact on the way that their city or county is governed. In a country of only 60 million people, a total of no more than 50 local councils, each possessing the same broadly defined legal powers, would seem appropriate. There is no obvious need for exact mathematical equality in population size between each unit of local government, and the current county council boundaries would provide a convenient starting point for redrawing local government boundaries. It would perhaps be unwise to have fewer than 50 sub-central elected authorities; a lesser figure might substantially reduce the probability that parties with disproportionately high levels of popular support in particular areas achieved effective levels of political power.

The question of precisely how much governmental power should be granted to local government is obviously a vexed one. The rationale underpinning these proposals is however clear – namely that a substantial degree of legal competence should be

3 See pp 398–400 above.
4 See pp 15–19 above. See also pp 378–382 above.

transferred from central government to the localities. Since much of the concern about the diminishing role of local authorities has arisen because of the Thatcher and Major governments' systematic removal of local autonomy since 1979, reinstating the pre-1980 allocation of powers would be an expedient solution to a contentious problem.

It would certainly seem essential that local councils should enjoy unrestrained power to levy local income and property taxes at whatever level their respective electorates were prepared to support. It is equally clear that local authorities could not be entirely self-financing. Again, for reasons both of expediency and principle, a pluralist constitutional settlement might sensibly adopt the principle that funds from central government to support locally provided services should be allocated in accordance with the statutory formulae in existence immediately prior to the passage of Local Government Planning and Land Act 1980.

Modern Britain's traditional fixation with the Commons as the centre of the constitutional order, and hence with MPs as the key players on the political stage, could be further reduced by granting councillors the same legal status and salary as members of the central legislature. The number of councillors in each authority might sensibly be fixed at a level of one per 20,000 citizens. Given the increased autonomy and power that councils would possess, a substantial amount of a councillor's activities would be taken up with constituency activities presently undertaken by MPs. An electorate of 20,000 is substantially smaller than is currently tended by most MPs; councillors should thus be able to deliver a considerably enhanced service to local voters. Each councillor should also be allocated sufficient funds to run an office and finance a modest level of research and/or administrative staff.

This internal federalisation of the United Kingdom's government structures would be intended to promote political diversity. Such diversity would be intended both to permit simultaneous expression of well-established differences of opinion on important political matters, and to encourage experimentation and innovation over social policy issues. These dual objectives accept that local authorities must be able to give (limited) vent to majoritarian sentiment. This would be facilitated if local councillors were elected through the 'single member constituencies first past the post' electoral system currently used for the Commons.

It is quite feasible that a geographically concentrated electoral majority might wish to support oppressive political initatives. Isolated minority groups should of course be 'protected' against such activities. However, such protection should not come from central government, for one then raises the prospect that the 'protection' will be (and/or be thought to be) prompted by partisan, party political objectives. Such protection would far better be achieved by subjecting all local authority actions to the supra-national constraints imposed by the convention and the EC treaties. The convention, like the justiciable provisions of EC law, would therefore have to be 'directly effective' in domestic courts.[5] Should we be able to pursue the 'revolutionary' route to reform, the provisions of the EC treaties and the convention would take their place as entrenched constitutional values.

The central legislature and executive

The provisions of the convention and the EC treaties would also have to be directly effective against the various institutions of the central legislature and executive. Increasing the autonomy of local government necessarily means that Parliament and central government would wield fewer powers. This would in turn mean that MPs and ministers could reasonably be expected to discharge their respective constitutional responsibilities with a greater degree of competence and assiduity than they currently manage to achieve. A 'revolutionary' settlement would further enhance this trend, since MPs would be aware that much of the partisan bickering which now occupies so much of the Commons' time would be utterly futile, given the enhanced majorities needed to alter entrenched political values.

Many of the Commons' present defects would automatically be ameliorated by reducing its potential workload. Pressure on the legislative timetable would be eased, and more time would be available on the floor of the house for MPs both to raise issues of public concern and to question government behaviour. Some rather more substantial provision would however have to be made to enhance the investigative competence of the Departmental Select Committees, by substantially increasing the financial resources available to them. Steps would also have to be taken to improve the capacity of individual MPs to contribute to the legislative process and the scrutiny of the executive. This end would perhaps best be achieved by granting each MP a research and administration allowance sufficient to employ several competent assistants on a full-time basis and also make occasional resort to expert advisers on particularly specialised questions.

---

5 As suggested in chapter 14, all the provisions of the convention would be regarded as justiciable for these purposes.

The pivotal element of these reform proposals, however, whether they be adopted as a 'revolution' or simply as ordinary legislation, is that members of the Commons should in future be elected on the basis of a party list system in each country of the United Kingdom, with each country allocated a number of MPs in strict accordance with its share of the population. This would ensure that no legislation could be enacted if the Bill concerned did not attract the support of MPs who collectively represented at least a majority of the voting population. In an entrenched system, it would ensure that Bills intended to affect constituent values could not pass through the Commons unless they were supported by MPs who collectively represented an overwhelming majority of the electorate.[6]

If its powers and composition were altered in these ways, a reformed Commons would require far fewer members. The argument in favour of a smaller lower house are strengthened when one recalls that many of the constituency responsibilities currently performed by MPs would in future be the responsibility of local councillors. Relatedly, in a constitutional context which placed more importance on the vertical separation of powers between central and local government than on the horizontal separation of powers within central government, the task of lobbying the central legislature or executive on behalf of local interests would better be performed by local councils than by MPs. There would seem to be no need for more than 400 MPs in a reformed House of Commons. The reduced powers of central government would also suggest that more stringent limits should be placed on the number of members of the Commons who may hold ministerial office: a maximum of 60 would seem a plausible figure, with an additional number not exceeding 20 to be drawn from the Lords.

Some suggestions for reforming the upper house of the central legislature were canvassed in chapter 6. The role envisaged for the Lords within this programme of reform would be in part to complement the functions performed by the Commons. This role would in itself demand that steps be taken to ensure that no single political party commanded majority support among its members. It is envisaged that the Lords would also exercise important powers in respect of the appointment of judges, a role which would make cross-party consensus even more important.

6 A subsidiary but welcome consequence of adopting a list system would be that one thereby abolishes the scope for electoral unfairness and partisan dispute engendered by the drawing and redrawing of constitutency boundaries; see pp 262–267 above.

A reformed House of Lords would be composed entirely of life peers. Given the much reduced competence of the central legislature, a second chamber need have no more than 200 members, each enjoying the same legal status, salary and other financial support afforded to members of the Commons. Life peers would be nominated by the leaders of political parties in accordance with their parties' cumulative average share of the vote in Commons elections since 1945. Should a life peer die or retire from office, she would be replaced by a nominee of the leader of whichever party's level of representation in the house diverged most from its average post-war electoral performance.

As suggested above, in the event of revolutionary reform a minority comprising more than one-third of the Lords' membership would be empowered to veto any proposed legislation which impinged upon constituent values. Should reform be introduced through ordinary legislation, there would seem little need to alter the current legislative powers of the upper house. A delaying power (by simple majority) of one year would be perfectly adequate to allow the Commons to reflect upon the merits of blocked Bills. It would however be necessary to empower the Lords to veto any Bill which altered the electoral system used to choose members of the Commons.

If these reforms were introduced, members of both houses would clearly be returned to office on the basis of their party affiliation rather than their status as individuals. Consequently, it would not be permissible for a member to change her party allegiance while retaining her seat in Parliament. Elections to the Commons would also have an entirely 'national' character, rather than being the aggregation of some 650 simultaneous local contests. Consequently, there would be an obvious need to impose limits on the amount of expenditure that parties could devote to their election campaign.

Ethical standards

Party swapping without resigning her seat is perhaps the most egregious way in which a member of the Commons can currently undermine the informed consent of her electors. It is not however the only way. The obvious shortcomings of the Nolan Committee's proposals to counter corruption and lack of financial candour among MPs were adverted to in chapter 8. The recommendations made here rest on the assumption that citizens forfeit any entitlement to financial privacy when they assume legislative roles within the state; citizens cannot make informed choices about their preferred representatives if occupants of elected political offices are permitted to conceal financial arrangements which might conceivably be thought to influence the discharge of their legislative or governmental functions.

Once again, these principles would ideally be introduced as entrenched values within a 'revolutionary' reform programme, but they might also usefully be enacted as ordinary legislation. The core of the proposals would be that all members of the central legislature and all councillors (and their husbands/ wives/ cohabitees) should be required to file their income tax returns for the five years before assumption of office, during their tenure of their seat, and for five years thereafter. A small grant, sufficient to enable each MP or councillor to employ a competent accountant to compile her income tax return should be added to the representative's research/administration allowance. The collected returns of all MPs and councillors would be available at a modest cost to any member of the public who wished to purchase it.

If the Inland Revenue concluded that an MP or councillor had not made an accurate return, her case would be referred to a High Court judge appointed for the duration of that parliamentary session by the Leader of the Opposition. If the judge considered the Inland Revenue's opinion well founded, she would be obliged to expel the member from the house or the council concerned. That member would not be permitted ever again to occupy a legislative position. Additionally, in respect of the Commons, the member's party would not be entitled to replace her with the next candidate on the party list.[7] In respect of councillors, a by-election would be held, at which neither the expelled councillor nor any member of her party would be permitted to stand. Such sanctions would ensure that the political parties themselves had a clear interest in policing the probity of their members' financial dealings. In a more general vein, reforms to the central legislature would also ensure that parliamentary privilege be explicitly redefined as a matter of common law. Such legislation would resolve the question of 'dualism' which has so plagued analysis of privilege.[8] Privilege would thus in future be subject to precisely the same degree of judicial oversight as central govern-

---

7 The statute could be similarly effective in the context of the current electoral system if it required that a by-election be held on the third Thursday after the expulsion. The expelled member's party would not be permitted to field a candidate at the by-election, nor would any individual who had been a member of the expelled MP's party be permitted to stand.

8 See pp 303 above.

ment's exercise of the royal prerogative, or the use by any public body of powers deriving from statute.

The independence of the judiciary

This programme of reform clearly envisages an enhanced constitutional role for the judiciary. In addition to exercising supervisory jurisdiction over the justiciable internal proceedings of the central legislature, the High Court would be responsible both for measuring the legality of all governmental behaviour against the requirements of the Convention, and for deciding if central government activities had intruded into the sphere of power reserved to local authorities (and vice versa). The scope for judges to be accused of partisan political bias would consequently increase. Certain steps would thus have to be taken to minimise the credibility of any such accusations.

The tenure of judicial office might usefully be strengthened by requiring that judges could only be dismissed by enhanced (two-thirds) majorities of both houses. But rather more extensive alterations should be made to the way in which High Court judges are appointed. This could perhaps be done most simply and effectively by subjecting the Prime Minister/Lord Chancellor's nominees to the scrutiny and approval of the second chamber. A special 'judicial committee' of the house, its membership reflecting the overall party balance, might sensibly be created to perform this task. Nominees who could not attract the support of a majority of the committee's members would not be permitted to assume office.

Certain measures would also be required to enhance the separation of powers between the judicial, executive and legislative branches of central government. In a purely symbolic vein, the House of Lords in its judicial capacity might simply be renamed as the Supreme Court. An initiative with rather more practical significance would be to render holders of judicial office (with the exception of the Lord Chancellor) ineligible to sit in the Lords. Since the Supreme Court would act as the final Court of Appeal, even greater care should be taken to minimise the possibility that its members have been selected for partisan political reasons. This objective might be achieved by providing that whenever a vacancy arose on the Supreme Court bench, both the Prime Minister and the Leader of the Opposition would be entitled to place a nominee before the judicial committee of the House of Lords. The committee might then examine both candidates in

whatever way it thought appropriate before determining (if necessary by a simple majority vote) which to appoint.

In the context of an entrenched constitution, the Supreme
Court would of course be acting as the guardian of the 'people's'
preferred constituent political values. Since this task would require
it to engage as much in discussions of moral legitimacy as of
simple legality, there would seem to be no particular need for all
of its members to be High Court judges or even lawyers. Indeed,
the presence of academics or non-lawyers within the court might
prove a useful spur to recent judicial trends towards expanding
the scope of justiciable controversies.

CONCLUSION

This book began its analysis of the British constitution from the
somewhat unusual starting point of Jefferson's Declaration of
Independence. It is readily apparent that many of the reform
proposals offered in the previous section draw heavily upon the
theoretical positions adopted by Madison and Hamilton in *The
Federalist Papers*. That such values might appear as self-evident
truths to the author of this book is however no guarantee even of
their defensibility, still less of their 'correctness'. I have discussed
elsewhere the merits and drawbacks of reshaping British public
law on an ad hoc basis in accordance with American principles.[9]
Whether to adopt those principles in a more systematic vein as the
inspiration for revolutionary constitutional reform is an obviously
contentious question, over which much ink might usefully be spilt.

Yet there is far less room to doubt the proposition that, at
present, it is something of a misnomer to speak of the *law* of the
British constitution. This misdescription does not simply arise
from the obvious fact that so much of the organisation and
behaviour of contemporary government rests on the non-justiciable basis of convention. More seriously, it derives from the
constant vulnerability of those principles which are expressed in
justiciable form to whichever political faction has temporary control of the House of Commons. To search for constitutional law
in a society which has thus far rejected the concept of subjecting
its government to constituent legal principles is to embark upon
a generally fascinating, often frustrating, but ultimately always
fallacious journey.

9 Loveland I (1995d) 'Introduction – should we take lessons from America?' in
Loveland (ed) (1995a) *op cit*.

Having begun that journey with Jefferson, we might, in the interests both of substantive and stylistic symmetry, end it with the words of Jefferson's great friend and colleague, James Madison:

> 'No doctrine can be sound that releases a legislature from the control of a constitution. The latter is as much a law to the former, as the acts of the former are to individuals; and although alterable by the people who formed it, it is not alterable by any other authority; certainly not by those chosen by the people to carry it in to effect. This is so vital a principle . . . that a denial of it cannot possibly last long or spread far.'[10]

Britain has of course denied the principle for over three hundred years. To many observers that may suggest the principle is a unnecessary ingredient of a democratic society. To others, it may in contrast indicate that fundamental reform is long overdue.

---

10 Padover S (ed) (1953) *The Complete Madison* p 344 (Easton Press, Norwalk, Conn).

Bibliography

Adonis, A, 'The House of Lords in the 1980s' (1988) Parliamentary
    Affairs 380–401.
    Parliament Today (1990) Manchester University Press
        (Manchester).
    Parliament Today (2nd edn, 1993) Manchester University Press
        (Manchester).
Ahier, J, and Flude, M (eds) *Contemporary Education Policy* (1983)
    Croom Helm (London).
Alder, J, *Constitutional and Administrative Law* (1994) Macmillan
    (London).
Alderman, R, and Smith, M, 'Can British Prime Ministers be given
    the push by their parties?' (1990) Parliamentary Affairs
    260–276.
Alderman, R, and Carter, N, 'A very Tory coup: the ousting of Mrs
    Thatcher' (1991) Parliamentary Affairs 125–139.
Allan, T, 'Parliamentary sovereignty: Lord Denning's dexterous
    revolution' (1983) Oxford Journal of Legal Studies 22–33.
    'Legislative supremacy and the rule of law: democracy and con-
        stitutionalism' (1985) Cambridge LJ 111–143.
    'Law, convention, prerogative: reflections prompted by the Can-
        adian constitutional case' (1986) Cambridge LJ 305–320.
    'Equality and moral independence: public law and private mora-
        lity', in Loveland, I (ed) *A Special Relationship?* (1995) Claren-
        don Press (Oxford).
Anderson, O, 'The Wensleydale peerage case and the position of
    the House of Lords in the mid-nineteenth century' (1967)
    English Historical Review 486–502.
Anson, W, *The Law and Custom of the Constitution* (5th edn, 1922)
    Clarendon Press (Oxford).
Arnstein W, *The Bradlaugh Case* (1983) University of Missouri Press
    (Columbia, Miss).

Arnull, A, 'The incoming tide: responding to *Marshall*' (1987) Public Law 383–399.

Ascher, K, 'The politics of administrative opposition – council house sales and the right to buy' (1983) Local Government Studies 12–20.

Audit Commission *The Administration of the Community Charge* (1990) HMSO (London).

Bagehot, W, *The English Constitution* (1963 ed by Crossman, R) Fontana (London).

Bailey, S, and Paddison, R (eds) *The Reform of Local Government Finance in Britain* (1988) Routledge (London).

Bailey, S, Harris, D, and Jones, B, *Civil Liberties* (3rd edn, 1991) Butterworths (London).

Bailyn, B, *The Ideological Origins of the American Revolution* (1967) HUP (Cambridge, Mass).

Baines, P, 'The history and rationale of the 1979 reforms', in Drewry, G (ed) *The New Select Committees* (1985) Clarendon Press (Oxford).

Baker, D, Gamble, A, and Ludlam, S, 'Whips or scorpions? The Maastricht vote and Conservative MPs' (1993) Parliamentary Affairs 147–166.

Baker, K, *The Turbulent Years* (1993) Faber & Faber (London).

Ball, W, Gulam, W, and Troyna, B, 'Pragmatism or retreat? Funding policy, local government, and the marginalisation of anti-racist education', in Ball, W, and Solomos, J (eds) *Race and Local Politics* (1990) Macmillan (London).

Ball, W, and Solomos J (eds) *Race and Local Politics* (1990) Macmillan (London).

Balsom, D, and McAllister, I, 'The Scottish and Welsh devolution referenda of 1979: constitutional change and popular choice' (1979) Parliamentary Affairs 394–409.

Barendt, E, *Freedom of Speech* (1987) Clarendon Press (Oxford).
'Spycatcher and freedom of speech' (1989) Public Law 204–212.
'Libel and freedom of speech in English law' (1993) Public Law 449–464.

Barker, R, 'Obedience, legitimacy and the state', in Harlow, C (ed) *Public Law and Politics* (1986) Sweet and Maxwell (London).

Bash, L, and Coulby, D (eds) *The Education Reform Act: Competition and Control* (1989) Cassell (London).

Bates, St, J, 'Scrutiny of administration', in Ryle, M, and Richards, P (eds) *The Commons under Scrutiny* (1988) Routledge (London).

Bealey, F, *Democracy in the Contemporary State* (1988) Clarendon Press (Oxford).

Beard, C, 'An economic interpretation of the Constitution', in Birmbaum, J, and Ollman, B (eds) *The United States Constitution* (1990) New York University Press (New York).

Bennet, P, and Pullinger, S, *Making the Commons Work* (1991) Institute for Public Policy Research (London).

Bevan, V, 'Is anybody there?' (1981) Public Law 431–453.

Biebr, R, 'The settlement of institutional conflicts on the basis of Article 4 of the Treaty' (1984) Common Market Law Review 505–523.

Bingham, T, 'The European Convention on Human Rights: time to incorporate' (1993) Law Quarterly Review 390–400.

Birmbaum, J, and Ollman, B (eds) *The United States Constitution* (1990) New York University Press (New York).

Blake, R, and Louis, W (eds) *Churchill* (1994) Clarendon Press (Oxford).

Boddy, M, and Fudge, C (eds) *Local Socialism* (1984) Macmillan (London).

Bogdanor, V, 'Freedom in education' (1976) Political Quarterly 149–159.

'The English constitution and devolution' (1979) Political Quarterly 36–49.

What is Proportional Representation? (1983) Martin Robertson (Oxford).

'Introduction', in Bogdanor, V (ed) *Constitutions in Democratic Politics* (1988) Dartmouth Publishing (Aldershot).

Bonner, D, and Stone, R, 'The Public Order Act 1986: steps in the wrong direction?' (1987) Public Law 202–230.

Borthwick, R, 'Public Bill Committees in the House of Lords' (1973) Parliamentary Affairs 440–453.

'Questions and debates', in Walkland, S (ed) *The House of Commons in the Twentieth Century* (1979) Clarendon Press (Oxford).

'The floor of the house', in Ryle, M, and Richards, P (eds) *The Commons under Scrutiny* (1988) Routledge (London).

Boulton, C (ed) *Erskine May's Treatise on the Law, Privileges, Proceedings and Usage of Parliament* (21st edn, 1989) Butterworths (London).

Bowley, M, *Housing and the State 1919–1945* (1985) Allen & Unwin (London).

Boyce, B, 'The democratic deficit of the European Community' (1993) Parliamentary Affairs 458–477.

Boyle, A, 'Political broadcasting, fairness and administrative law' (1986) Public Law 562–596.

Bradley, A, 'Police powers and the prerogative' (1988) Public Law 298–303.

'The UK before the Strasbourg court', in Finnie, W, Himsworth, C, and Walker, N (eds) *Edinburgh Essays in Public Law* (1991) Edinburgh University Press (Edinburgh).

Bradley, K, 'Maintaining the balance: the role of the Court of Justice in defining the institutional position of the European Parliament' (1987) Common Market Law Review 41–64.

Branson, N, *Poplarism* (1979) Lawrence and Wishart (London).

Brazier, M, *Street on Torts* (9th edn, 1993) Butterworths (London).

Brazier R, 'Choosing a Prime Minister' (1982) Public Law 395–417.

Constitutional Texts: Materials on Government and the Constitution (1990) OUP (Oxford).

'The downfall of Margaret Thatcher' (1991) Modern Law Review 471–491.

Constitutional Reform: Re-shaping the British Political System (1991) OUP (Oxford).

'It is a constitutional issue: fitness for Ministerial office in the 1990s' (1994) Public Law 431–451.

Bridges, L, et al *Legality and Local Politics* (1987) Avebury (Aldershot).

Briggs, A (ed) *Chartist Studies* (1962) Macmillan (London).

Brock, M, *The Great Reform Act* (1973) Hutchinson (London).

Brogan, H, *History of the USA* (1986) Pelican (Harmondsworth).

Brown, K (ed) *The First Labour Party* (1985) Croom Helm (London).

Brown, L, and Kennedy, T, *The Court of Justice of the European Communities* (1994) Sweet and Maxwell (London).

Brown, R, 'The Beard thesis attacked: a political approach', in Levy, L (ed) *The Making of the Constitution* (1987) OUP (New York).

Brown, W, 'The Hare system in Tasmania' (1899) Law Quarterly Review 51–70.

Browne-Wilkinson, Lord, 'The infiltration of a Bill of Rights' (1992) Public Law 397–410.

Budgen, N, 'Confidence in crisis' (1992) Guardian, 24 November.

Bull, D, 'School admissions: a new appeals procedure' (1980) Journal of Social Welfare Law 209–233.

Burton, I, and Drewry, G, 'Public legislation: a survey of the session of 1971–1972' (1972) Parliamentary Affairs 145–185.

'Public legislation: a survey of the sessions of 1975/76 and 1976/77' (1978) Parliamentary Affairs 140–162.

Bush, M, 'The Act of Proclamations: a reinterpretation' (1983) American Journal of Legal History 33–53.

Butler, D, *The Electoral System in Britain 1918–1951* (1953) Clarendon Press (Oxford).

'The Australian crisis of 1975' (1976) Parliamentary Affairs 201–210.

Butler, D, Adonis, A, and Travers, T, *Failure in British Government: the Politics of the Poll Tax* (1994) OUP (Oxford).

Butler, D, and Bogdanor, V (eds) *Democracy and Elections* (1994) CUP (Cambridge).

Butler, D, and Butler, G, *British Political Facts 1900–1985* (1986) Macmillan (London).

Butler, D, and Kavanagh, D, *The British General Election of 1979; 1983; 1987; 1992* respectively (1980; 1984; 1988; 1993) Macmillan (London).

Butler, D, Penniman, H, and Ranney, A, *Democracy at the Polls* (1981) American Enterprise Institute for Public Policy Research (Washington DC).

Butler, D, and Sloman, A, *British Political Facts* (1975) Macmillan (London).

Buxton, R, *Local Government* (2nd edn, 1973) Penguin (Harmondsworth).

Cannon, J, *Parliamentary Reform 1640–1832* (1973) CUP (Cambridge).

Castle, S, 'Divided they dither and drift' (1994) Independent on Sunday, 27 November.

Centre for Contemporary Cultural Studies *Unpopular Education* (1981) Hutchinson (London).

Chapman, R, and Hunt, M (eds) *Open Government* (1987) Routledge (London).

Chester, N, 'Questions in the house', in Walkland, S, and Ryle, M (eds) *The Commons in the Seventies* (1977) Martin Robertson (London).

Chester, N, and Bowring, M, *Questions in Parliament* (1962) OUP (London).

Clark, A, *Diaries* (1993) Weidenfeld and Nicolson (London).

Coleman, D, and Salt, J, *The British Population* (1992) OUP (Oxford).

Coopers and Lybrand *Local Management of Schools* (1988) Coopers and Lybrand (London).

Coppel, J, and O'Neill, A, 'The European Court of Justice: taking rights seriously?' (1994) Legal Studies 227–245.

Corbett, R, 'The 1985 intergovernmental conference and the

Single European Act', in Pryce, R (ed) *The Dynamics of European Union* (1985) Croom Helm (London).

'Testing the new procedures; the European Parliament's first experiences with its new "Single Act" powers' (1989) 7 Journal of Common Market Studies 362–372.

Corwin, E, 'The "higher law" background of American constitutional law (parts I and II)' (1928) Harvard Law Review 149–175 and 365–409.

Coulby, D, 'From educational partnership to central control', in Bash, L, and Coulby, D (eds) *The Education Reform Act: Competition and Control* (1989) Cassell (London).

Cowen, D, 'Legislature and judiciary: parts I and II' (1952) Modern Law Review 282–296 and (1953) Modern Law Review 273–298.

Cowling, M, *1867: Disraeli, Gladstone and Revolution* (1967) CUP (Cambridge).

Craig, J, 'Parliament and boundary commissions' (1959) Public Law 23–45.

Craig, P, 'Sovereignty of the United Kingdom Parliament after *Factortame*' (1991) Yearbook of European Law 221–255.

'Once upon a time in the west: direct effect and the federalisation of EEC law' (1992) Oxford Journal of Legal Studies 453–479.

'*Francovich*, remedies and the scope of damages liability' (1993) 109 Law Quarterly Review 595–621.

Crosby, S, 'The single market and the rule of law' (1991) European Law Review 451–465.

Crosland, A, 'The transition from capitalism', in Crossman, R (ed) *New Fabian Essays* (1952) Turnstile (London).

Cross, C, *The Fascists in Britain* (1961) Barrie Books (London).

Cross, J, 'Withdrawal of the Conservative party whip' (1967) Parliamentary Affairs 169–175.

Crossman, R, (ed) *New Fabian Essays* (1952) Turnstile (London).
Diaries (1979) Mandarin (London).

Cullingworth, J, *Essays on Housing Policy* (1979) Allen & Unwin (London).

Curtin, D, 'The province of government: delimiting the direct effect of directives in the common law context' (1990) European Law Review 195–223.

Dale, R, 'Thatcherism and education', in Ahier, J, and Flude, M (eds) *Contemporary Education Policy* (1983) Croom Helm (London).

Dauses, M, 'The protection of fundamental rights in the Community legal order' (1985) European Law Review 398–417.

Davies, H, and Stewart, J, *The Growth of Government by Appointment: Implications for Democracy* (1994) Local Government Management Board (Birmingham).

'A new agenda for local governance' (1994) Public Money and Management (October) 29–36.

Denning, Lord, '*Re Parliamentary Privilege Act* 1770' (1985) Public Law 80–92.

de Smith, S, 'Boundaries between parliament and the courts' (1955) Modern Law Review 281–286.

'The constitution and the Common Market: a tentative appraisal' (1971) Modern Law Review 597–614.

Constitutional and Administrative Law (5th edn by Brazier, R, and Street, H, 1985) Penguin (London).

Constitutional and Administrative Law (7th edn by Brazier, R, 1994) Penguin (London).

de Smith, S, Woolf, H, and Jowell, J, *Judicial Review of Administrative Action* (5th edn, 1995) Sweet and Maxwell (London).

Dicey, A, *The Law of the Constitution* (10th edn, 1959) Macmillan (London).

Dickman, J, 'Debt and the poll tax' (1989) Municipal Review (May).

Dike, C, 'The case against Parliamentary sovereignty' (1976) Public Law 283–297.

Diplock, Lord, 'The common market and the common law' (1972) Law Teacher 3–12.

DoE *Local Government in England* (1971) (Cmnd 4584) HMSO (London).

Report of the Committee of Inquiry into Local Government Finance (1976) (Cmnd 6453) HMSO (London).

Housing Policy: a Consultative Document (1977) HMSO (London).

Local Government Finance (1977) HMSO (London).

Streamlining the Cities (1983) (Cmnd 9063) HMSO (London).

Rates (1983) (Cmnd 9008) HMSO (London).

Paying for Local Government (1986) HMSO (London).

The Conduct of Local Government Business (1986) (Cmnd 9797) HMSO (London).

Doherty, M, 'Prime Ministerial power and ministerial responsibility in the Thatcher era' (1988) Parliamentary Affairs 49–67.

Donoughmore, Lord, *Report of the Committee on Minister's Powers* (1932) (Cmnd 4060) HMSO (London).

Drewry, G, 'The National Audit Act – half a loaf' (1983) Public Law 531–537.

(ed) *The New Select Committees: a Study of the 1979 Reforms* (1985) Clarendon Press (Oxford).

'Select committees and backbench power', in Jowell, J, and Oliver, D (eds) *The Changing Constitution* (1985) OUP (Oxford).

'Leaking in the public interest' (1985) Public Law 203–212.

'Legislation' in Ryle, M, and Richards, P (eds) *The Commons Under Scrutiny* (1988) Routledge (London).

'Mr Major's Charter: empowering the consumer' (1993) Public Law 248–256.

Drewry, G, and Butcher, T, *The Civil Service Today* (1988) Basil Blackwell (Oxford).

Du Bois, W, 'Slavery and the founding fathers', in Birmbaum, J, and Ollman, B (eds) *The United States Constitution* (1990) New York University Press (New York).

Dunleavy, P, Jones, G, and O'Leary, B, 'Prime Ministers and the Commons: patterns of behaviour 1868–1987' (1990) Public Administration 123–140.

Economist 'On the low road' (1974) The Economist, 4 May.

Edelman, M, *The Symbolic Uses of Politics* (1964) University of Illinois Press (Urbana).

Edward, D, 'The impact of the Single European Act on the institutions' (1987) Common Market Law Review 19–30.

Ehlermann, C, 'Applying the new budgetary procedure for the first time' (1975) Common Market Law Review 325–343.

'The internal market following the Single European Act' (1987) Common Market Law Review 361–409.

Elcock, H, *Local Government* (2nd edn, 1986) Methuen (London).

Ellis, D, 'Collective ministerial responsibility and collective solidarity' (1980) Public Law 367–396.

Elton, G, *The Tudor Revolution in Government* (1953) CUP (Cambridge).

'Henry VIII's Act of Proclamations' (1960) English Historical Review 208–222.

Emiliou, N, 'Subsidiarity: panacea or fig leaf?', in O'Keefe, D, and Twomey, P (eds) *Legal Issues of the Maastricht Treaty* (1994) Wiley Chancery Law (London).

Erskine May, *see*: Boulton, C (ed) *above*.

European Council *Speeches and Statements made on the Occasion of the Signing of the Single European Act* (1986) (Brussels: EC).

Ewing, K, *The Funding of Political Parties in Britain* (1987) Clarendon Press (Oxford).

Ewing, K, and Gearty, C, *Civil Liberties under Thatcher* (1990) OUP (Oxford).

Fast Facts 'Housing action trusts: an end of term report' (1990) ROOF 12 (November/December).

'The top twenty percentage council rent increases 1990/91' (1990) ROOF 16 (July/August).

Feldman, D, *Civil Liberties and Human Rights in England and Wales* (1993) Clarendon Press (Oxford).

Fennel, P, '*Roberts v Hopwood*: the rule against socialism' (1986) Journal of Law and Society 401–422.

Finer, S, 'The individual responsibility of Ministers' (1956) Public Administration 377–396.

Finnie, W, Himsworth, C, and Walker, N (eds) *Edinburgh Essays in Public Law* (1991) Edinburgh University Press (Edinburgh).

Fitzpatrick, B, 'The significance of EEC directives in UK sex discrimination law' (1989) Oxford Journal of Legal Studies 336–355.

Forrest, R, and Murie, A, *Selling the Welfare State* (1988) Routledge (London).

Forwood, N, and Clough, M, 'The Single European Act and free movement' (1986) *European Law Review* 383–408.

Fowler, N, *Ministers Decide* (1988) Chapman (London).

Freedland, M, 'Privatising Carltona: Part II of the Deregulation and Contracting Out Act 1994' (1995) Public Law 21–27.

French, D, 'Spy fever in Britain 1900–1915' (1978) Historical Journal 355–370.

Friedmann, W, '*Trethowan*'s case, parliamentary sovereignty and the limits of legal change' (1950) Australian Law Journal 103–108.

Fry, G, 'The Sachsenhausen concentration camp case and the convention of ministerial responsibility' (1970) Public Law 336–357.

Gamble, A, *Britain in Decline* (1981) Papermac (London).

Ganz, G, 'The depoliticisation of local authorities: the Local Government and Housing Act 1989, Part I' (1990) Public Law 224–242.

Gash, N, *Politics in the Age of Peel* (1953) Longman (London).

Genn, H, and Richardson, G (eds) *Administrative Law and Government Action* (1994) Clarendon Press (Oxford).

George, V, and Wilding, P, *Ideology and State Welfare* (1976) RKP (London).

Golby, M, 'Parents as school governors', in Munn, P (ed) *Parents and Schools* (1993) Routledge (London).

Gordon, P, 'A dirty war: the new right and local authority anti-racism', in Ball, W, and Solomos, J (eds) *Race and Local Politics* (1990) Macmillan (London).

Gough, I, 'Thatcherism and the welfare state', in Hall, S, and Jacques, M (eds) *The Politics of Thatcherism* (1983) Lawrence and Wishart (London).

Gould, M, '*M v Home Office*: government and the judges' (1993) Public Law 568–578.

Gravells, N, 'Disapplying an Act of Parliament pending a preliminary ruling: constitutional enormity or common law right?' (1989) Public Law 568–586.

Grief, N, 'The domestic impact of the ECHR as mediated through Community law' (1991) Public Law 555–567.

Griffith, J, *Central Departments and Local Authorities* (1966) Allen & Unwin (London).

Parliamentary Scrutiny of Government Bills (1974) Allen & Unwin (London).

The Politics of the Judiciary (1977) Fontana (London).

The Politics of the Judiciary (2nd edn, 1981) Fontana (London).

'Judicial decisionmaking in public law' (1985) Public Law 564–582.

Judicial Politics Since 1920: a Chronicle (1993) Blackwell (Oxford).

Griffith, J, and Ryle, M, *Parliament: Functions, Practice and Procedures* (1989) Sweet and Maxwell (London).

Griswold, E, 'The "coloured vote case" in South Africa' (1952) 65 Harvard LR 1361–1374.

Gyford, J, *The Politics of Local Socialism* (1985) Allen & Unwin (London).

Hall, S, 'The great moving right show', in Hall, S, and Jacques, M (eds) *The Politics of Thatcherism* (1983) Lawrence and Wishart (London).

Hall, S, and Jacques, M (eds) *The Politics of Thatcherism* (1983) Lawrence and Wishart (London).

Hall, W, 'Contract compliance at the GLC' (1986) Local Government Studies 17–24.

Hampson, W, *Local Government and Urban Politics* (2nd edn, 1991) Longman (London).

Hamson, C, 'The real lesson of Crichel Down' (1954) Public Administration 383–400.

Harlow, C (ed) *Public Law and Politics* (1986) Sweet and Maxwell (London).

'A special relationship? American influences on judicial review in England', in Loveland, I (ed) *A Special Relationship?* (1995) Clarendon Press (Oxford).

Harlow, C, and Rawlings, R, *Law and Administration* (1984) Weidenfeld and Nicolson (London).

Harris, N, *Law and Education: Regulation, Consumerism and the Education System* (1993) Sweet and Maxwell (London).

Hart, H, *The Concept of Law* (2nd edn, 1994) Clarendon Press (Oxford).

Hart, J, *Proportional Representation: Critics of the British Electoral System 1820–1945* (1992) Clarendon Press (Oxford).

Hartley, T, *The Foundations of European Community Law* (2nd edn, 1988) Clarendon Press (Oxford).

'Constitutional and institutional aspects of the Maastricht Agreement' (1993) International and Comparative Law Quarterly 213–237.

The Foundations of European Community Law (3rd edn, 1994) Clarendon Press (Oxford).

Hattersley, R, 'The beggaring of PM's question time' (1992) Guardian, 28 January.

Hawes, D, 'Parliamentary select committees: some case studies in contingent influence' (1992) Policy and Politics 227–235.

Hay, J, *The Origins of the Liberal Welfare Reforms 1906–1914* (1975) Macmillan (London).

Hayek, F, von *The Road to Serfdom* (1944) RKP (London).

Hencke, D, 'Ministers face reprimand over wasteful projects' (1994) Guardian, 7 July.

'Fury as Ritz MP avoids penalty' (1995) Guardian, 8 June.

Hencke, D, and Bowcott, O, 'MPs' fury as Wiggin escapes' (1995) Guardian, 23 May.

Hennessy, P, 'Helicopter crashes into Cabinet: Prime Minister and constitution hurt' (1986) Journal of Law and Society 423–432.

Cabinet (1986a) Basil Blackwell (Oxford).

Never Again (1992) Jonathan Cape (London).

Heuston, R, *Essays in Constitutional Law* (2nd edn, 1964) Stevens (London).

'*Liversidge v Anderson* in retrospect' (1970) Law Quarterly Review 33–68.

Hewart, Lord, *The New Despotism* (1929) Lawrence and Wishart (London).

Hill, D, 'A job to do' (1991) New Statesman and Society, 8 March.

Himsworth, C, 'Poll tax capping and judicial review' (1991) Public Law 76–92.

'The delegated powers scrutiny committee' (1995) Public Law 34–44.

Hobsbawm, E, *Industry and Empire* (1969) Penguin (Harmondsworth).

Hogg, Q, *The Case for Conservatism* (1947) Penguin (West Drayton).

Holden, B, *Understanding Liberal Democracy* (1988) Phillip Allan (Oxford).

Hood-Phillips, O, 'A Garland for the Lords: Parliament and Community law again' (1982) Law Quarterly Review 524–526.

Horne, A, *Macmillan 1957–1986* (1987) Macmillan (London).

Horwitz, H, 'Parliament and the Glorious Revolution' (1974) Bulletin of the Institute of Historical Research 36–52.

House of Commons Foreign Affairs Committee *British North American Acts: the Role of Parliament* (1981) HMSO (London).

Hughes, D, and Pollard, D, *Cases and Materials on Constitutional and Administrative Law* (1990) Butterworths (London).

Hume, D, 'Of the original contract', in Locke, J, *Social Contract: Essays by Locke, Hume and Rousseau* (1978) OUP (London).

    Political Writings (1994) (edited by Warner, D, and Livingston, D) Hackett Publishing Co (Cambridge).

Hutton, R, *The Restoration* (1985) Clarendon Press (Oxford).

Institute for Public Policy Research *A Written Constitution for the UK* (1991) IPPR (London).

Institute of Fiscal Studies *Local Government Finance: the 1990 Reforms* (1990) IFS (London).

Irving, R, 'The United Kingdom referendum, June 1975' (1975) European Law Review 3–12.

Irwin, H, 'Opportunities for backbenchers', in Ryle, M, and Richards, P (eds) *The Commons Under Scrutiny* (1988) Routledge (London).

Jackman, R, 'The Rates Bill: a measure of desperation' (1984) Political Quarterly 161–170.

Jackson, P, 'The royal prerogative' (1964) Modern Law Review 709–717.

    'War Damage Act 1965' (1965) Modern Law Review 574–576.

Jenkins, J, 'The green sheep in Colonel Gadaffi Drive' (1987) New Society, 9 January.

Jenkins, R, 'Equality', in Crossman, R (ed) *New Fabian Essays* (1952) Turnstile (London).

    Mr Balfour's Poodle: an Account of the Struggle Between the House of Lords and the Government of Mr Asquith (1968) Heinemann (London).

    A Life at the Centre (1991) Pan (London).

    'Churchill: the government of 1951–1955', in Blake, R, and Louis, W (eds) *Churchill* (1994) Clarendon Press (Oxford).

Jennings, I, *The Law and the Constitution* (5th edn, 1959) Hodder and Stoughton (London).

    Cabinet Government (3rd edn, 1959) CUP (Cambridge).

Principles of Local Government Law (4th edn, 1960) University of London Press (London).

Jensen, M, 'The Articles of Confederation', in Birmbaum, J, and Ollman, B (eds) *The United States Constitution* (1990) New York University Press (New York).

Johnson, N, 'Departmental select committees', in Ryle, M, and Richards, P (eds) *The Commons under Scrutiny* (1988) Routledge (London).

Jones, A, *The Politics of Reform 1884* (1972) CUP (Cambridge).

Jones, G, 'The Prime Minister and parliamentary questions' (1973) Parliamentary Affairs 260–272.

'Herbert Morrison and poplarism' (1973) Public Law 11–31.

Jones, H, 'The rule of law and the welfare state' (1958) Columbia LR 143–156.

Jowell, J, and Lester, A, 'Proportionality: neither novel nor dangerous', in Jowell, J, and Oliver, D (eds) *New Directions in Judicial Review* (1988) Stevens and Sons (London).

Jowell, J, and Oliver, D (eds) *The Changing Constitution* (1st edn, 1985); (2nd edn, 1989); (3rd edn, 1994) Clarendon Press (Oxford).

New Directions in Judicial Review (1988) Stevens and Sons (London).

Judson, M, 'Henry Parker and the theory of parliamentary sovereignty', in Wittke, C (ed) *Essays in History and Political Theory in Honour of Charles Howard McIlwain* (1936) HUP (Cambridge, Mass).

Kavanagh, D, and Seldon, A (eds) *The Major Effect* (1994) Macmillan (London).

Kay, A, Legg, C, and Foot, J, *The 1980 Tenant's Rights in Practice* (1985) City University (London).

Keenan, P, 'Some legal consequences of Britain's entry into the European Common Market' (1962) Public Law 327–343.

Keir, D, *The Constitutional History of Modern Britain* (8th edn, 1966) Adam and Charles Black (London).

Cases in Constitutional Law (6th edn, 1978) Clarendon Press (Oxford).

Keith-Lucas, B, 'Poplarism' (1962) Public Law 52–80.

Kelly, A, Harbison, W, and Belz, H, *The American Constitution: its Origins and Development* (Volumes I and II) (7th edn, 1991) W W Norton (New York).

Kent, S, *Sex and Suffrage in Britain 1860–1914* (1989) Princeton University Press (New Jersey).

Knewstub, N, 'Ousted Tory MP lambasts government arrogance' (1992) Guardian, 14 July.

Koopmans, T, 'Federalism: the wrong debate' (1992) Common Market Law Review 1047–1052.

Laffin, M, *Professionalism and Policy: the Role of the Professions in the Central-local Government Relationship* (1986) Gower (Aldershot).

Laffin, M, and Young, K, *Professionalism in Local Government* (1990) Longman (Harlow).

Lane, R, 'New Community competences under the Maastricht Treaty' (1993) Common Market Law Review 939–979.

Large, D, 'The decline of the "Party of the Crown" and the rise of parties in the House of Lords, 1783–1837' (1963) English Historical Review 669–695.

Laski, H, 'Judicial review of social policy in England' (1926) Harvard LR 832–848.

Laslett, P, 'The social and political theory of Two Treatises of Government', in Laslett, P (ed) *Locke – Two Treatises of Government* (1988) CUP (Cambridge).

'Two Treatises of Government and the revolution of 1688', in Laslett, P (ed) *Locke – Two Treatises of Government* (1988) CUP.

(ed) *Locke – Two Treatises of Government* (1988) CUP (Cambridge).

Lasok, D, and Bridge, J, *Law and Institutions of the European Communities* (5th edn, 1991) Butterworths (London).

Laundy, P, 'The Speaker and his office in the twentieth century', in Walkland, S (ed) *The House of Commons in the Twentieth Century* (1979) Clarendon Press (Oxford).

Laws, J, 'Is the High Court the guardian of fundamental constitutional rights?' (1993) Public Law 59–79.

Lawson, N, *The View from No 11* (1992) Bantam (London).

Leach, S, 'Strengthening local democracy? the government's response to Widdicombe', in Stewart, J, and Stoker, G (eds) *The Future of Local Government* (1989) Macmillan (London).

Lee, S, 'Prerogative and public law principles' (1985) Public Law 186–193.

'Law and the constitution', in Kavanagh, D, and Seldon, A (eds) *The Major Effect* (1994) Macmillan (London).

Leigh, I, 'A tapper's charter' (1986) Public Law 8–18.

'Spycatcher in Strasbourg' (1992) Public Law 200–208.

Le May, G, 'Parliament, the Constitution and the doctrine of the mandate' (1957) South African Law Journal 33–42.

Leneman, L, 'When women were not "persons": the Scottish women graduates case, 1906–1908' (1991) Juridical Review 109–118.

Leopold, P, 'References in court to Hansard' (1981) Public Law 316–321.

'Parliamentary privilege and an MP's threats' (1984) Public Law 547–550.

'Leaks and squeaks in the Palace of Westminster' (1986) Public Law 368–374.

'The freedom of peers from arrest' (1989) Public Law 398–406.

Lester, A, 'Fundamental rights: the United Kingdom isolated' (1984) Public Law 46–72.

Levy, L, 'Introduction – the making of the Constitution 1776–1789', in Levy, L (ed) *The Making of the Constitution* (1987) OUP (New York).

(ed) *The Making of the Constitution* (1987) OUP (New York).

Lewin, J, 'The struggle for law in South Africa' (1956) Political Quarterly 176–181.

Liddington, J, and Norris, J, *One Hand Tied Behind Us* (1979) Virago (London).

Loach, J, *Parliament under the Tudors* (1990) Clarendon Press (Oxford).

Lock, G, 'Information for Parliament', in Ryle, M, and Richards, P (eds) *The Commons under Scrutiny* (1988) Routledge (London).

Locke, J, *Two Treatises of Government* (1988) CUP (Cambridge).

Loughlin, M, 'Municipal socialism in a unitary state', in McAuslan, P, and McEldowney, J (eds) *Law, Legitimacy and the Constitution* (1985) Sweet and Maxwell (London).

'The restructuring of central–local government legal relations' (1985) Local Government Studies 59–73.

Local Government in the Modern State (1986) Sweet and Maxwell (London).

Public Law and Political Theory (1992) Clarendon Press (Oxford).

Loveland, I, 'The restructuring of central–local government relations', in Jowell, J, and Oliver, D (eds) *The Changing Constitution* (1994) Clarendon Press (Oxford).

'Labour and the constitution: the "right" approach to reform' (1992) Parliamentary Affairs 173–187.

'Square pegs, round holes: the "right" to council housing in the post-war era' (1992) Journal of Law and Society 339–364.

'Racial segregation in state schools: the parent's right to choose?' (1993) Journal of Law and Society 341–355.

'Defamation of government: taking lessons from America?' (1994) Legal Studies 61–80.

Housing Homeless Persons: Administrative Law and Practice (1995a) Clarendon Press (Oxford).

(ed) *A Special Relationship?* (1995b) Clarendon Press (Oxford).
'The criminalisation of racist violence', in Loveland, I (ed) *A Special Relationship?* (1995c) Clarendon Press (Oxford).
(ed) *Frontiers of Criminality* (1995) Sweet and Maxwell (London).

Luba, J, 'Legal Eye' (1991) ROOF (January/February).

Lustgarten, L, *The Governance of Police* (1989) Sweet and Maxwell (London).

Lustgarten, L, and Leigh, I, *In from the Cold: National Security and Parliamentary Democracy* (1994) Clarendon Press (Oxford).

MacCormick, N, 'Does the United Kingdom have a constitution?' (1978) 29 Northern Ireland Law Quarterly 1–20.

Mackintosh, J, *The British Cabinet* (1962) Stevens and Sons (London).
'The report of the Royal Commission on the constitution 1969–1973' (1974) Parliamentary Affairs 115–123.

Madgwick, P, 'Resignations' (1966) Parliamentary Affairs 59–76.

Magnus, P, *Gladstone* (1963) John Murray (London).

Maidment, R, *The Supreme Court and the New Deal* (1992) Open University Press (Buckingham).

Maier, P, 'John Wilkes and American disillusionment with Britain' (1963) William and Mary Quarterly 373–395.

Maitland, F, *The Constitutional History of England* (1908) CUP (Cambridge).

Malpass, P, and Murie, A, *Housing Policy and Practice* (1987) Macmillan (London).

Mandler, P, *Aristocratic Government in the Age of Reform* (1990) Clarendon Press (Oxford).

Marshall, G, 'What is Parliament? The changing concept of Parliamentary sovereignty' (1954) Political Studies 193–209.
'The House of Commons and its privileges', in Walkland, S (ed) *The House of Commons in the Twentieth Century* (1979) Clarendon Press (Oxford).
Constitutional Conventions (1984) Clarendon Press (Oxford).
'Ministers, civil servants and open government', in Harlow, C (ed) *Public Law and Politics* (1986) Sweet and Maxwell (London).
'The end of Prime Ministerial government?' (1991) Public Law 1–6.
'Ministerial responsibility, the Home Office, and Mr Baker' (1992) Public Law 7–12.

Marshall, G, and Loveday, B, 'The police: independence and accountability', in Jowell, J, and Oliver, D (eds) *The Changing Constitution* (1994) Clarendon Press (Oxford).

Mason, D, *Revising the Rating System* (1985) Adam Smith Institute (London).

Mather, F, 'The government and the Chartists', in Briggs, A (ed) *Chartist Studies* (1962) Macmillan (London).

Matthew, C, *Gladstone 1809–1874* (1986) Clarendon Press (Oxford).

Maude, A, and Szemerey, J, *Why Electoral Reform? The Case for Electoral Reform Examined* (1981) Conservative Political Centre (London).

McAuslan, P, 'Administrative law, collective consumption and judicial policy' (1983) Modern Law Review 1–21.

'The Widdicombe Report: local government business or politics' (1987) Public Law 154–162.

McAuslan, P, and McEldowney, J (eds) *Law, Legitimacy and the Constitution* (1985) Sweet and Maxwell (London).

McEldowney, J, 'Dicey in historical perspective', in McAuslan, P, and McEldowney, J (eds) *Law, Legitimacy and the Constitution* (1985) Sweet and Maxwell (London).

'The contingencies fund and the parliamentary scrutiny of public finance' (1988) Public Law 232–245.

Public Law (1994) Sweet and Maxwell (London).

McGhie, J, 'Tory backbenchers to ask Speaker to spare them from their whips' (1992) Observer, 12 July.

McKay, D, *American Politics and Society* (2nd edn, 1989) Basil Blackwell (Oxford).

McKie, D, 'Labour triumph in boundary change review' (1994) Guardian, 11 August.

Merret, S, *State Housing in Britain* (1979) RKP (London).

Miers, D, 'Citing Hansard as an aid to interpretation' (1983) Statute LR 98–102.

Miliband, R, and Smith, J (eds) *Socialist Register* (1975) Merlin (London).

Miller, J, 'The Glorious Revolution: "contract" and "abdication" reconsidered' (1982) The Historical Journal 541–555.

The Glorious Revolution (1983) Longman (London).

Mitchell, A, 'Clay Cross' (1974) Political Quarterly 165.

Montesquieu, C, *The Spirit of the Laws* (1989) CUP (Cambridge).

Morris, G, and Fredman, S, 'Judicial review and civil servants: contracts of employment declared to exist' (1991) Public Law 485–490.

Mount, F, *The British Constitution Now: Recovery or Decline?* (1992) Heinemann (London).

Munn, P (ed) *Parents and Schools* (1993) Routledge (London).

Munro, C 'Elections and expenditure' (1976) Public Law 300–304.

Studies in Constitutional Law (1987) Butterworths (London).

Murdie, A, 'Bailiffs, Henry III, the community charge and all that' (1990) Municipal Journal, 17–23 August.

Nally, S, and Dear, J, 'No surrender' (1990) Municipal Journal, 12–18 October.

Nicol, W, 'The Luxembourg compromise' (1984) Journal of Common Market Studies 35–43.

Nicol, W, and Simon, T, *Understanding the New European Community* (1994) Harvester Wheatsheaf (London).

Nixon, J, and Nixon, N, 'The social services committee' (1983) Journal of Social Policy 331–355.

Norton, P, 'Government defeats in the House of Commons: myth and reality' (1978) Public Law 360–378.

'The organisation of parliamentary parties', in Walkland, S (ed) *The House of Commons in the Twentieth Century* (1979) Clarendon Press (Oxford).

Dissension in the House of Commons 1974–1979 (1980) Macmillan (London).

' "Dear Minister" ... The importance of MP to minister correspondence' (1982) Parliamentary Affairs 59–72.

The Commons in Perspective (1985) Martin Robertson (London).

'Opposition to government', in Ryle, M, and Richards, P (eds) *The Commons under Scrutiny* (1988) Routledge (London).

The British Polity (2nd edn, 1991) Longman (London).

O'Keefe, D, and Twomey, P (eds) *Legal Issues of the Maastricht Treaty* (1994) Wiley Chancery Law (London).

O'Leary, B, 'Why was the GLC abolished?' (1987) International Journal of Urban and Regional Research 192–217.

'British farce, French drama and tales of two cities' (1987) Public Administration 369–389.

O'Leary, C, *The Elimination of Corrupt Practices in British General Elections 1868–1911* (1962) Clarendon Press (Oxford).

Oliver, D, 'Why electoral reform? The case for electoral reform examined' (1982) Public Law 236–239.

Government in the United Kingdom: the Search for Accountability, Effectiveness and Citizenship (1991) Open University Press (Milton Keynes).

'Written constitutions: principles and problems' (1992) Parliamentary Affairs 135–152.

Ousley, H, 'Local authority race initiatives', in Boddy, M, and Fudge, C (eds) *Local Socialism* (1984) Macmillan (London).

Owens, R, 'If the HAT fits' (1991) ROOF 17 (November/ December).

Padover, S (ed) *The Complete Madison* (1953) Easten Press (Norwalk, Conn).

Palmer, S, 'In the interests of the state' (1988) Public Law 523–535.
'Tightening secrecy law: the Official Secrets Act 1989' (1990) Public Law 243–256.

Pannick, D, 'The Law Lords and the needs of contemporary society' (1984) Political Quarterly 318–328.
'No Logic behind gagging terrorists' empty rhetoric' (1994) The Times, 2 August.

Pedley, R, 'Lord Hailsham's legacy' (1958) Journal of Education (January) 4–5.
The Comprehensive School (1966) Penguin (Harmondsworth).

Pescatore, P, 'The protection of human rights in the European Communities' (1972) Common Market Law Review 73–79.
'The doctrine of direct effect: an infant disease of Community Law' (1983) European Law Review 155–177.

Peterson, J, 'Subsidiarity: a definition to suit any vision' (1994) Parliamentary Affairs 116–132.

Phelan, D, 'Right to life of the unborn v promotion of trade in services' (1992) Modern Law Review 670–689.

Pimlott, B, *Harold Wilson* (1992) Harper Collins (London).

Plucknett, T, 'Dr Bonham's Case and judicial review' (1928) Harvard LR 30–70.
Taswell-Langmead's English Constitutional History (11th edn, 1960) Sweet and Maxwell (London).

Plumb, J, 'Elections to the Convention Parliament of 1689' (1937) Cambridge Historical Journal 235–254.

Pryce, R (ed) *The Dynamics of European Union* (1985) Croom Helm (London).

Pugh, M, *Women's Suffrage in Britain 1867–1928* (1980) The Historical Association.
'Labour and women's suffrage', in Brown, K (ed) *The First Labour Party* (1985) Croom Helm (London).

Pulzer, P, 'Germany', in Butler, D, and Bogdanor, V (eds) *Democracy and Elections* (1983) CUP (Cambridge).

Punnet, R *British Government and Politics* (1968) Heinemann (London).

Raab, C, 'Parents and schools: what role for education authorities?', in Munn, P (ed) *Parents and Schools* (1993) Routledge (London).

Radcliffe, Lord, *Report on Ministerial Memoirs* (1976) (Cmnd 6386) HMSO (London).

Ranson, S, 'From 1944–1988: education, citizenship and democracy' (1988) Local Government Studies 1–19.

Ranson, S, and Thomas, H, 'Educational reform: consumer democracy or social democracy', in Stewart, J, and Stoker, G (eds) *The Future of Local Government* (1989) Macmillan (London).

Rawlings, H, *Law and the Electoral Process* (1988) Sweet and Maxwell (London).

Rawlings, R, 'Legal politics: the UK and ratification of the Treaty on European Union (part one)' (1994) Public Law 254–278. 'Legal politics: the UK and ratification of the Treaty on European Union (part two)' (1994) Public Law 367–391.

Raworth, P, 'A timid step forwards: Maastricht and the democratisation of the EC' (1994) European Law Review 16–33.

Raz, J, 'The rule of law and its virtue' (1977) Law Quarterly Review 195–211.

Rhodes, R, *The National World of Local Government* (1977) Allen & Unwin (London).

Richards, P, *Parliament and Conscience* (1970) Allen & Unwin (London).

Richardson, T, 'The War Crimes Act 1991', in Loveland, I (ed) *Frontiers of Criminality* (1995) Sweet and Maxwell (London).

Ridley, N, *My Style of Government* (1991) Fontana (London).

Robertson, A, and Merrill, J, *Human Rights in Europe* (3rd edn, 1994) Manchester University Press (Manchester).

Robinson, R, 'The House of Commons and public money', in Ryle, M, and Richards, P (eds) *The Commons under Scrutiny* (1988) Routledge (London).

Rose, H, 'The Immigration Act 1971: a case study in the work of Parliament' (1973) Parliamentary Affairs 69–91.

Rousseau, J, *The Social Contract* (ed and tr C Betts) (1987) OUP (Oxford).

Rover, C, *Women's Suffrage and Party Politics in Britain 1866–1914* (1967) RKP (London).

Rude, G, *Wilkes and Liberty* (1962) Clarendon Press (Oxford).

Russell, C, *The Crisis of Parliaments* (1971) Clarendon Press (Oxford).

Ryle, M, and Richards, P (eds) *The Commons under Scrutiny* (1988) Routledge (London).

Scarman, Lord, 'Human rights in an unwritten constitution' (1987) Denning LJ 129. 'Points of common law' (1995) Guardian, 8 May.

Scraton, P, ' "If you want a riot, change the law": the implications of the 1985 White Paper on public order' (1985) Journal of Law and Society 385–393.

Sedley, S, 'Governments, constitutions and judges', in Genn, H, and Richardson, G (eds) *Administrative Law and Government Action* (1994) Clarendon Press (Oxford).

Seymour, C, *Electoral Reform in England and Wales* (1970) David and Charles (Newton Abbot).

Seymour-Ure, C, 'The misuse of the question of privilege in the 1964–5 session of Parliament' (1964) Parliamentary Affairs 380–388.

  'Proposed reforms of parliamentary privilege: an assessment in the light of recent cases' (1970) Parliamentary Affairs 221–231.

Shannon, R, *Gladstone Vol 1* (1982) Hamish Hamilton (London).

Sharp, A, *Political Ideas of the English Civil War* (1983) Longman (London).

Sharpe, J, 'Theories and value of local government' (1970) Political Studies 153–174.

Shaw, J, *EC Law* (1993) Macmillan (London).

Shell, D, 'The House of Lords and the Thatcher government' (1985) Parliamentary Affairs 16–32.

  The House of Lords (1992) Harvester Wheatsheaf (London).

Silk, P, *How Parliament Works* (1992) Longman (London).

Sills, P, 'Report of the Select Committee on Parliamentary Privilege' (1968) Modern Law Review 435–439.

Simon, B, *Bending the Rules* (1988) Lawrence and Wishart (London).

Simpson, A, *In the Highest Degree Odious* (1991) Clarendon Press (Oxford).

Skidelsky, R, 'Great Britain', in Woolf, S (ed) *European Fascism* (1968) Weidenfeld and Nicolson (London).

Sklair, L, 'The struggle against the Housing Finance Act', in Miliband, R, and Smith, J (eds) *Socialist Register* (1975) Merlin (London).

Slaughter, T, ' "Abdicate" and "contract" in the Glorious Revolution' (1981) The Historical Journal 323–337.

Smith, E, *The House of Lords in British Politics and Society 1815–1911* (1992) Longman (London).

Smith, T, 'The Union of 1707 as fundamental law' (1957) Public Law 99–121.

Speck, W, *Reluctant Revolutionaries* (1986) Clarendon Press (Oxford).

Steiner, J, 'Coming to terms with EC directives' (1990) Law Quarterly Review 144–159.

  'From direct effect to *Francovich*: shifting means of enforcement of Community Law' (1993) European Law Review 3–22.

Stellman, H, 'Israel: the 1984 election and after' (1985) Parliamentary Affairs 73–85.

Stewart, J, *Defending Public Accountability* (1993) Demos (London).

Stewart, J, and Stoker, G (eds) *The Future of Local Government* (1989) Macmillan (London).

Stockdale, E, 'The unnecessary crisis: the background to the Parliamentary Papers Act 1840' (1989) Public Law 30–49.

Szyszczak, E, 'Sovereignty: crisis, compliance, confusion, complacency' (1990) European Law Review 480–488.

'Interpretation of Community law in the courts' (1993) European Law Review 214–225.

Taylor and DES *A New Partnership for our Schools* (1977) HMSO (London).

Taylor, P, and Gudgin, G, 'The myth of non-partisan cartography' (1976) Urban Studies 13–25.

Thatcher, M, 'Address to the College of Europe, Bruges' (1988) The Times, 21 September.

Thomas, R, 'The British Official Secrets Act 1911–1939 and the Ponting case', in Chapman, R, and Hunt, M (eds) *Open Government* (1987) Routledge (London).

Thompson, E, *Whigs and Hunters* (1975) Penguin (London).

Thompson, H, and Game, C, 'Section 137: propoganda on the rates?' (1985) Local Government Studies 11–18.

Thomson, A, 'Youngest peer steps into the limelight' (1995) The Times, 5 April.

Thorne, S, 'Dr Bonham's Case' (1938) Law Quarterly Review 543–552.

Titmuss, R, 'Welfare rights, law and discretion' (1971) Political Quarterly 133–131.

Toth, A, 'The legal status of declarations attached to the SEA' (1986) Common Market Law Review 803–812.

'Is subsidiarity justiciable?' (1994) European Law Review 268–285.

Travis, A, 'Howard package left limping by Lords onslaught' (1994) Guardian, 19 July.

Trinadade, F, 'Parliamentary sovereignty and the primacy of Community law' (1972) Modern Law Review 375–402.

Turbeville, A, *The House of Lords in the Eighteenth Century* (1927) Clarendon Press (Oxford).

The House Lords in the Age of Reform (1958) Faber and Faber (London).

Turpin, C, *British Government and the Constitution: Text, Cases and Materials* (1st edn, 1985); (2nd edn, 1990) Weidenfeld and Nicolson (London); (3rd edn, 1995) Butterworths (London).

Underdown, D, *Revel, Riot, and Rebellion* (1985) Clarendon Press (Oxford).

Vile, M, *Constitutionalism and the Separation of Powers* (1967) Clarendon Press (Oxford).

Vincent-Jones, P, 'The hippy convoy and criminal trespass' (1986) Journal of Law and Society 343–370.

Wade, H, 'The basis of legal sovereignty' (1955) Cambridge Law Journal 172–197.

'Constitutional and administrative aspects of the *Anisminic* case' (1969) Law Quarterly Review 198–212.

'Sovereignty and the European Communities' (1972) Law Quarterly Review 1–5.

'Judicial control of the prerogative' (1977) Law Quarterly Review 325–327.

Constitutional Fundamentals (1980) Stevens (London).

'The civil service and the prerogative' (1985) Law Quarterly Review 190–199.

Wade, H, and Forsyth, C, *Administrative Law* (7th edn, 1994) Clarendon Press (Oxford).

Walker, C, 'Review of the prerogative: the remaining issues' (1987) Public Law 63–84.

Walkland, S (ed) *The House of Commons in the Twentieth Century* (1979) Clarendon Press (Oxford).

Walkland, S, and Ryle, M (eds) *The Commons in the Seventies* (1977) Martin Robertson (London).

Wallington, P, and McBride, J, *Civil Liberties and a Bill of Rights* (1976) Cobden Trust (London).

Warburton, M, and Malpass, P, 'Riding the rent rocket' (1991) ROOF 27 (July/August).

Ward, J, *Chartism* (1973) Harper Row (New York).

Ward, M, 'Priced out' (1988) Housing 9 (October).

Watkins, A, 'Mrs Thatcher and the Spanish fishermen' (1991) Observer, 30 June.

'Why young Tony should keep his winning smile' (1994) Independent on Sunday, 19 June.

Weare, V, 'The House of Lords – prophecy and fulfilment' (1964) Parliamentary Affairs 422–433.

Webster, P, 'Major faces Tory backlash over Nolan' (1995) The Times, 19 May.

Webster, P, Wilkinson, P, and Gibb, F, ' "Women only" candidate shortlists ruled illegal' (1996) The Times, 9 January.

Weiler, J, 'The Community system: the dual character of supranationalism' (1981) Yearbook of European Law 267–306.

'Eurocracy and distrust' (1986) Washington Law Review 1103.

Weiler, J, and Lockhart, N, ' "Taking rights seriously": the European Court and its fundamental rights jurisprudence' (1995) (Parts I and II) 32 Common Market Law Review 51–94 and 579–627.

Welfare, D, 'The Lords in defence of local government' (1992) Parliamentary Affairs 205–219.

Weston, C, *English Constitutional Theory and the House of Lords* (1965) RKP (London).

White, M, 'Low acts of attrition' (1994) Guardian, 17 February.

'MPs vote to reform working hours' (1994) Guardian, 20 December.

'Cautious Hunt rests the temperature as "bureaucratic" rules for MPs alarm Tories' (1995) Guardian, 19 May.

White, M, and Norton-Taylor, R, 'Commons watchdogs lack full set of teeth' (1995) Guardian, 22 March.

Wilson, H, *Final Term* (1979) Weidenfeld and Nicolson (London).

Wilson, T, 'Local freedom and central control – a question of balance', in Bailey, S and Paddison, R (eds) *The Reform of Local Government Finance in Britain* (1988) Routledge (London).

Winter, J, 'Direct applicability and direct effect: two distinct and different concepts in Community law' (1972) Common Market Law Review 425–438.

Winterton, G, 'The British grundnorm: parliamentary sovereignty re-examined' (1976) Law Quarterly Review 591–617.

'Parliamentary supremacy and the judiciary' (1981) Law Quarterly Review 265–275.

Wittke, C (ed) *Essays in History and Political Theory in Honour of Charles Howard McIlwain* (1936) HUP (Cambridge, Mass).

The History of English Parliamentary Privilege (1970) Da Capo Press (New York).

Wolffe, W, 'Values in conflict: incitement to racial hatred and the Public Order Act 1986' (1987) Public Law 85–95.

Wood, N, 'Tories may lose eight seats in capital boundary changes' (1994) The Times, 11 August.

Woodward, R, 'Mobilising opposition: the campaign against housing action trusts in Tower Hamlets' (1991) Housing Studies 44–56.

Woolf, S (ed) *European Fascism* (1968) Weidenfeld and Nicolson (London).

Young, H, *One of Us* (1991) Pan (London).

Zander, M, *The Law-making Process* (3rd edn, 1994) Butterworths (London).

Index